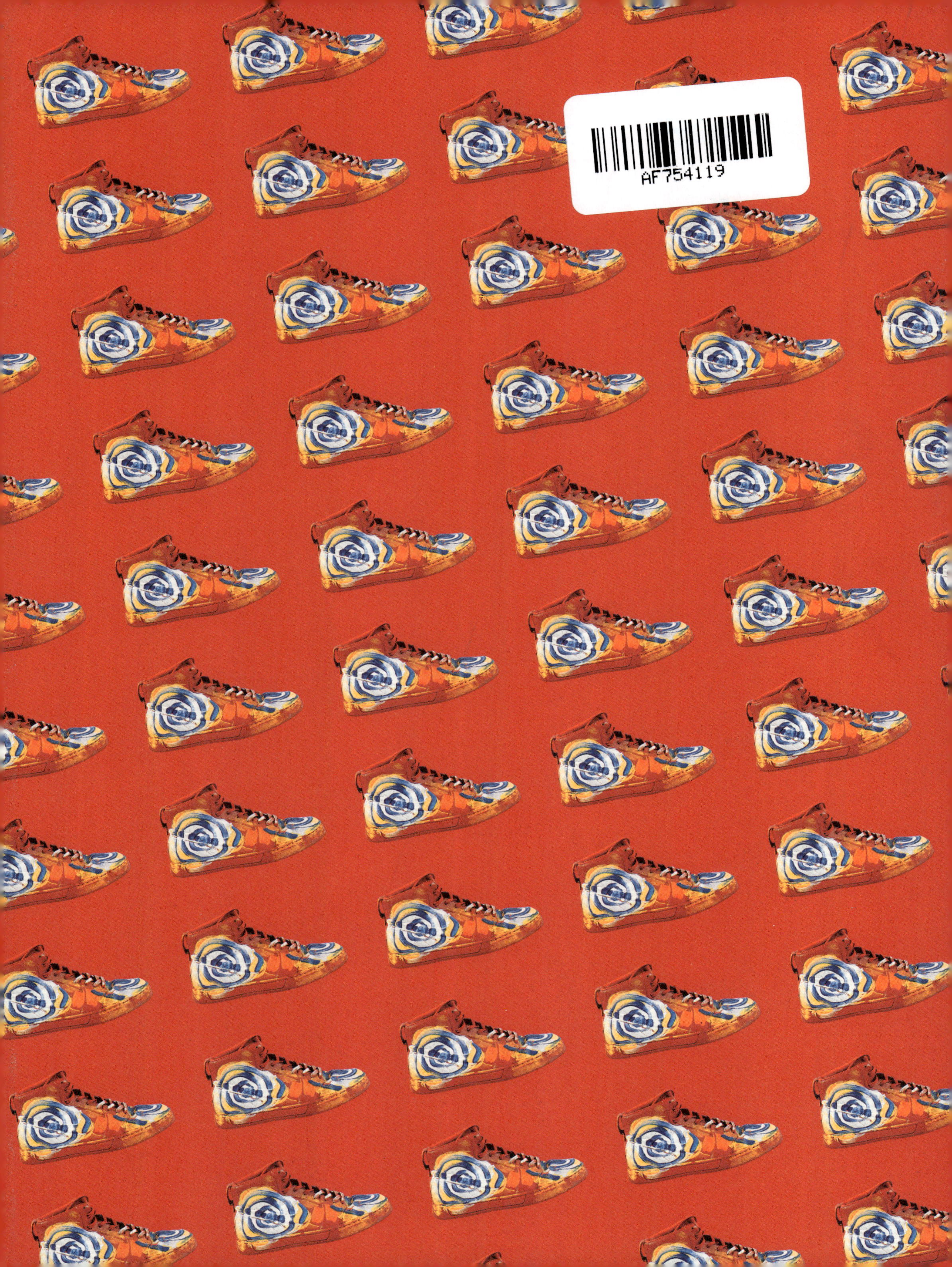

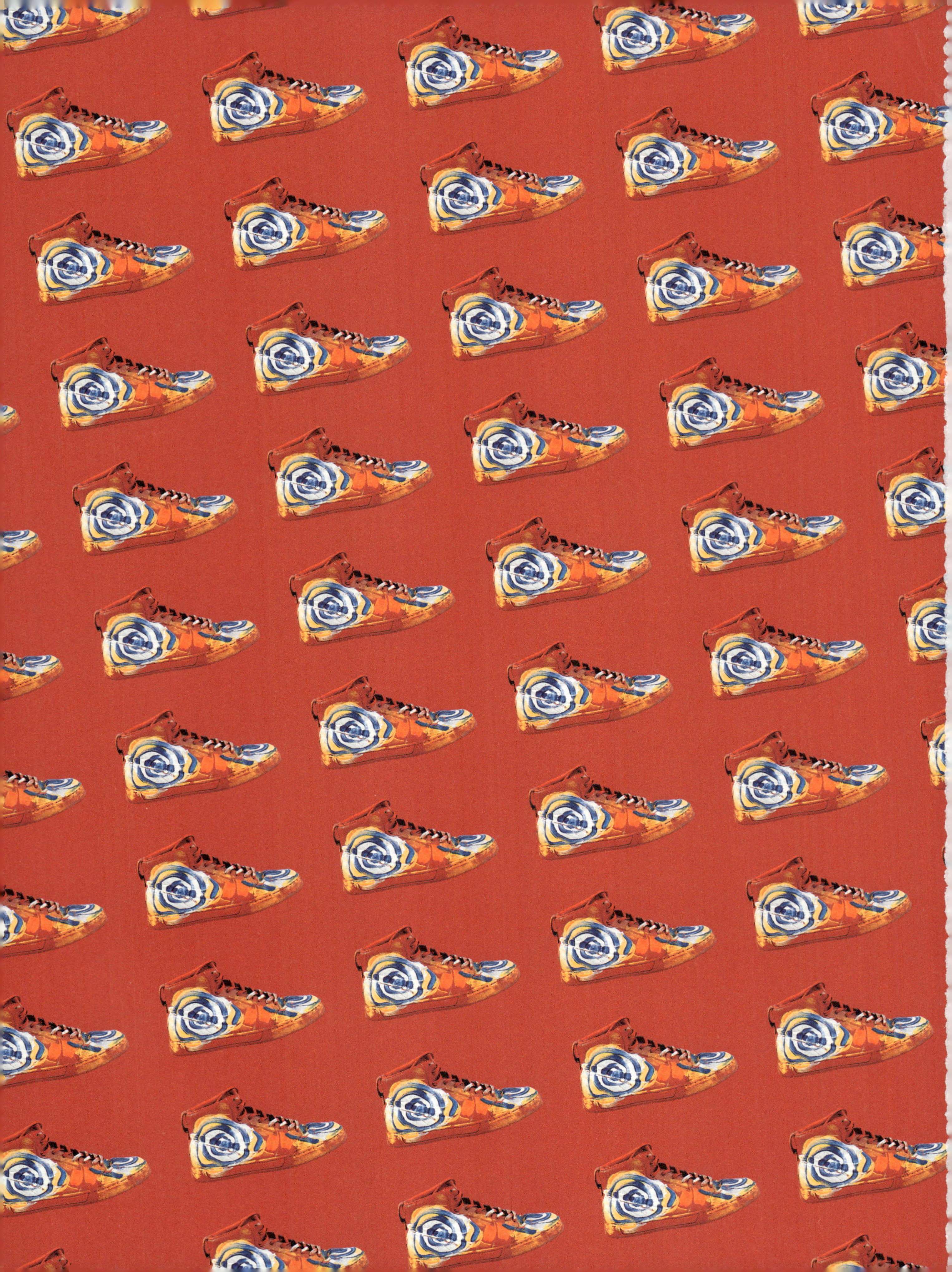

RONNIE WOOD ARTIST

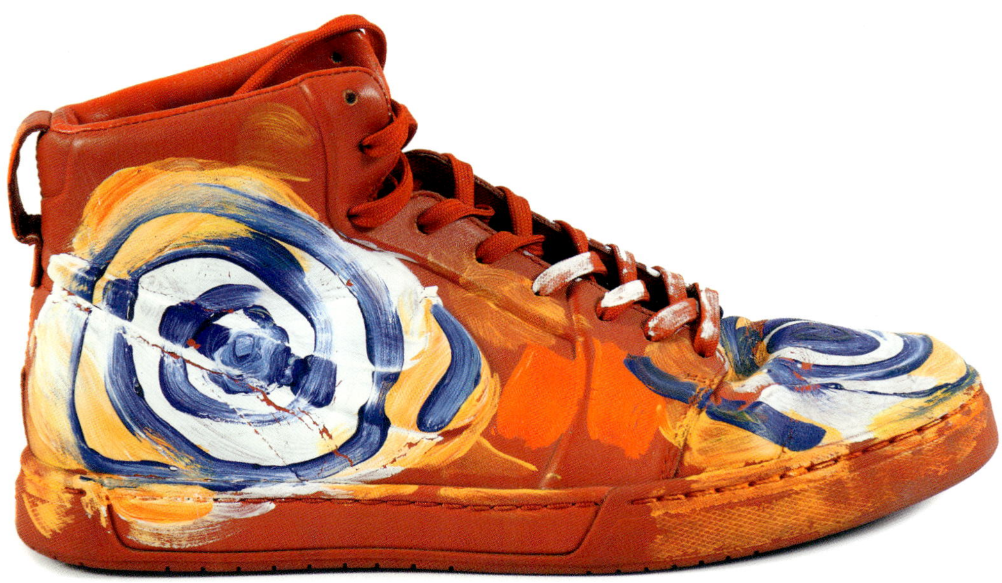

*"Dedicated to my mother Mercy Leah Elizabeth,
my father Archie, and my brothers Ted and Art,
for their relentless encouragement throughout my life."*

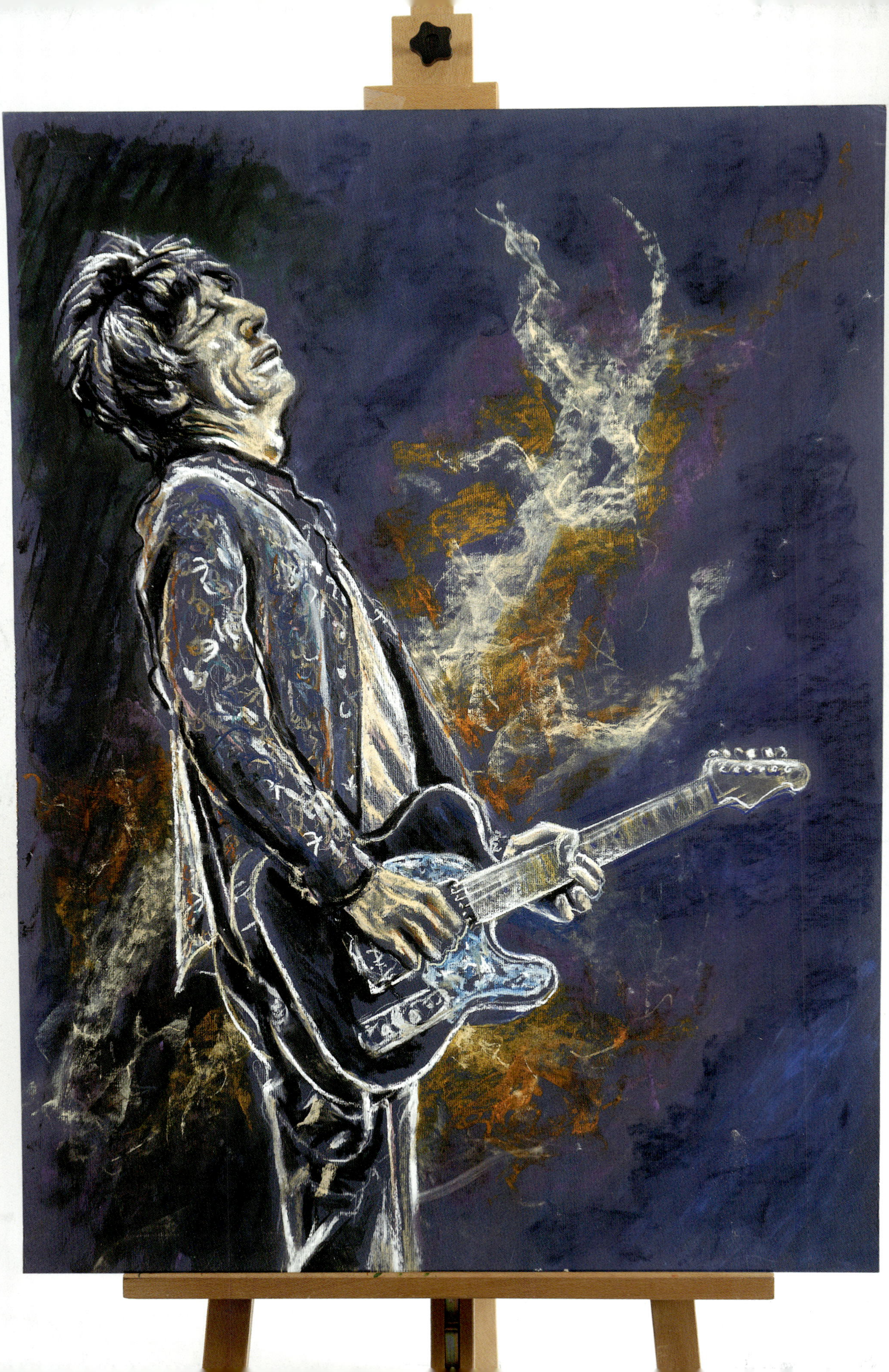

RONNIE WOOD
ARTIST

intro EMMANUEL GUIGON

outro KEITH RICHARDS

with 377 illustrations

Thames & Hudson

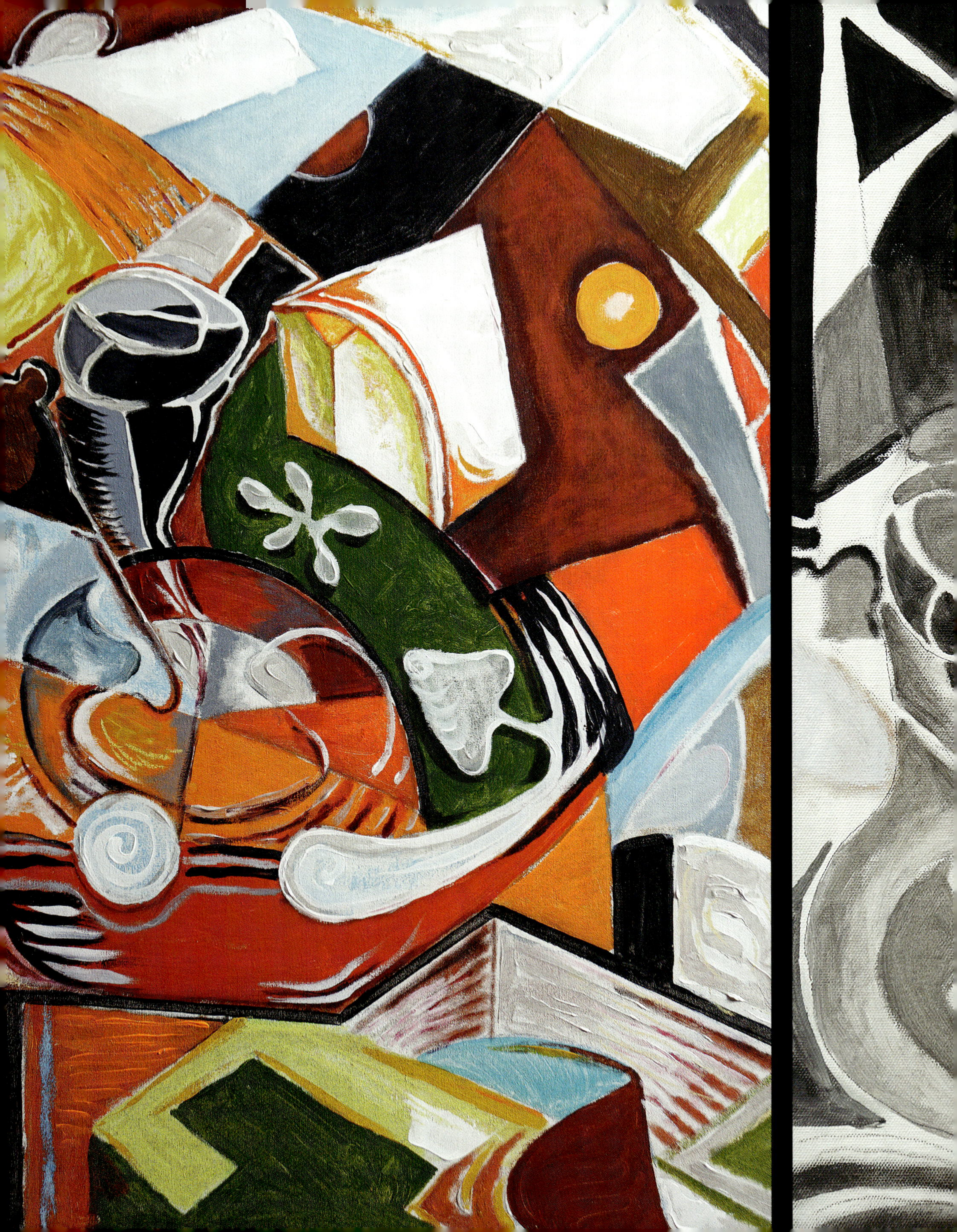

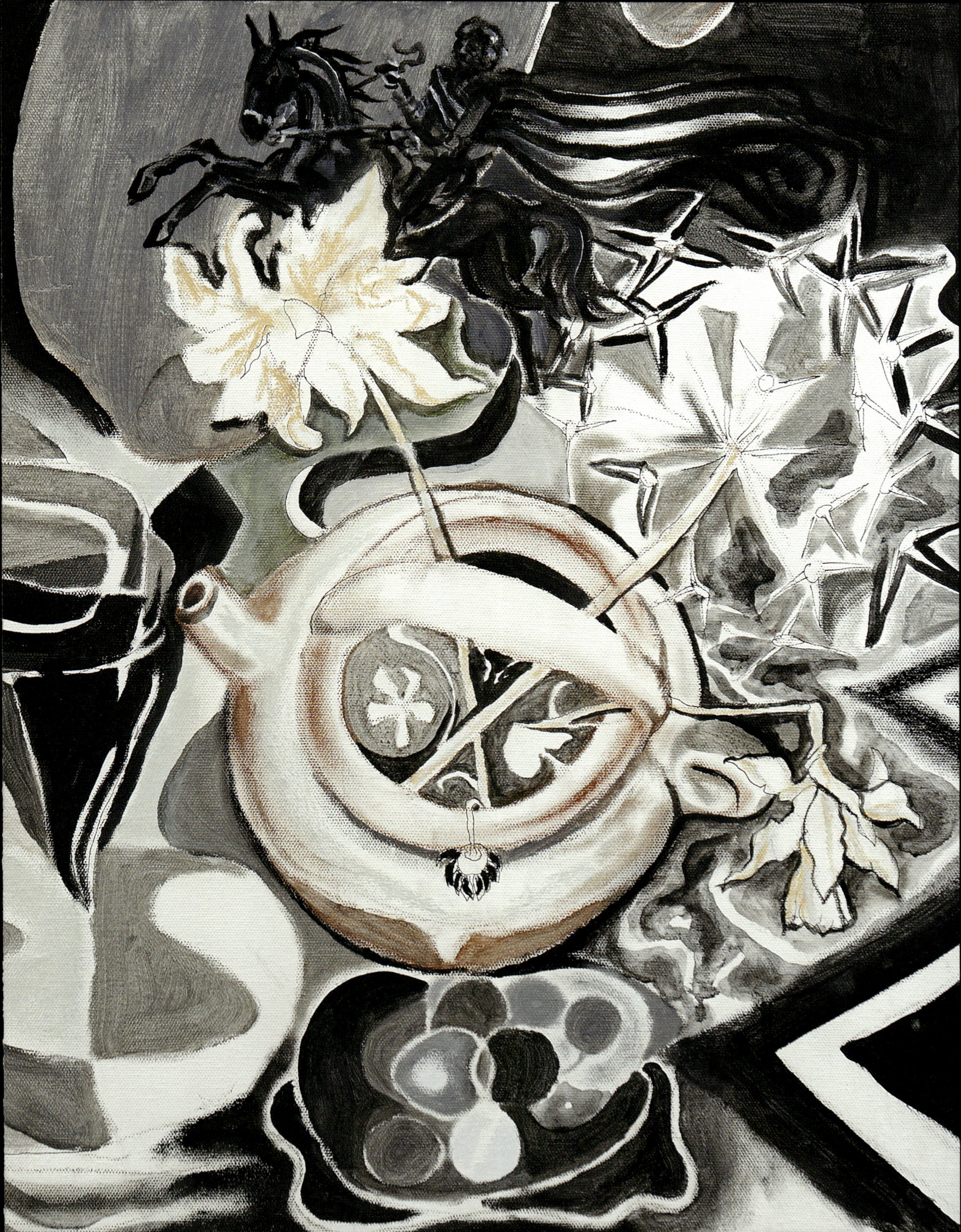

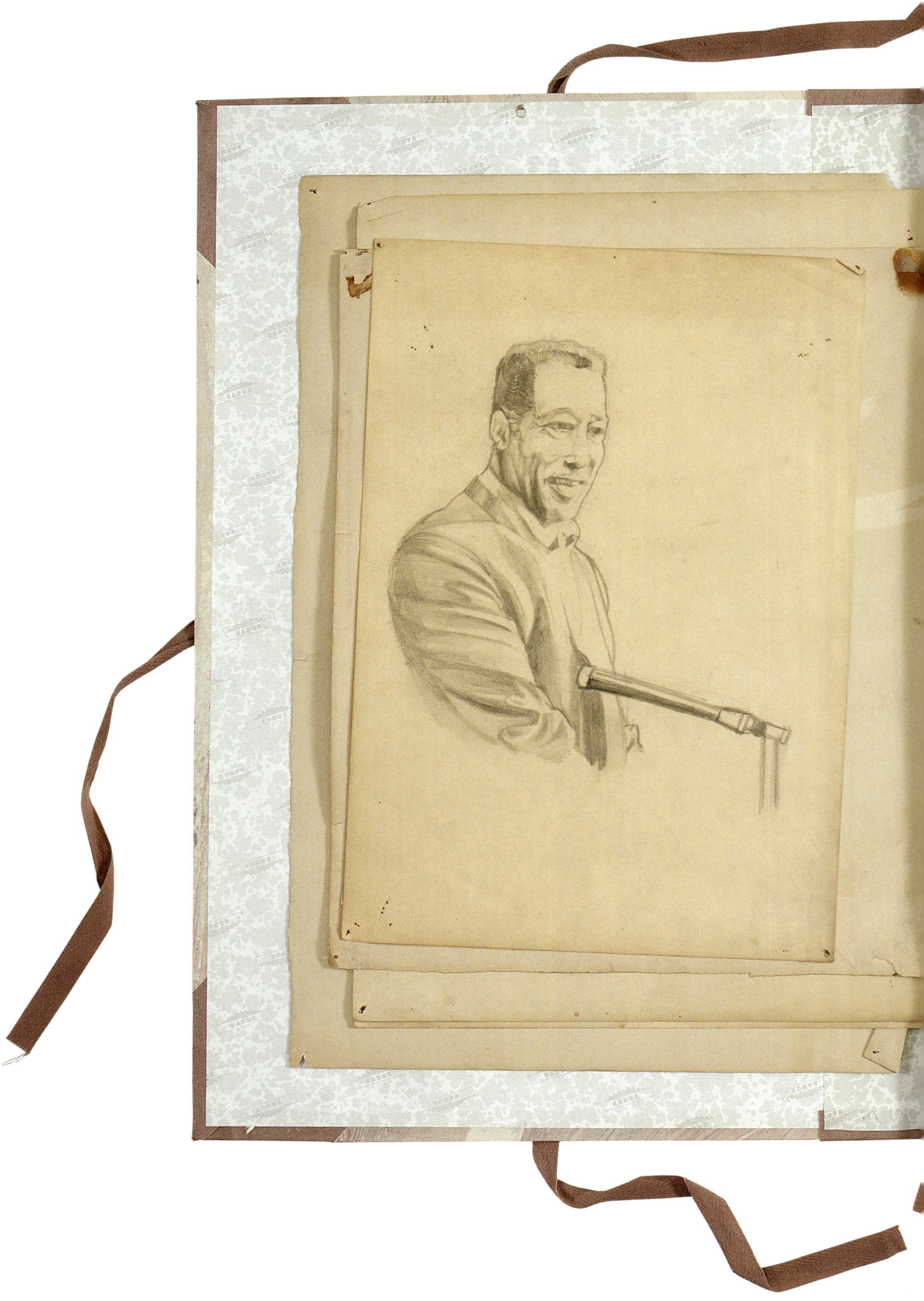

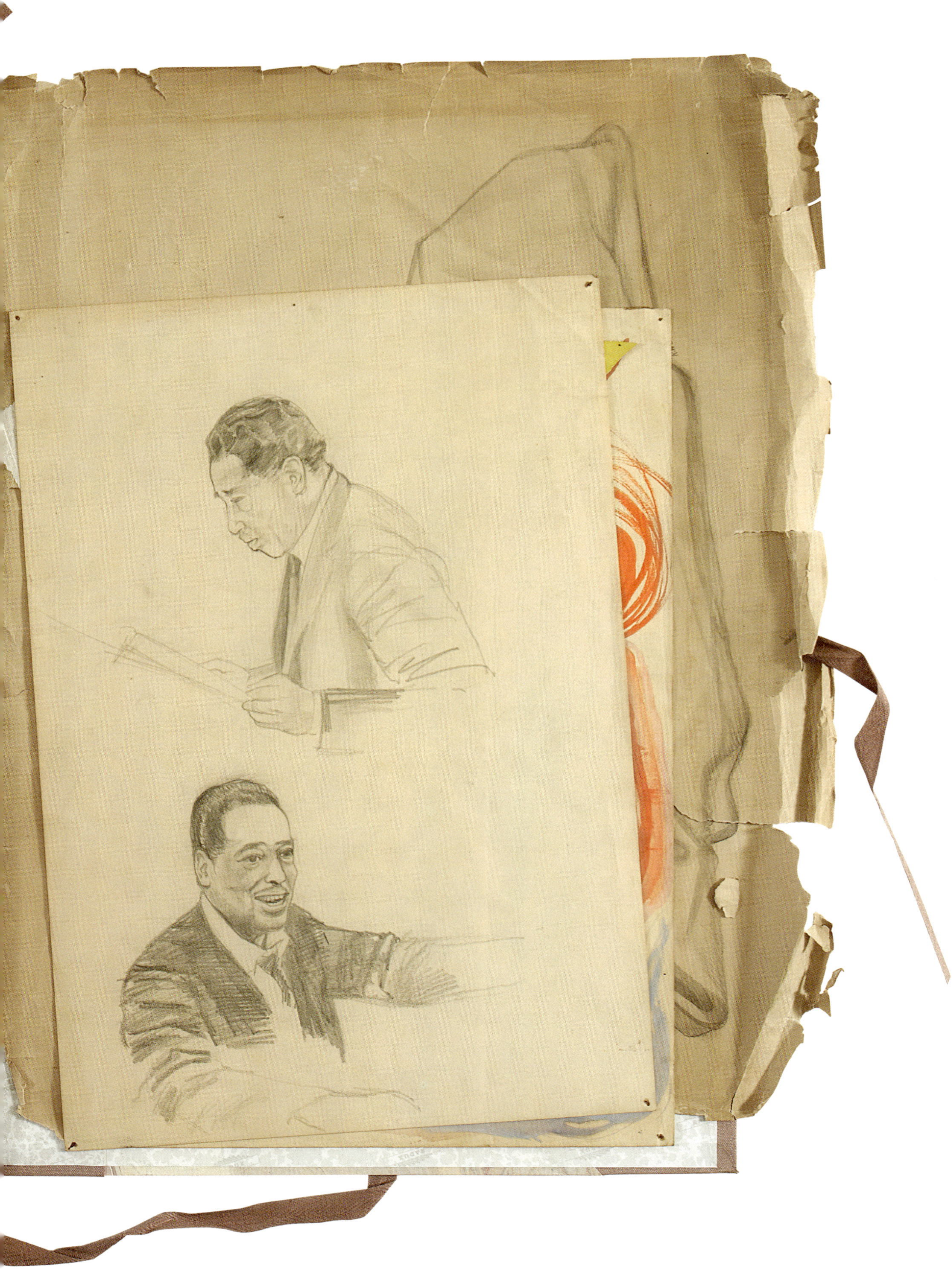

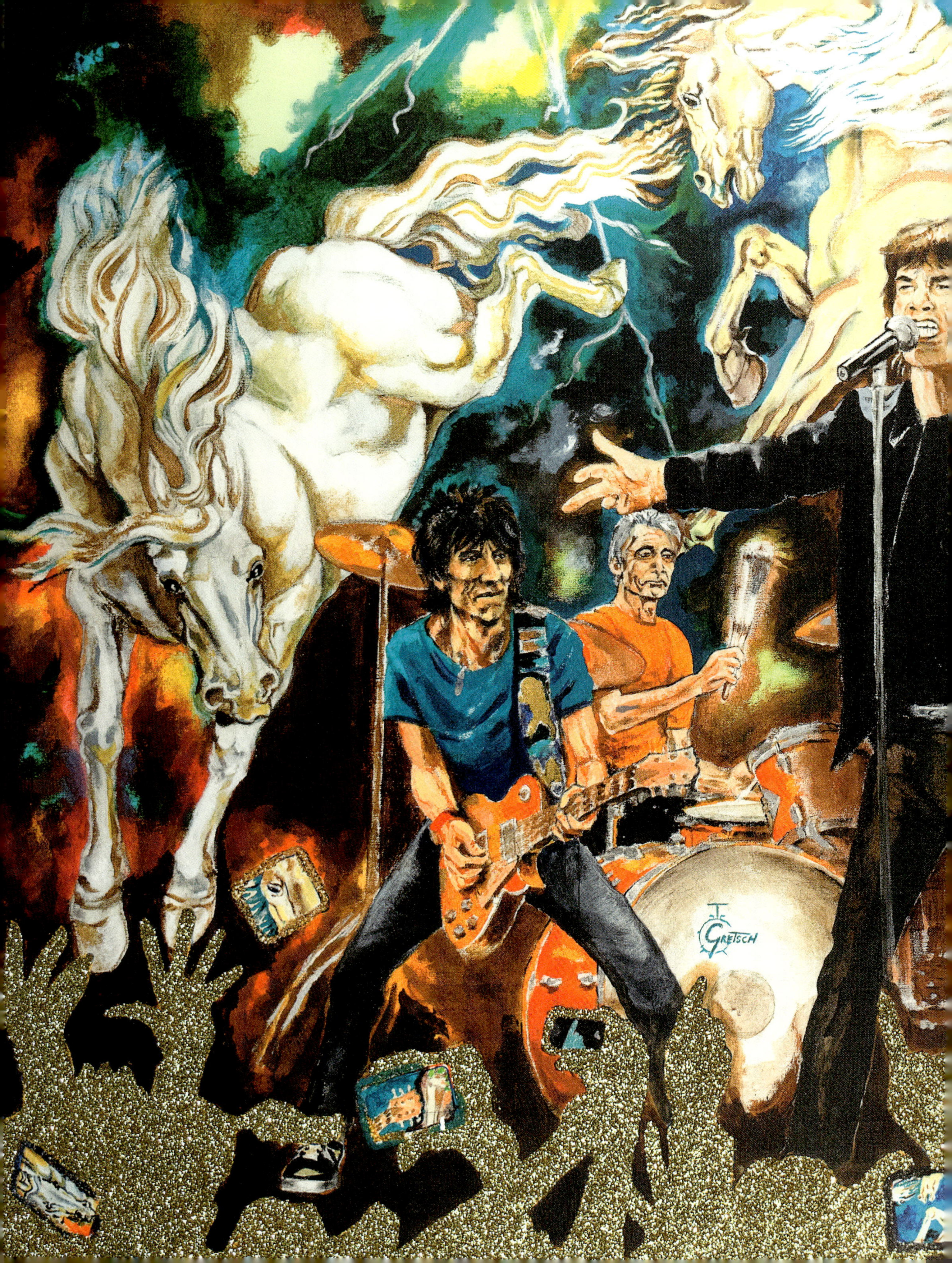
GRETSCH

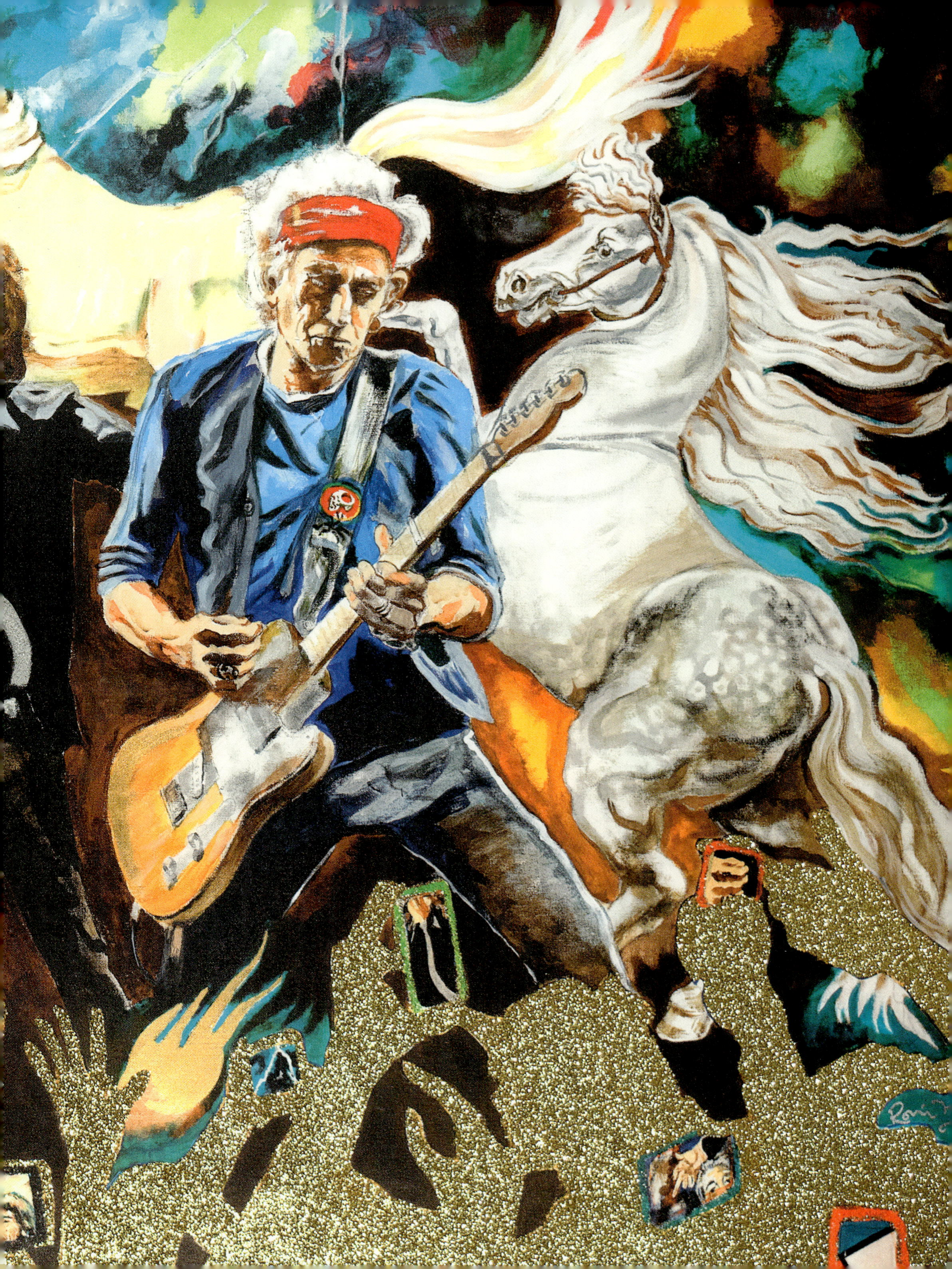

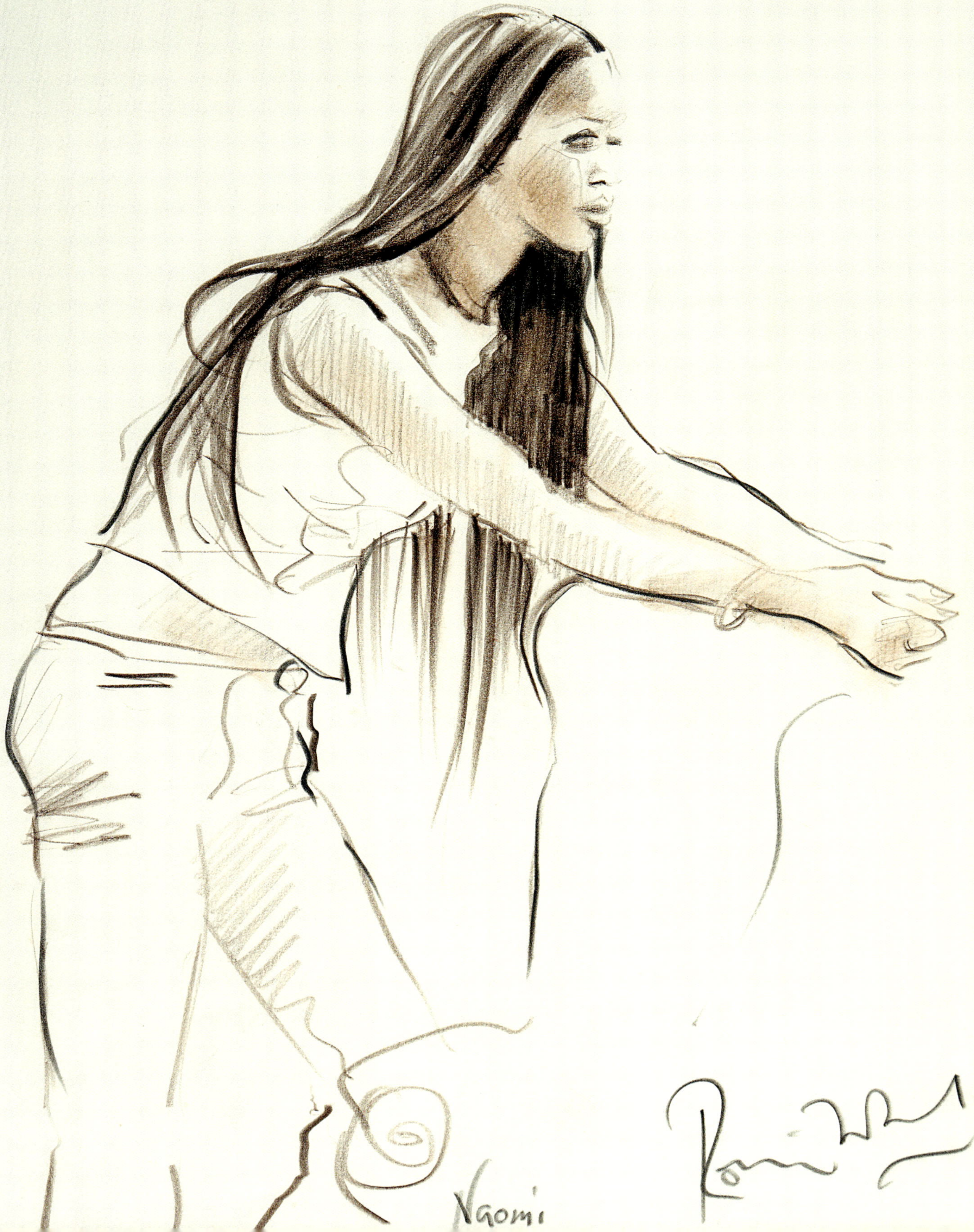
Naomi

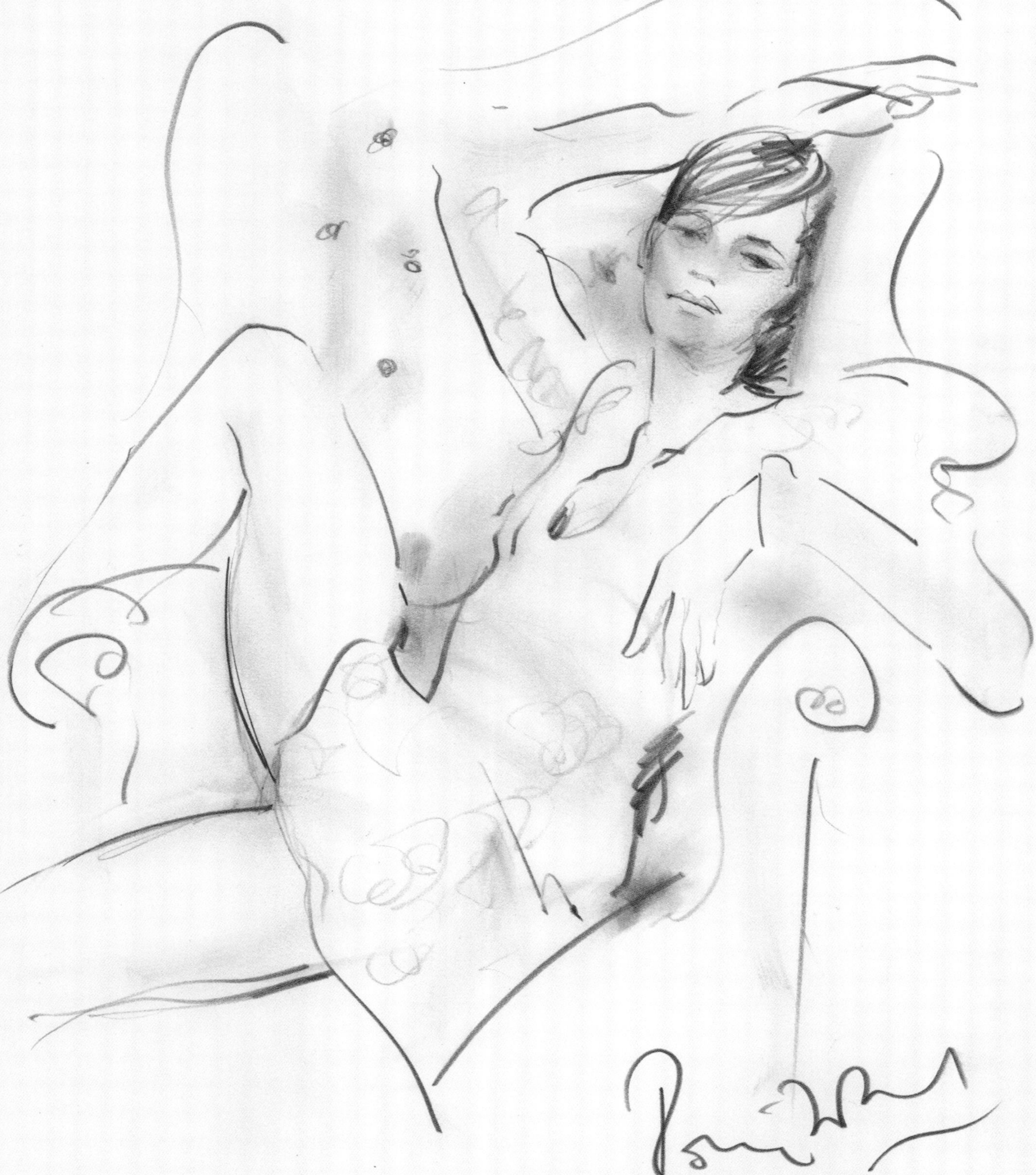

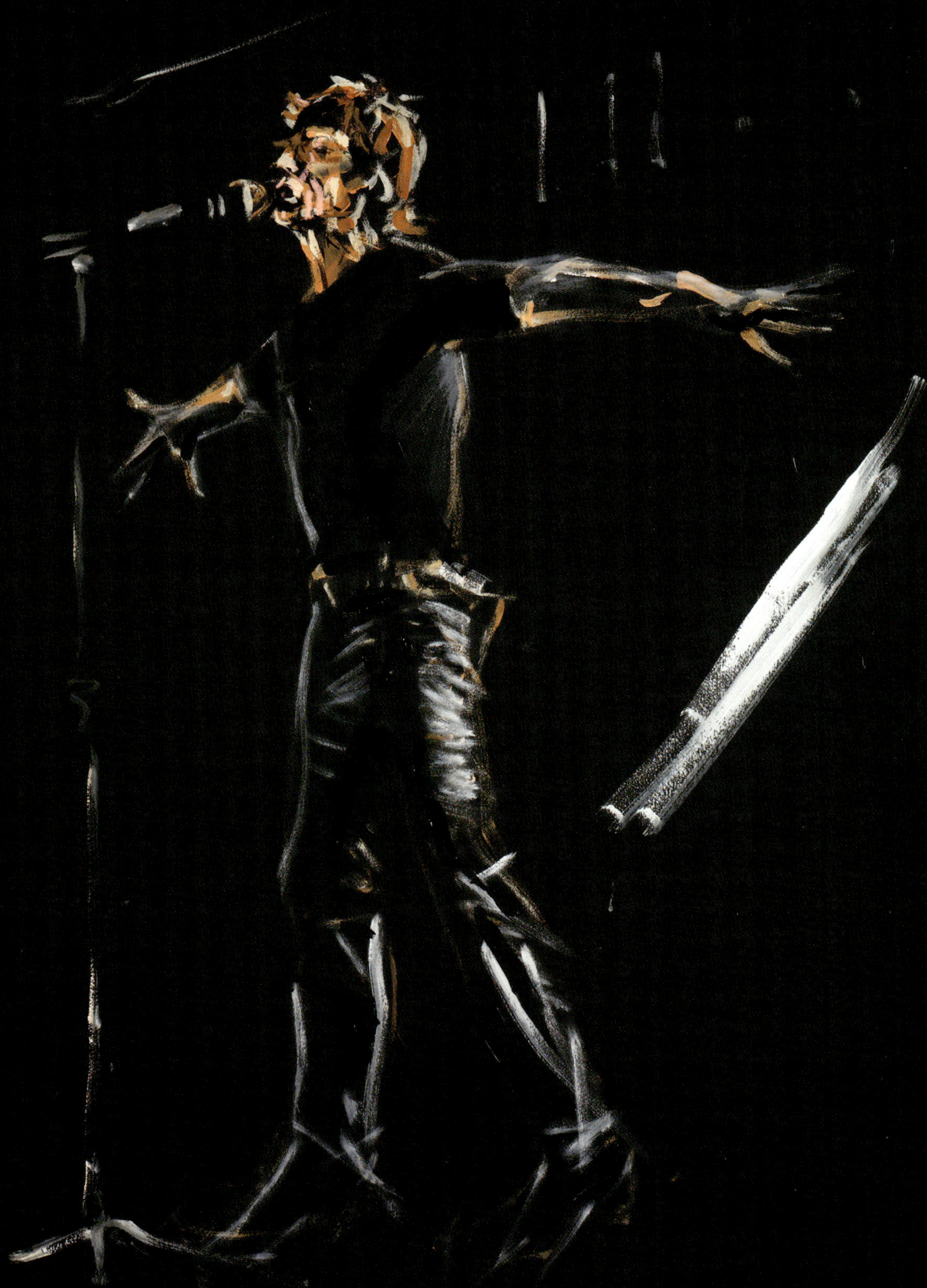

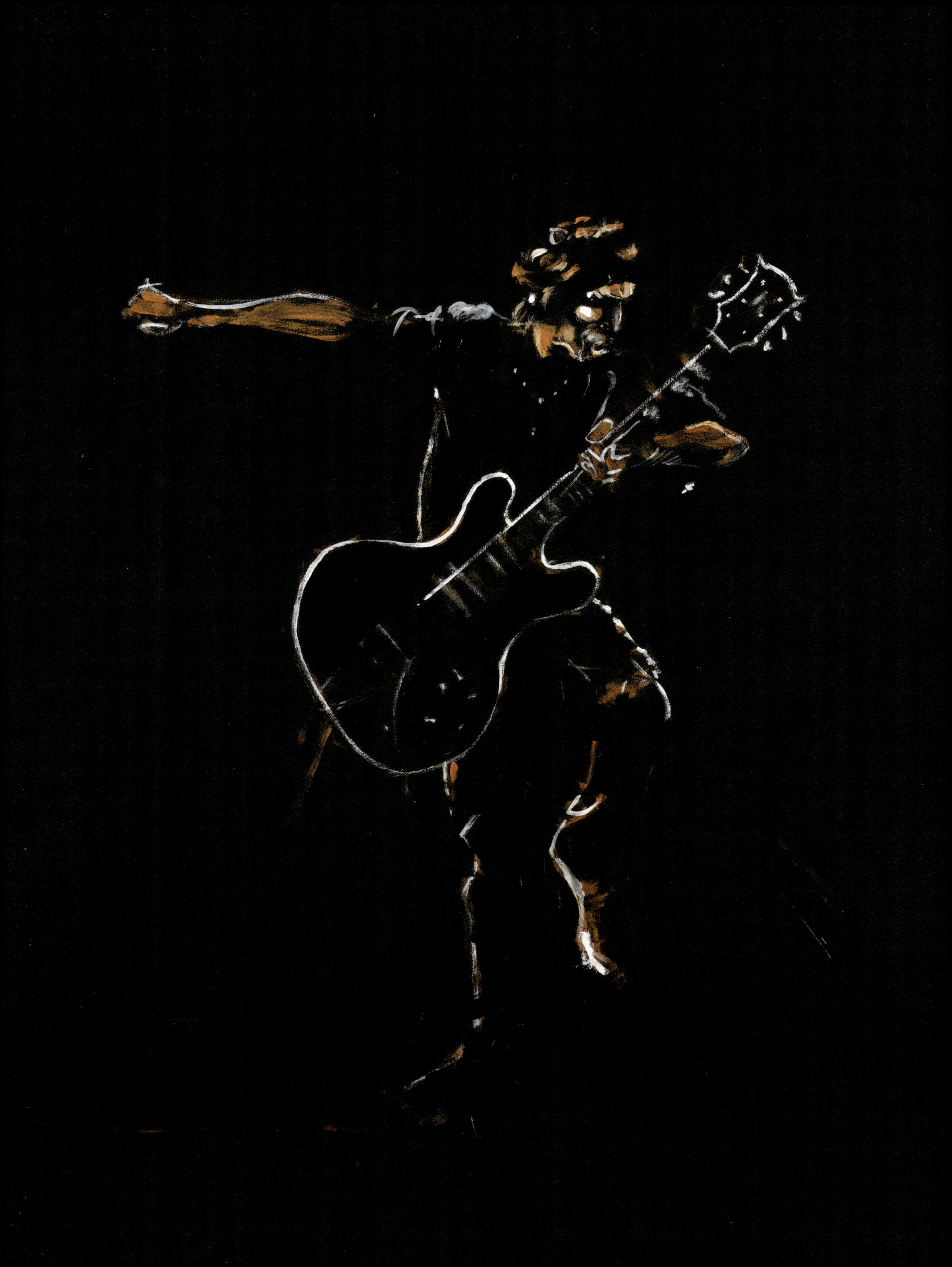

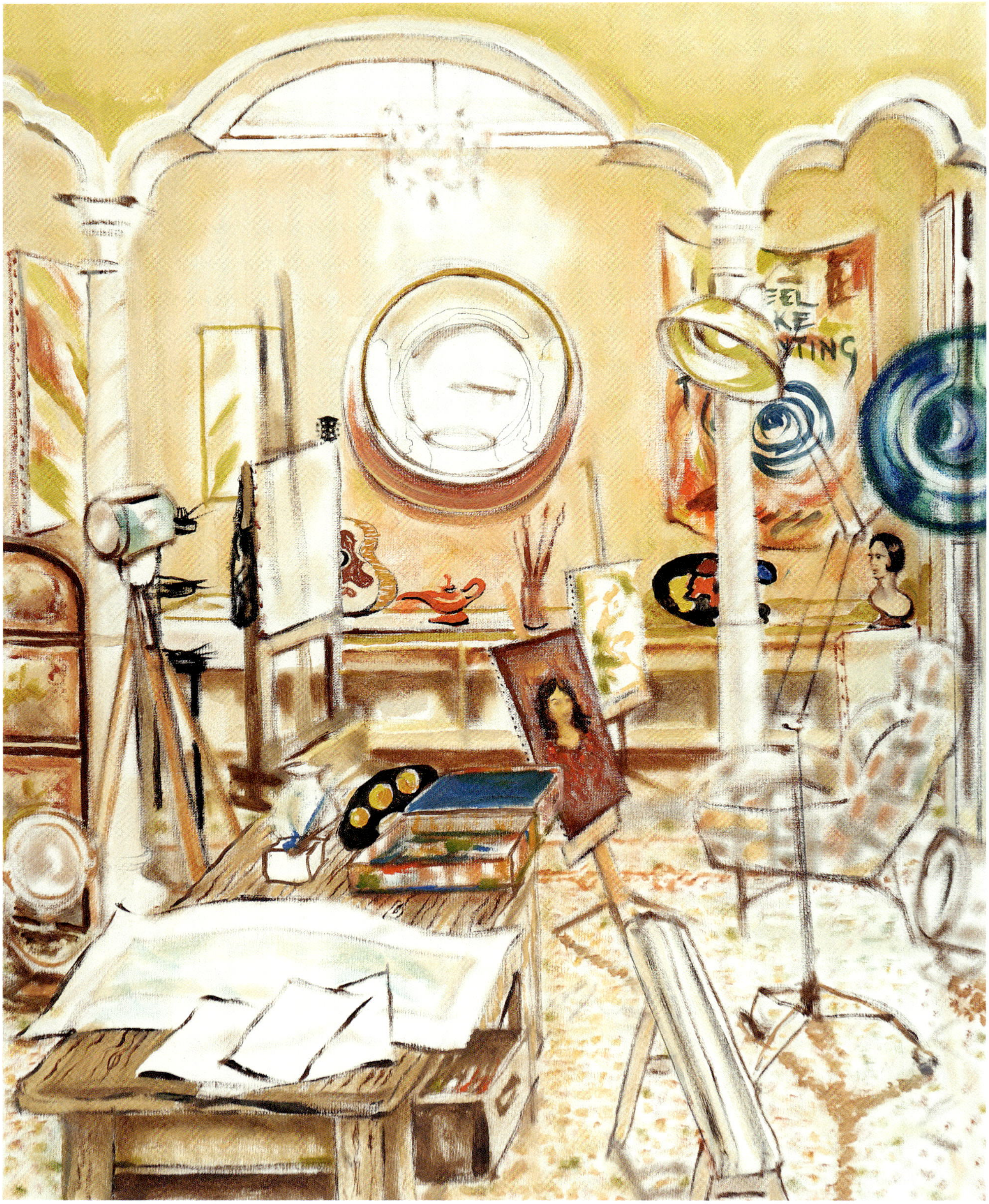

ABOVE: *My Barcelona Studio* | 2015 | acrylic on canvas | 73 × 60 cm
PAGE 1: *Painted Sneaker* | 2009 | acrylic on leather | size 9 (UK)
PAGE 2: *Self-Portrait II* | 2016 | pastel on board | 84 × 59 cm
PAGE 4: *Recurring Things* | 2016 | acrylic and pastel on paper | 112 × 74 cm
PAGES 4–5: *Allium Spikes* | 2015 | acrylic and pastel on paper | 112 × 74 cm
PAGES 6–7: *Duke Ellington* | 1962–64 | pencil on paper | 35 × 25 cm
PAGES 8–9: *Renaissance Horses* | 2013 | acrylic and pastel on paper 121 × 185 cm
PAGE 10: *Naomi Campbell* | 2002 | coloured pencil on paper | 42 × 29 cm
PAGE 11: *Kate Moss* | 2002 | coloured pencil on paper | 42 × 29 cm
PAGE 12: *Full Stretch* | 2007 | acrylic and pastel on paper | 112 × 74 cm
PAGE 13: *The Doctor* | 2007 | acrylic and pastel on paper | 112 × 74 cm

CONTENTS

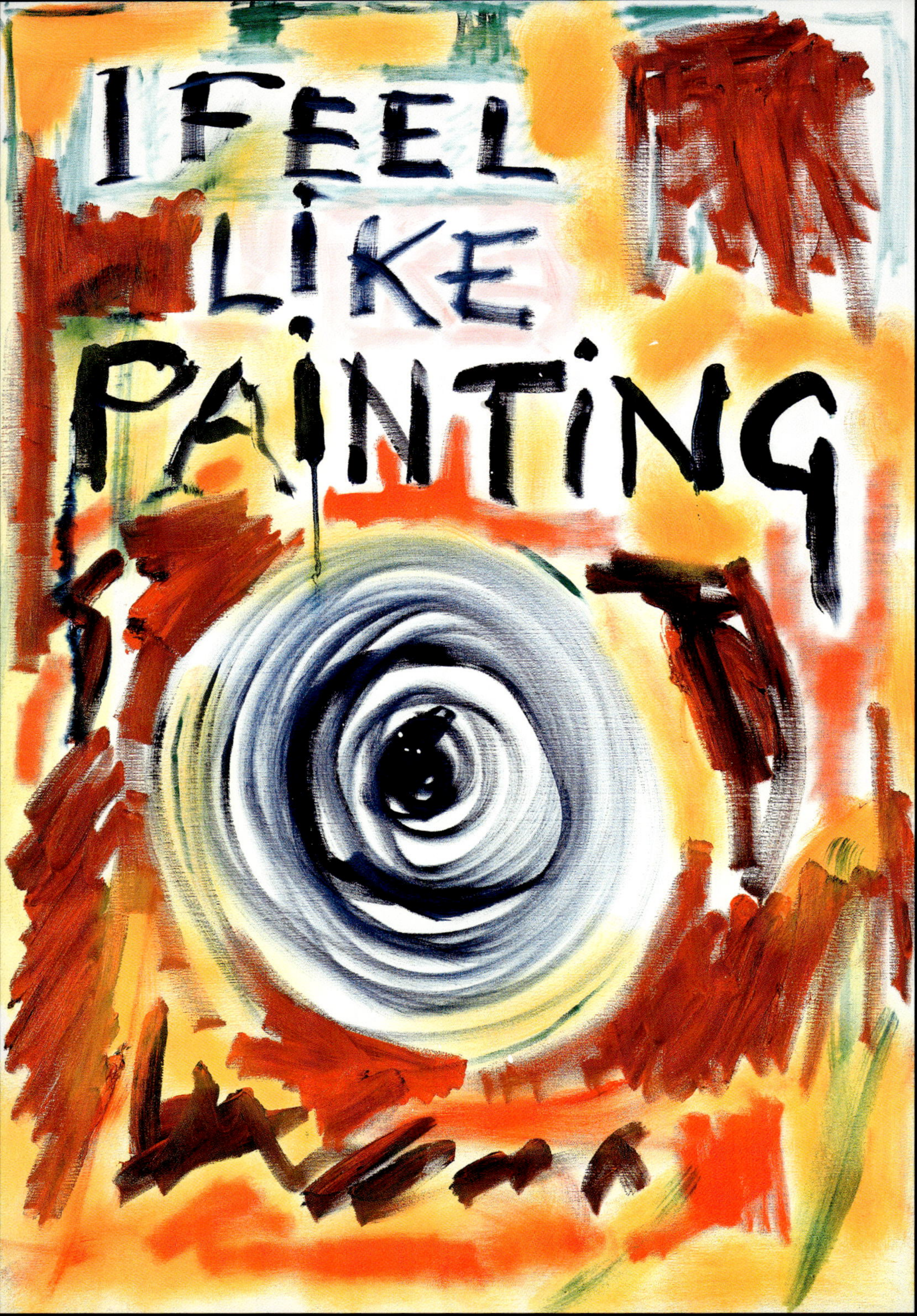
I FEEL
LIKE
PAINTING

INTRO
EMMANUEL GUIGON

Museu Picasso, Barcelona

People who think in conventional ways sometimes do not like mixing art forms. They strive to organize well-defined fields. But perhaps other pleasures spring up in other places: in scattered things, in sketchy descriptions. Miles away from certainties, far from the beaten track, a meditation on art and beauty can aim to roam freely. This is where you find poet-painters and painter-poets. There are musician-painters. Ingres, of course, and his famous violin. And musician-painters. From an early age, Ronnie Wood never ceased to draw and paint. *Nulla dies sin linea*. Not a day went by without a line. He never ceased to take a keen interest in painting. For him this was a personal passion, as witnessed by this book. On 13 February 2017, Ronnie Wood visited the Picasso Museum in Barcelona, where he stays from time to time, accompanied by Sally and their twins. We lingered in front of the museum's masterpieces from the artist's blue period and pink period – Ronnie once even painted a portrait of Picasso – *La belle Margot*, *Señora Canals*, *L'Arlequin* and the extraordinary series of the *Meninas* painted by Picasso in 1957 after Velázquez. But he enthused about the sketches, the small pictures of Catalan landscapes, extremely sensitive and delicate. He had the enchanted eye of someone who truly looks. And of a connoisseur. A few days later, we met in his Barcelona apartment-studio, in a magnificent building from Gaudí's day. By a strange coincidence, we are neighbours. There I discover dozens of Ronnie's paintings: portraits of the Rolling Stones and of his musician friends, a sort of snapshot of ephemeral moments of his life, his concert tours, his rehearsals, captured in mid-air. They are like a diary of "lived moments" that add up to a manifestation and a tribute to energy – where, in his own way, he casts panic in the middle of ceremoniousness. But there are also more intimate works, still lifes and landscapes that I like particularly, views from balconies or the street seen from a window. In these he celebrates the pavings; he pays homage to the land and the places. The starting point is always emotion. Perhaps the power of these simple images resides in the way they recall this self-evident reality: painting, even when it defines itself stridently as form and colour, cannot claim to cut forever the umbilical cord that ties it to the world and to everyday life. Ronnie Wood is a painter of fleeting instants. All that matters is the truth of the image, the tremors of time.

Emmanuel Guigon, Barcelona

OPPOSITE: *I Feel Like Painting* | 2009 | acrylic on canvas | 99 × 61 cm

OVERLEAF: *Life Lines – A Day at a Time* | 2001 | mixed media on paper | 60 × 90 cm

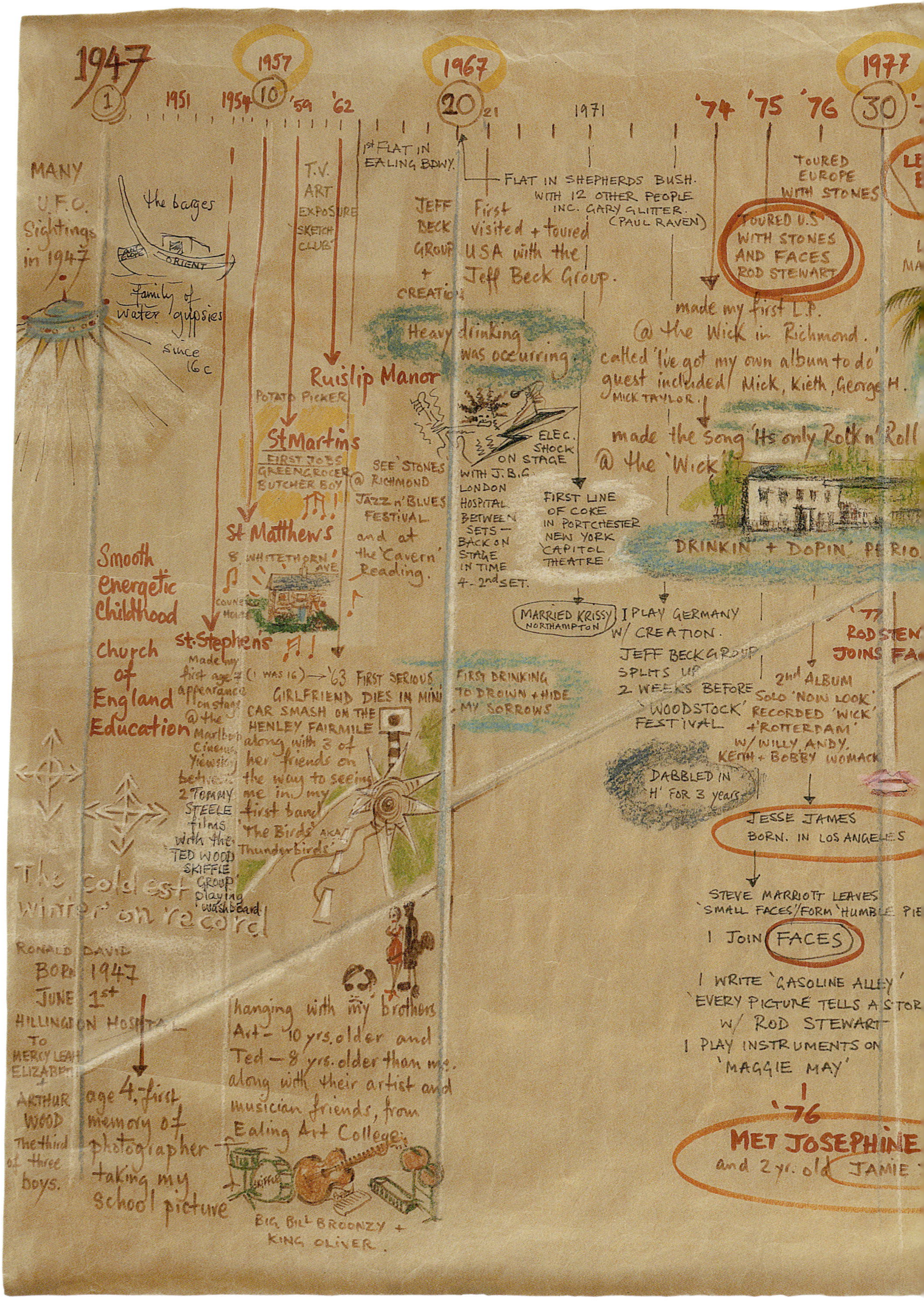

1947
1
1951
1954
1957
10
'59
'62
1967
20
21
1971
'74
'75
'76
1977
30
MANY U.F.O. Sightings in 1947
the barges
ORIENT
Family of water gypsies since 16 c
T.V. ART EXPOSURE SKETCH CLUB
1st FLAT IN EALING BDWY.
FLAT IN SHEPHERDS BUSH. WITH 12 OTHER PEOPLE INC. GARY GLITTER. (PAUL RAVEN)
JEFF BECK GROUP + CREATION
First visited + toured USA with the Jeff Beck Group.
TOURED EUROPE WITH STONES
TOURED U.S. WITH STONES AND FACES ROD STEWART
made my first L.P. @ the Wick in Richmond. called 'I've got my own album to do' guest included Mick, Kieth, George H. MICK TAYLOR.
made the song 'It's only Rock n' Roll' @ the 'Wick'
Heavy drinking was occuring.
Ruislip Manor
POTATO PICKER
St Martin's
FIRST JOBS GREENGROCER BUTCHER BOY
SEE STONES @ RICHMOND JAZZ n' BLUES FESTIVAL and at the 'Cavern' Reading.
ELEC. SHOCK ON STAGE WITH J.B.G. LONDON HOSPITAL BETWEEN SETS – BACK ON STAGE IN TIME 4 – 2nd SET.
FIRST LINE OF COKE IN PORTCHESTER NEW YORK CAPITOL THEATRE
DRINKIN' + DOPIN' PERIO
St Matthew's
8 WHITETHORN AVE
COUNCIL HOUSE
Smooth energetic Childhood
Church of England Education
St. Stephens
Made my first age 7 appearance on stage @ the Marlboro Cinema, Yiewsley between 2 TOMMY STEELE films with the TED WOOD SKIFFLE GROUP playing washboard
(I WAS 16) → '63 FIRST SERIOUS GIRLFRIEND DIES IN MINI CAR SMASH ON THE HENLEY FAIRMILE along with 3 of her friends on the way to seeing me in my first band 'The Birds' AKA Thunderbirds'
FIRST DRINKING TO DROWN + HIDE MY SORROWS
MARRIED KRISSY NORTHAMPTON
I PLAY GERMANY W/ CREATION.
JEFF BECK GROUP SPLITS UP 2 WEEKS BEFORE 'WOODSTOCK' FESTIVAL
'77 ROD STEW JOINS FA
2nd ALBUM SOLO 'NOW LOOK' RECORDED 'WICK' + ROTTERDAM' W/ WILLY, ANDY, KEITH + BOBBY WOMACK
DABBLED IN 'H' FOR 3 years
JESSE JAMES BORN. IN LOS ANGELES
STEVE MARRIOTT LEAVES 'SMALL FACES'/FORM 'HUMBLE PIE
I JOIN FACES
I WRITE 'GASOLINE ALLEY' 'EVERY PICTURE TELLS A STOR W/ ROD STEWART
I PLAY INSTRUMENTS ON 'MAGGIE MAY'
'76
MET JOSEPHINE and 2 yr. old JAMIE
The coldest winter on record
RONALD DAVID BORN 1947 JUNE 1st HILLINGDON HOSPITAL To MERCY LEAH ELIZABETH + ARTHUR WOOD The third of three boys.
age 4 – first memory of photographer taking my school picture
hanging with my brothers Art – 10 yrs. older and Ted – 8 yrs. older than me, along with their artist and musician friends, from Ealing Art College.
BIG BILL BROONZY + KING OLIVER.

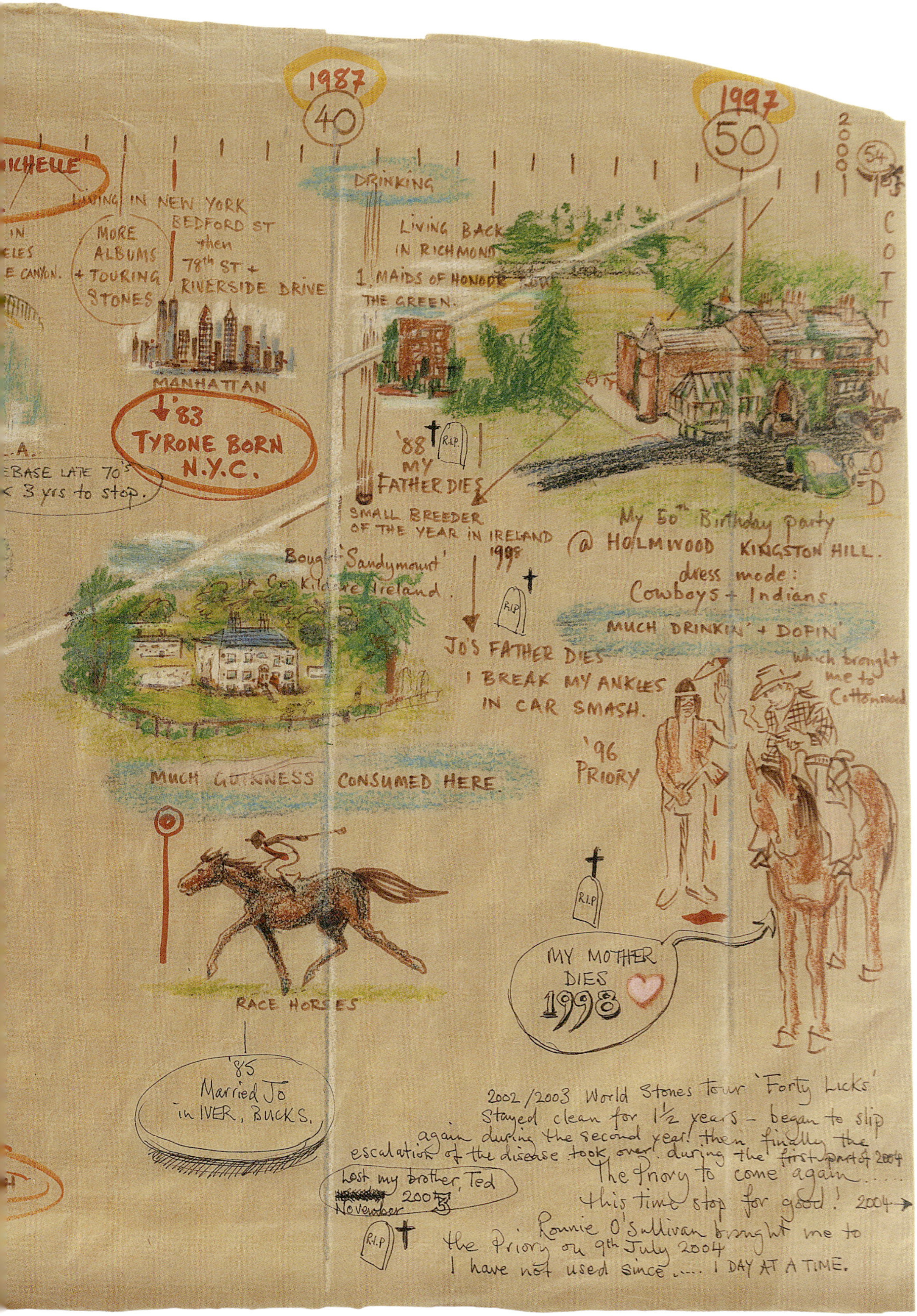

1987
40
1997
50
2000
54
'05
MICHELLE
LIVING IN NEW YORK
BEDFORD ST
then
78th ST + RIVERSIDE DRIVE
IN
ELES
E CANYON.
MORE ALBUMS + TOURING STONES
MANHATTAN
'83
TYRONE BORN
N.Y.C.
.A.
EBASE LATE 70's
x 3 yrs to stop.
DRINKING
LIVING BACK IN RICHMOND
1, MAIDS OF HONOUR ROW
THE GREEN.
'88 MY FATHER DIES
R.I.P.
SMALL BREEDER OF THE YEAR IN IRELAND 1998
COTTONWOOD
My 50th Birthday party
@ HOLMWOOD KINGSTON HILL.
dress mode:
Cowboys + Indians.
MUCH DRINKIN' + DOPIN'
which brought me to Cottonwood
Bought 'Sandymount' in Co. Kildare Ireland.
JO'S FATHER DIES
I BREAK MY ANKLES IN CAR SMASH.
'96 PRIORY
MUCH GUINNESS CONSUMED HERE.
RACE HORSES
MY MOTHER DIES 1998
'85
Married Jo in IVER, BUCKS.
2002/2003 World Stones tour 'Forty Licks'
Stayed clean for 1½ years – began to slip again during the second year! then finally the escalation of the disease took over! during the first part of 2004
The Priory to come again.....
this time stop for good! 2004 →
Lost my brother, Ted
November 2003
Ronnie O'Sullivan brought me to the Priory on 9th July 2004
I have not used since..... 1 DAY AT A TIME.

RONNIE WOOD
A LIFE IN ART

"From the moment I get up in the morning, I see everything as a painting."

I was born into a family of bargees, and my brothers and I were the first members of our family, in living memory, to have been born on dry land. The only art in my parent's life was the painting on the side of their barge; neither Mum nor Dad could draw, but both my brothers went to art school as teenagers and became commercial artists. They loved jazz, and with the blues being a close relative of jazz, music was always in our house. It was a natural progression as I grew up that I should be drawn to both art and music.

My brother Art was ten years older than me and Ted was eight years older; they both had bands. Art's was an R&B band, while Ted's was a jazz band. Art and Ted grew up during the war, so as kids they had no TV to watch and drawing became their way of expressing themselves. It was inevitable that "little Ronnie" followed them, nicking their paints to try and do my own thing. They especially loved drawing horses and, like them, I've always loved to paint horses.

When I went to school I loved my art classes; as a young kid, when my mum went to my school, they'd say, "You're the mother of the artist." Before I reached my teens, some of my drawings featured on the BBC's *Sketch Club* and one of them even won a prize, which furthered my interest in art. It means that I've been painting and drawing for seven decades, which is even longer than I've been playing music. But when I was young, I never really thought about the art that I did; I just did it. Later I went to Ealing Art School, after studying history of art at A level.

My brothers were the first to tell me about the old masters, showing me their work, and I've found their influence creeping into my own pieces – Caravaggio, Braque, Goya, Munch, Matisse, Rembrandt and Picasso. It's the same as playing music; I listen to guitarists like Grant Green, Matt "Guitar" Murphy, Big Bill Broonzy, Hubert Sumlin, Hop Wilson and Elmore James, and their playing styles influence my own playing. Ultimately, it all comes out as your own style.

After art school, I became a sign writer for a while, but only briefly. I learnt a lot from that job, especially the discipline that is involved. I tried getting a job at Pinewood Studios to paint scenery, but I couldn't get in because the union controlled everything; it was a closed shop.

When I was seventeen, I formed The Birds with some local friends. We got a record deal and released a number of singles, but we had no hits. In 1967 I joined the Jeff Beck Group as the bass player; Rod Stewart was the singer. Two years later, Rod and I joined forces with some of the Small Faces to become the Faces. During this time, my art was less to the fore as I was trying to make it in music, but as the Faces began to find success, I found more time for my art.

As a guitarist, I'm known for playing the slide guitar and very much as a rock guitar player – a defined genre. My art allows me to explore more. I break the confines

OVERLEAF: *Family on Barge in Paddington Basin* | 1999 | acrylic on canvas | 82 × 127 cm

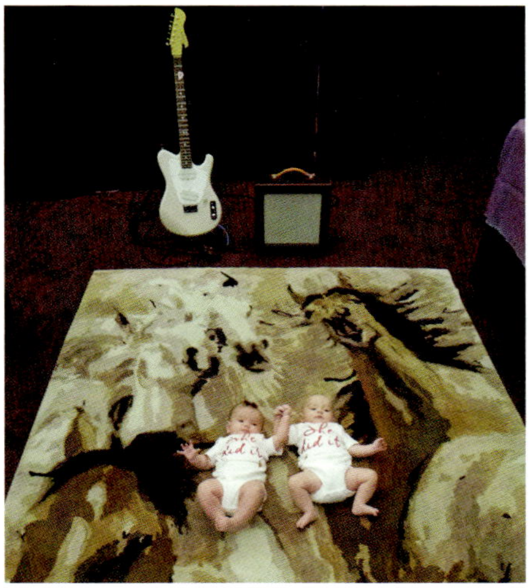

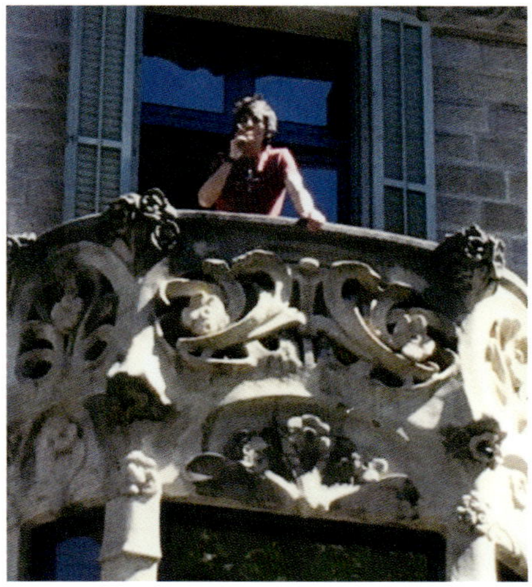

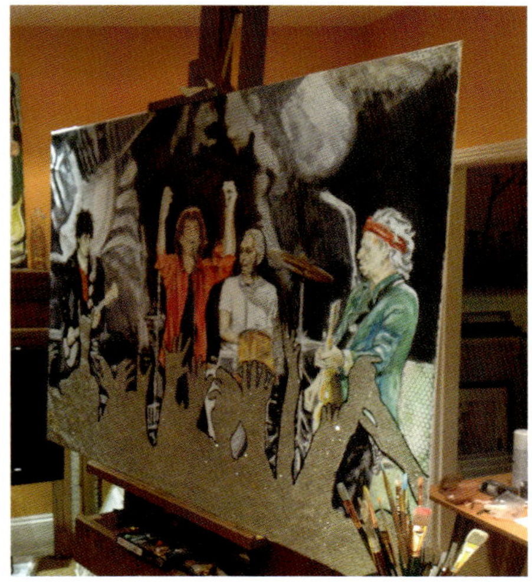

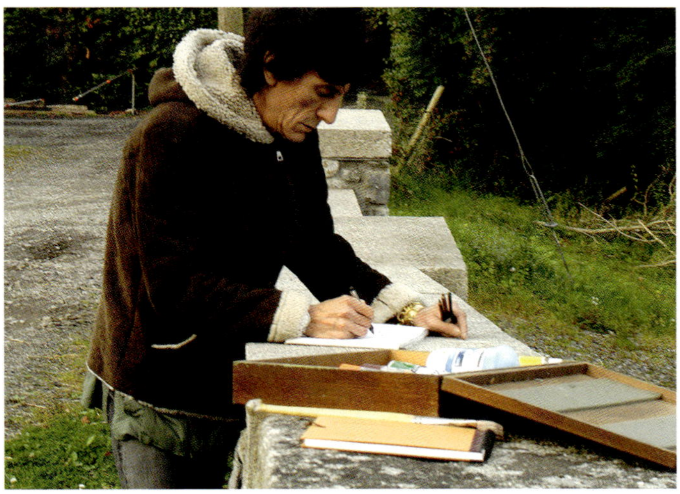

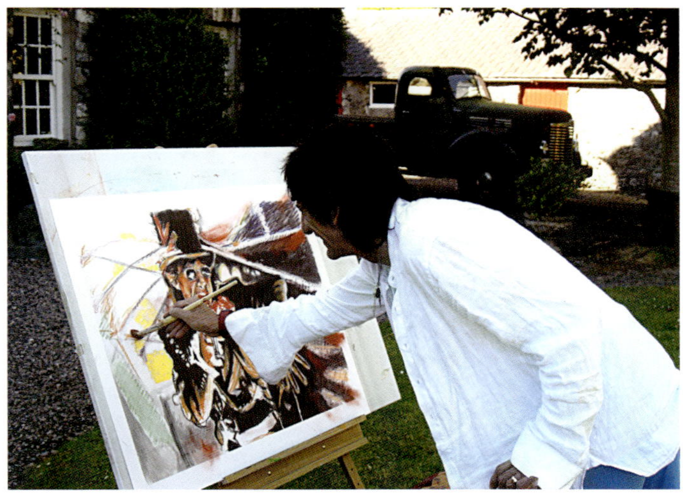

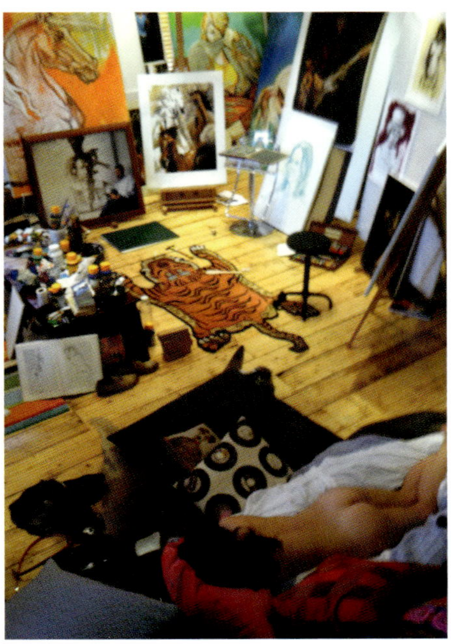

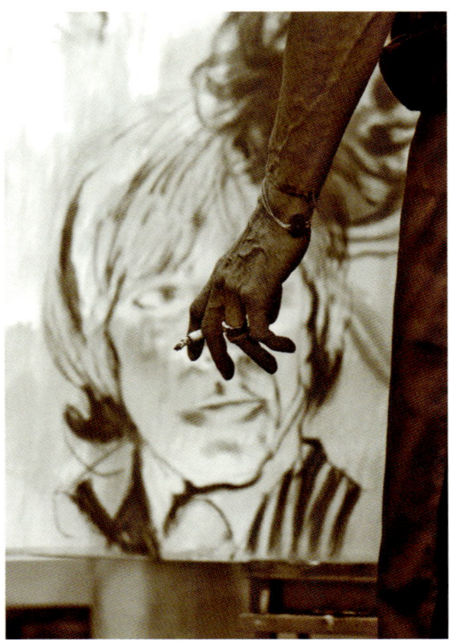

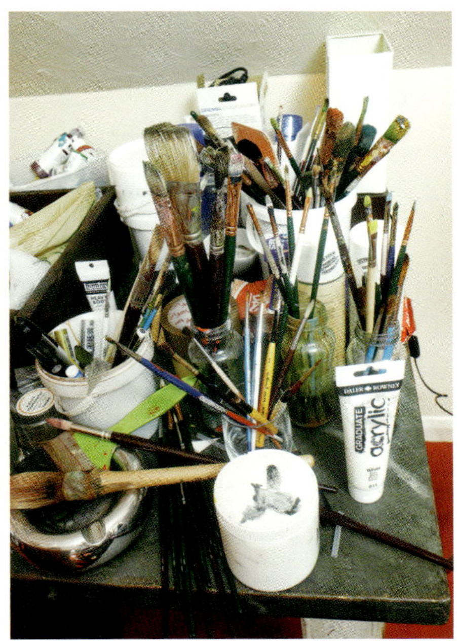
acrylic

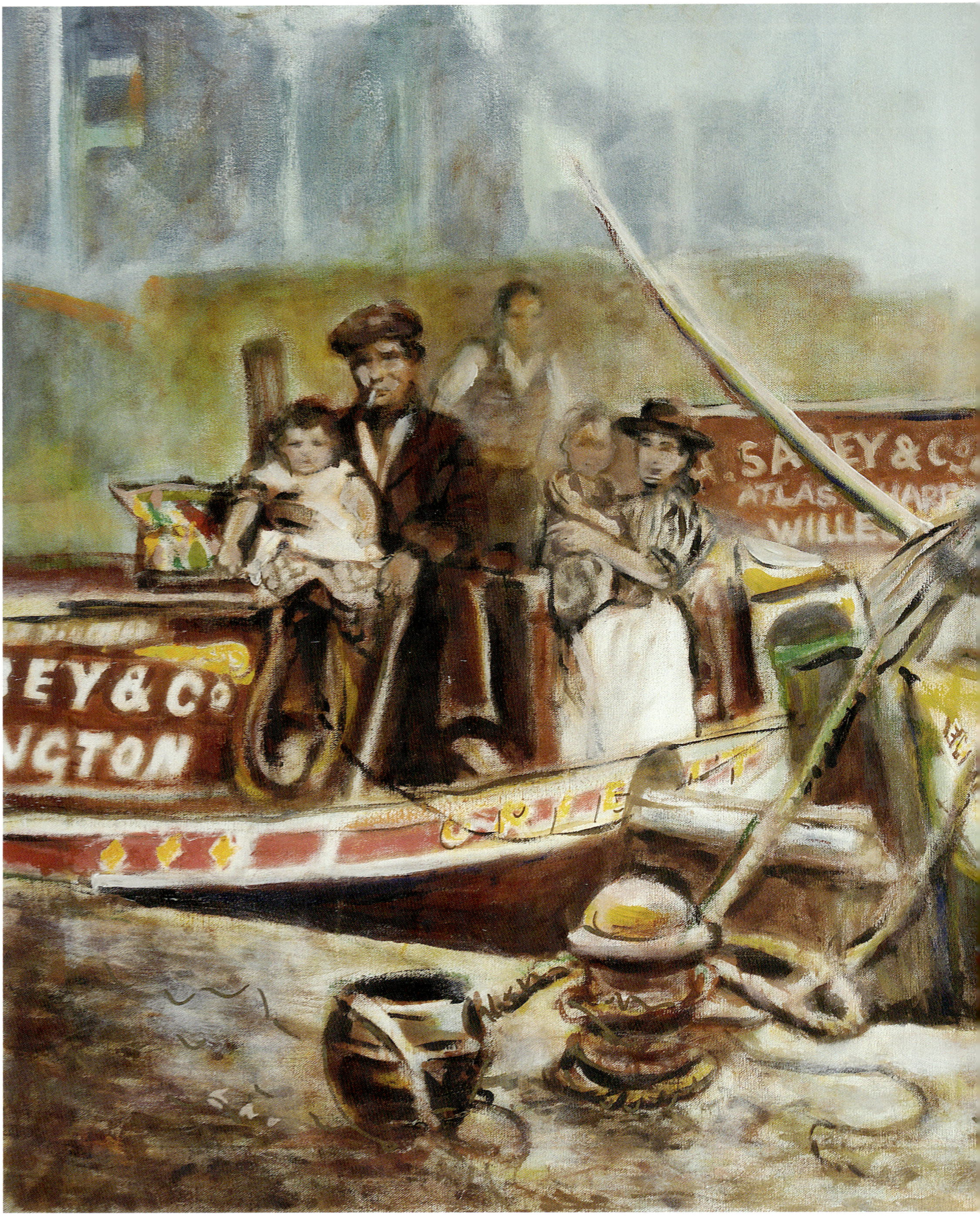
BEY&Co
NCTON
ATLAS
WILLE

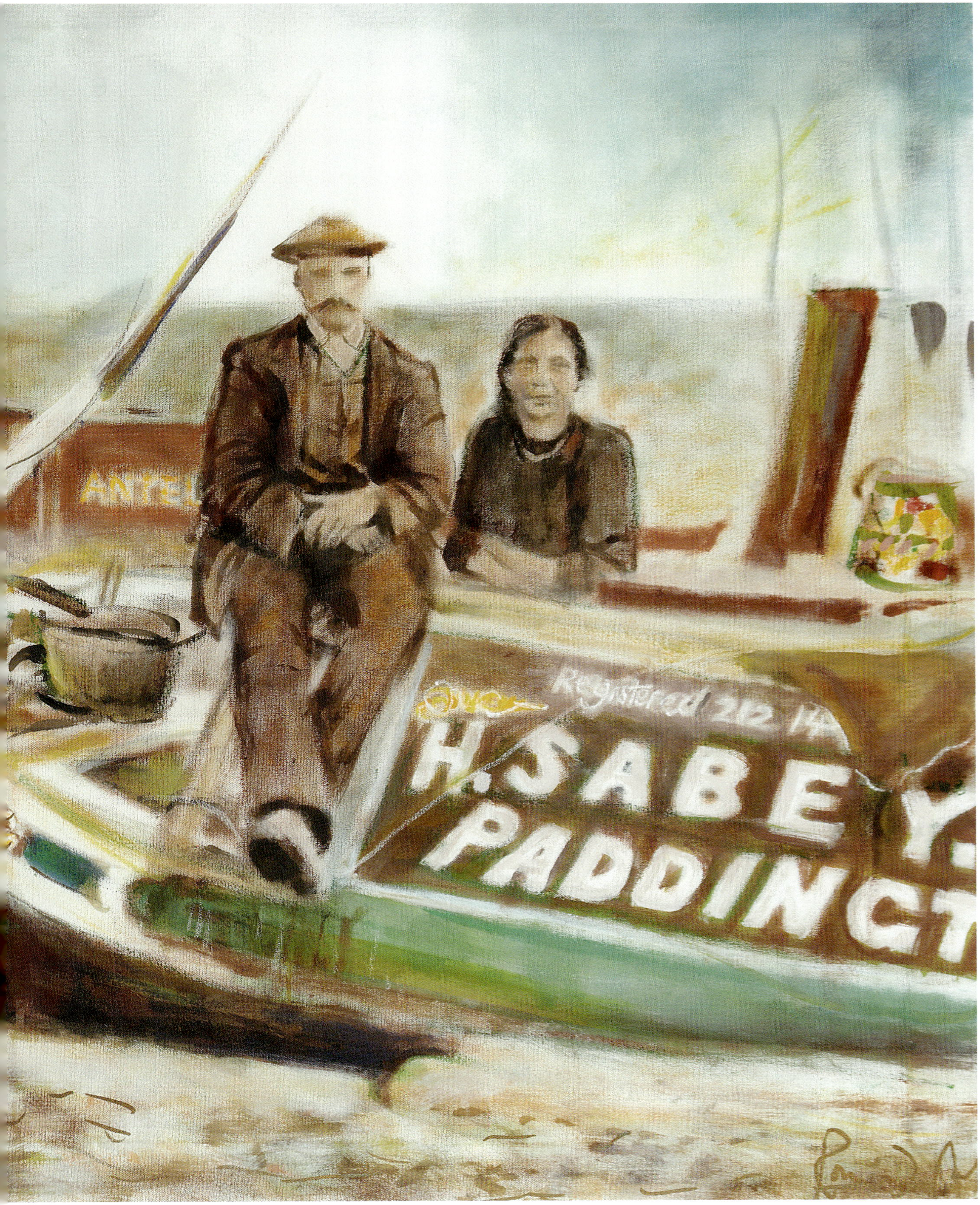
ANTEL
Registered 212 14
H.SABEY.
PADDINGT

of a chord sequence with my art; I'm able to do whatever I want without having to think about being a part of a band, restricted by what a particular song needs. But as I always say, being a Gemini, I'm also a nice bunch of guys to work with. My twins are Gemini too, which makes us a double Gemini family.

In 1973 I worked with Mick Jagger on the song "It's Only Rock 'n' Roll (But I Like It)" and over the next couple of years I got closer to the Stones and then joined the band. Keith and I formed a partnership and soon developed 'the ancient art of weaving', which describes how the two of us play together in a seamless way.

For me, art and music are so similar; sometimes putting more time into a song or picture does not necessarily make it better. Having said that, I have gone back to a painting that I started and at the time was unable to finish, but after returning to it, it has worked out fine. Both art and music hold their position in my life. They bounce off one another and make me the person I am. Sometimes I hit a streak that overtakes everything and I just have to paint. Music sometimes calls me and I take the painting with me, and equally it happens in reverse. But more often than not they are both happening at the same time. I paint to music, and sometimes when I'm playing, in my head I'm doing it to a painting.

When I paint the Stones, I often use photographs of us on stage, then I try to add to the perspective of my memory by sketching my subjects from life to give them unique takes. But I also love getting among the elements. One day in Ireland, I was painting outside and went in to get a jacket and the easel blew over and the painting ended up with cow's hoof prints on it. I just left them in to become part of the picture.

I'm always looking for new inspiration for my art – colour fills my life. Even the decoration in my homes is a riot of colour. I paint the walls, everything, and I've even turned some of my art into mosaics for our bathroom. I've turned paintings into carpets, stained glass and bronzes, and have collaborated on marine chronometers for Bremont and even a Rolls-Royce Wraith; Liberty and Co has used my paintings to create scarves, bags and clothes. I've done art for albums, including the cover of an Eric Clapton album, and I do the Stones' set lists as little works of art.

Putting this book together has been the culmination of a lifetime of art. There are people who think I just paint the Stones, but as you will see that is far from true.

Art fills my life, art is my life and art will continue to be my life.

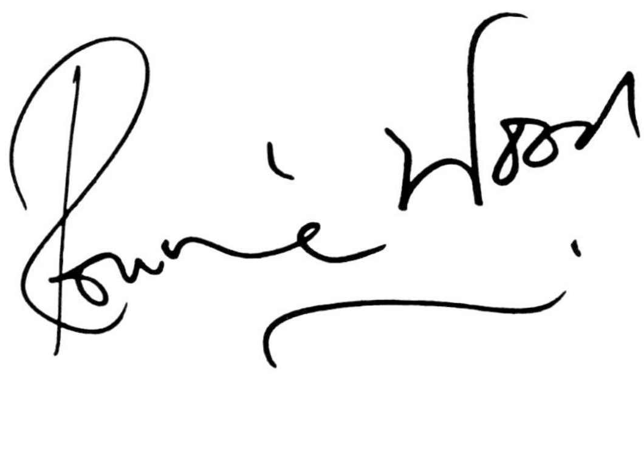

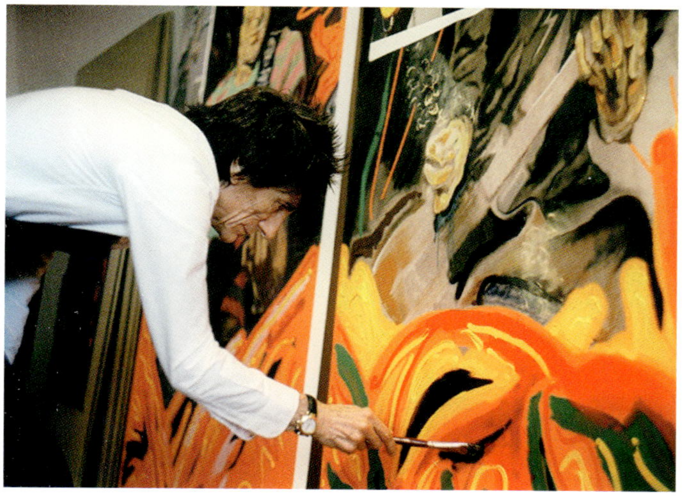

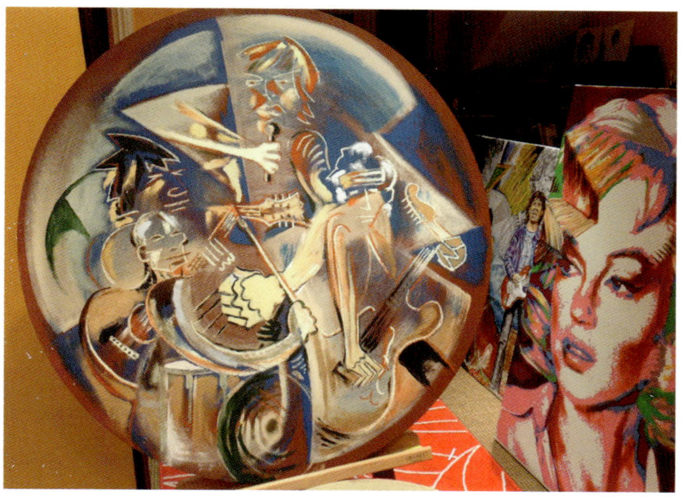

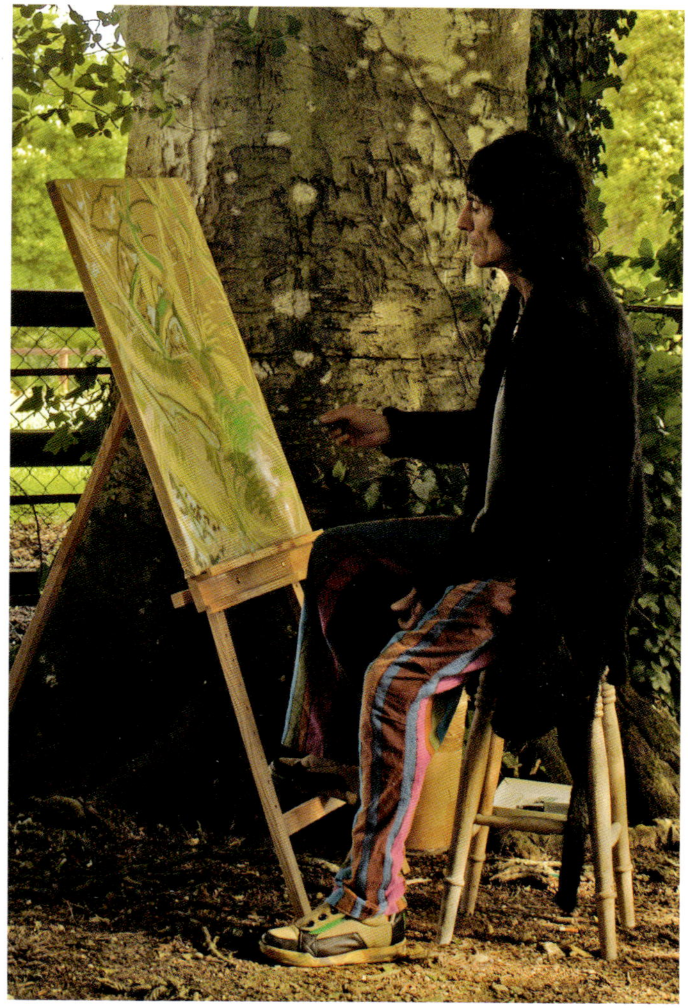

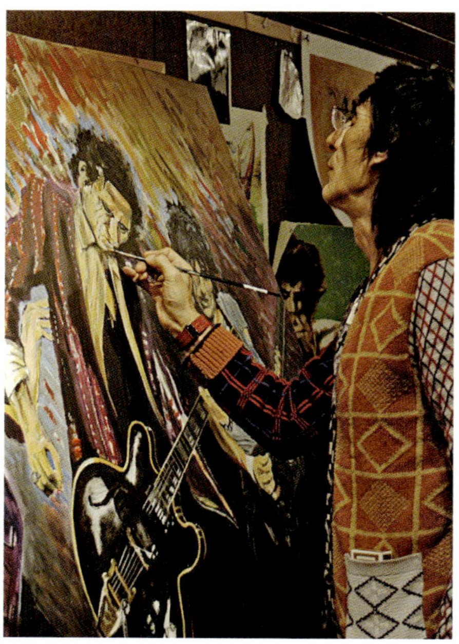

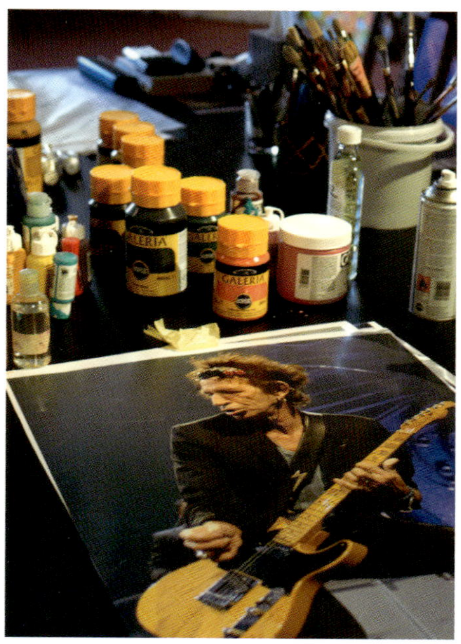
GALERIA

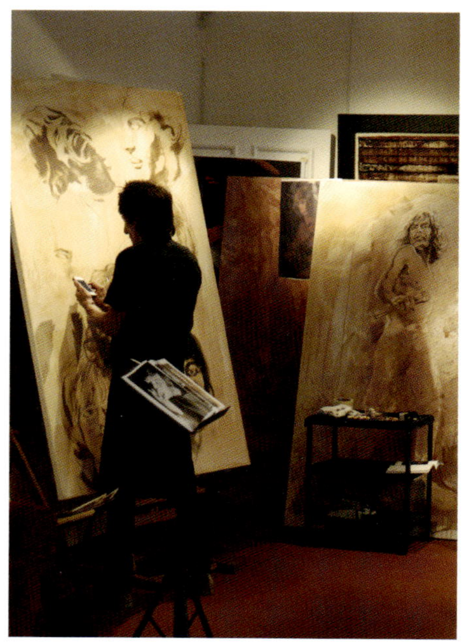

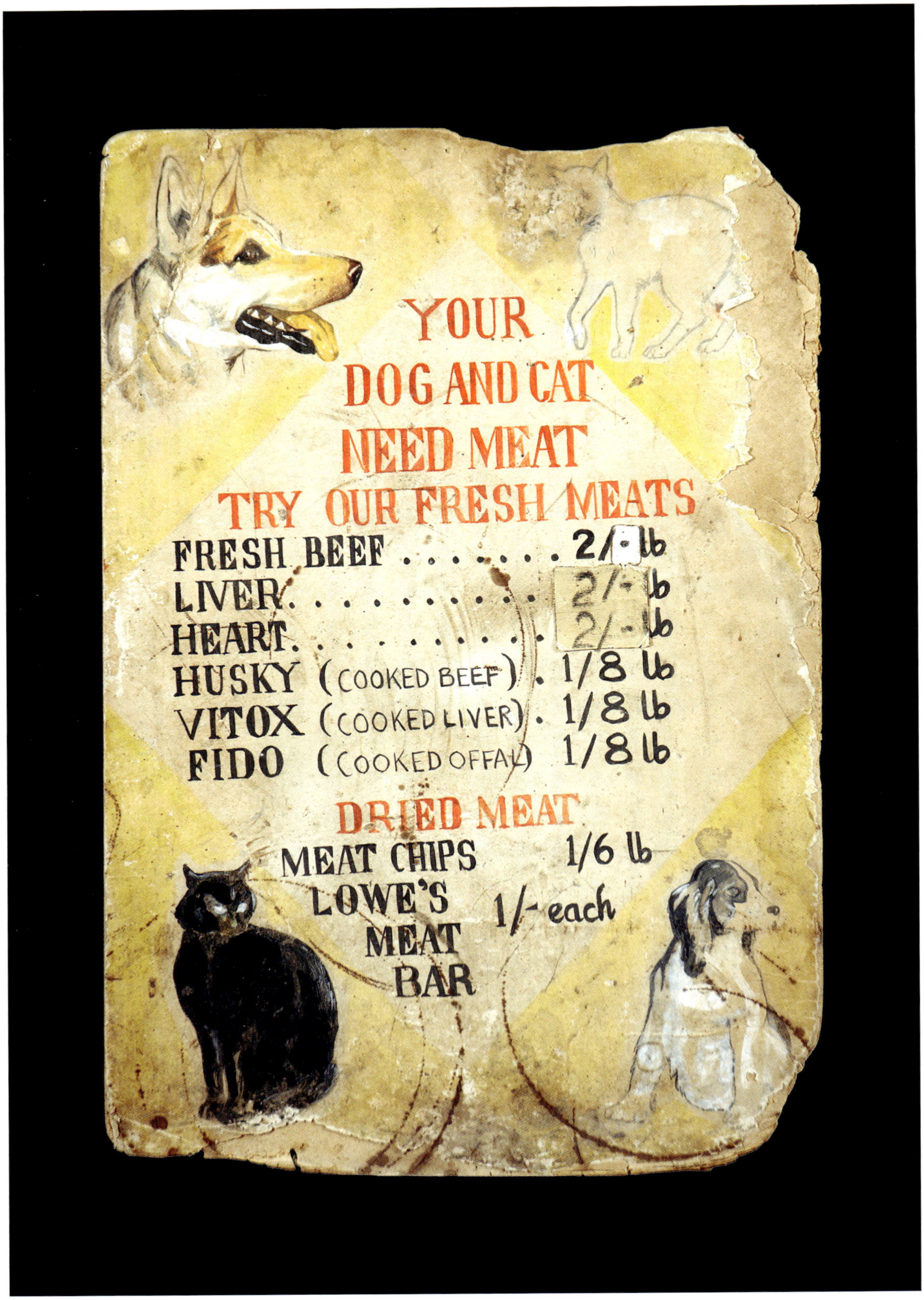
YOUR
DOG AND CAT
NEED MEAT
TRY OUR FRESH MEATS
FRESH BEEF ....2/- lb
LIVER..........2/- lb
HEART..........2/- lb
HUSKY (COOKED BEEF). 1/8 lb
VITOX (COOKED LIVER). 1/8 lb
FIDO (COOKED OFFAL) 1/8 lb
DRIED MEAT
MEAT CHIPS 1/6 lb
LOWE'S MEAT BAR 1/- each

EARLY WORK

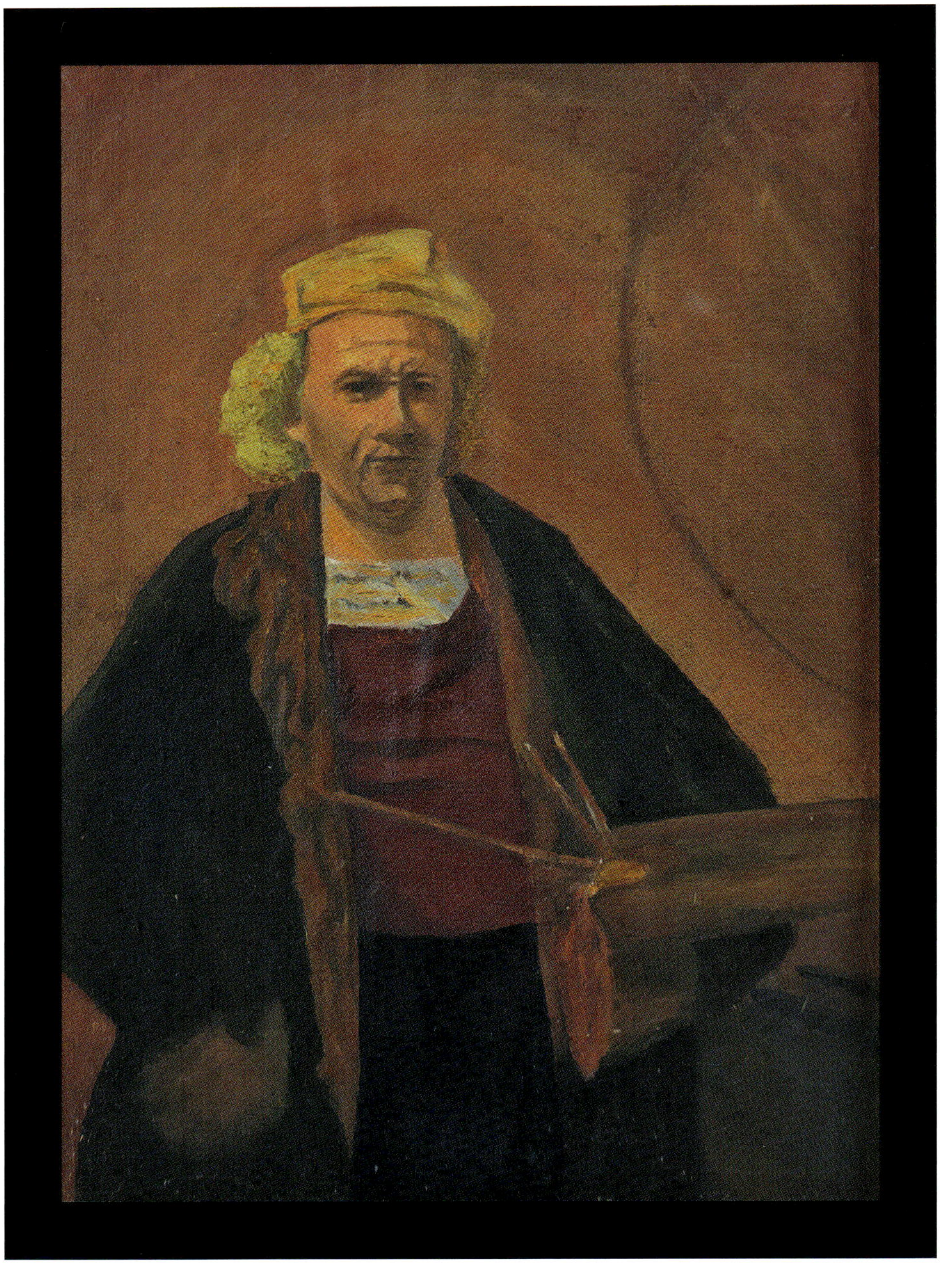

"When it awakens, the expression of art strives and claws to come out, sometimes possessing your every waking moment."

PREVIOUS PAGE: *Pet Shop Advert* (My first commission) | 1959 | acrylic on board | 57 × 39 cm
ABOVE: *After Rembrandt* | 1959 | oil on canvas | 33 × 24 cm
OPPOSITE: *Abstract* | 1965 | oil on canvas | 60 × 50 cm

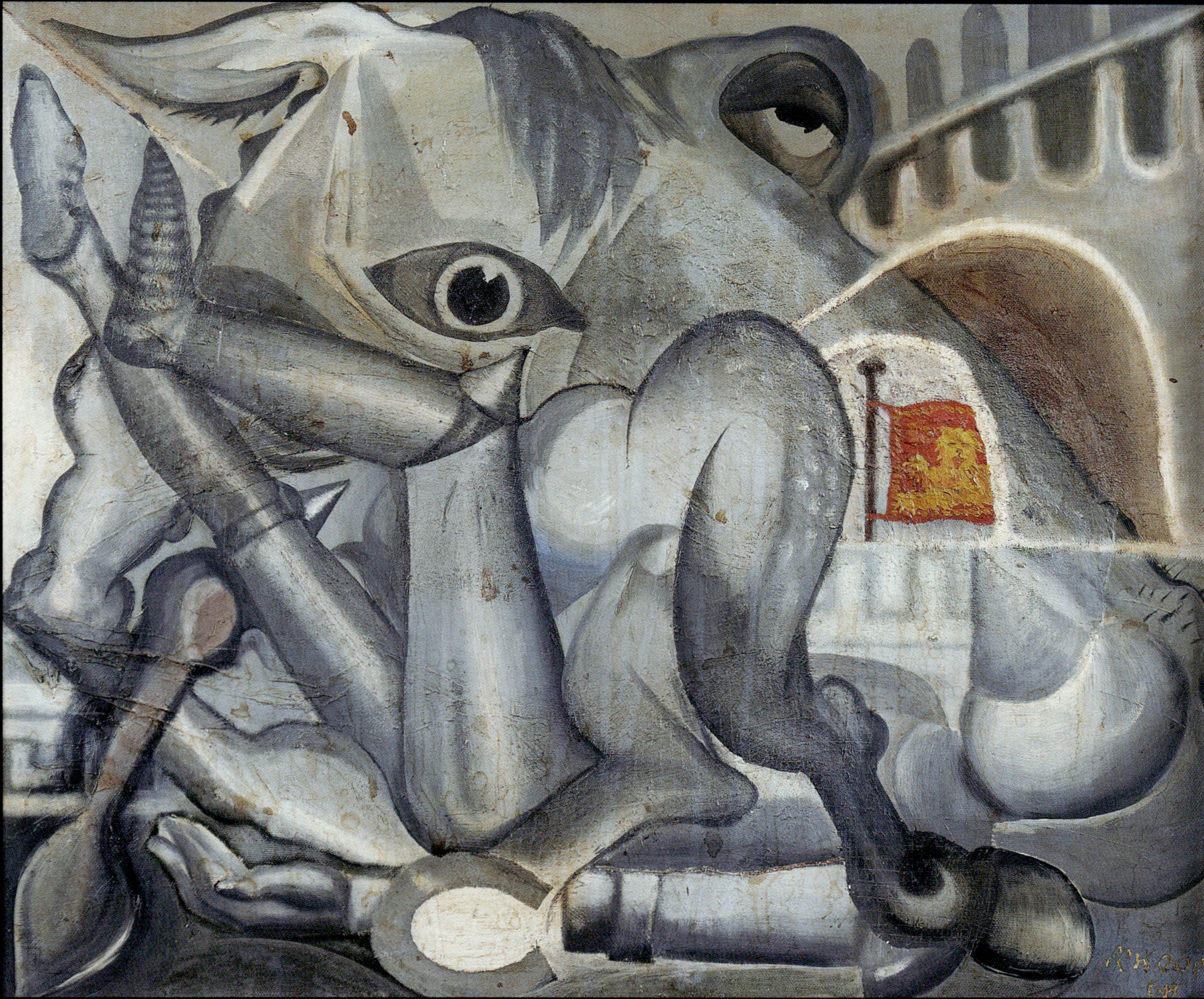

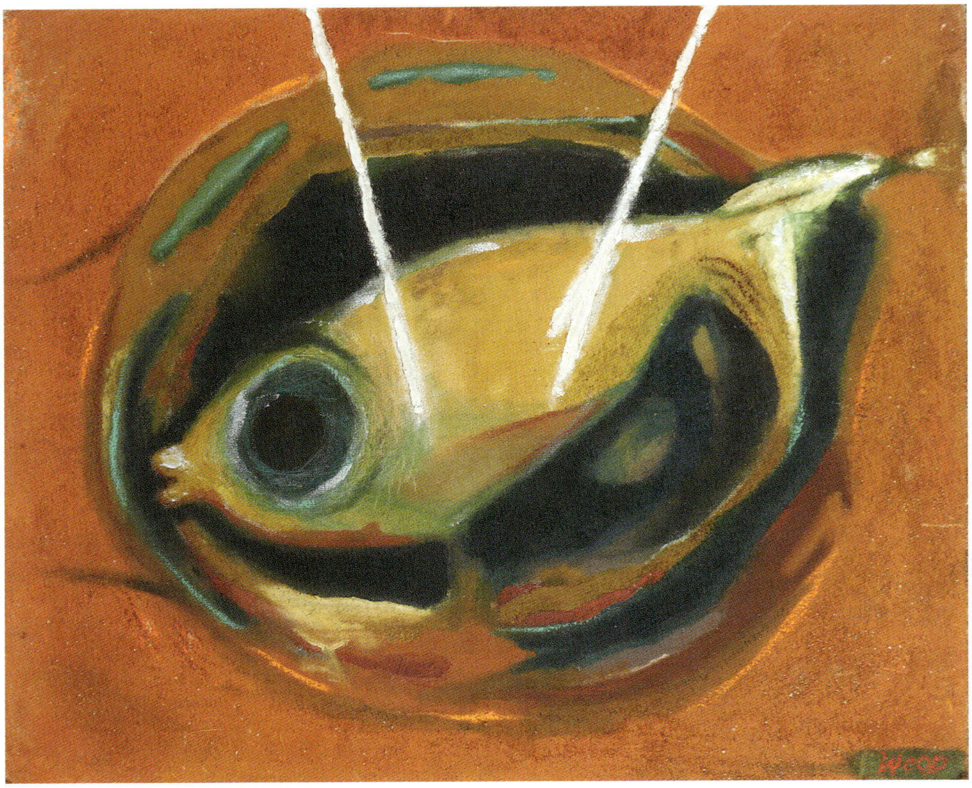

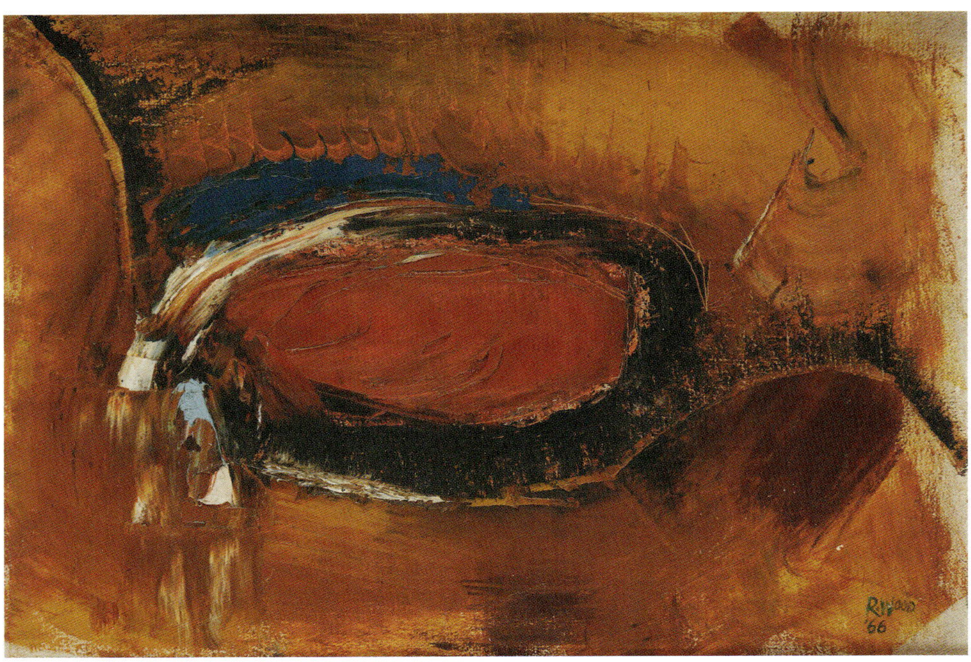

"Ali McKenzie, the vocalist with The Birds, is the present owner of my pet shop advert and my abstract opposite was bought by Mrs Packham, my music teacher."

TOP: *Fish* | 1966 | oil on canvas | 76 × 60 cm
ABOVE: *Abstract Still Life* | 1966 | oil on canvas | 50 × 75 cm
OPPOSITE: *Mrs Packham's Abstract* | 1963 | mixed media on canvas | 90 × 50 cm approx

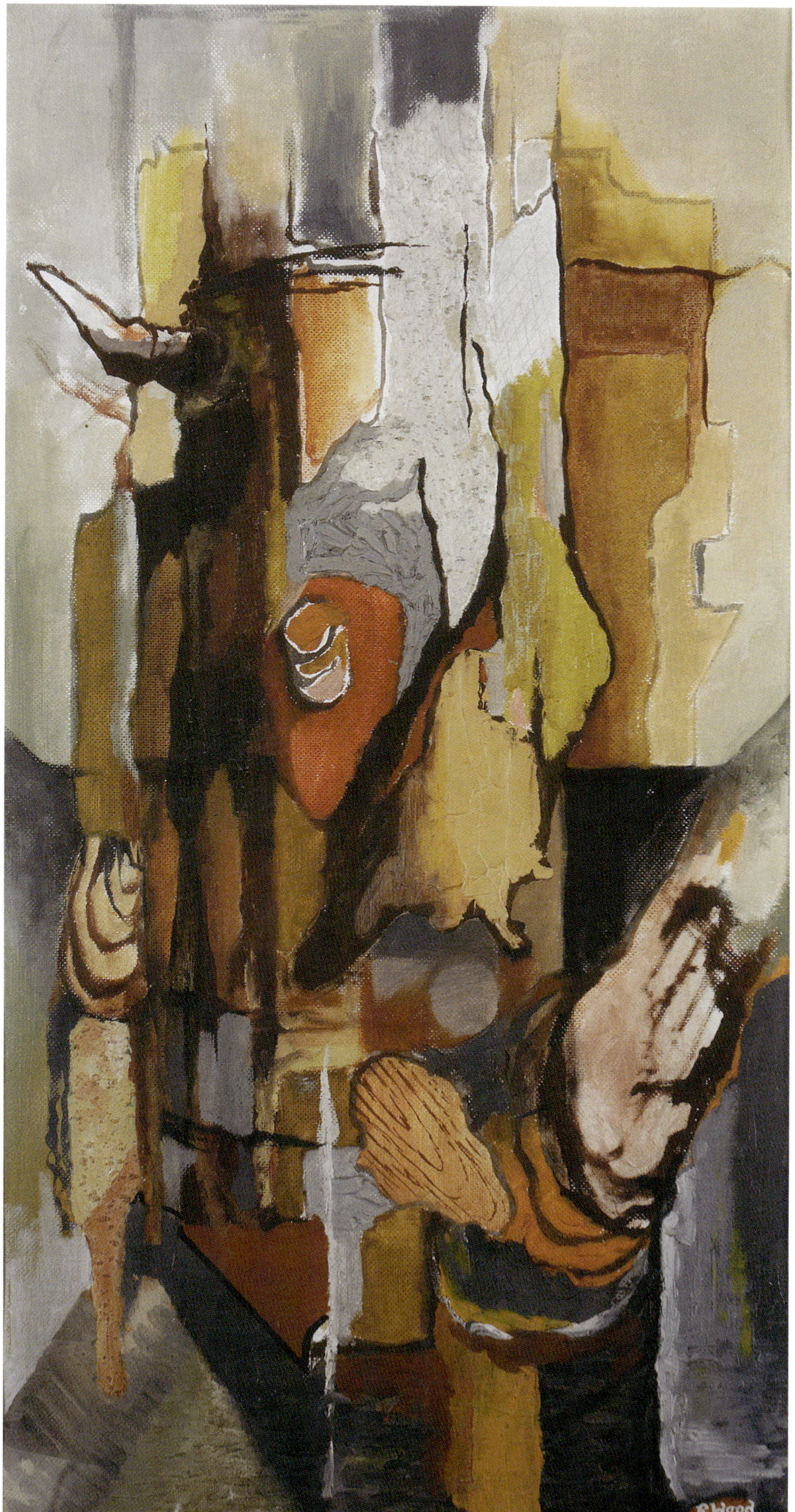
R. Wood
1963.

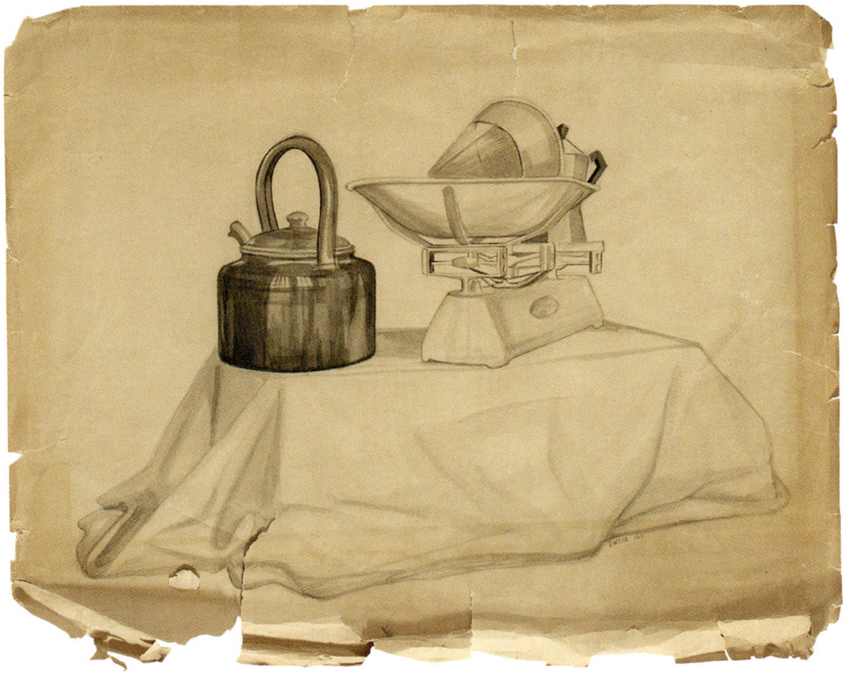

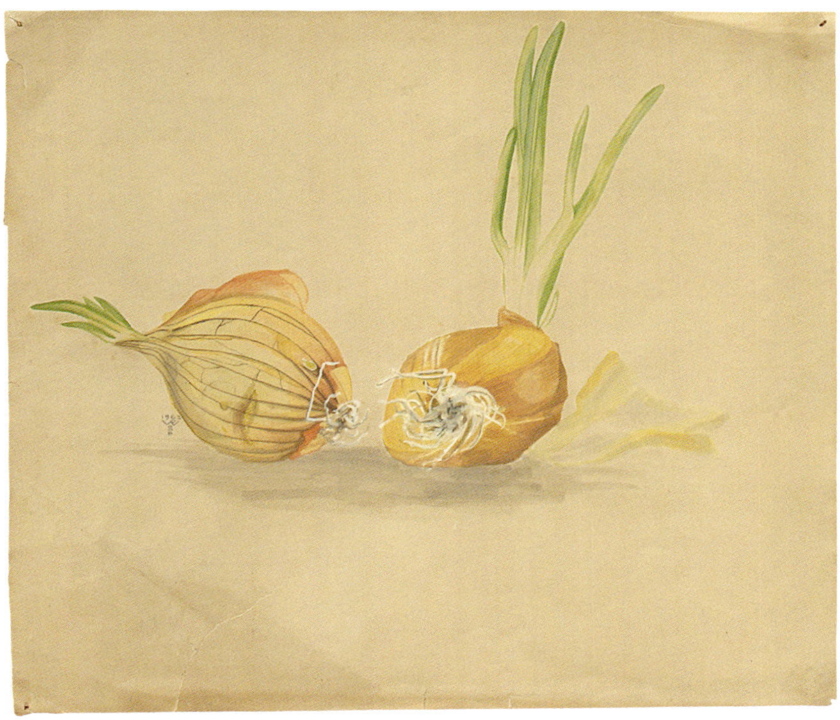

TOP: *Study of Kettle* | 1963 | pencil on paper | 35 × 45 cm
ABOVE: *Onions* | 1963 | watercolour on paper | 26 × 31 cm
OPPOSITE ABOVE LEFT: *Foreshortening the Reclining Man* | 1963 | pencil on paper | 38 × 28 cm
OPPOSITE ABOVE RIGHT: *Tal Farlow & Barney Kessel* | 1963 | pen on paper | 35.5 × 25 cm
OPPOSITE BELOW LEFT: *A Jug* | 1963 | pencil on paper | 32 × 22 cm
OPPOSITE BELOW RIGHT: *Dick Ashby Driving The Birds' Van* | 1963 | pencil on paper | 38 × 28 cm

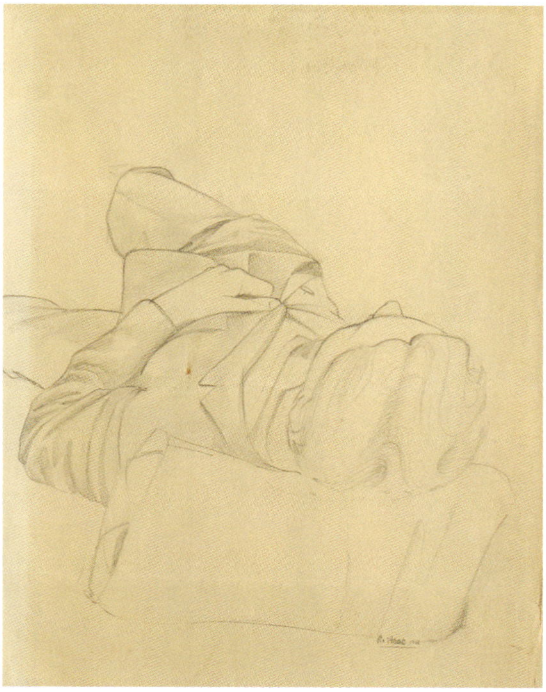

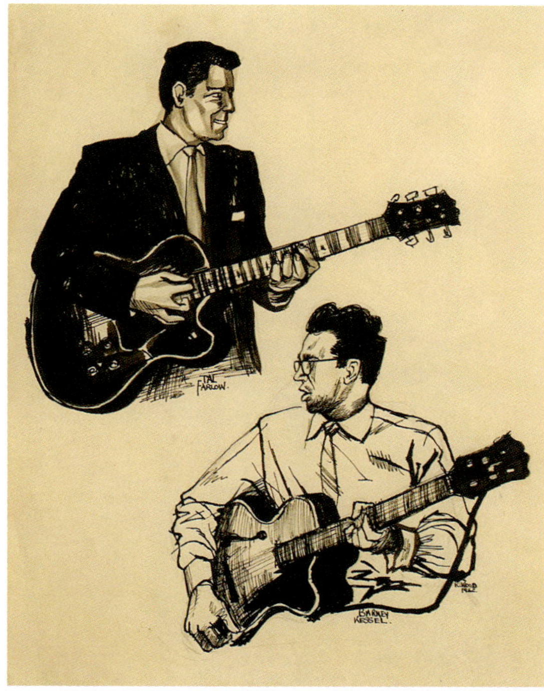

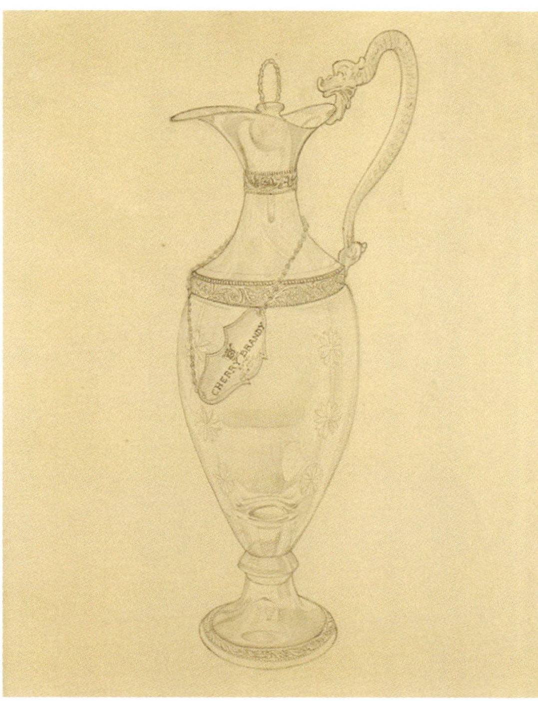

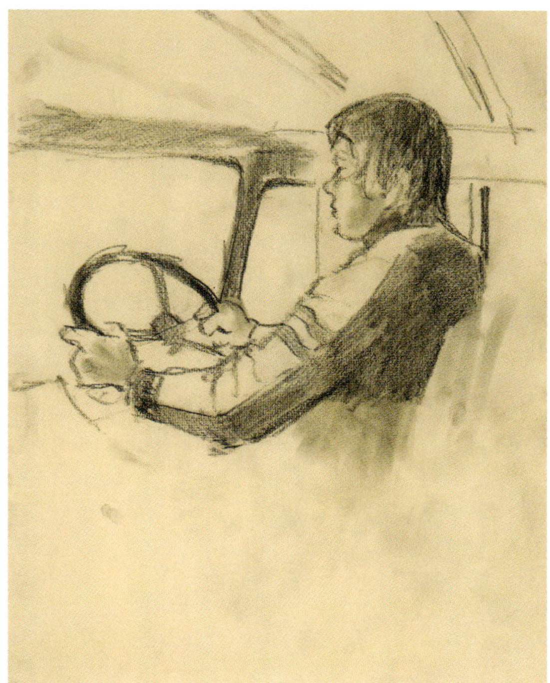

"I used photos from my brother's copy of the Jazz Times *to do the images of Tal Farlow and Barney Kessel. Dick Ashby went on to become the Bee Gees' manager."*

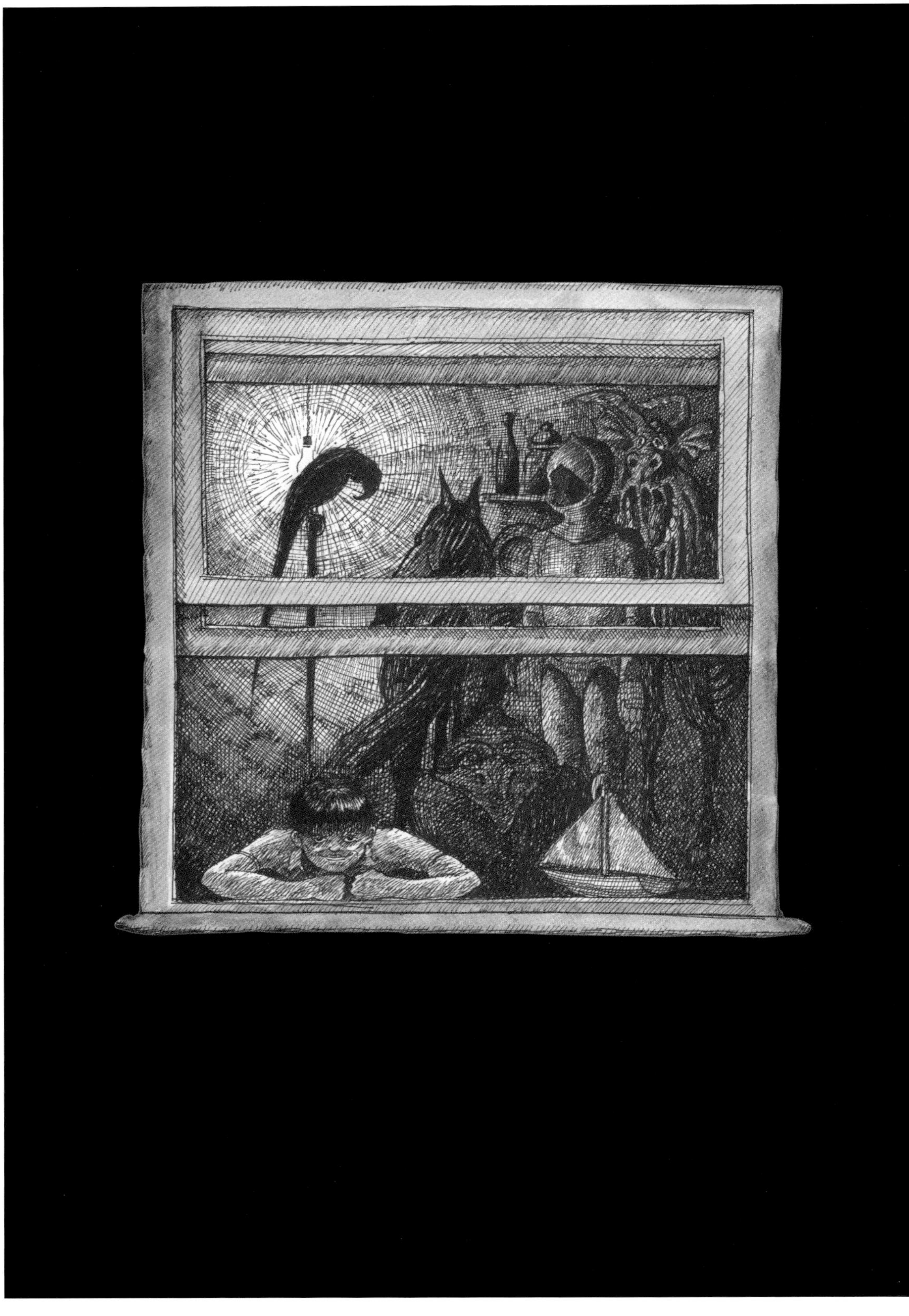

2

FACES

"The Wick Studio in Richmond was where I recorded my first album, and is also the studio where the basic track was laid down for 'It's Only Rock 'n' Roll (But I Like It)' in 1973. Me and David Bowie were on backing vocals."

PREVIOUS PAGE: *Something Wicked This Way Comes* | 1970–74 | pen and ink on paper | 38 × 42 cm
BELOW: *Wick Studios Logo* | 1973 | pen and ink on paper | 20 × 30 cm
OPPOSITE: *Faces UK Tour Advert for the* Melody Maker | 1972 | pen on paper | 45 × 35.5 cm

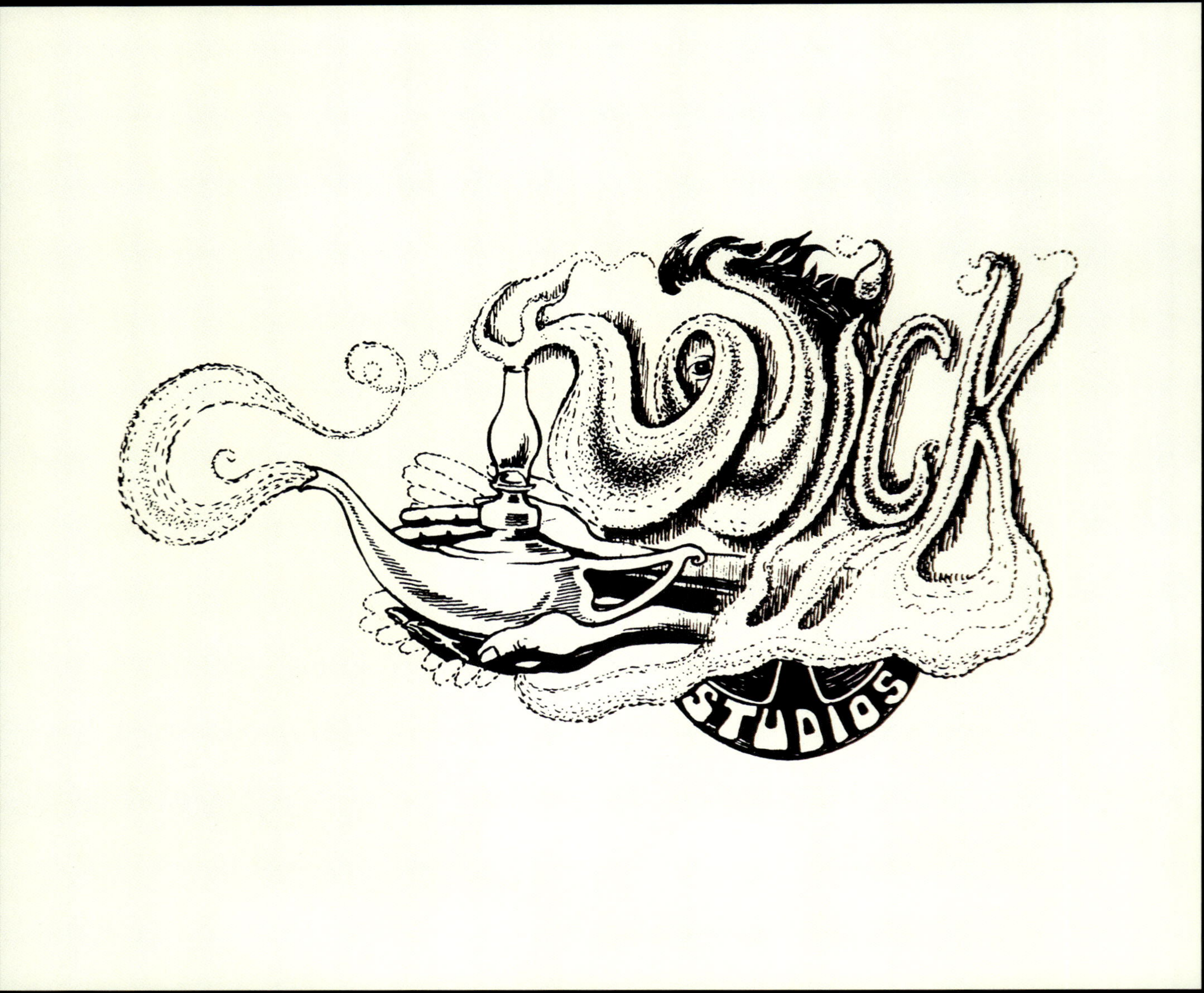

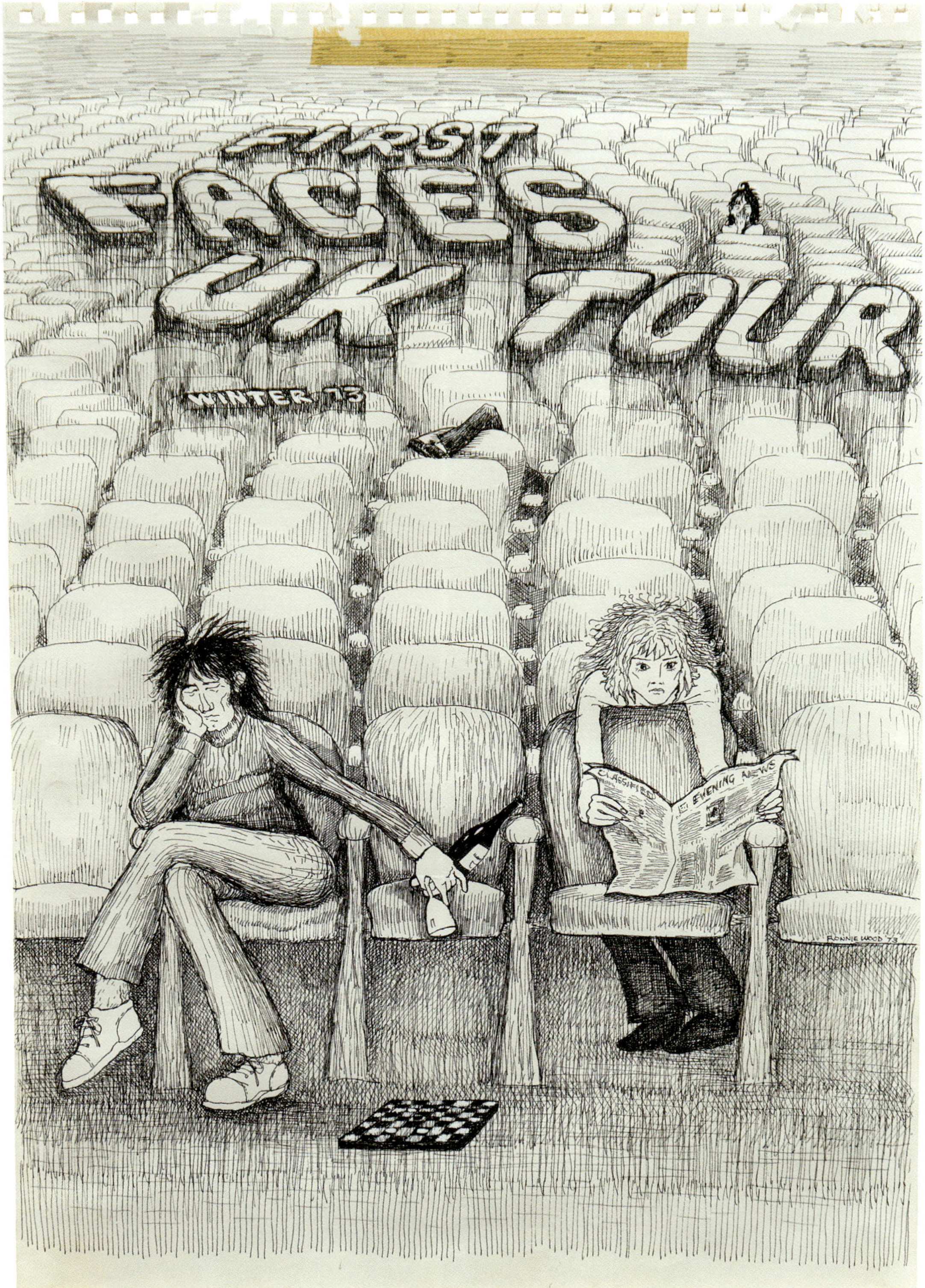
FIRST
FACES
UK TOUR
WINTER '73
EVENING NEWS
CLASSIFIED
RONNIE WOOD '73

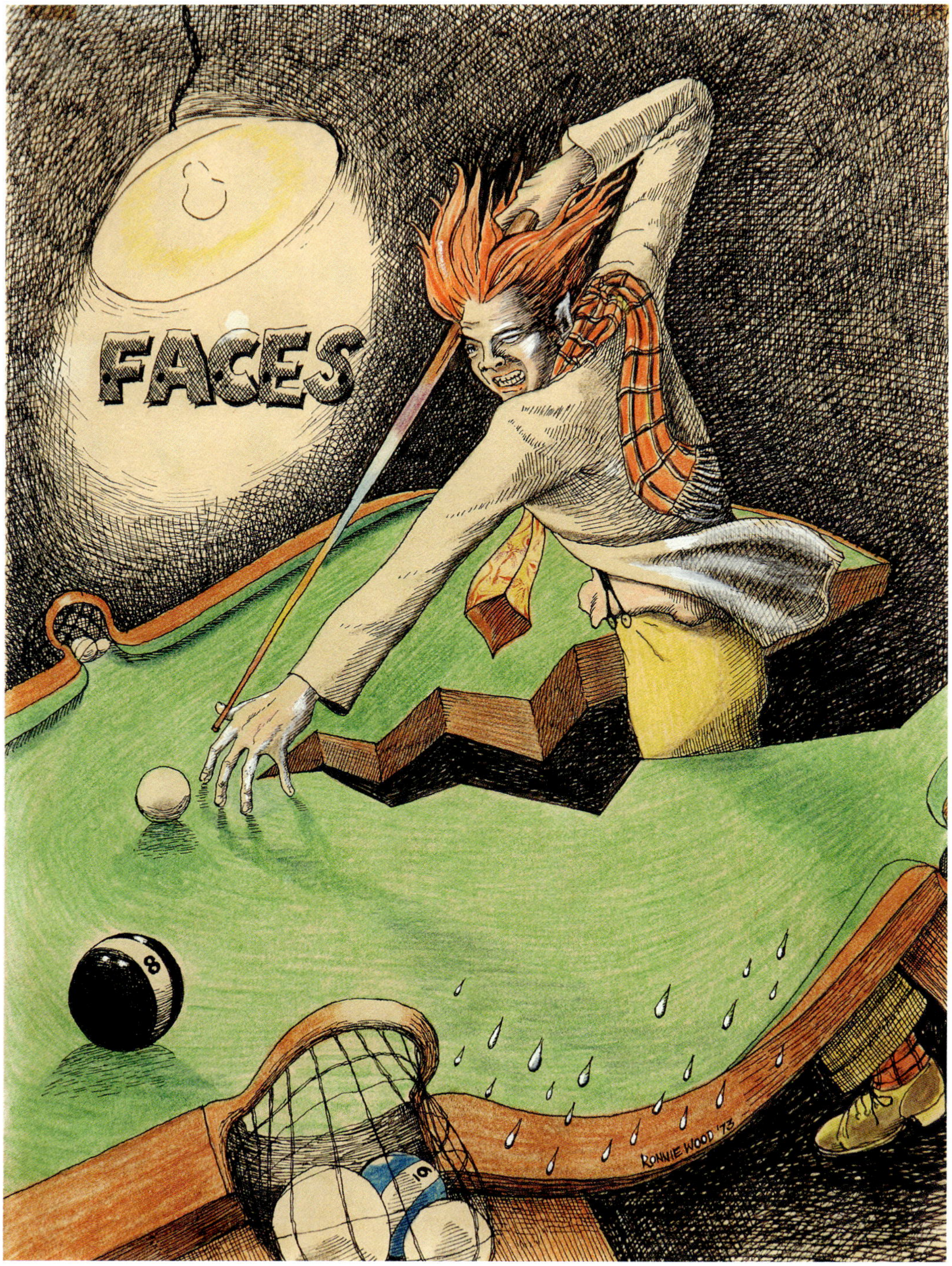

ABOVE: *Faces Poster, inspired by 'Pool Hall Richard'* | 1973 | mixed media on paper | 20 × 30 cm approx
OPPOSITE: *Faces Poster* | 1974 | pen and pastel on paper | 45 × 35 cm approx

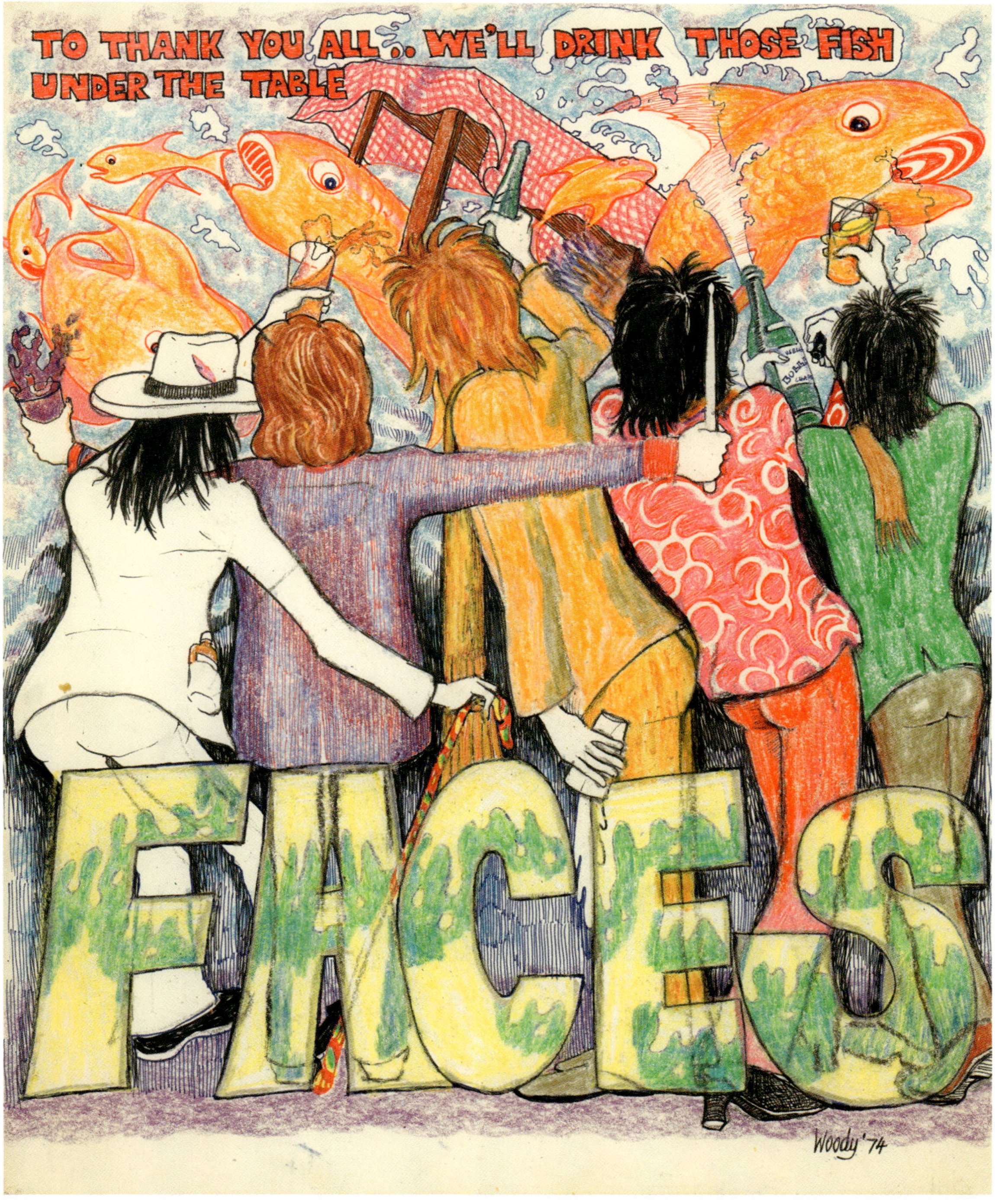

"The picture opposite illustrates 'Pool Hall Richard', a song that Rod and I wrote that the Faces released as a single in 1973."

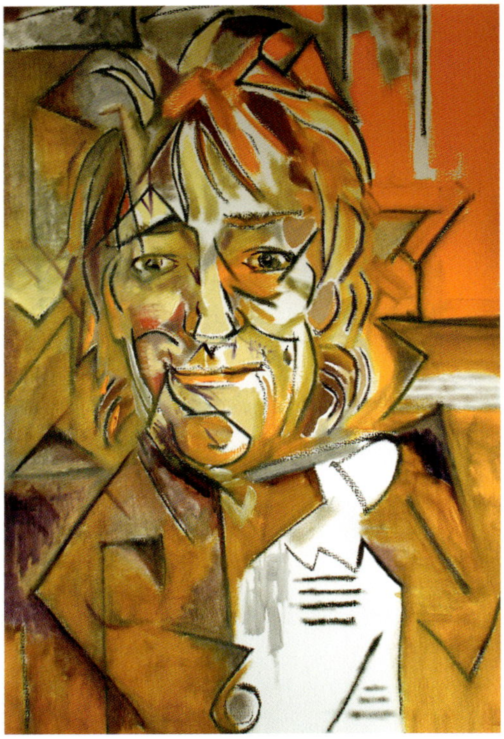

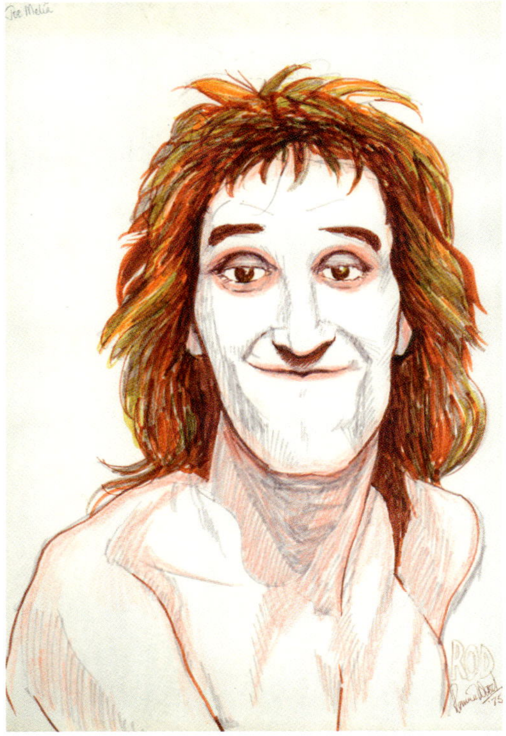

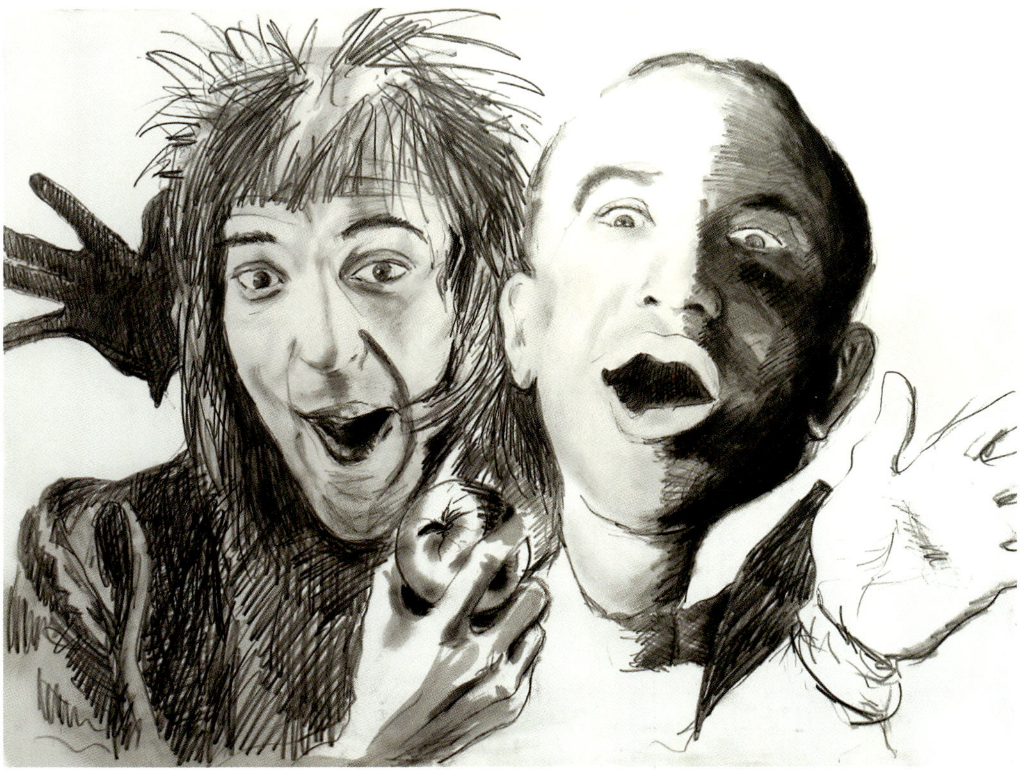

"Rod Stewart's first inspiration was Al Jolson, so it seemed perfect to paint the pair of them together."

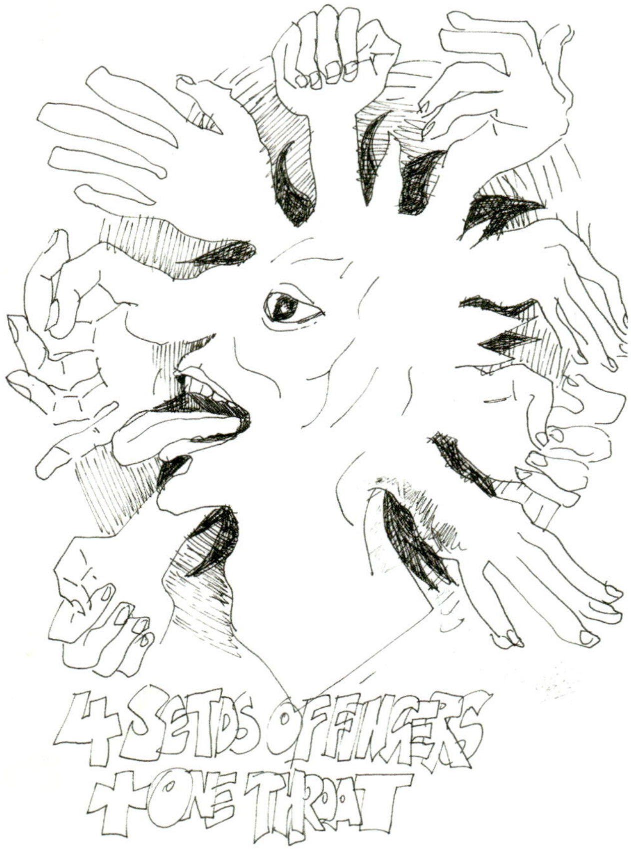

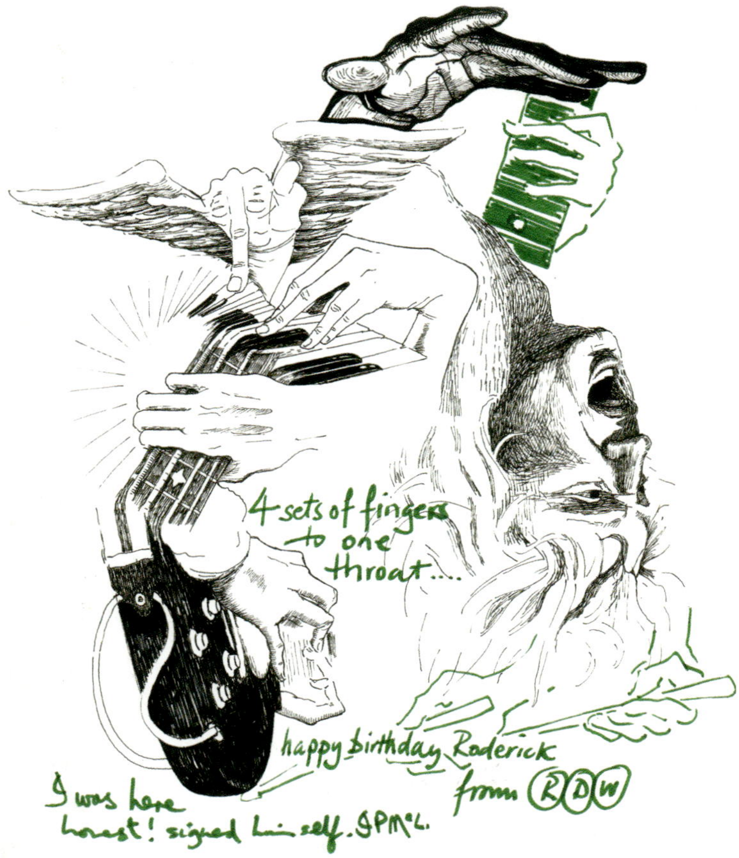

OPPOSITE ABOVE LEFT: *Abstract Rod* | 2009 | acrylic on canvas | 61 × 38 cm
OPPOSITE ABOVE RIGHT: *Rod* | 1975 | coloured pencil on paper | 57 × 51 cm
OPPOSITE BELOW: *Rod and Al Jolson* | 1987 | pen and ink on paper | 76 × 112 cm
ABOVE LEFT: *Four + One* | 1970–74 | pen on paper | 29.5 × 21 cm
ABOVE RIGHT: *Happy Birthday Roderick* | 1970–74 | pen and ink on paper | 42 × 35.5 cm

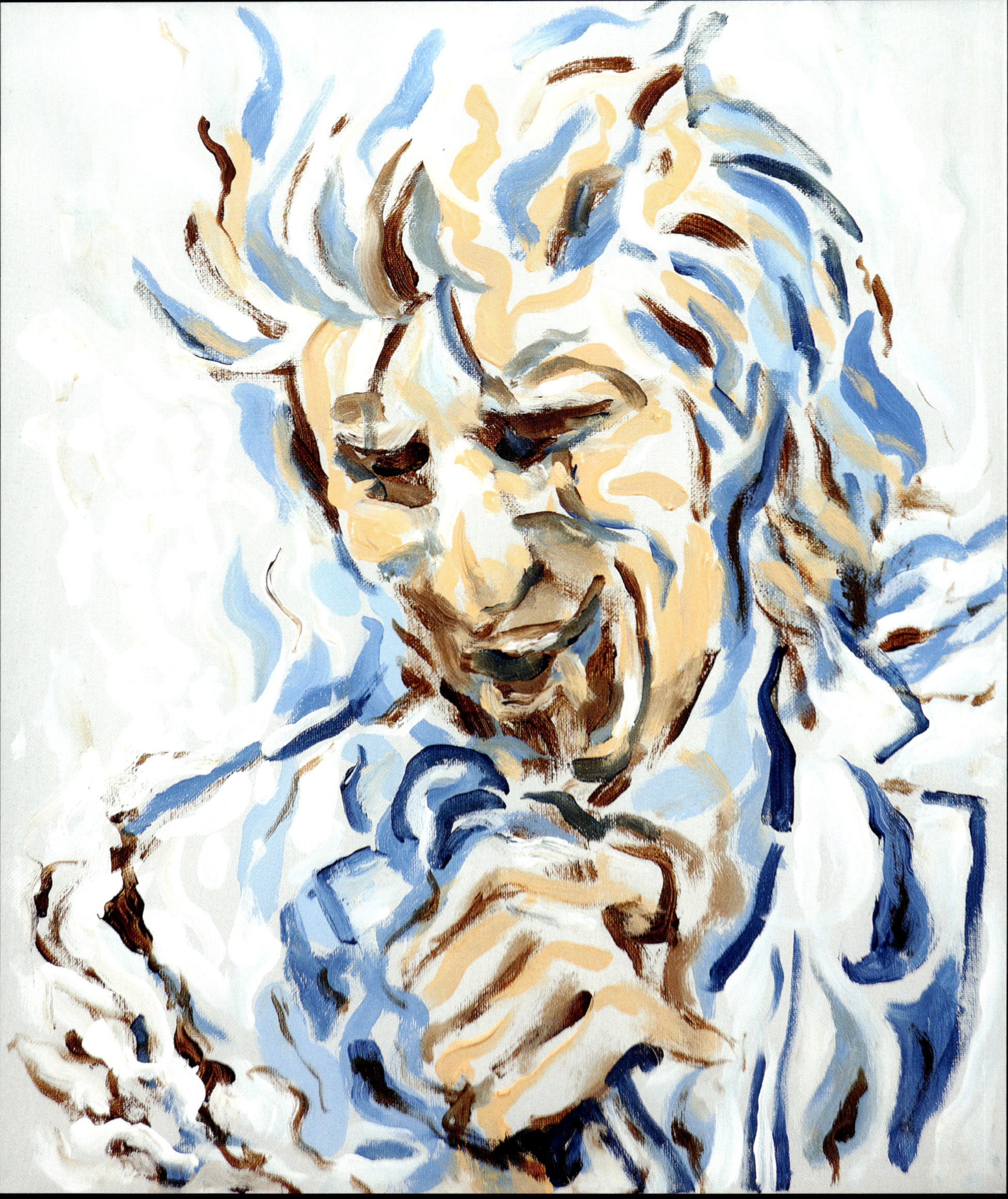

'The blues-shouting Rod, morphing into the 'Great American Song Book' Rod, nicely juxtaposed with Jeff Beck whose band I joined in 1967."

OPPOSITE: *Morphing Rod* | 2016 | acrylic on canvas | 46 × 40 cm
BELOW: *Jeff Beck* | 2004 | oil on canvas | 127 × 98 cm

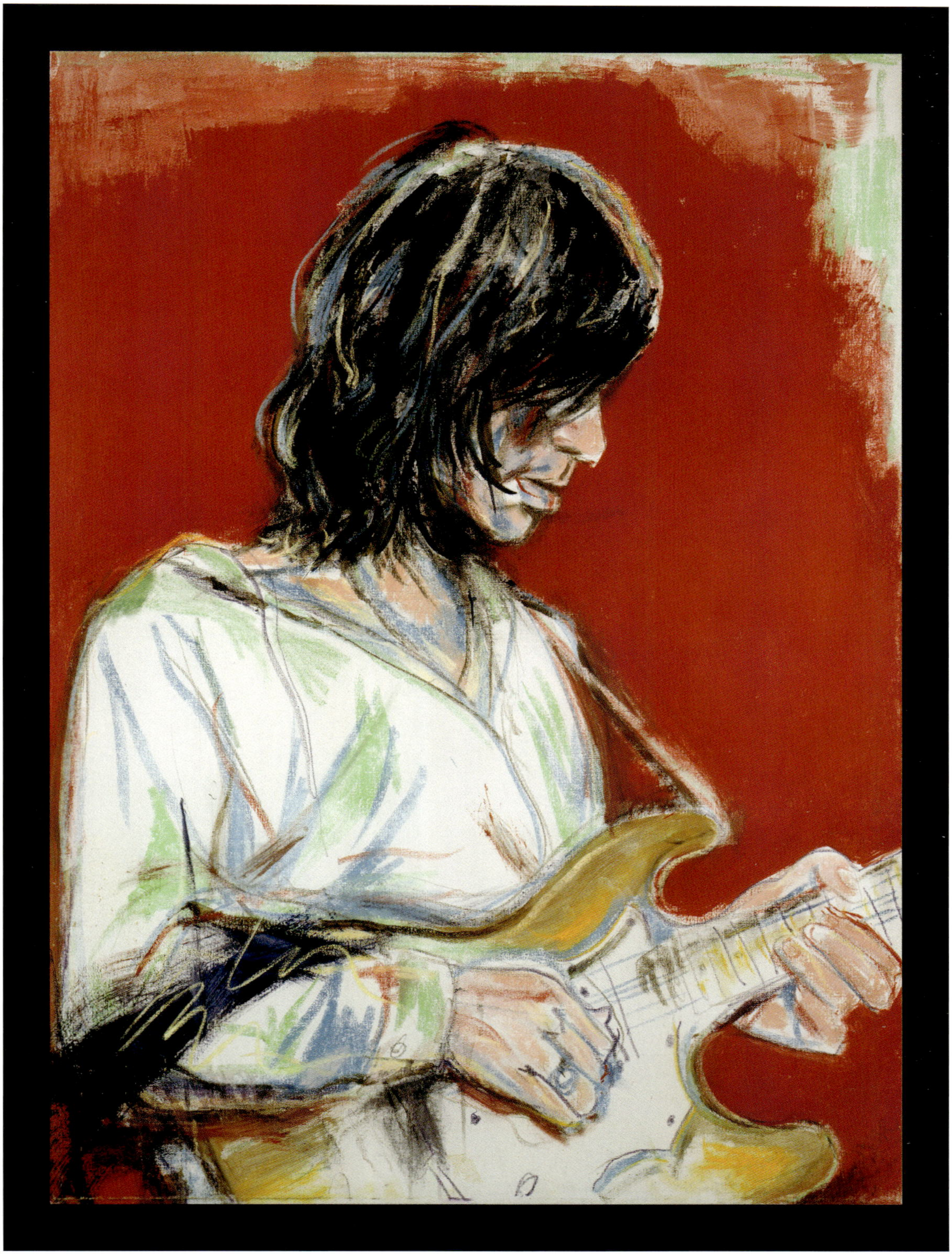

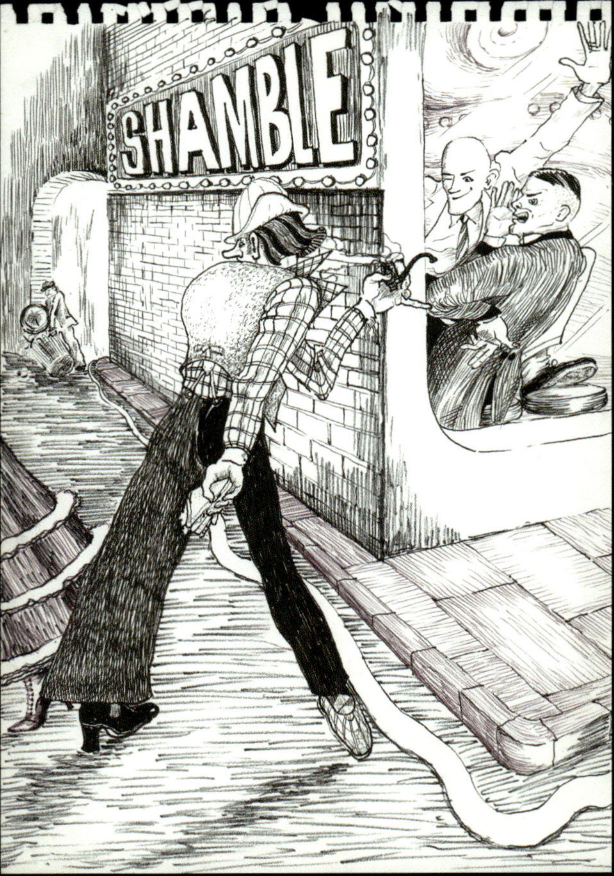
SHAMBLE

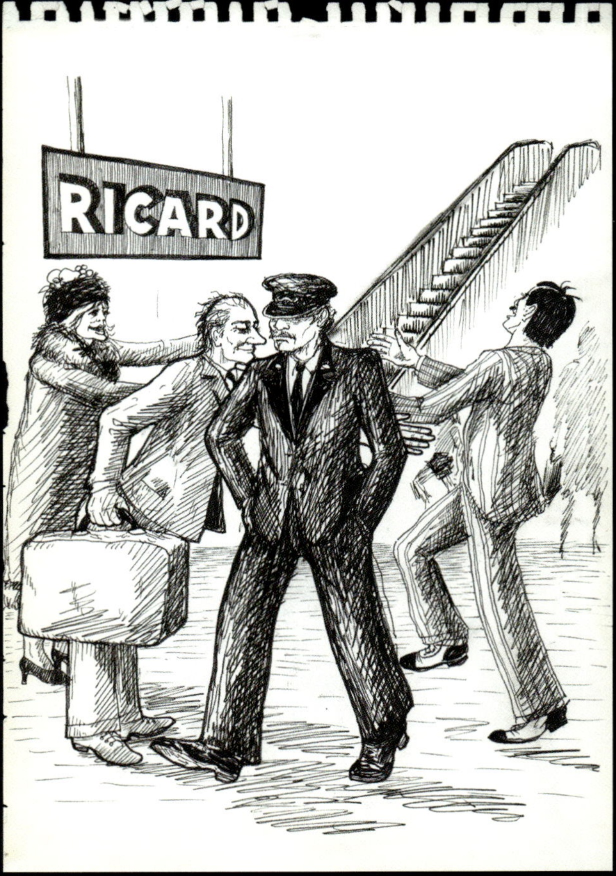
RICARD

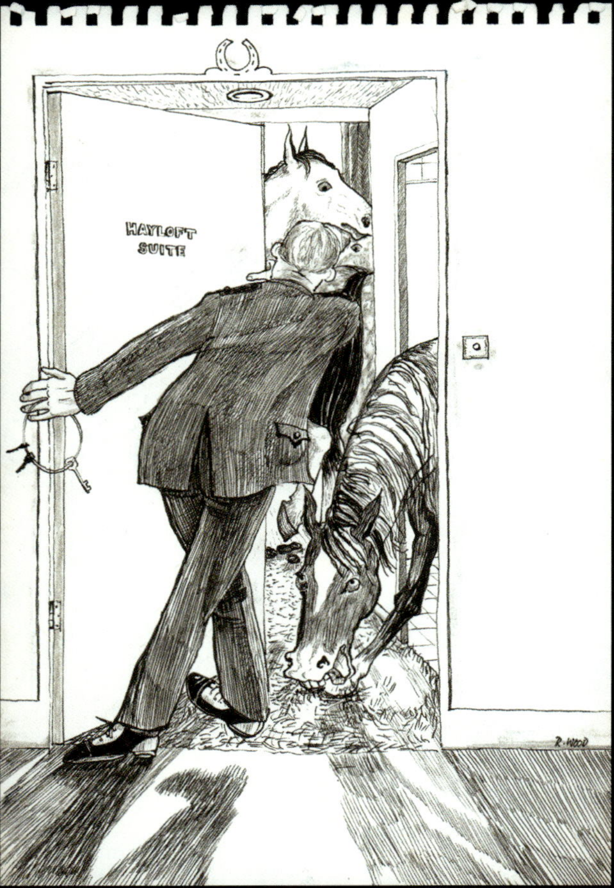
HAYLOFT
SUITE

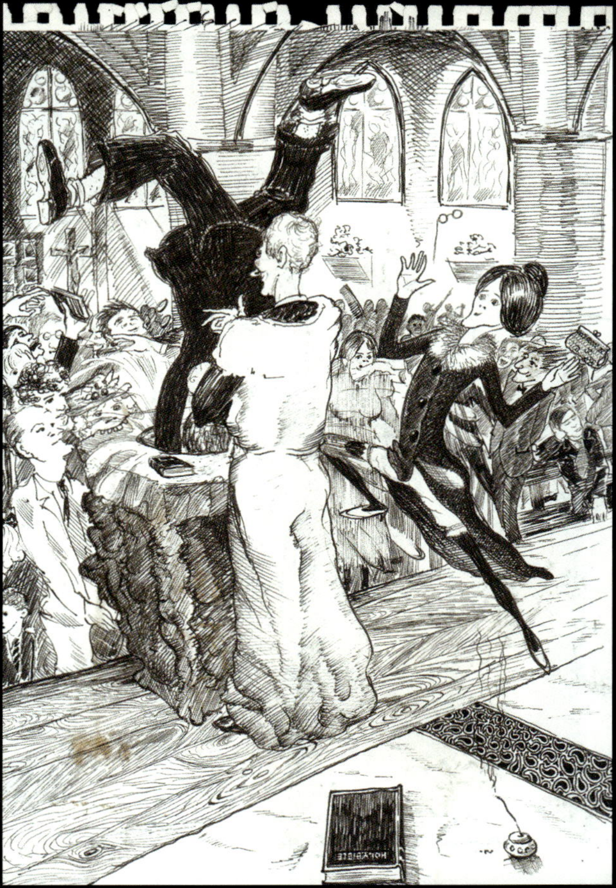

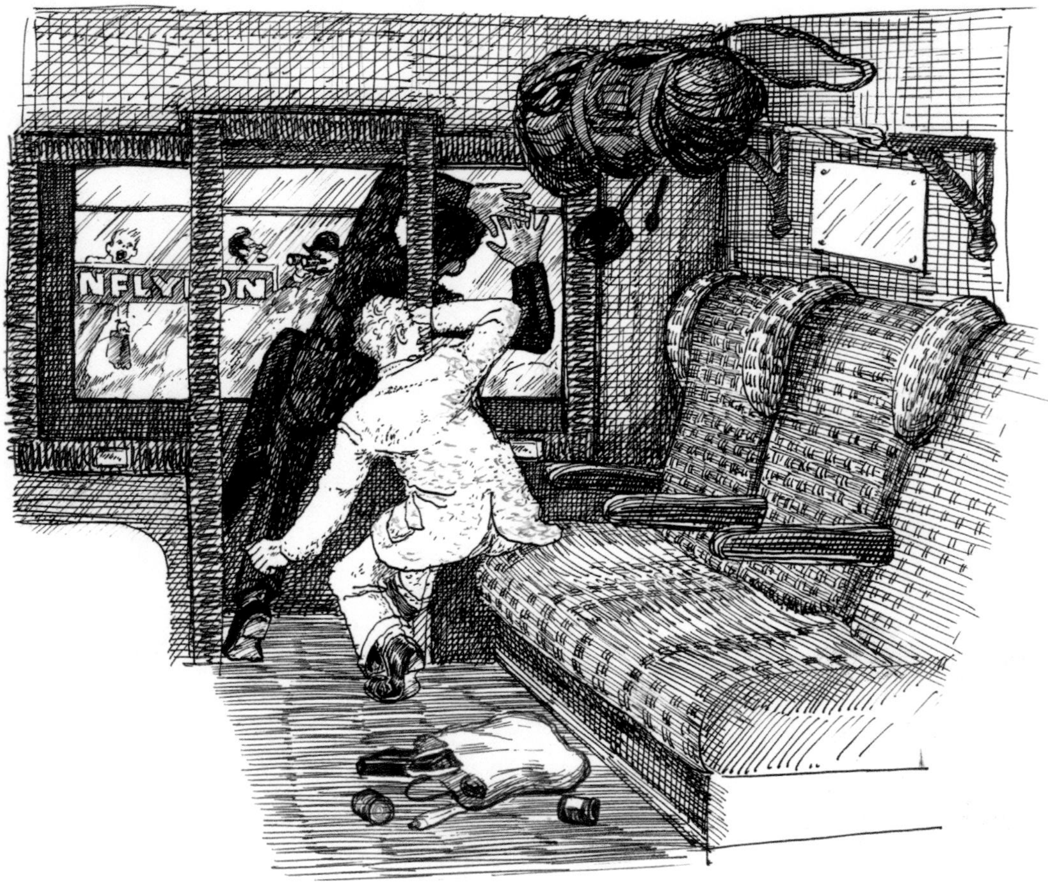

"'Dunflynnon from Dunflannon, my train pulled in and gave a stealthy jog' is the opening line to one of the poems in A Variety of Annoyances. *It commemorates the Faces' first visit to Scotland in 1972."*

OPPOSITE ABOVE LEFT: *A Variety of Annoyances* | 1970–74 | pen and ink on paper | 31 × 24 cm
OPPOSITE ABOVE RIGHT: *A Variety of Annoyances (My first visit abroad)* | 1970–74 | pen and ink on paper | 31 × 24 cm
OPPOSITE BELOW LEFT: *A Variety of Annoyances* | 1970–74 | pen and ink on paper | 29 × 21 cm
OPPOSITE BELOW RIGHT: *A Variety of Annoyances (A new member in the family)* | 1970–74 | pen and ink on paper | 31 × 24 cm
ABOVE: *A Variety of Annoyances* | 1970–74 | pen and ink on paper | 31 × 24 cm

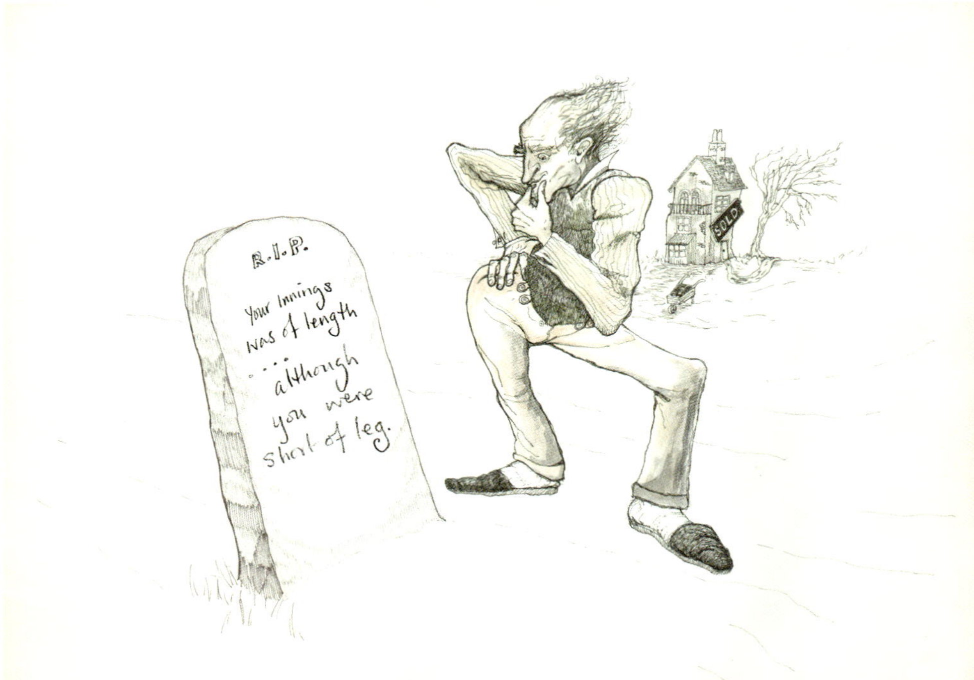

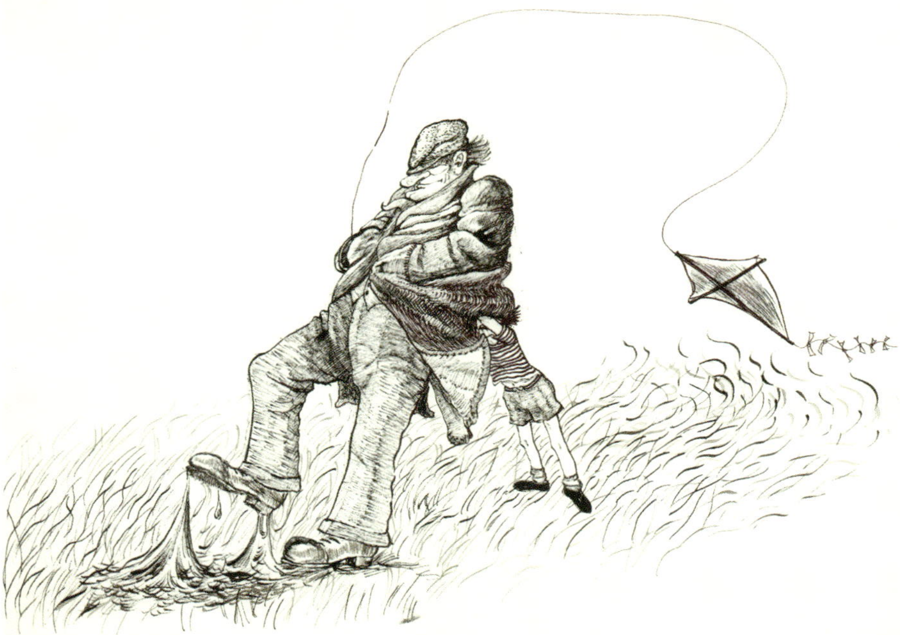

TOP: *A Variety of Annoyances (Grave for Father's Day)* | 1970–74 | pen and ink on paper | 35 × 51 cm
ABOVE: *A Variety of Annoyances (Father's Day)* | 1970–74 | pen and ink on paper | 35 × 51 cm
OPPOSITE ABOVE: *A Variety of Annoyances (My idol)* | 1970–74 | pen and ink on paper | 42 × 59 cm
OPPOSITE BELOW: *A Variety of Annoyances (My idol)* | 1970–74 | pen and ink on paper | 35 × 51 cm

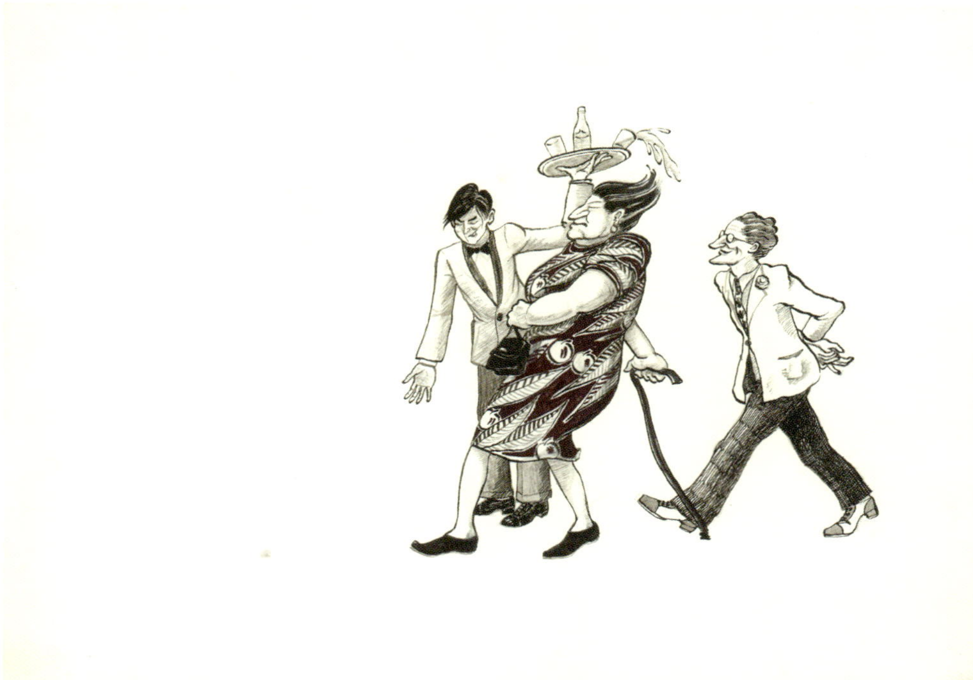

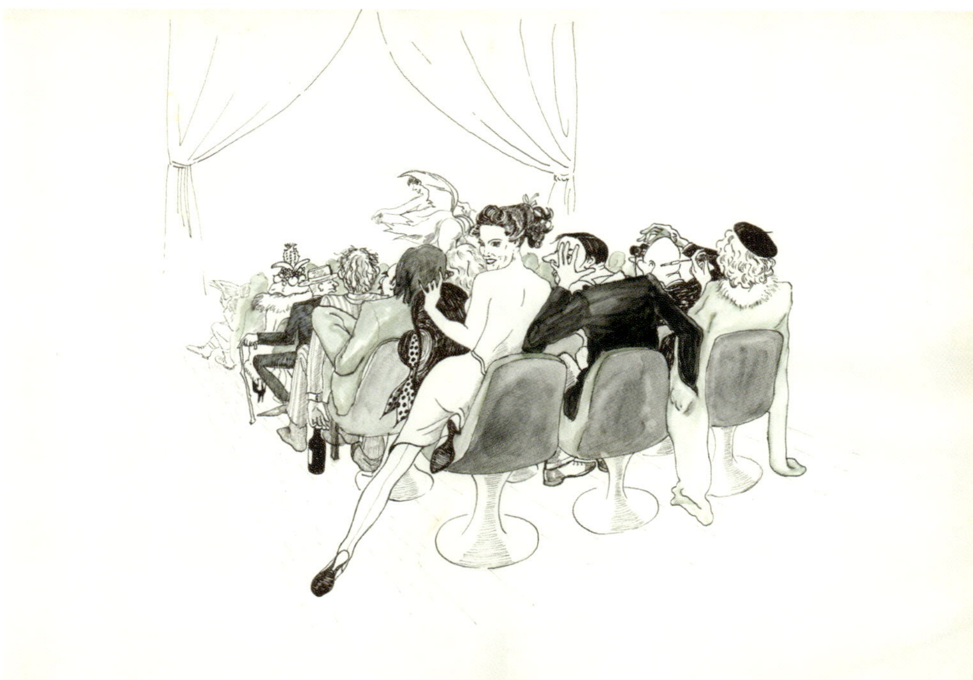

"I drew these, and Rod and I wrote the poems for the unpublished A Variety of Annoyances, *while we were on the road with the Faces; we had a language that he and I used that was in the style of Stanley Unwin."*

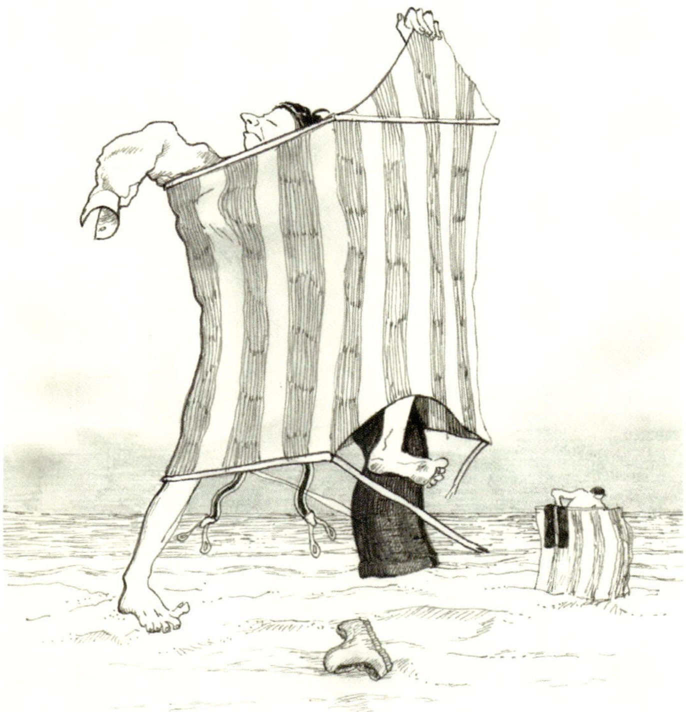

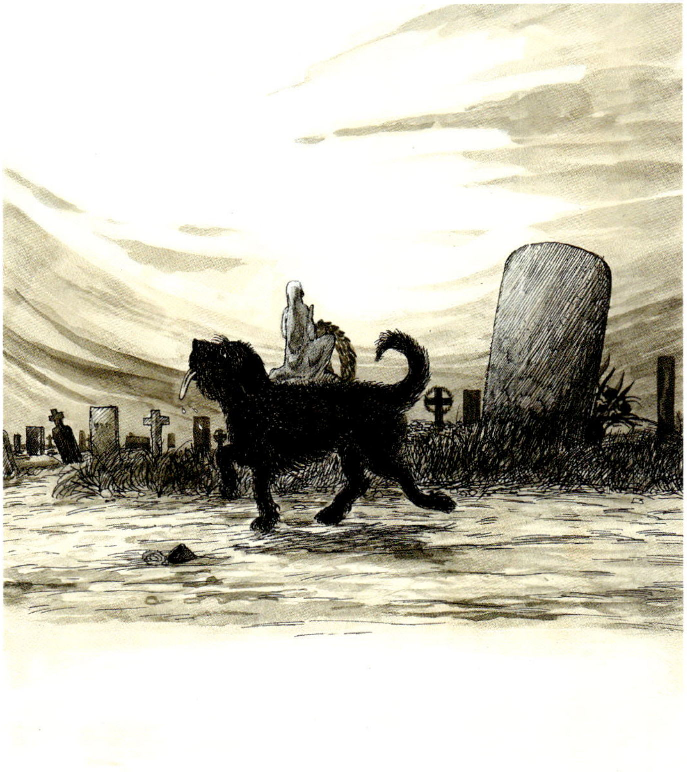

"A Variety of Annoyances was displayed at the Butler Institute of American Art in Youngstown, Ohio. Opposite is a drawing I did at a Pueblo Indian reservation; while I was there I didn't see a single person."

ABOVE LEFT: *A Variety of Annoyances (A trip to the seaside)* | 1970–74 | pen and ink on paper | 22.5 × 17 cm
ABOVE RIGHT: *A Variety of Annoyances (Spot the dog)* | 1970–74 | pen and ink on paper | 22.5 × 17 cm
OPPOSITE: *Pueblo Indian Cart* | 1970–74 | pen on paper | 59 × 42 cm

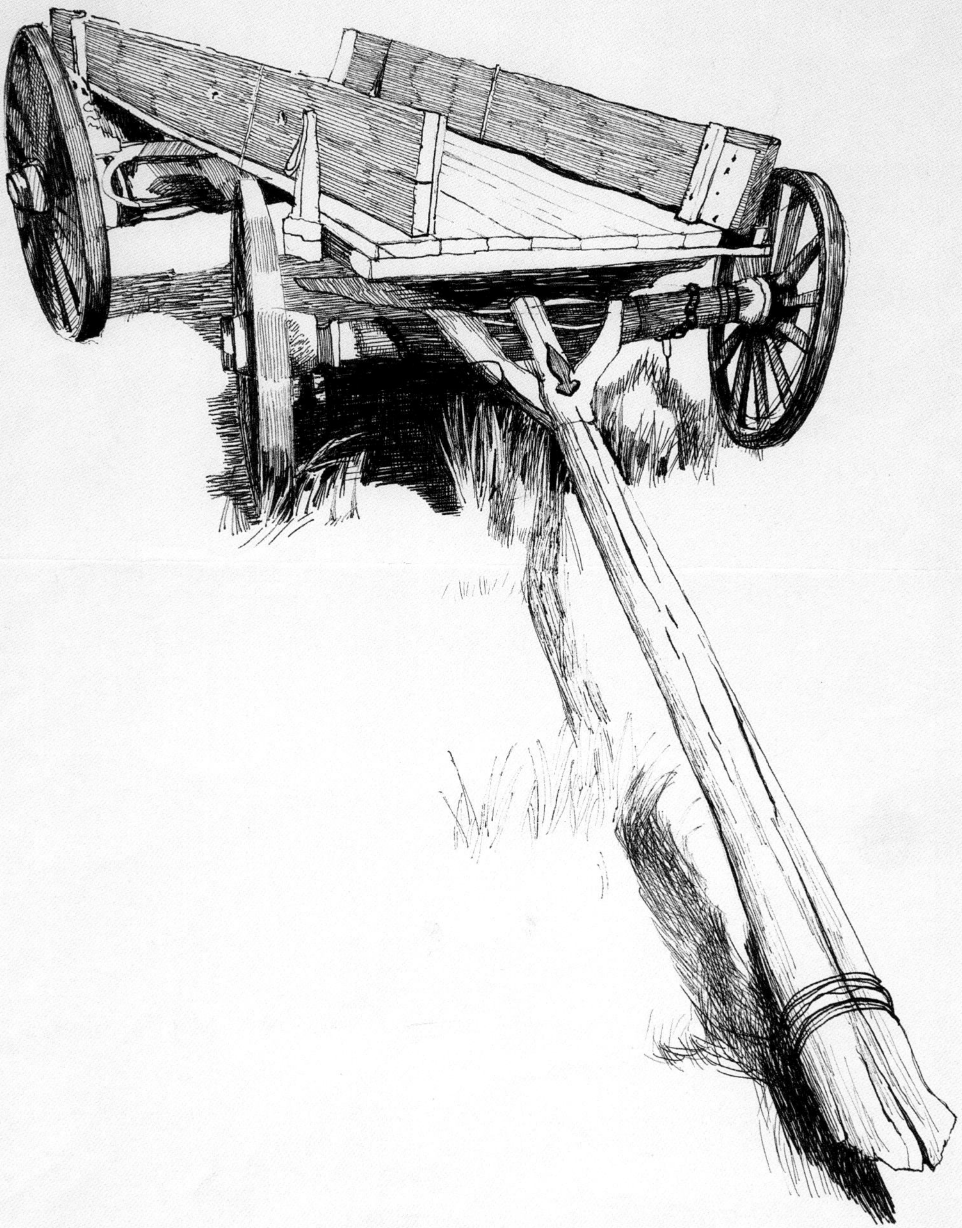

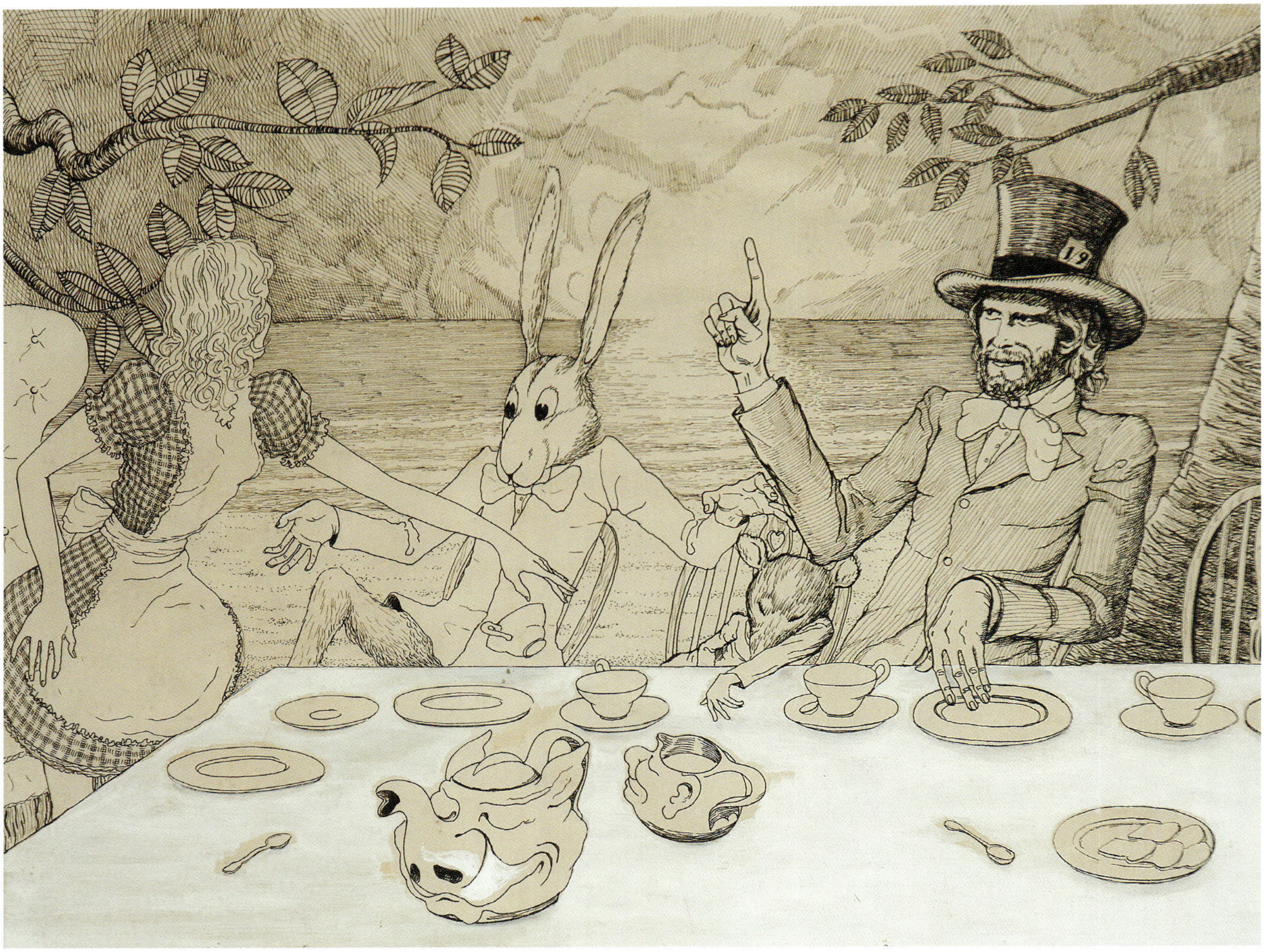

"This was a preliminary sketch I did for the cover of Long John Baldry's album Everything Stops for Tea; *Elton John produced side one of the original album and Rod Stewart side two."*

Everything Stops for Tea (detail) | 1972 | drawing with additional wash | 59 × 41 cm

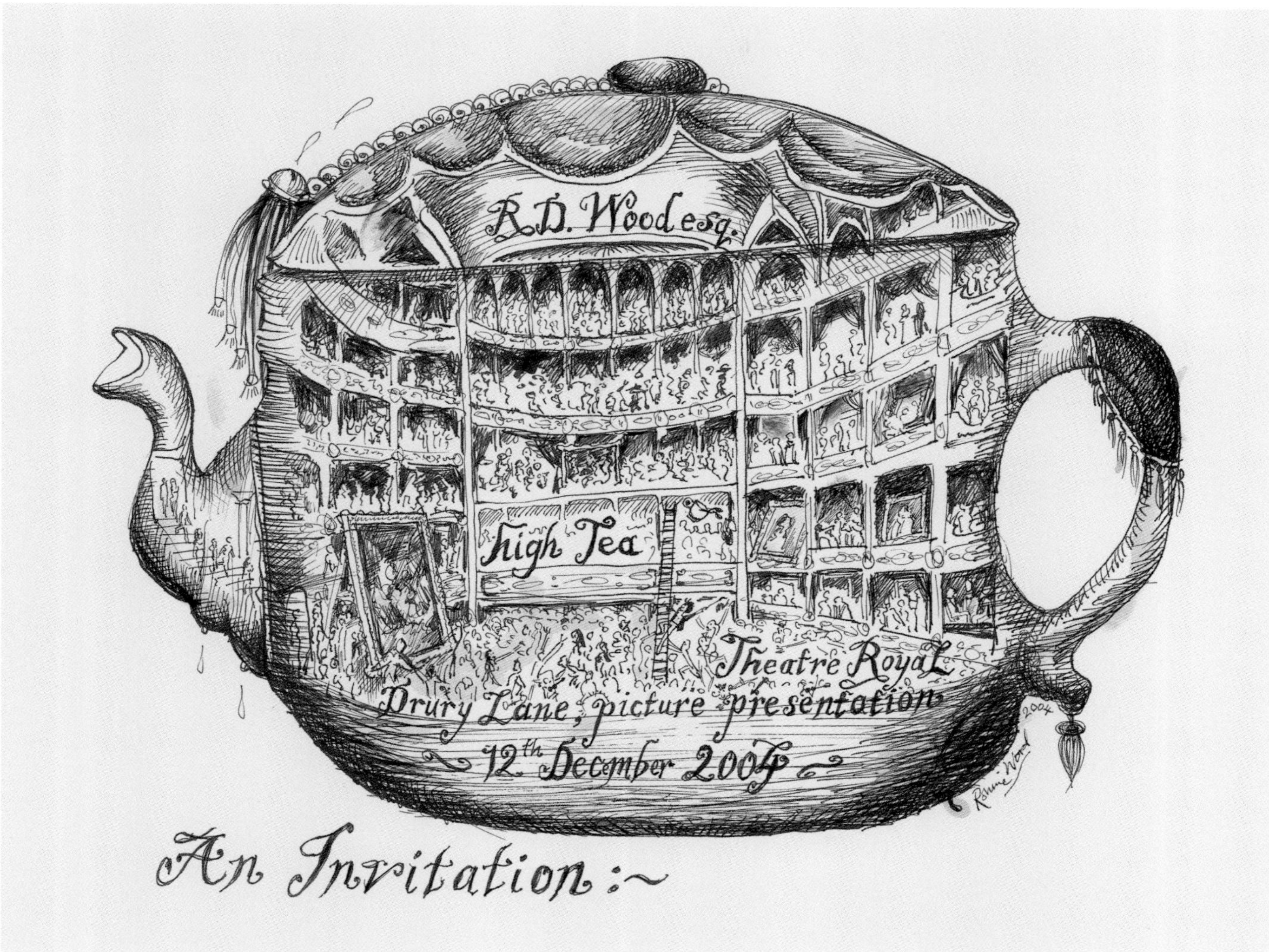

"This invitation was for an event at the Theatre Royal, Drury Lane, featuring my solo music and an exhibition of my art. Slash came and played guitar with me, and Bernard Fowler, who sings backing vocals with the Stones, helped out too."

Theatre Royal Invitation | 2004 | pen and ink | 21 × 28 cm

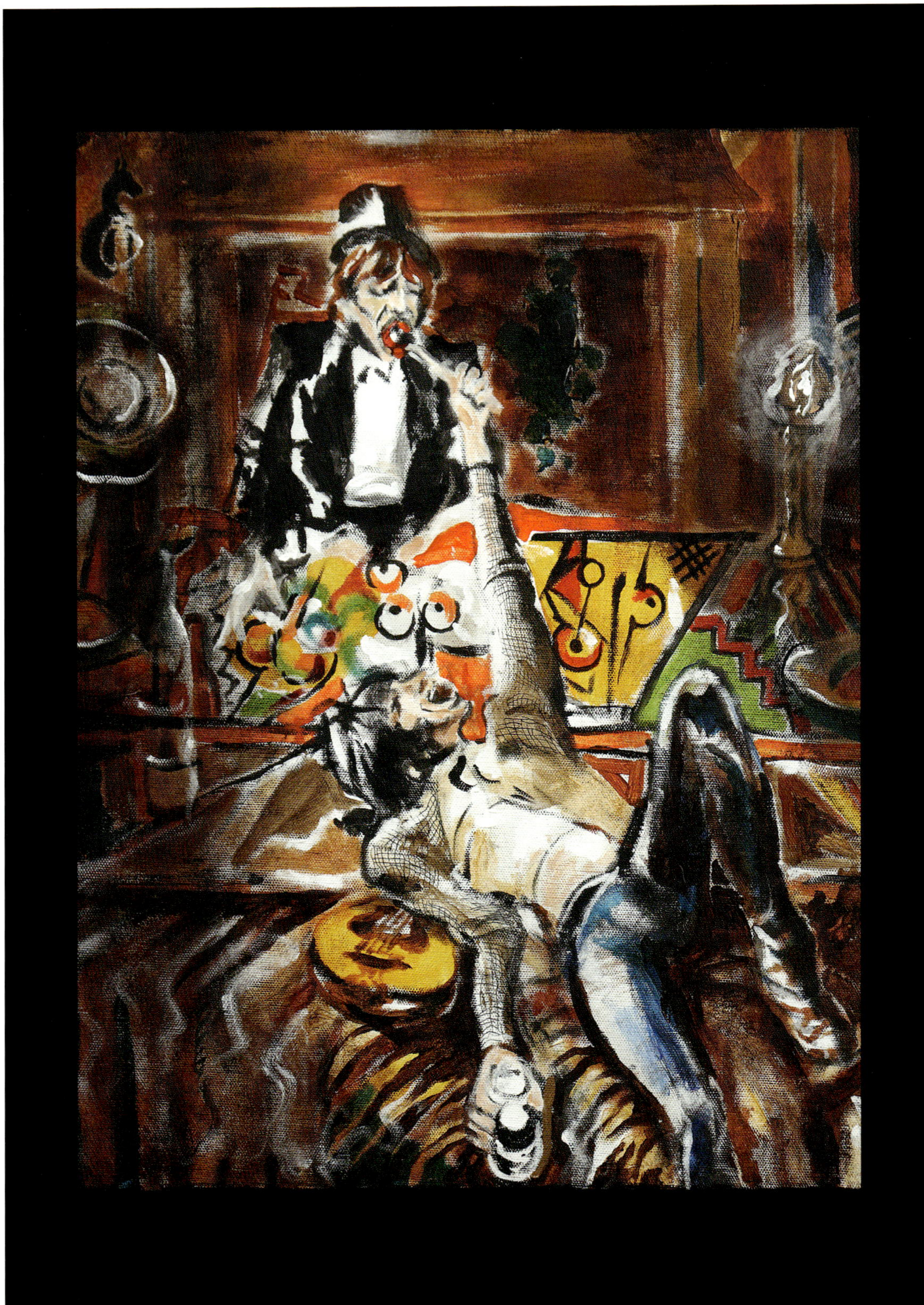

3

THE ROLLING STONES

"I painted these in the studio at the bottom of my garden in Wimbledon, mostly during parties. I was influenced by Rembrandt and Caravaggio in the colours I chose for these paintings; I was bringing some Renaissance influences to my rock 'n' roll life."

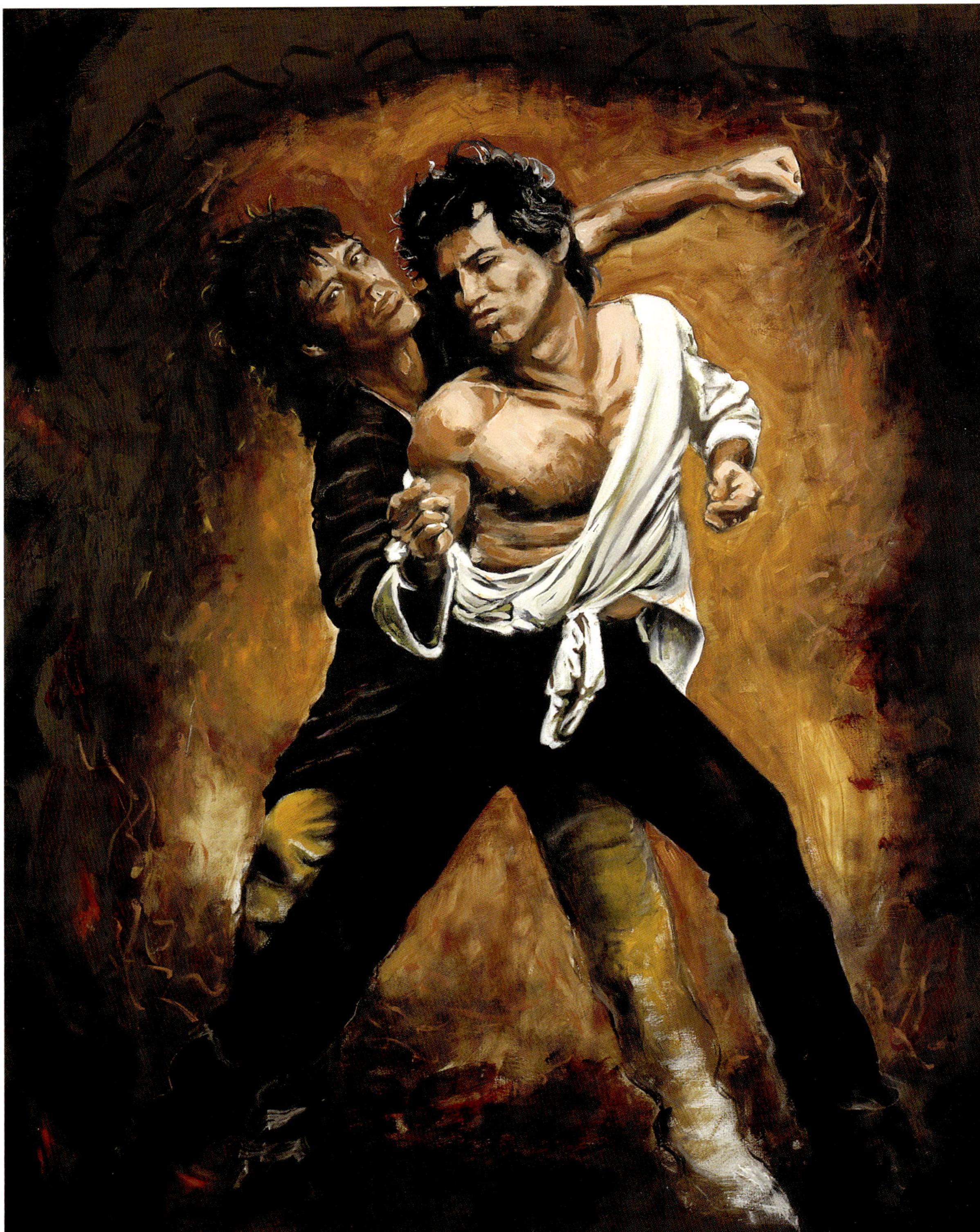

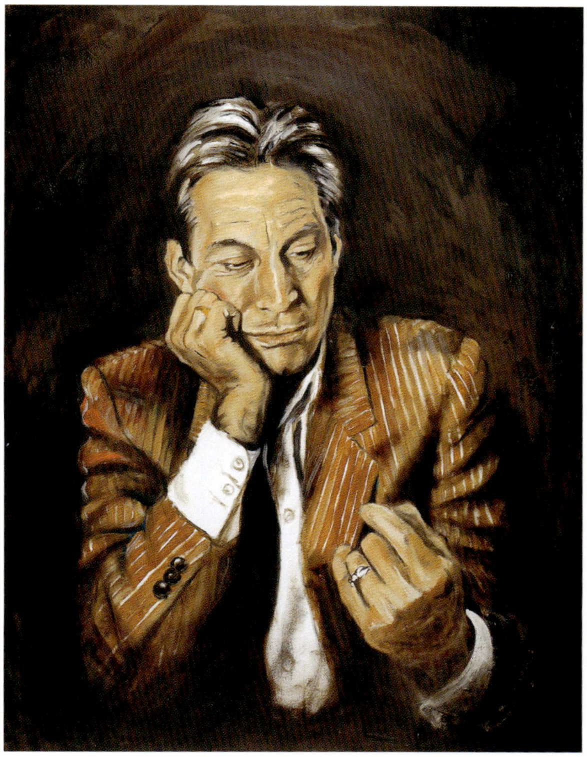

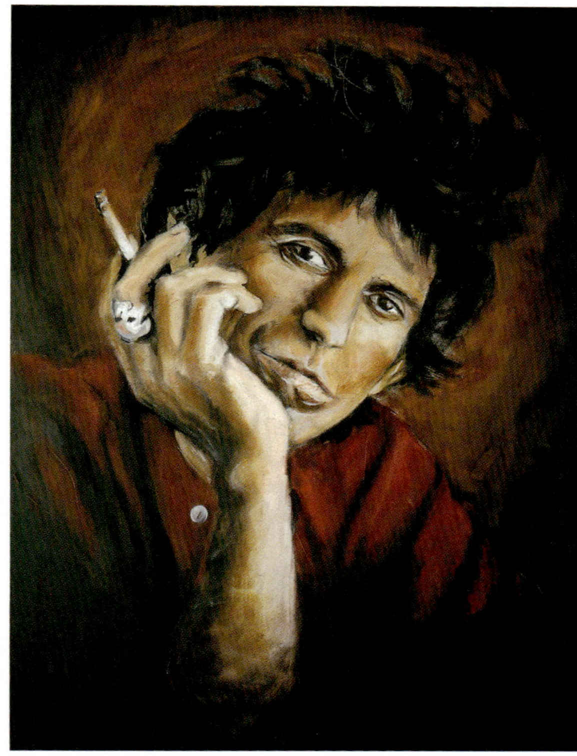

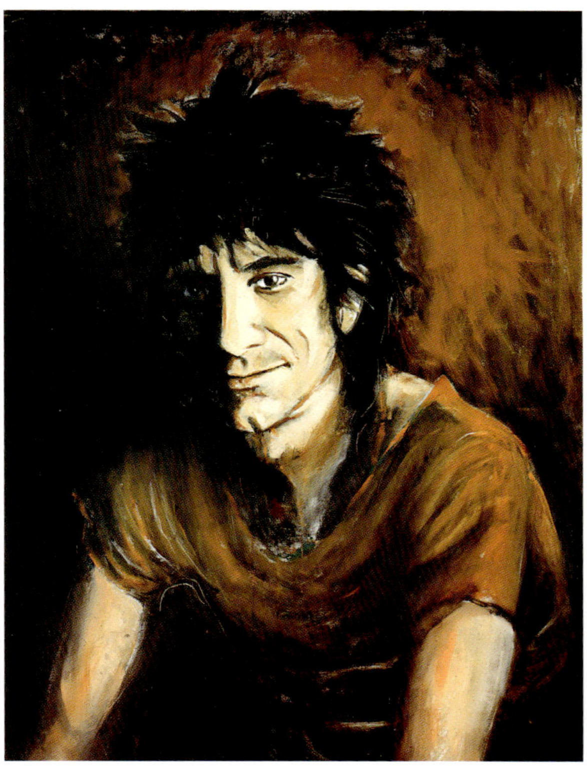

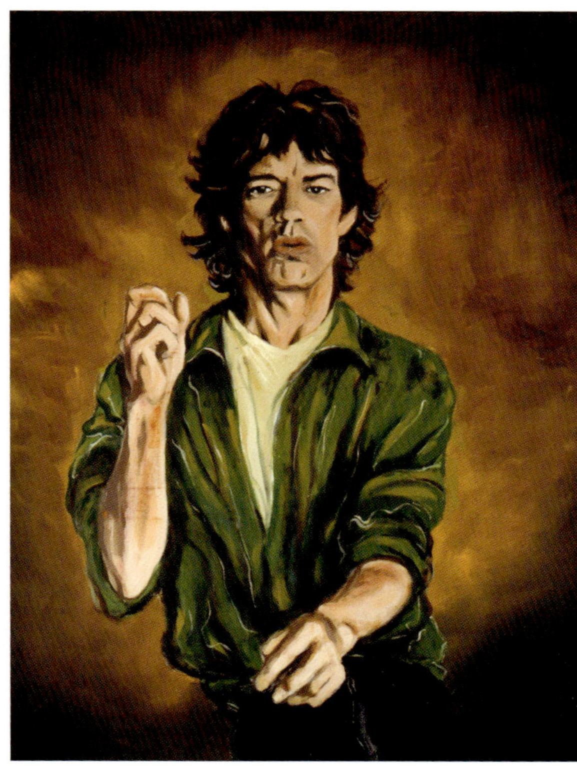

PREVIOUS PAGE: *Beggars Banquet Study* (detail) | 2016 | acrylic on canvas | 51 × 51 cm
OPPOSITE: *Keith and Mick Staged* | 1989 | oil on canvas | 152.5 × 122 cm
TOP LEFT: *Charlie* | 1989 | oil on canvas | 152.5 × 122 cm
TOP RIGHT: *Keith* | 1989 | oil on canvas | 152.5 × 122 cm
ABOVE LEFT: *Ronnie* | 1989 | oil on canvas | 152.5 × 122 cm
ABOVE RIGHT: *Mick* (detail) | 1989 | oil on canvas | 152.5 × 122 cm

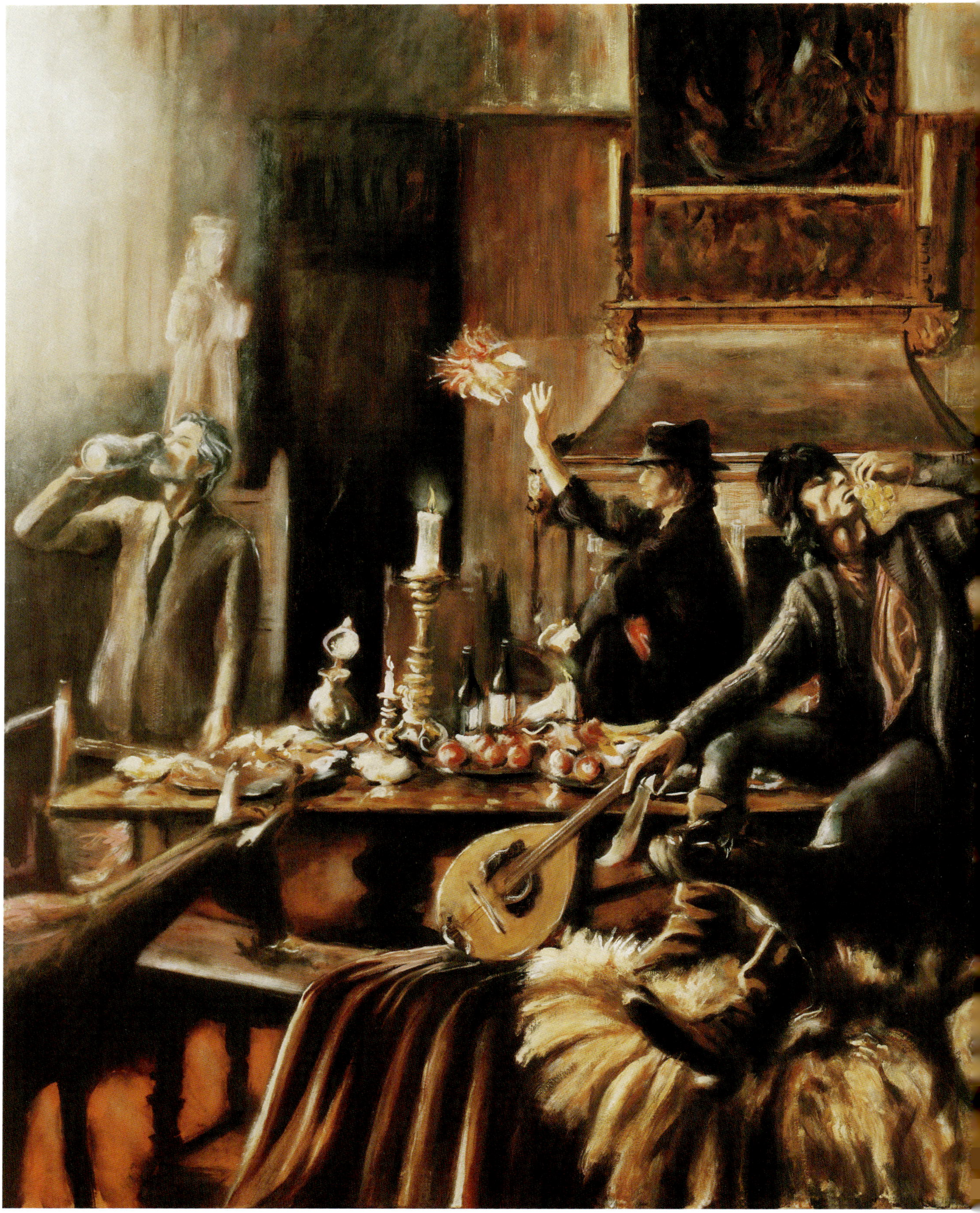

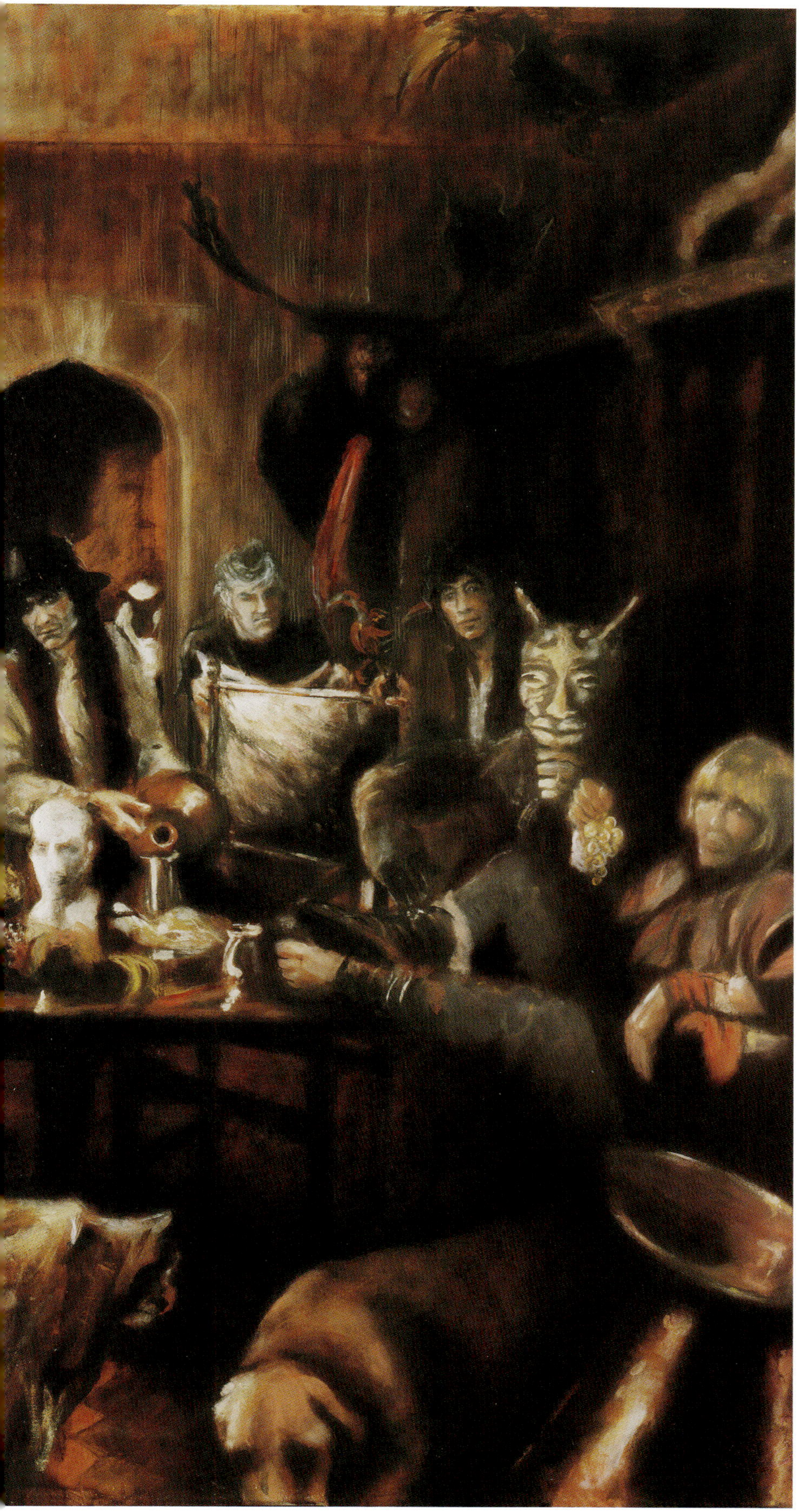

"This is my reimagining of the Beggars Banquet *gatefold. I took artistic licence: I put myself in the picture, showed Mick Taylor leaving the band and added Ian Stewart in the background reading the paper."*

Beggars Banquet | 1989
oil on canvas | 178 × 244 cm

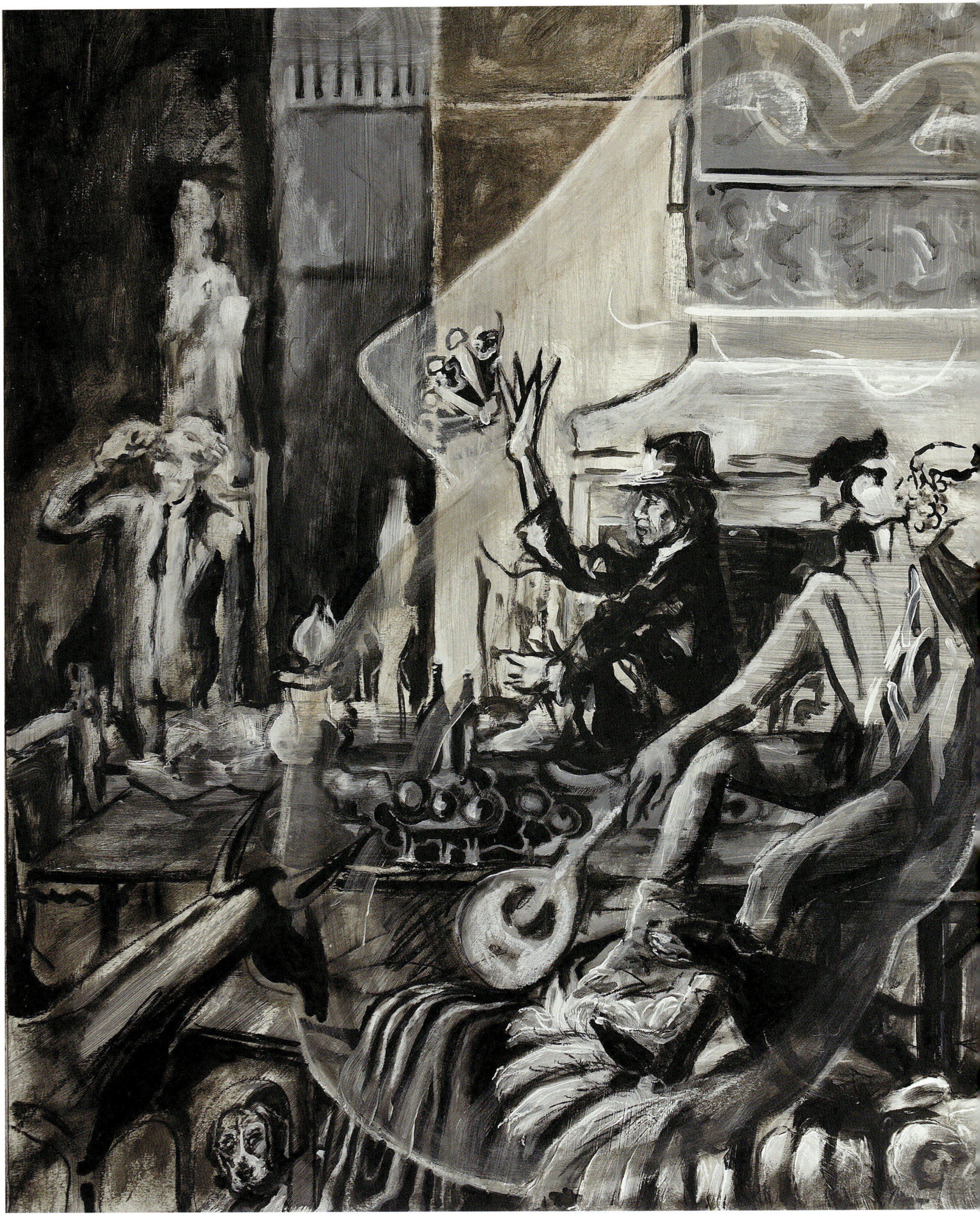

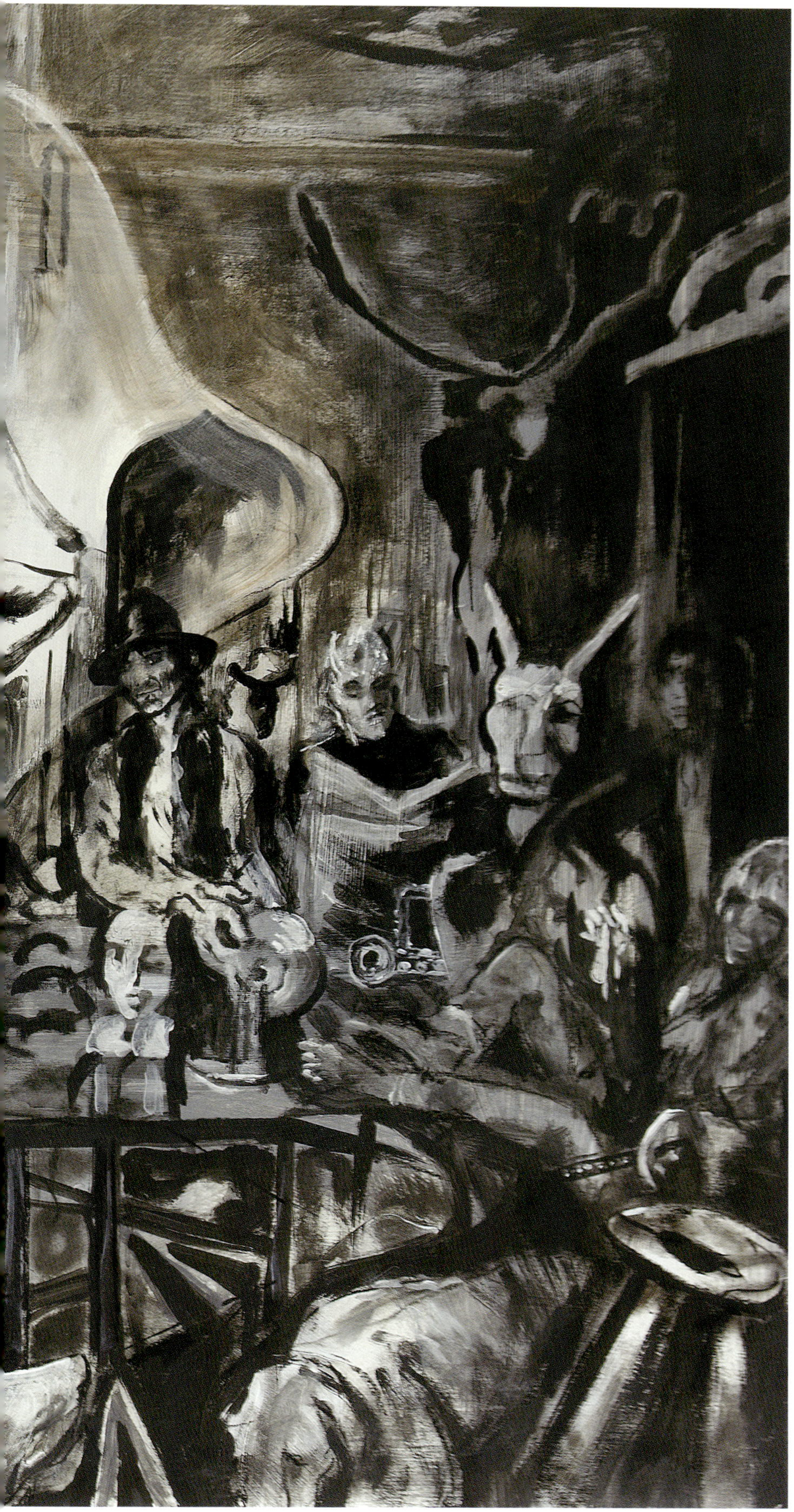

"This is me revisiting my reimagining of the Beggars Banquet *gatefold. I've even included Dolly, our dog, bottom left."*

Study for Beggars Banquet | 2016
acrylic on canvas | 92 × 122 cm

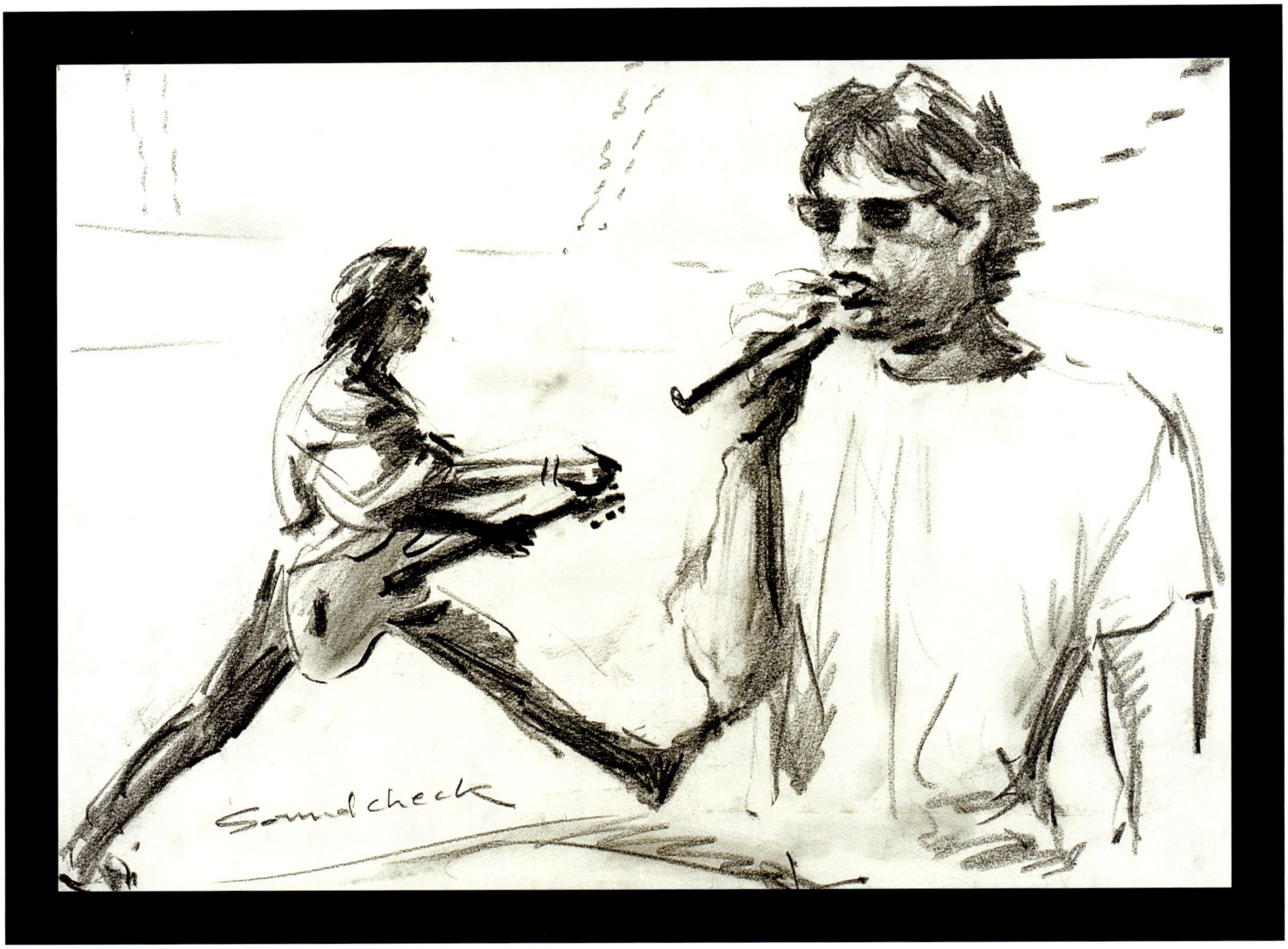

"Opposite, I used a photograph of Keith taken during our 1981 US tour in Philadelphia; he's playing his customized Fender Telecaster."

ABOVE: *Early Mick Drawing* | *c.* 1980 | pencil on paper | 40 × 50 cm
OPPOSITE: *Keith Richards on Stage* | 1987 | mixed media on paper | 112 × 76 cm

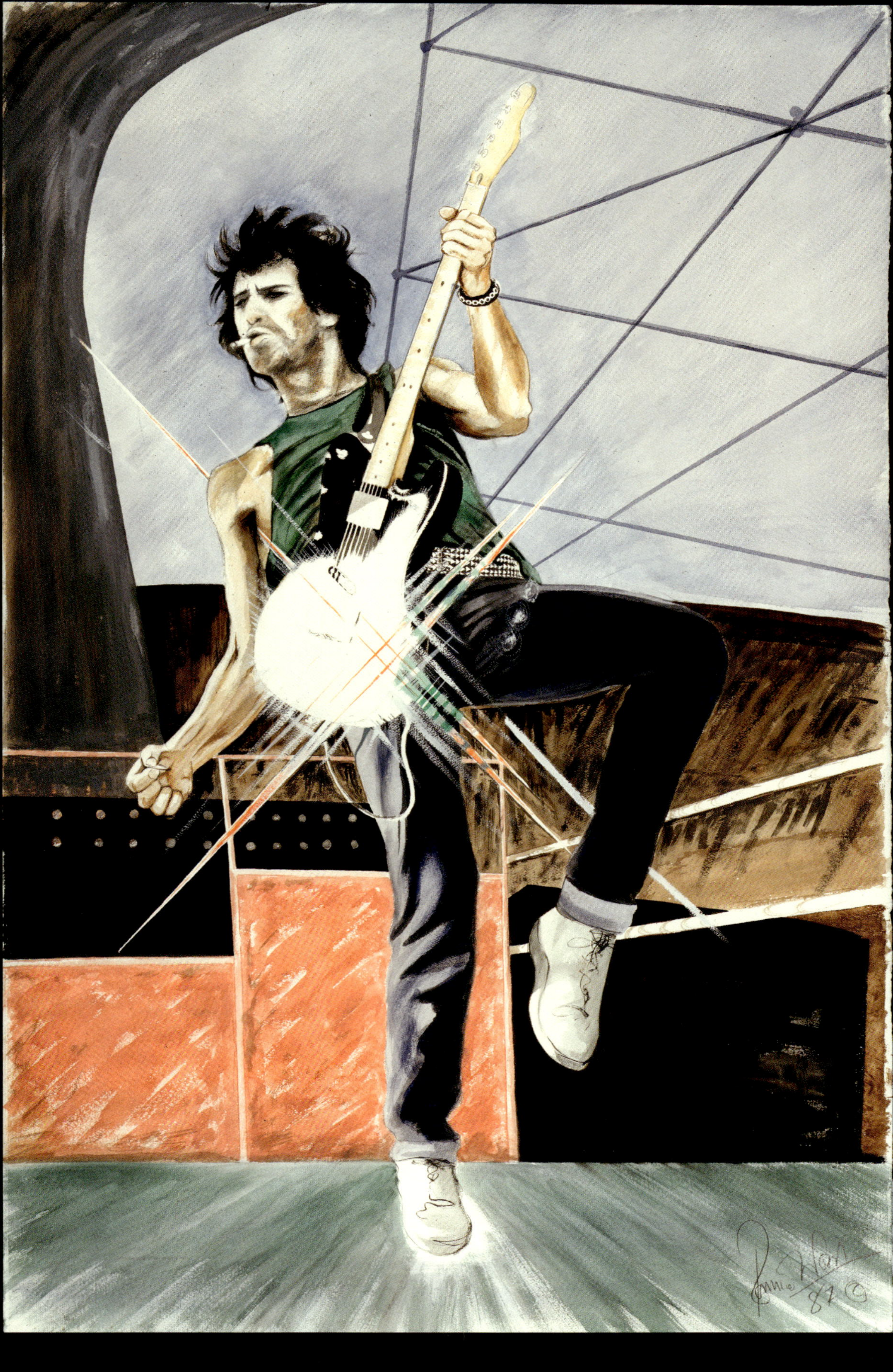

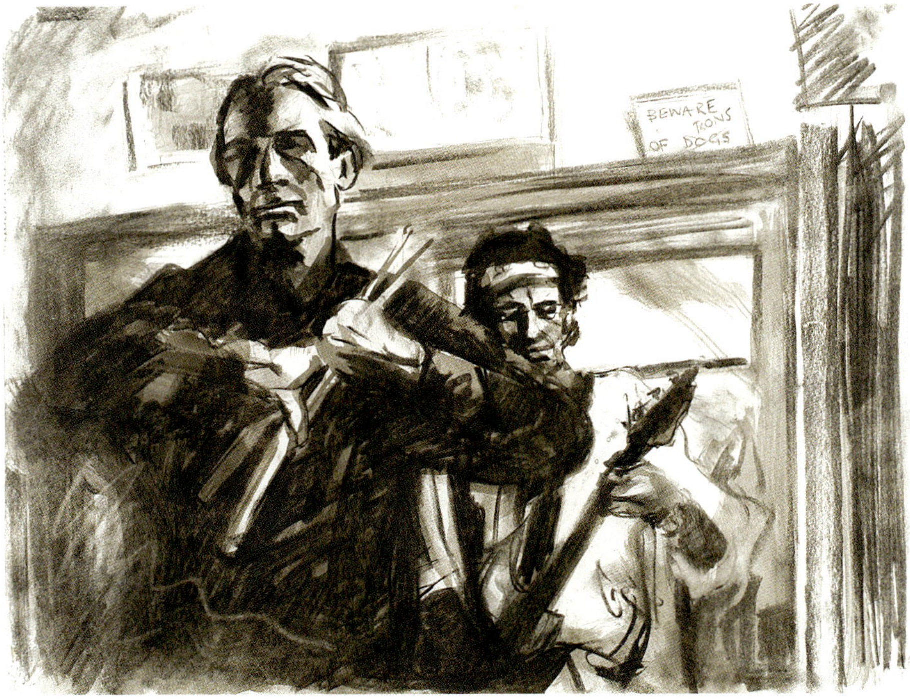

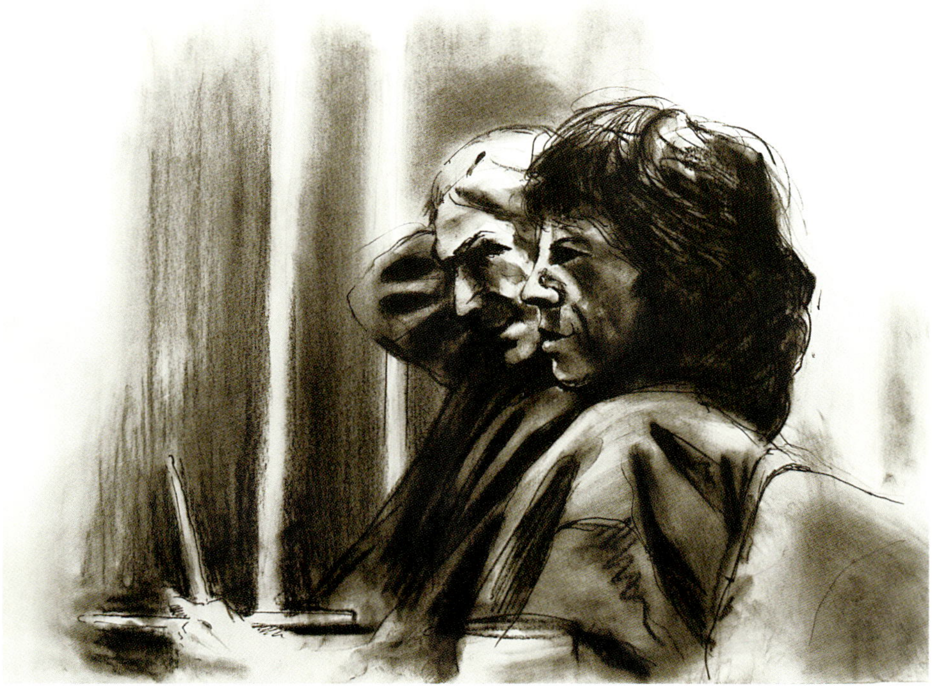

"These were drawn in the summer of 1993 while we were working on tracks for the Voodoo Lounge *album in my studio at Sandymount in Ireland."*

TOP: *Charlie and Keith Relaxing* | 1993 | mixed media on paper | 58 × 76 cm
ABOVE: *Charlie and Mick Relaxing* | 1993 | mixed media on paper | 58 × 76 cm

BELOW LEFT: *Rehearsing at Sandymount, Charlie* | 1993 | mixed media on paper | 64 × 54 cm
BELOW RIGHT: *Rehearsing at Sandymount, Charlie & Ronnie* | 1993 | mixed media on paper | 54 × 64 cm
BOTTOM LEFT: *Rehearsing at Sandymount, Charlie & Ronnie* | 1993 | mixed media on paper | 64 × 54 cm
BOTTOM RIGHT: *Rehearsing at Sandymount, Mick* | 1993 | mixed media on paper | 64 × 54 cm

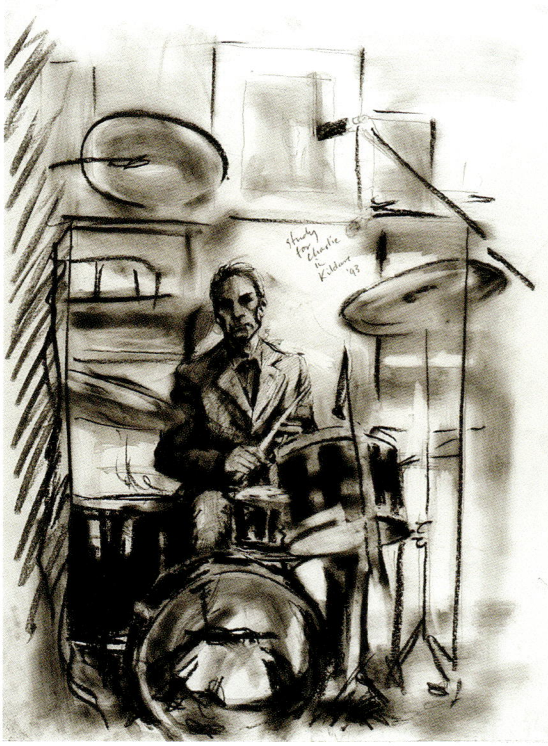

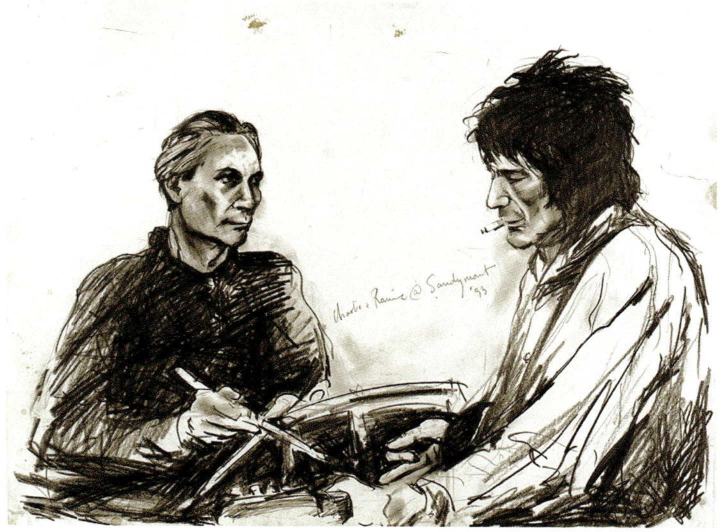

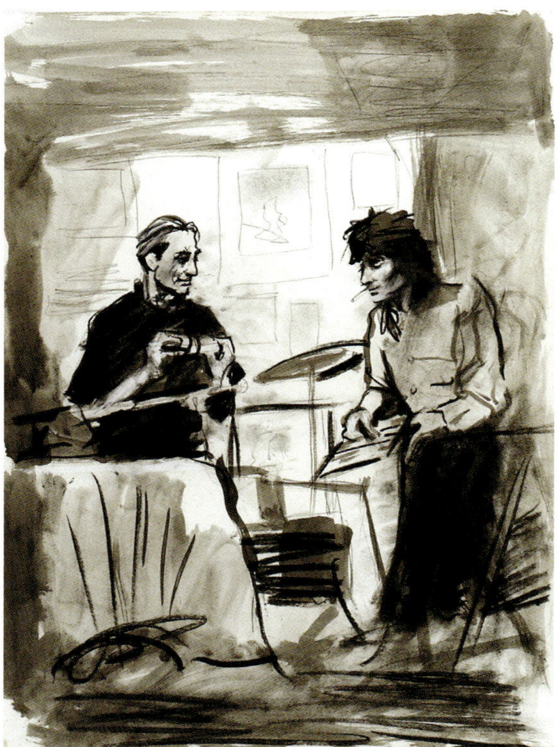

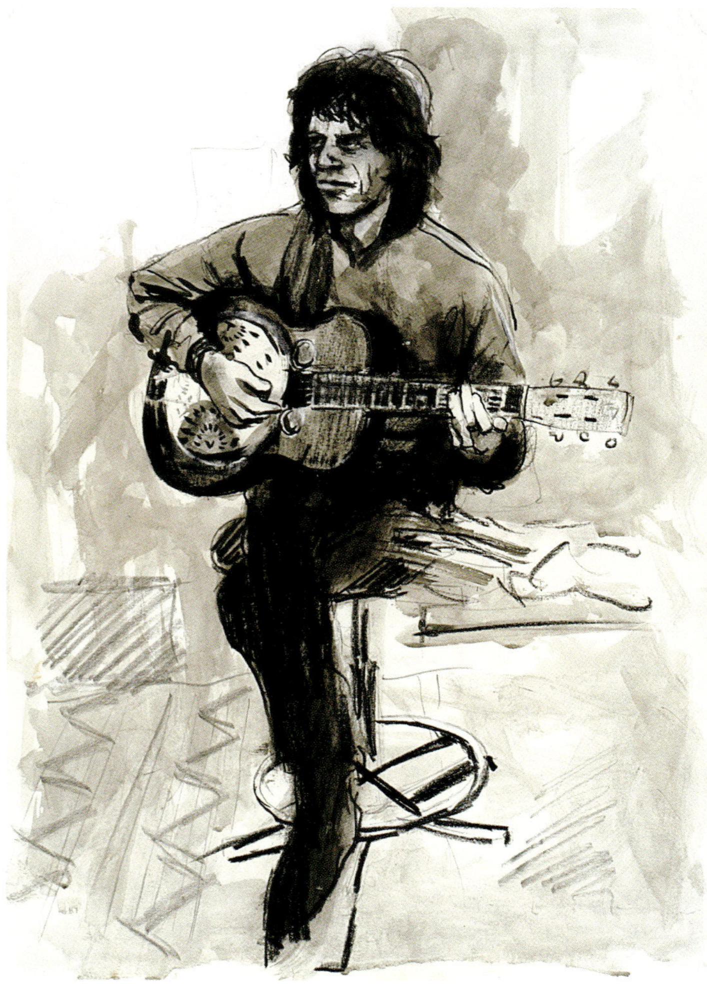

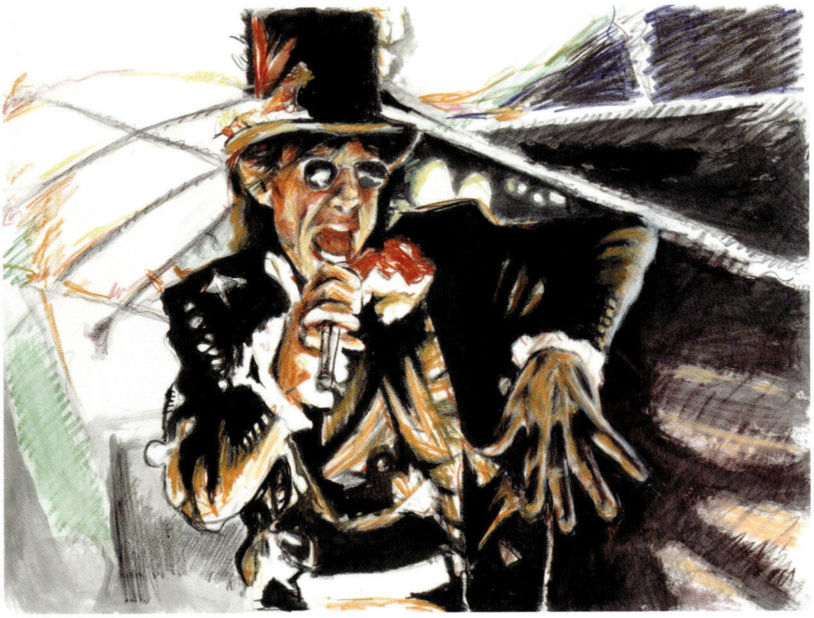

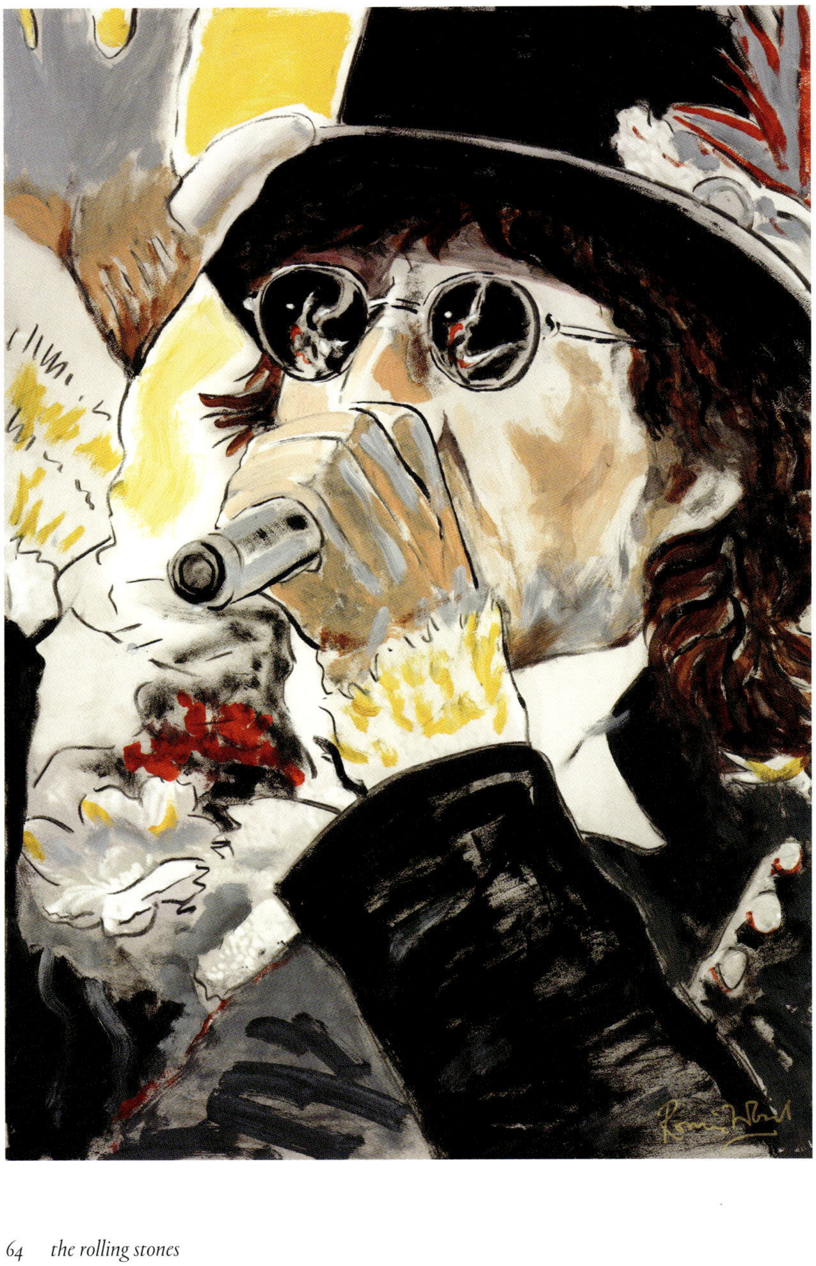

"Here's Mick in the great outfit he wore for our Voodoo Lounge tour that ran from August 1994 to August 1995. I made the four studies opposite during rehearsals for the Voodoo Lounge tour."

OPPOSITE ABOVE: *Sympathy for the Devil* | 1996 | mixed media on paper | 56 × 80 cm

OPPOSITE BELOW: *Jagger Sympathy* | 2010 | mixed media on board | 81 × 60 cm

BELOW LEFT: *Ronnie Voodoo* | 1996 | pastel on paper | 64.5 × 48.5 cm

BELOW CENTRE: *Charlie Voodoo* | 1996 | pastel on paper | 64.5 × 48.5 cm

BELOW RIGHT: *Keith Voodoo* | 1996 | pastel on paper | 64.5 × 48.5 cm

BOTTOM: *Mick Voodoo* | 1996 | pastel on paper | 48.5 × 64.5 cm

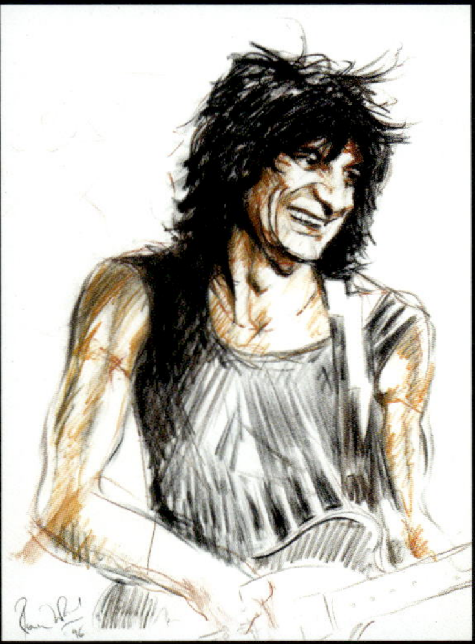

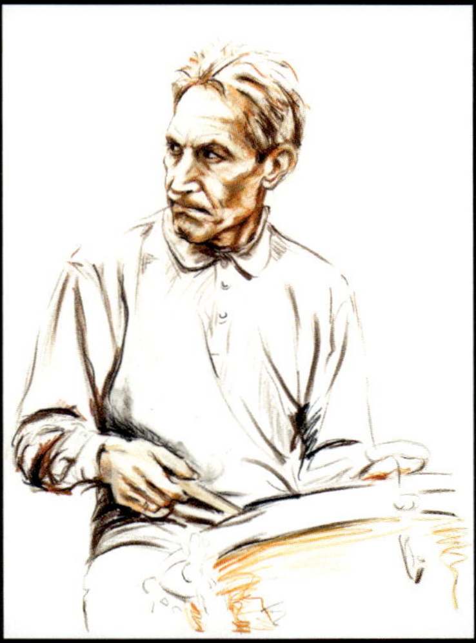

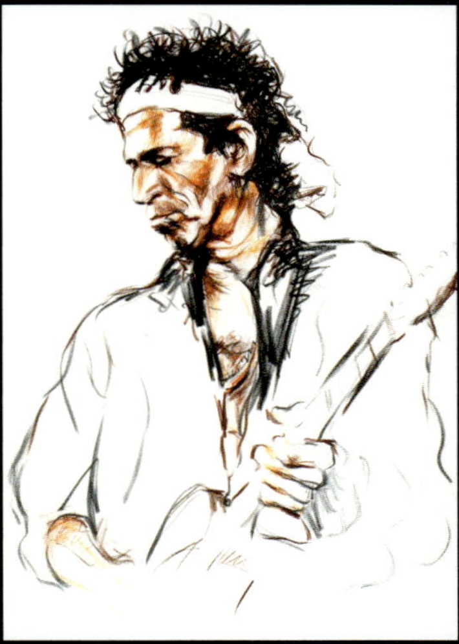

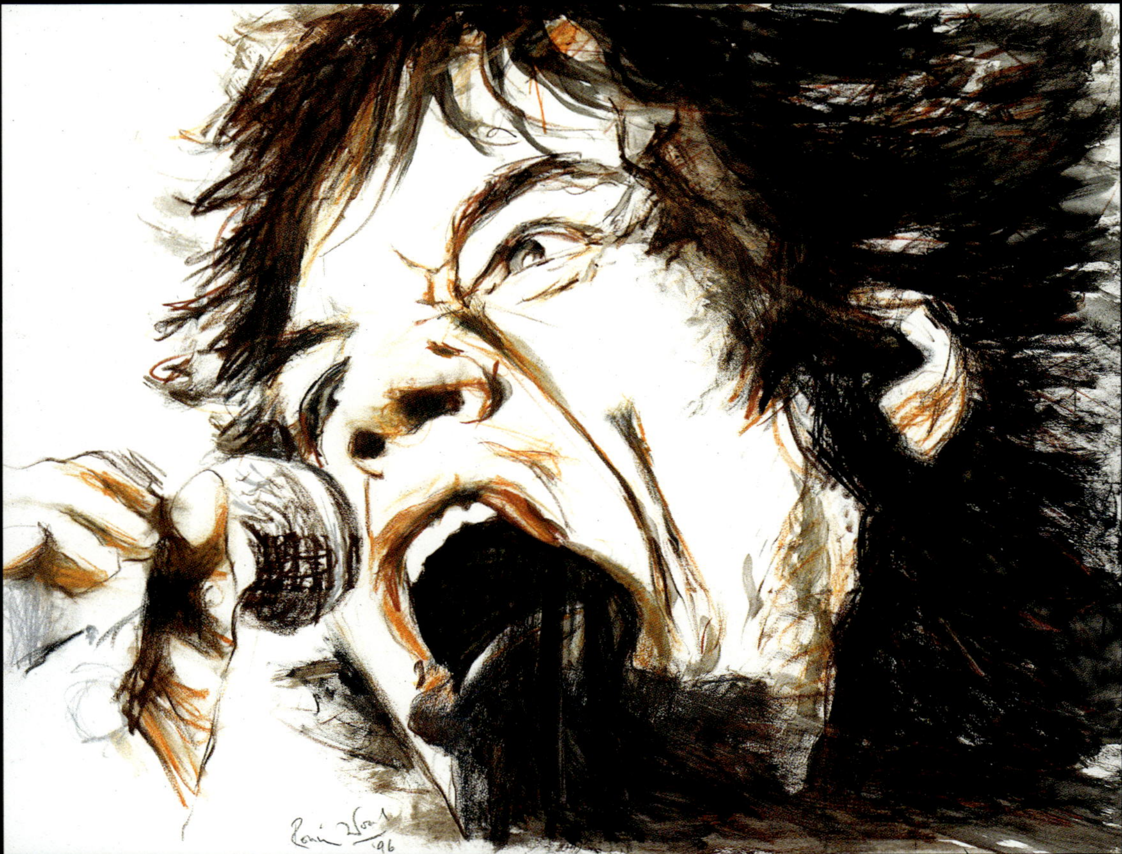

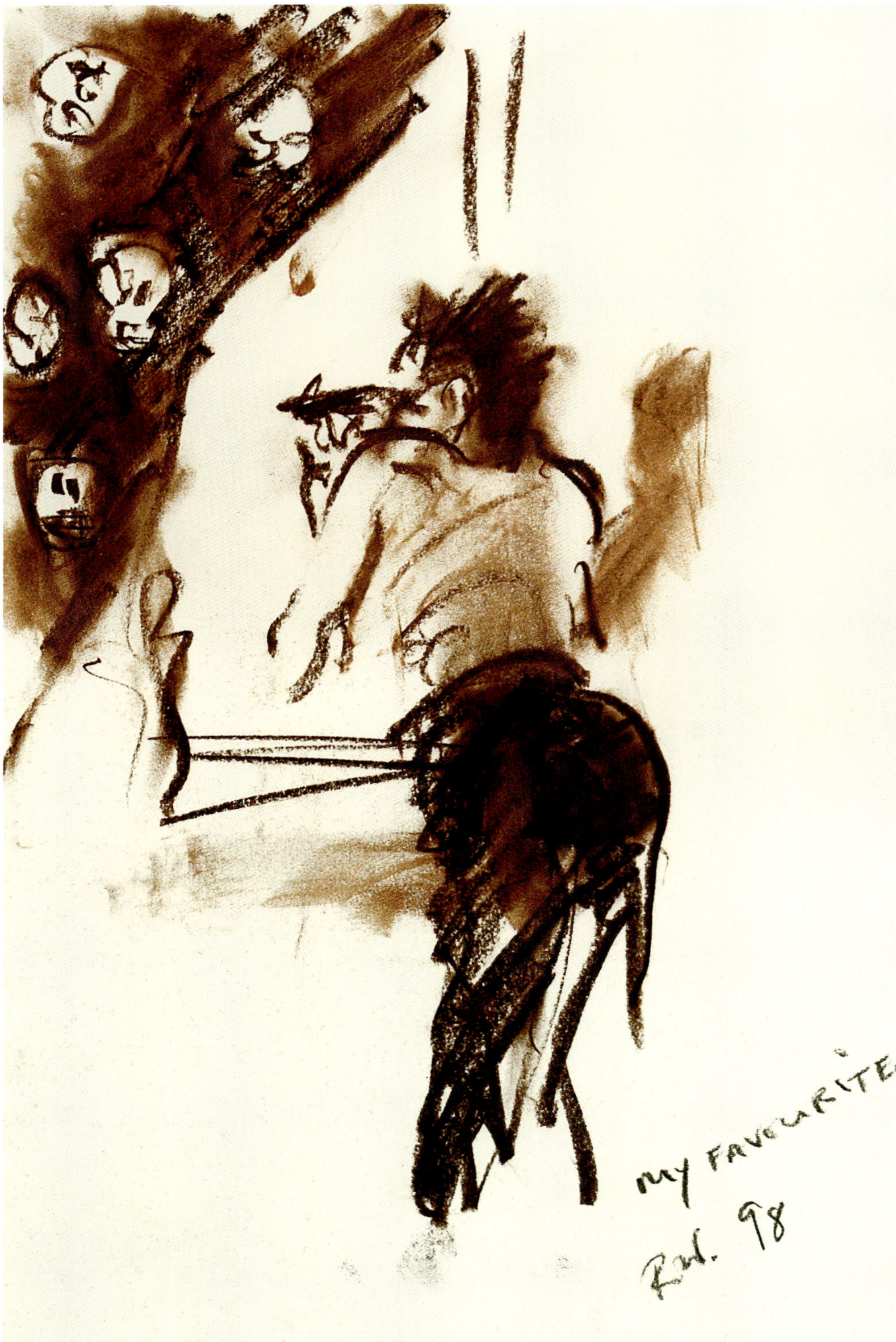

"Keith peering out of his window at the Baltschug Kempinski Hotel in Moscow."

ABOVE: *Keith* | 1998 | pastel on paper | 30 × 22 cm
OPPOSITE: *Abstract Keith (Barcelona)* | 2016 | acrylic on canvas | 46 × 40 cm

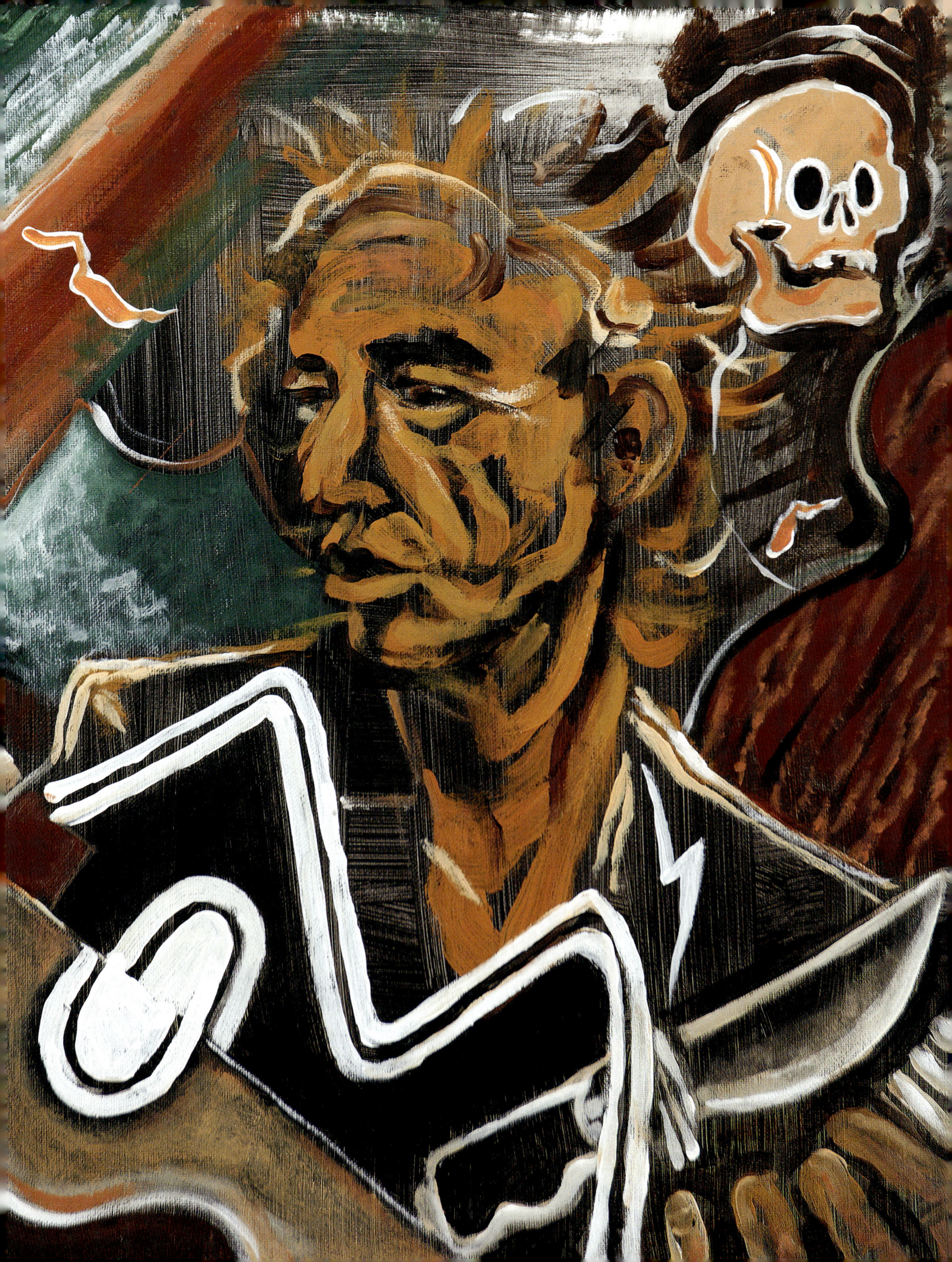

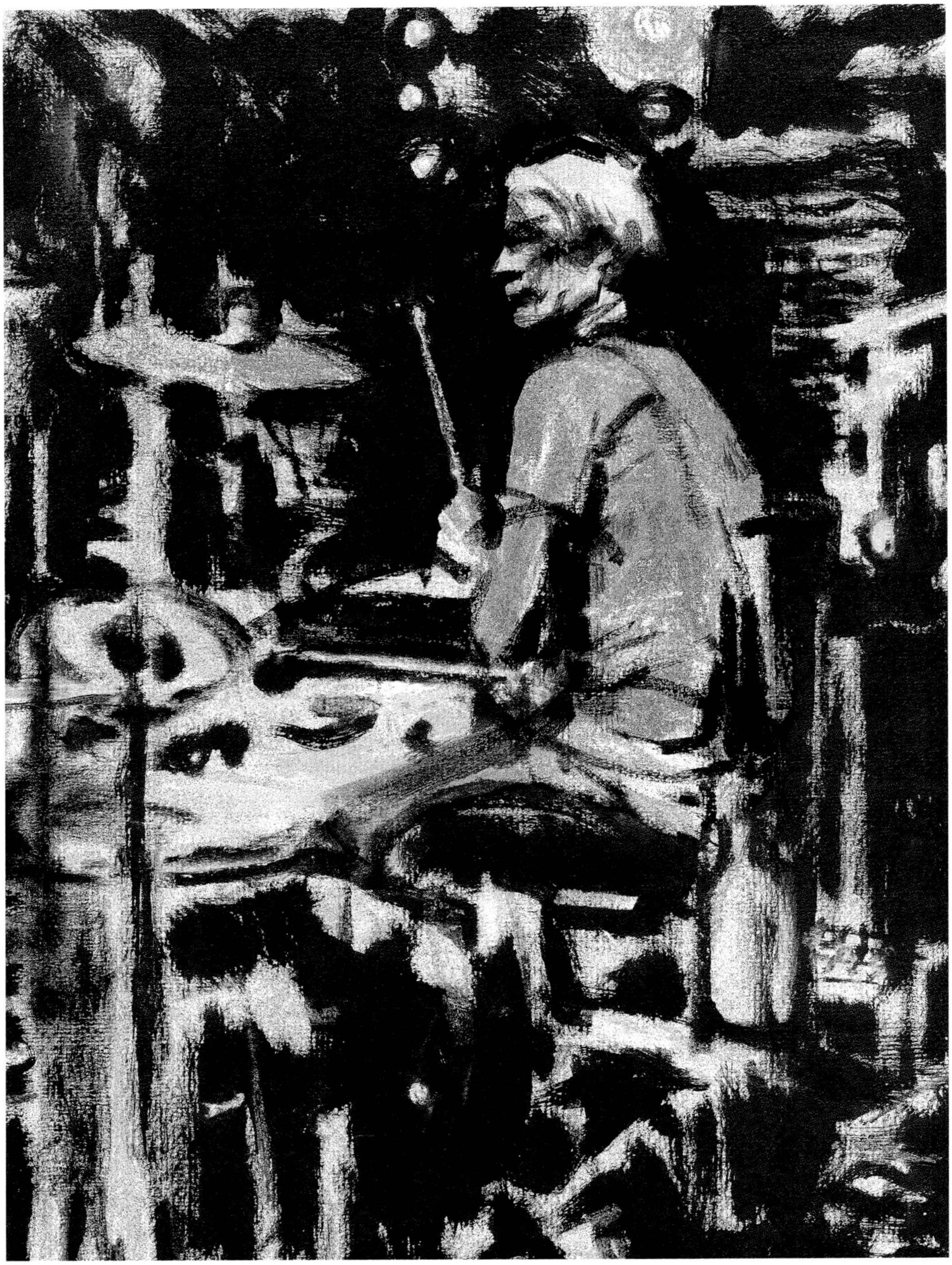

ABOVE: *Charlie with Drums* | 2002 | dry point etching | 34.4 × 29 cm
OPPOSITE LEFT: *Study for Keith* | 2002 | dry point etching | 53 × 39 cm
OPPOSITE RIGHT: *Study for Mick* | 2002 | dry point etching | 52 × 39.5 cm

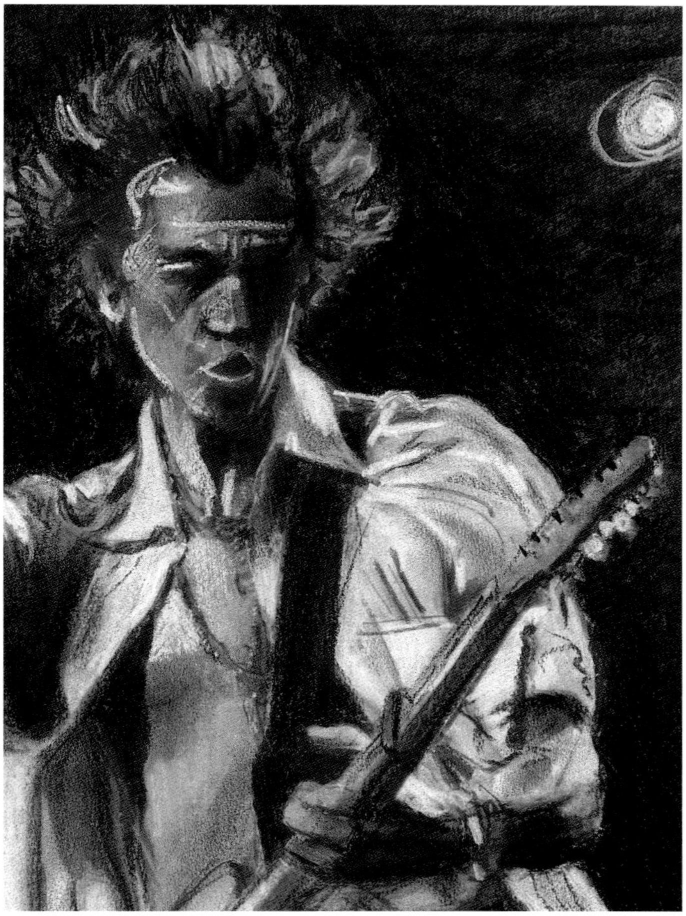 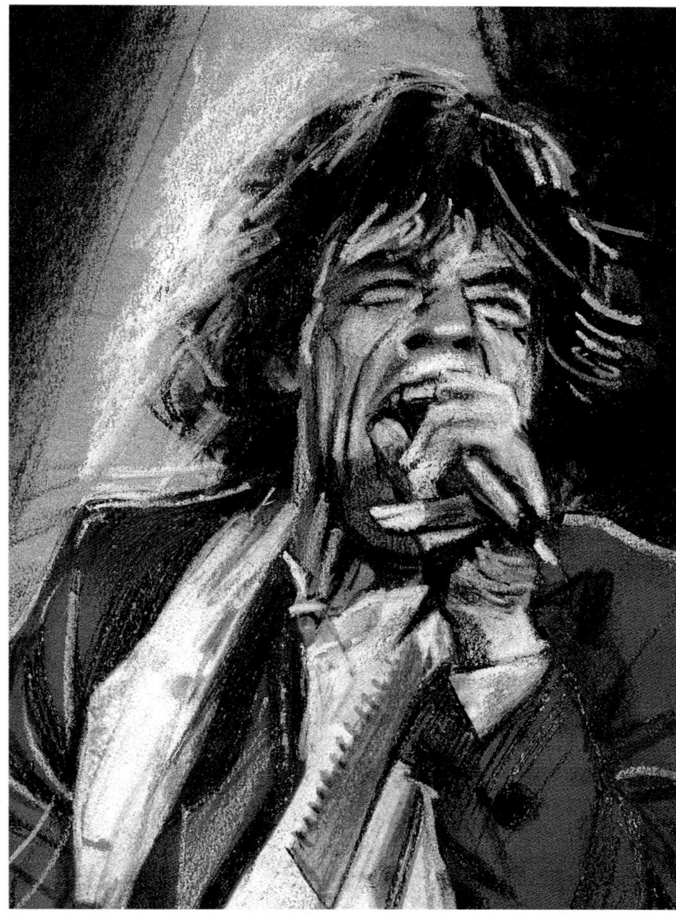

"Opposite, Charlie in my studio at Sandymount in Ireland; above are studies of Mick and Keith on stage during the Licks tour."

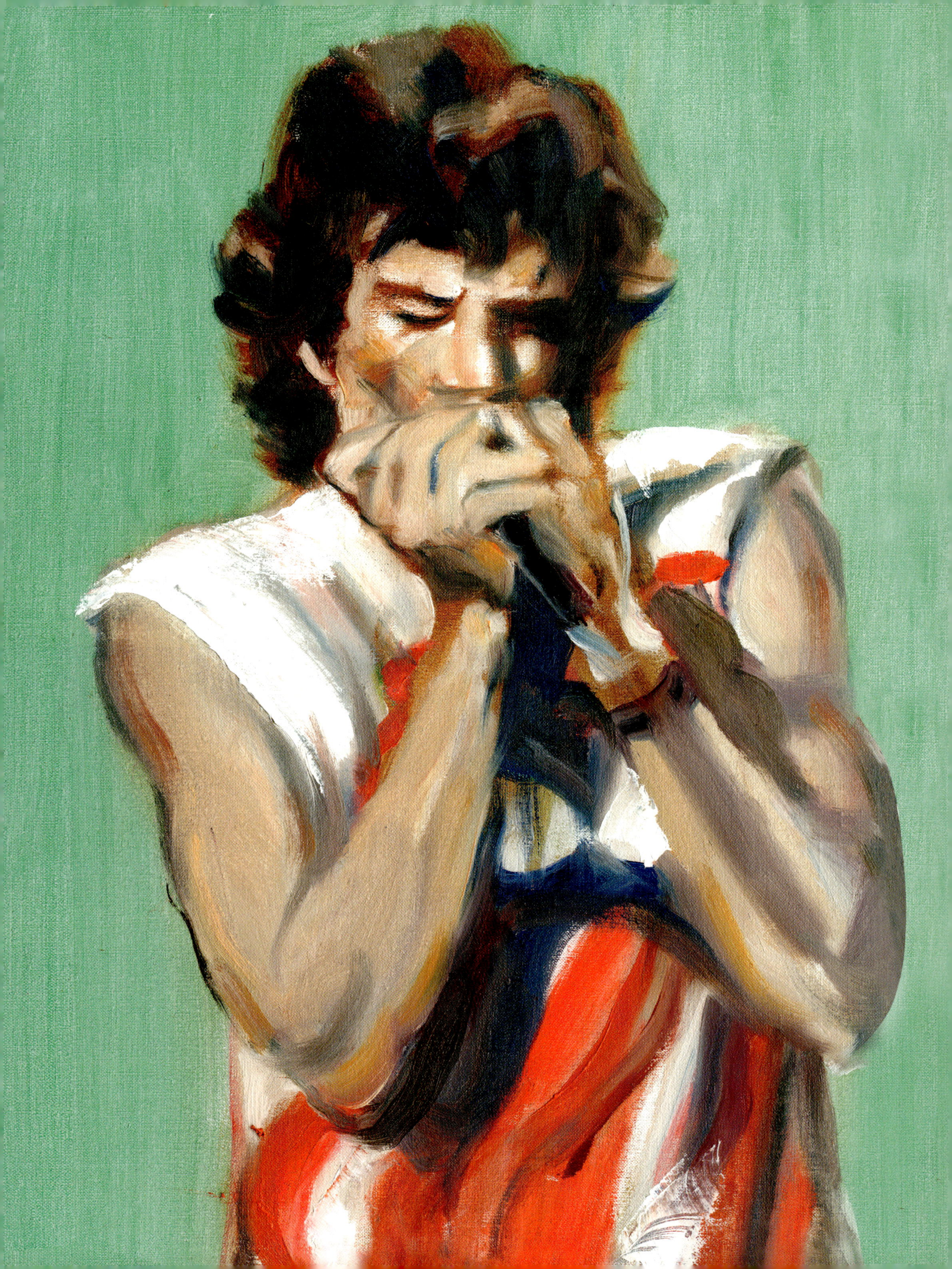

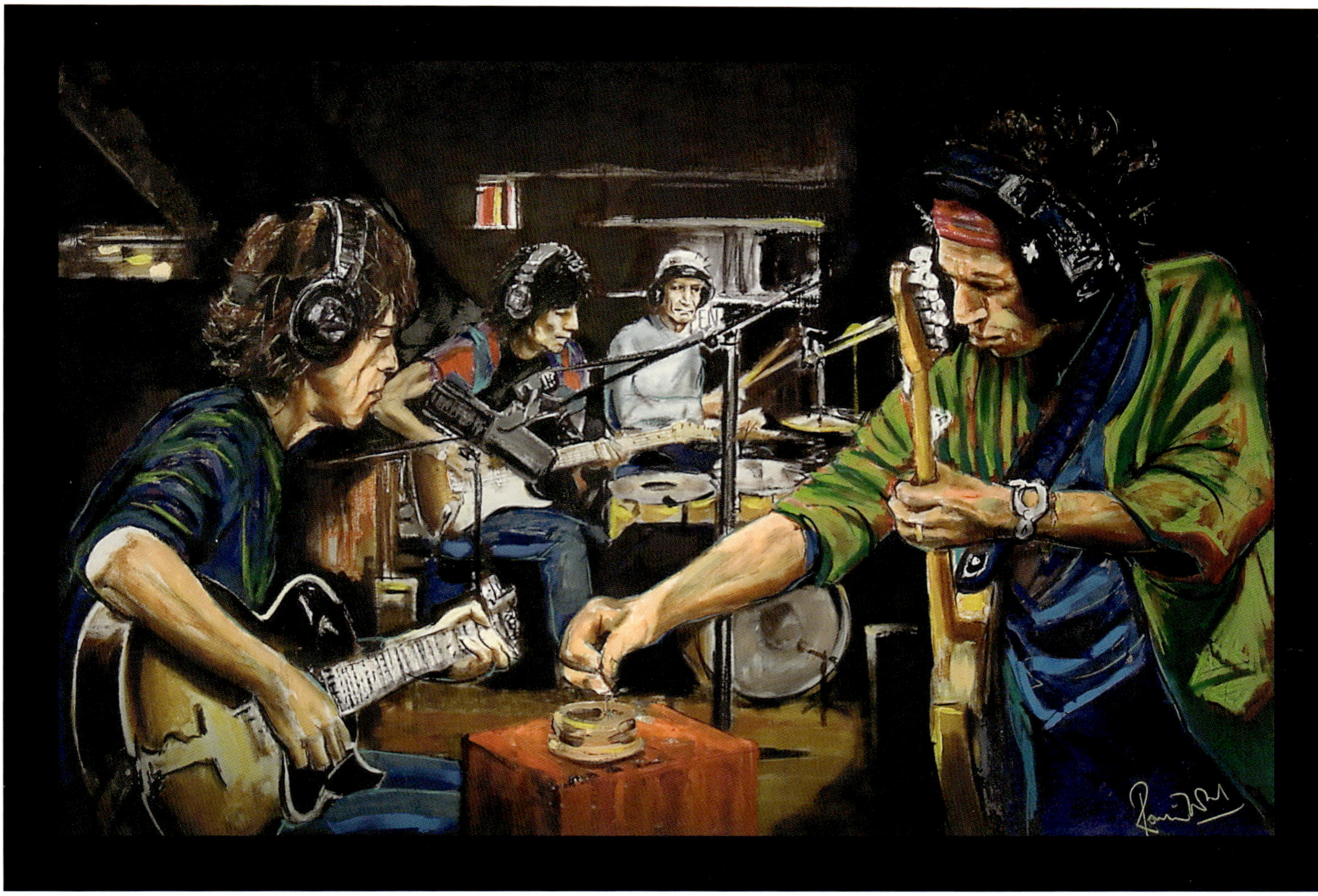

"Conversation Piece *shows us recording 'Don't Stop' at Guillaume Tell Studios in Suresnes, France. It came out as a single and then we played it throughout our Forty Licks tour."*

OPPOSITE: *Mick with Harmonica* | 2003 | oil on canvas | 41 × 30.5 cm
ABOVE: *Conversation Piece* | 2005 | acrylic on canvas | 91.5 × 122 cm

BELOW: *Preparatory Sketch for Flatbed Original* | 2004 | pencil on paper | 28 × 42 cm
RIGHT: *Flatbed Original* | 2005 | mixed media on canvas | 91.5 × 122 cm
OVERLEAF: *Forty Licks* | 2004 | mixed media on canvas | 91.5 × 122 cm

"In May 1975, we went down Fifth Avenue on a flatbed truck and played 'Brown Sugar' to promote our Tour of the Americas; this was my first tour with the Stones."

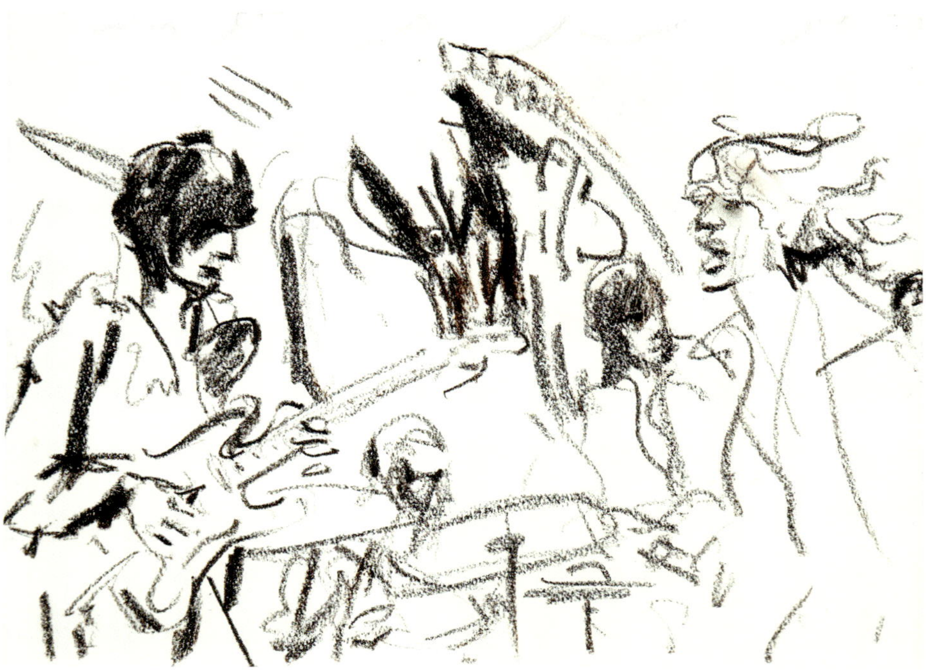

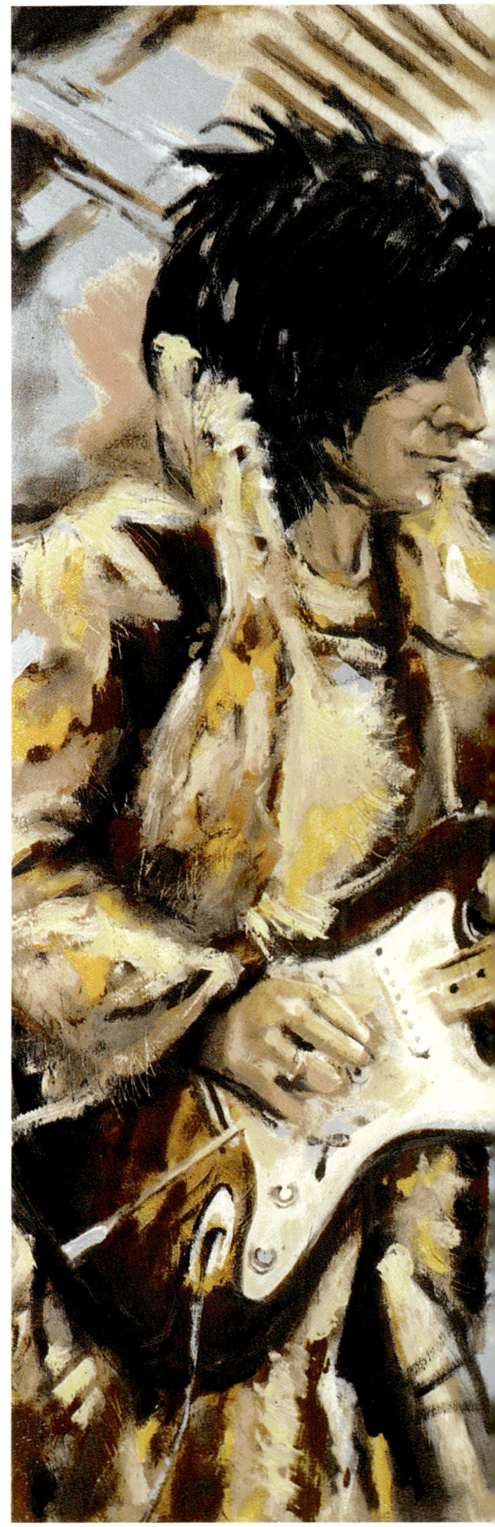

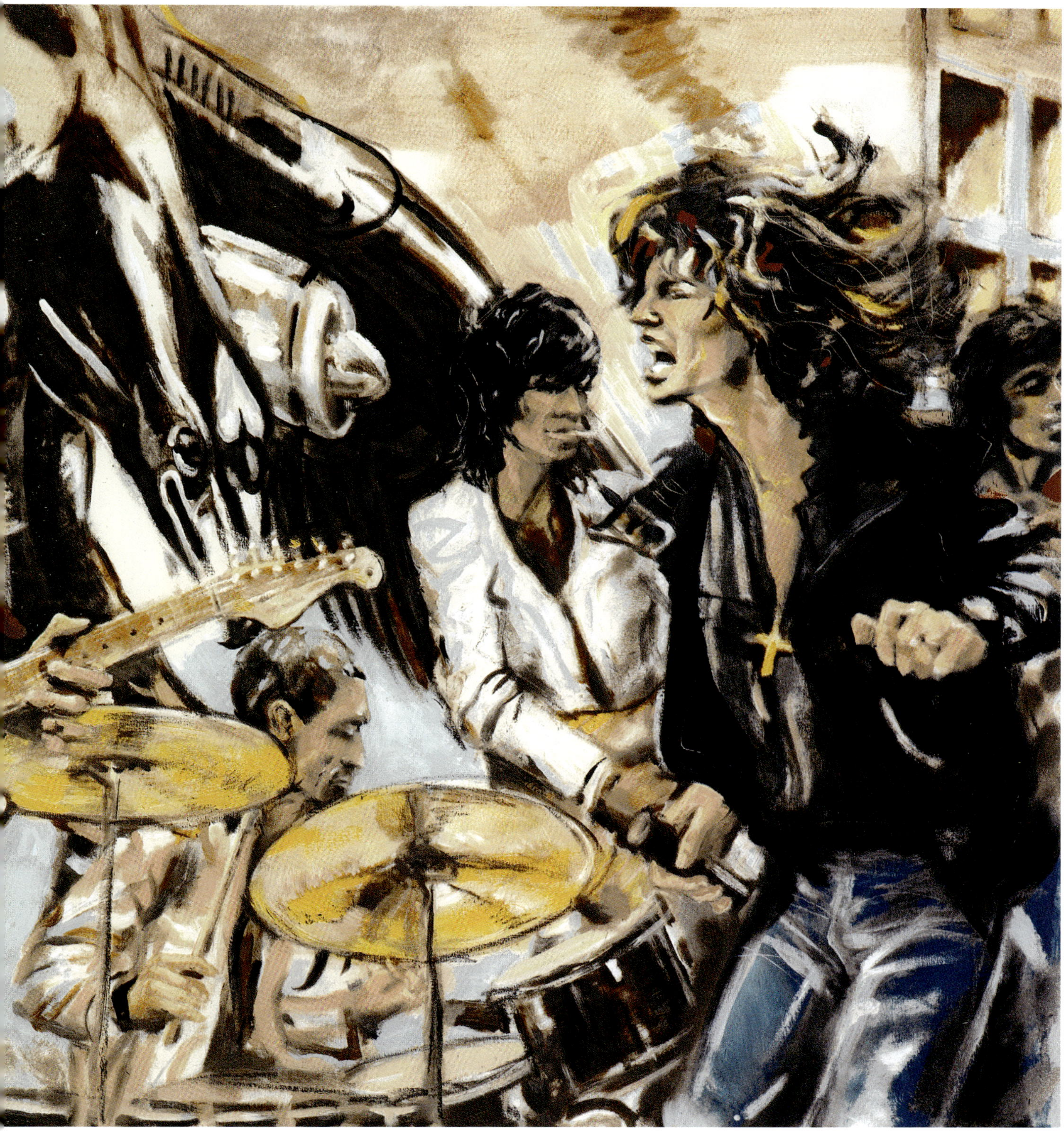

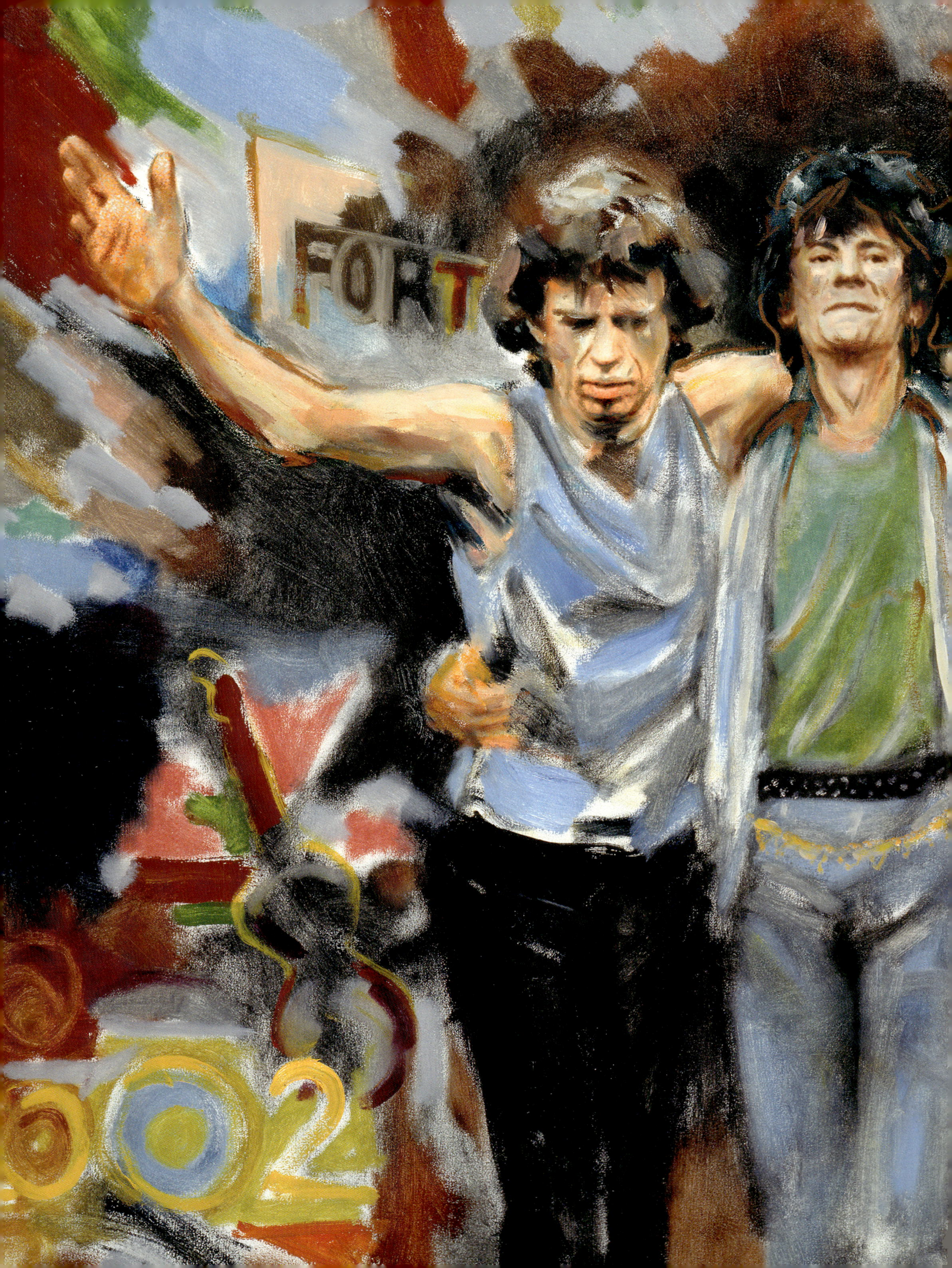
FORT

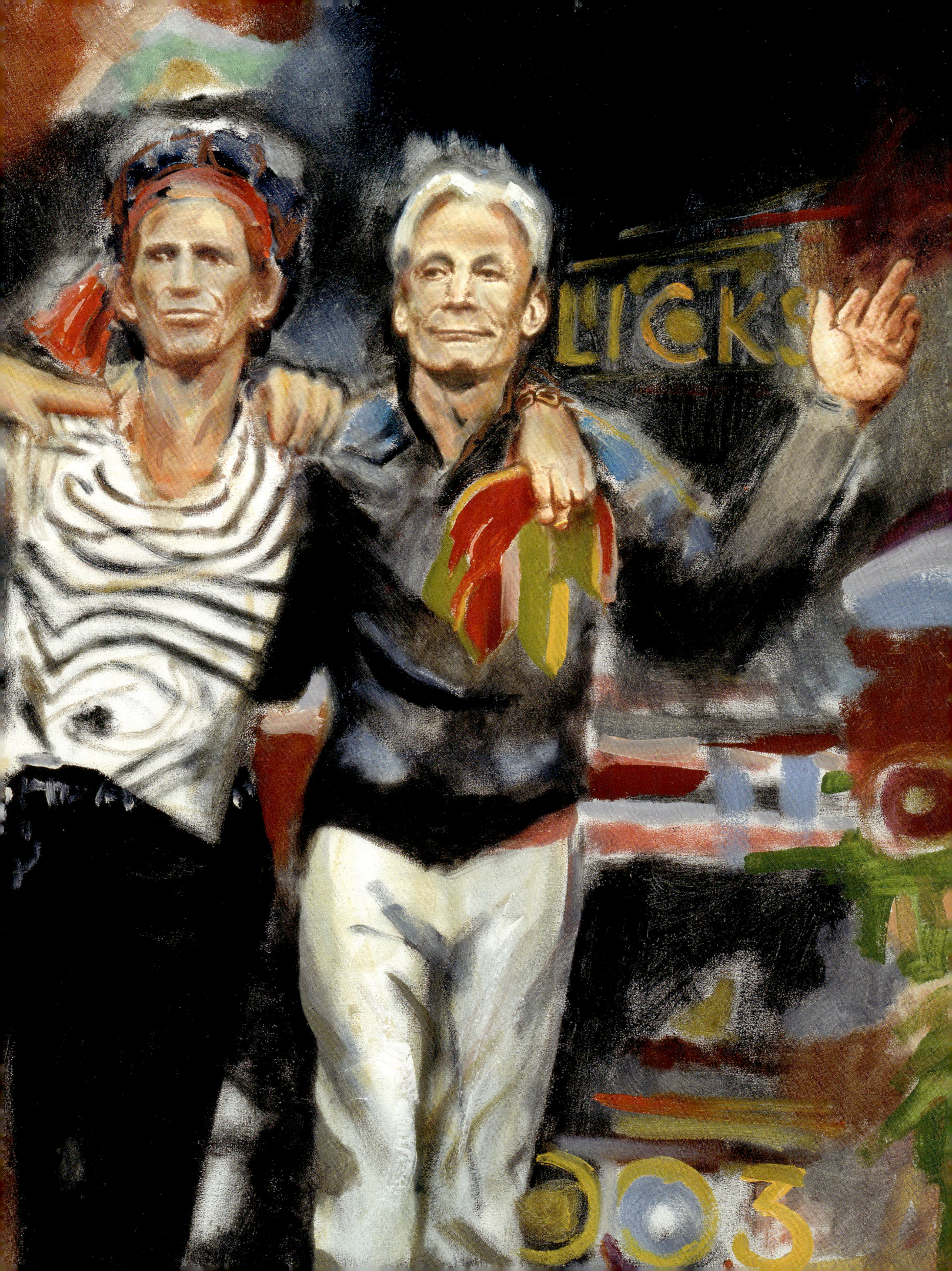

LICKS
003

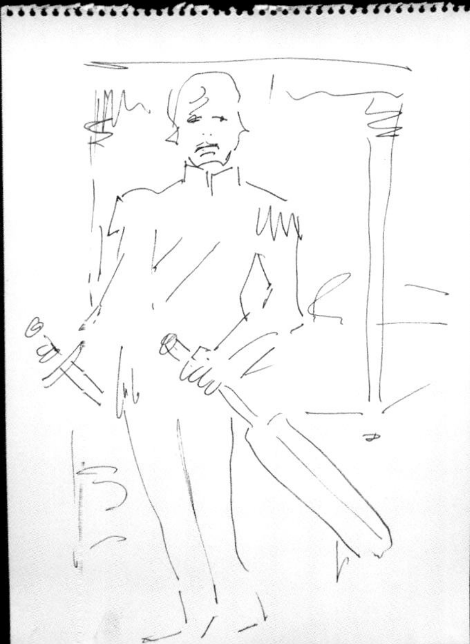

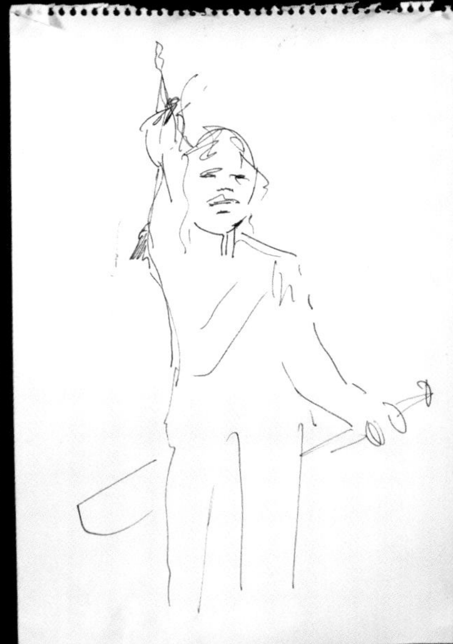

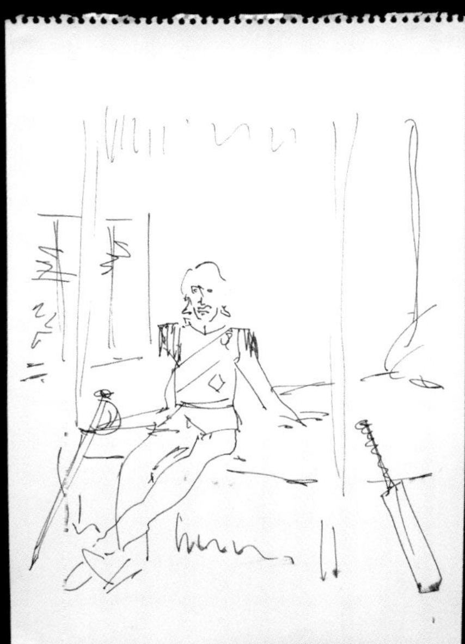

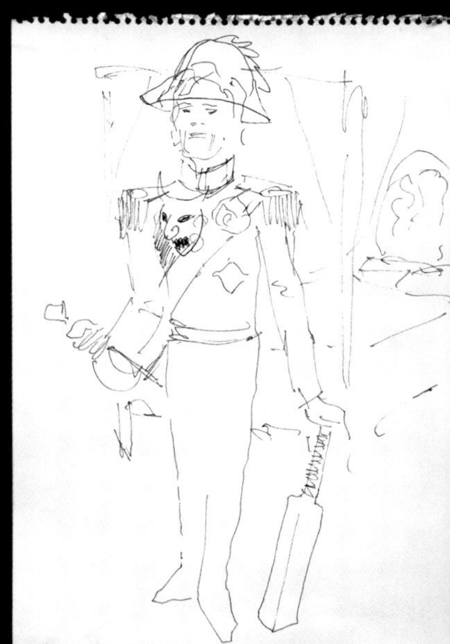

"In 2002, Mick was given a knighthood for 'services to popular music' in the Queen's Birthday Honours and this is my take on it,

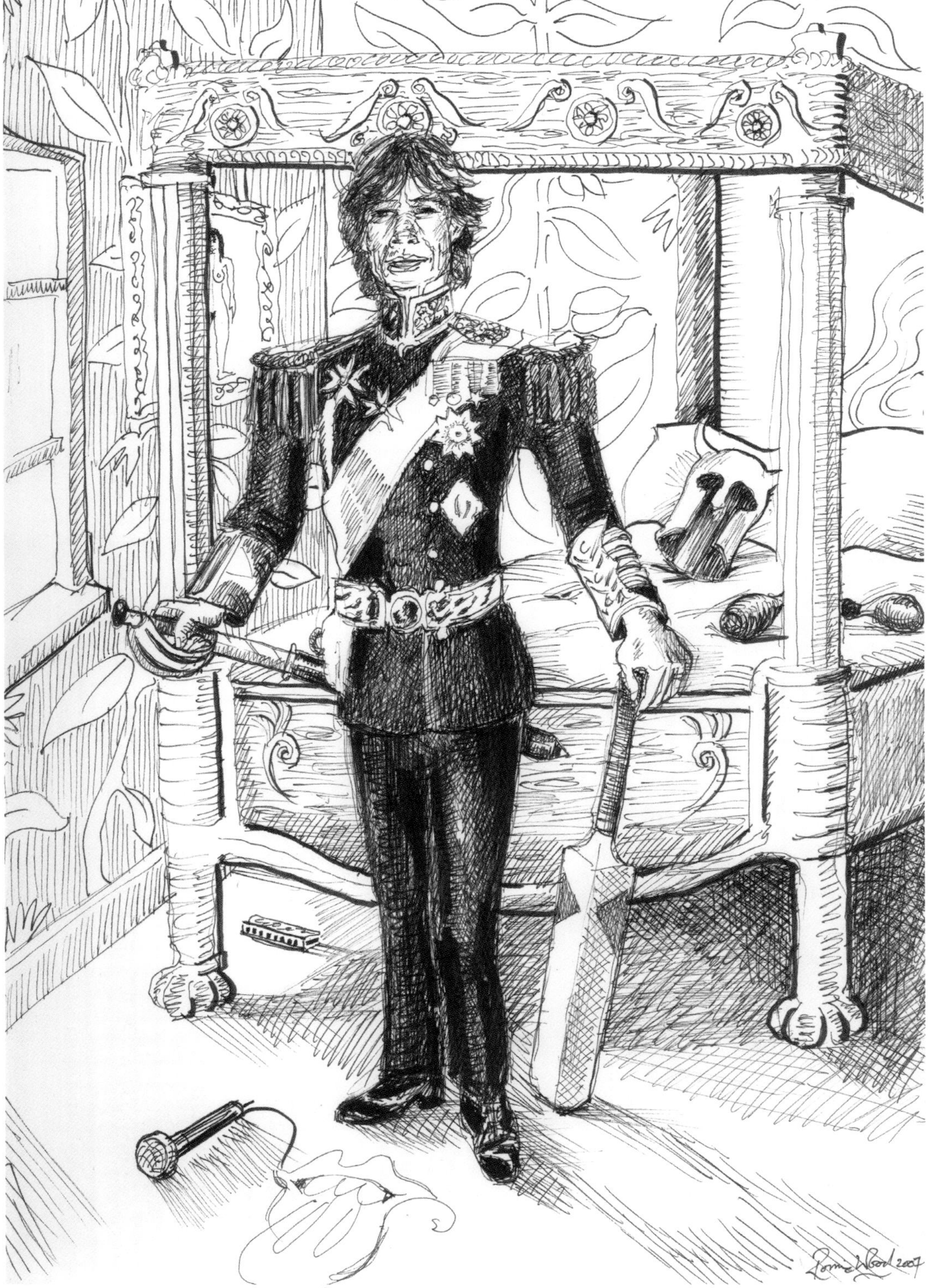

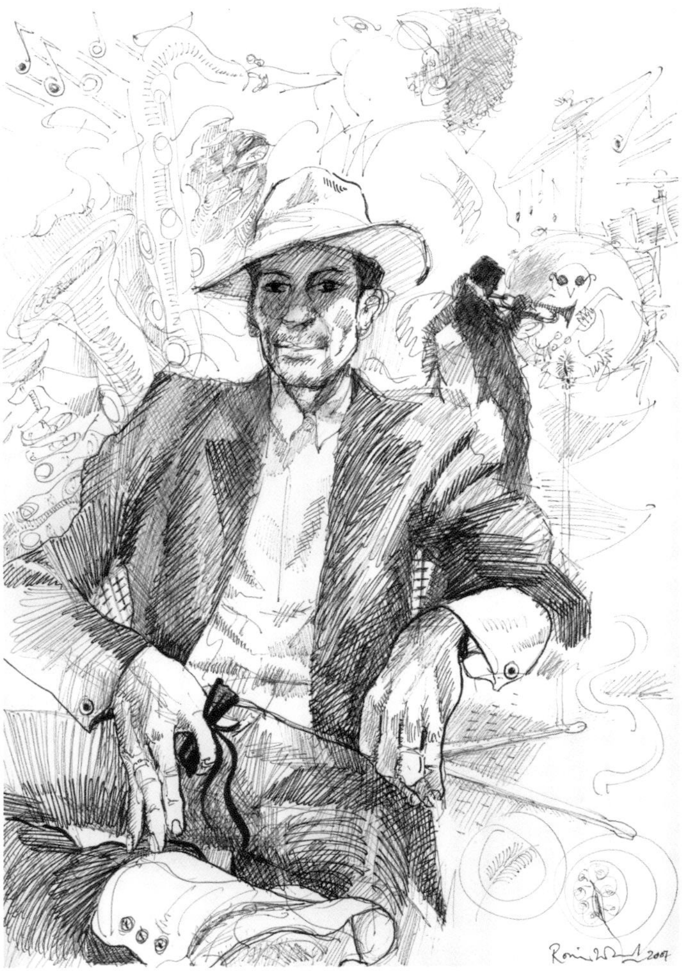

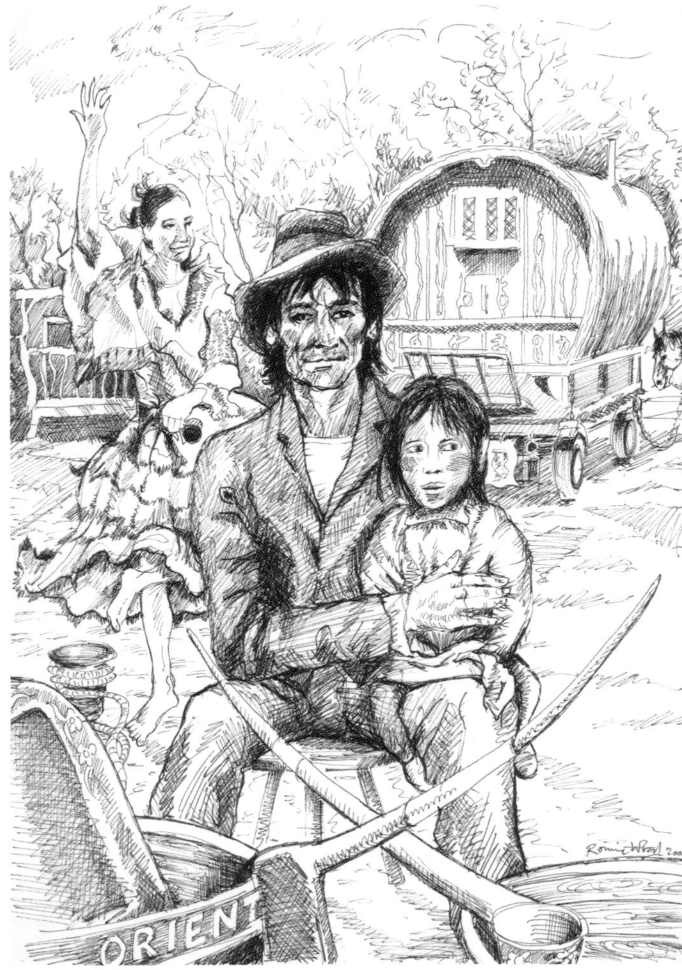

"Three studies from 2007 featuring Charlie doing his 'jazz thing', Keith channelling his inner pirate and me tracing my gypsy roots."

ABOVE LEFT: *Charlie* | 2007 | pen and ink | 42 × 29.5 cm
ABOVE RIGHT: *Ronnie* | 2007 | pen and ink | 42 × 29.5 cm
OPPOSITE: *Keith as Pirate* | 2007 | pen and ink | 42 × 29.5 cm

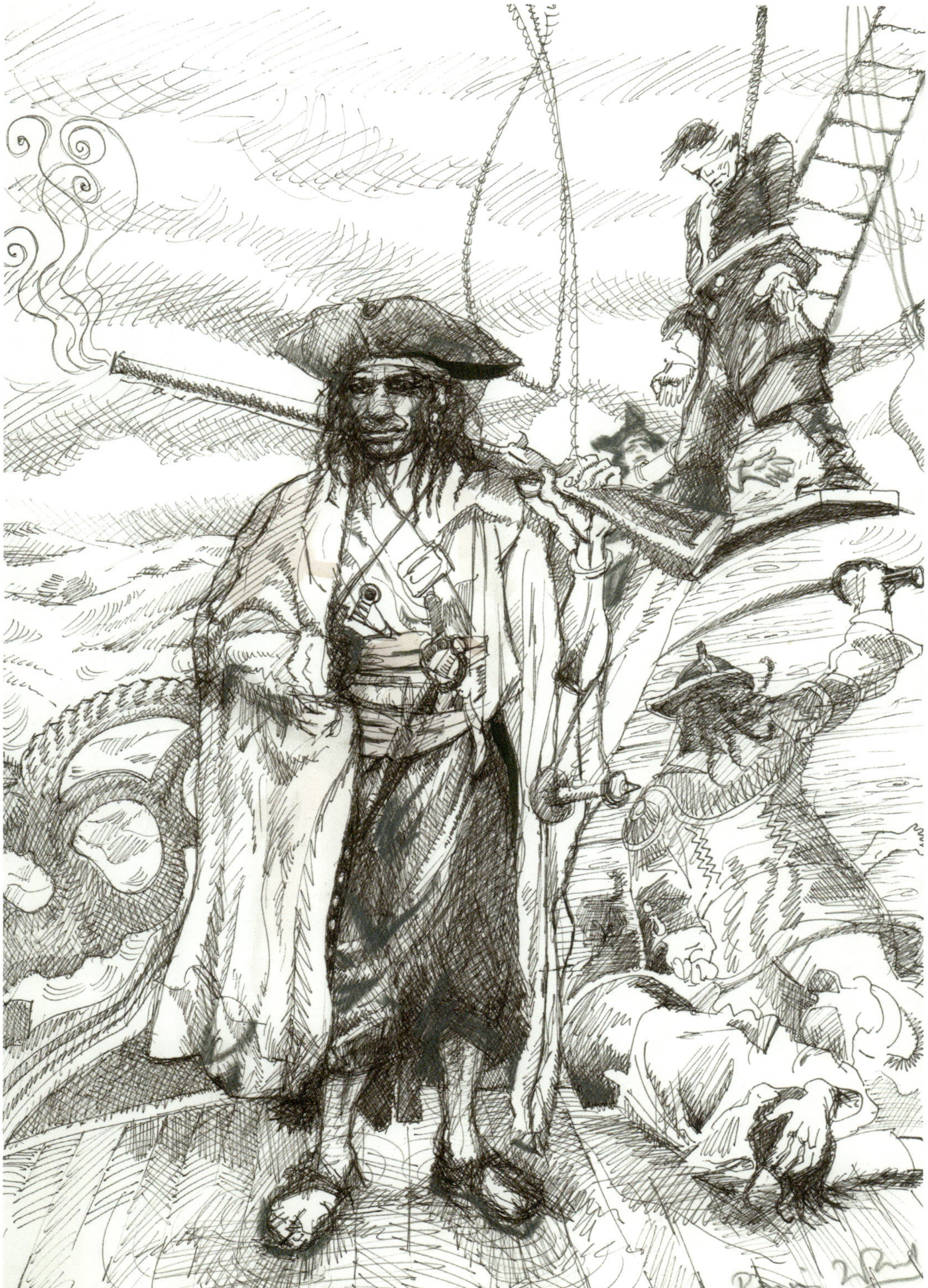

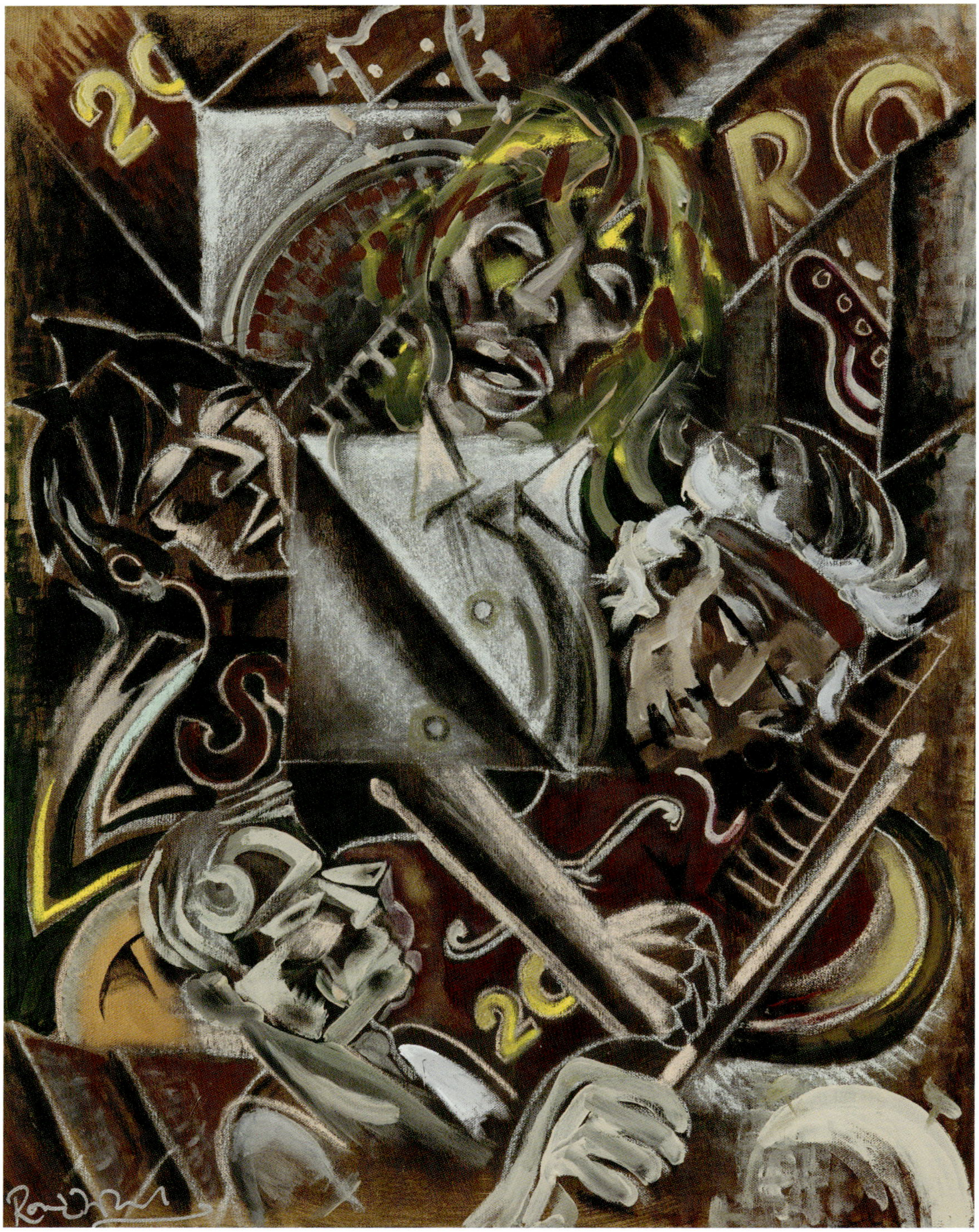

"In these studies of the band on stage I was trying a different style, using the light as the key element."

ABOVE: *Stage Studies* | 2013 | acrylic and pastel on canvas | 75 × 60 cm
OPPOSITE: *Charlie and Darryl* | 2007 | pastel on paper | 112 × 74 cm

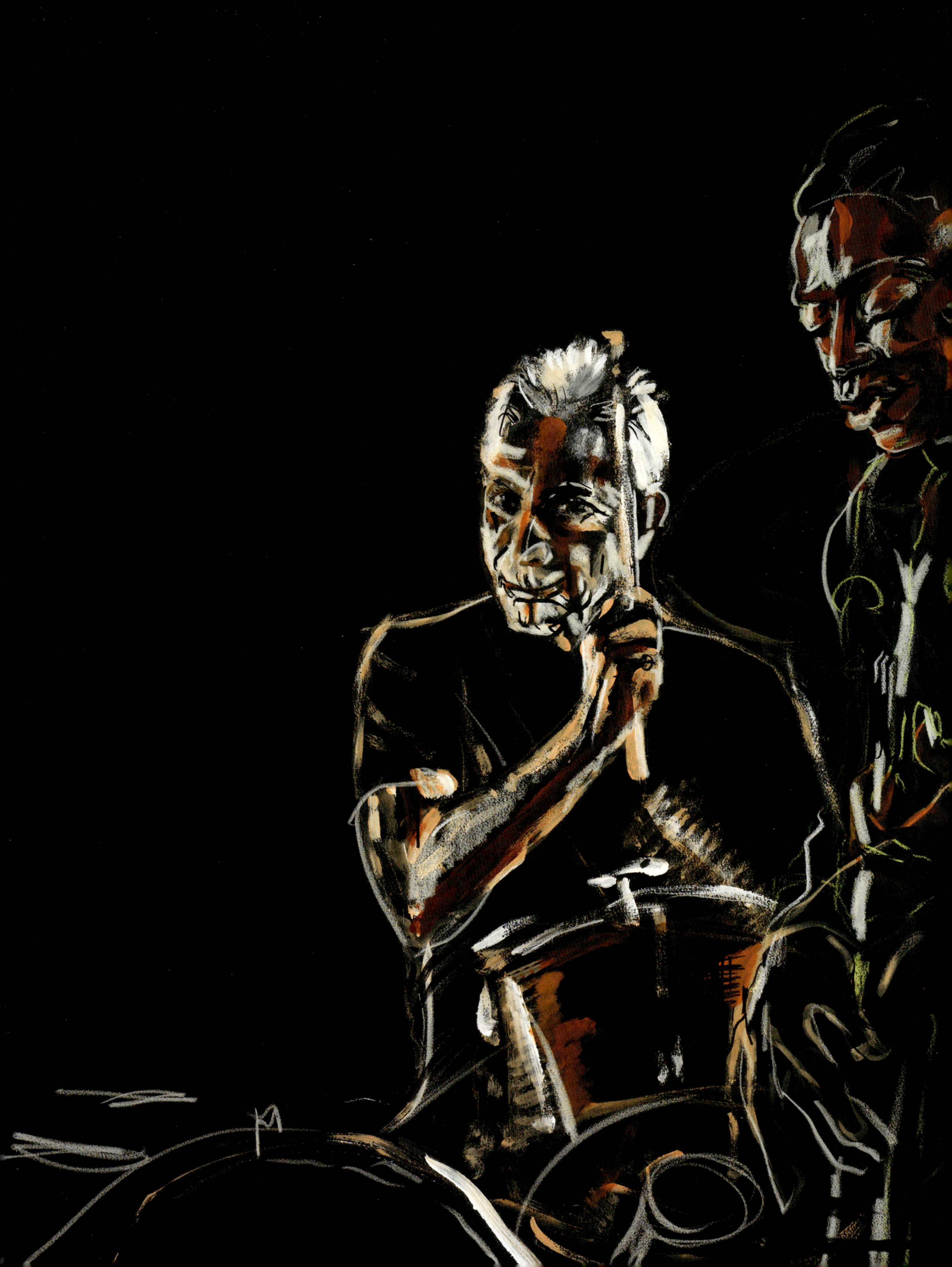

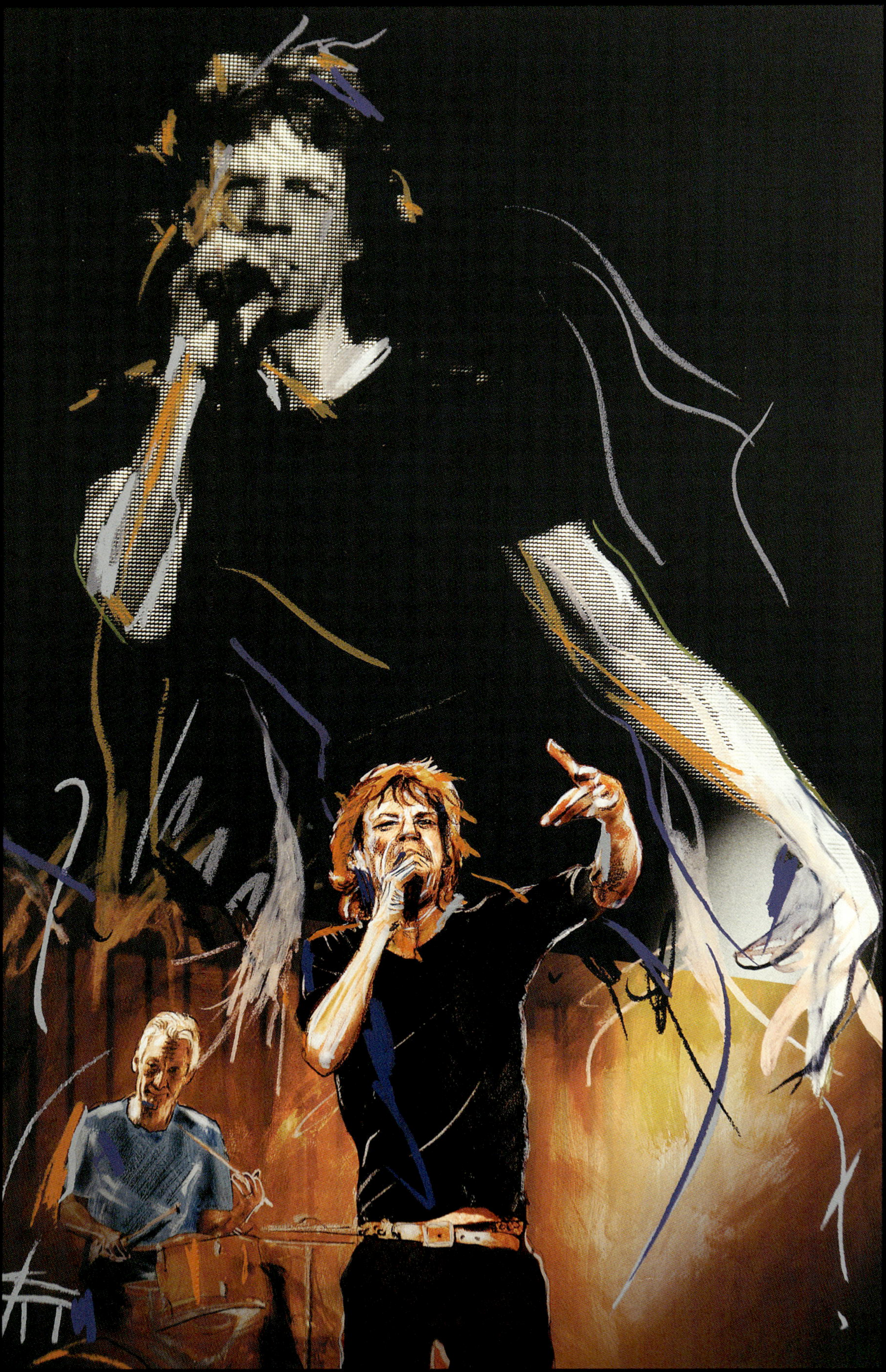

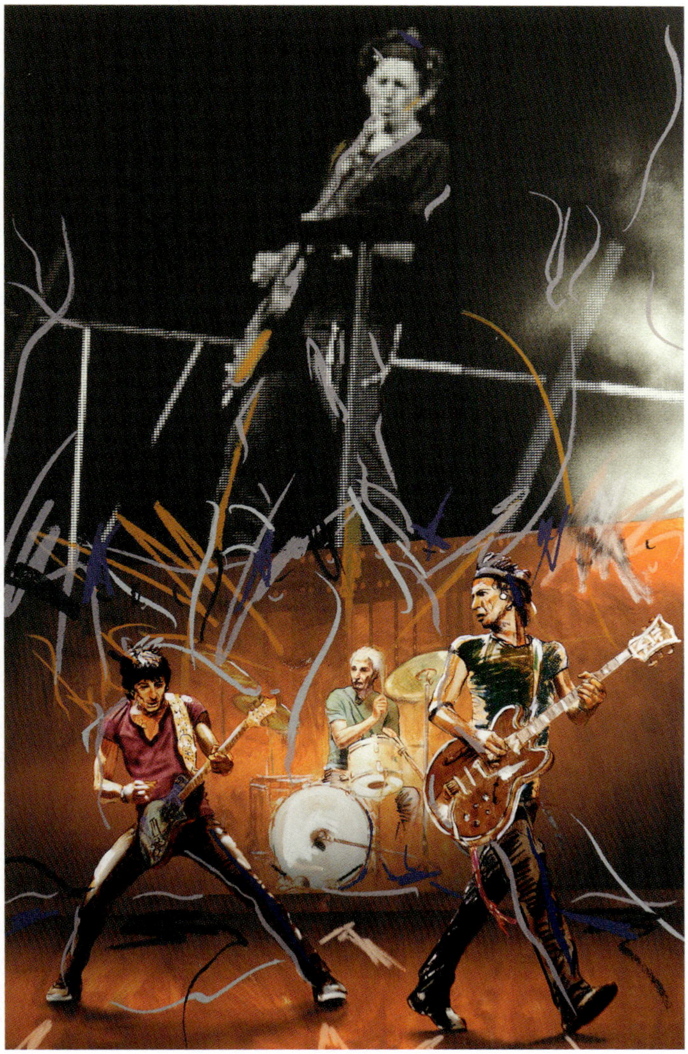

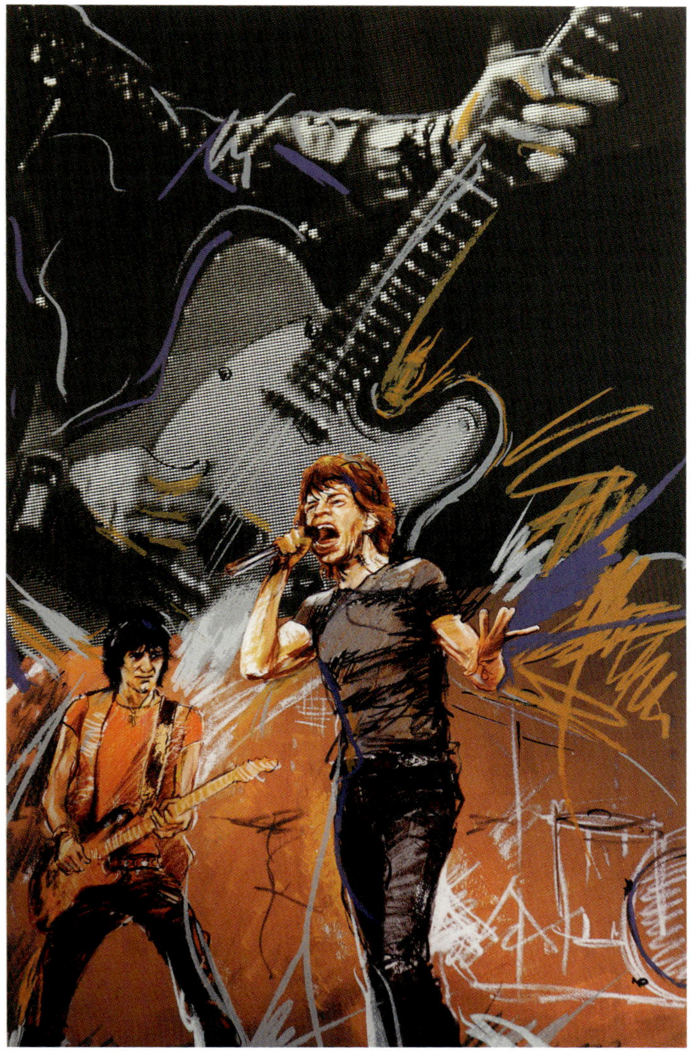

"I was trying something different again here: using the massive screens that we have on tour as the backdrop gives these images a very different quality."

OPPOSITE: *Play On Hands* | 2007 | inkjet and screen print | 75 × 50 cm
ABOVE LEFT: *Twang* | 2007 | inkjet and screen print | 75× 50 cm
ABOVE RIGHT: *Weaving* | 2007 | inkjet and screen print | 75 × 50 cm
OVERLEAF: *Pensive (Keith Richards)* (detail) | 2007 | acrylic on canvas | 122 × 183 cm

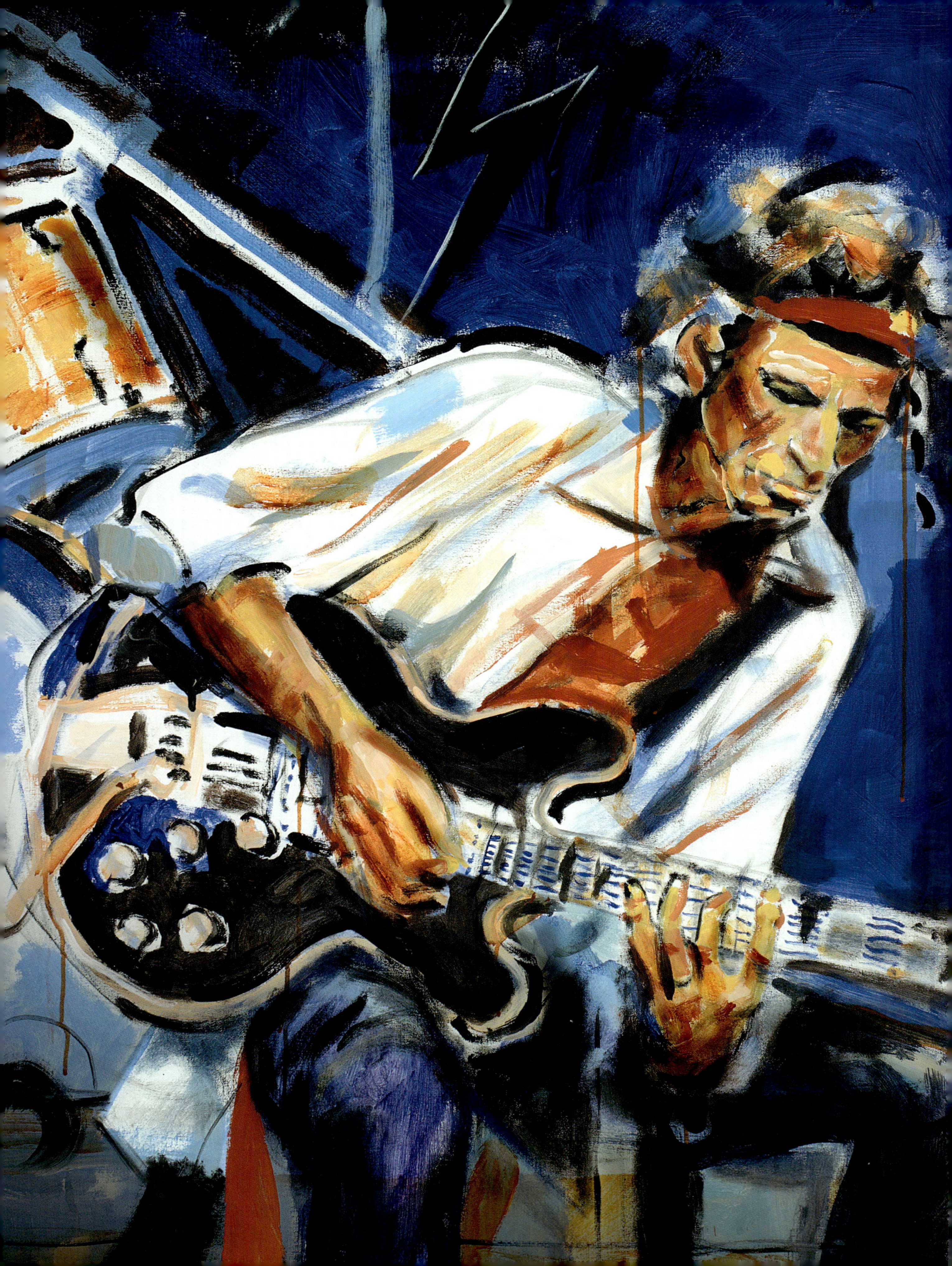

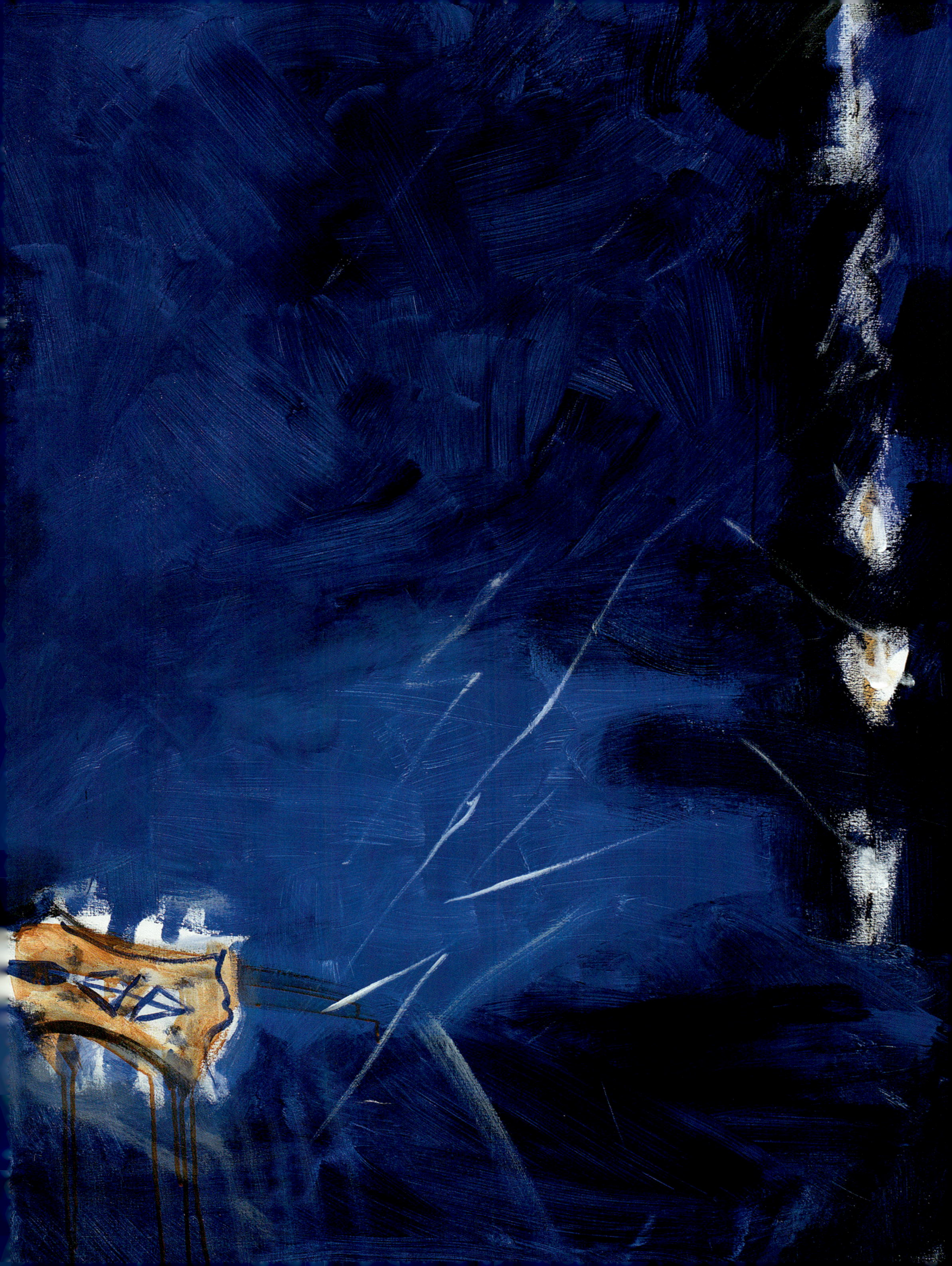

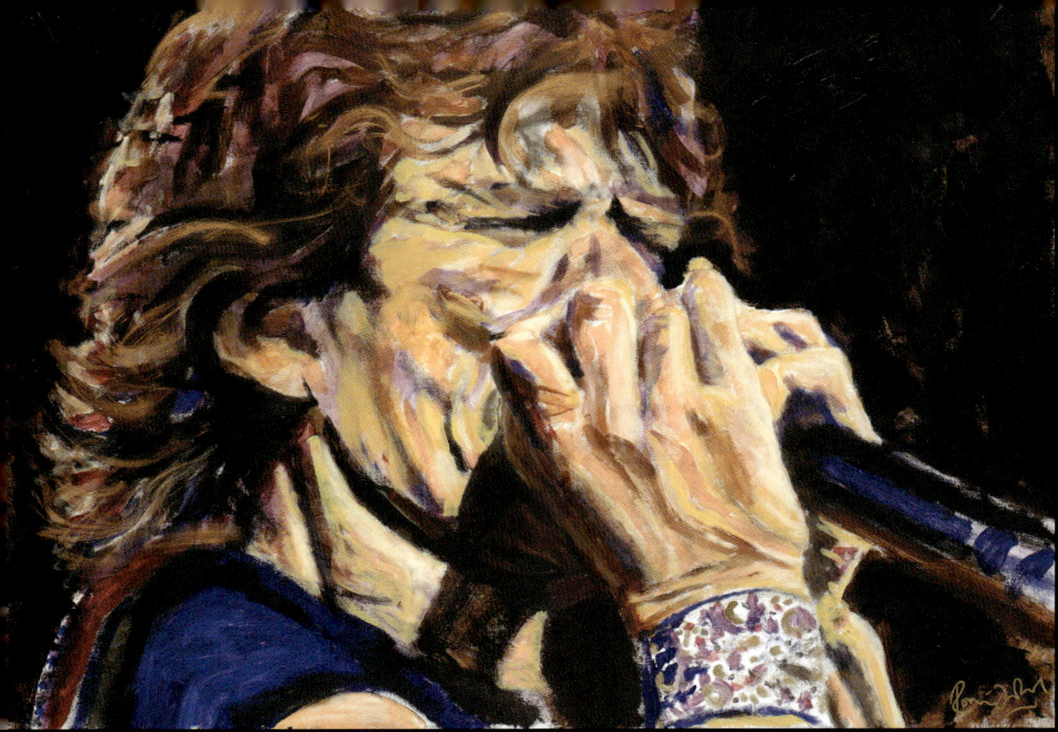

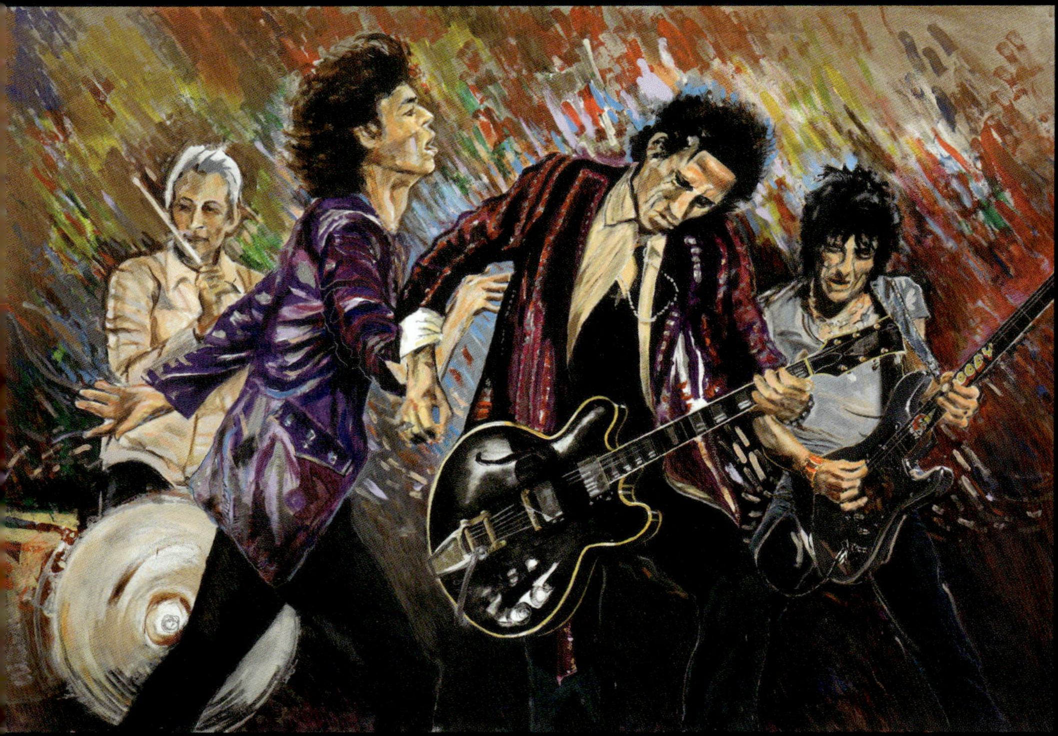

I was experimenting with mixed media in this self-portrait, which was bought by a Scandinavian collector.”

TOP: *Mick Harmonica* | 2009 | acrylic on canvas | 91.5 × 122 cm
ABOVE: *Rolling Stones* | 2009 | acrylic on canvas | 122× 91.5 cm
OPPOSITE: *Ronnie* | 2009 | mixed media on canvas | 183 × 122 cm

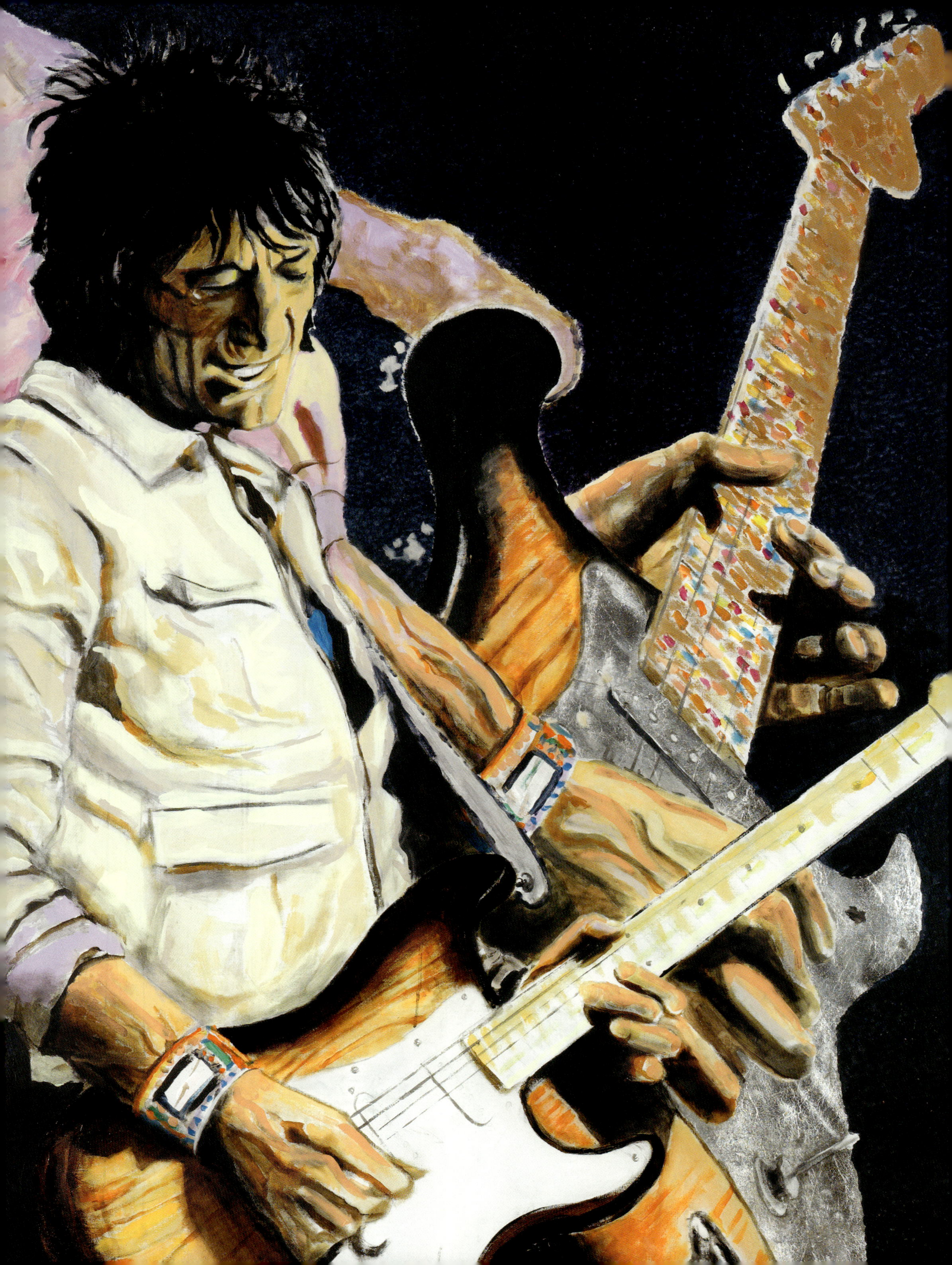

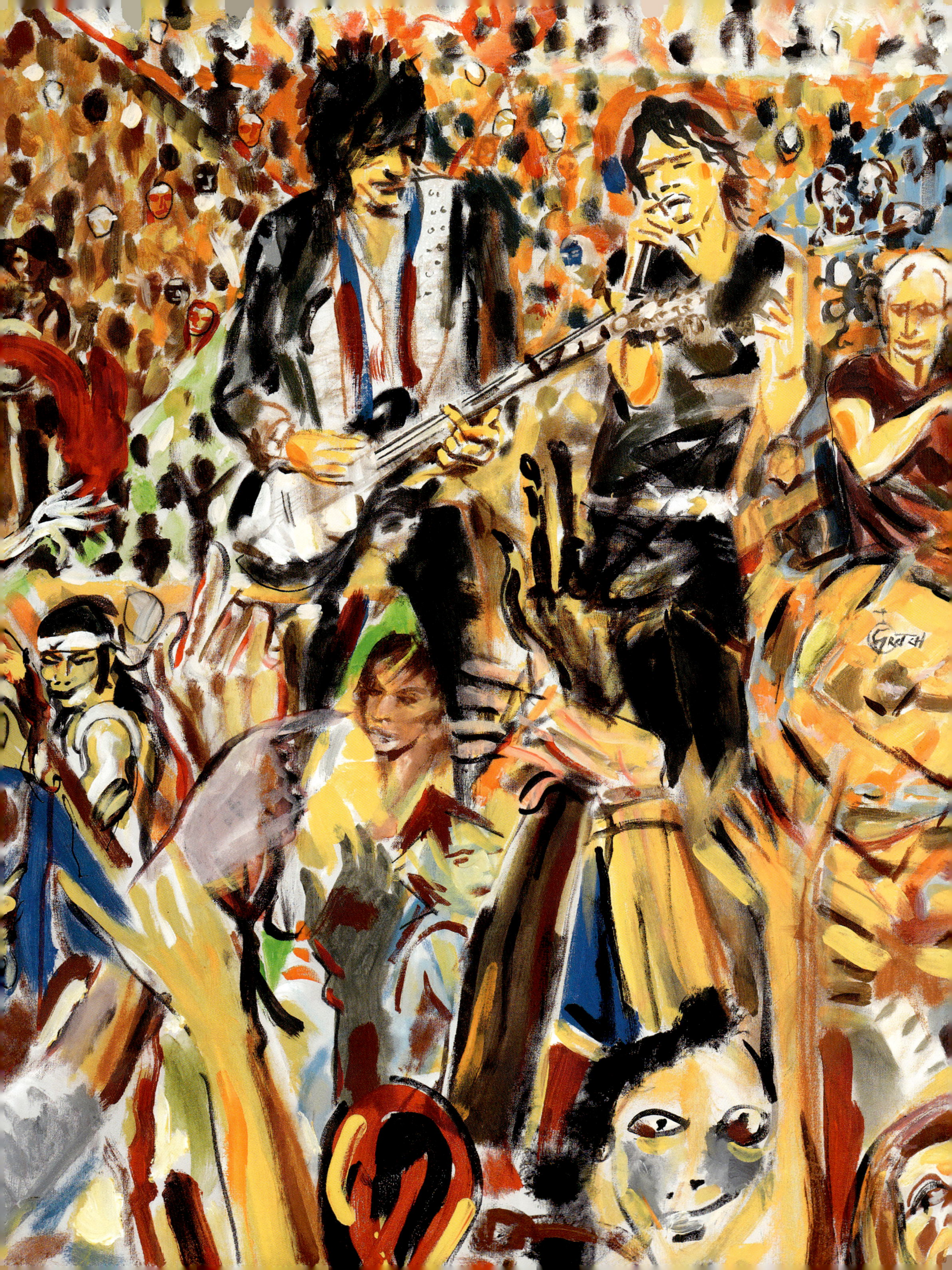

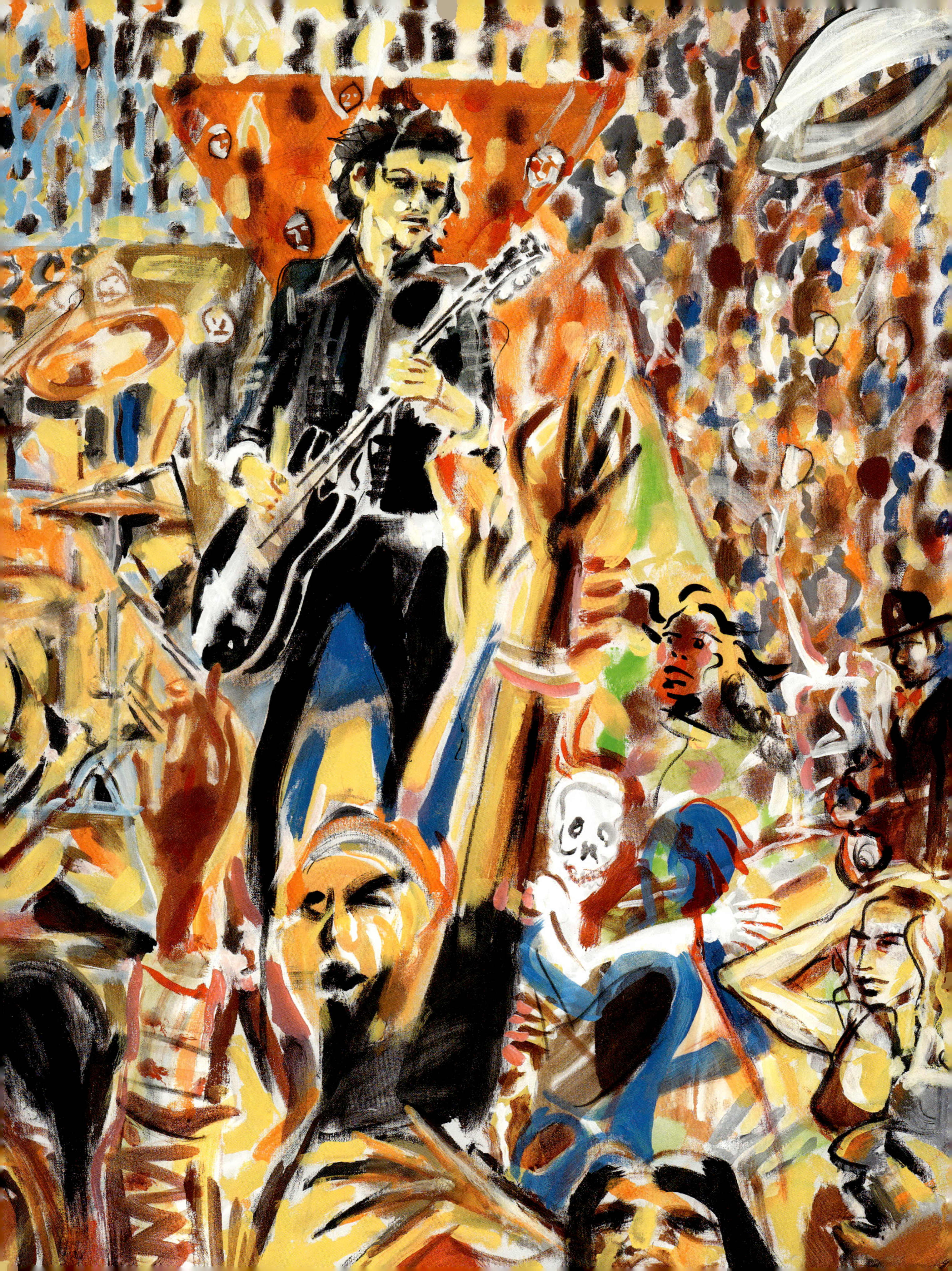

"The previous page shows half-time at the Super Bowl which we played in 2006. Bill Clinton has this hanging in his office. In the top painting opposite, I used bank notes I'd collected while on tour."

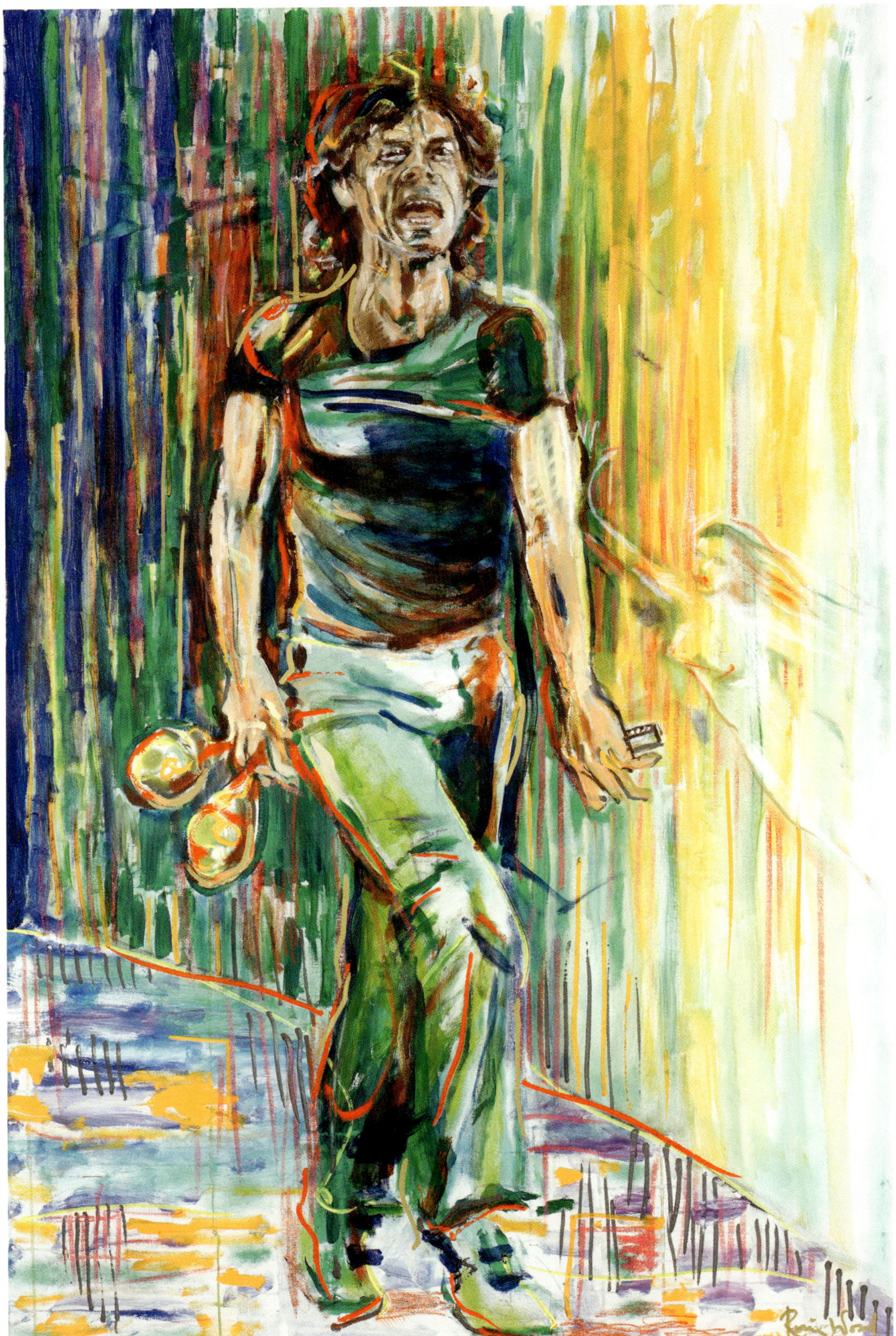

PREVIOUS PAGE: *B-Stage (Rolling Stones at the Super Bowl)* | 2006
acrylic on canvas | 91 × 122 cm
OPPOSITE: *Mick with Maracas* | 2009 | acrylic on canvas | 183 × 122 cm
BELOW: *Stones 1990* | 2013 | mixed media on canvas | 121 × 185 cm
BOTTOM: *Stones 1990* | 2013 | acrylic on canvas | 120 × 182 cm

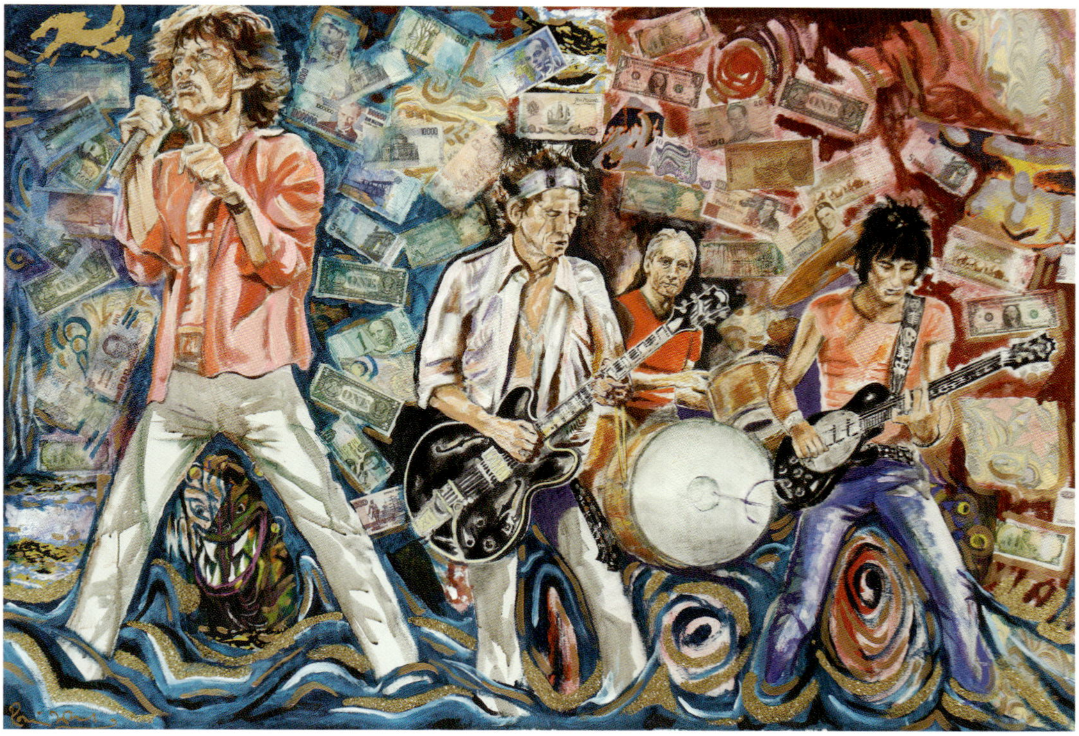

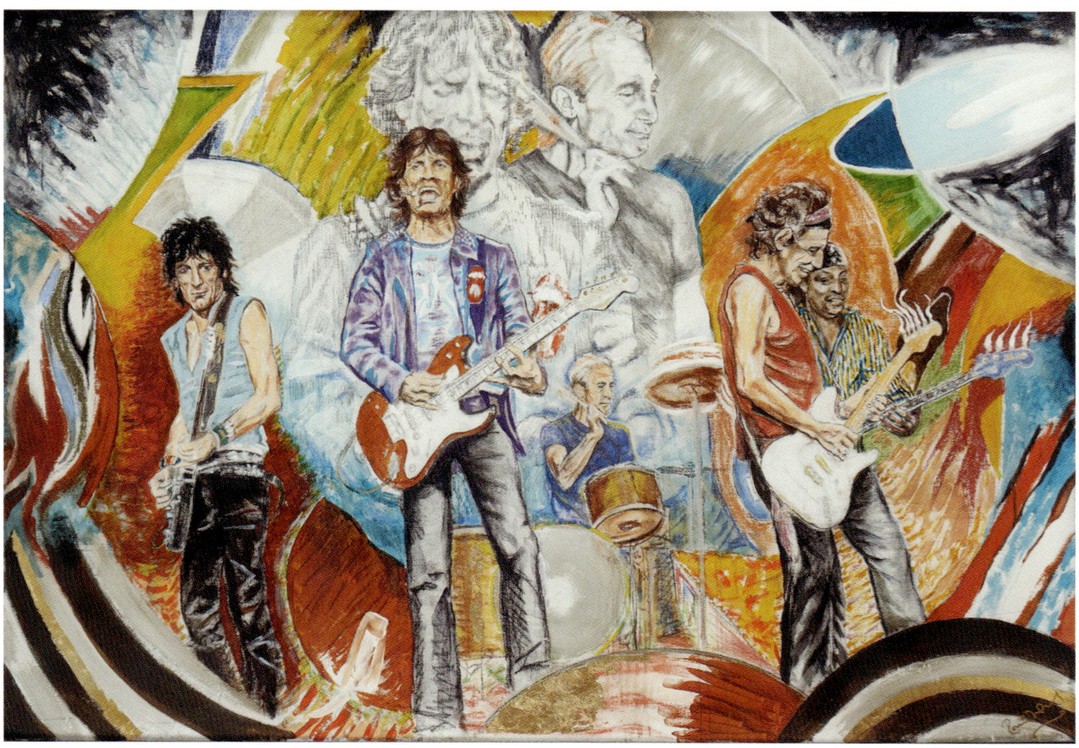

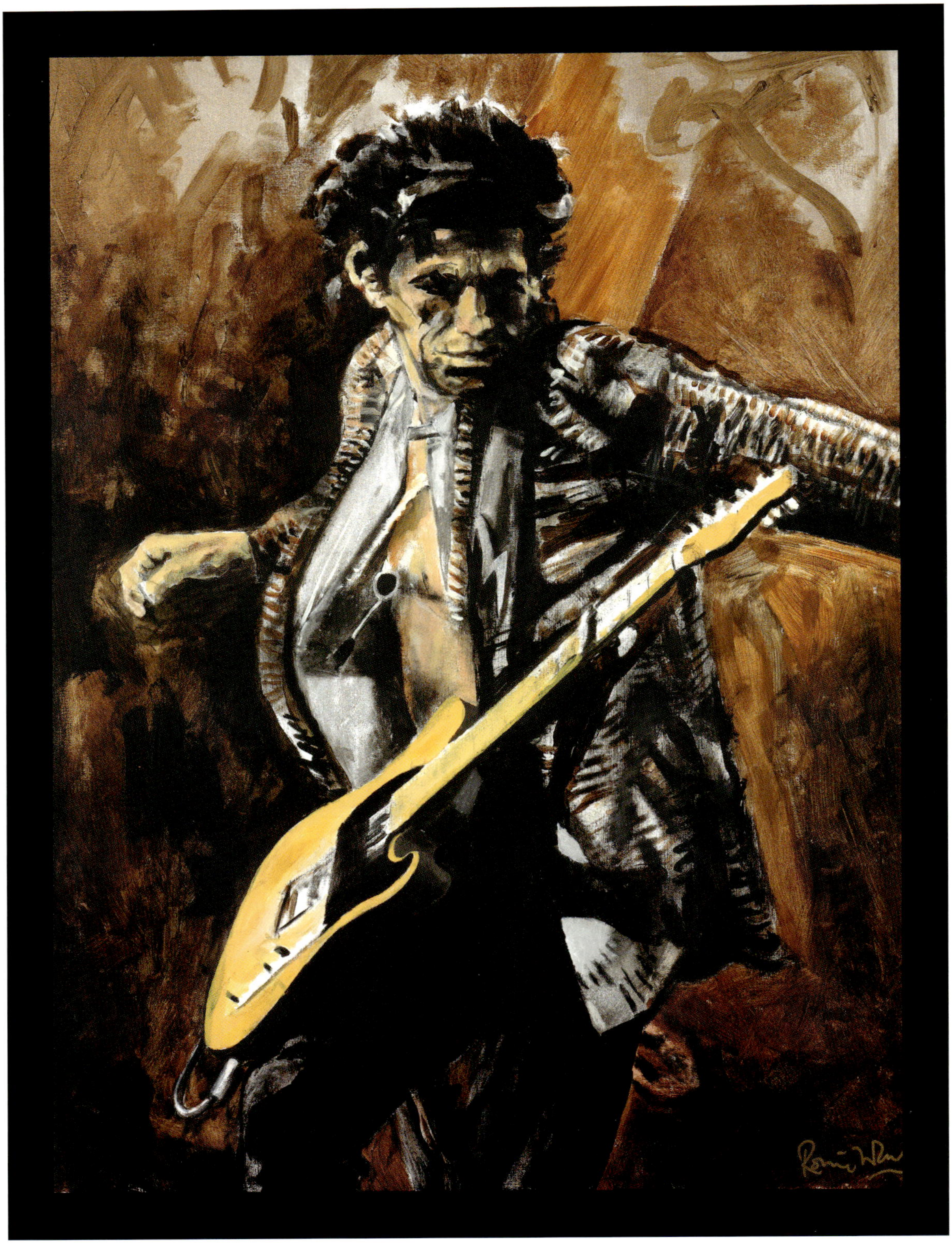

"When Keith and I play together we call our guitar interplay 'the ancient art of weaving'; it's sometimes difficult for us to tell which of us is playing which note when we listen to the playback."

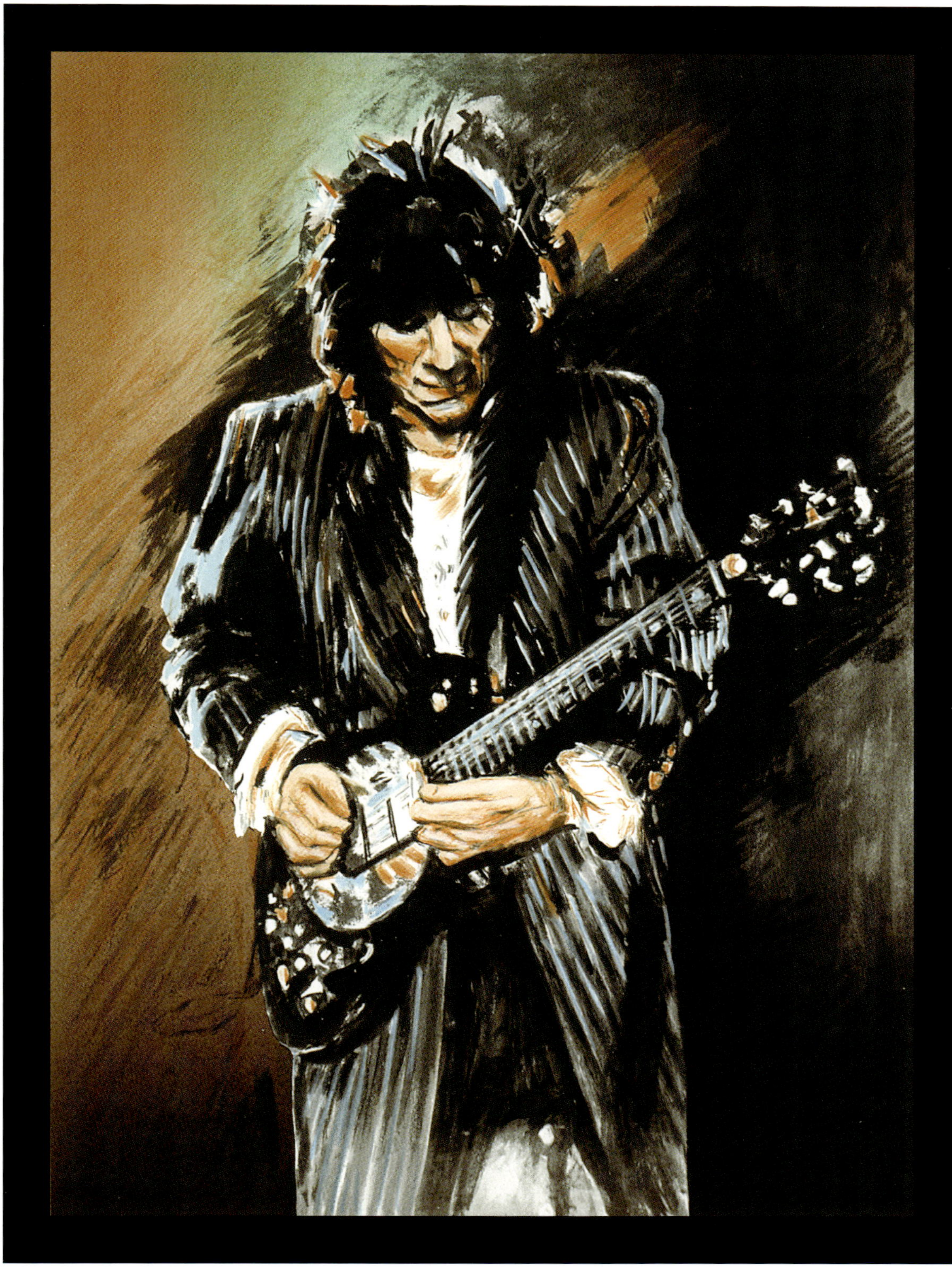

OPPOSITE: *Richards* | 2010 | acrylic on canvas | 122 × 91.5 cm
ABOVE: *Slide on This* | 1996 | mixed media on canvas | 53.5 × 39.7 cm

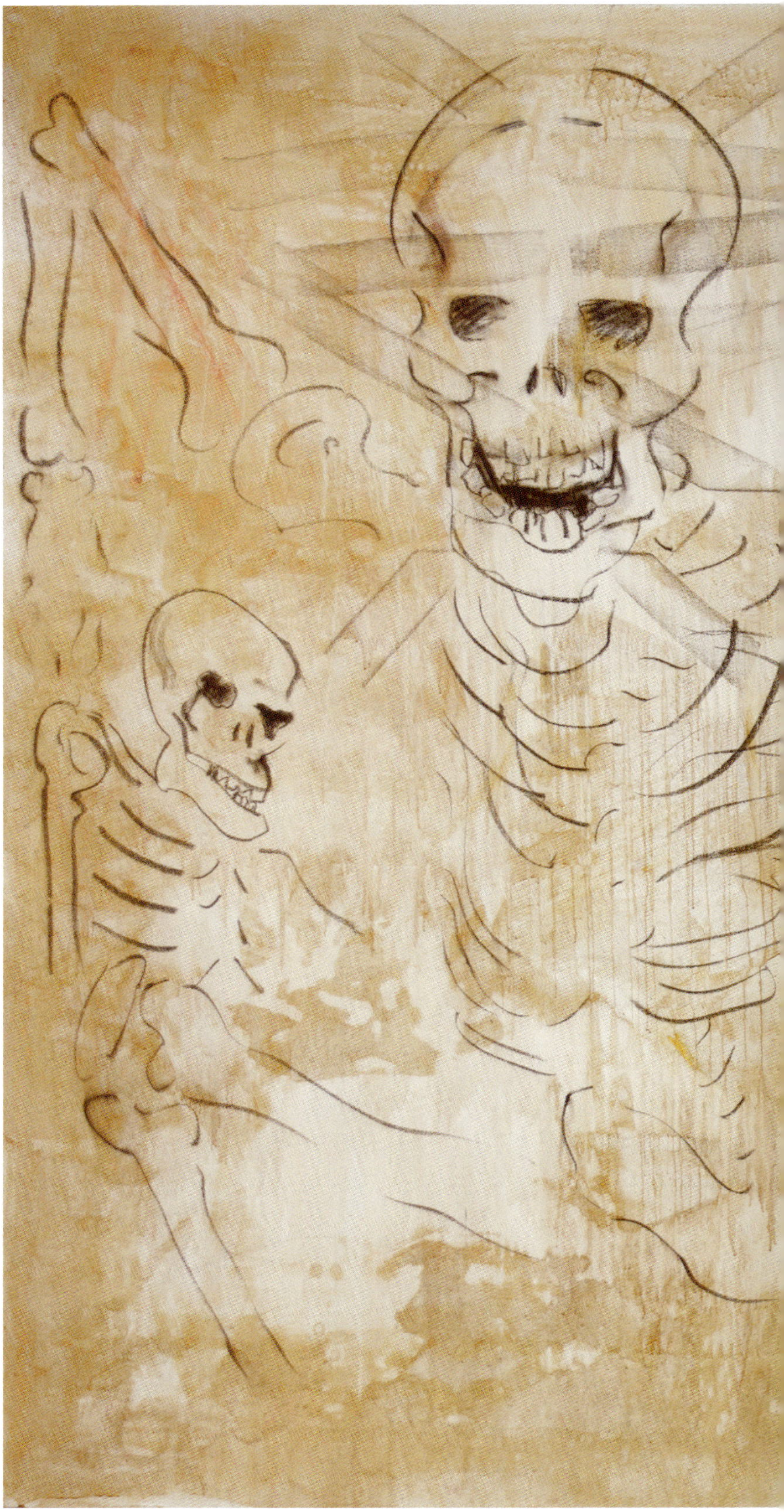

"This was painted in my studio at the Bruton Street Gallery in London. I used a reference image from the band's 1971 UK tour."

Mick | 2012 | mixed media on canvas | 152 × 305 cm

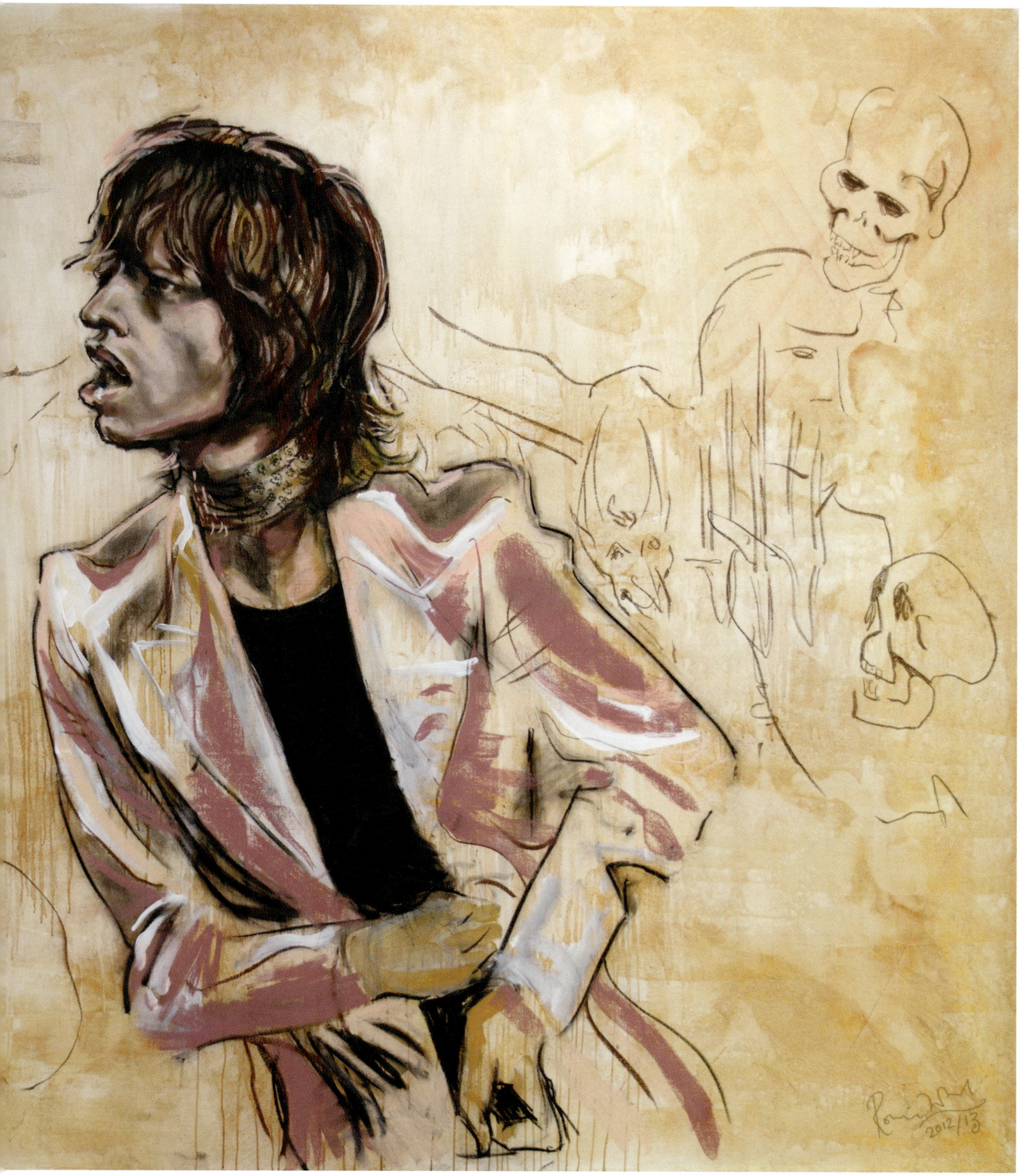

"Charlie has an idiosyncratic way of holding his hands which I've caught perfectly here."

BELOW: *Idiosyncratic Jazz Man* | 2011 | mixed media on paper | 100 × 75 cm
OPPOSITE: *Touch* | 2002 | acrylic and ink on paper | 90 × 60 cm

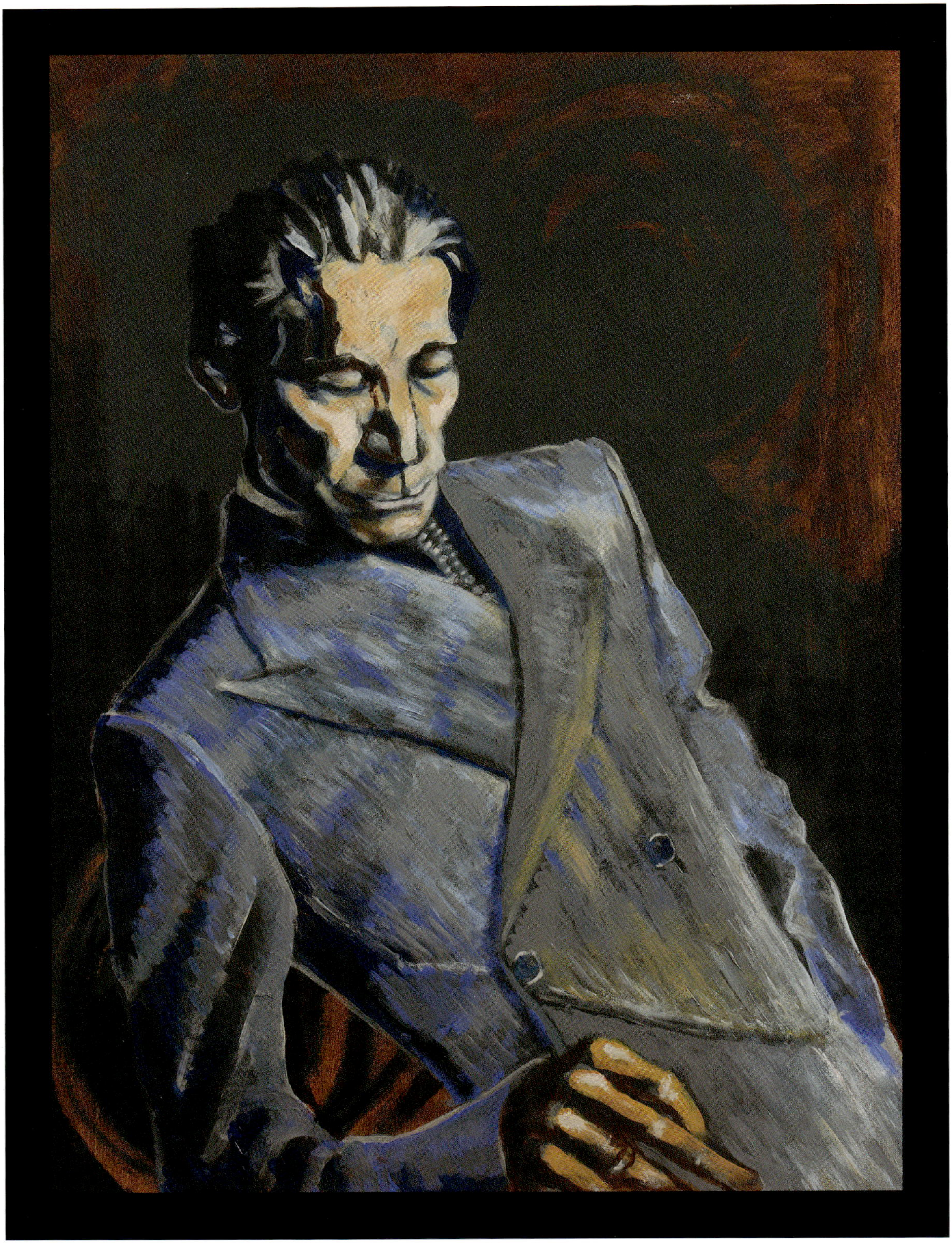

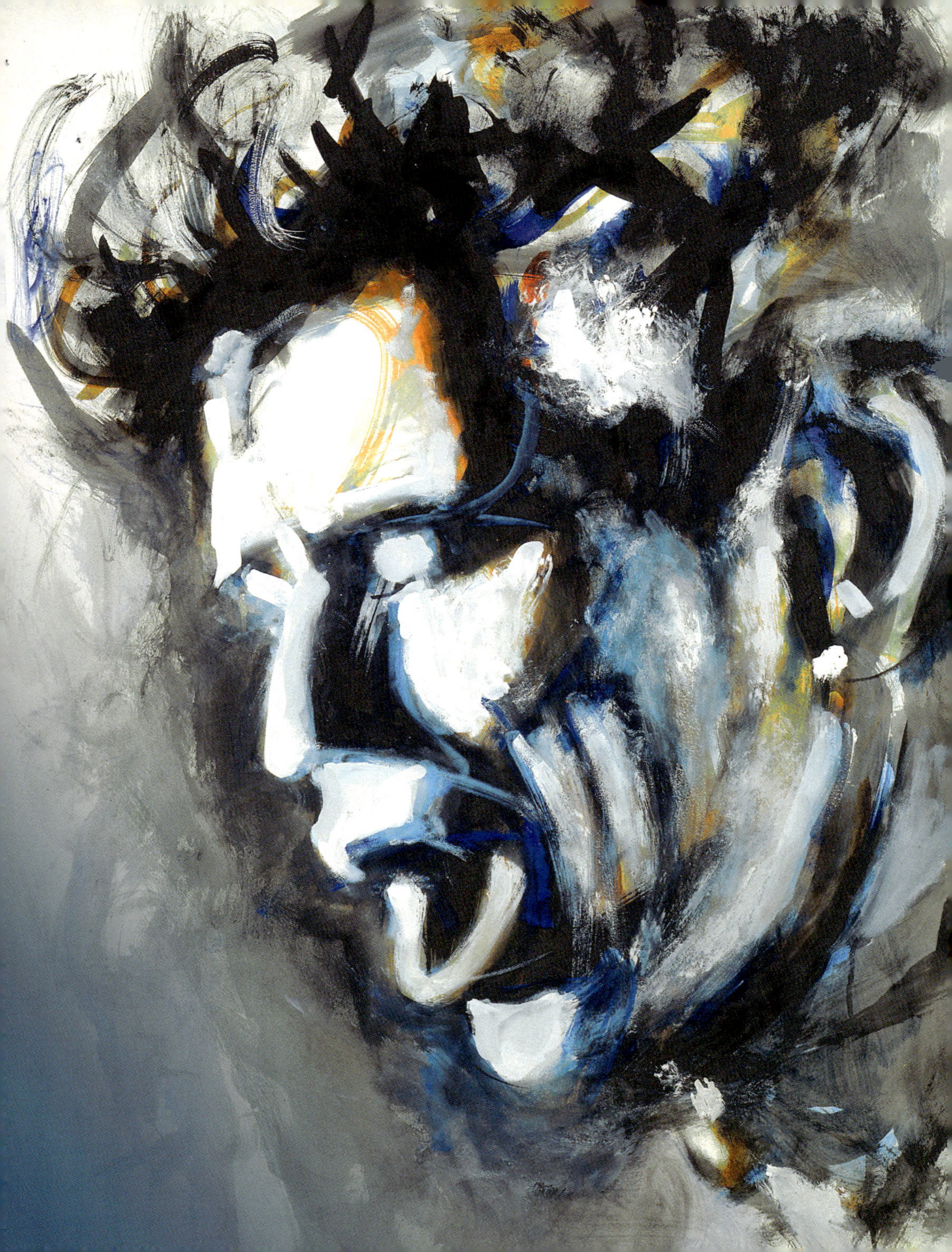

BELOW LEFT: *Charlie: Rehearsal in Paris* | 2014 | ink on paper | 31 × 23 cm
BELOW RIGHT,: *Keith: Rehearsal in Paris* | 2014 | ink on paper | 23 × 31 cm
BOTTOM RIGHT: *Pensive Mick: Rehearsal in Paris* | 2014 | ink on paper | 23 × 31 cm
OPPOSITE ABOVE LEFT: *Mick Taylor and Bobby Keys: Rehearsal in Paris* | 2014 | ink on paper | 31 × 23 cm
OPPOSITE BELOW LEFT: *Bernard Fowler and Lisa Fischer: Rehearsal in Paris* | 2014 | ink on paper | 23 × 31 cm
OPPOSITE RIGHT: *Ronnie: Rehearsal in Paris* | 2014 | ink on paper | 31 × 23 cm

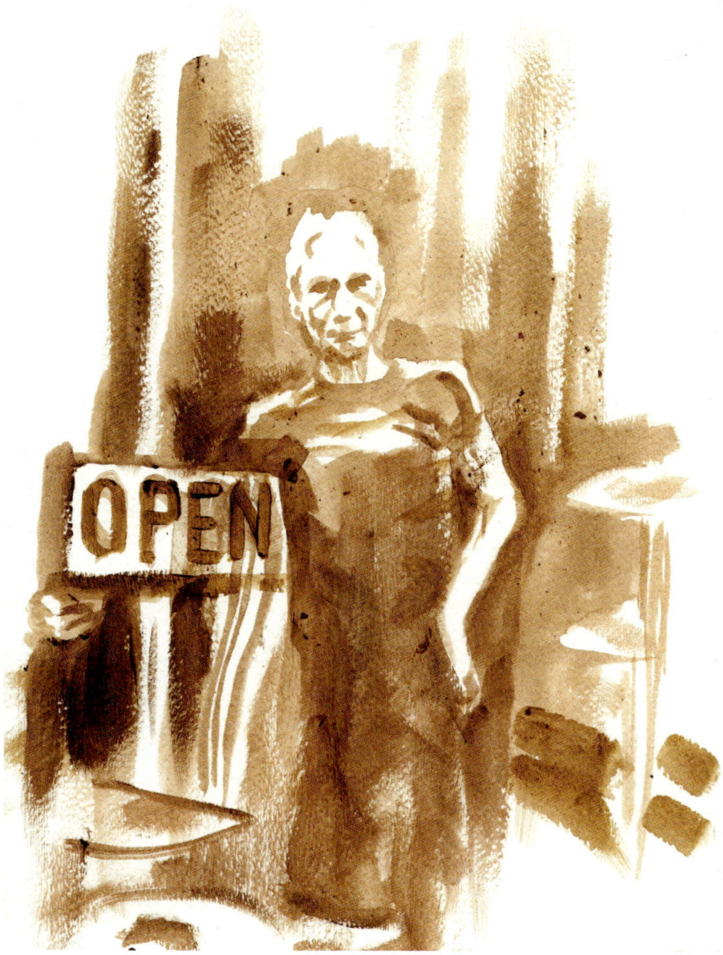

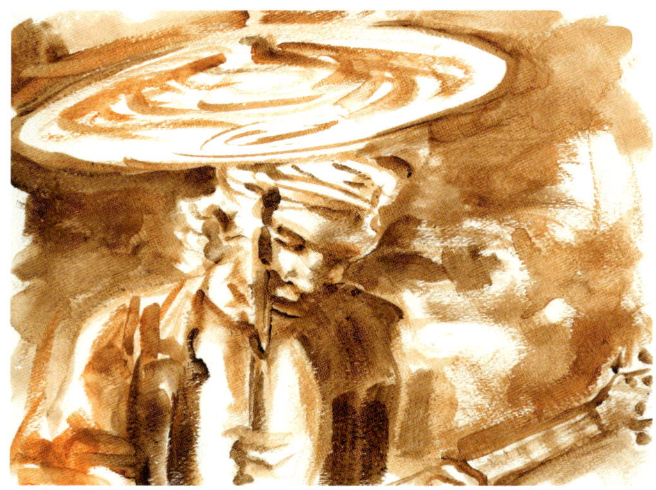

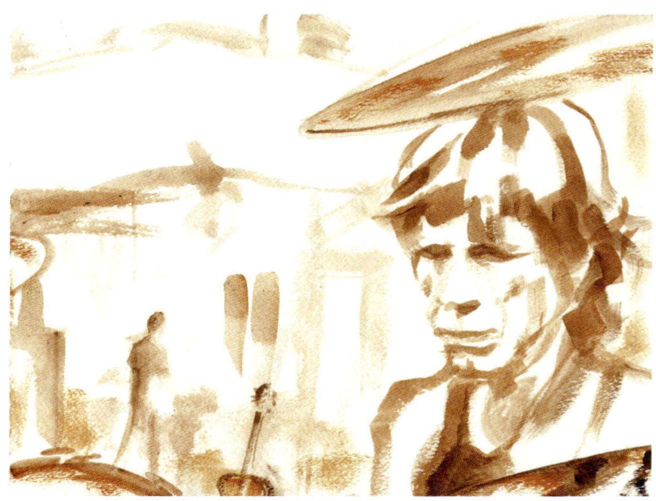

"These are some of my favourites, especially the one of Mick; it captures him perfectly. They were done in February 2014 at a studio near Paris while we rehearsed for the 50 and Counting tour."

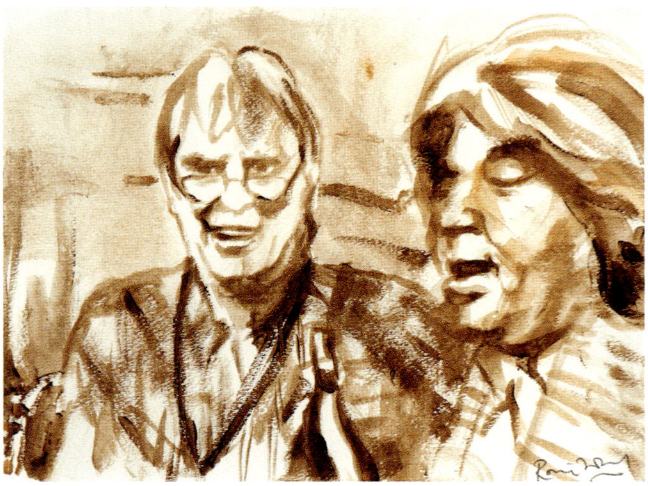

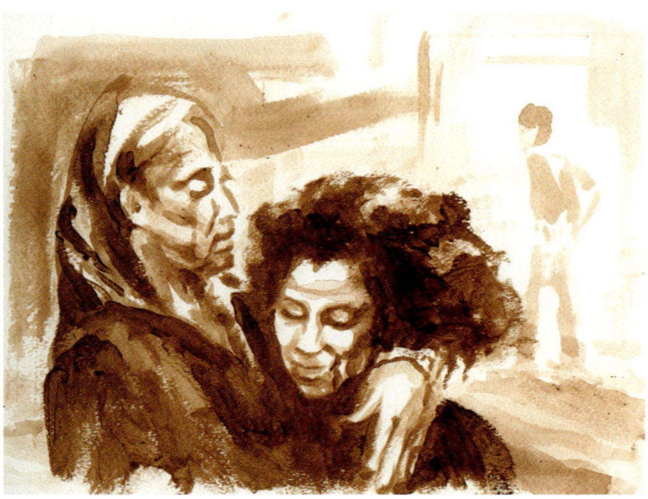

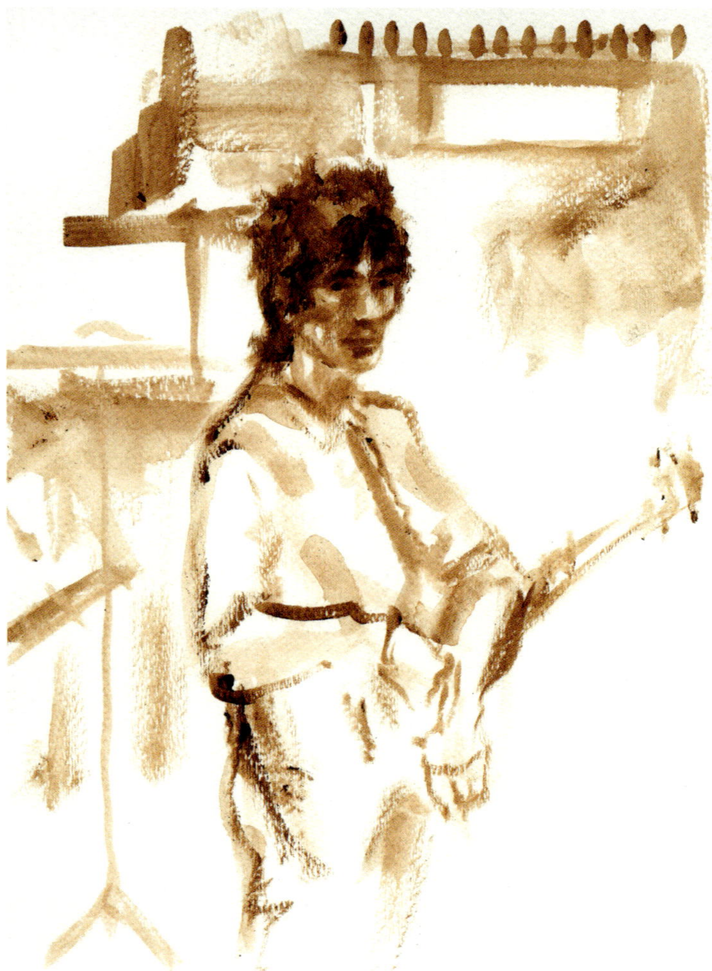

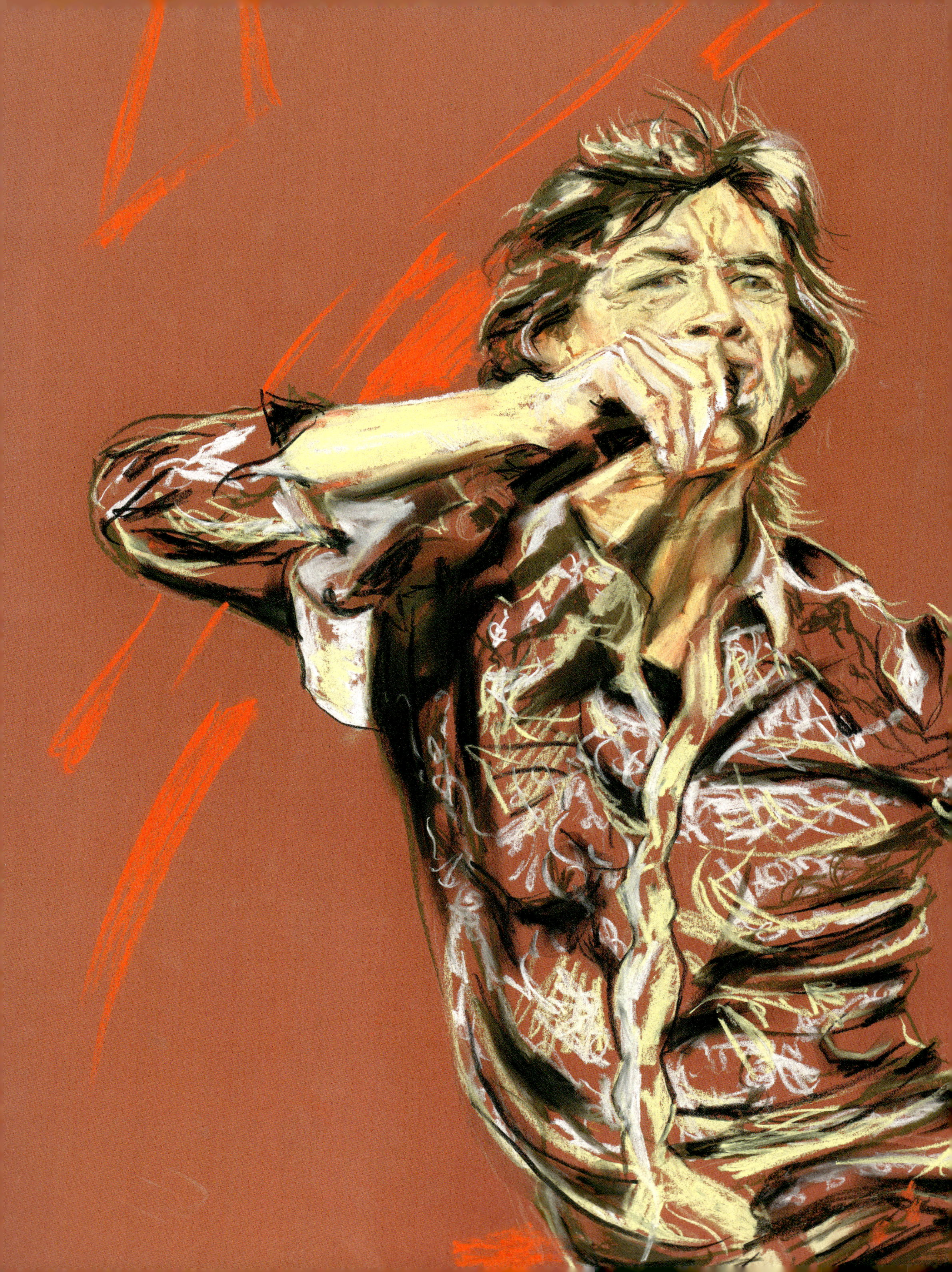

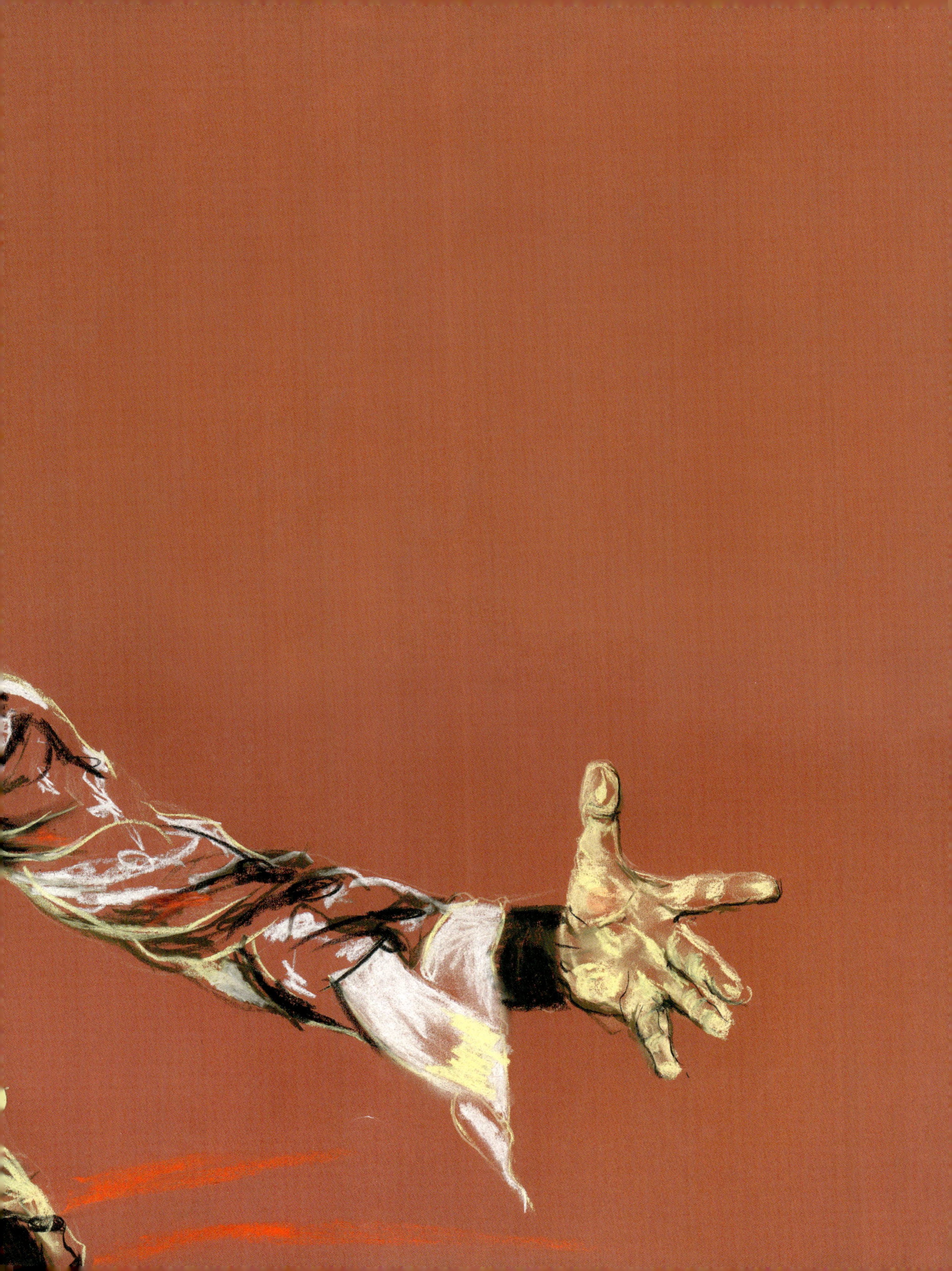

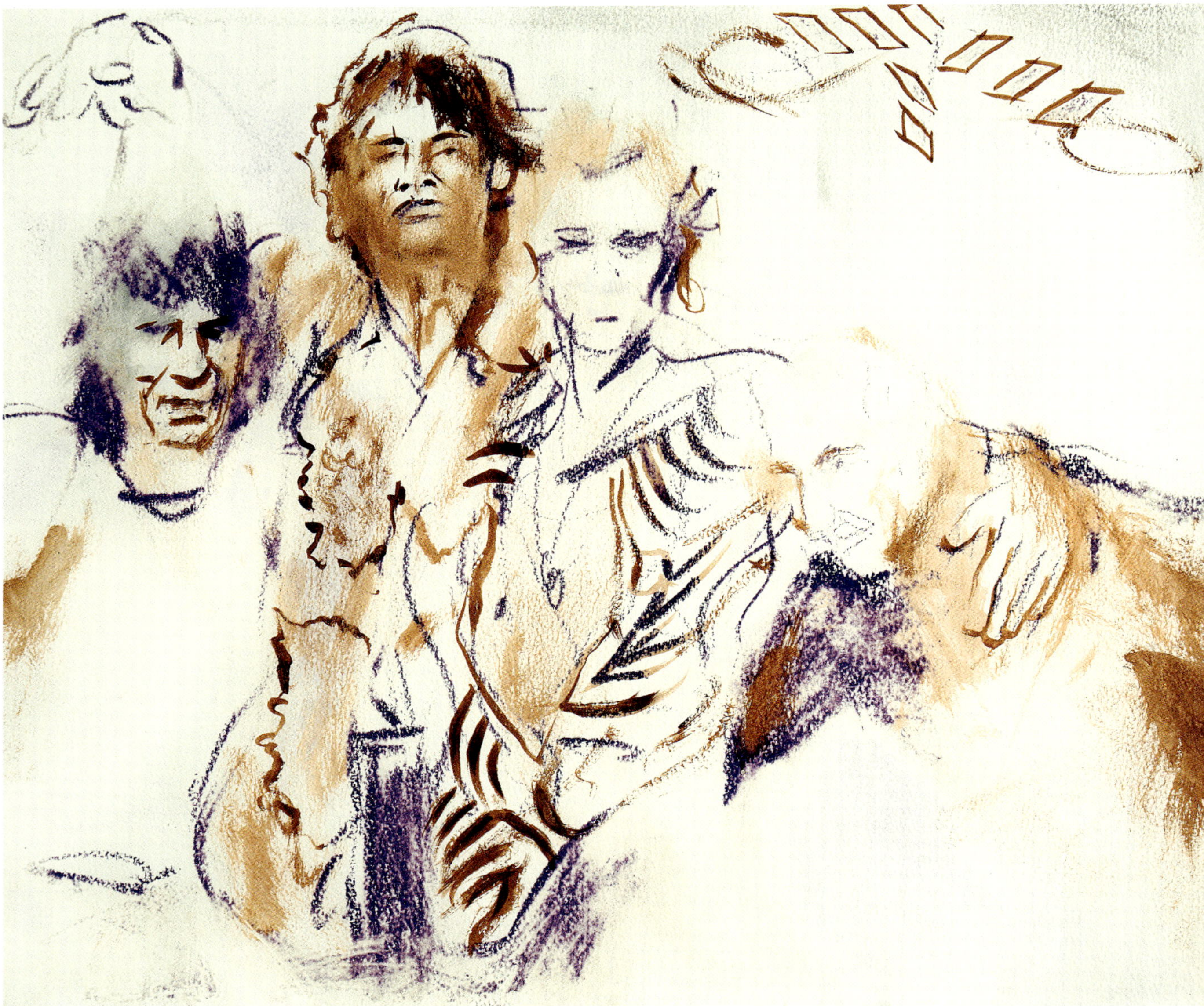

"The pastel of Mick on the previous page is the most recent I have done of him. The mixed media opposite was inspired by the Caravaggio paintings that were discovered in a loft in France. Like Caravaggio, I painted a new work over an existing painting."

PREVIOUS PAGES: *Mick* | 2016 | pastel on board | 59 × 84 cm
ABOVE: *Stones* | 2004 | pastel on paper | 39.5 × 48 cm
OPPOSITE ABOVE: *Stones Raw Panel* | 2013 | mixed media on canvas | 60 × 95 cm
OPPOSITE BELOW: *Stones Through the Ages* | 2013 | mixed media on canvas | 127 × 108.5 cm

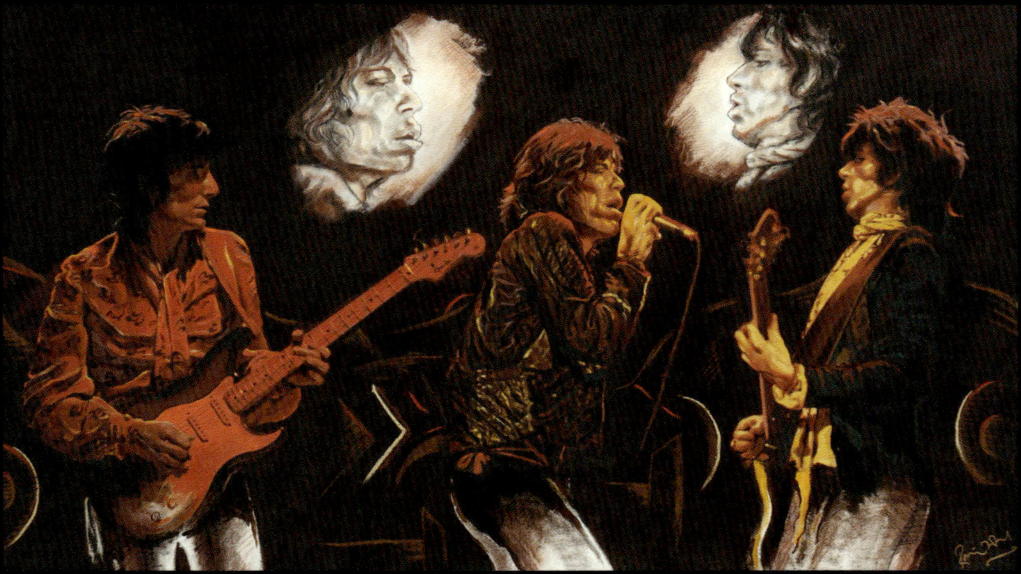

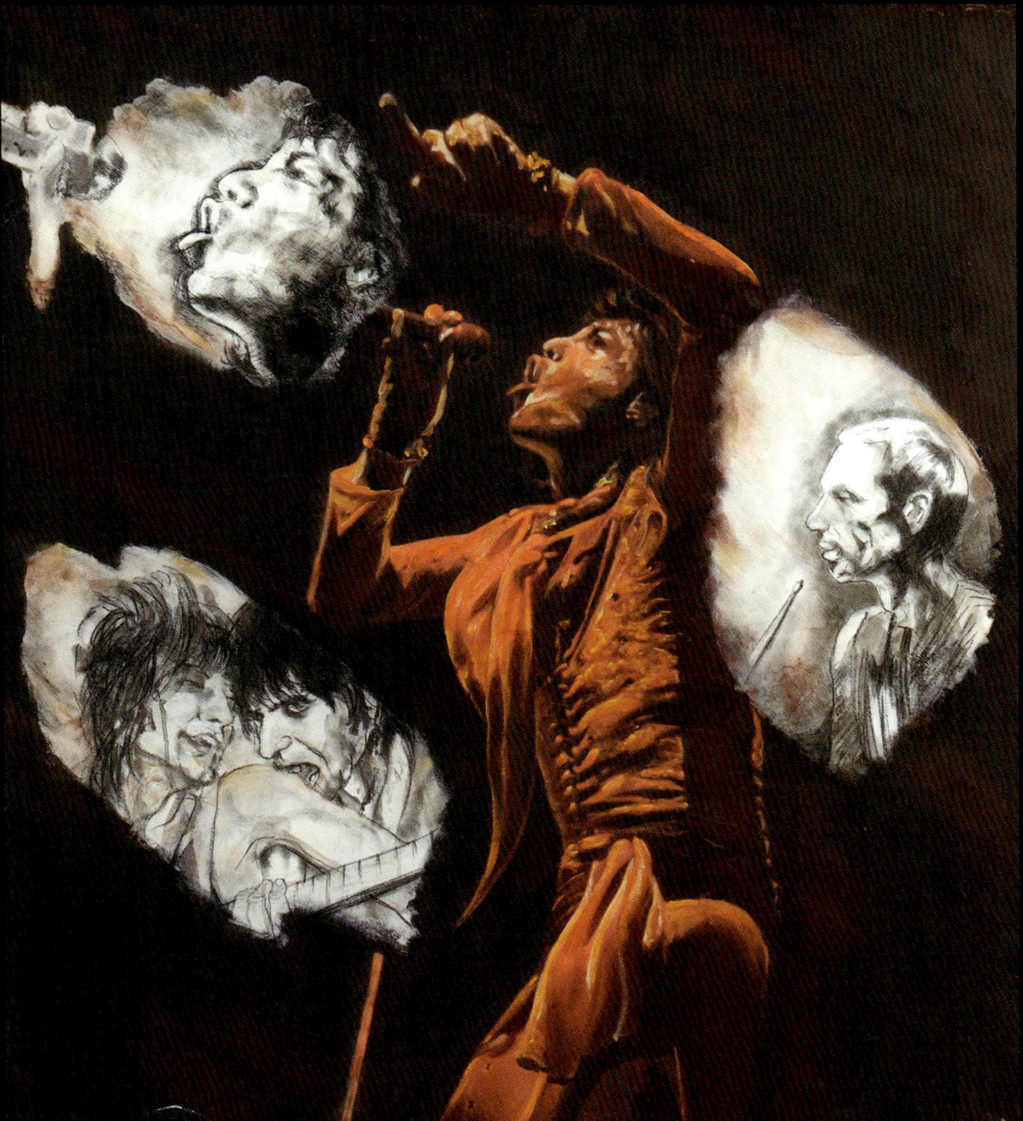

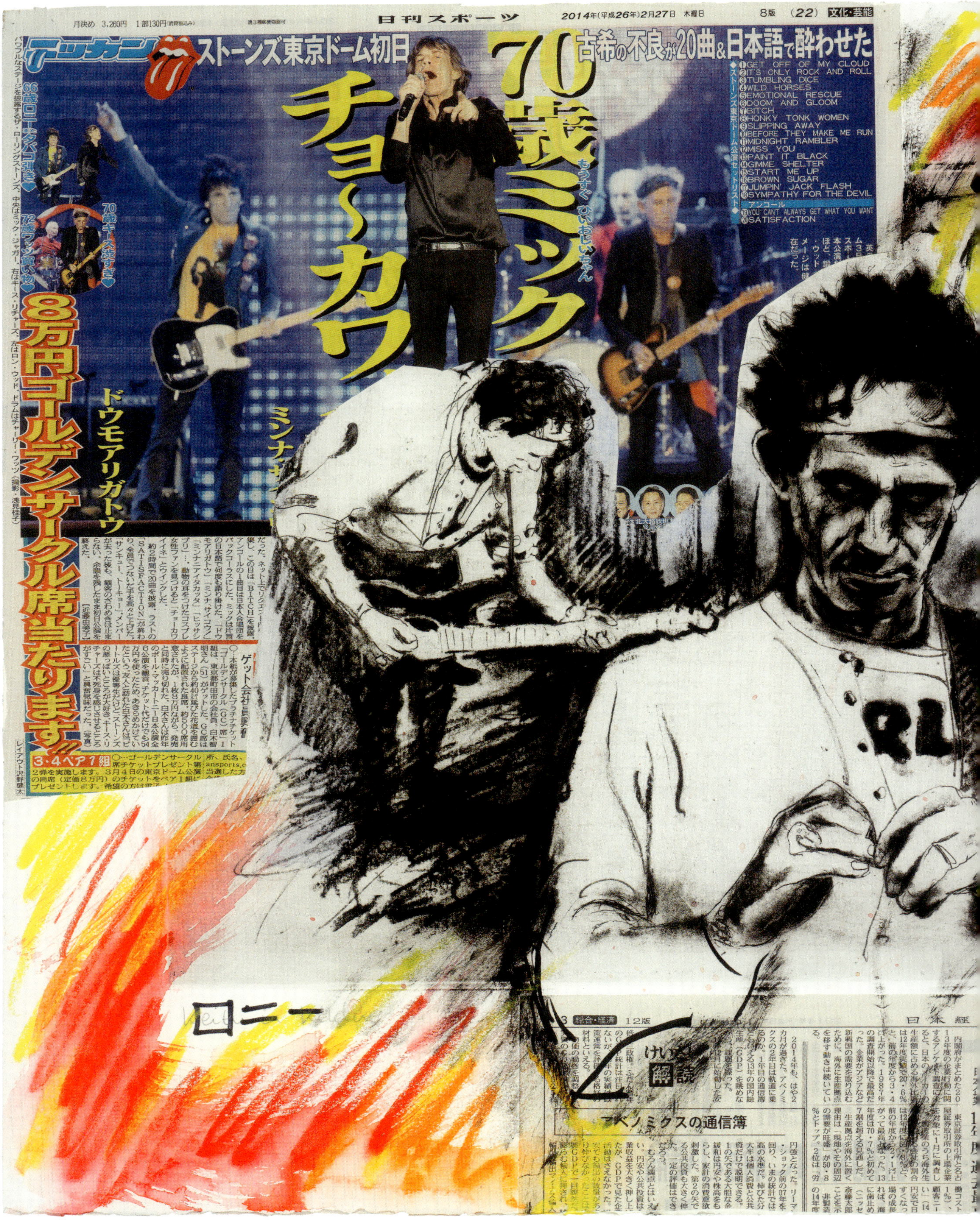
日刊スポーツ
2014年(平成26年)2月27日 木曜日
ストーンズ東京ドーム初日
古希の不良が20曲&日本語で酔わせた
70歳ミック
チョ～カワ
GET OFF OF MY CLOUD
IT'S ONLY ROCK AND ROLL
TUMBLING DICE
WILD HORSES
EMOTIONAL RESCUE
DOOM AND GLOOM
BITCH
HONKY TONK WOMEN
SLIPPING AWAY
BEFORE THEY MAKE ME RUN
MIDNIGHT RAMBLER
MISS YOU
PAINT IT BLACK
GIMME SHELTER
START ME UP
BROWN SUGAR
JUMPIN' JACK FLASH
SYMPATHY FOR THE DEVIL
アンコール
YOU CAN'T ALWAYS GET WHAT YOU WANT
SATISFACTION
ドウモアリガトウ
8万円ゴールデンサークル席当たります!!
ロニー
アベノミクスの通信簿

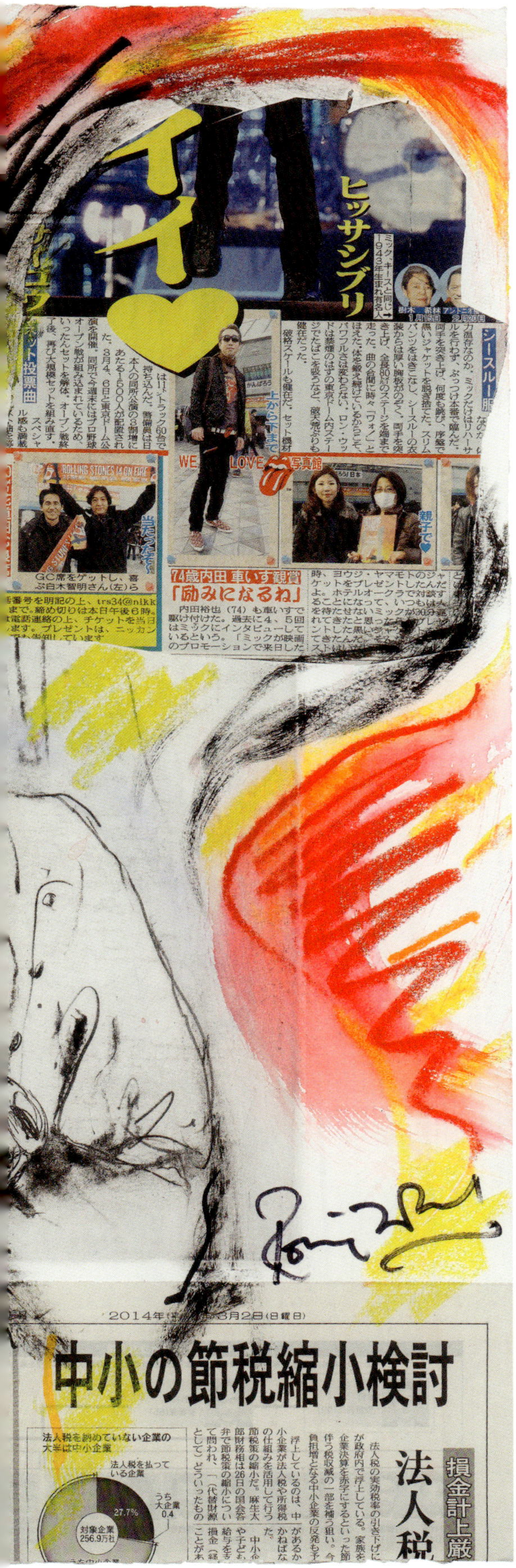

"Here is one of a series of mixed media works made while we were in Japan in 2014. Overleaf is my latest image of Keith in action."

THIS PAGE: *Japan (3)* | 2014 | monoprint | 54 × 64 cm
OVERLEAF: *Keith in Action* | 2015 | oil on canvas | 92 × 120 cm
PAGES 108–109: *The Rolling Stones Set Lists (Burbank 19 April 2013, Paris 11 February 2014, Oslo 21 May 2014, Mexico City 17 March 2016, Havana 25 March 2016)* 2013–16 | pen on paper | various dimensions

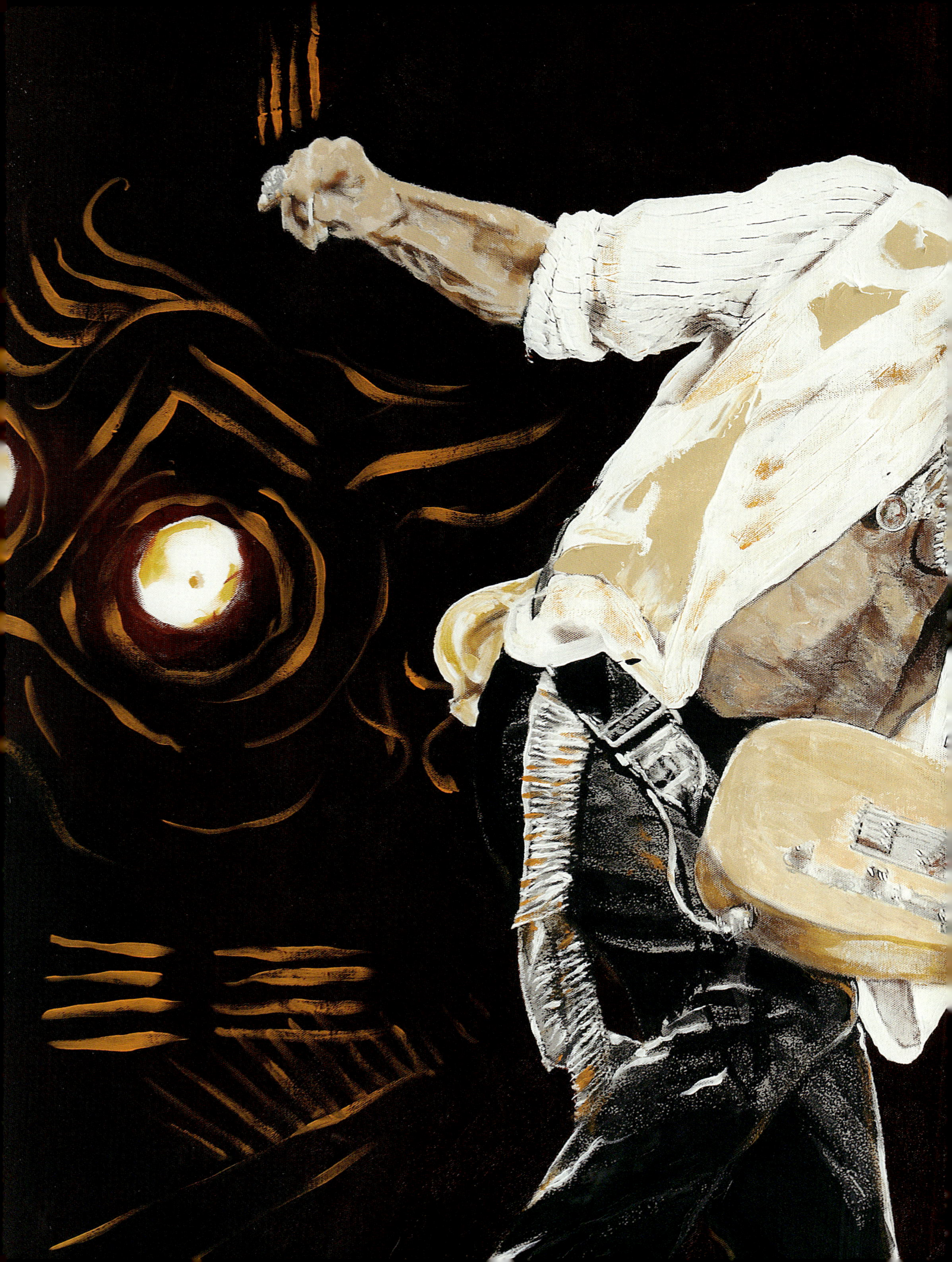

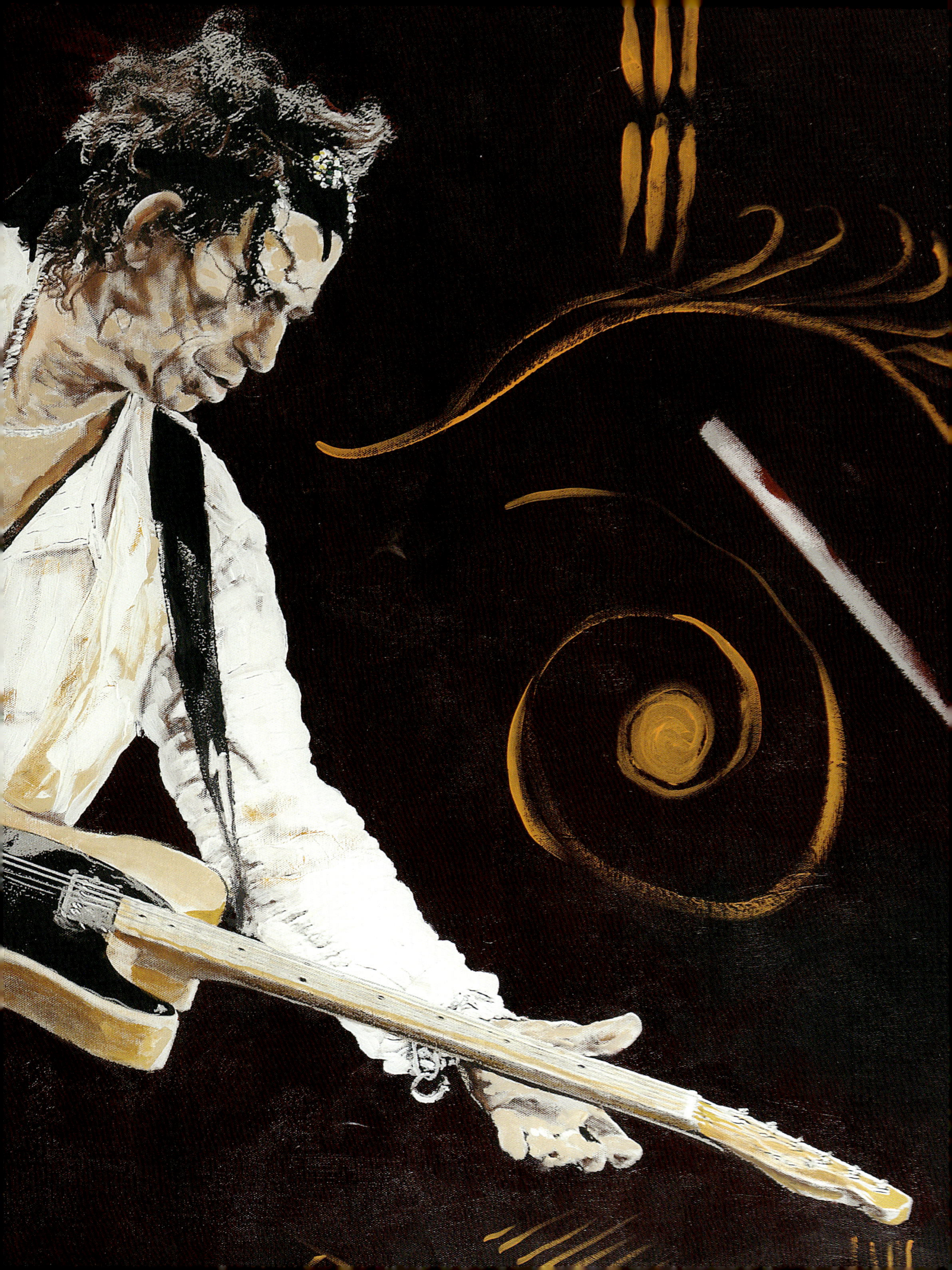

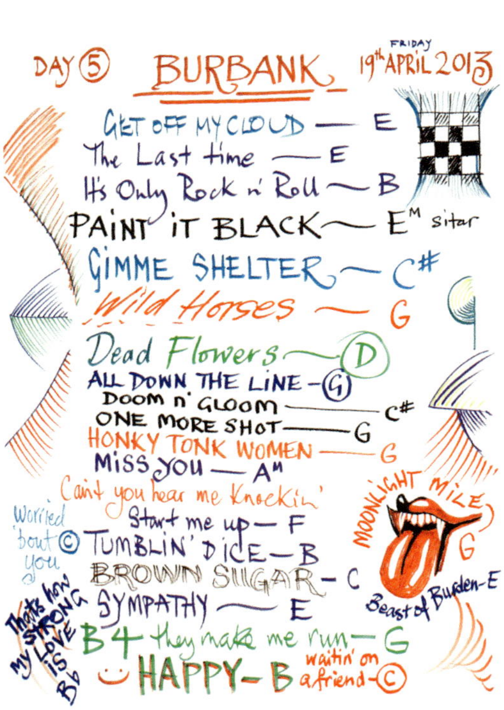

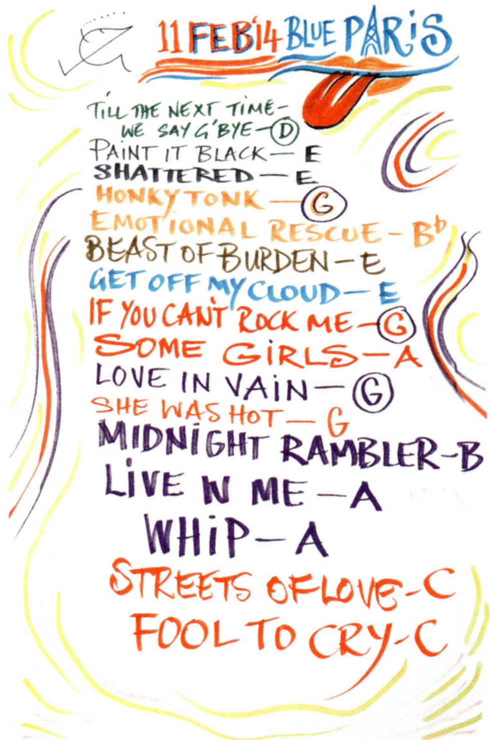

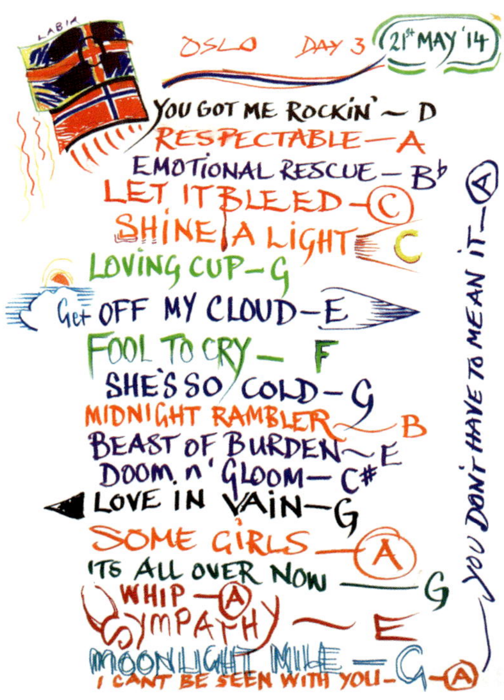

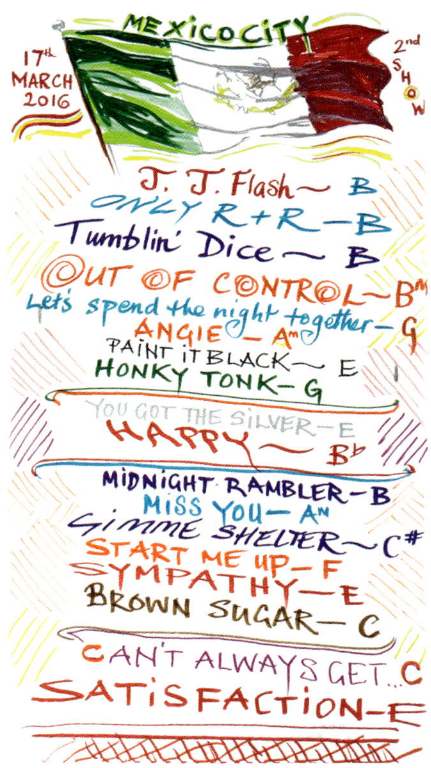

"A few of my set lists. I do these for all our rehearsal days as well as for our live shows."

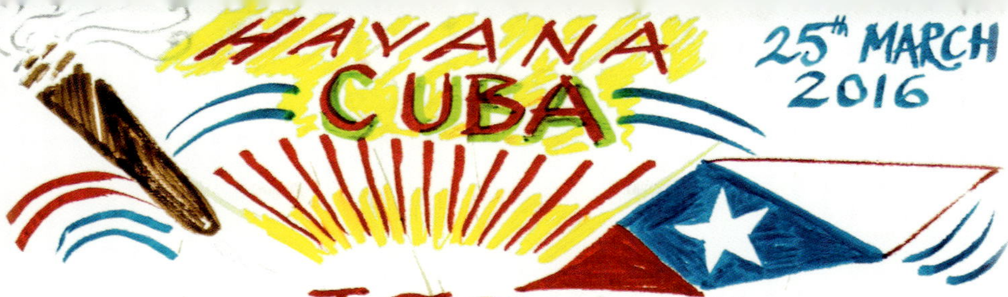

25th MARCH 2016

J.J.F. — B
IT'S ONLY R+R — B
Tumblin' Dice — B
OUT OF CONTROL – Bm
all down the line ~ G
ANGIE — Am
PAINT IT BLACK ~ E
Honky Tonk Women ~ G

You GOT THE SILVER – E
B4 they make me run ~ G

MIDNIGHT RAMBLER – B
MISS YOU ~ Am
Gimme Shelter — C#
START ME UP – F
SYMPATHY — E
BROWN SUGAR – C

Can't always get... ©
SATISFACTION – E

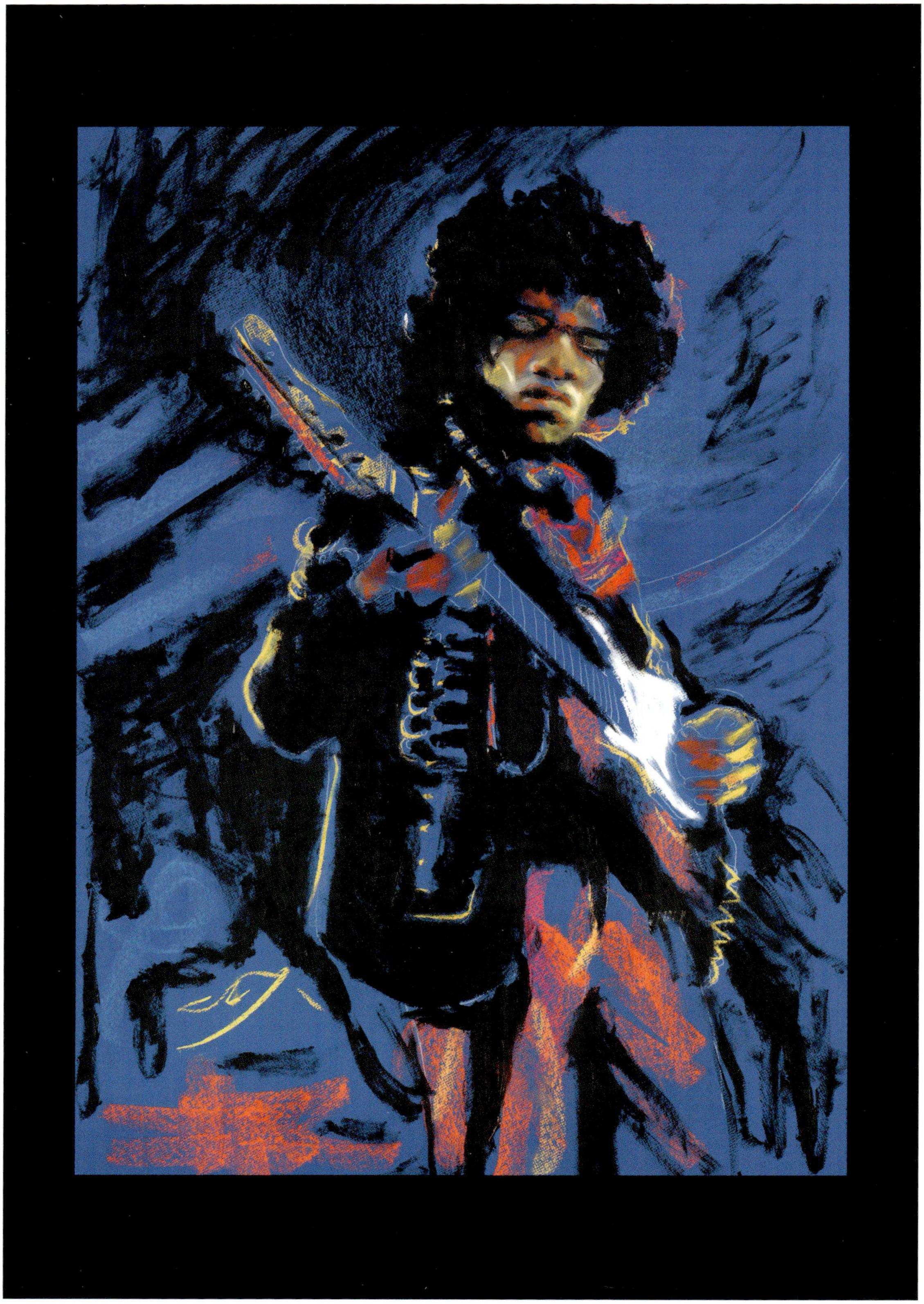

4

ICONS

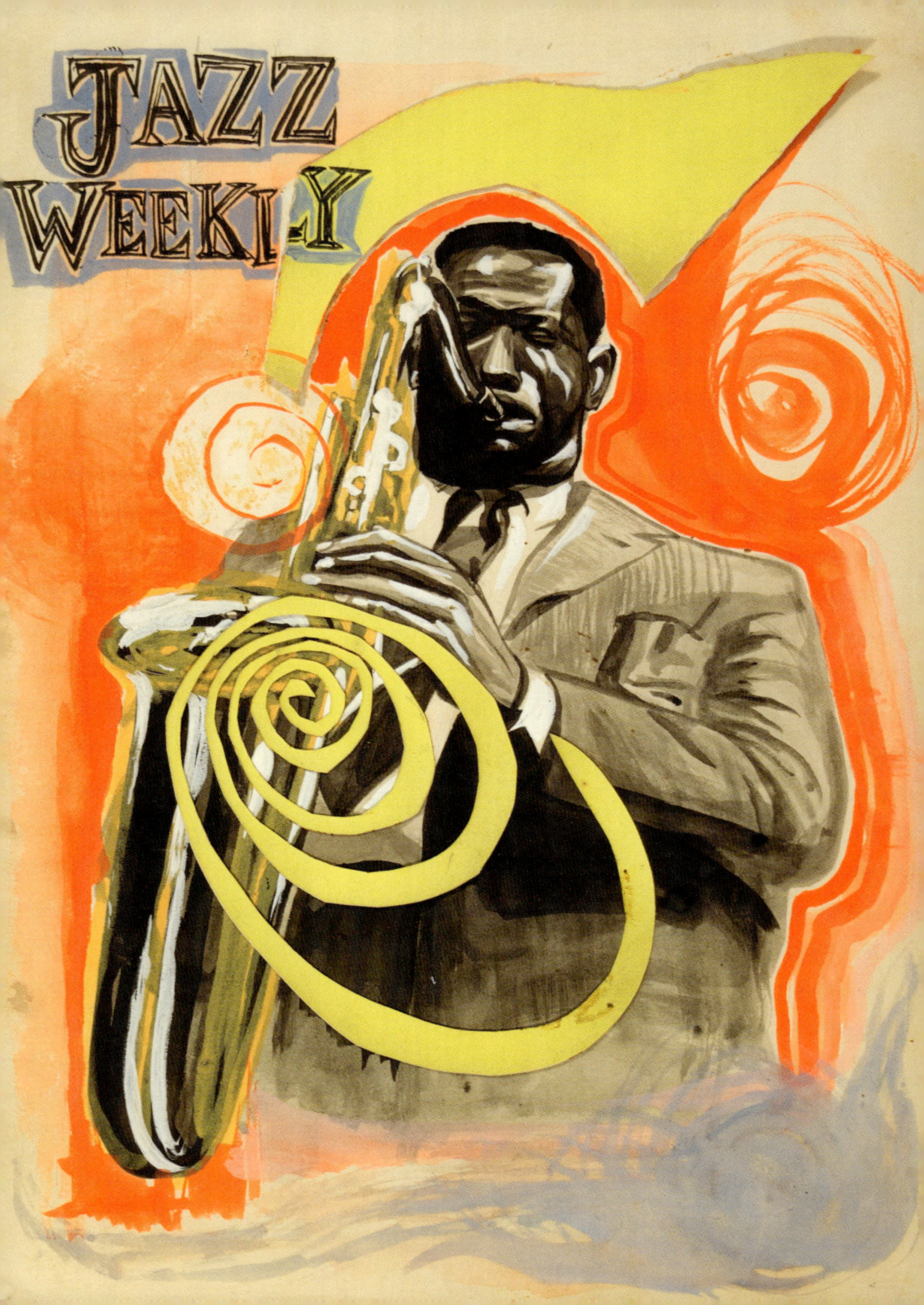
JAZZ
WEEKLY

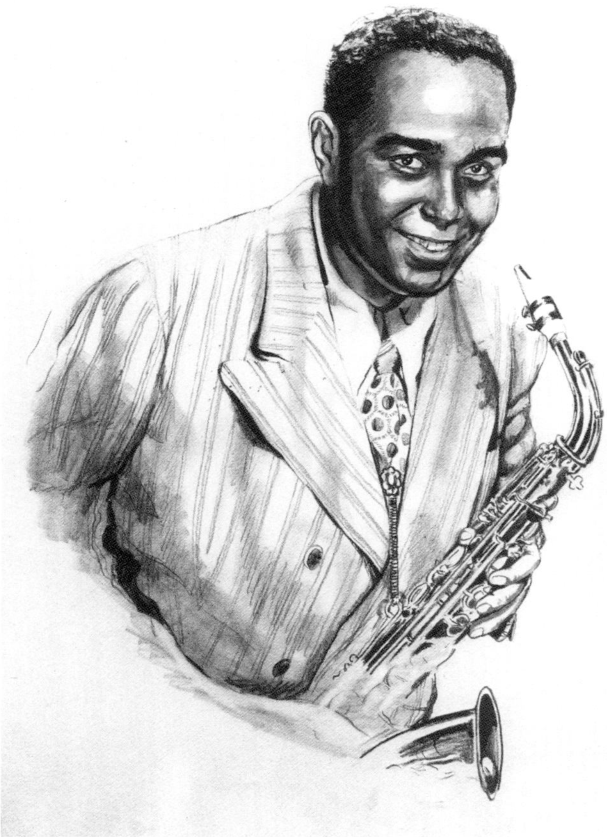

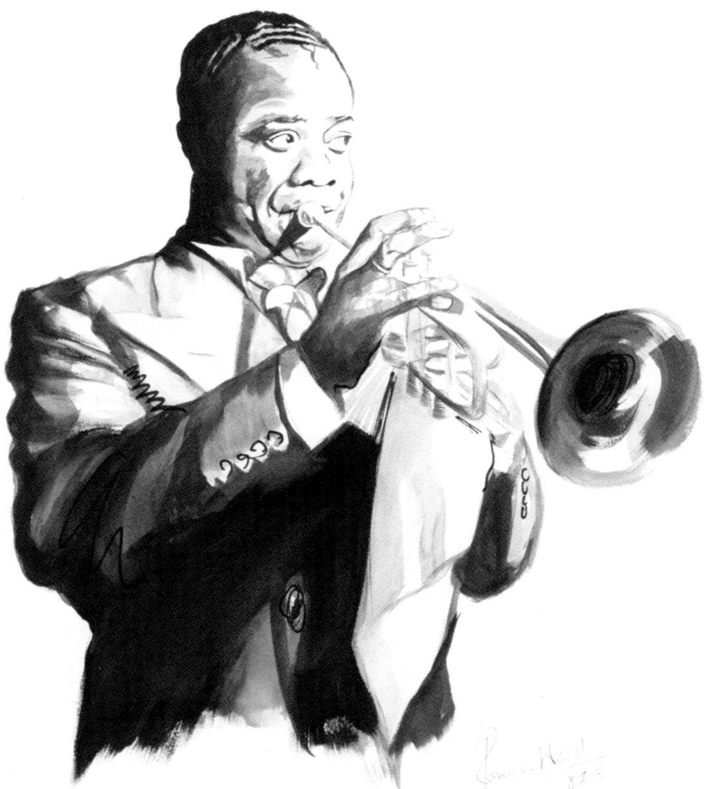

"Being around my brothers who loved jazz inspired me to paint these jazz icons. I relaunched my art career in 1987 with the Decades *series."*

PREVIOUS PAGE: *Electric Blue Hendrix* | 2008 | pastel on board | 81 × 60 cm
OPPOSITE: *1960s Jazz Weekly* | 1963 | mixed media on paper | 35 × 25 cm
ABOVE LEFT: *Charlie Parker (Study for Decades)* | 1987 | pen and pencil on paper | 50 × 35 cm
ABOVE RIGHT: *Louis Armstrong (Study for Decades)* | 1987 | ink and pen on paper | 65 × 42 cm

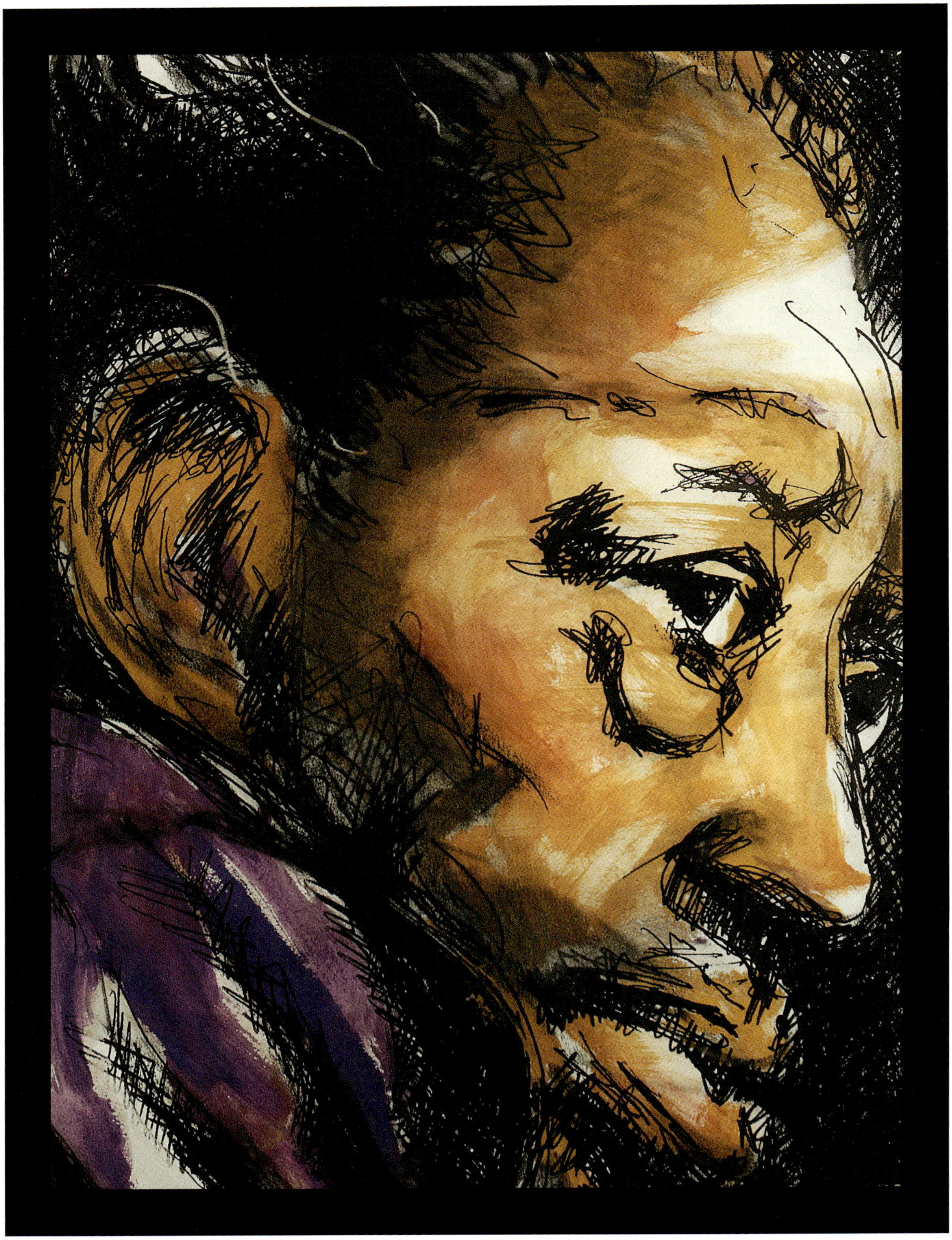

ABOVE: *Duke Ellington (Jazz Series)* | 2007 | intaglio and inkjet | 72 × 53 cm
OPPOSITE: *Miles Davis* | 2007 | intaglio and inkjet | 72 × 53.3 cm

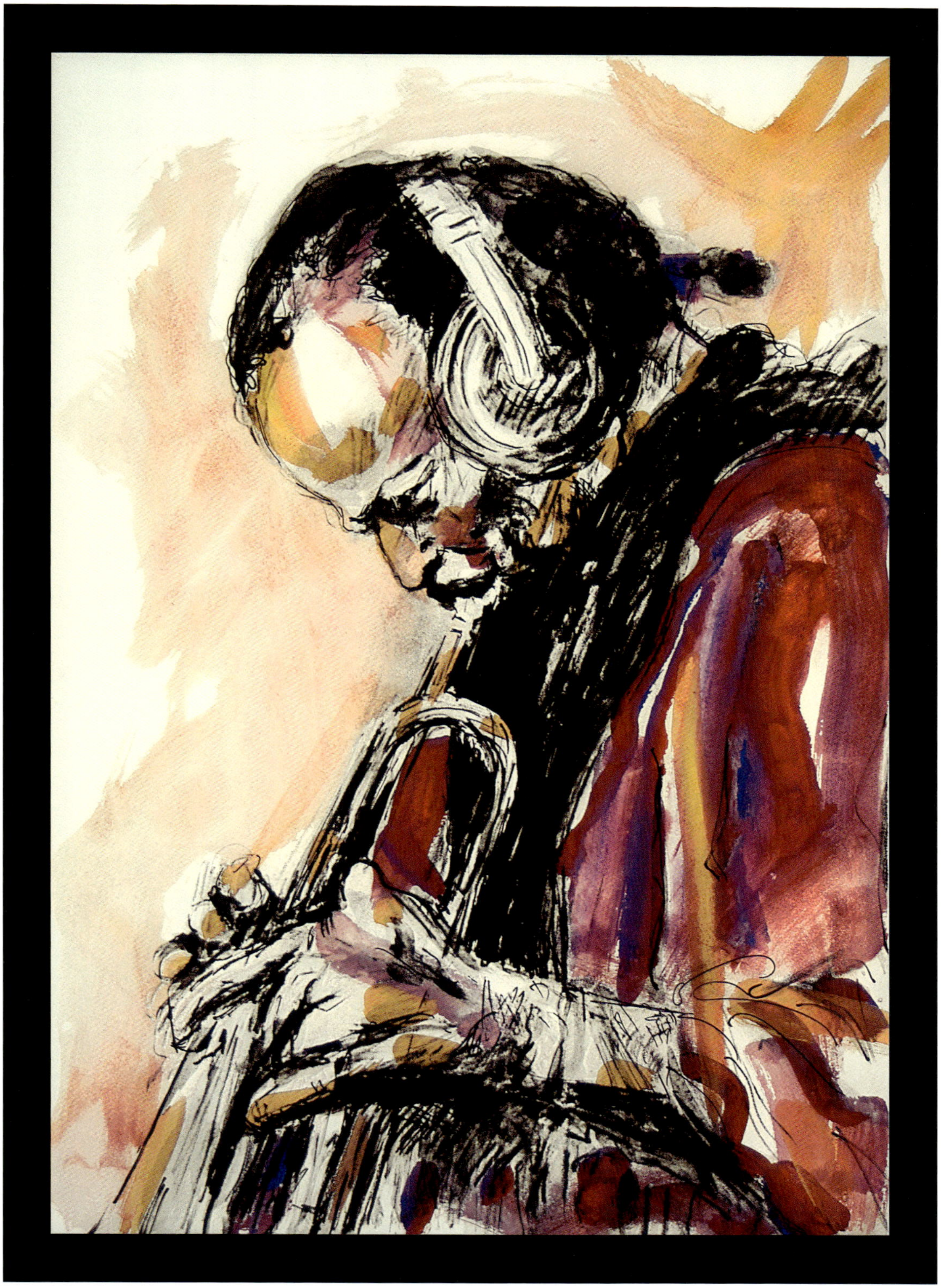

"**Miles Davis** *was exhibited in the Museum of Contemporary Art in Chicago, after which it sadly went missing.*"

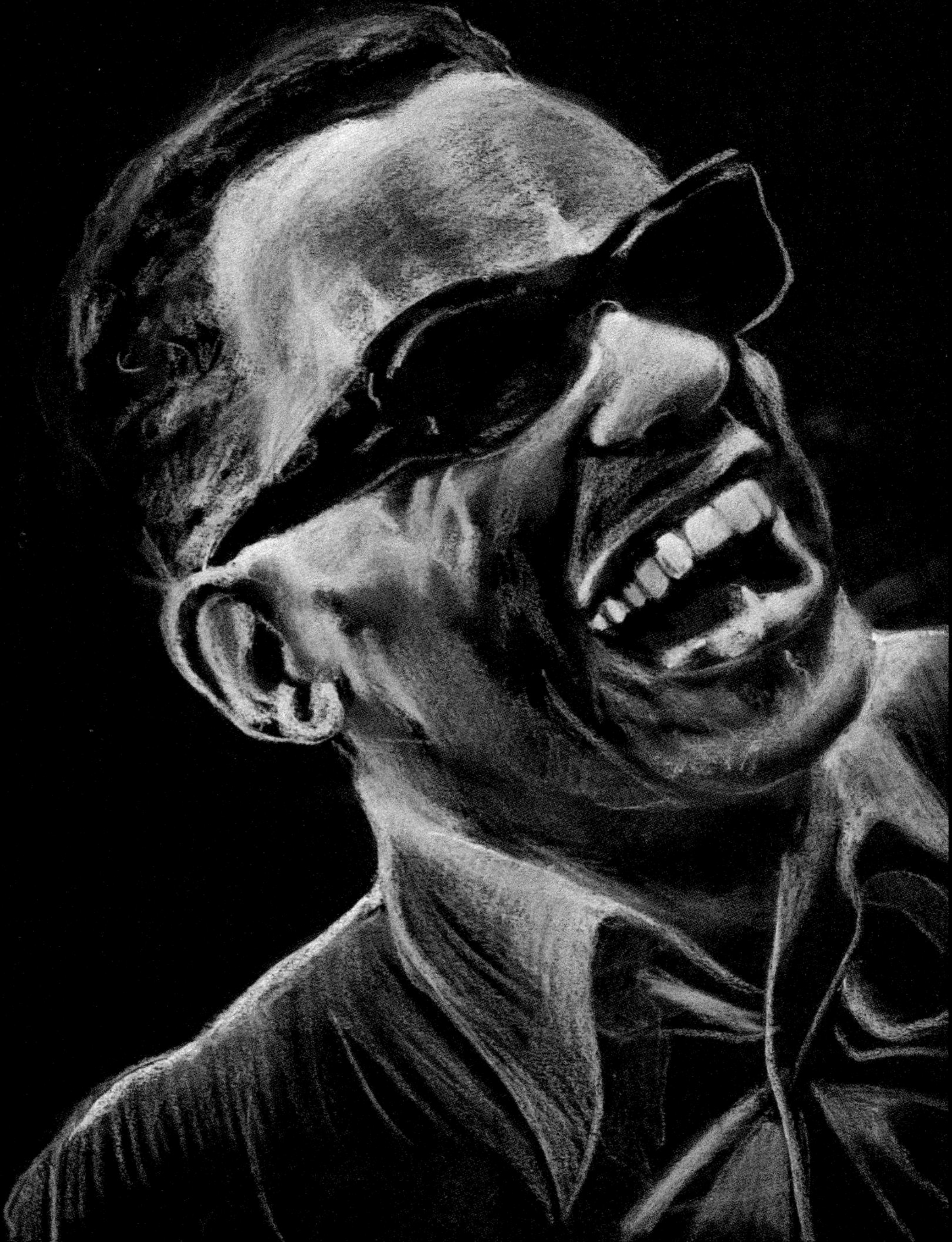

"Brother Ray was created in my Holland Park Studio."

ABOVE: *Ray Charles* | 2015 | pastel on paper | 37 × 29.5 cm
OPPOSITE ABOVE: *Lady Day (Billie Holiday)* | 1991 | pastel on paper | 40 × 30 cm
OPPOSITE BELOW: *Billie Holiday and Bessie Smith* | 1991 | pastel on paper | 45 × 60 cm

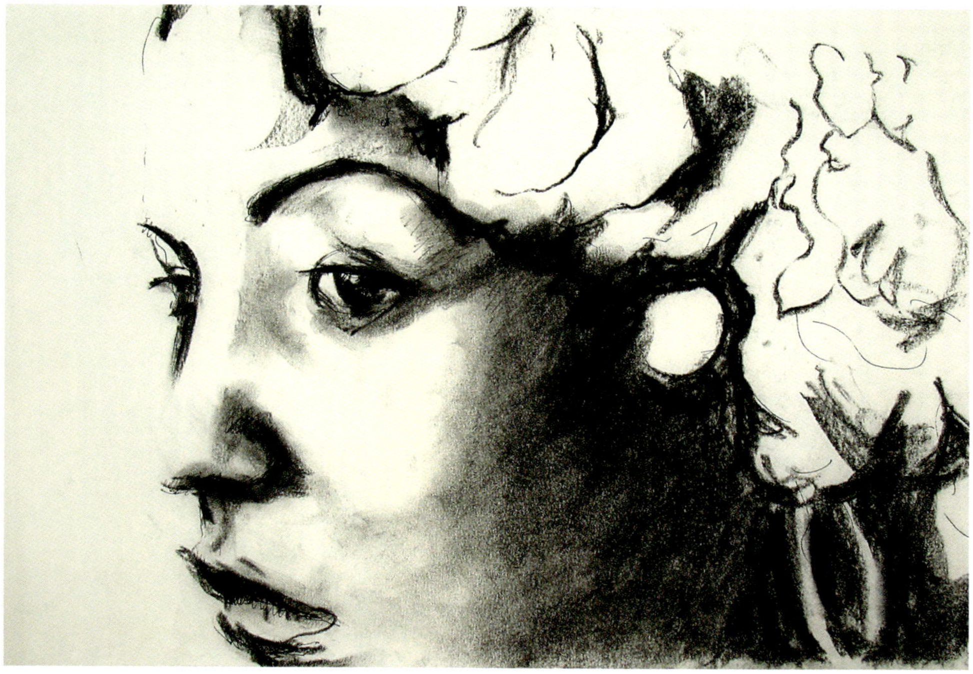

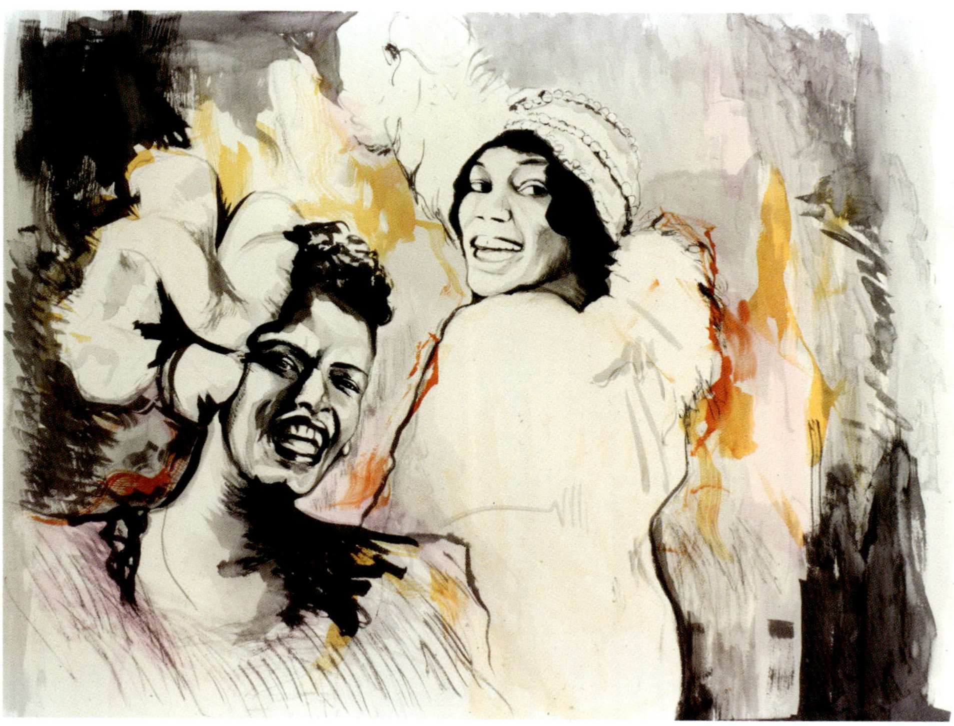

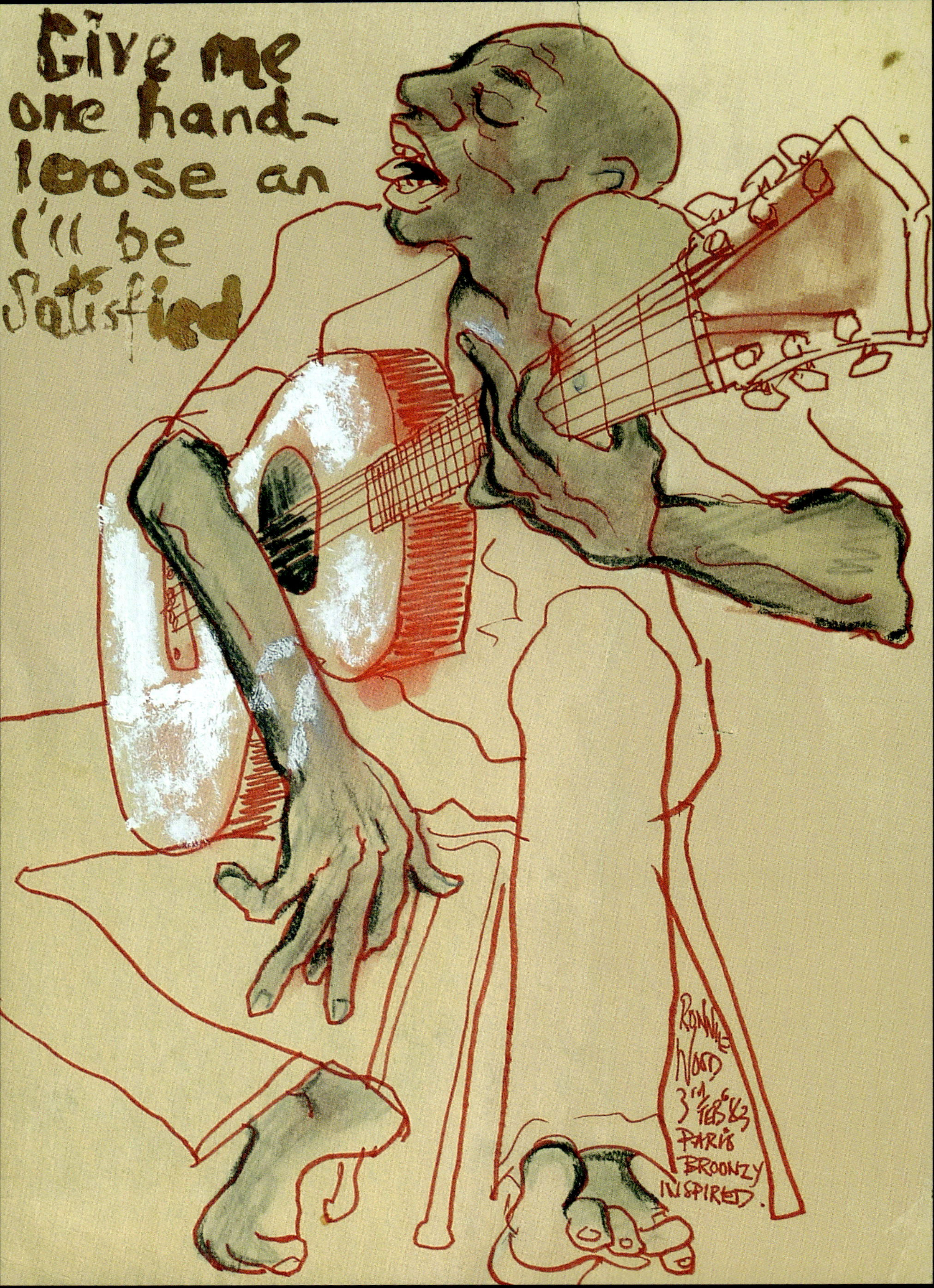
Give me
one hand-
loose an
I'll be
Satisfied
Ronnie
Wood
3rd Feb '83
Paris
Broonzy
Inspired.

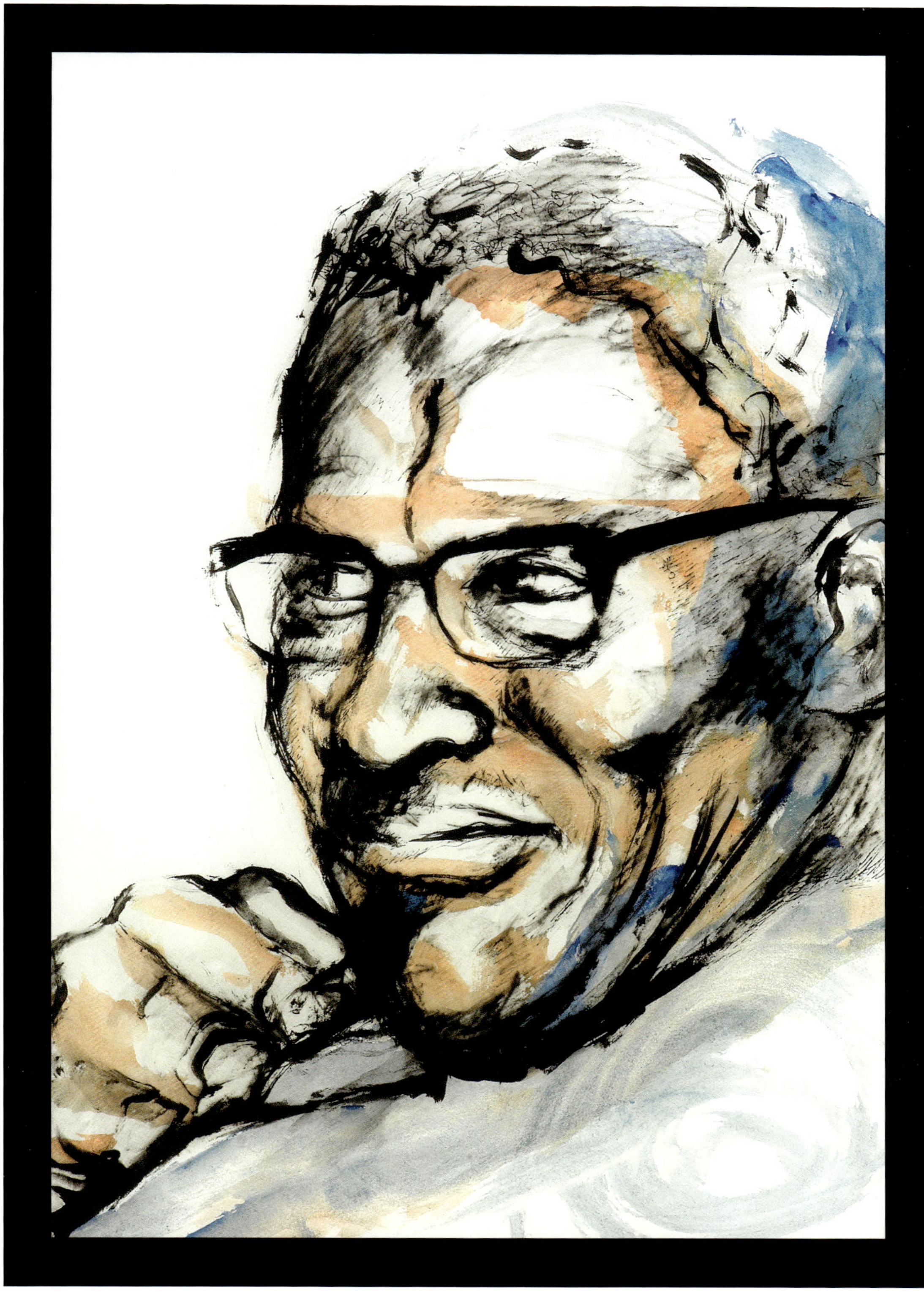

"I found out recently that 'Give me one hand loose' is a line from a Charlie Feathers song."

OPPOSITE: *Give Me One Hand Loose...* | 1983 | acrylic, pen and ink on paper | 29 × 21 cm
ABOVE: *Howlin' Wolf (Jazz Series, No. 12)* | 1987 | intaglio print | 72 × 53 cm

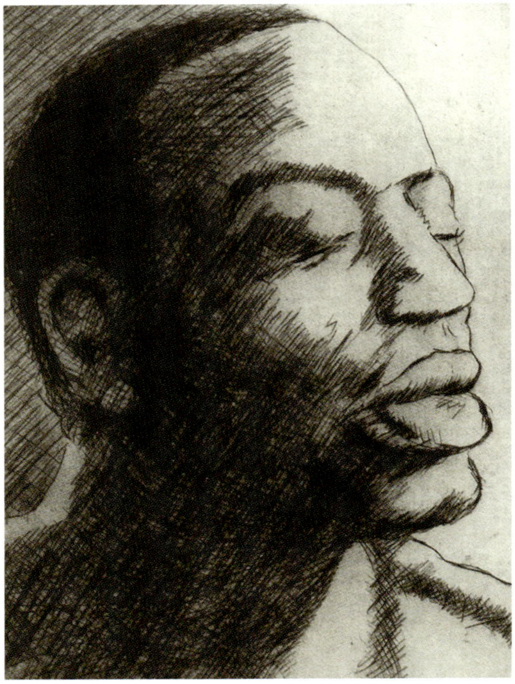

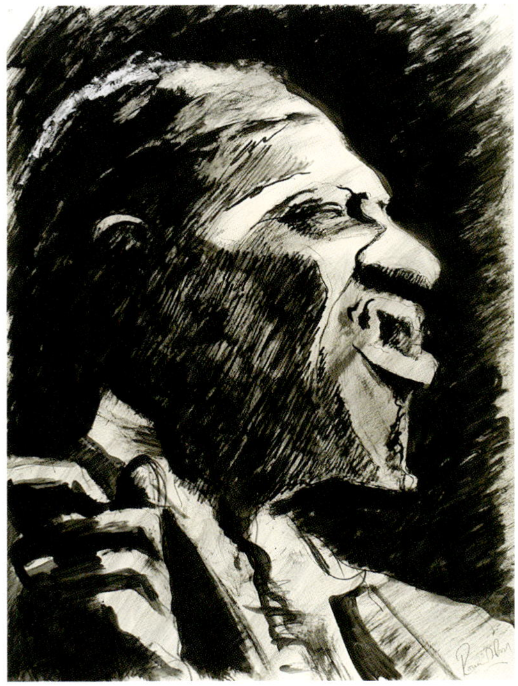

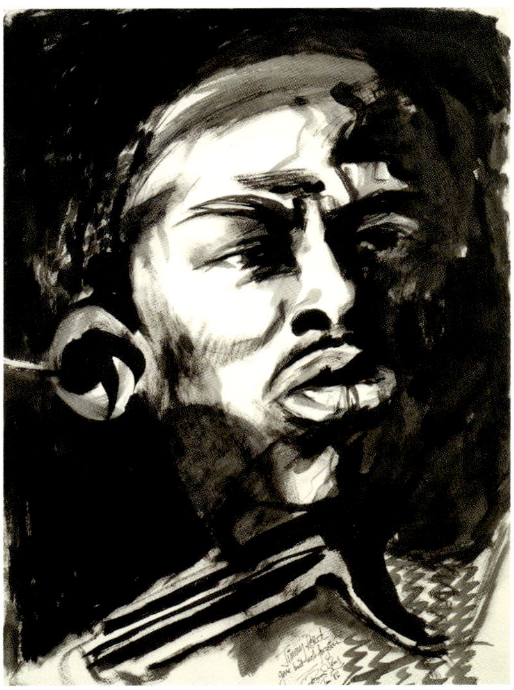

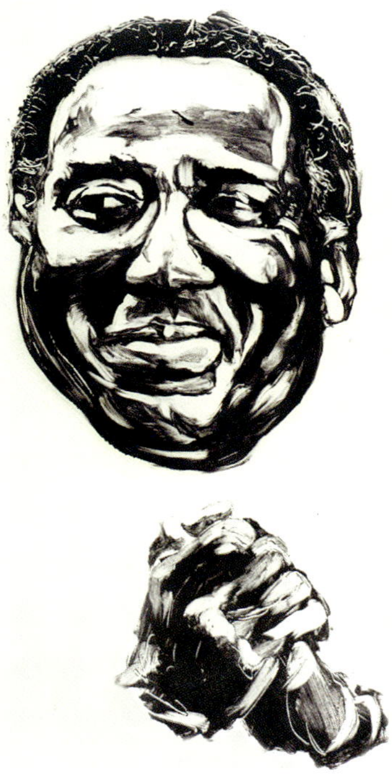

"In these pieces, I used different approaches to reflect the many different styles in which the blues can be played. The Muddy Waters *is a monoprint, using oil on metal and then pressed on paper."*

TOP LEFT: *Big Bill Broonzy* | 1987 | drypoint | 35 × 27.8 cm
TOP RIGHT: *Sonny Boy Williamson II* | 1987 | pen and ink on paper | 76 × 56 cm

ABOVE LEFT: *Jimmy Reed* | 1987 | ink on paper | 76 × 56 cm
ABOVE RIGHT: *Muddy Waters* | 1987 | monoprint | 76 × 56 cm
OPPOSITE: *Robert Johnson* | 2007 | etching | 72 × 53 cm

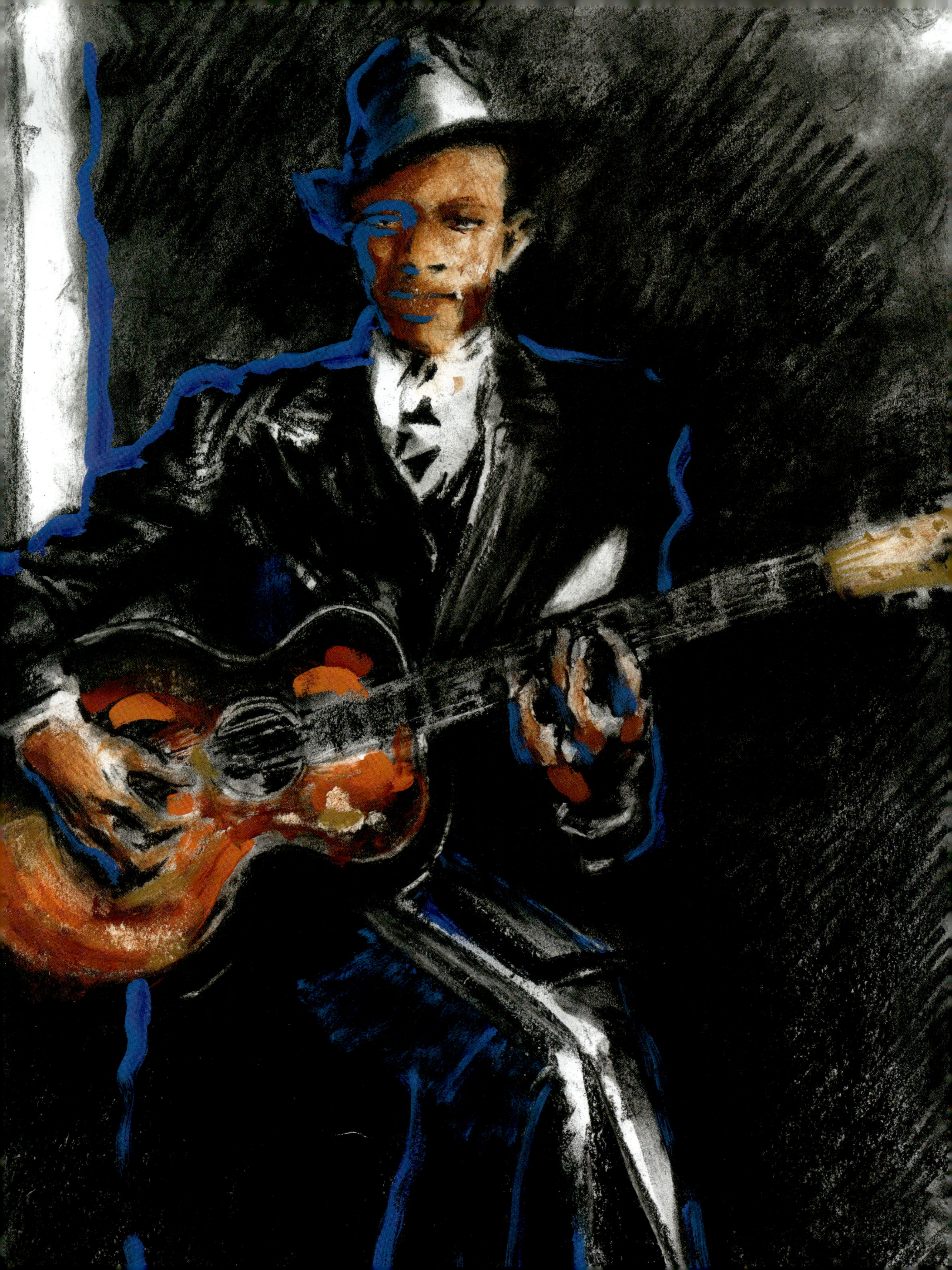

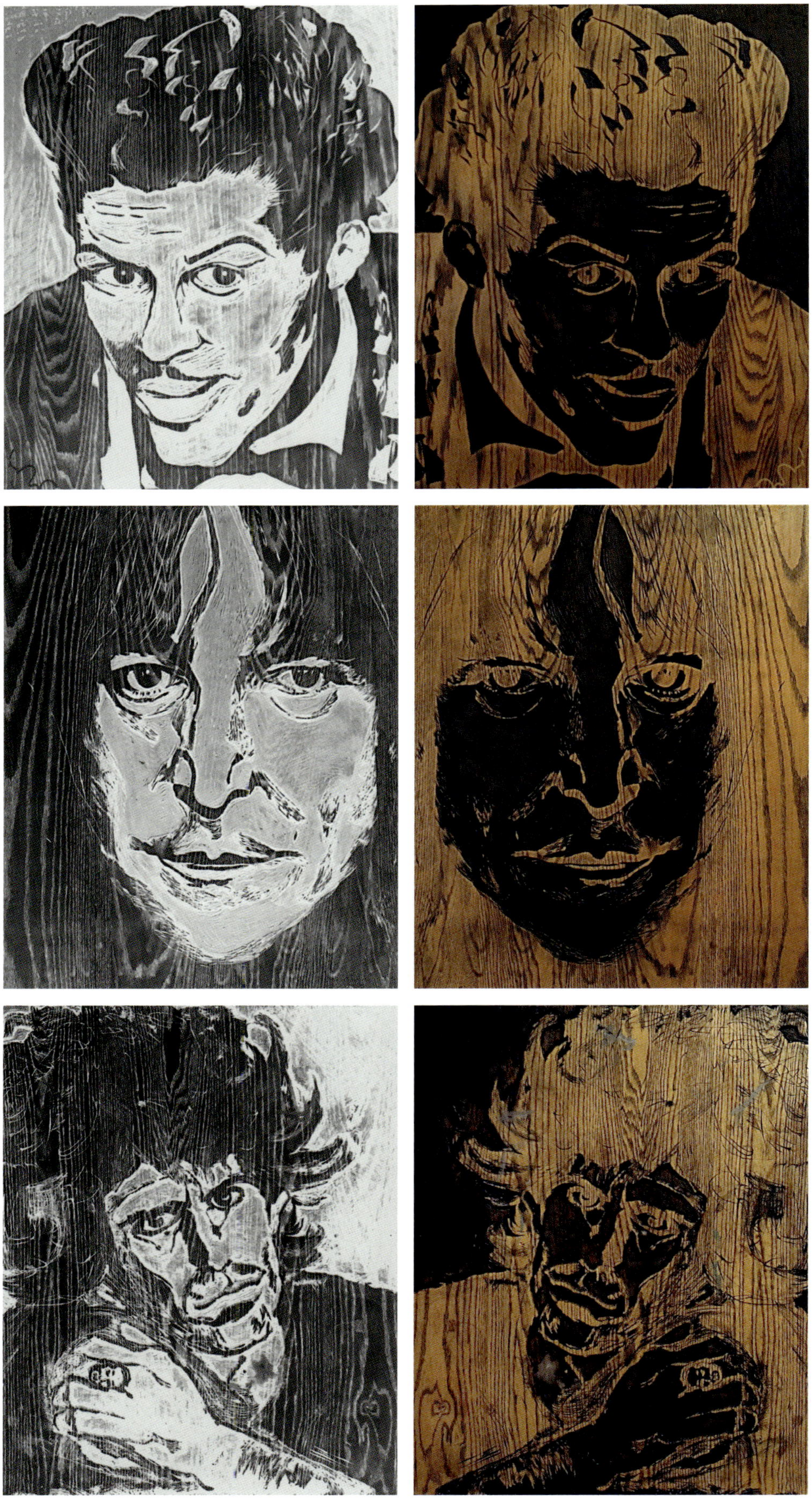

LEFT: *Prints and Woodblocks (Chuck Berry, John Lennon, Keith Richards)* 1984–87 | woodcut and woodblock 79.3 × 64.2 cm each

OPPOSITE ABOVE: *Elvis, Scotty Moore and Bill Black* | 1970 | pen and ink on paper | 52 × 73 cm

OPPOSITE BELOW: *Elvis* | 1984 monotype | 76 × 56 cm

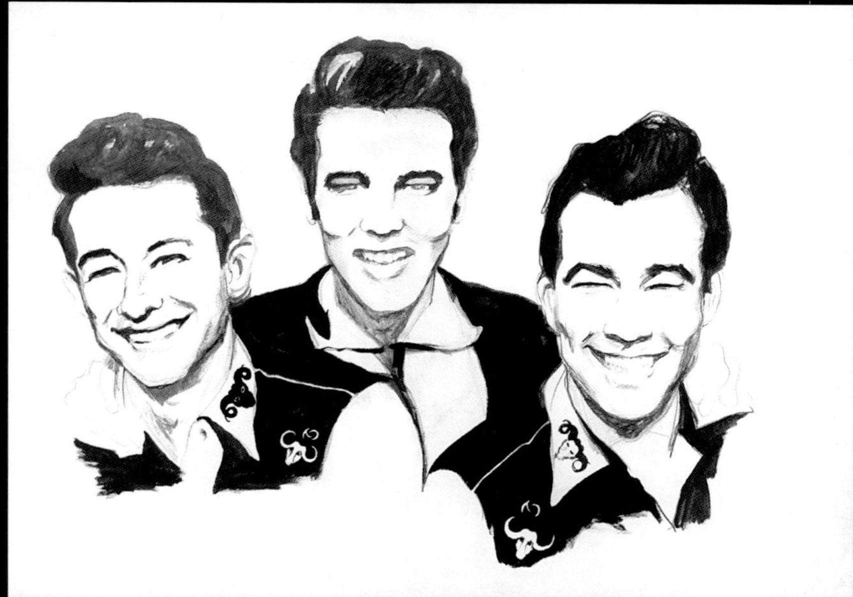

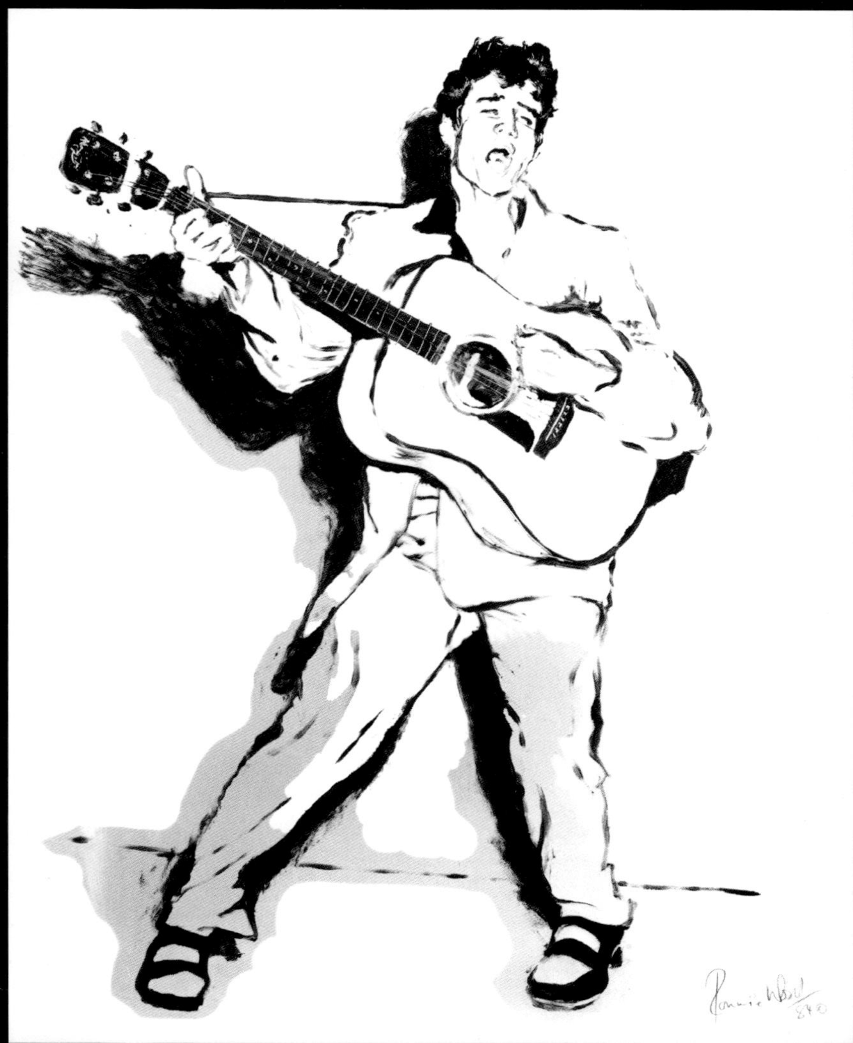

"The woodcuts opposite hung in the theatre in Drury Lane for a long time. Later, when I lived in Kingston, I turned them into coffee tables!"

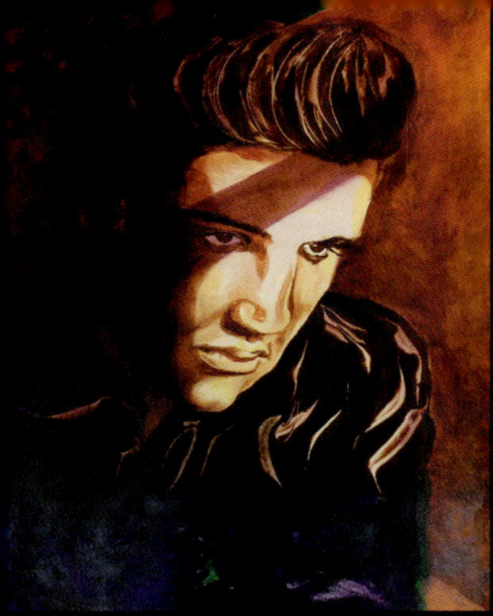
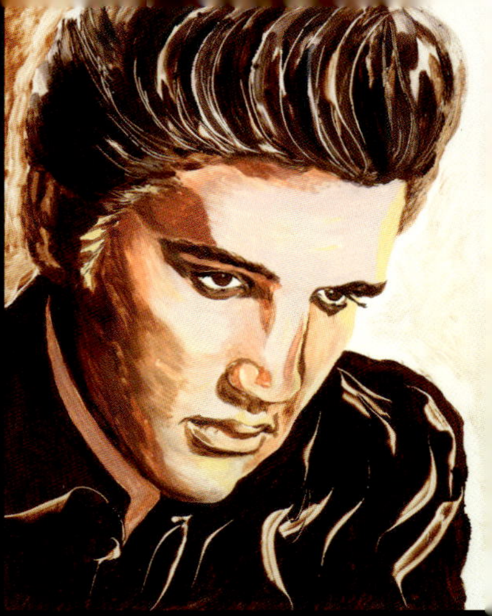
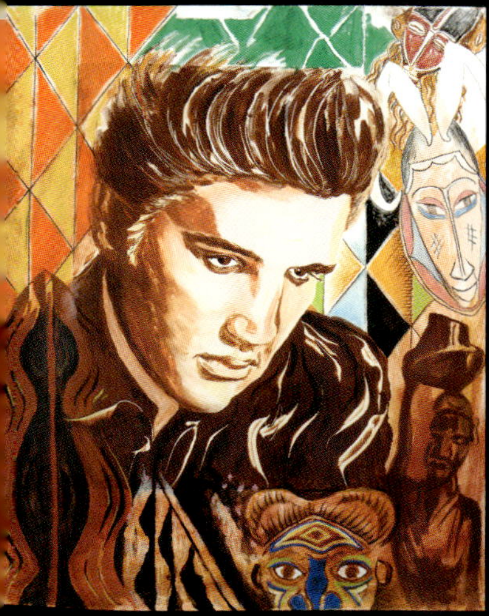
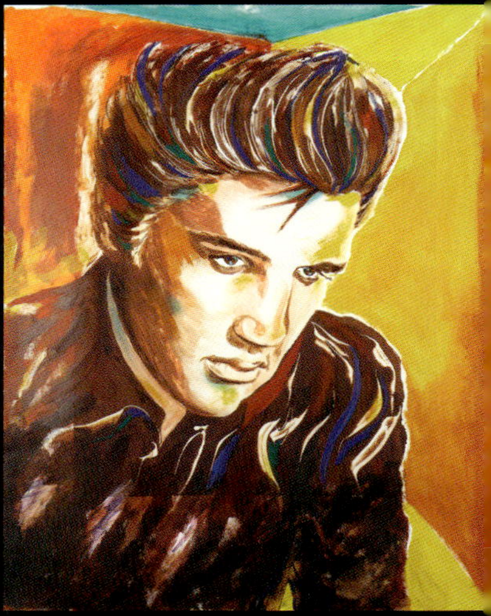
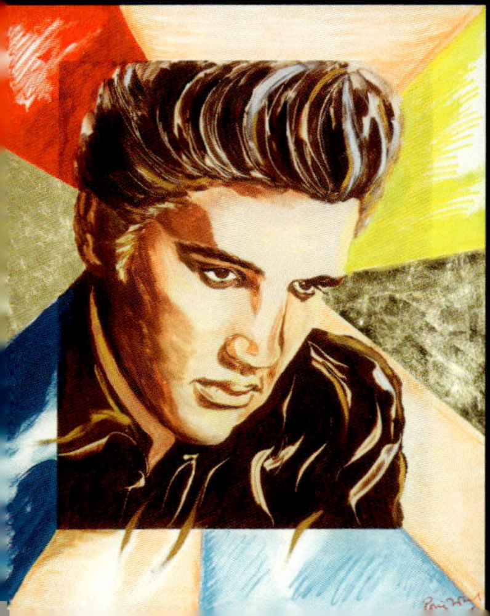
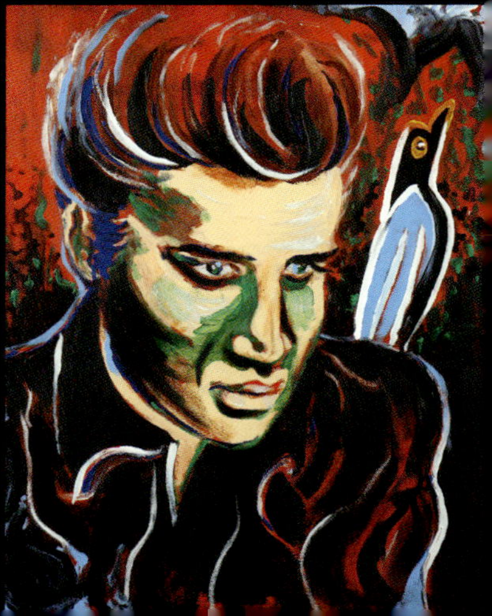

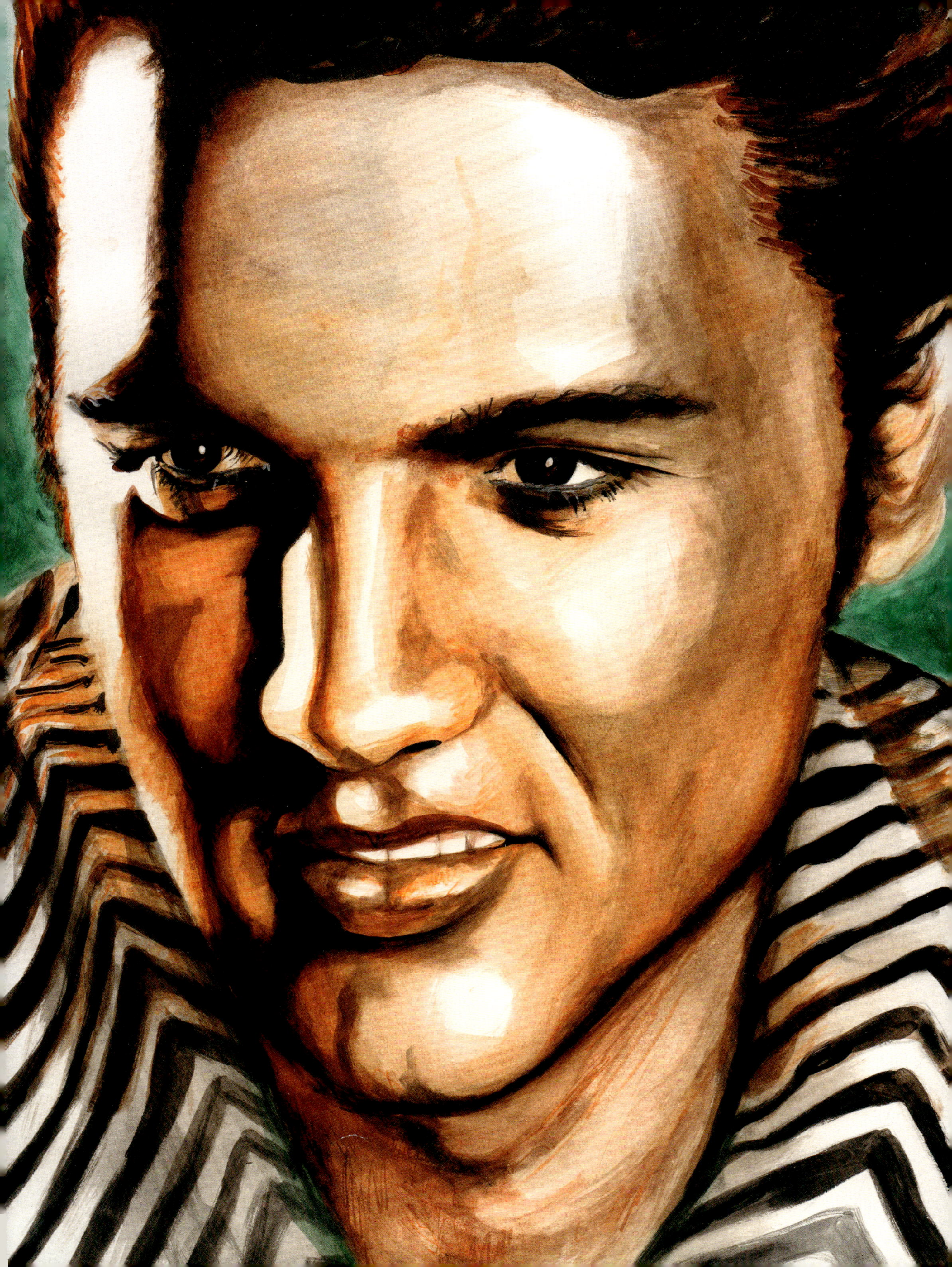

he gave me a song called 'Seven Days' and we've always kept in touch. I saw him at Desert Trip in Coachella in 2016 when he gave us presents for our twins."

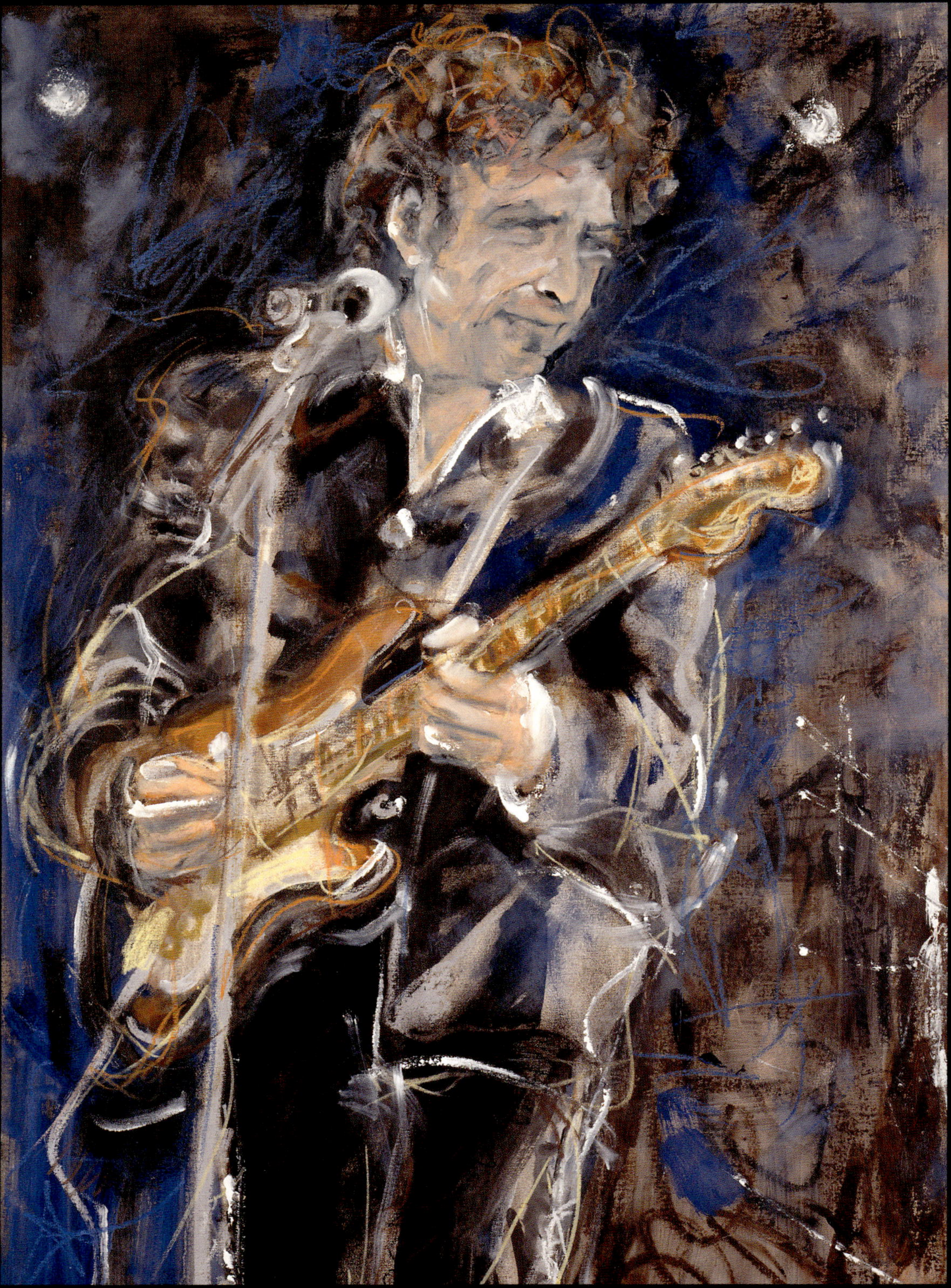

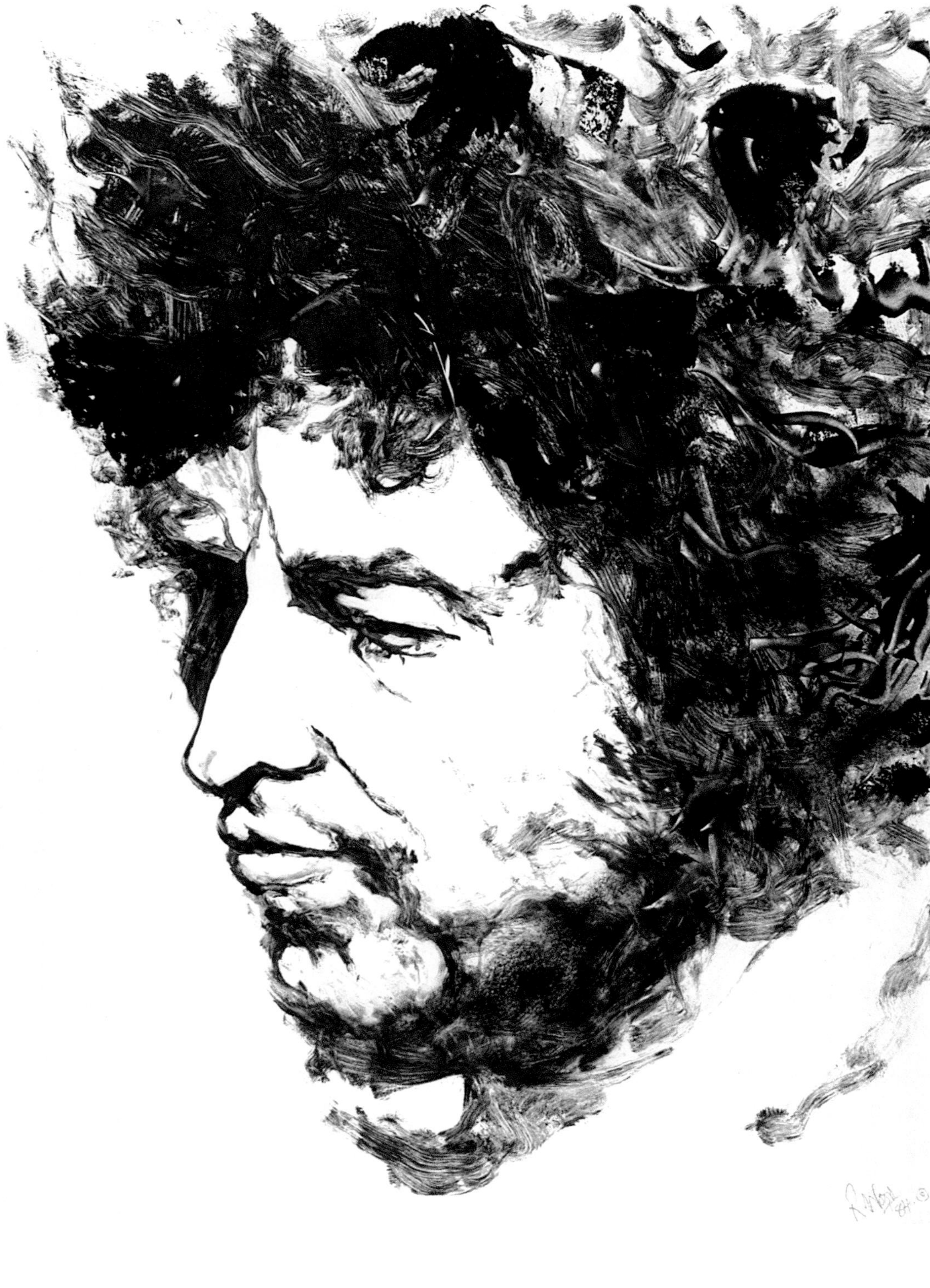

PREVIOUS PAGE LEFT: *Elvis Monoprints* | 2013 | print with mixed media | 102.5 × 87.5 cm
PREVIOUS PAGE RIGHT: *Elvis* | 1985 | acrylic on paper | 112 × 76 cm
OPPOSITE: *Dylan* | 2002 | inkjet and pastel on paper | 112 × 74 cm
ABOVE: *Dylan* | 1984 | monoprint | 53 × 44 cm

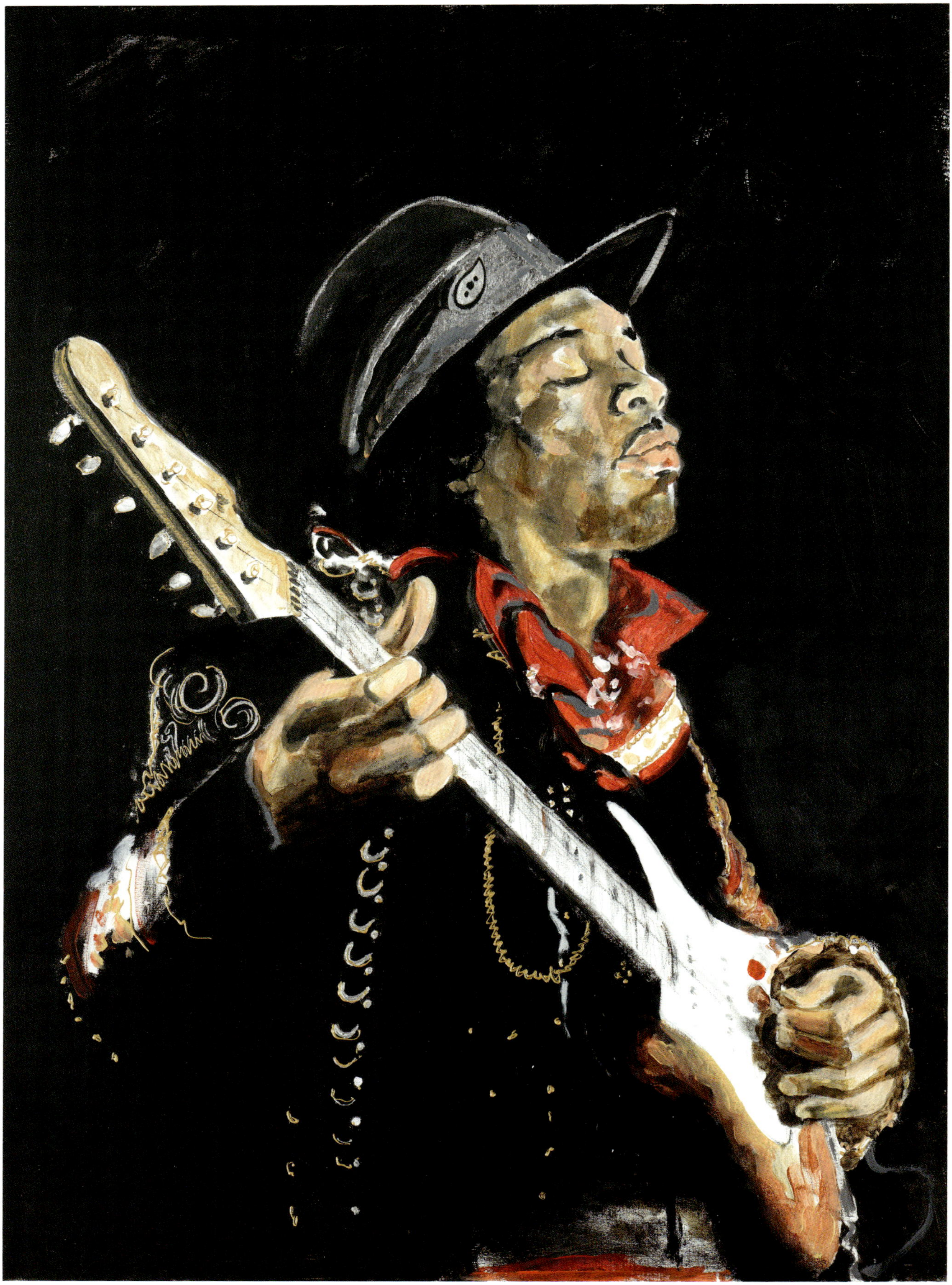

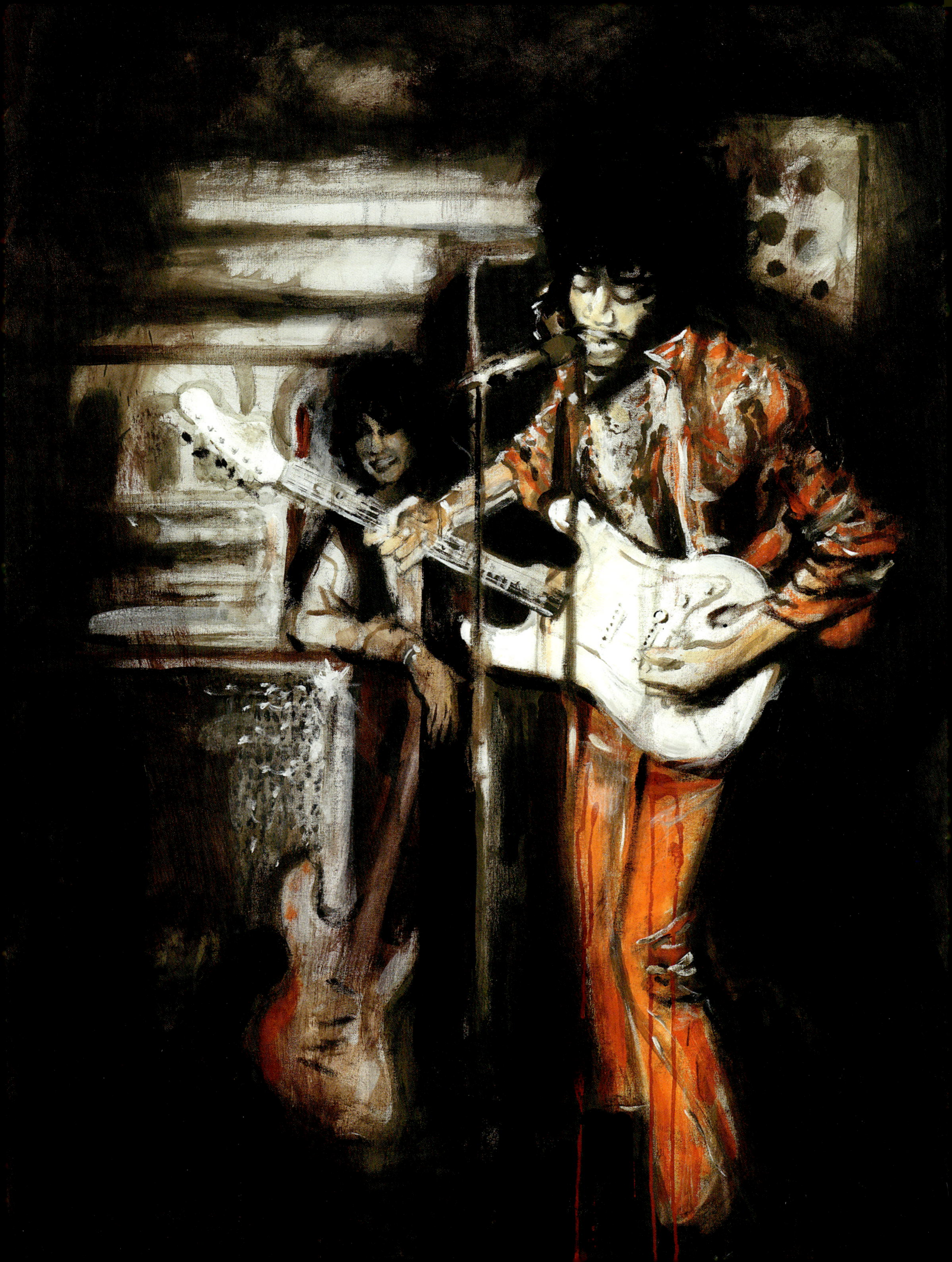

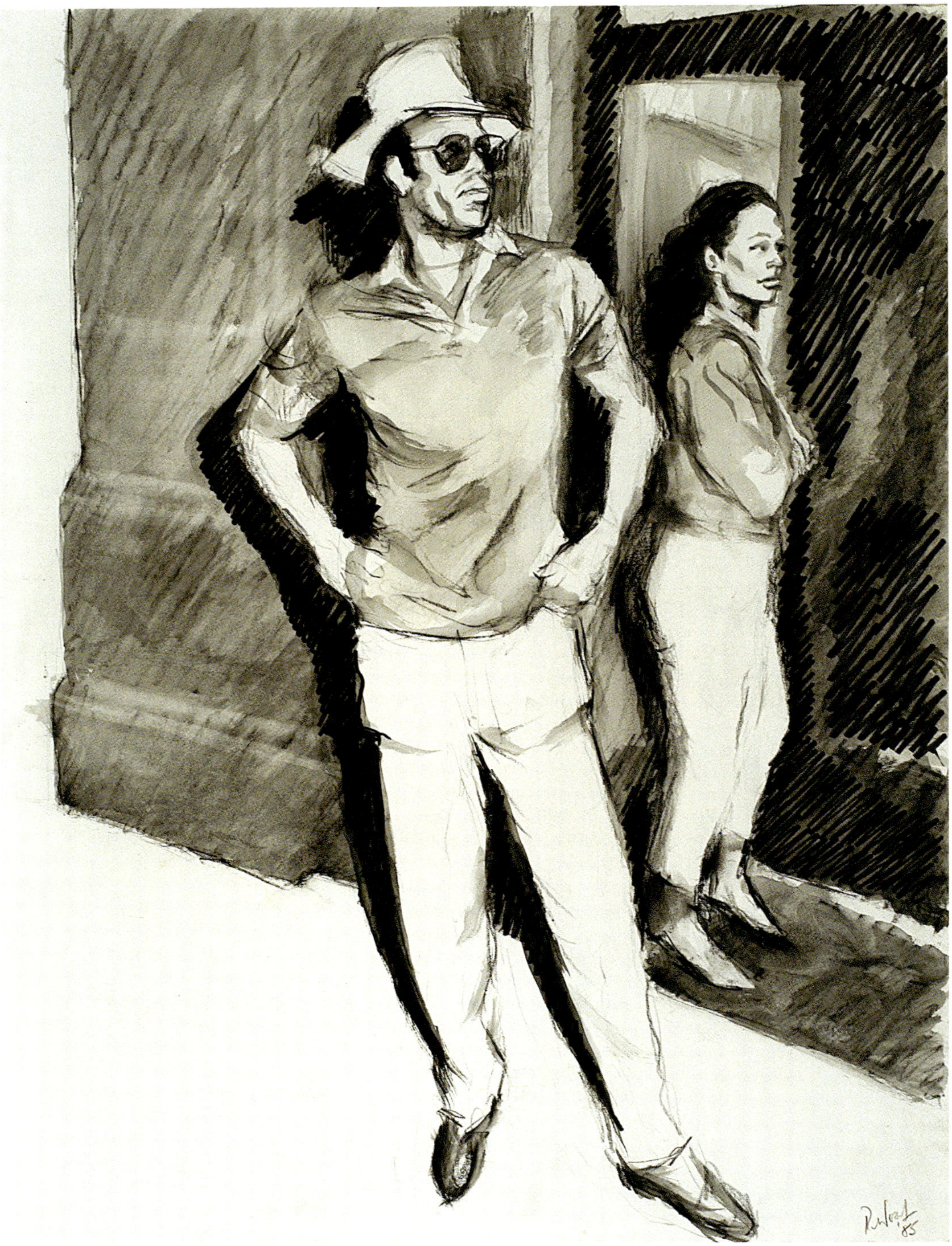

PREVIOUS PAGE LEFT: *Jimi Hendrix* | 2009 | oil on canvas | 112 × 91.5 cm
PREVIOUS PAGE RIGHT: *Jimi and Me at Scene* | 2005 | oil on canvas | 107 × 80 cm
ABOVE: *Bobby Womack* | 1985 | pen and ink on paper | 48 × 31 cm
OPPOSITE: *Eric Lost in the Blues* | 1994 | pencil on paper | 60 × 45 cm

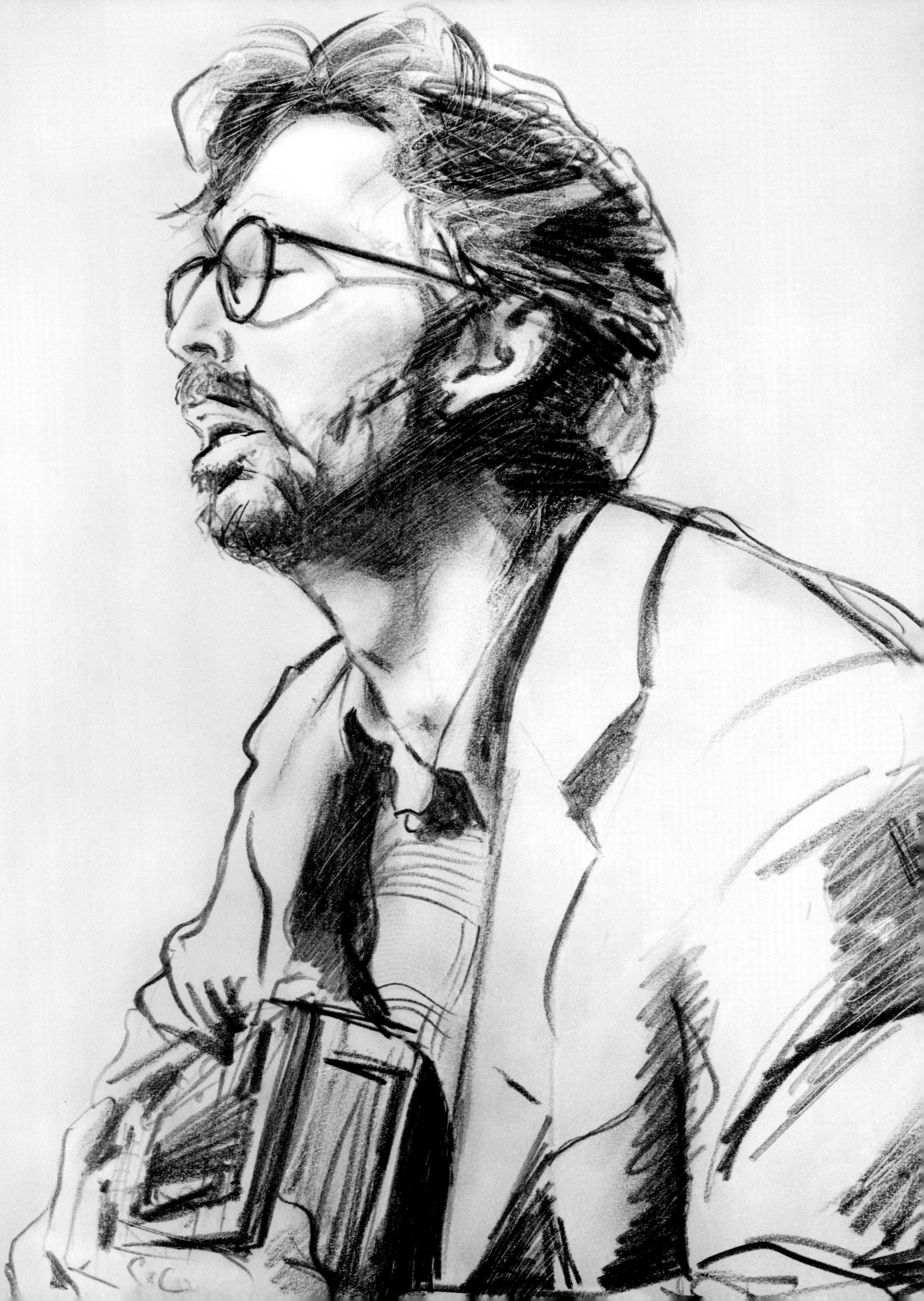

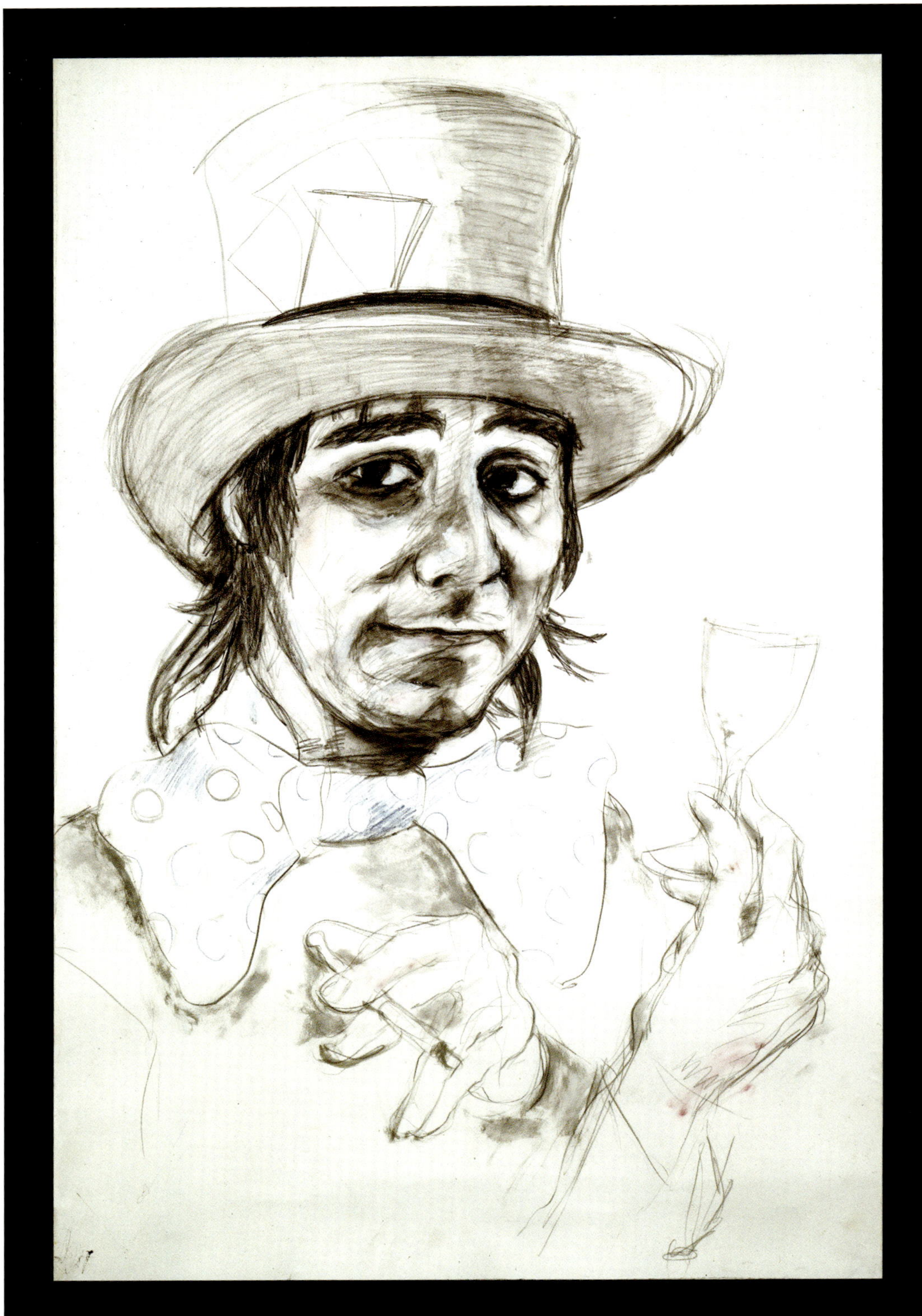

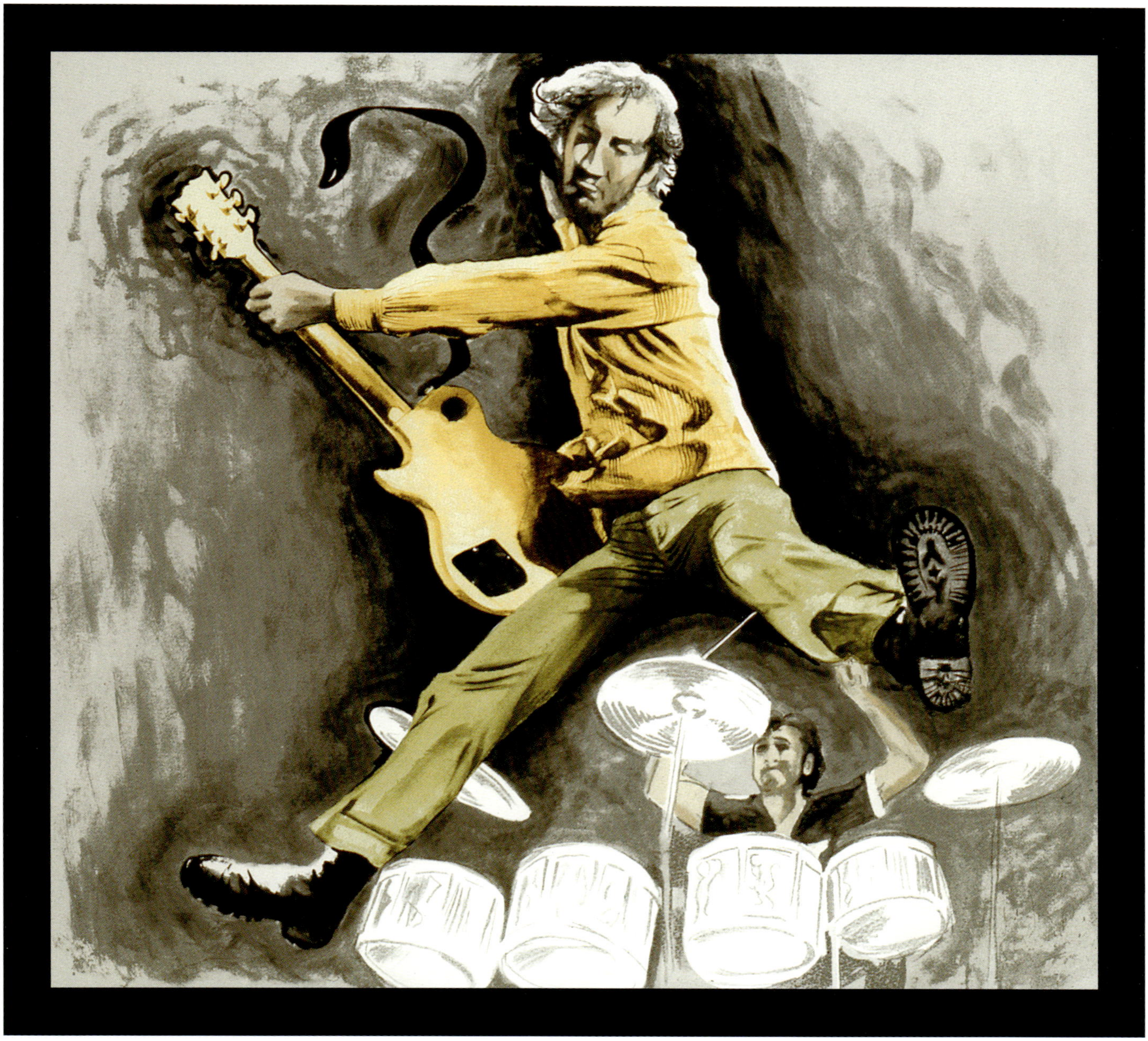

"Some of the best times I ever had with Keith Moon were with Lionel Bart; Keith was the real life Artful Dodger."

OPPOSITE: *Keith Moon (The Mad Hatter)* | 1993 | pencil on paper | 62 × 45 cm
ABOVE: *Pete Townshend & Keith Moon* | 1997 | screen print | 51 × 58.5 cm

BELOW: *Stevie Ray Vaughan* | 2005 | mixed media on paper | 53 × 70 cm
OPPOSITE: *Slash* | 2009 | acrylic on canvas | 112 × 91.5 cm

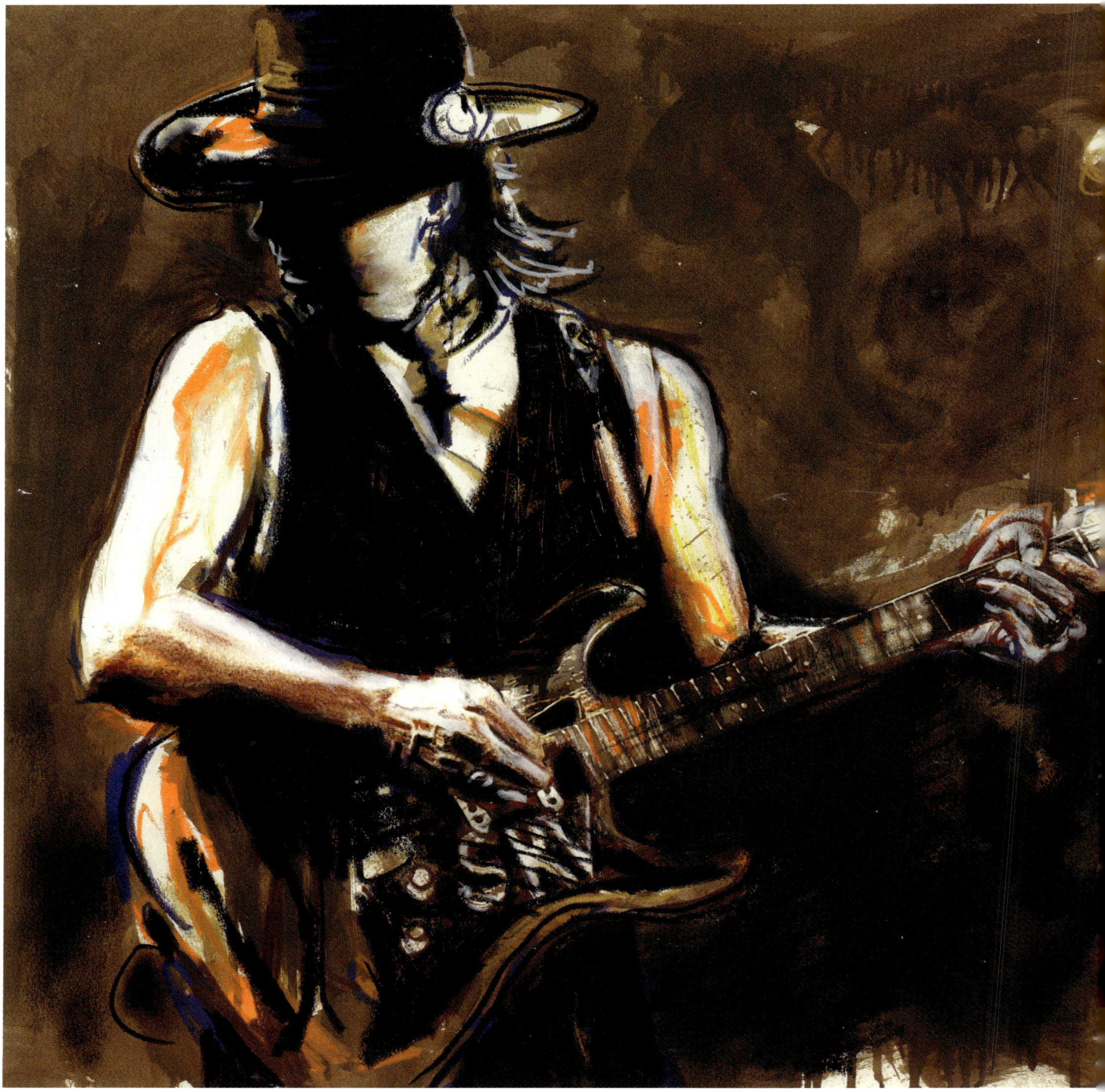

"In the early 1970s I met Slash when he was in his early teens at Seymour Cassel's house in Hollywood; Slash's mother was a friend of Seymour. Slash would look over my shoulder as I played guitar; now I learn from him."

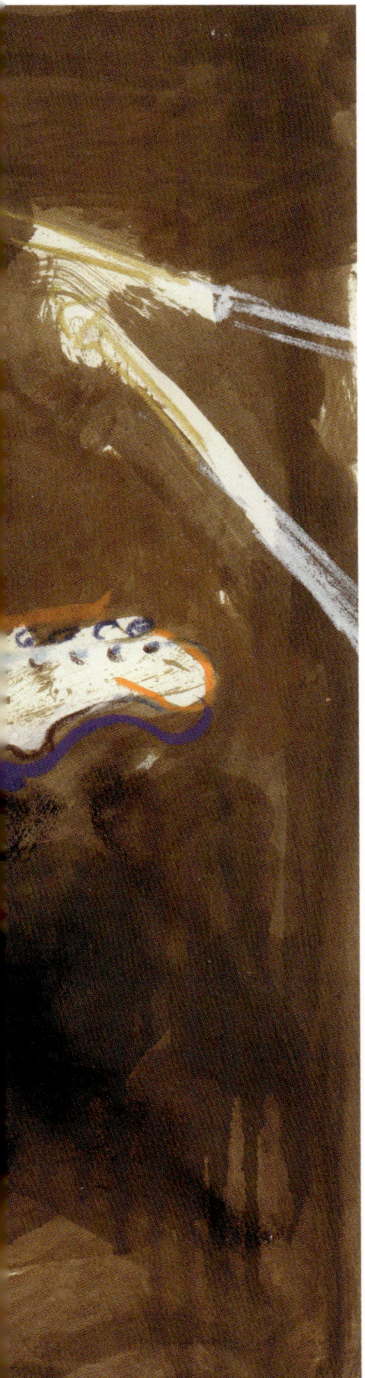

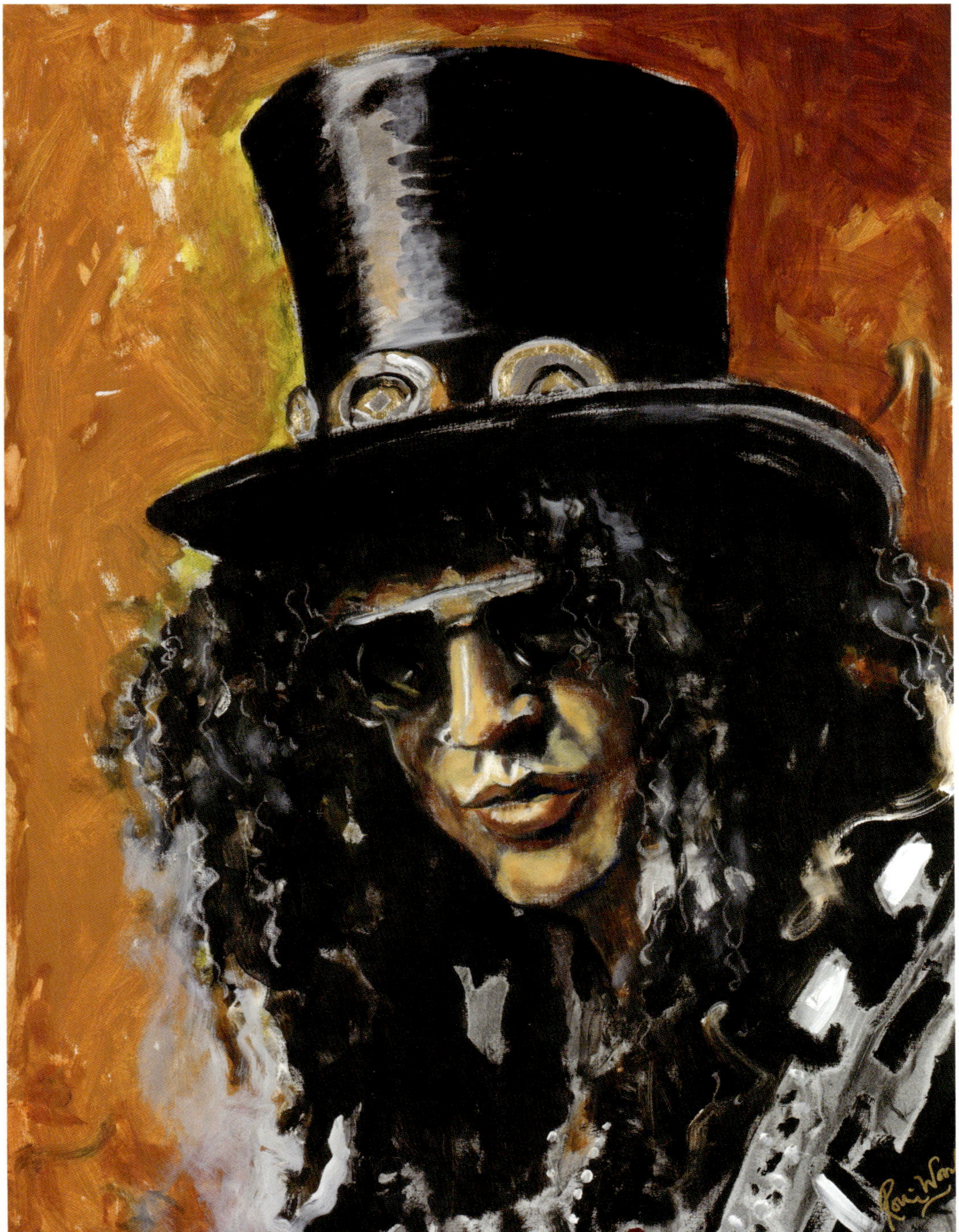

BELOW: *John Lydon Drawing Study* | 1987 | pen and ink on paper | 76 × 112 cm
OPPOSITE ABOVE: *Drawing Study for Decades Project (80s)* | 1987 | acrylic and pastel on paper | 67 × 98 cm
OPPOSITE BELOW: *Drawing Study for Decades Project (80s)* | 1987 | acrylic and pastel on paper | 67 × 98 cm

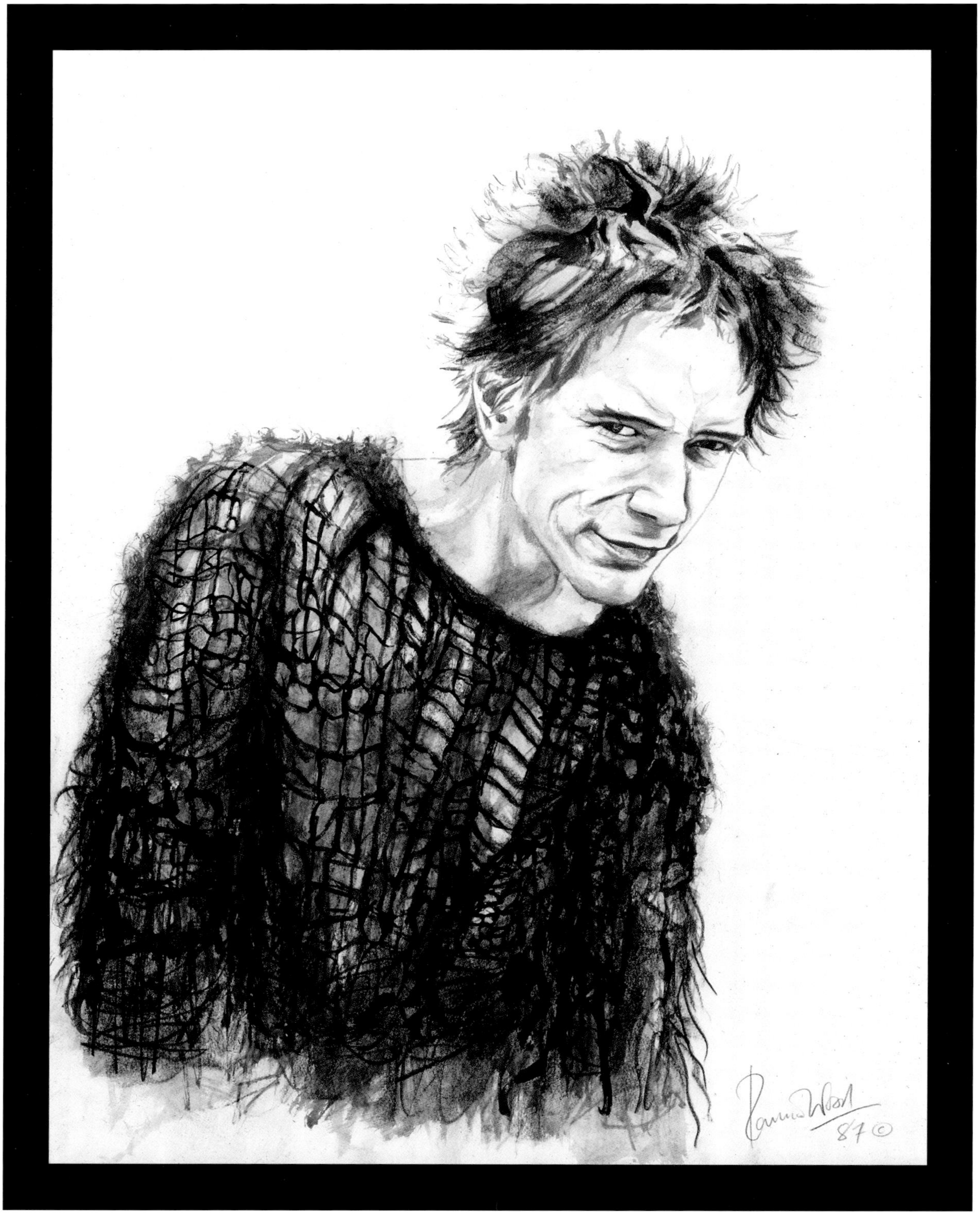

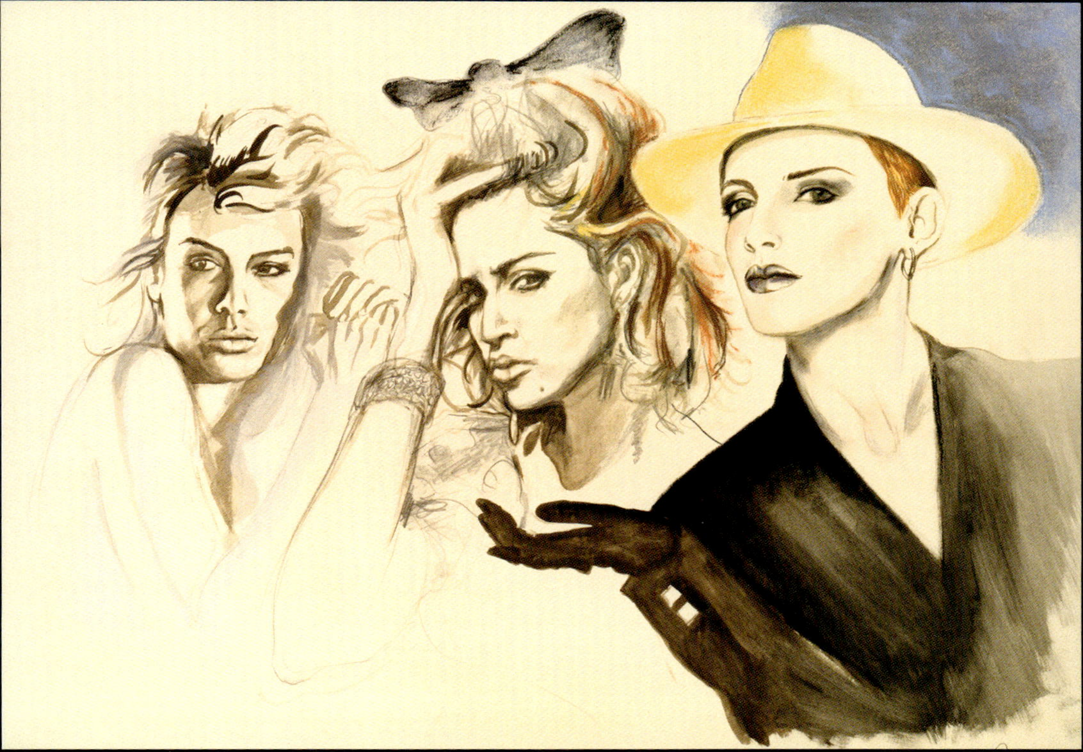

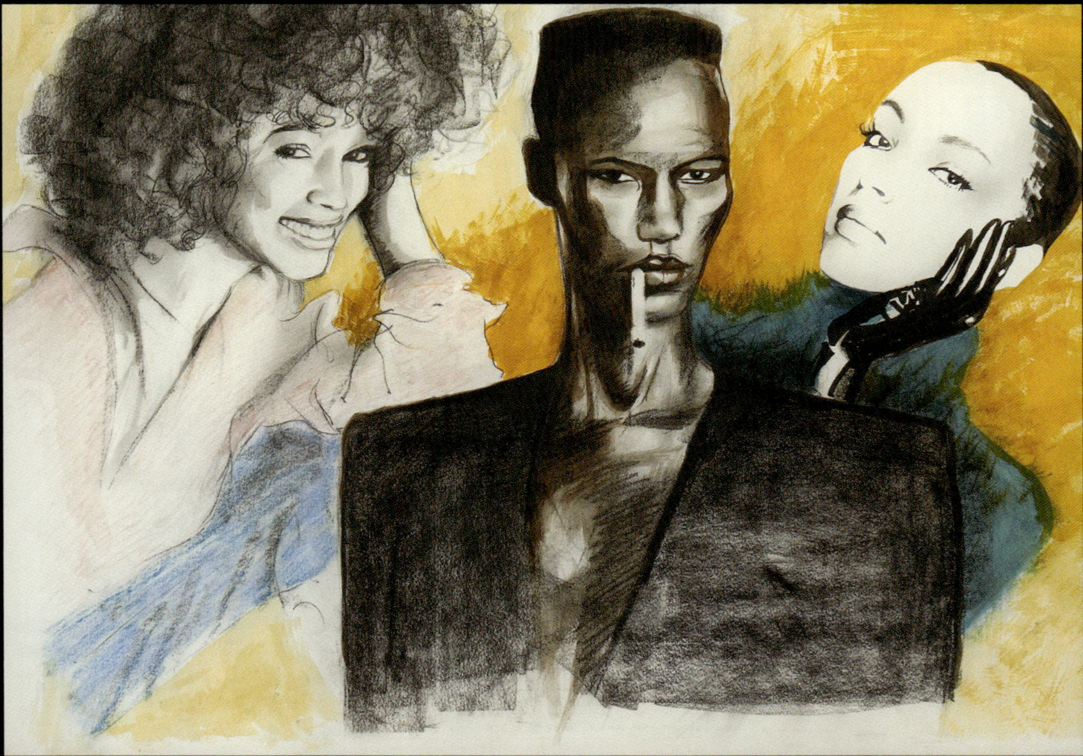

"I put together singers who were representative of their decade, so here we have Kim Wilde,

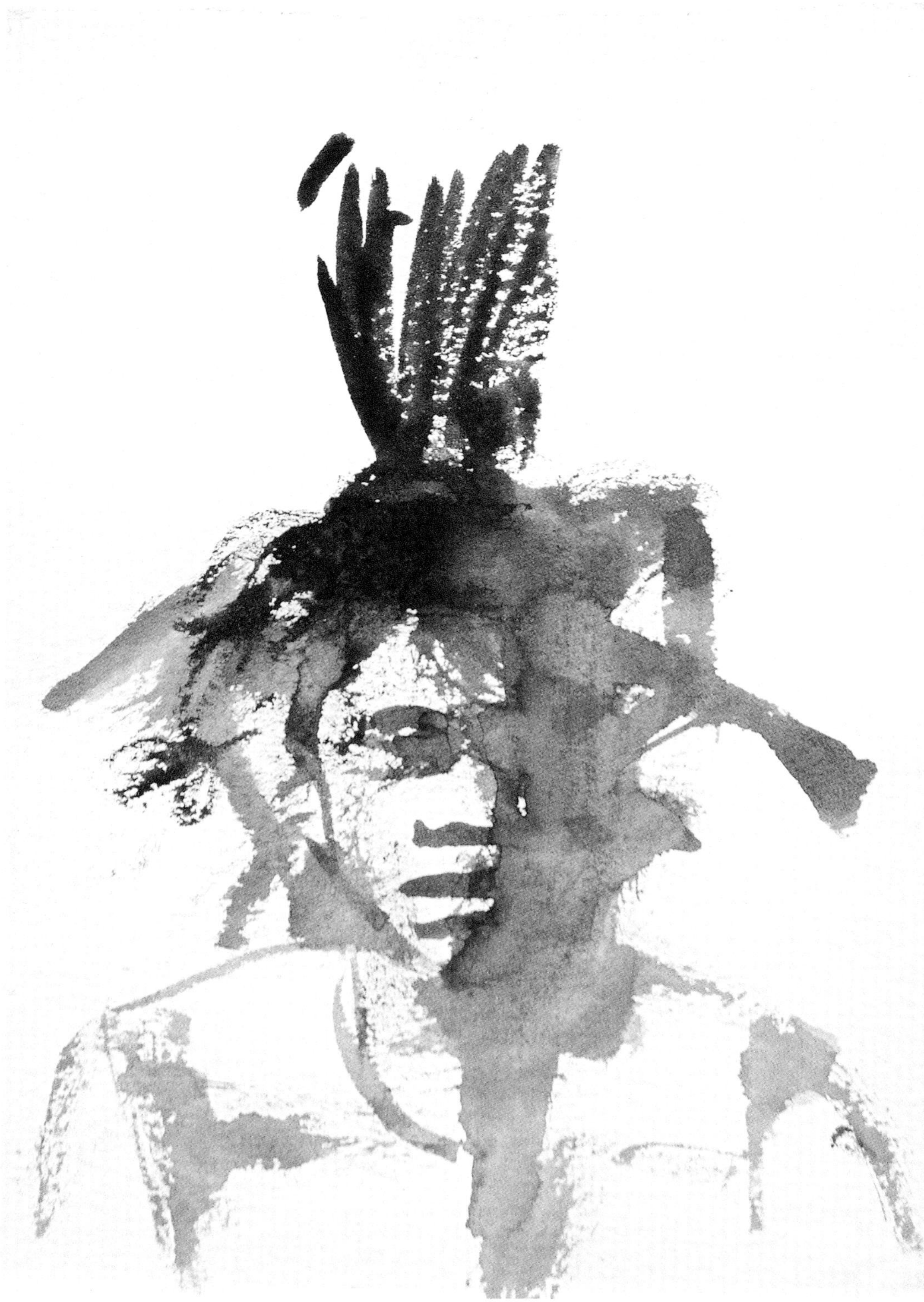

"Formula One's Eddie Jordan has the original of Bongo Man."

ABOVE: *Bongo Man* | 2000 | pen and ink on paper | 12.5 × 7 cm
OPPOSITE ABOVE: *Abstract Bongo Man* | 2003 | oil on canvas | 50 × 76 cm
OPPOSITE BELOW: *Bob Marley* | 2005 | pen and ink on paper | 77 × 70 cm

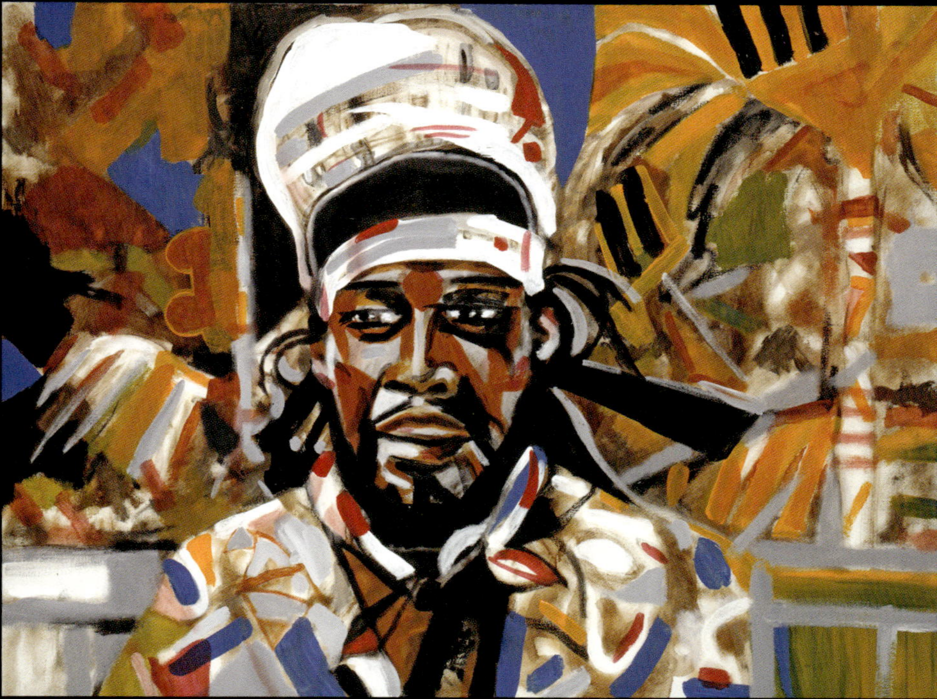

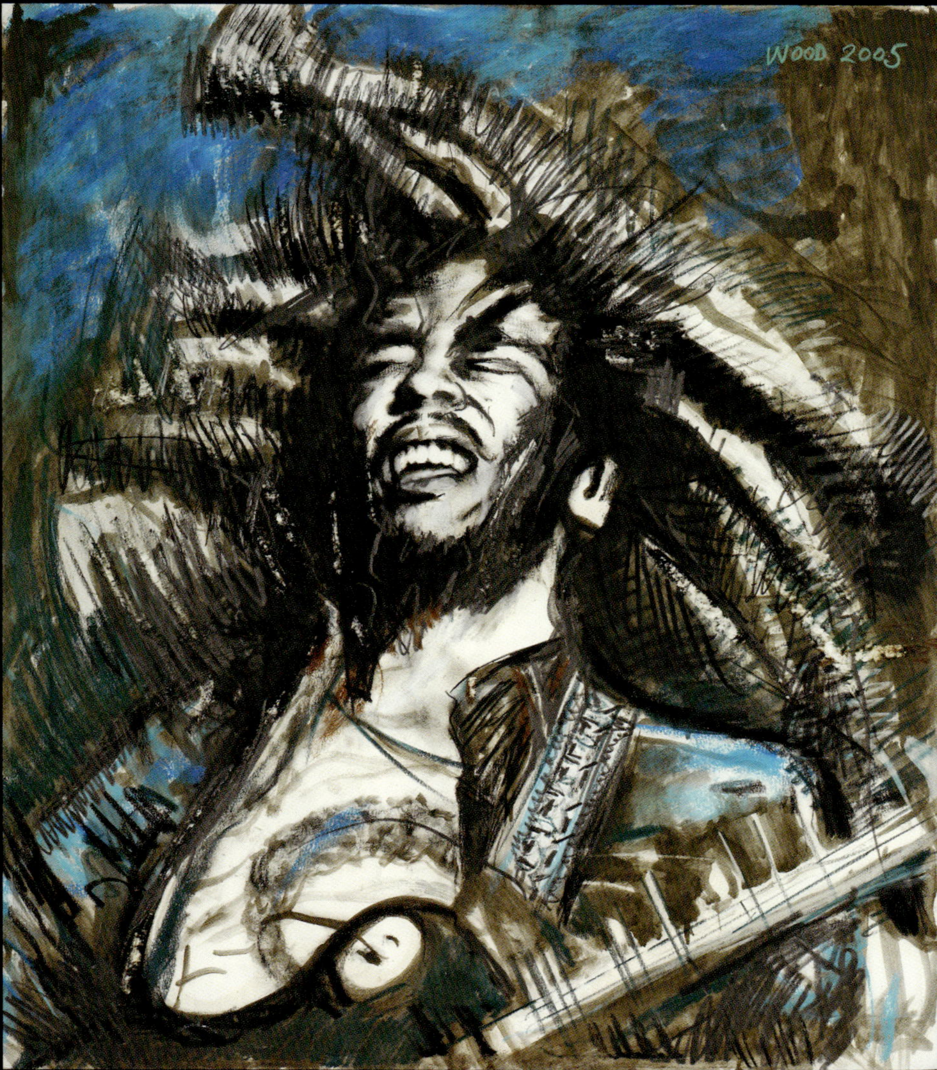
WOOD 2005

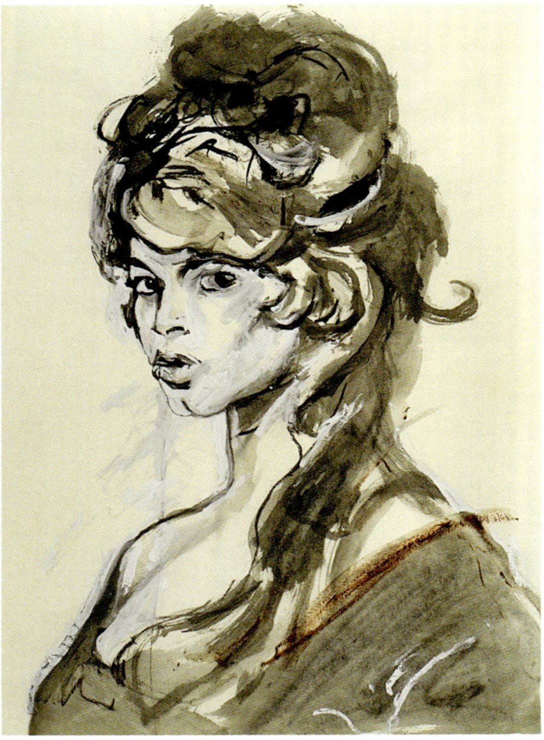

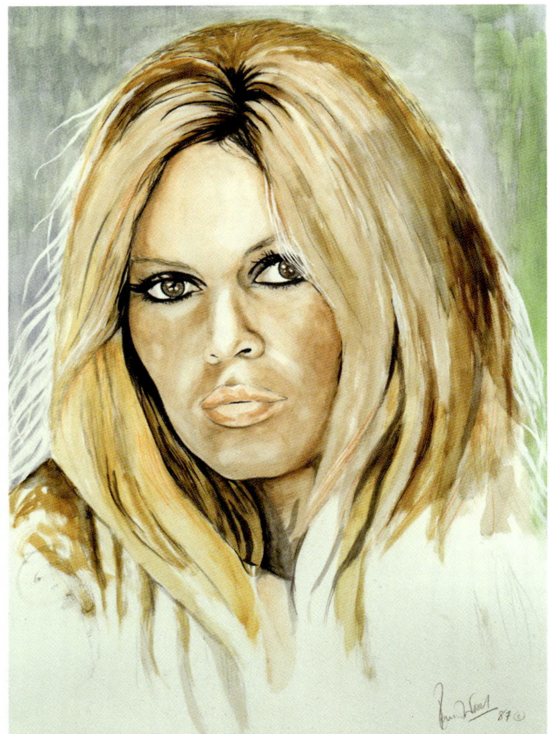

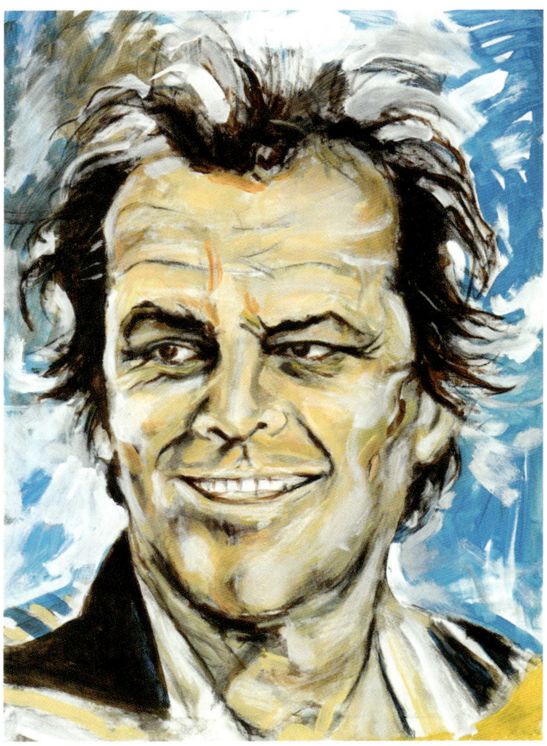

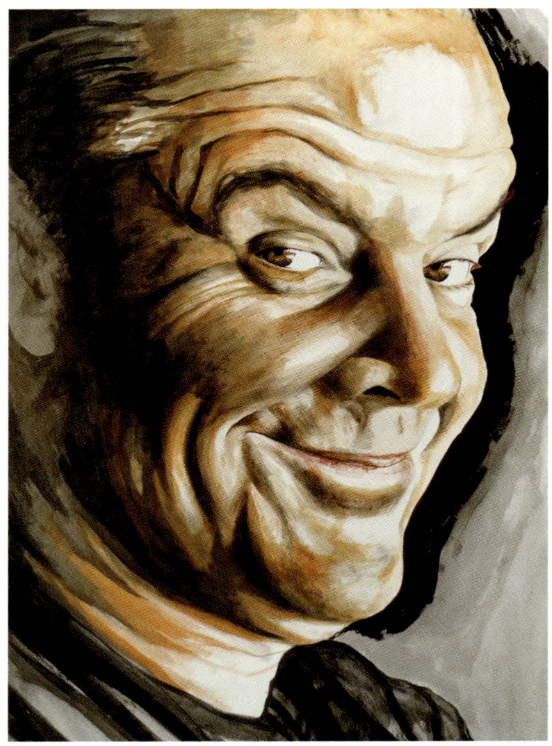

"If you capture a person's eyes then the rest of the painting takes care of itself."

OPPOSITE ABOVE LEFT: *Brigitte Bardot* | 1987 | pen, ink and wash on paper | 60 × 40 cm
OPPOSITE ABOVE RIGHT: *Brigitte Bardot* | 1987 | pen, ink and colour wash on paper | 112 × 76 cm
OPPOSITE BELOW LEFT: *Jack Nicholson* | 2009 | acrylic on canvas | 122 × 91.5 cm
OPPOSITE BELOW RIGHT: *Jack, The Eyes Have It* | 1987 | watercolour on paper | 70 × 46 cm
BELOW: *Al Pacino* (detail) | 2009 | acrylic on canvas | 122 × 91.5 cm
BOTTOM: *De Niro* | 2009 | acrylic on canvas | 91.5 × 122 cm

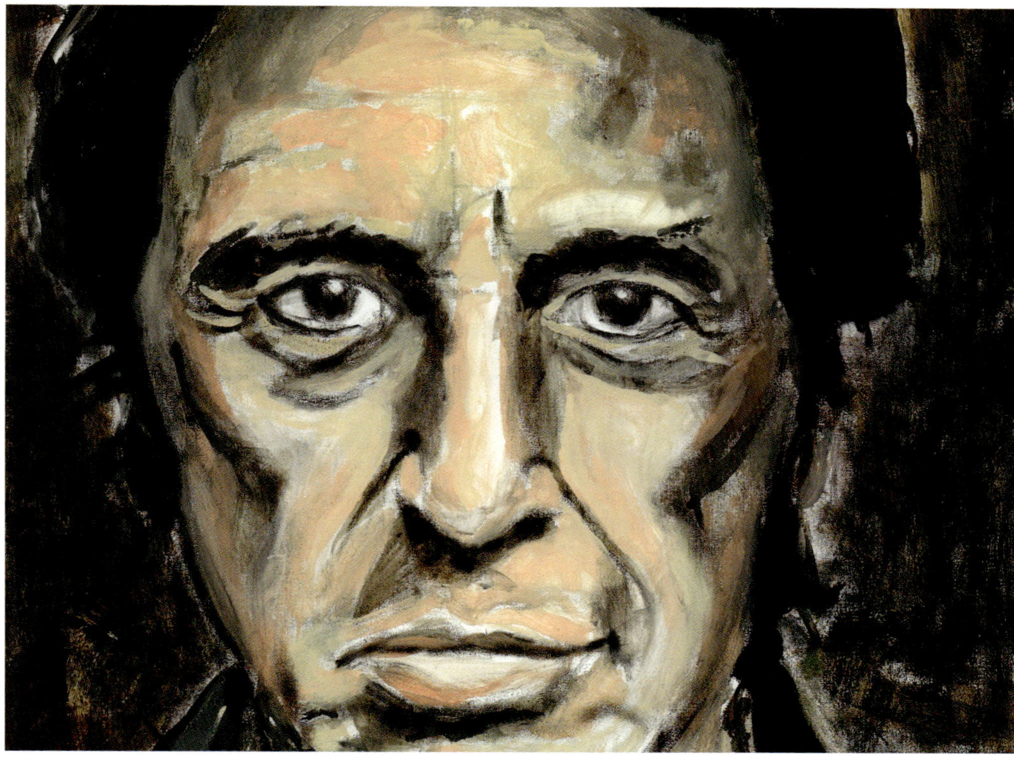

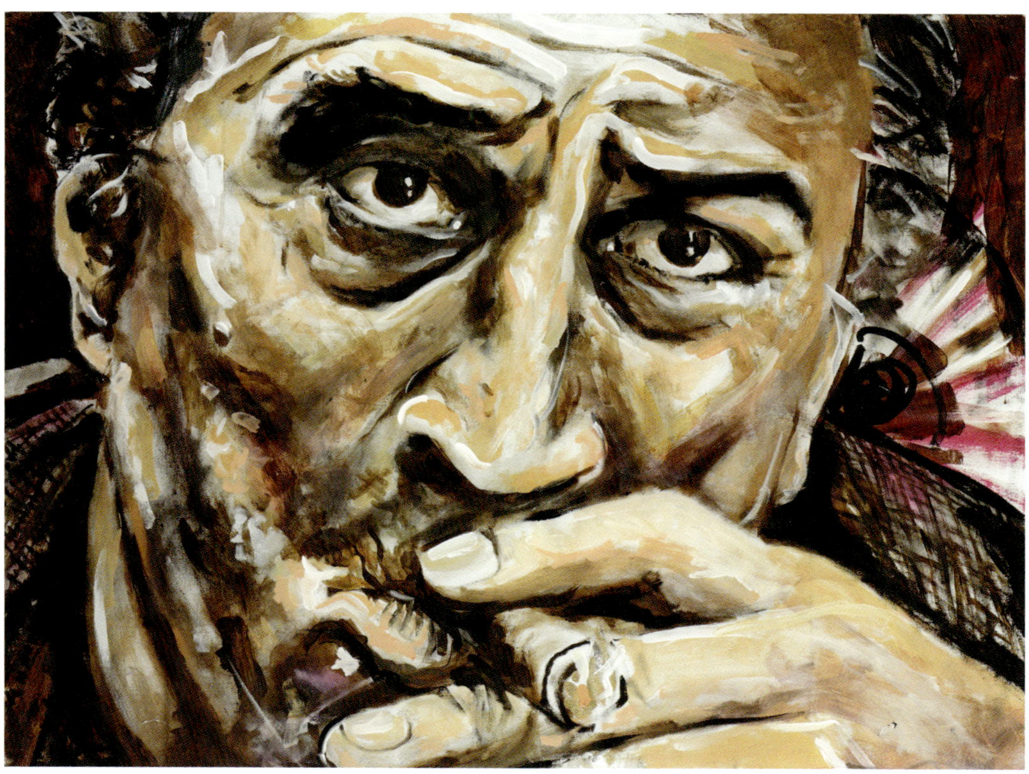

BELOW: *Marilyn* | 2004 | acrylic on paper | 62 × 45 cm
OPPOSITE LEFT: *James Dean* | 2000 | pen and ink wash on paper | 51 × 36 cm
OPPOSITE ABOVE RIGHT: *Paul Newman* | 2000 | pen and ink wash on paper | 51 × 36 cm
OPPOSITE BELOW RIGHT: *Charlie Chaplin* | 2000 | pen and ink wash on paper | 51 × 36 cm

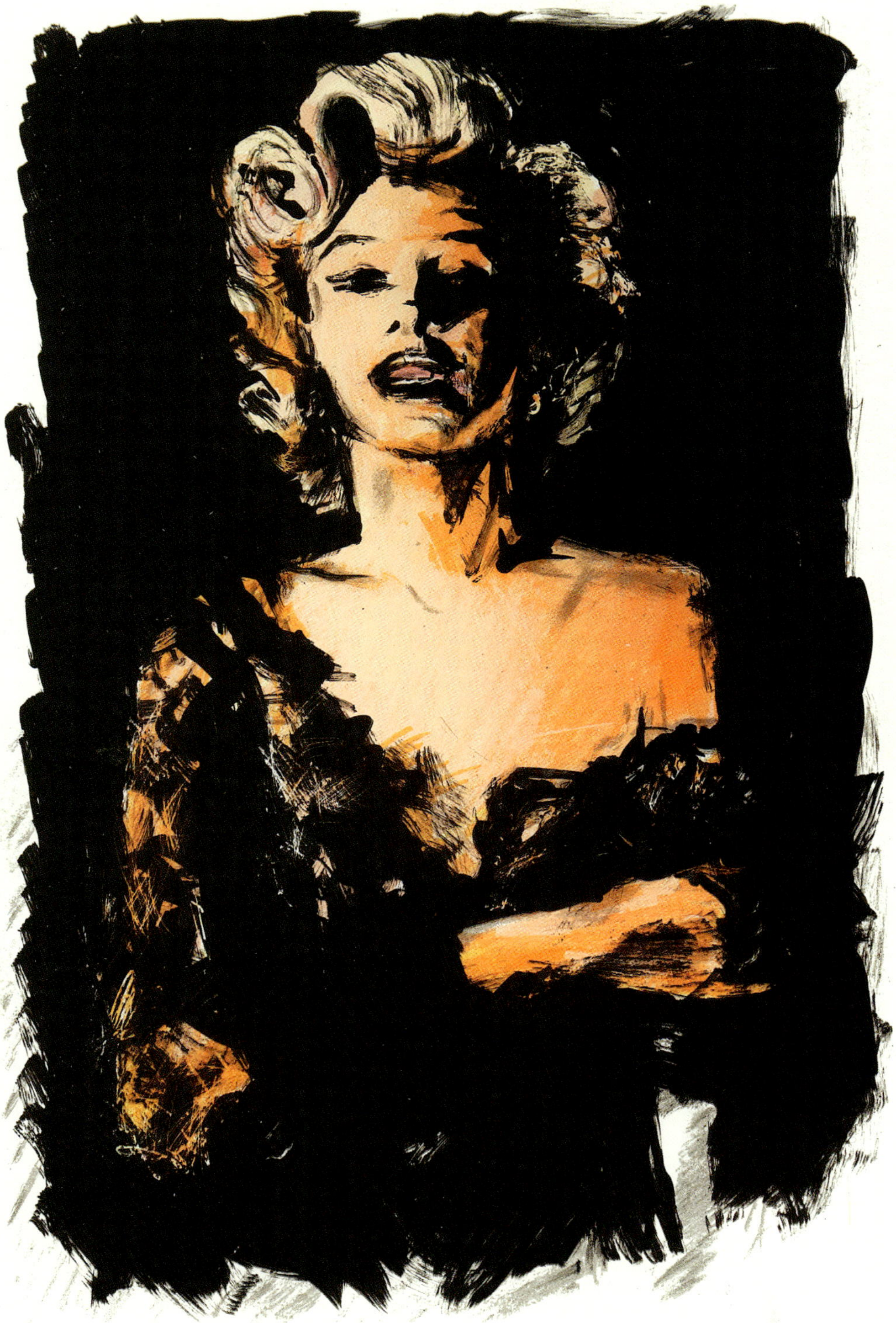

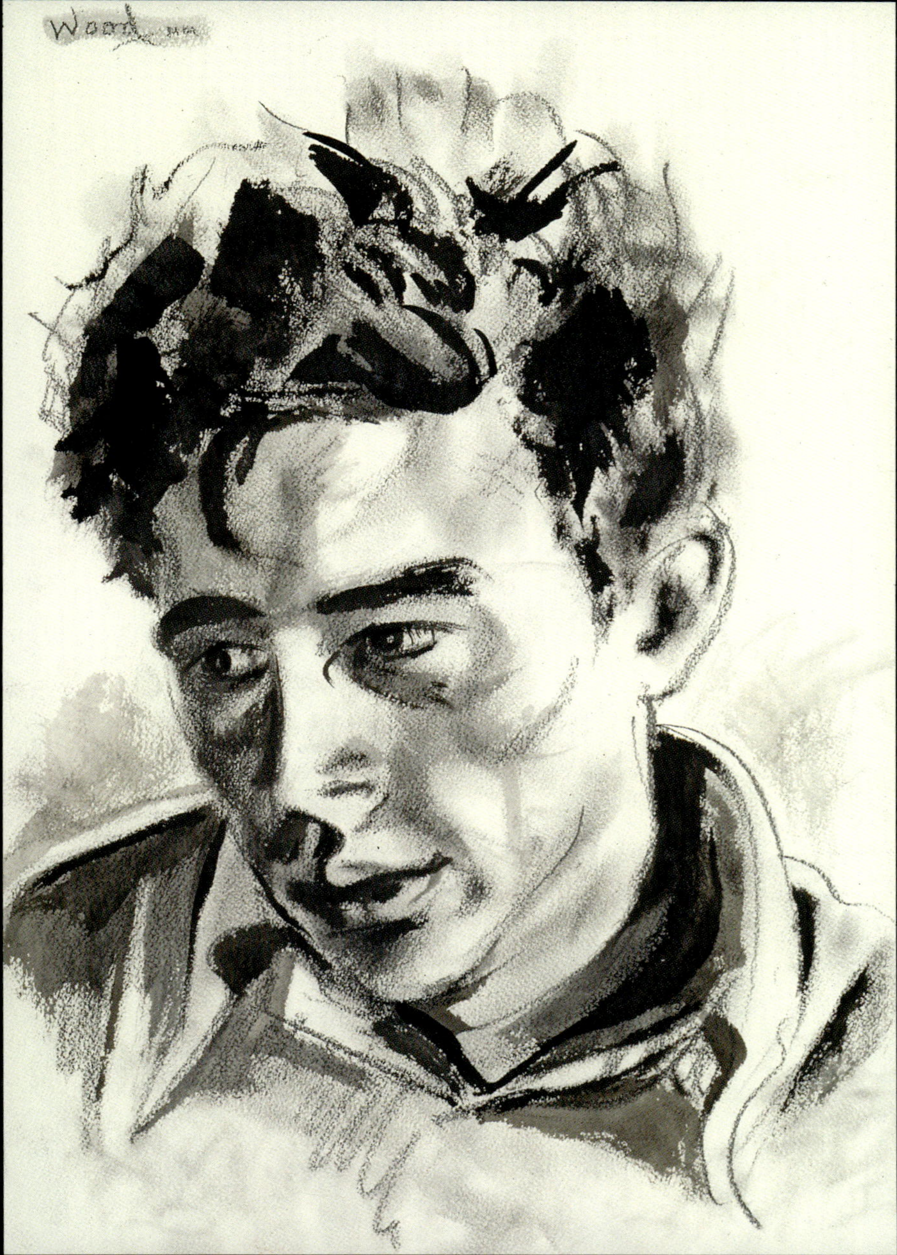

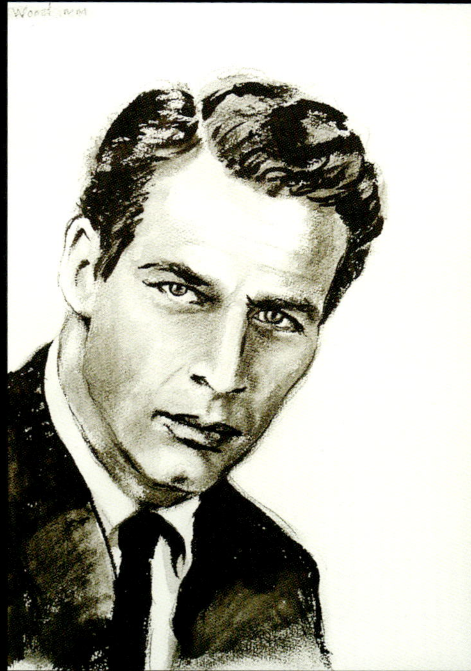

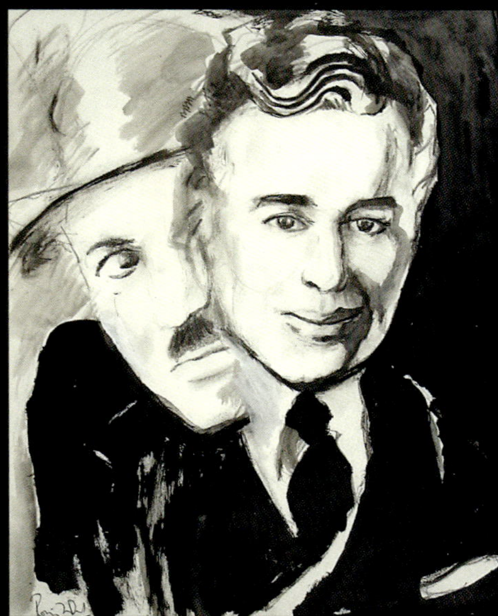

"I tried to do something different with Charlie Chaplin here, portraying him as the young actor and the older director."

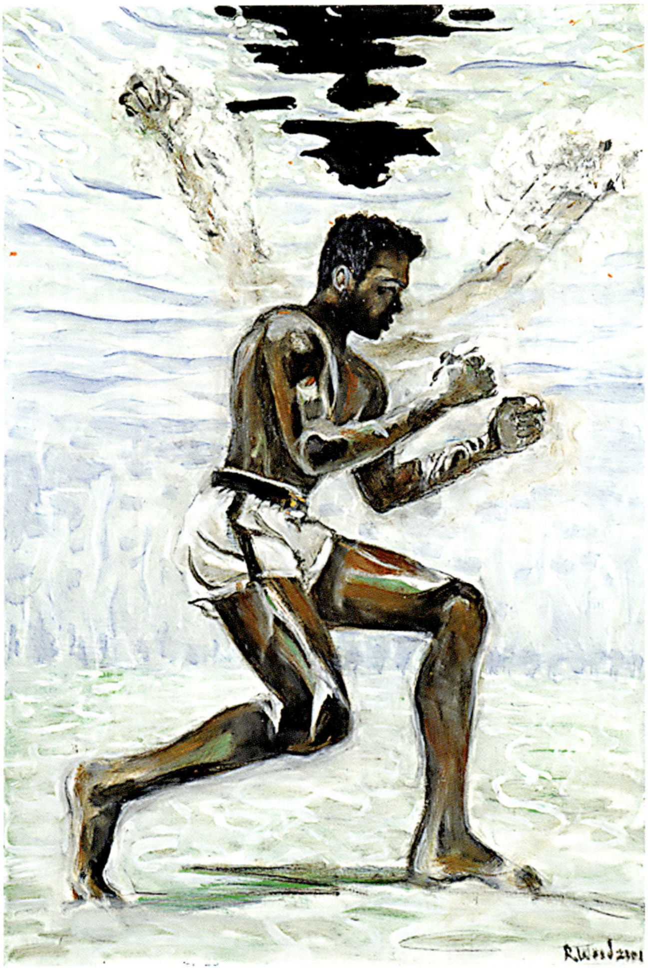

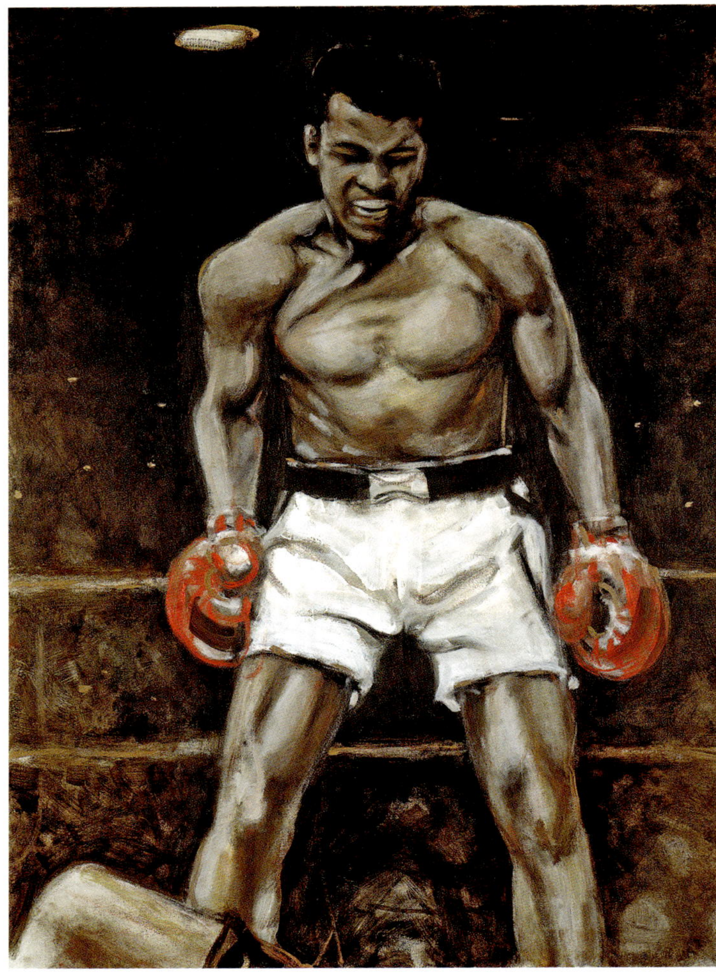

"When I was with Ali at a hotel in New York he said, let's go downstairs and both walk down Fifth Avenue. If you walk down one side and I walk down the other we'll stop the traffic!"

ABOVE LEFT: *Ali Training Underwater* | 2001 | oil on canvas | 122 × 91.5 cm
ABOVE RIGHT: *Ali vs Liston* | 2001 | oil on canvas| 122 × 91.5 cm
OPPOSITE: *The Softer Side of Ali* | 2001 | oil on canvas| 122 × 91.5 cm

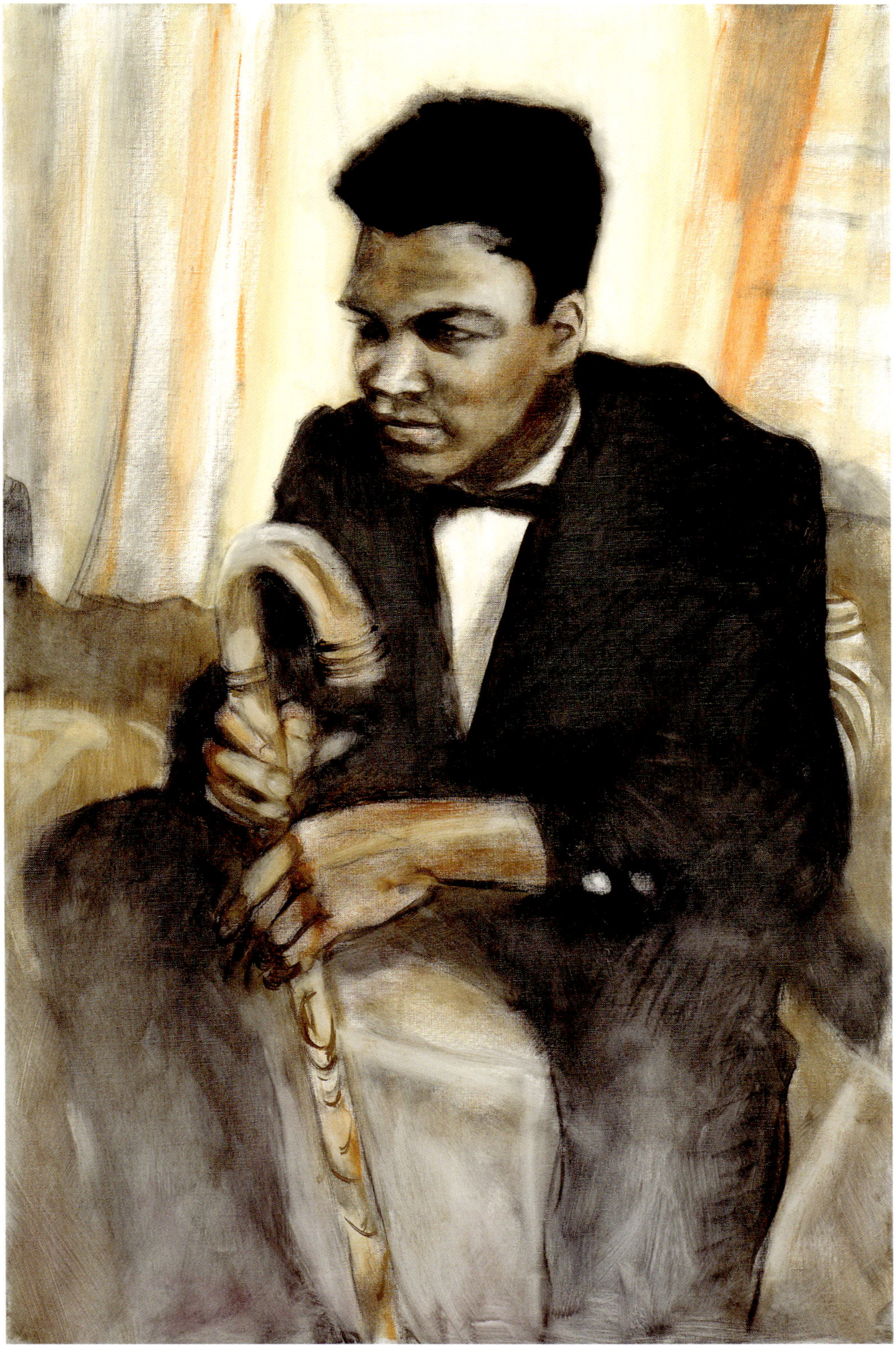

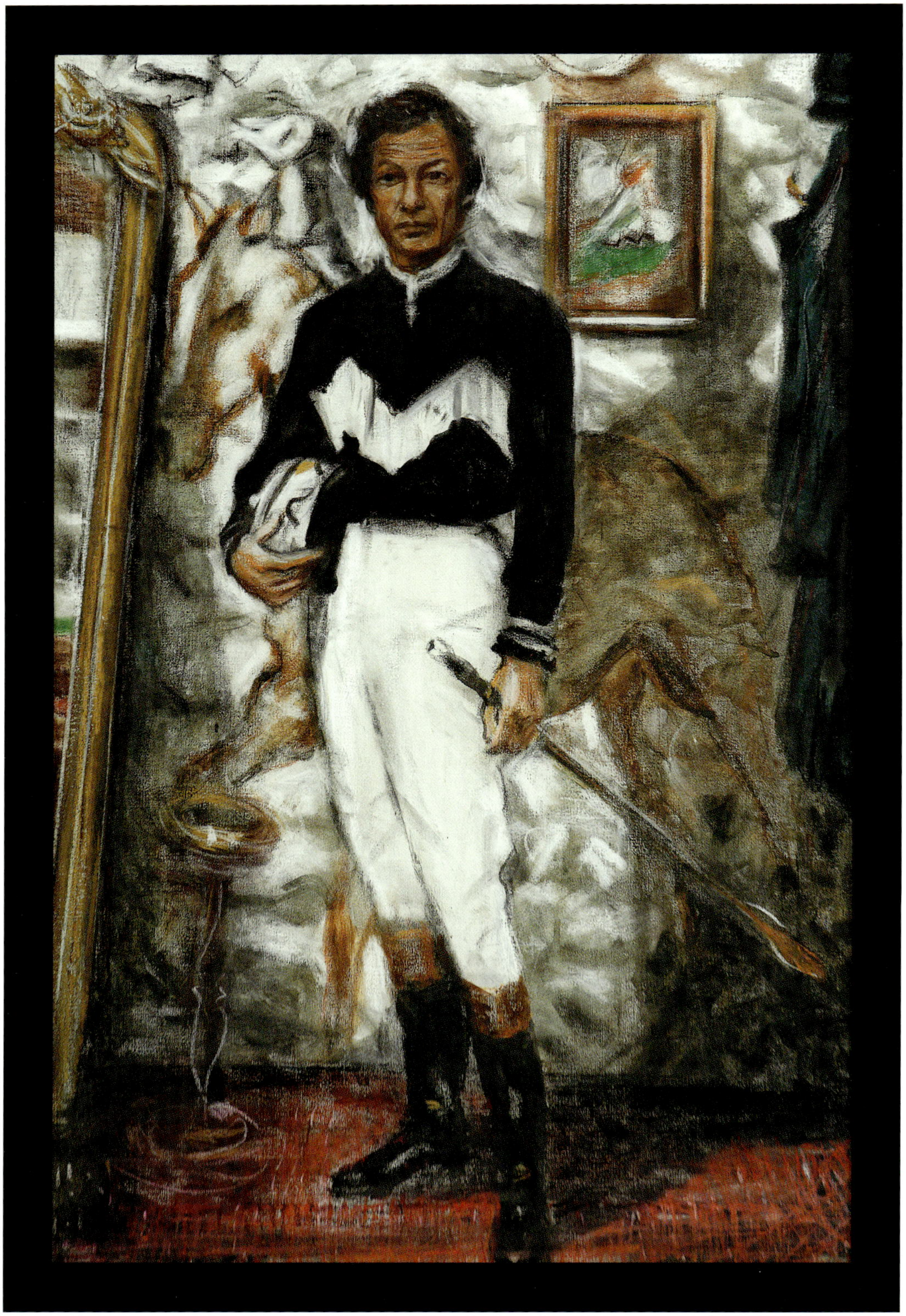

ABOVE: *Lester Piggot* | 2004 | acrylic on canvas | 91 × 60.5 cm
OPPOSITE ABOVE LEFT: *Alex Higgins* | 1986 | pen, ink and gouache on paper | 24 × 20 cm
OPPOSITE BELOW LEFT: *Ronnie O'Sullivan* | 2017 | pen, ink and gouache on paper | 26 × 21 cm
OPPOSITE RIGHT: *Jimmy White* | 2000 | pen and ink wash on paper | 51 × 36 cm

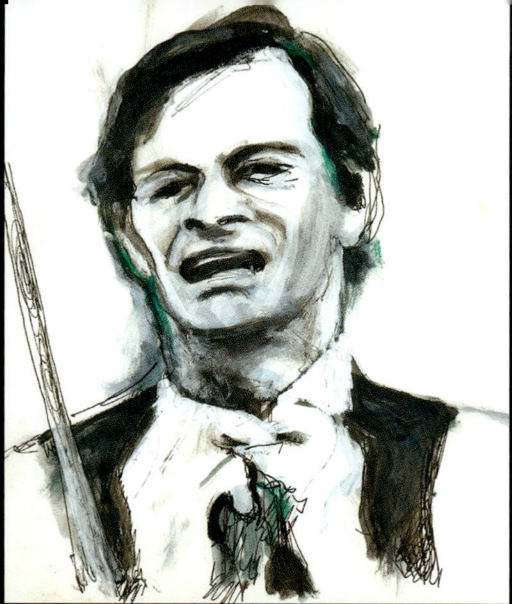

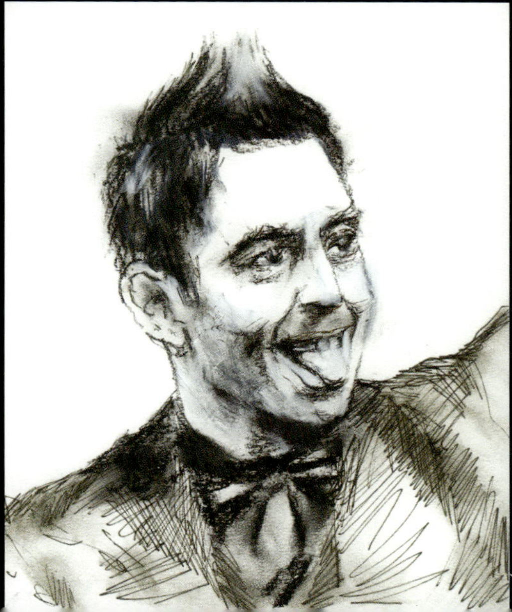

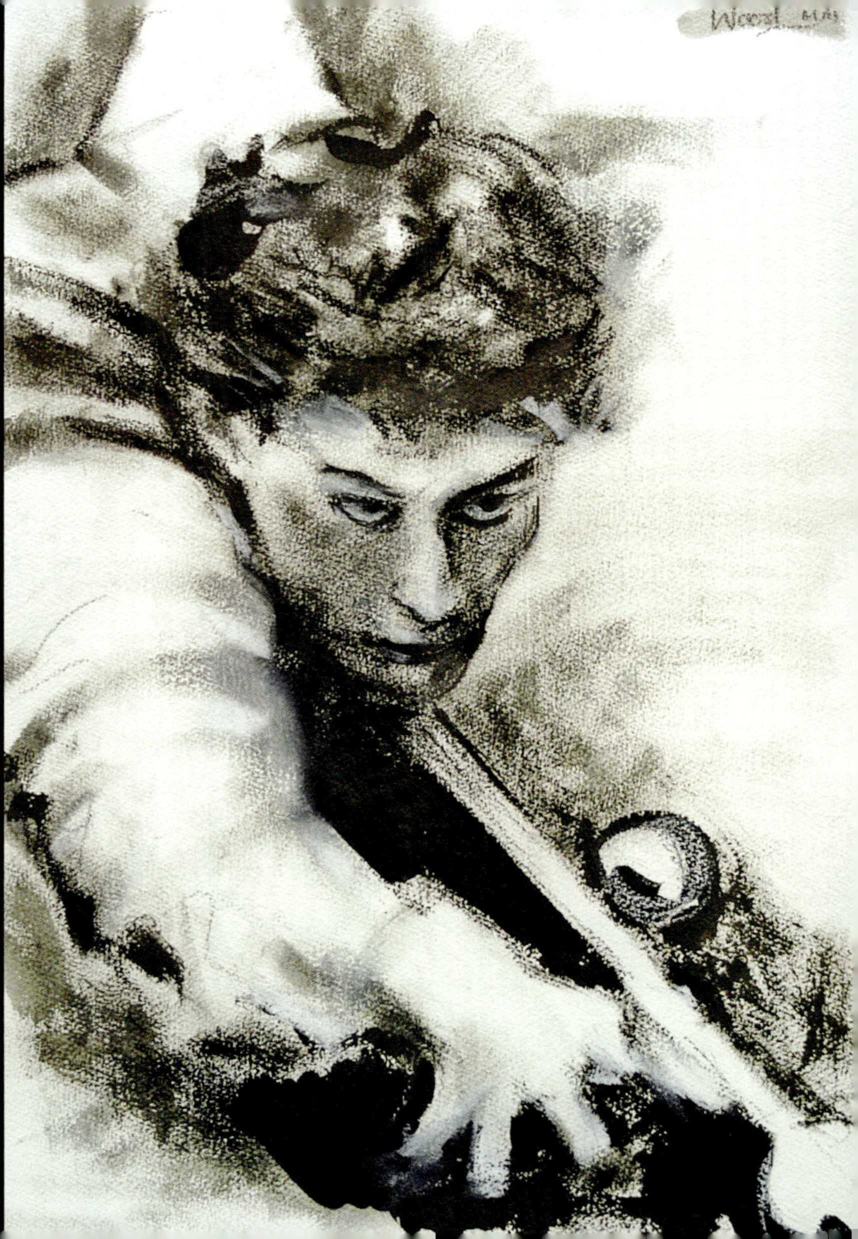

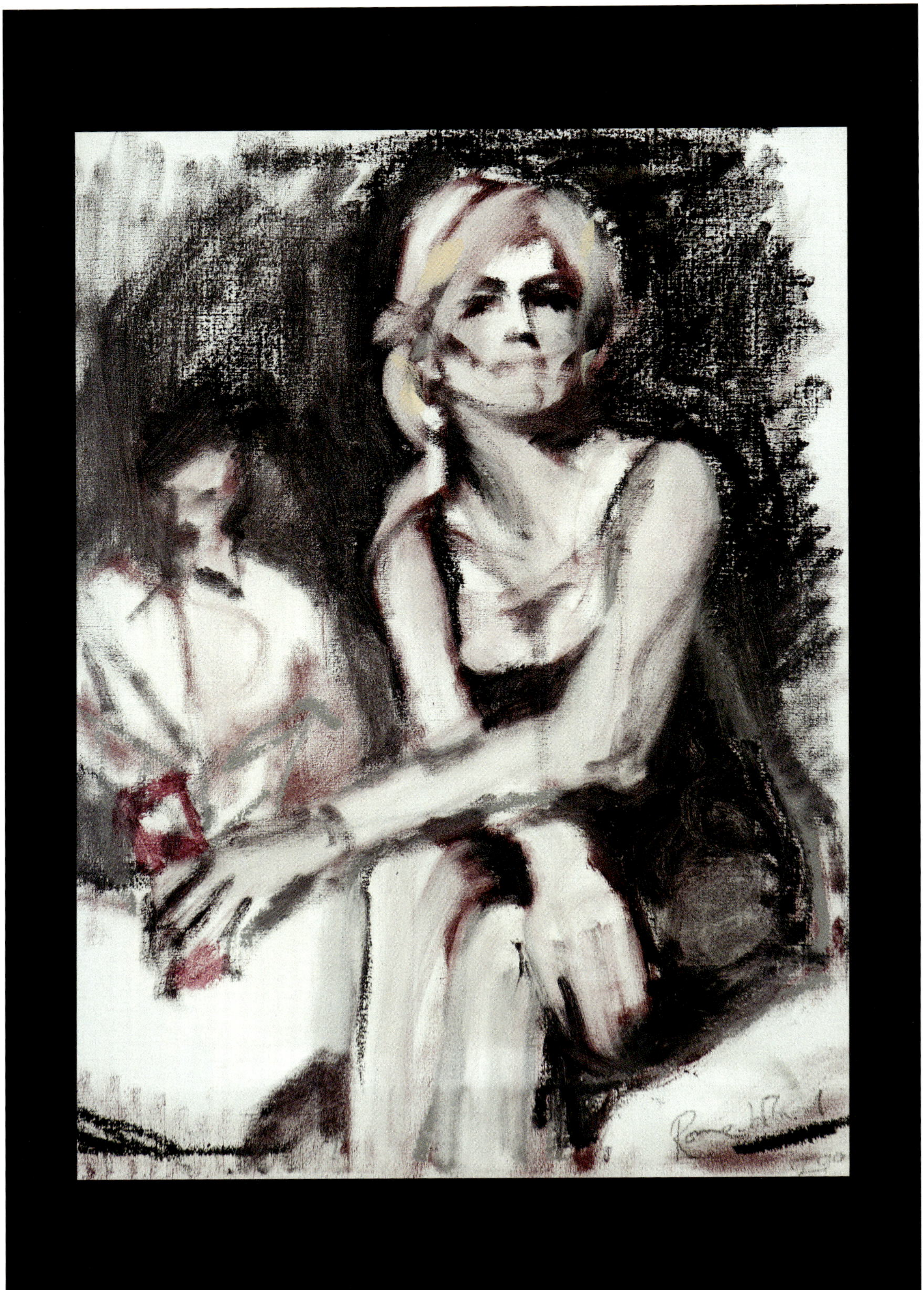

5

PORTRAITS

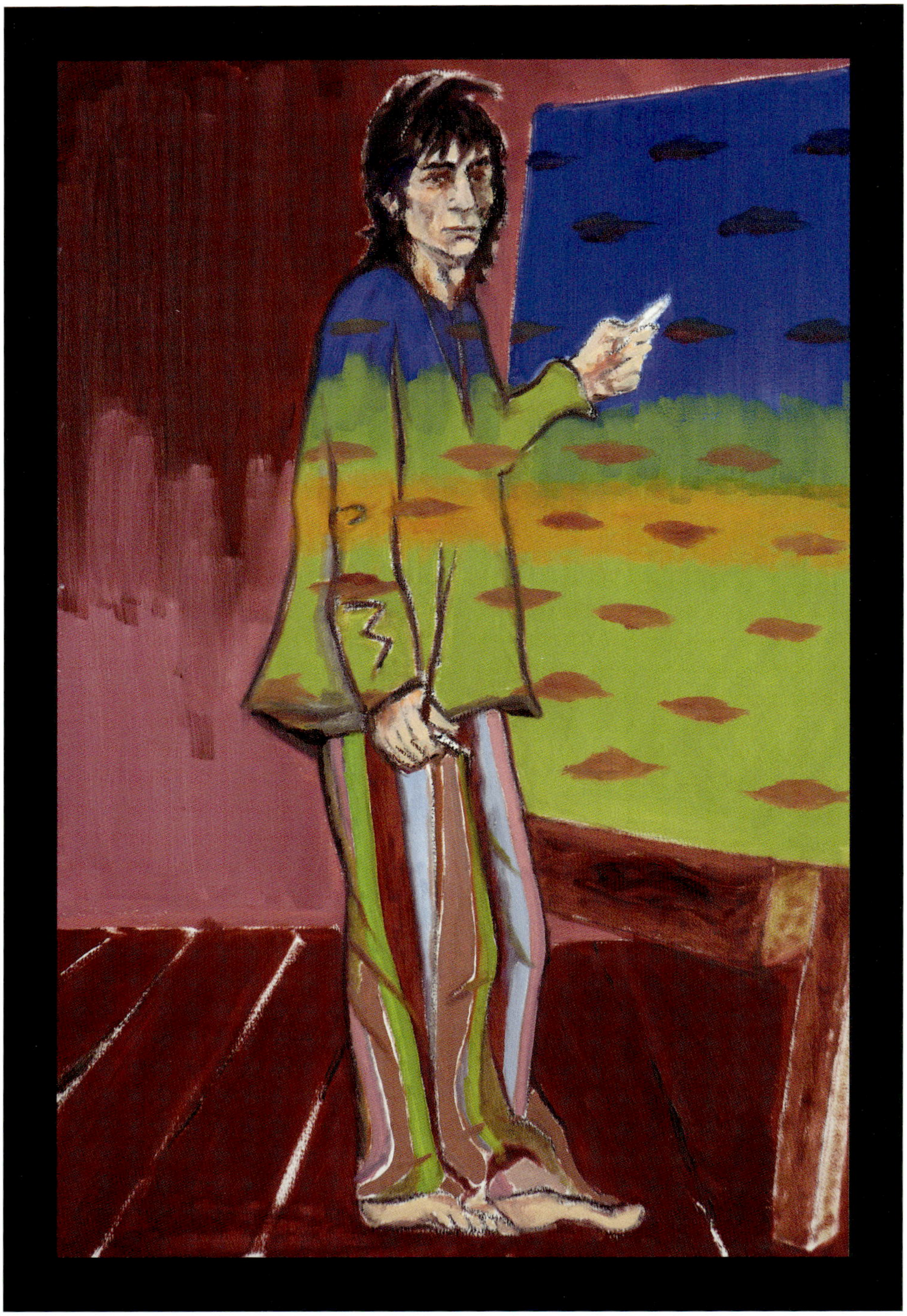

PREVIOUS PAGE: *Patti Hansen* | 2000 | acrylic on canvas | 50 × 40 cm
ABOVE: *Mirror Image* | 2016–17 | acrylic on canvas | 92 × 61 cm
OPPOSITE: *In Transition* | 2016–17 | acrylic on canvas | 150 × 113 cm

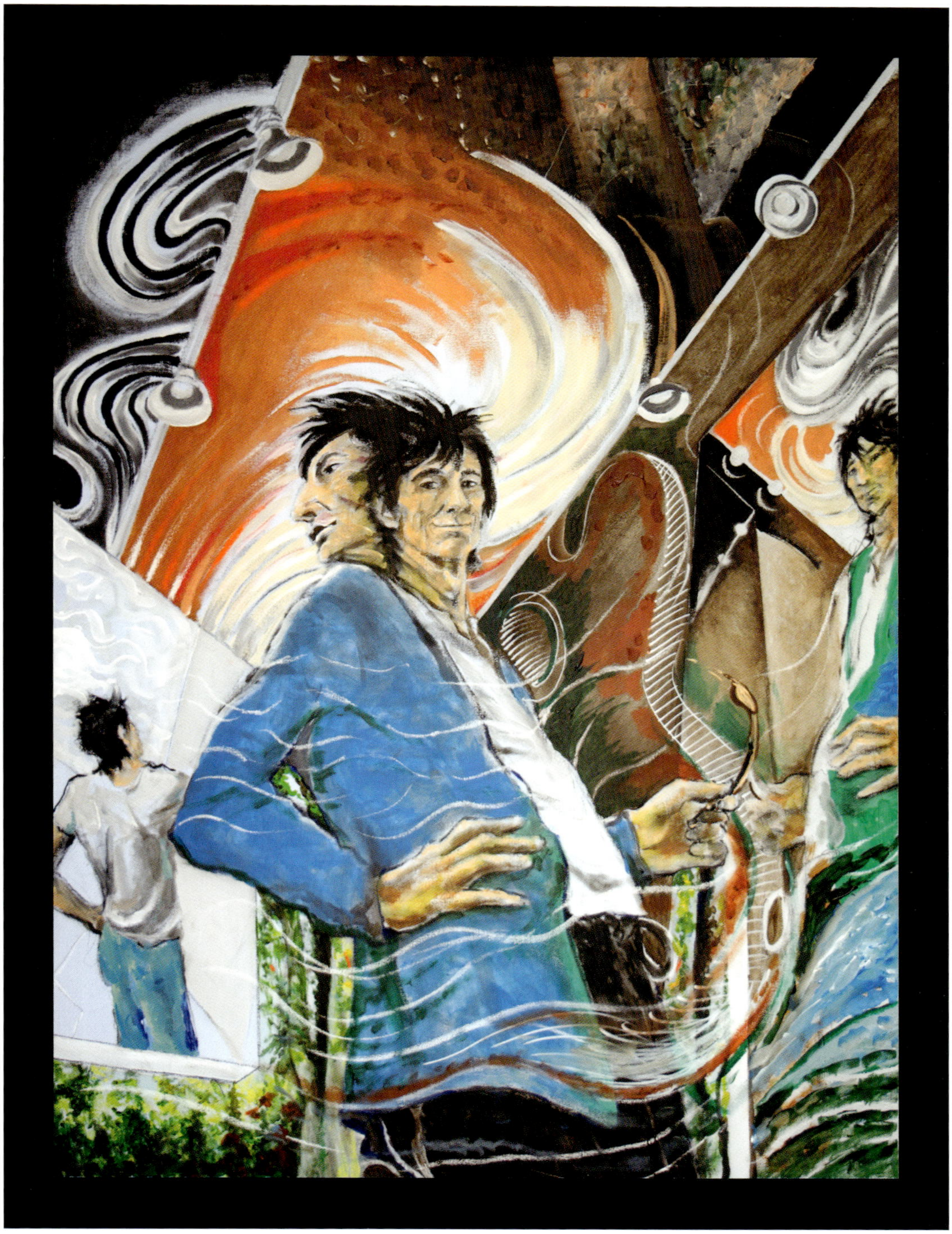

"I was trying to paint Jerry Hall from the theatre production of The Graduate *(previous page), but she turned into Patti Hansen, with Manuel from* Fawlty Towers *in the background. That's the power of art!"*

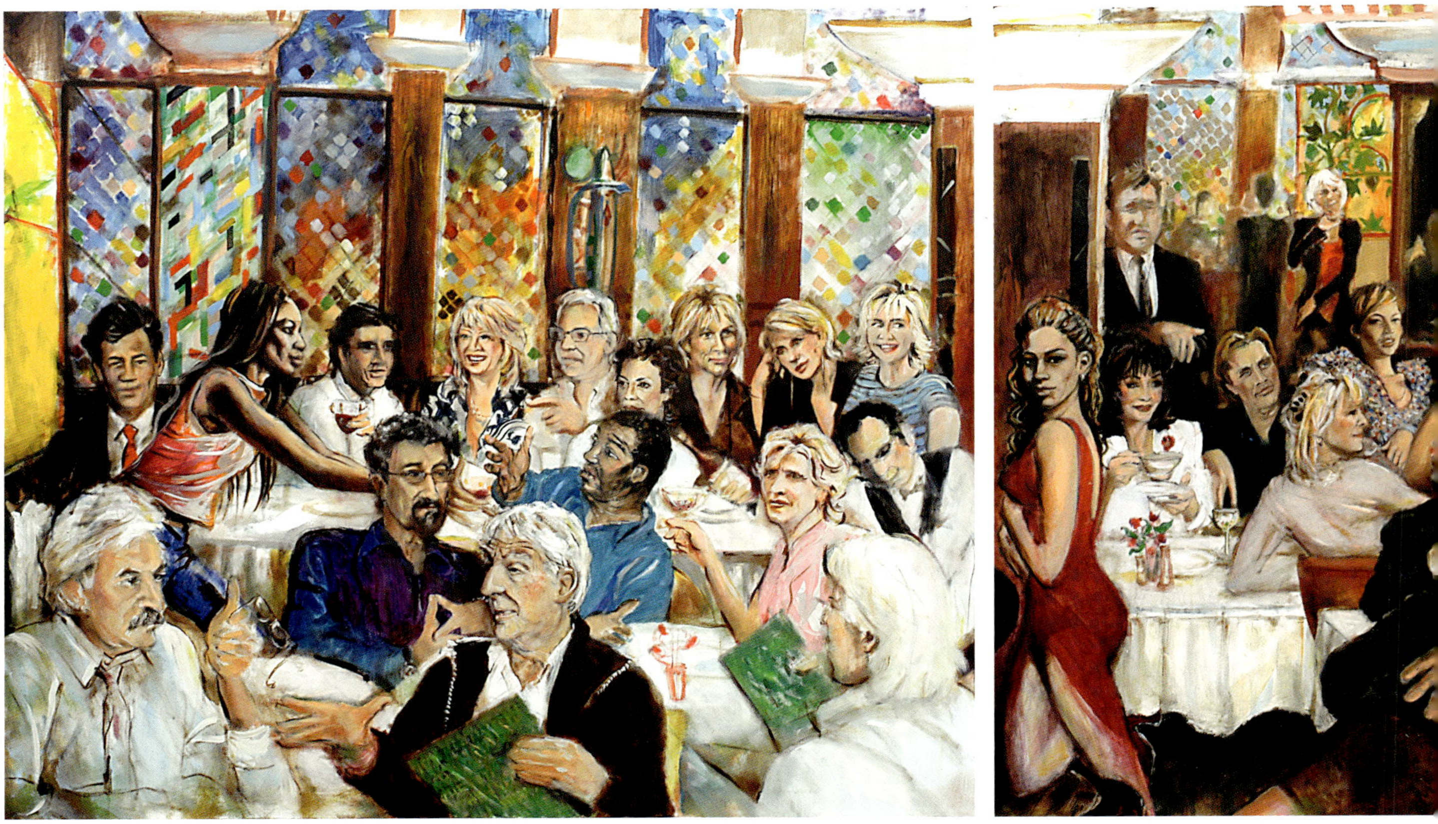

"This is my triptych for The Ivy, night going into day. It was commissioned by Andrew Lloyd-Webber and is from his personal collection. He wanted a cross-section of people, representing every facet of the arts at the time. All of the subjects came to my studio so I could sketch them before painting them. Alternative Ivy *is from my imagination, and includes many of the people I have painted who have since passed away."*

ABOVE: *The Ivy (triptych)* | 2004 | oil on canvas | 152.5 × 183 cm (each panel)
OPPOSITE: *Alternative Ivy* | 2001 | oil on canvas | 61 × 91.5 cm

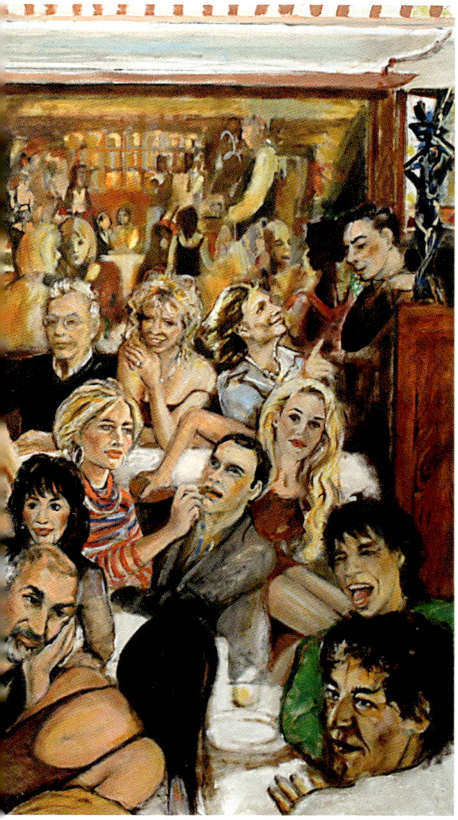

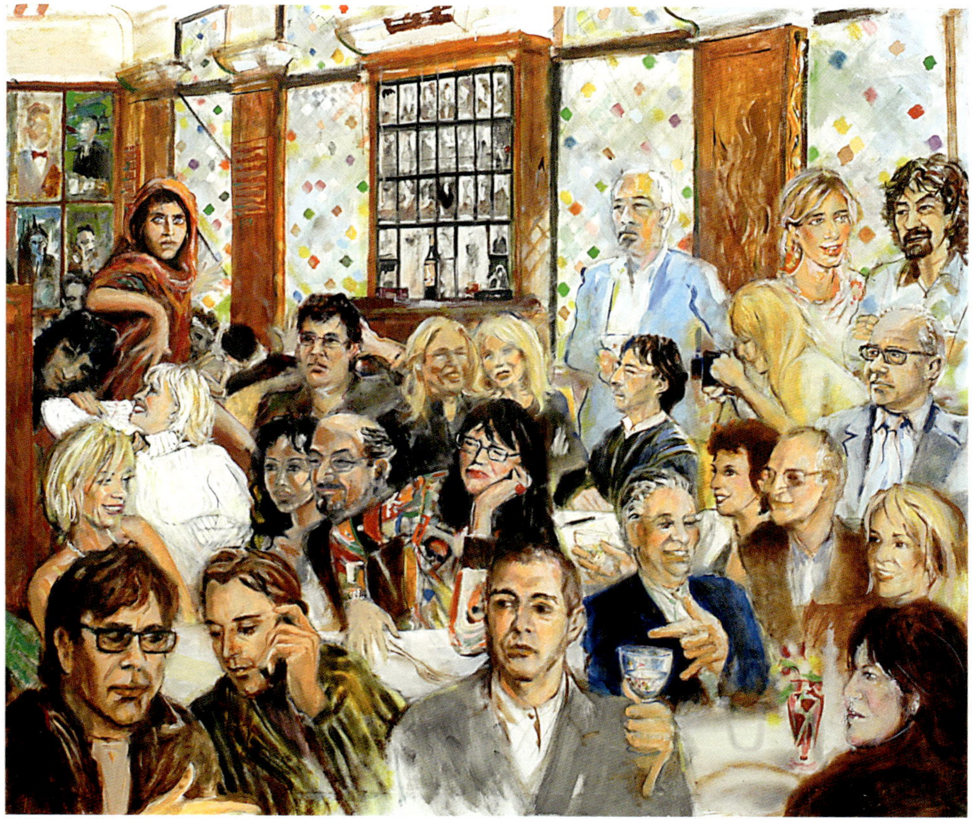

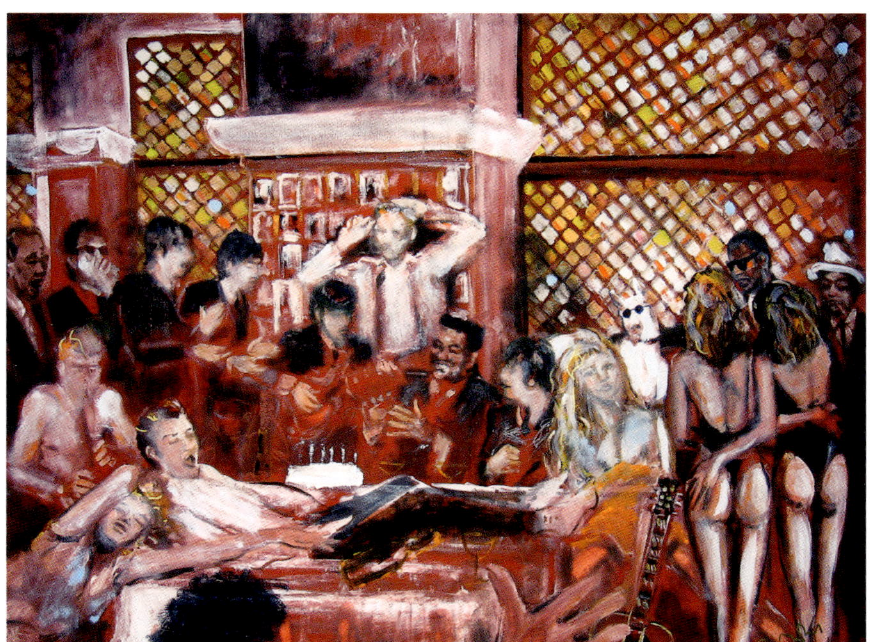

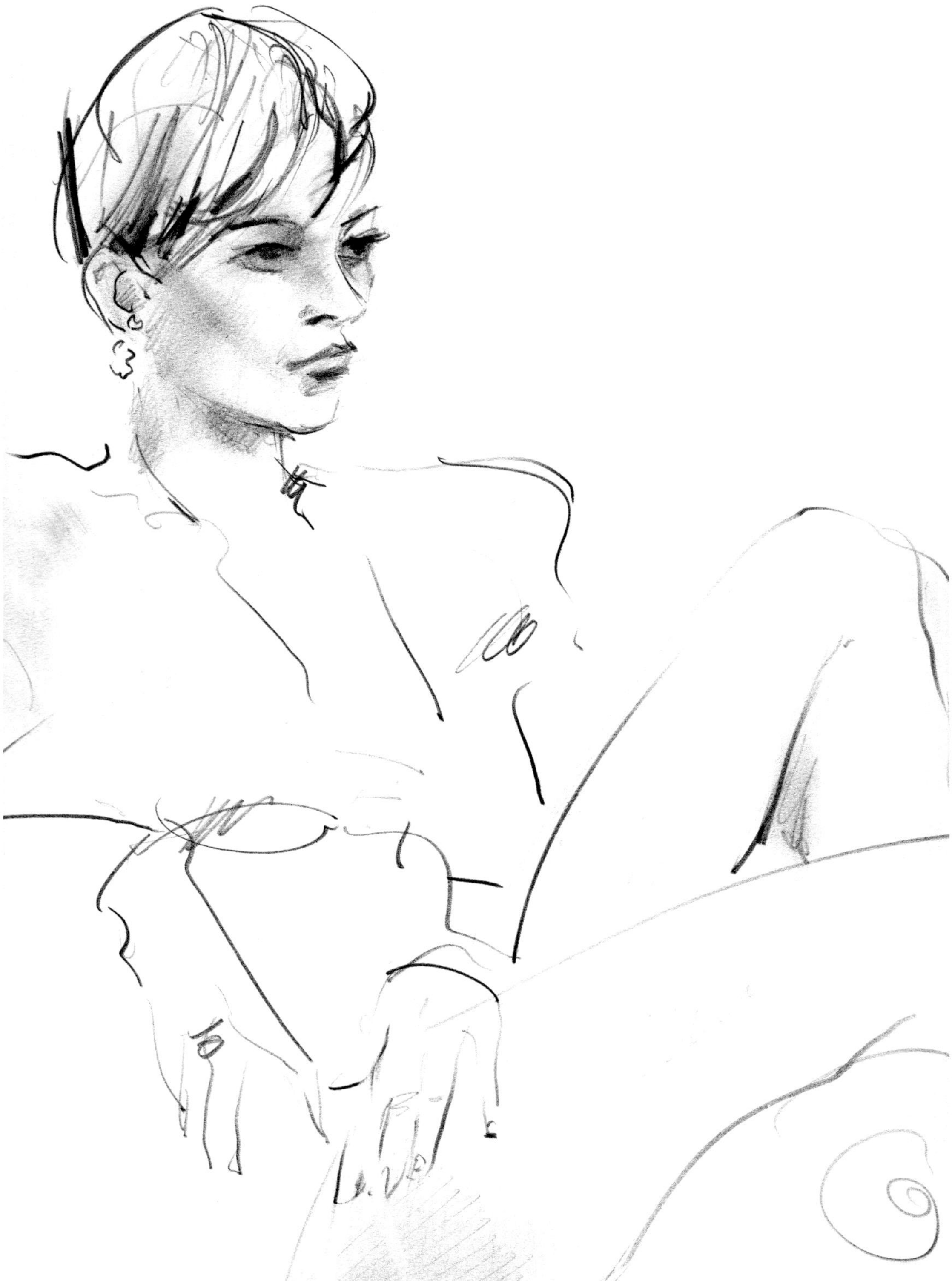

ABOVE: *Long Lost Kate* | 2001 | pencil on paper | 42 × 29 cm
OPPOSITE ABOVE: *Sketch for The Ivy* | 2001–04 | pen and ink on paper | 42 × 59 cm
OPPOSITE BELOW: *Sketch for The Ivy* | 2001–04 | coloured pencil on paper | 42 × 59 cm

"I did the sketches inside The Ivy and the drawing of Kate was done in my studio as it was one of the more detailed references for the triptych."

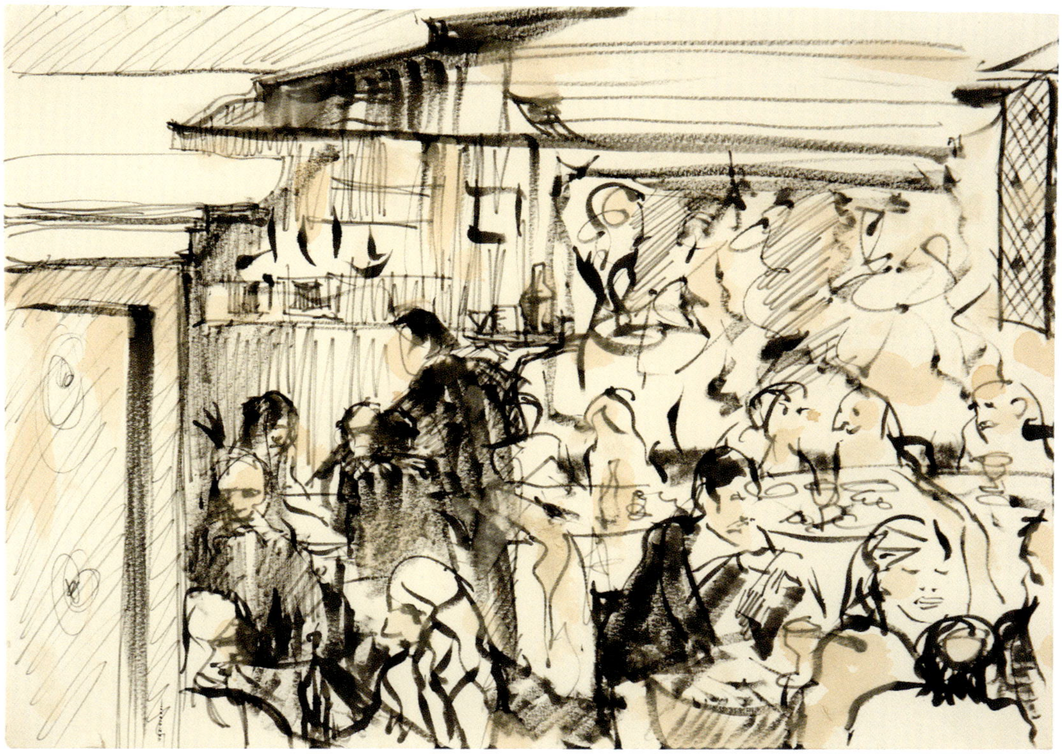

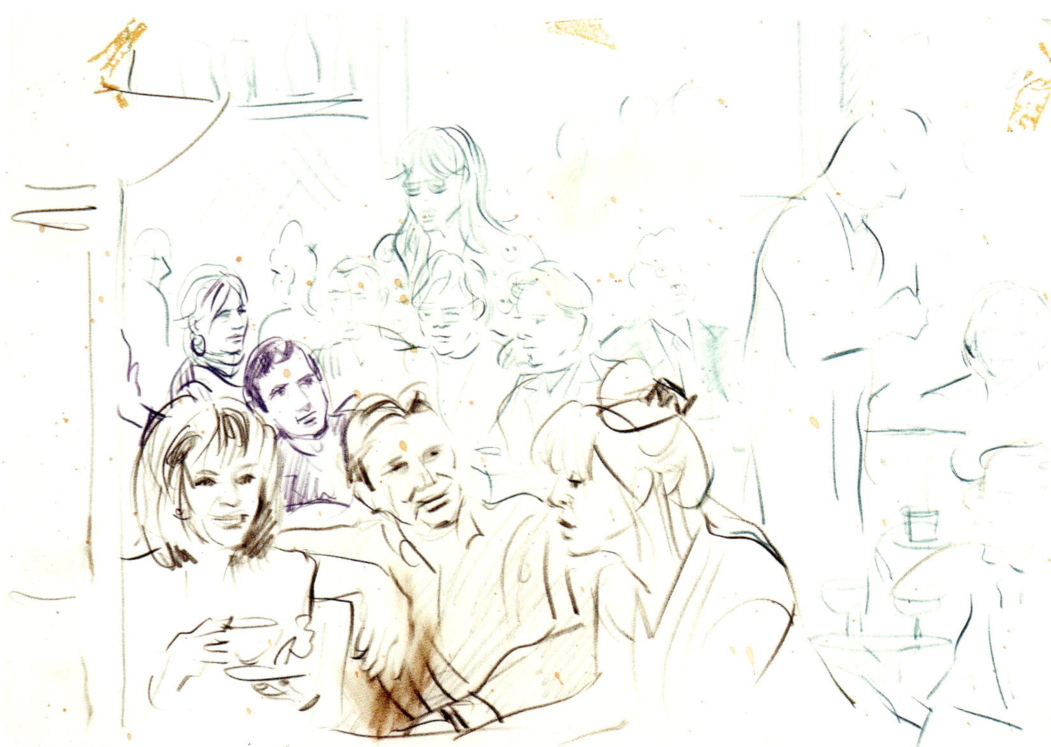

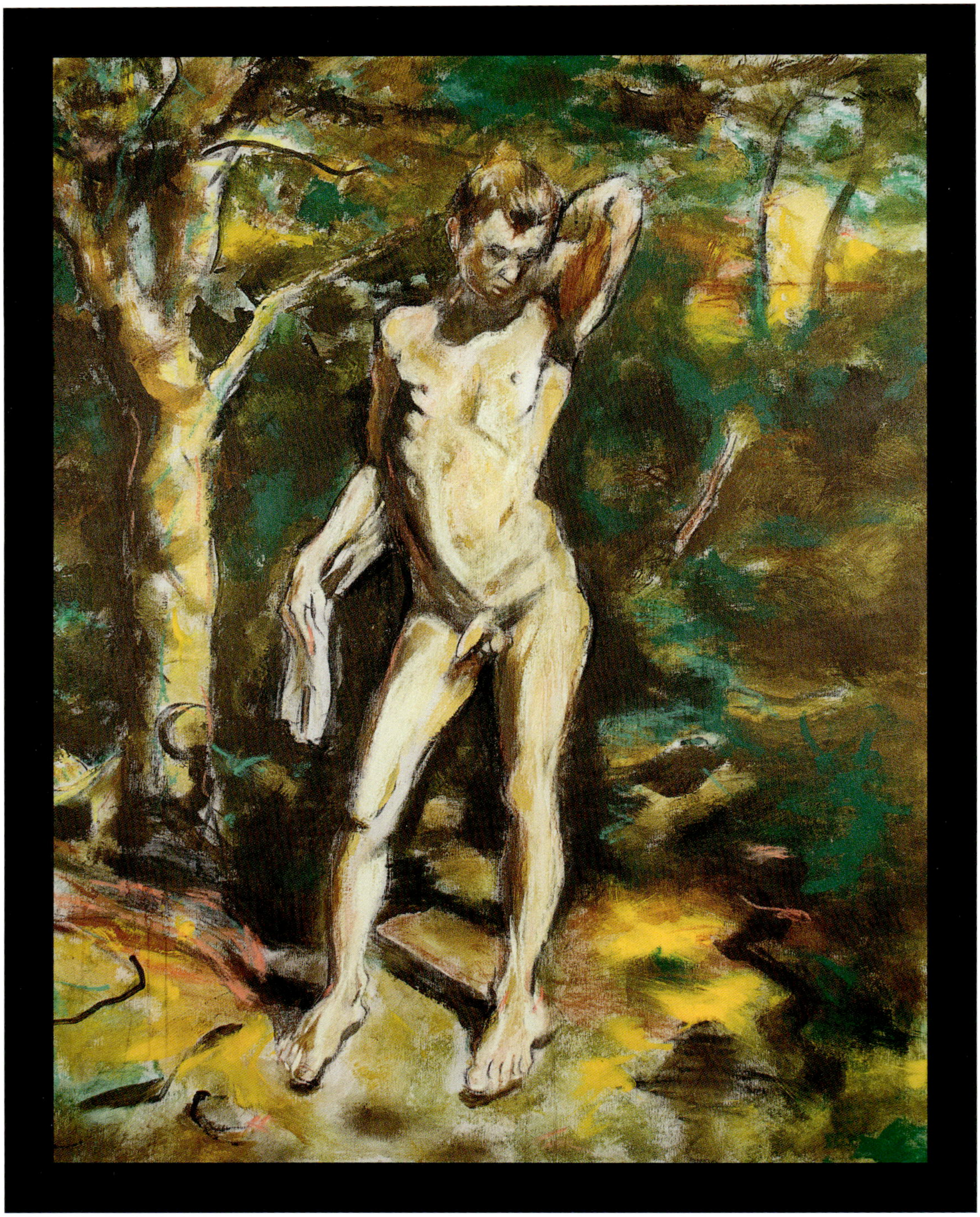

"Here I'm paying tribute to the Irish artist William Orpen by painting this study of Boy Under the Apple Tree. *I now own the original."*

ABOVE: *Orpen Study* | 2004 | oil on canvas | 152.5 × 122 cm
OPPOSITE: *Barnado's* | 1990 | oil on canvas | 153 × 92 cm

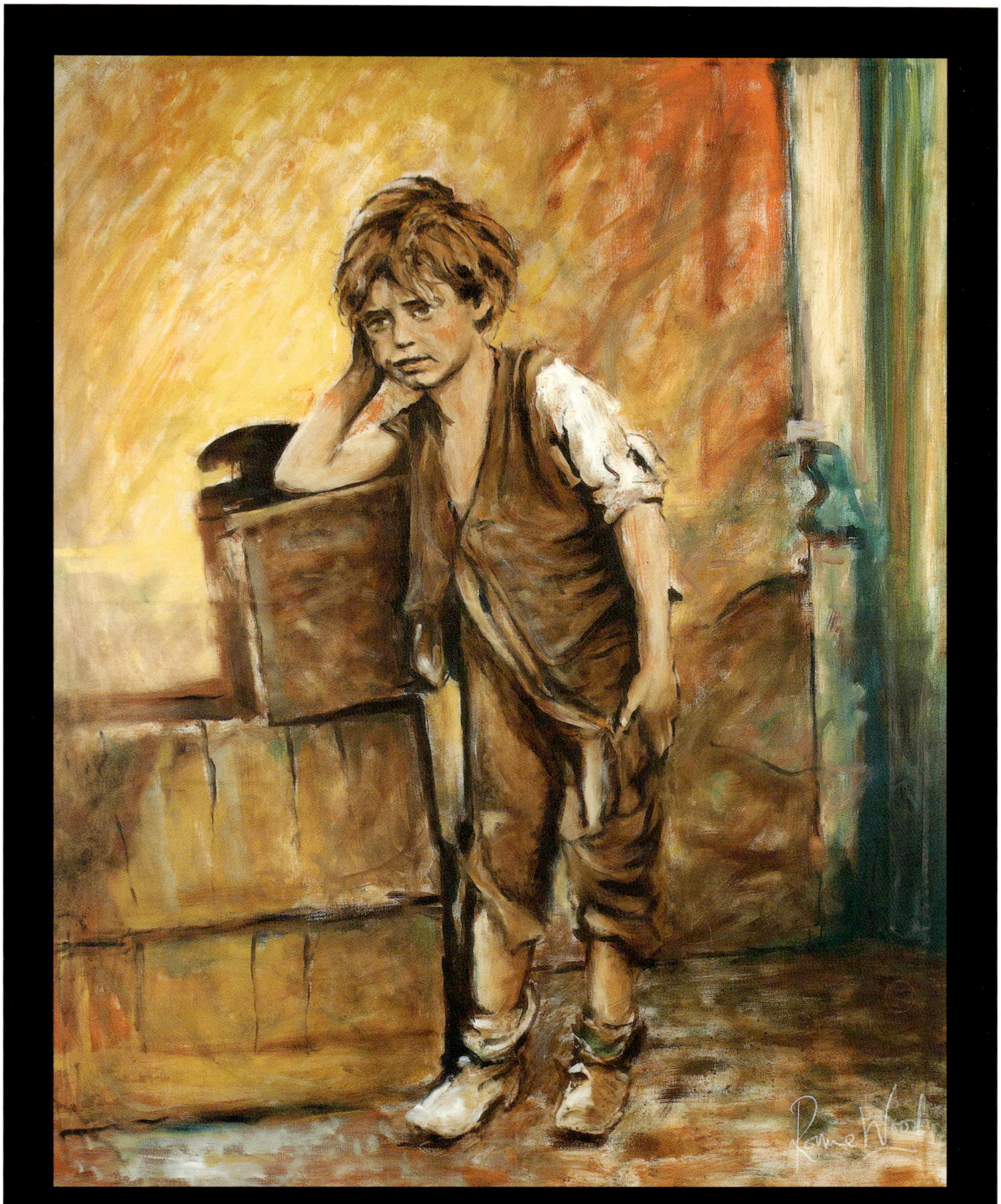

"This painting helped raise money for vulnerable children who are cared for by the Barnardo's charity."

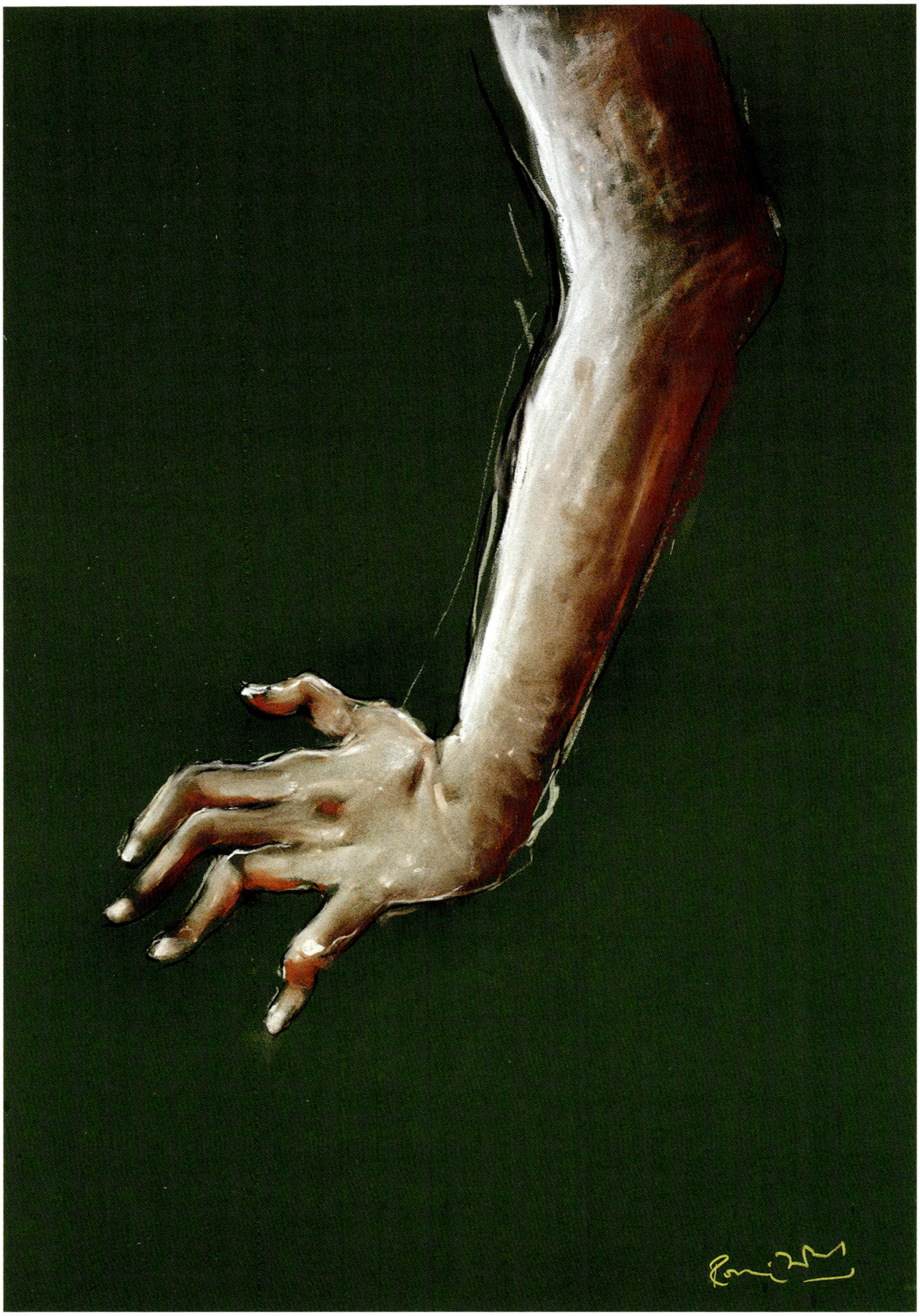

"I love to focus on hands and often make a feature them in my art. Hands are so expressive, but they're also a challenge."

OPPOSITE: *Arm Study* | 2009 | pastel on board | 84 × 59 cm
BELOW: *Hand (Study 3)* | 2015 | pencil on paper | 29.7 × 42 cm
BOTTOM: *Hand (Study 4)* | 2015 | pencil on paper | 29.7 × 42 cm

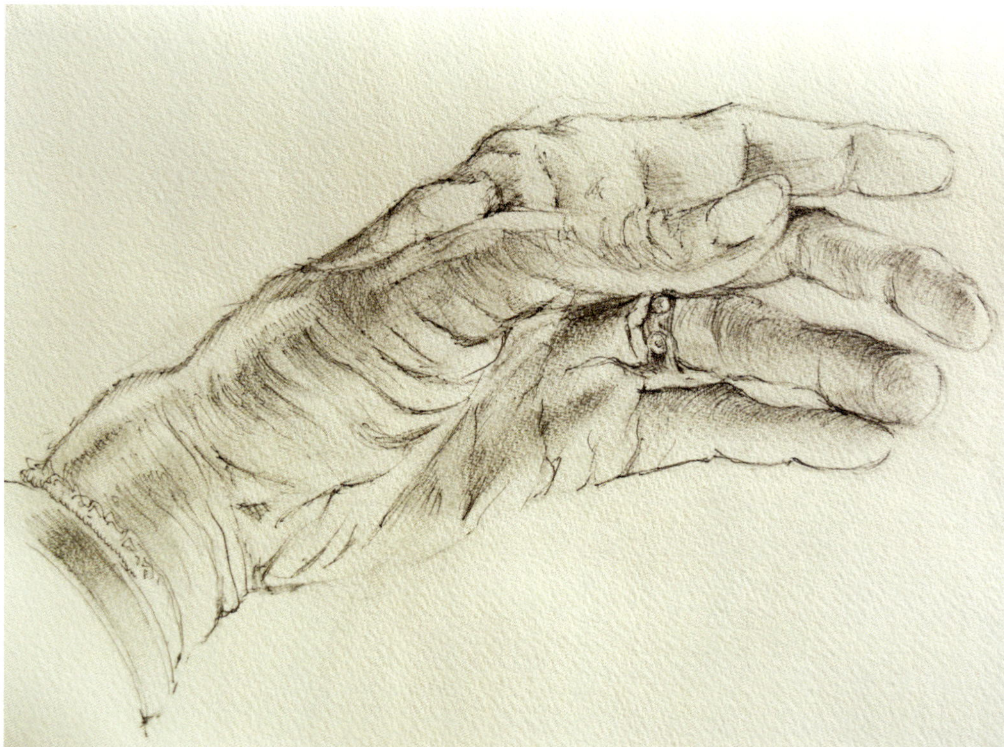

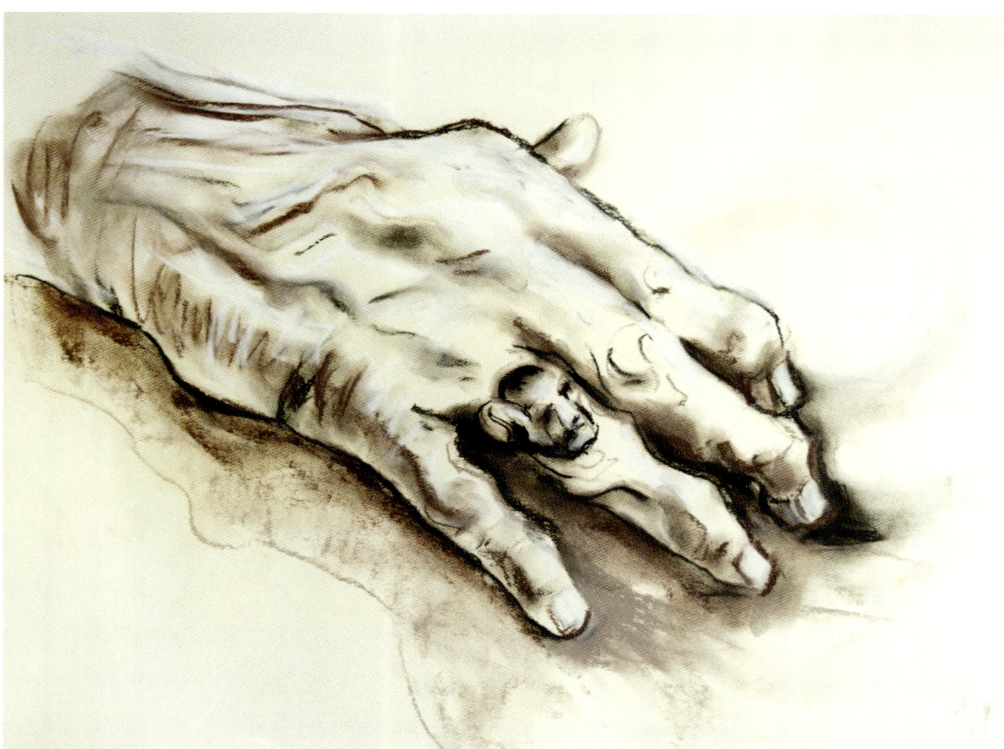

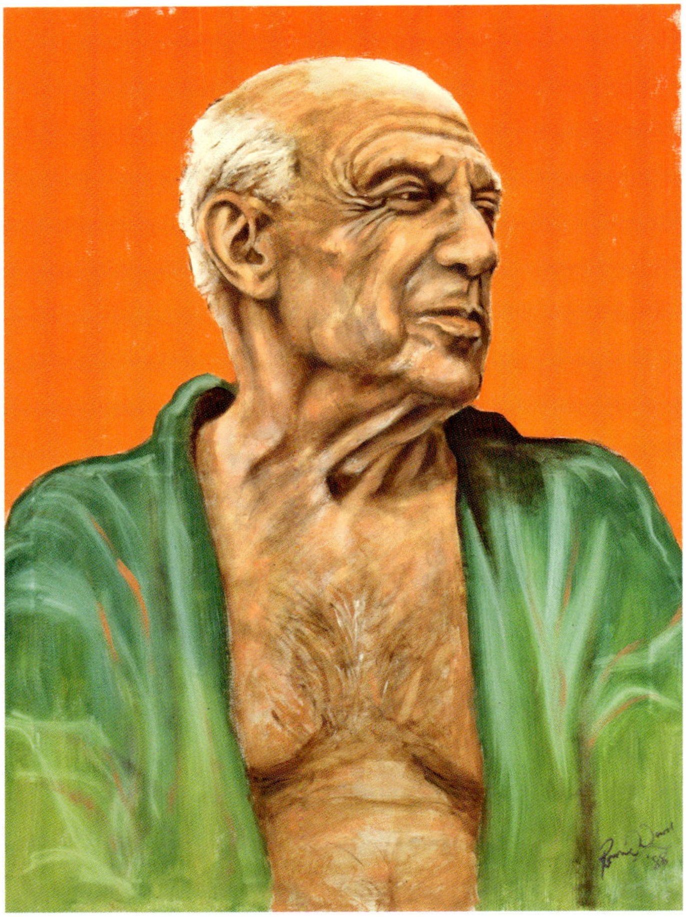

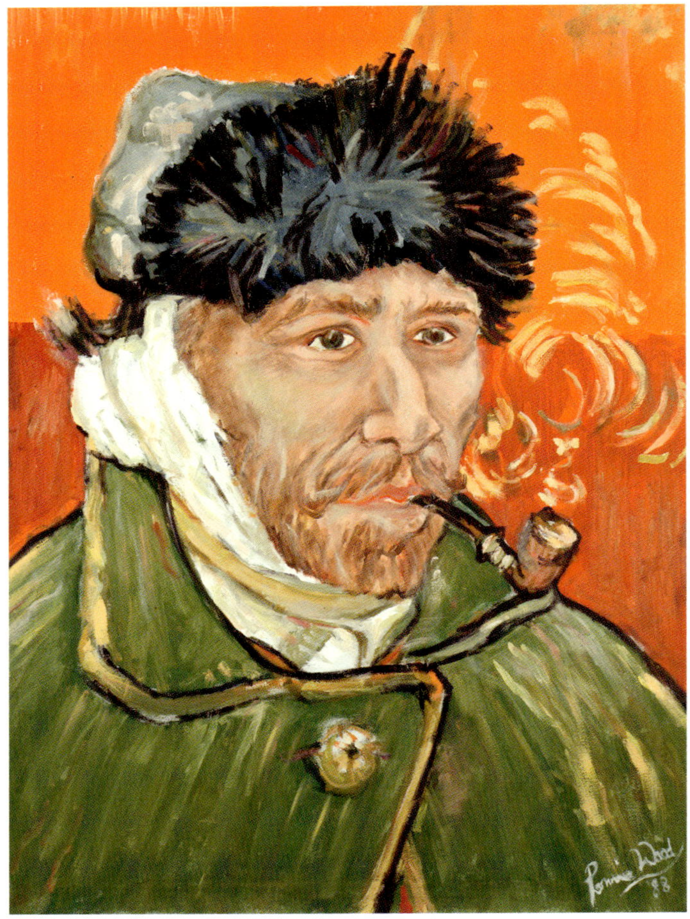

"The old masters have always inspired me.
I like to pay homage to them in my work."

ABOVE LEFT: *Picasso Study in Oil* | 1989 | oil on canvas | 122 × 91.5 cm
ABOVE RIGHT: *Van Gogh Study in Oil* | 1989 | oil on canvas | 122 × 91.5 cm
OPPOSITE: *Bar Orpen* | 2004 | oil on canvas | 91 × 71 cm

"I'm a big fan of William Orpen;
I even named my bar after him!"

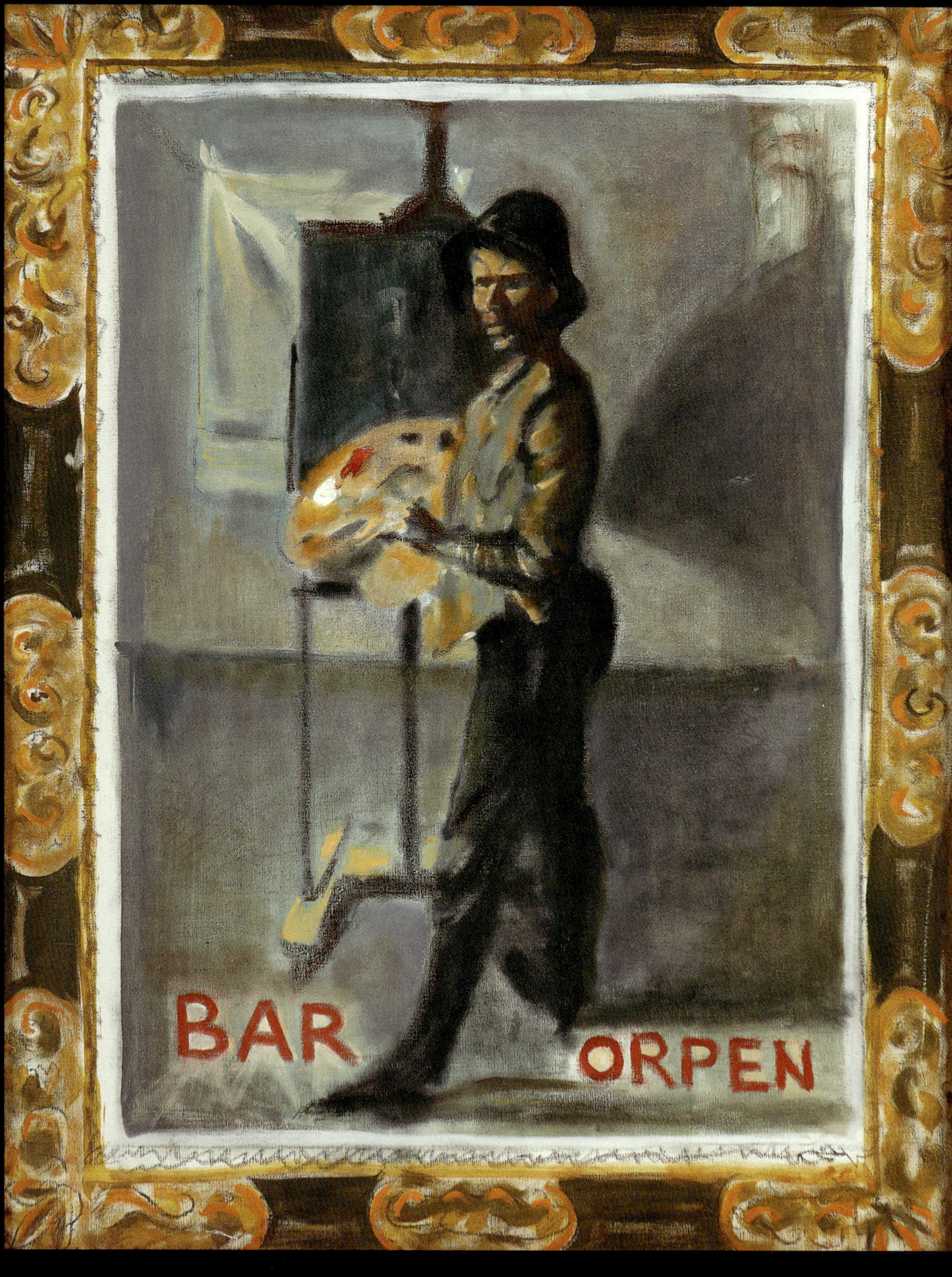

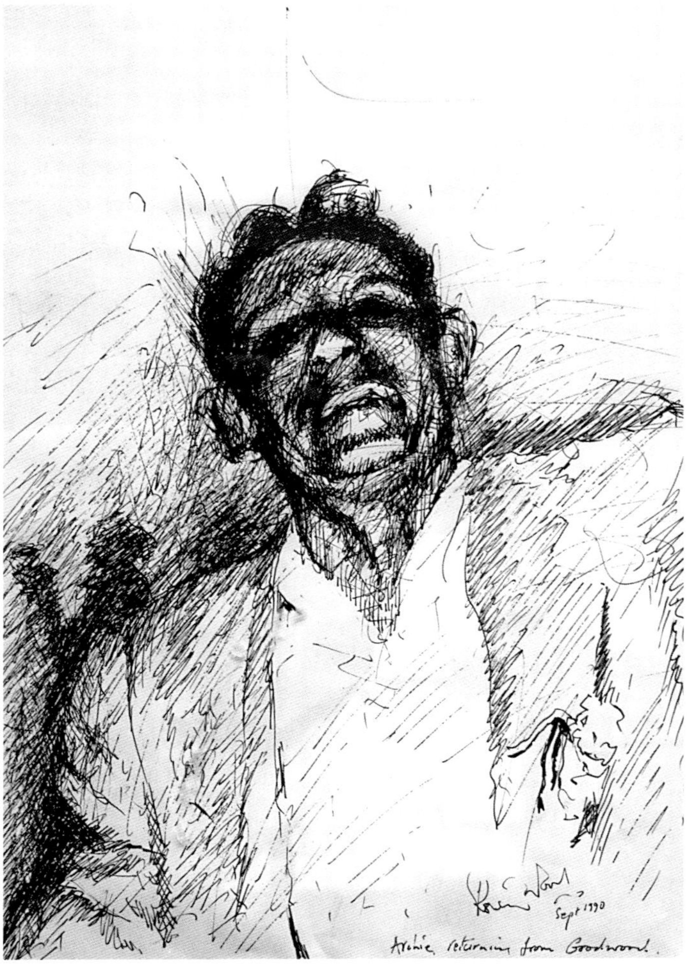

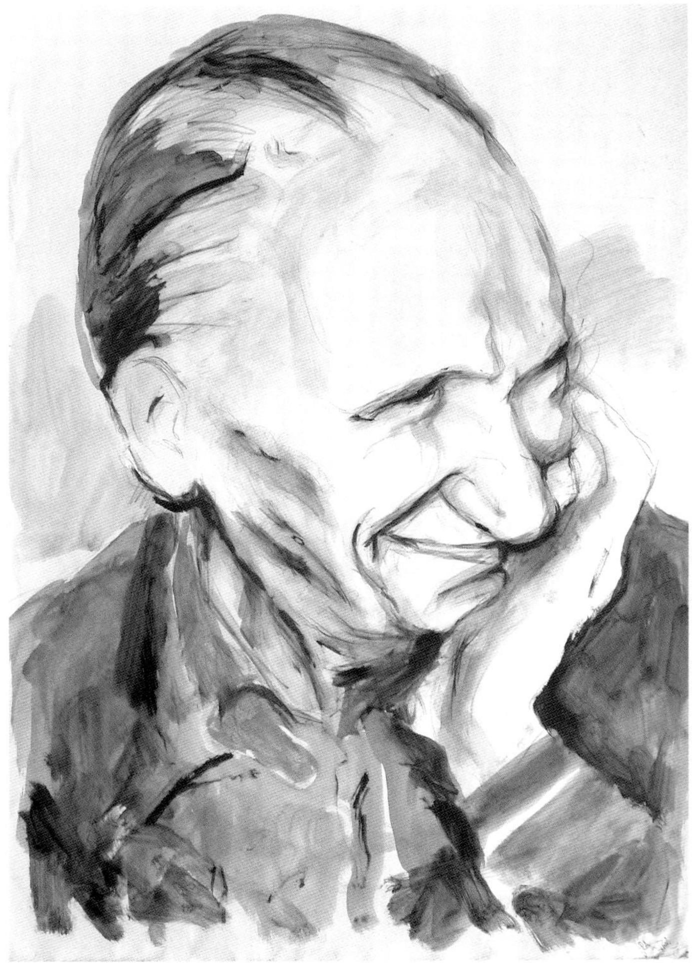

"Like so many artists, I love to paint from life. My family were among the first people I ever painted, as they were always around."

ABOVE LEFT: *Archie Returning From Goodwood* | 1990 | pen and ink on paper | 112 × 74 cm
ABOVE RIGHT: *Dad* | *c.* 1990 | pencil and acrylic wash on paper | 110.5 × 76 cm
OPPOSITE: *Mum* | 1979 | pen and ink on paper | 50 × 39 cm

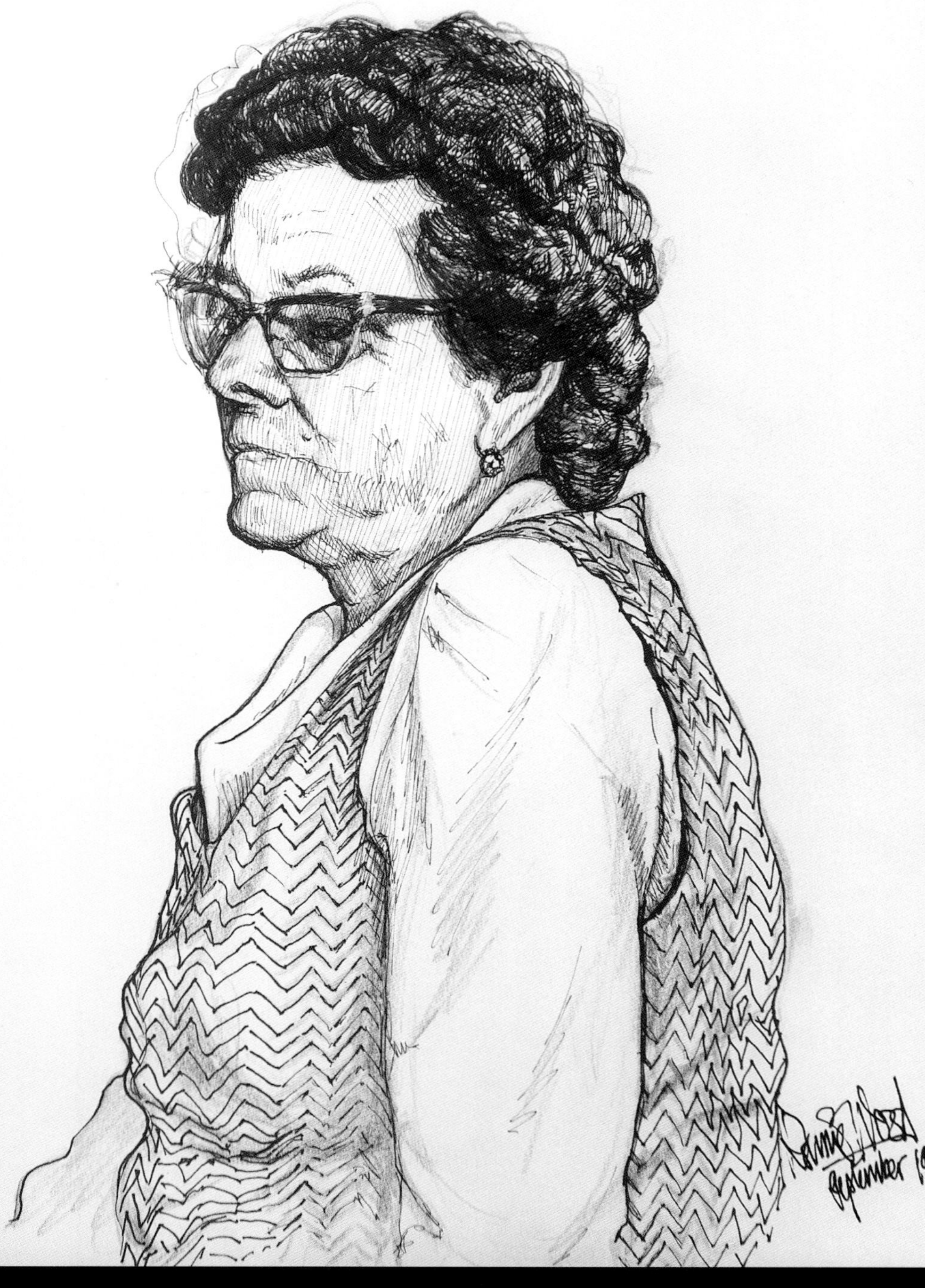
September 1979

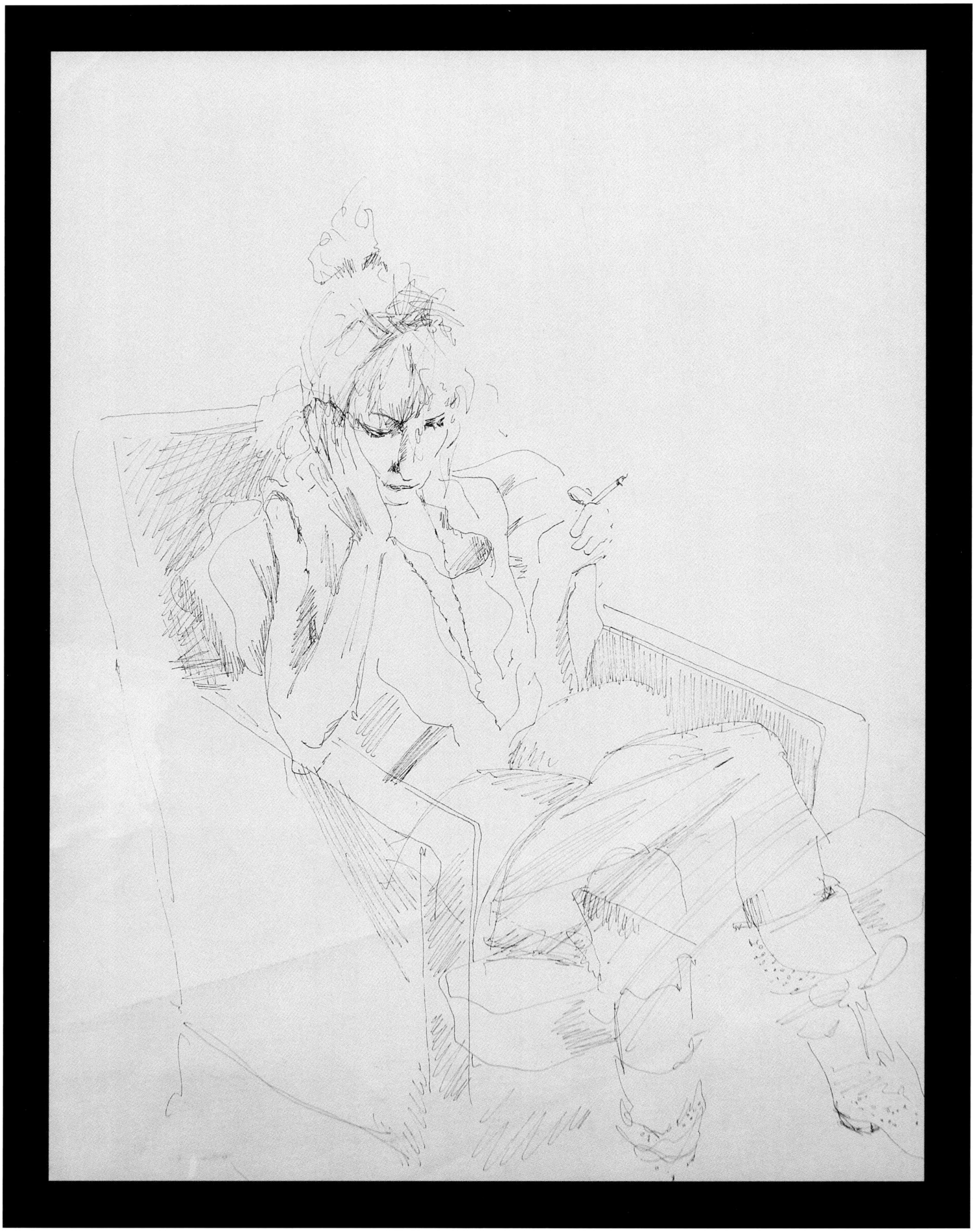

"My son, Tyrone, took the photograph that inspired The Flame; *it is the painting that encouraged fine art publishers Washington Green to begin working with me. The drawing opposite is of Billy Idol's girlfriend, and was completed in my New York apartment, on Riverside Drive/ West End Avenue."*

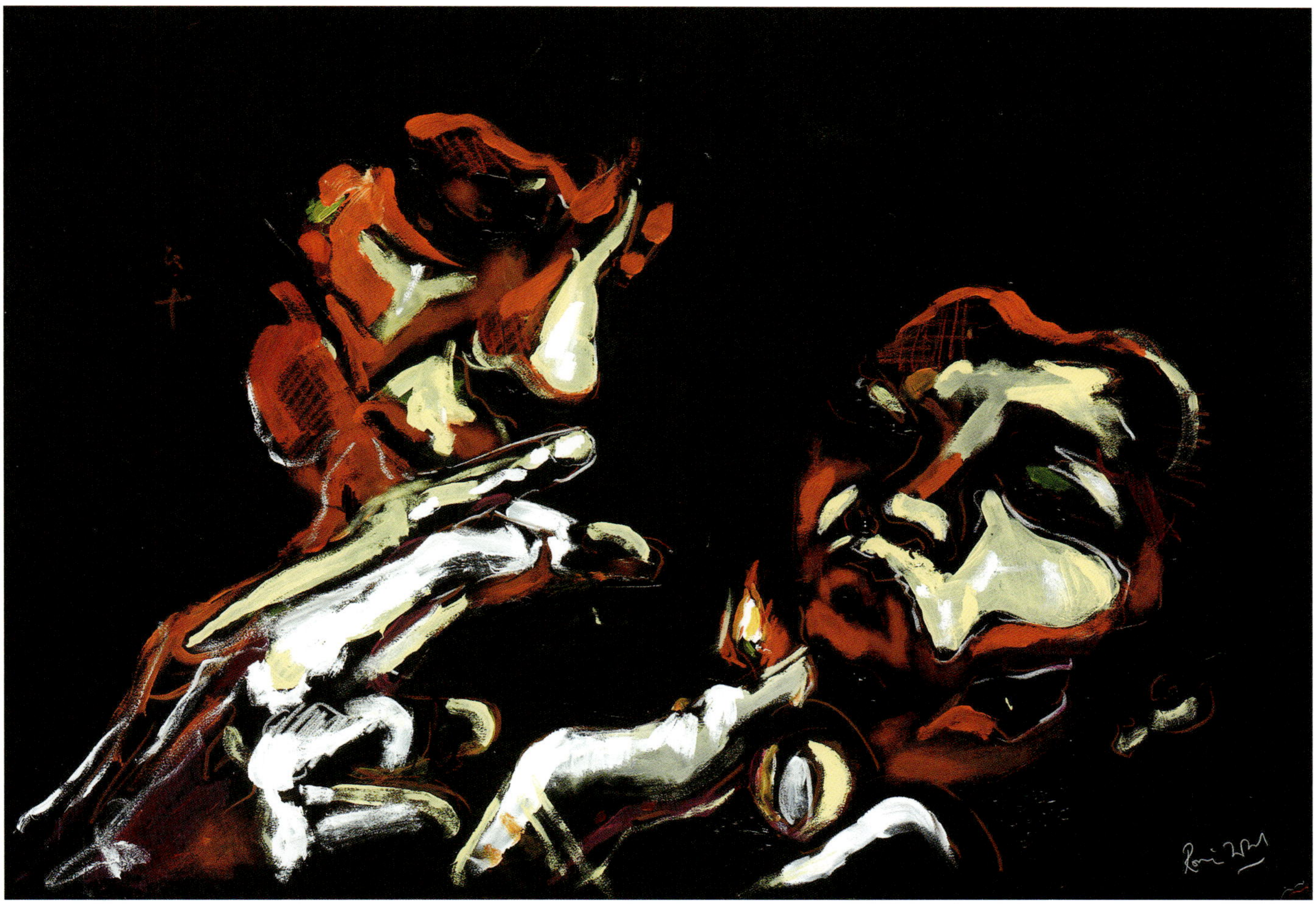

OPPOSITE: *Woman in New York* | 1987 | pen on paper | 44 × 59 cm
ABOVE: *The Flame* | 2008 | oil on canvas | 72 × 97 cm

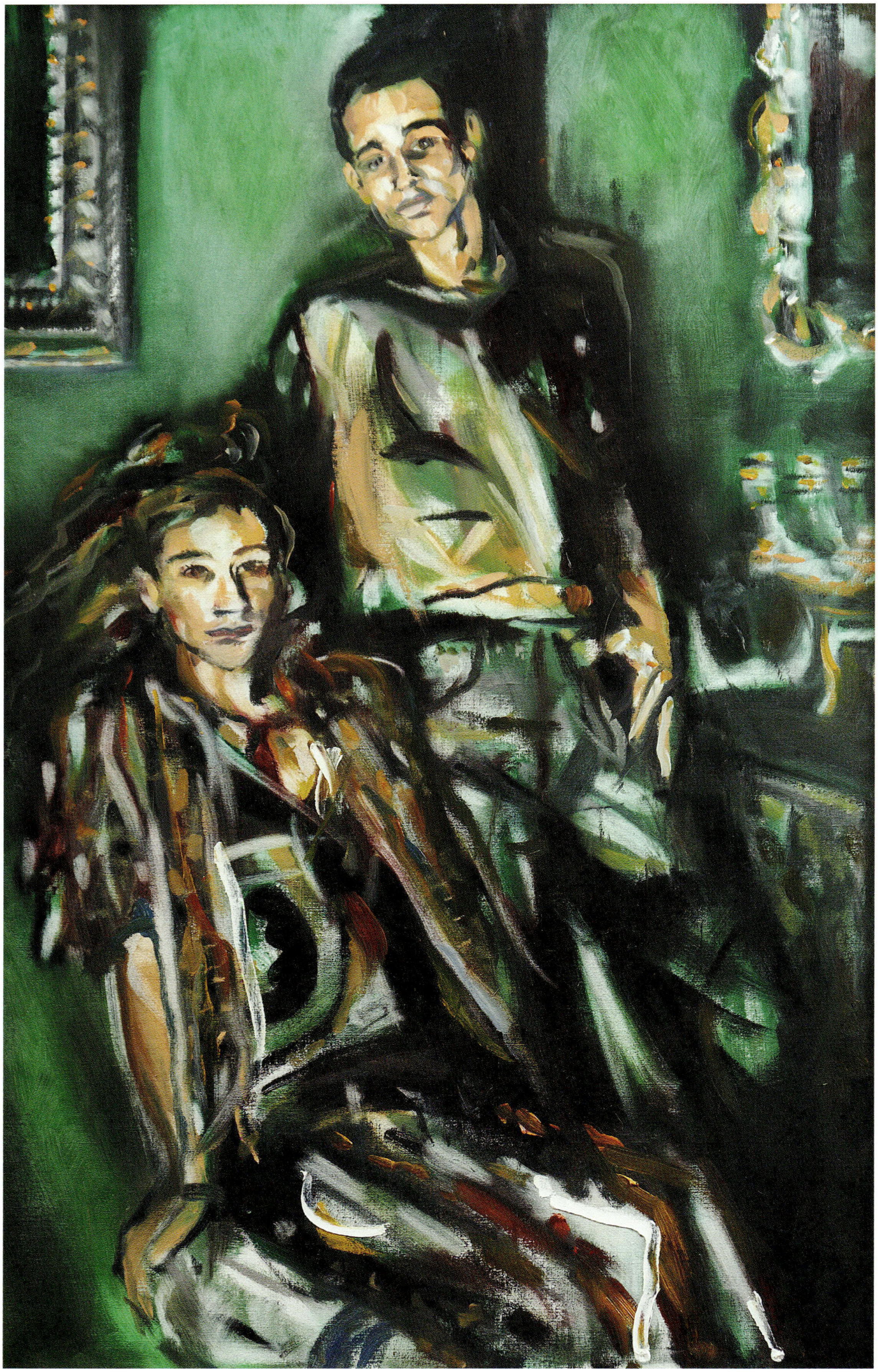

"The painting of my daughter Leah and son Tyrone is from a photograph taken by fashion photographer Mario Testino. The painting of Jesse and Arthur was composed while looking out of my studio window in Kingston, near London. Although the palm tree – pure artistic licence – makes it look more like Kingston, Jamaica!"

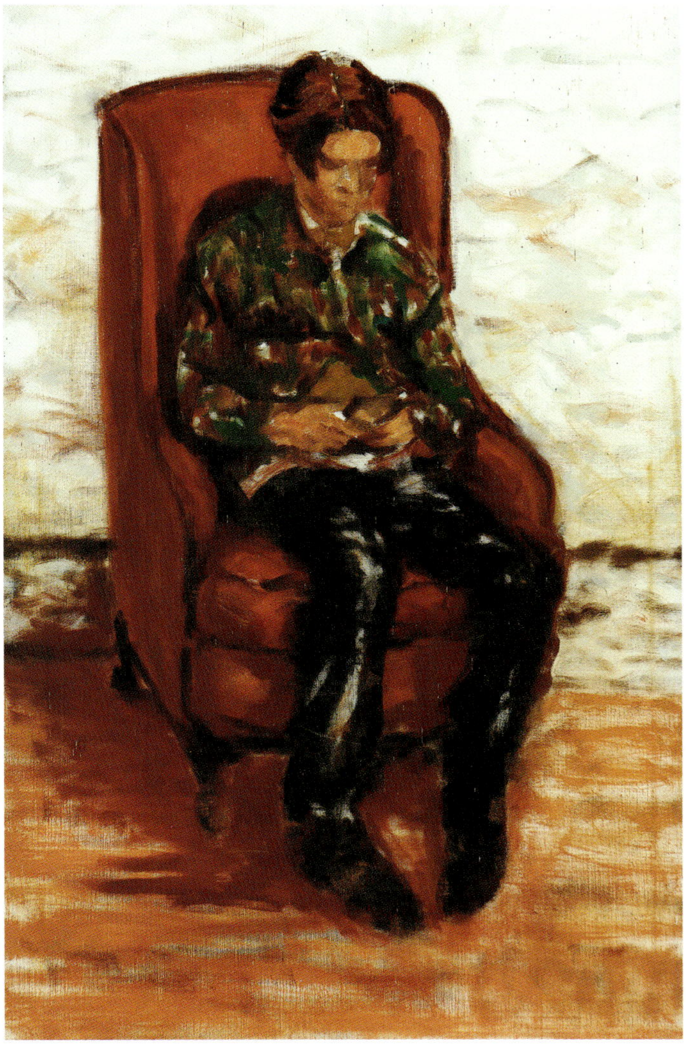

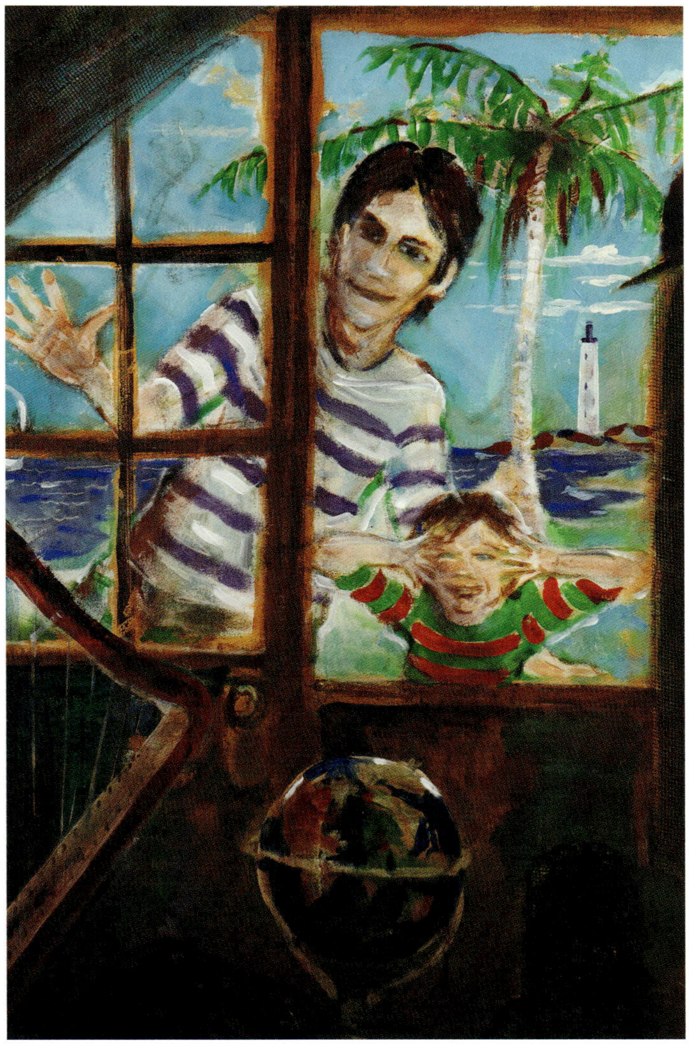

OPPOSITE: *Leah and Tyrone* | 2001 | oil on canvas | 107 × 60 cm
ABOVE LEFT: *Jesse in his Teens* | 1990 | oil on canvas | 92 × 61 cm
ABOVE RIGHT: *Jesse and his son, Arthur* | 2005 | oil on canvas | 91.5 × 61 cm

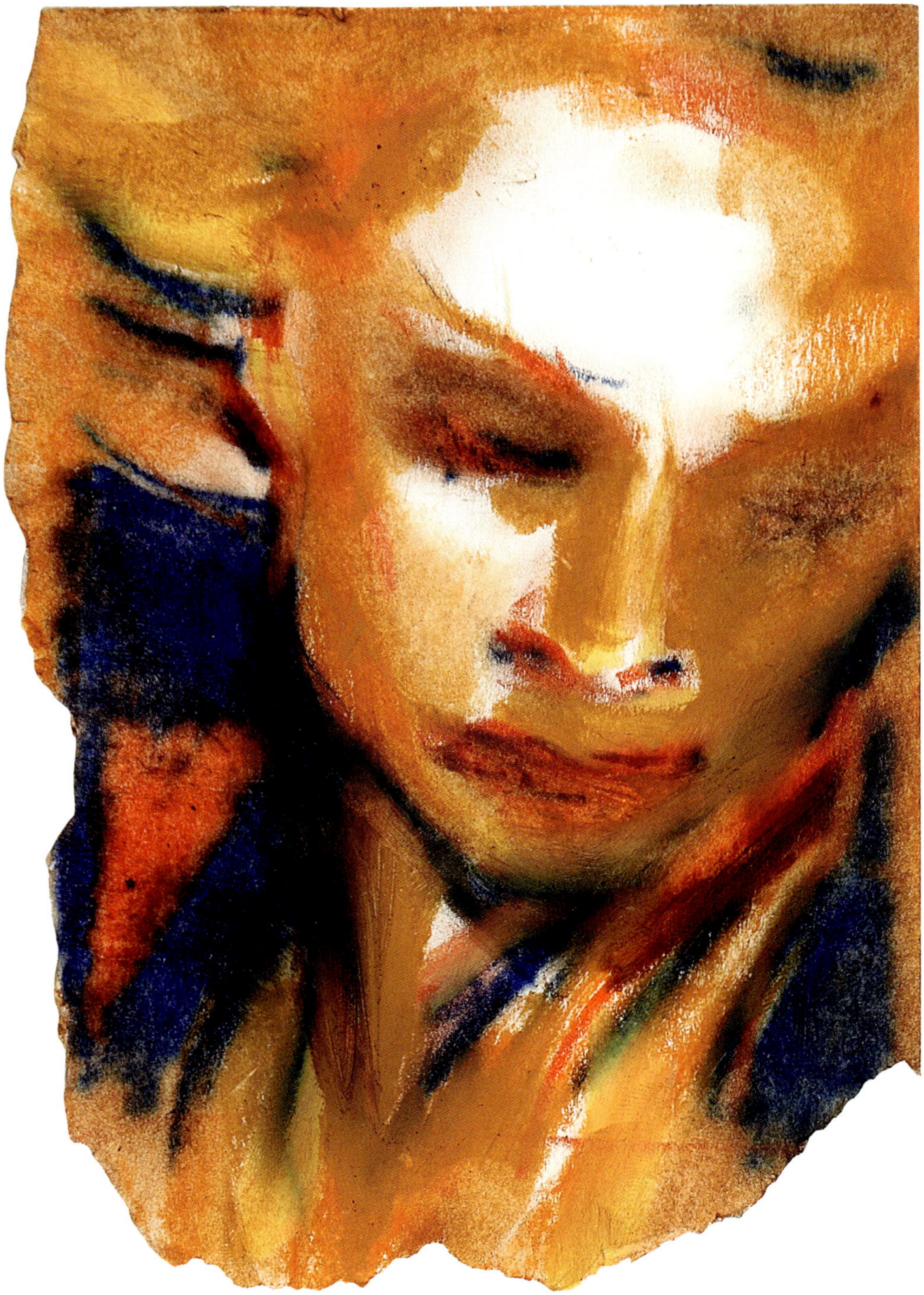

"This sketch I did of Jo is on a tiny, postage-stamp-size piece of paper, shown large here."

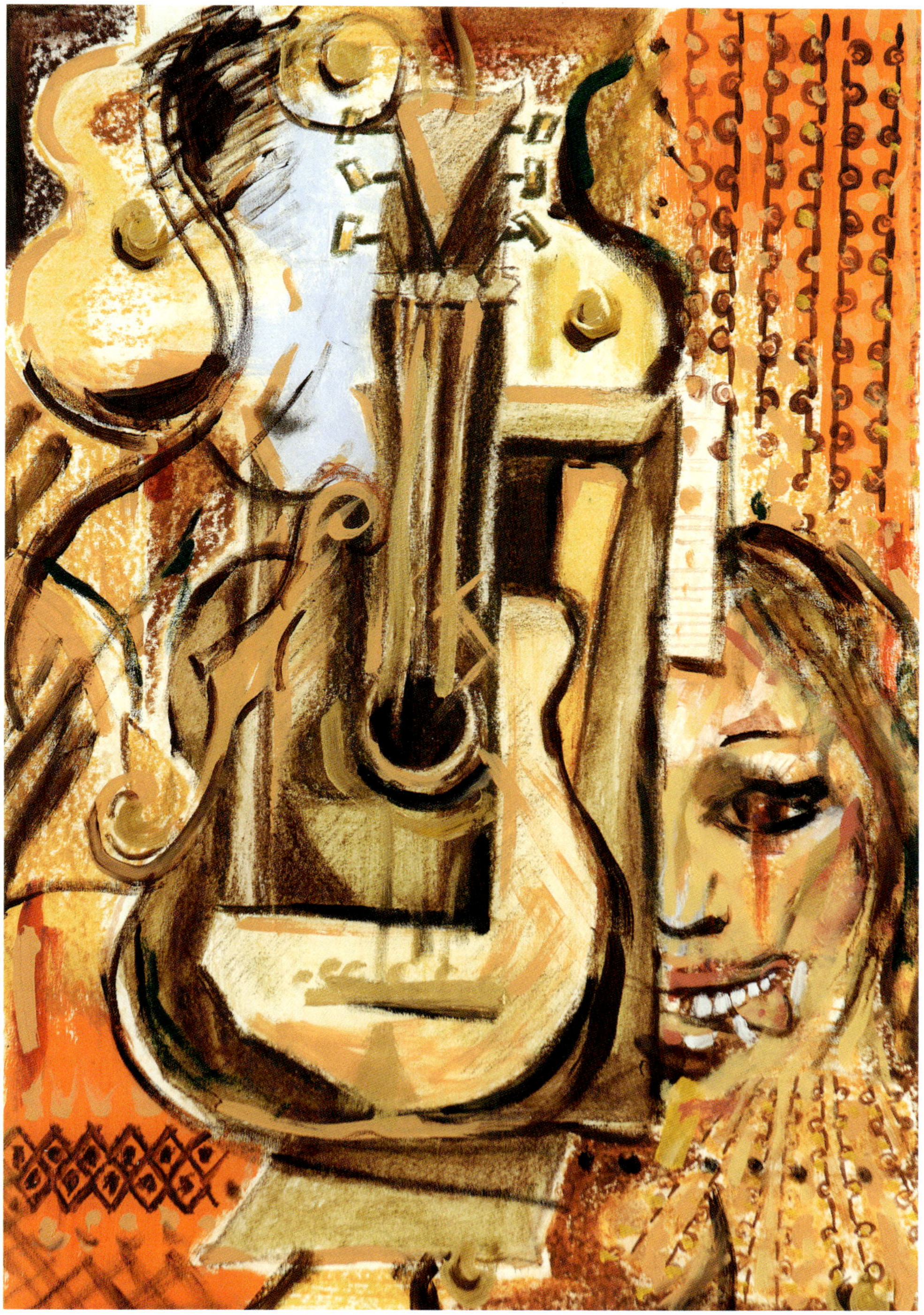

OPPOSITE: *Jo* | 2008 | acrylic on paper | 16 × 12 cm
ABOVE: *Sad Guitar* | 2005 | oil on canvas | 90 × 64 cm

BELOW: *Sophisticado* | 2007 | pastel on paper | 29 × 21 cm
OPPOSITE: *Special Sally* | 2007 | pastel on paper | 29 × 21 cm

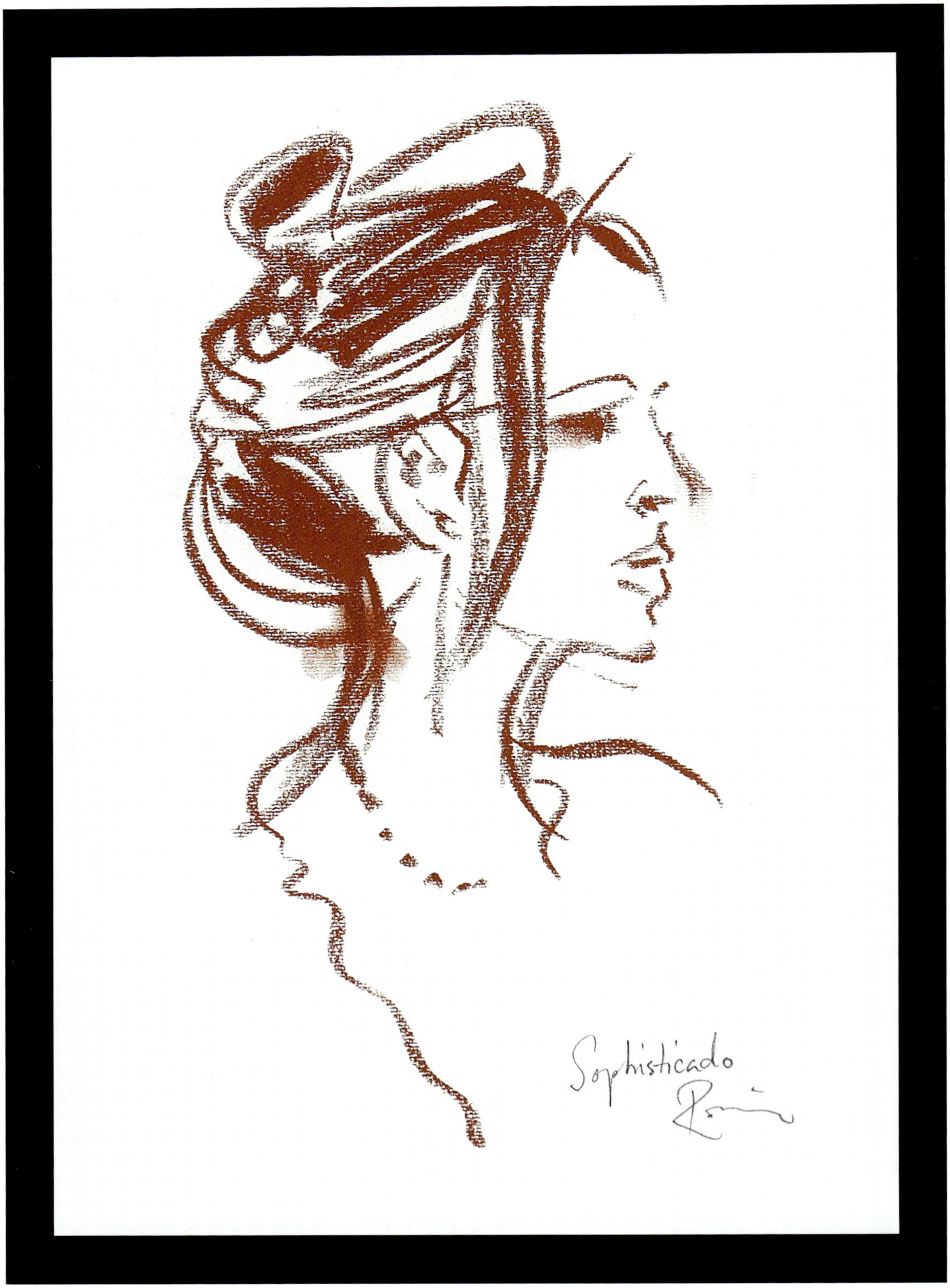

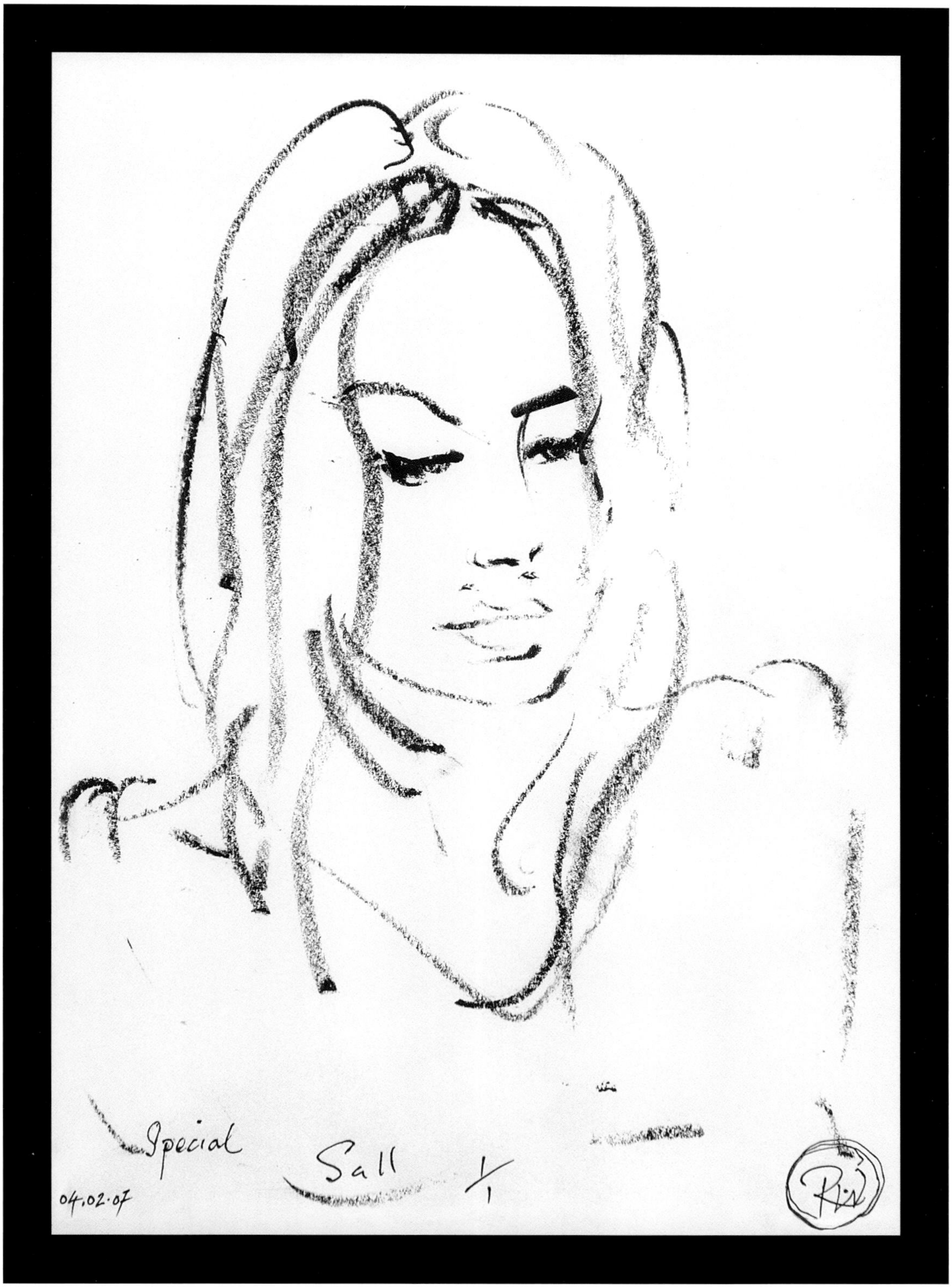
Special
Sall
1/1
04.02.07

'These capture my wife, Sally, during what was a very special time for us both.'

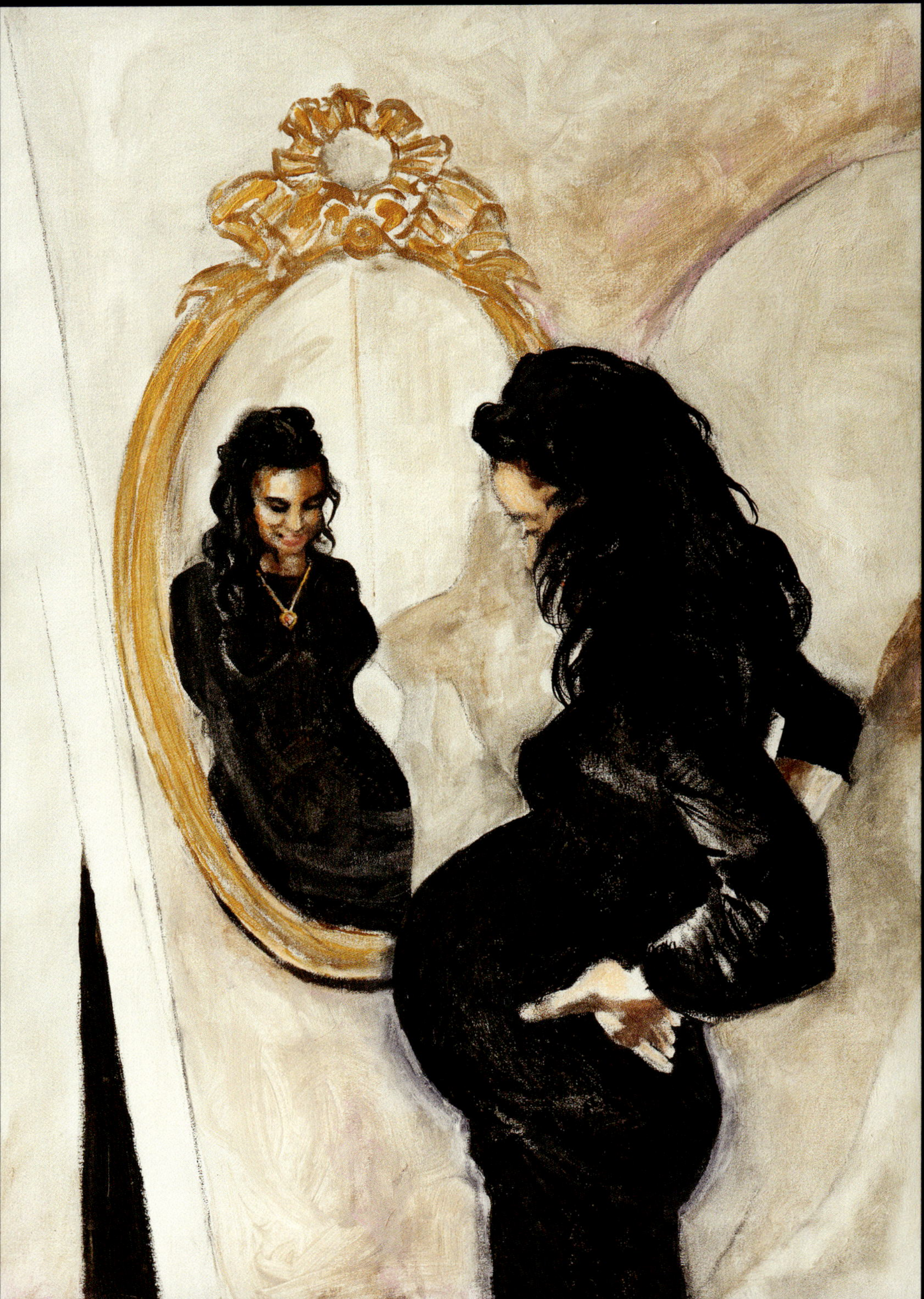

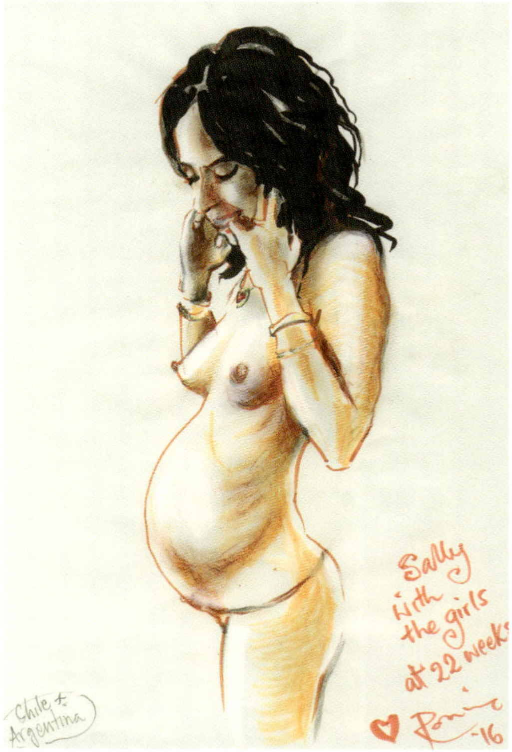

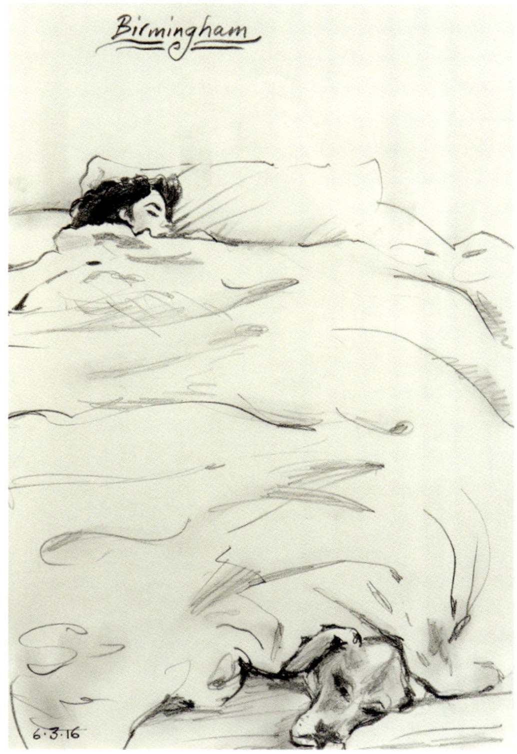

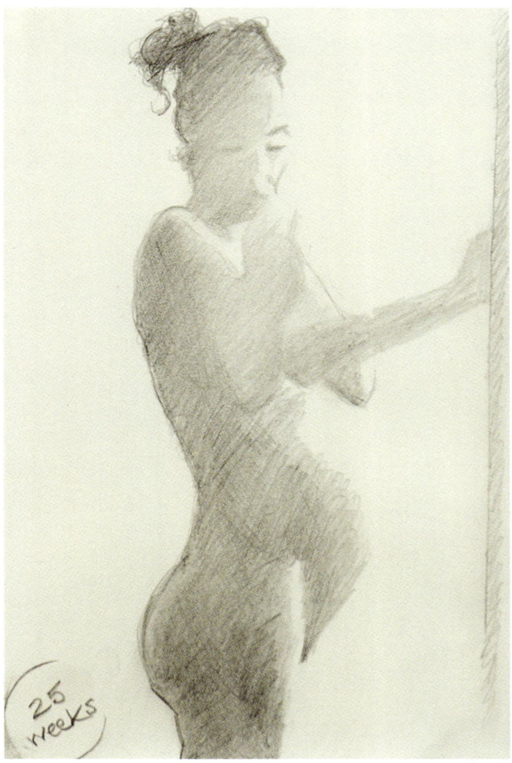

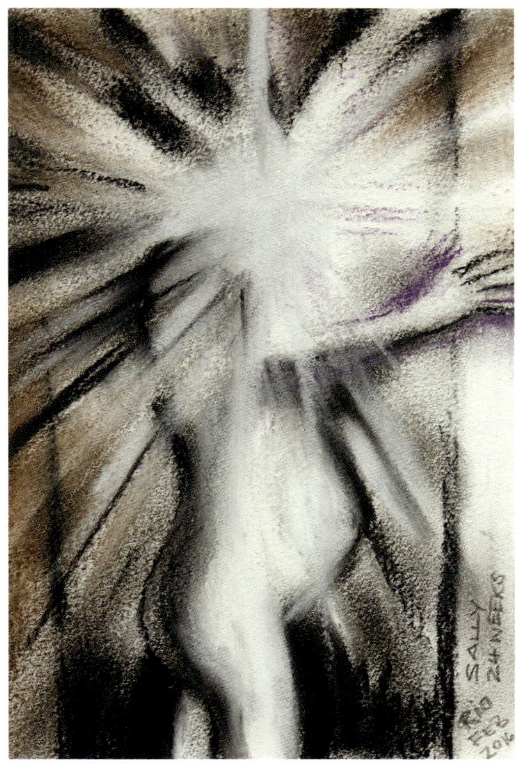

OPPOSITE: *Sally* | 2016 | mixed media on canvas | 70.3 × 50 cm
TOP LEFT: *Sally With the Girls at Twenty Two Weeks* | 2016 | mixed media on paper | 29 × 21 cm
TOP RIGHT: *Birmingham* | 2016 | pencil and pastel on paper | 29 × 21 cm
ABOVE LEFT: *Twenty Five Weeks* | 2016 | pencil on paper | 29 × 21 cm
ABOVE RIGHT: *Sally Twenty Four Weeks* | 2016 | mixed media on paper | 29 × 21 cm

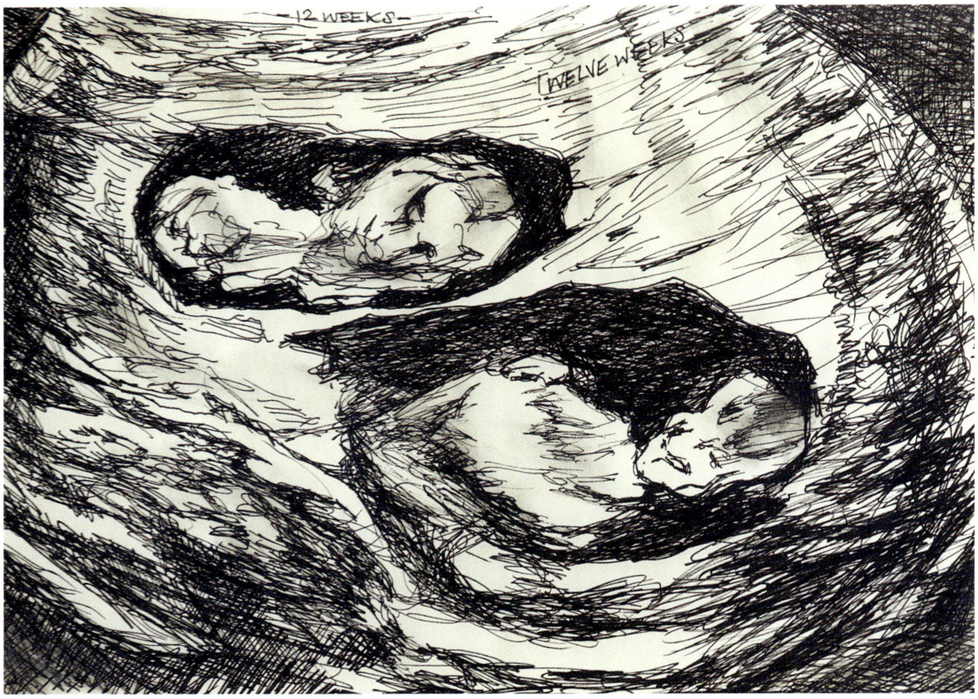

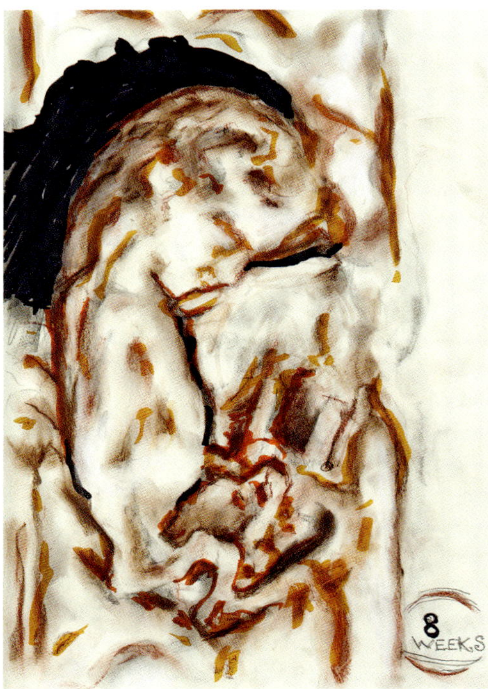

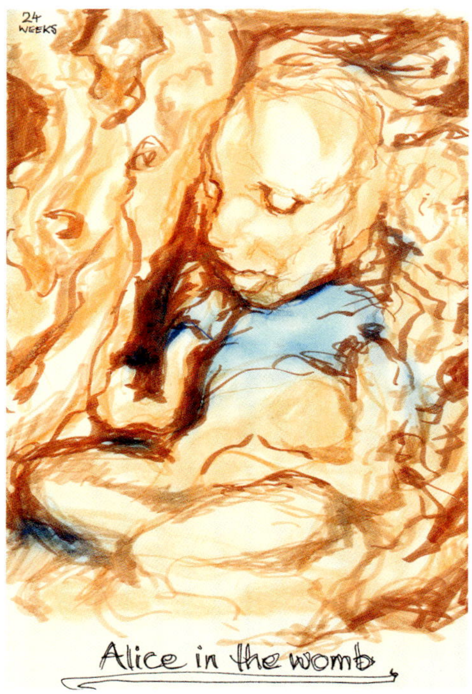

"From works in progress, to masterpieces, our beautiful Alice and Gracie."

TOP: *Twelve Weeks* | 2015 | pen on paper | 21 × 29 cm
ABOVE LEFT: *Eight Weeks* | 2015 | mixed media on paper | 29 × 21 cm
ABOVE RIGHT: *Alice in the Womb* | 2016 | mixed media on paper | 29 × 21 cm
OPPOSITE: *The Girls* | 2016 | acrylic on canvas | 80 × 60 cm approx

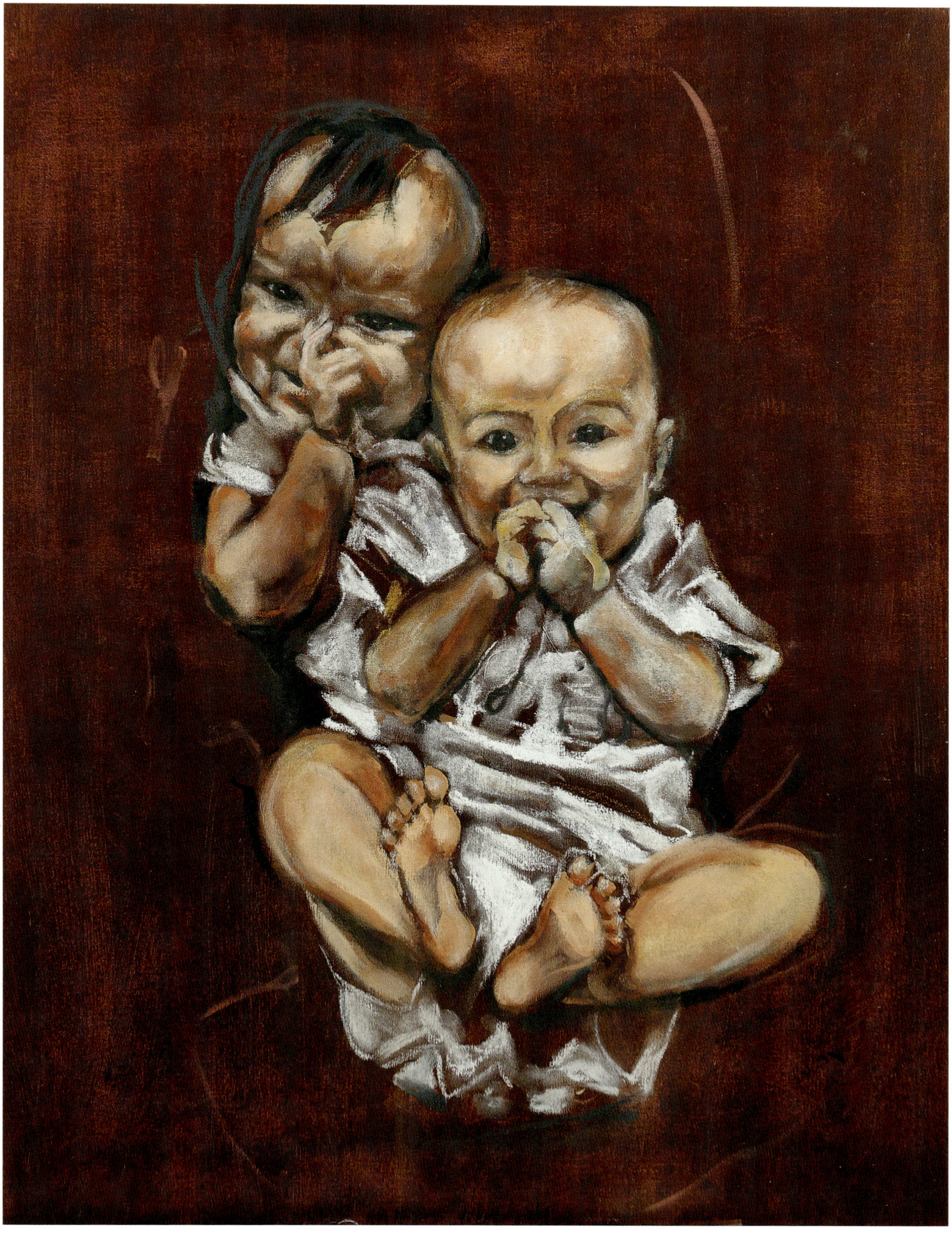

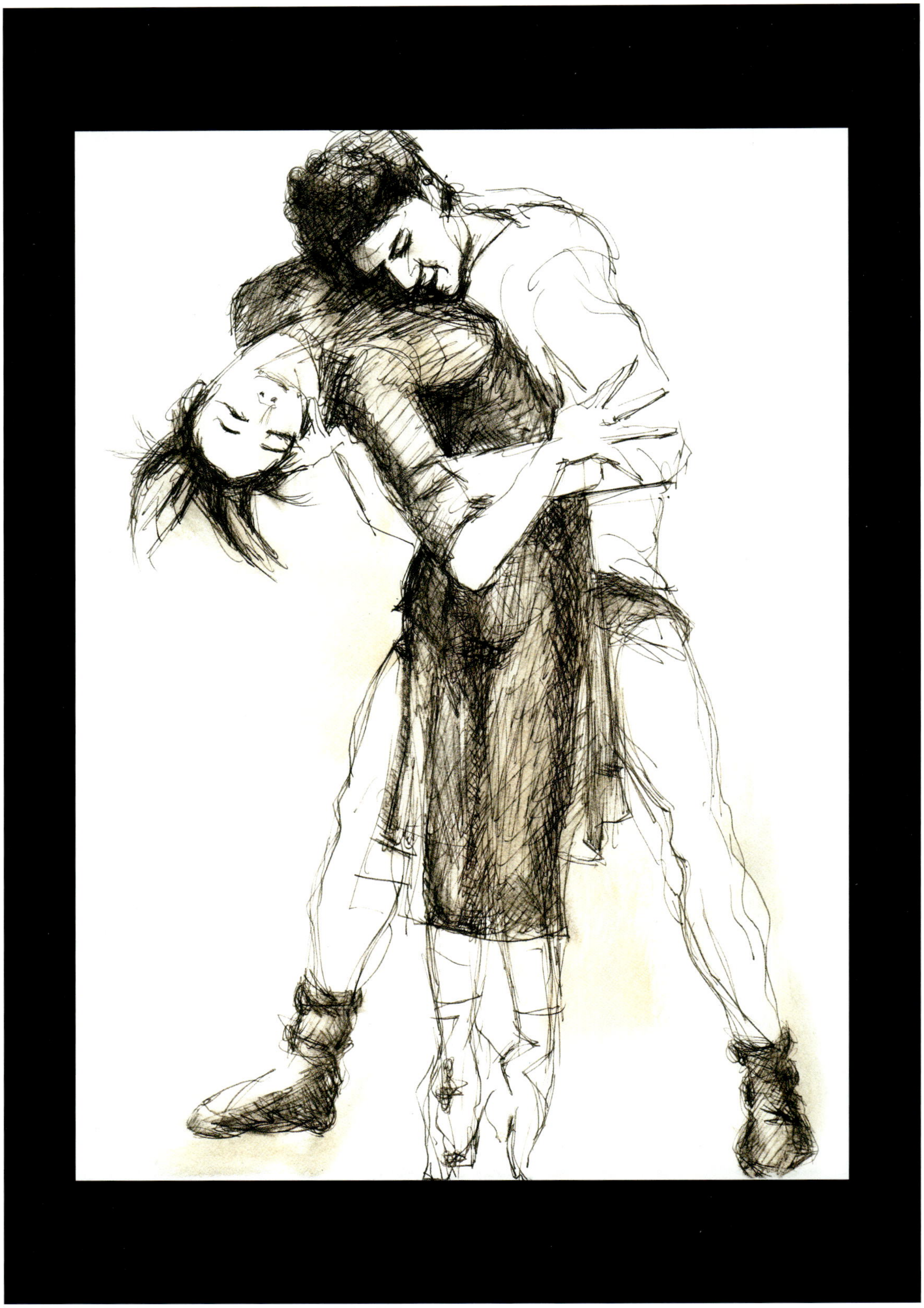

6

BALLET

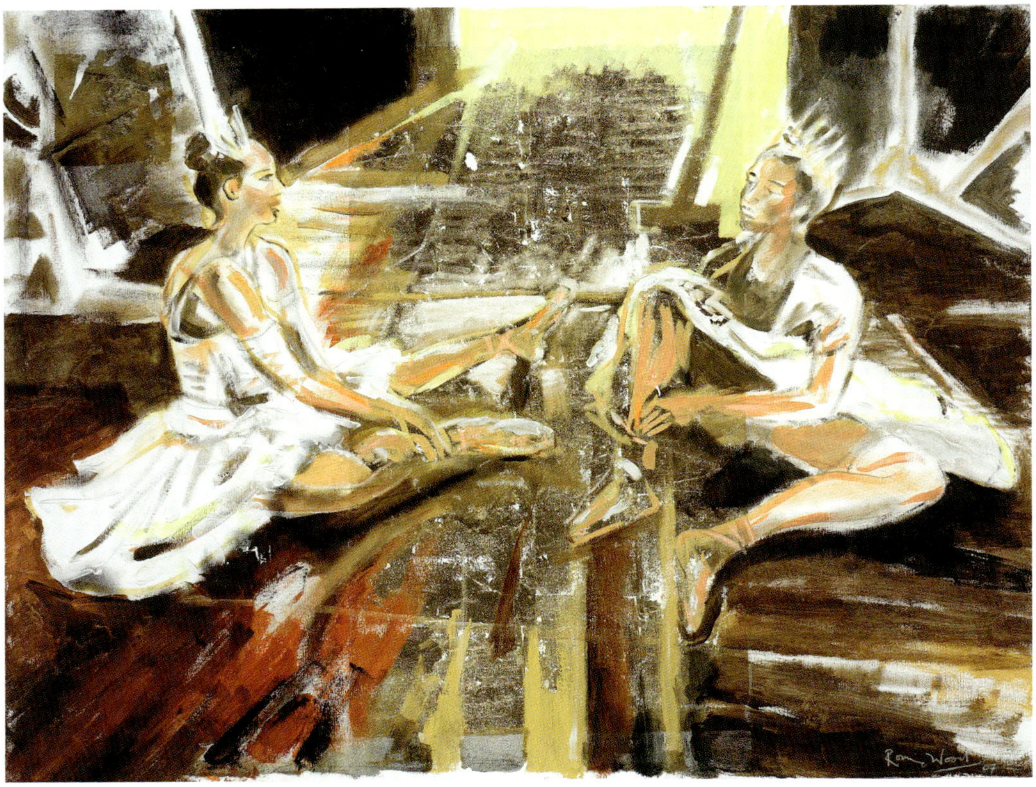

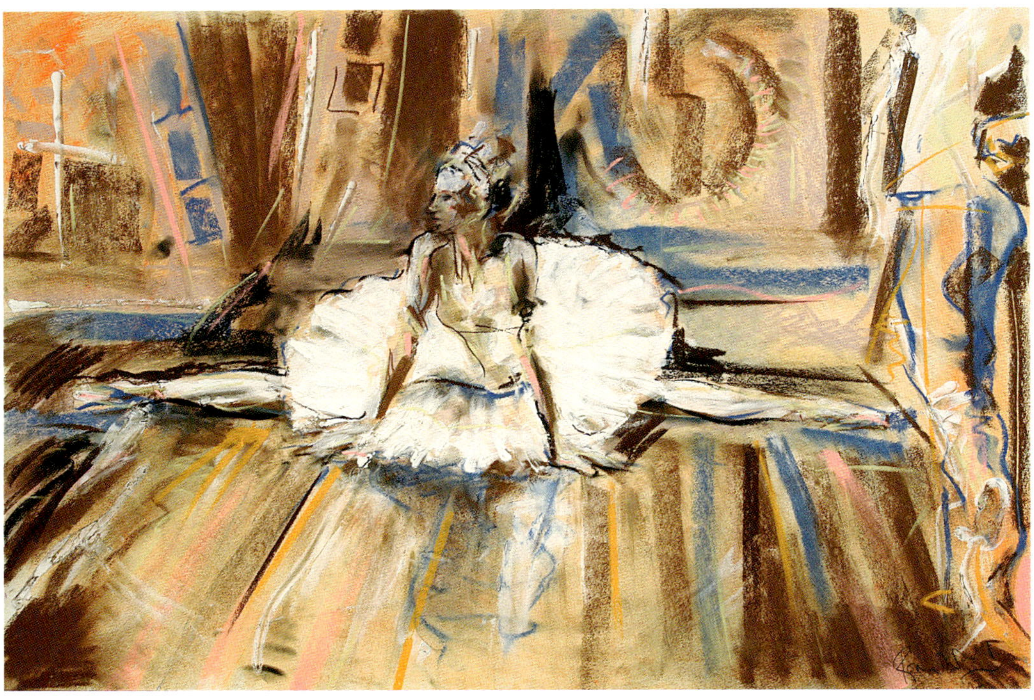

PREVIOUS PAGE: *Tamara & Jonathan, First Day Rehearsal* | 2007 | pen and ink on paper | 48 × 36 cm
TOP: *Study in the Wings* | 2007 | mixed media on paper | 76 × 112 cm
ABOVE: *Tamara* | 2007 | acrylic and pastel on paper | 69 × 104 cm
OPPOSITE: *Triple Bill* | 2007 | acrylic and gold leaf on paper | 122 × 73.5 cm

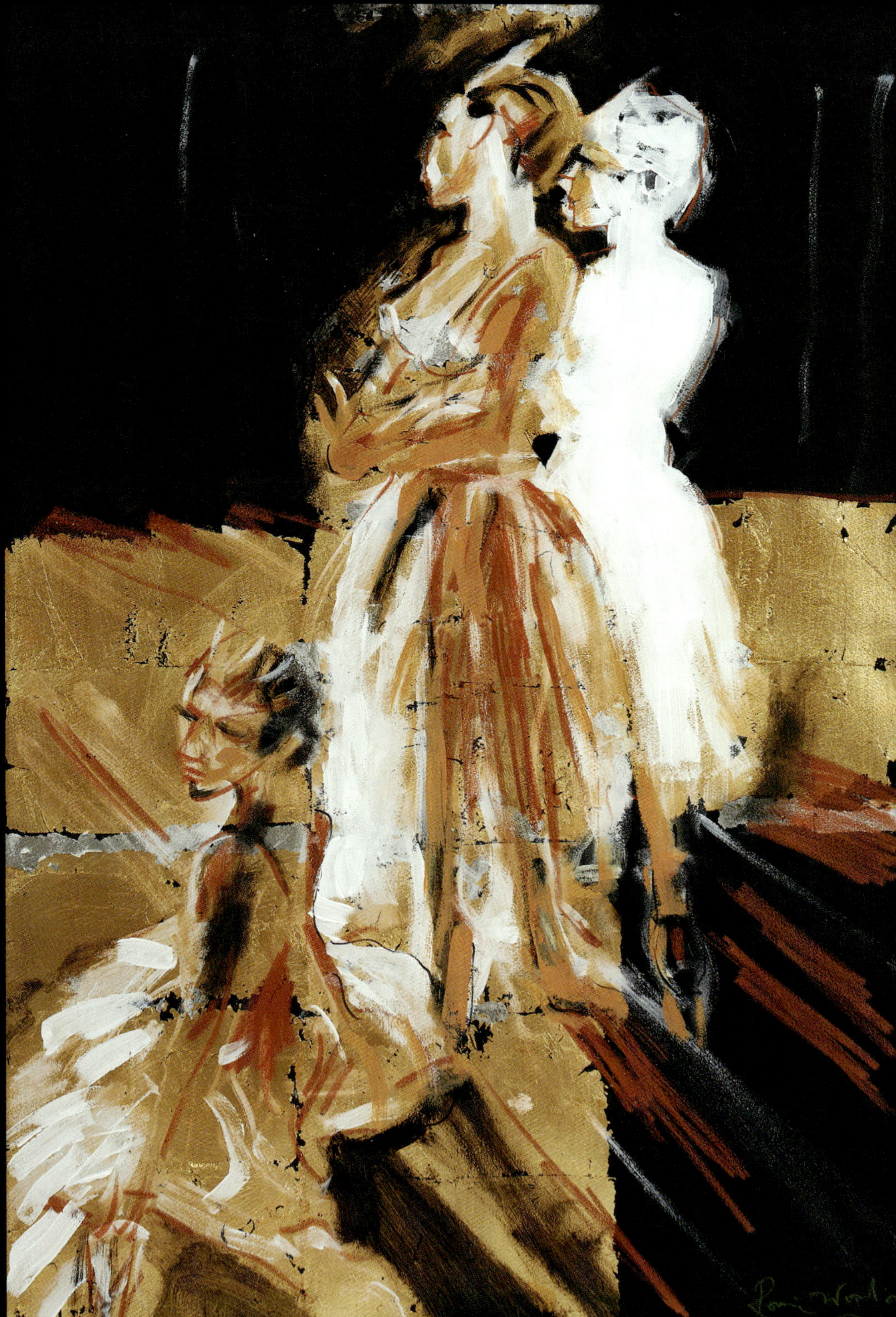

"I was commissioned by ITV's The South Bank Show *to paint the dancers at the Royal Ballet."*

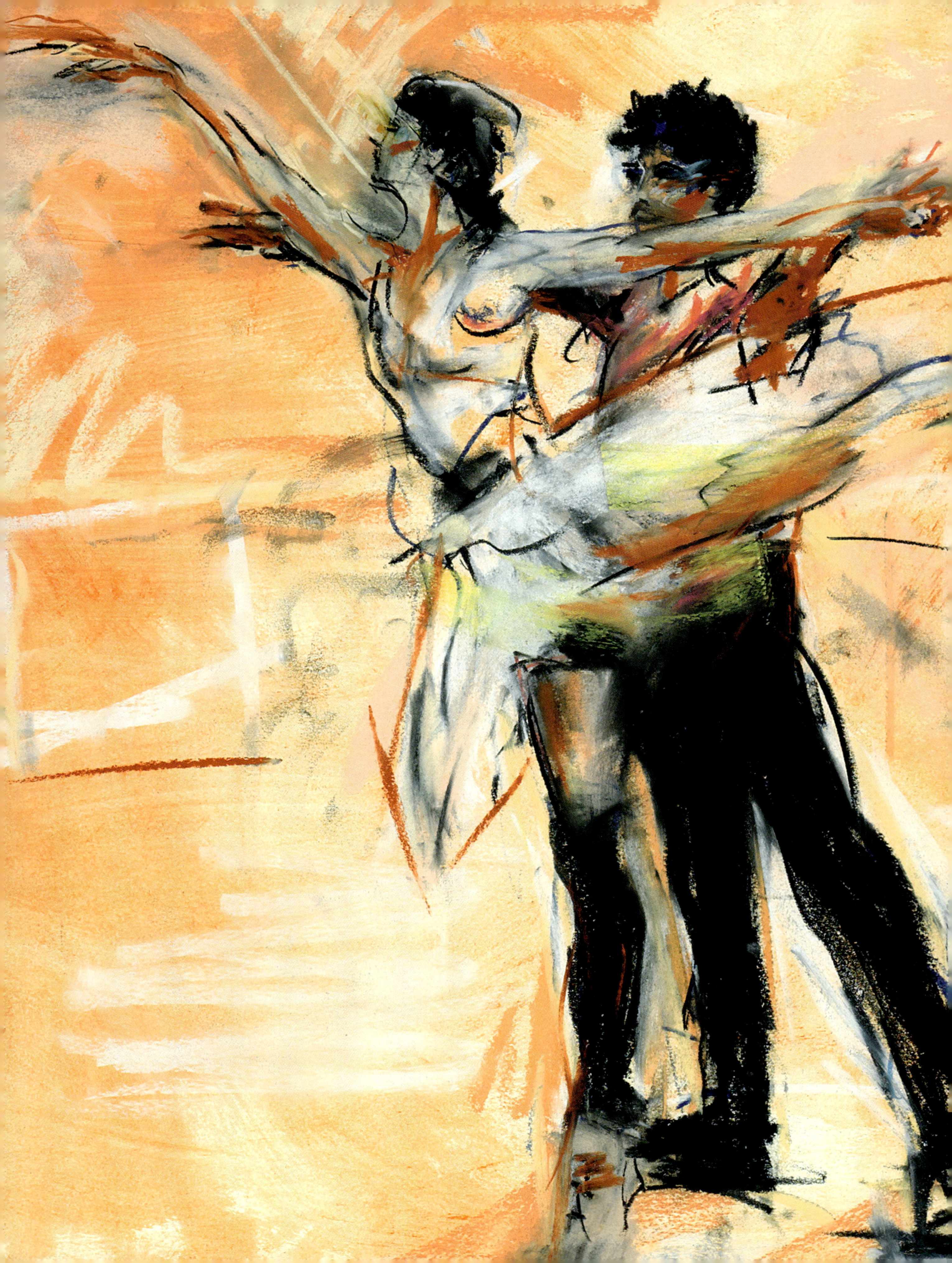

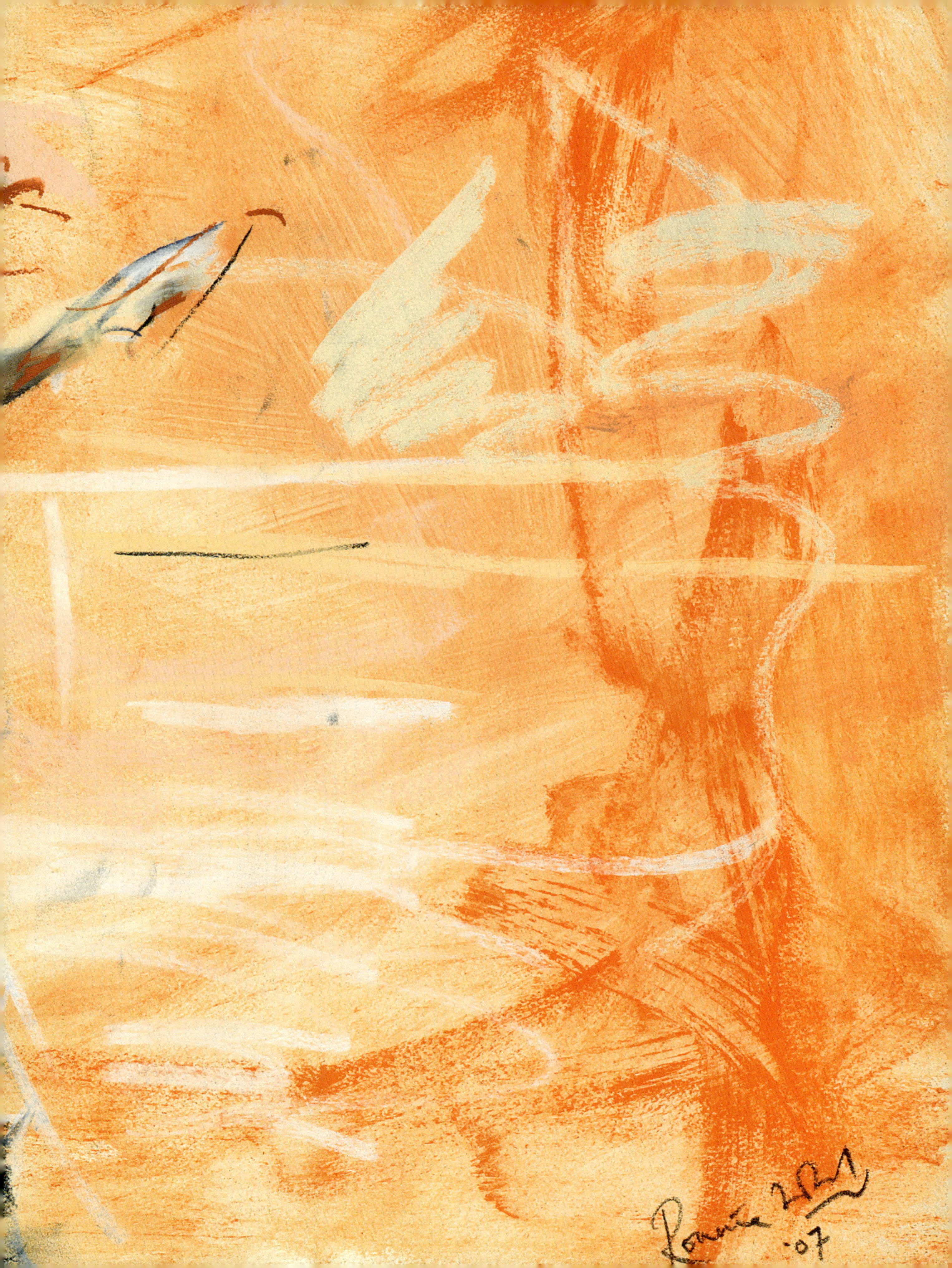

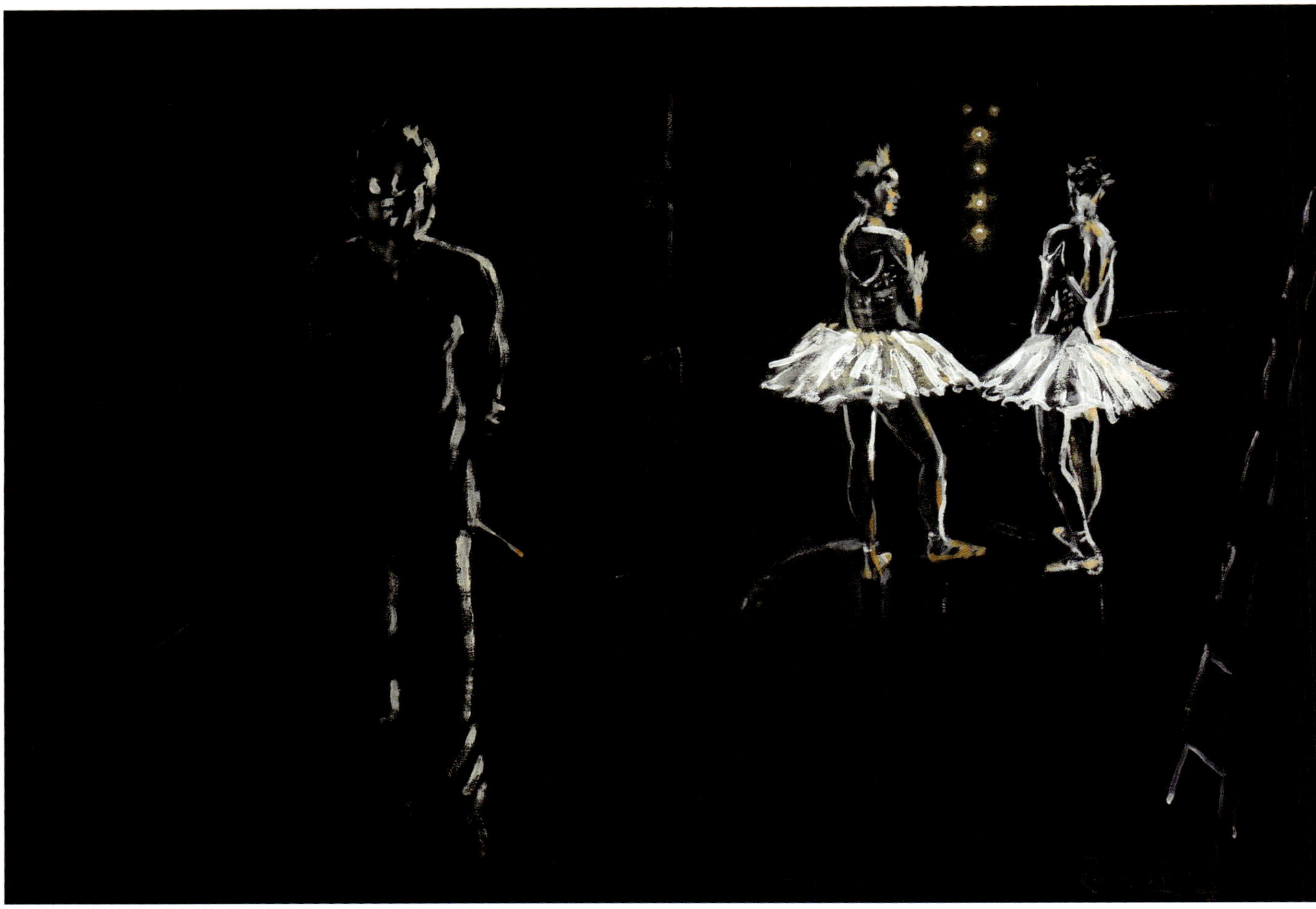

PREVIOUS PAGE: *Darcey Bussell and Carlos Acosta* (detail) | 2007 | acrylic and pastel on paper | 69 × 104 cm
ABOVE: *In the Wings With Brush* | 2007 | mixed media on paper | 56 × 76 cm
OPPOSITE: *Study for Painting III* | 2007 | mixed media on paper | 56 × 76 cm

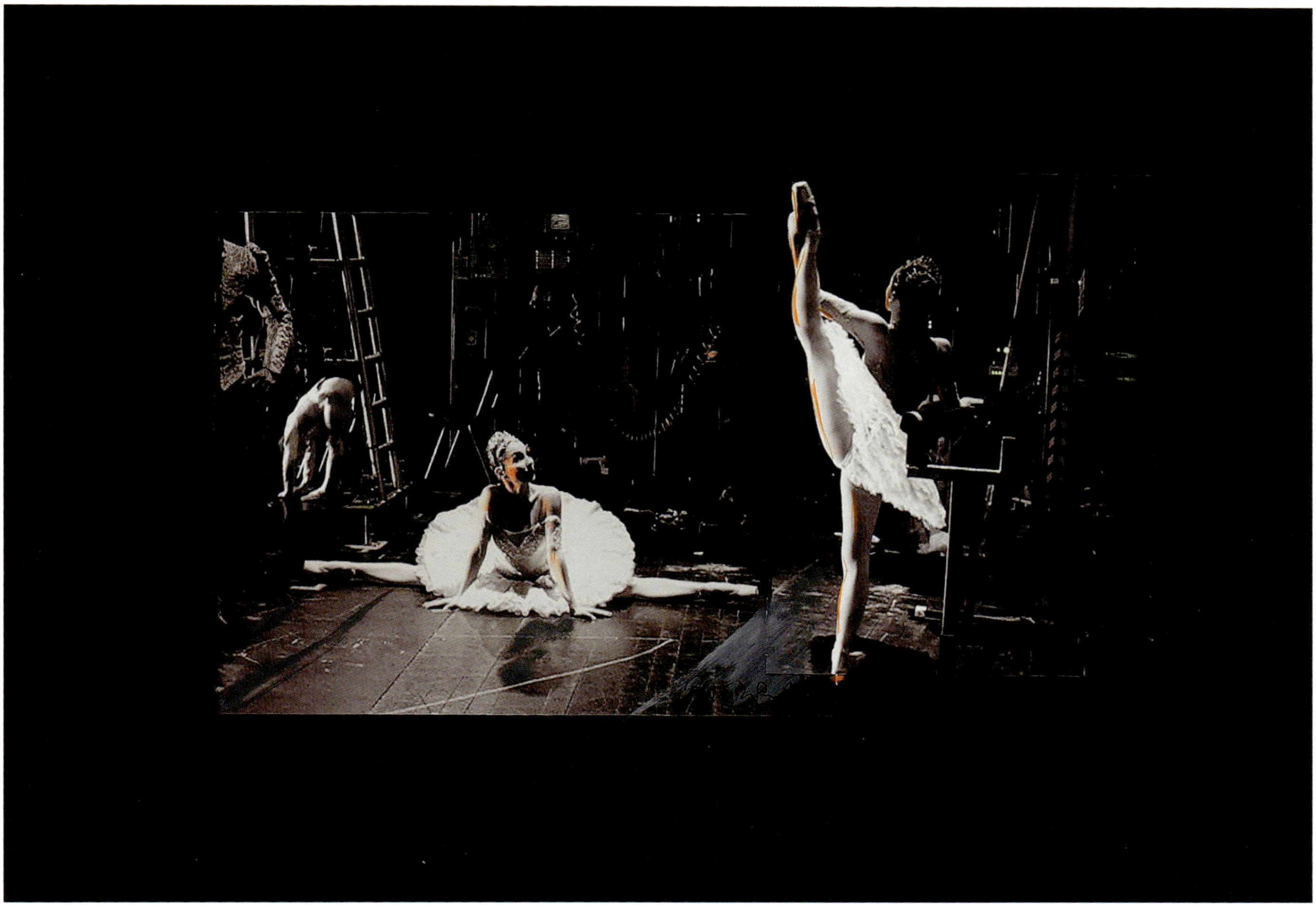

"I used my original photographs, taken from the wings, and then painted on them. So much of what makes these work for me is the light."

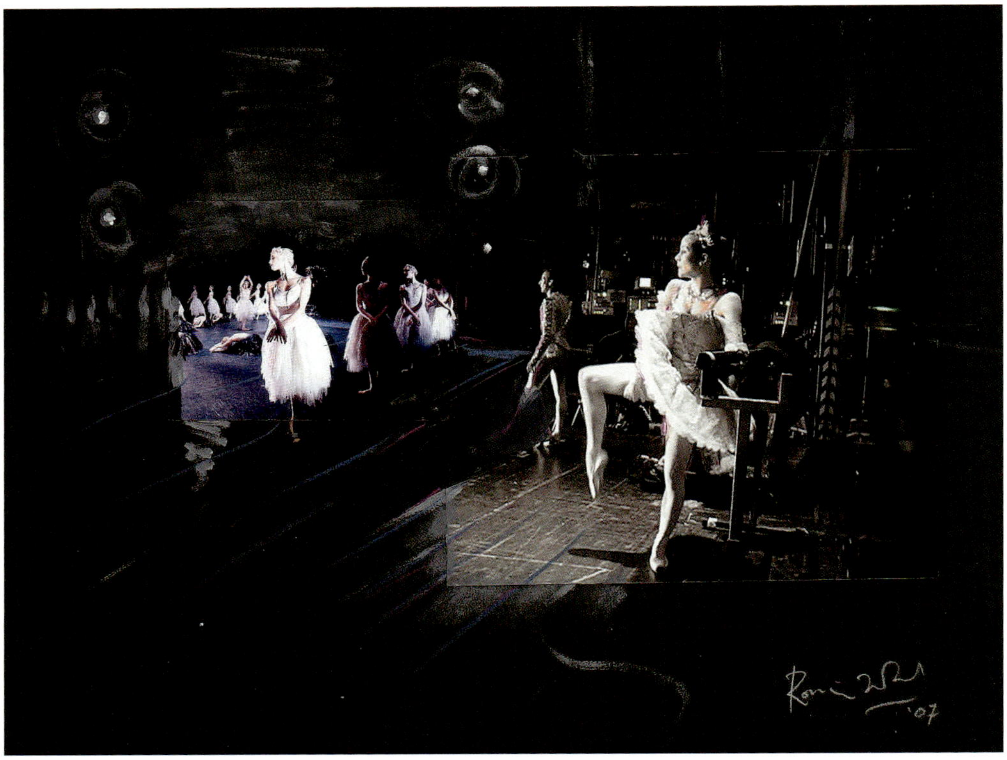

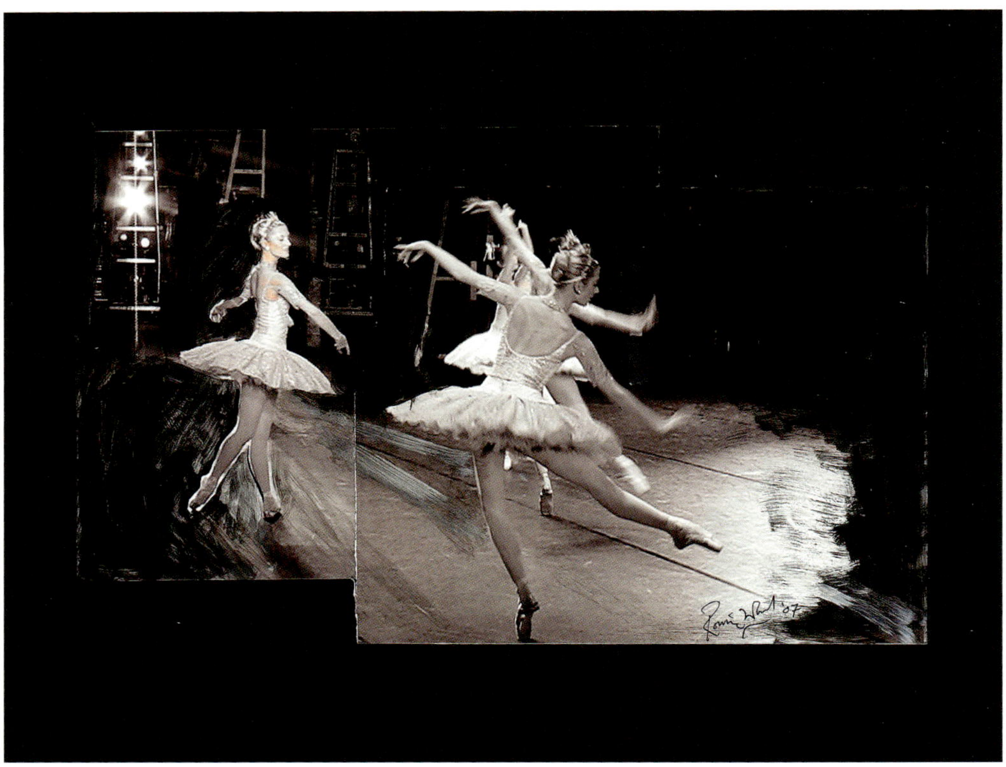

TOP: *Study for Painting I* | 2007 | mixed media on paper | 56 × 76 cm
ABOVE: *Study for Painting IV* | 2007 | mixed media on paper | 56 × 76 cm

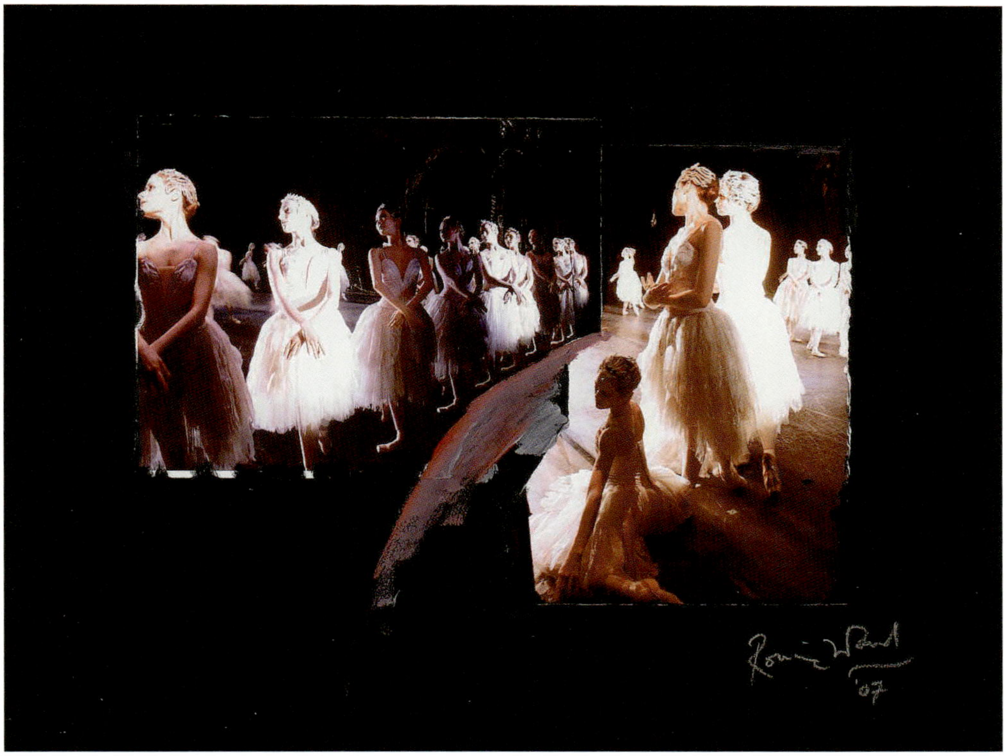

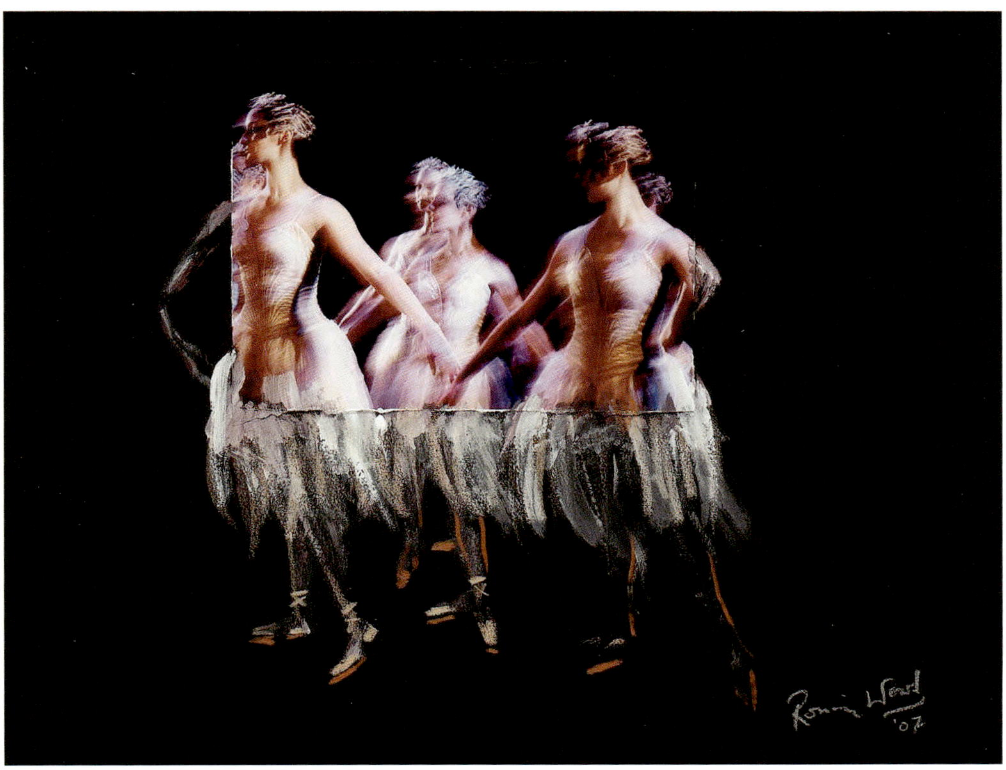

TOP: *Study for Painting II* | 2007 | mixed media on paper | 56 × 76 cm
ABOVE: *Study for Painting V* | 2007 | mixed media on paper | 56 × 76 cm

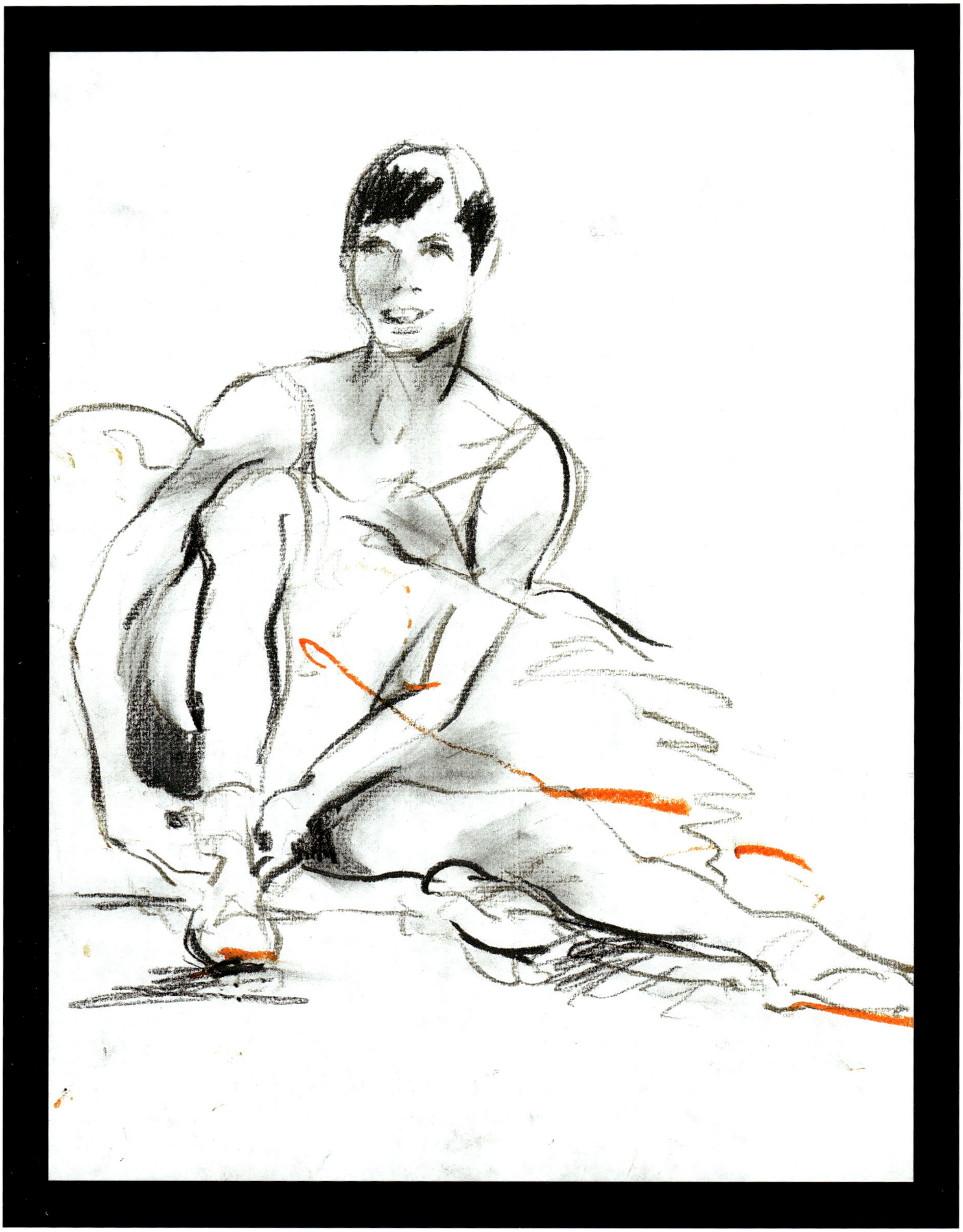

ABOVE: *Darcey – Study II* | 2007 | pencil on paper | 29.5 × 23 cm
OPPOSITE: *Darcey – Study I* | 2007 | pencil on paper | 29.5 × 23 cm

"I did these very quickly – in five minutes – to capture the moment and, in the case of Study I, *the movement as well. Sometimes the moment escapes me, other times I overdo it, but here, I think I've nailed it."*

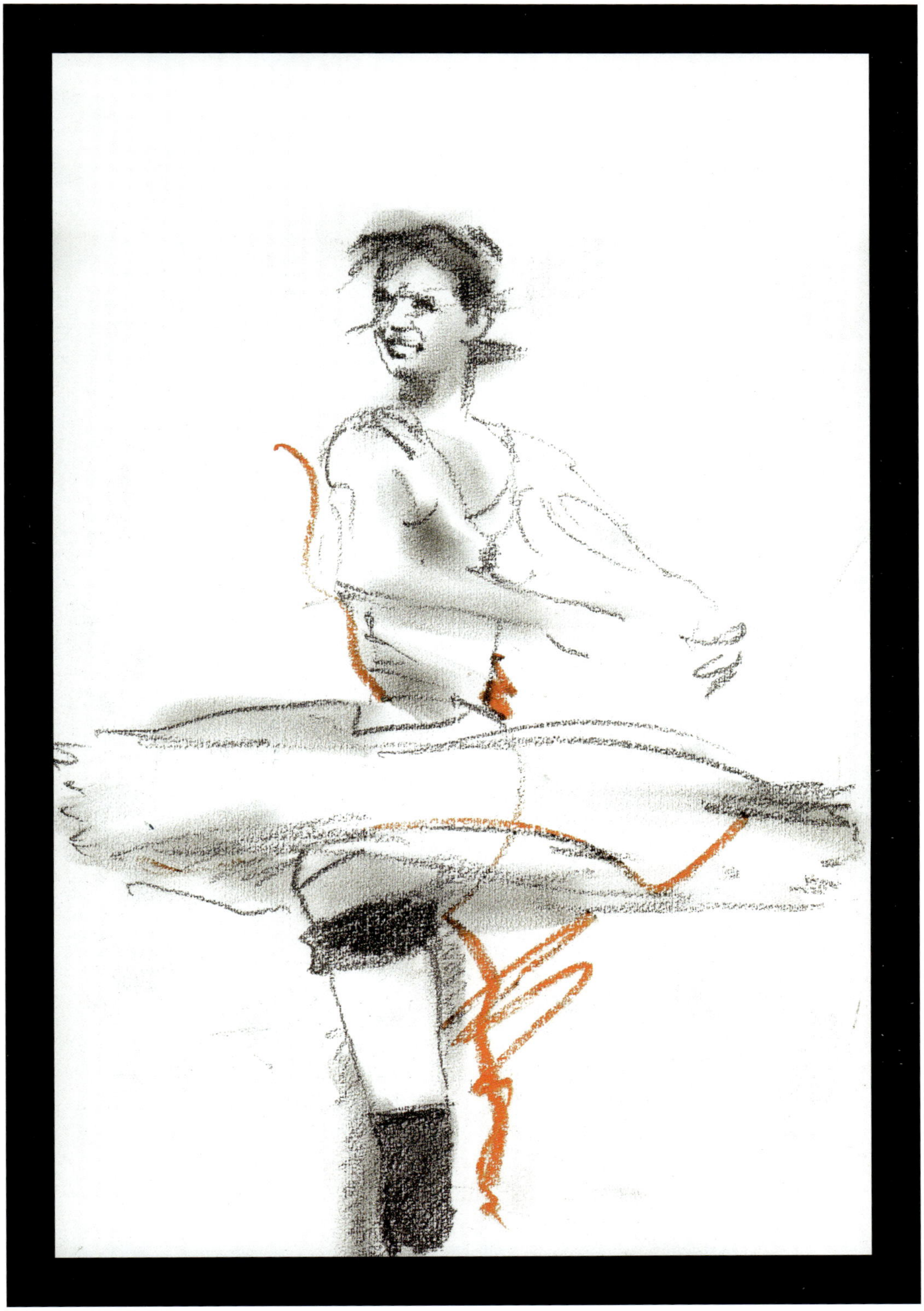

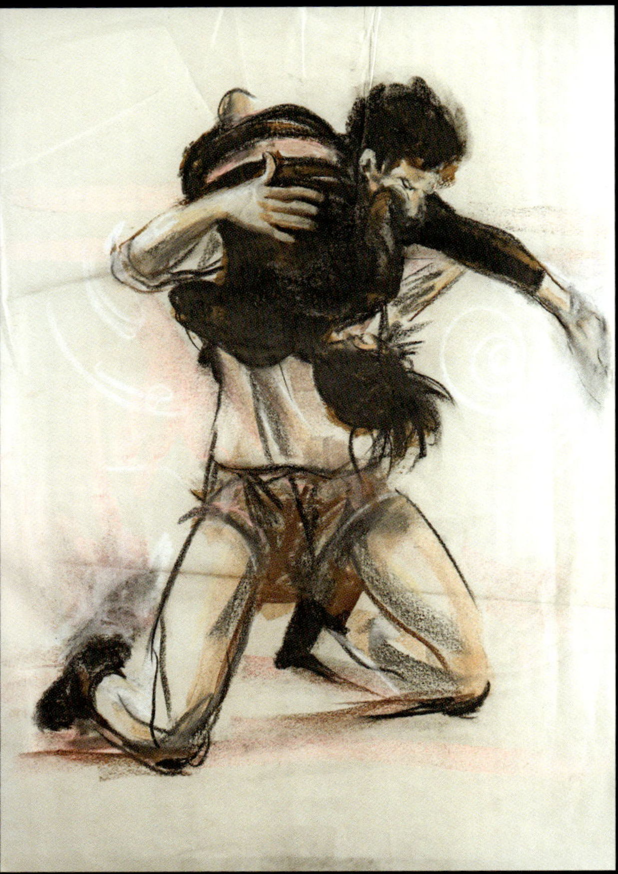
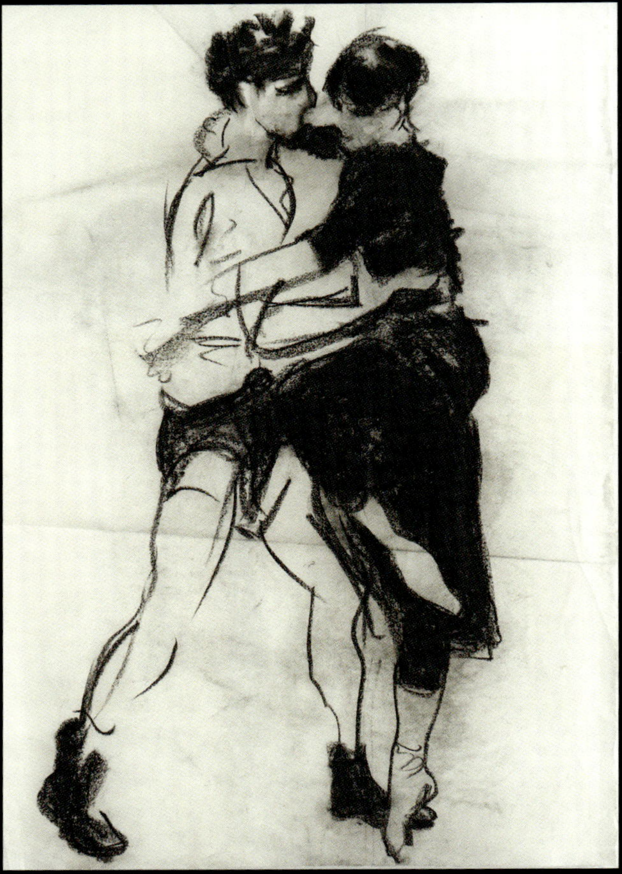
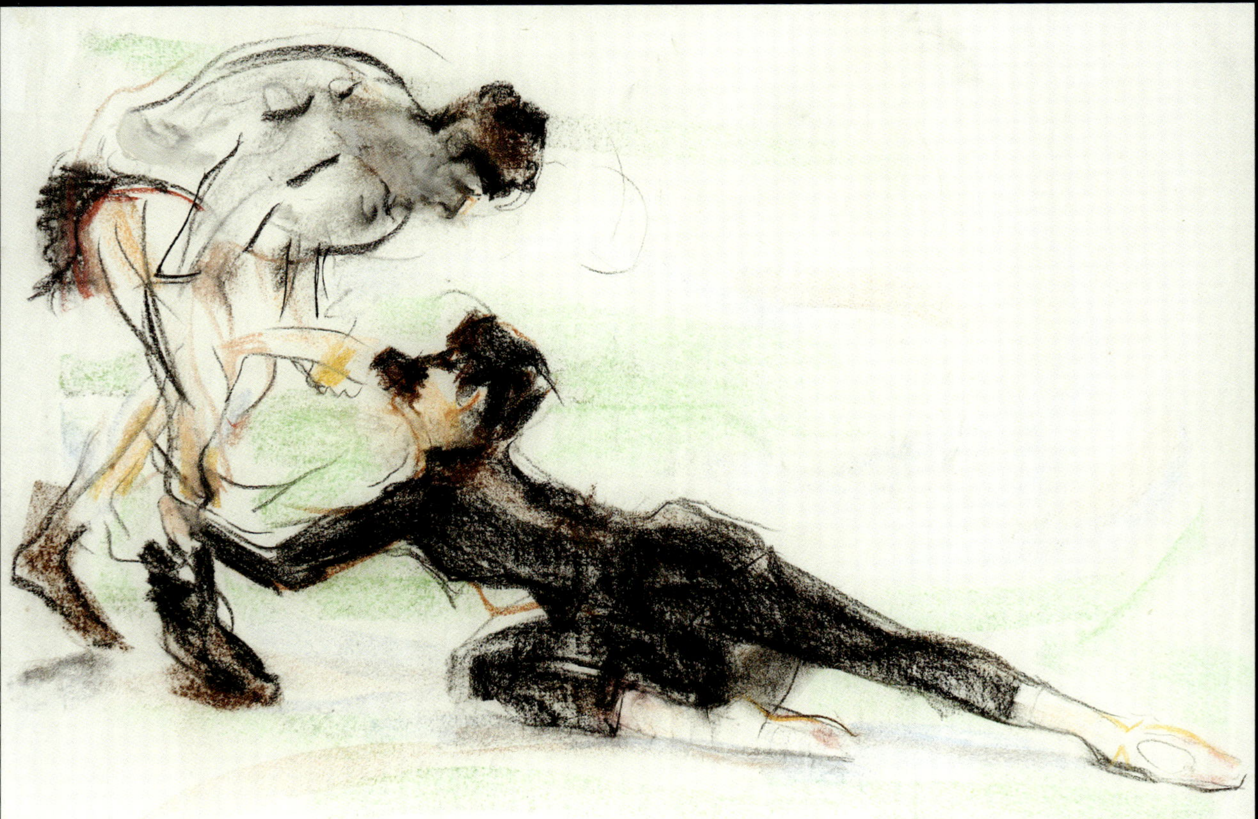

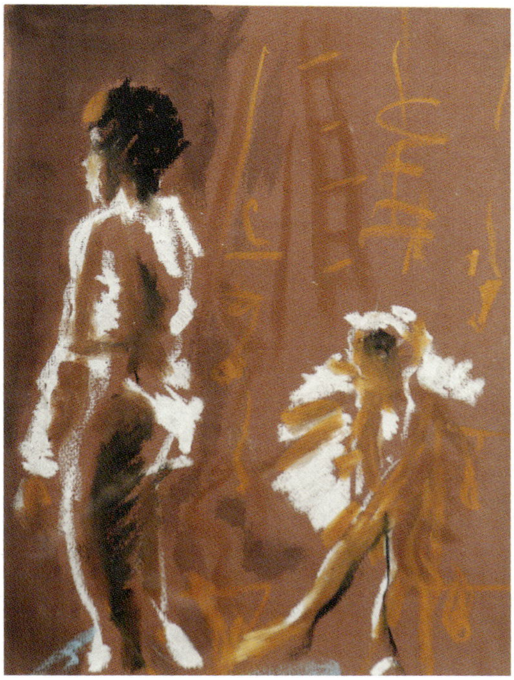

"The great thing about doing ballet is that it is live – the dancers are there and then they are gone. You have to work fast to get it done."

OPPOSITE ABOVE LEFT: *Tamara Rojo & Jonathan Cope II* | 2007 | charcoal on paper | 105 × 73 cm
OPPOSITE ABOVE RIGHT: *Tamara Rojo & Jonathan Cope I* | 2007 | charcoal on paper | 93 × 63 cm
OPPOSITE BELOW: *Tamara Rojo & Jonathan Cope III* | 2007 | charcoal on paper | 93 × 63 cm
LEFT: *Study in the Wings* | 2007 | acrylic and pastel on paper | 30 × 23 cm
BELOW: *Study in the Wings II* | 2007 | acrylic and pastel on paper | 23 × 30 cm

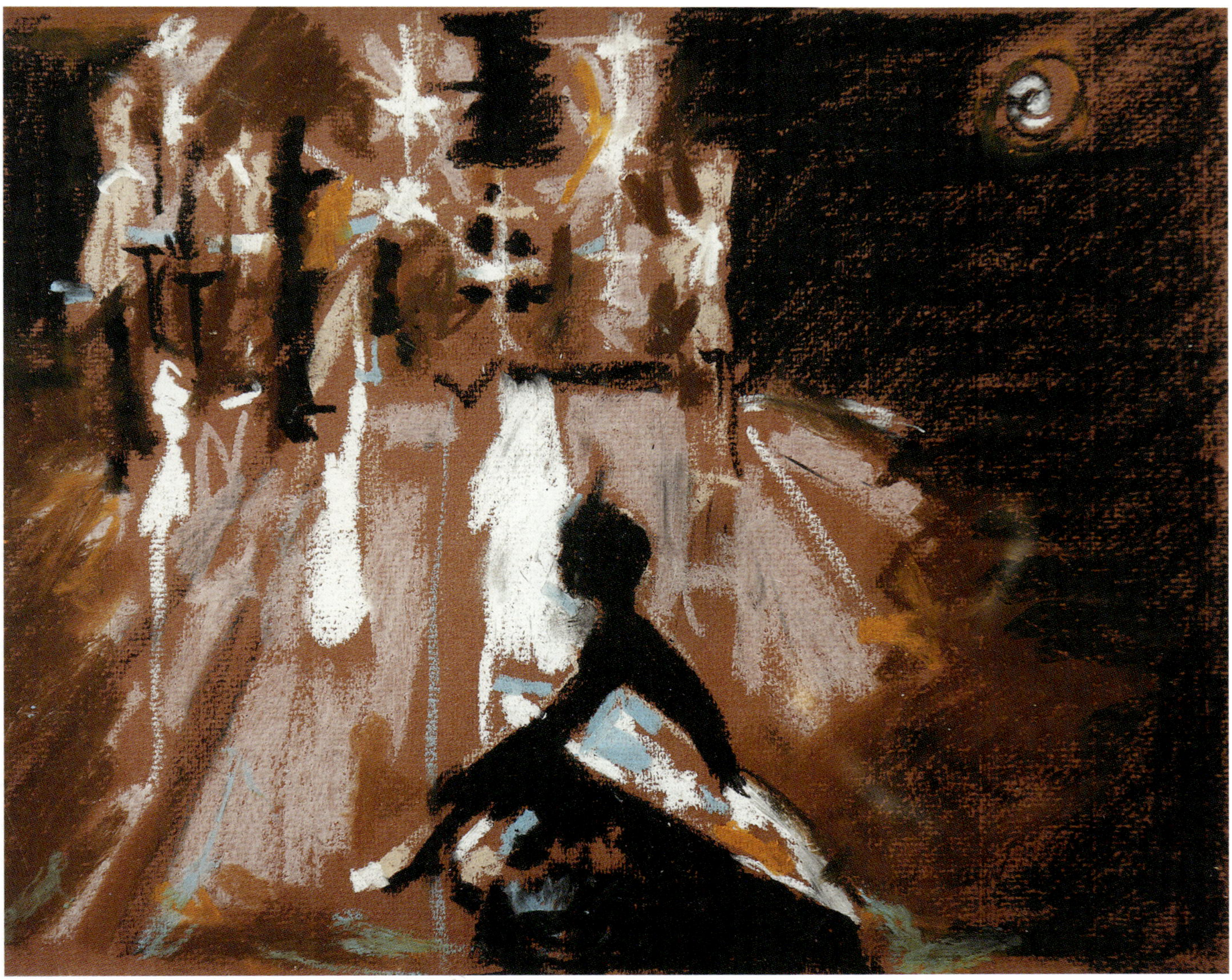

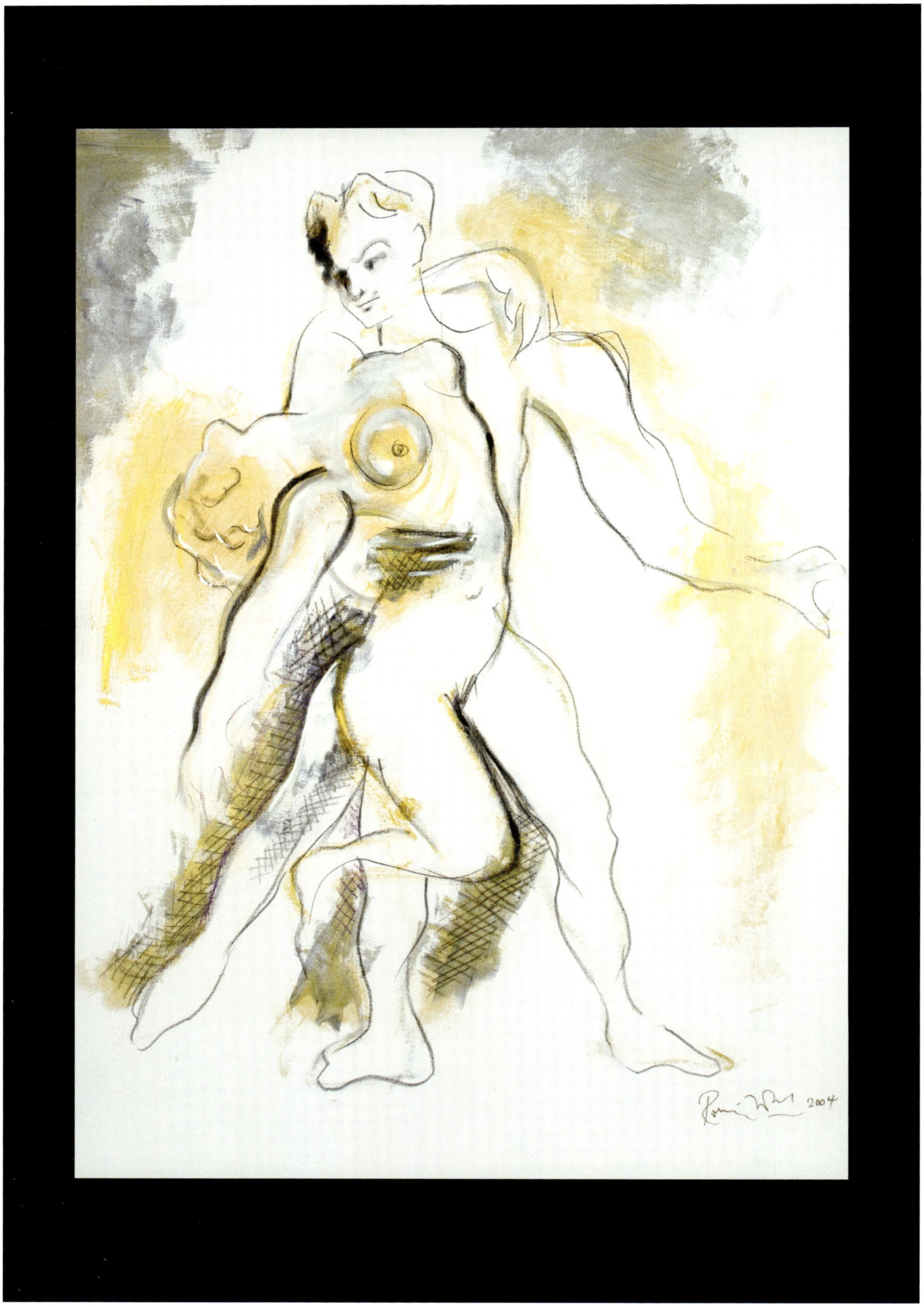
2004

7

NUDES

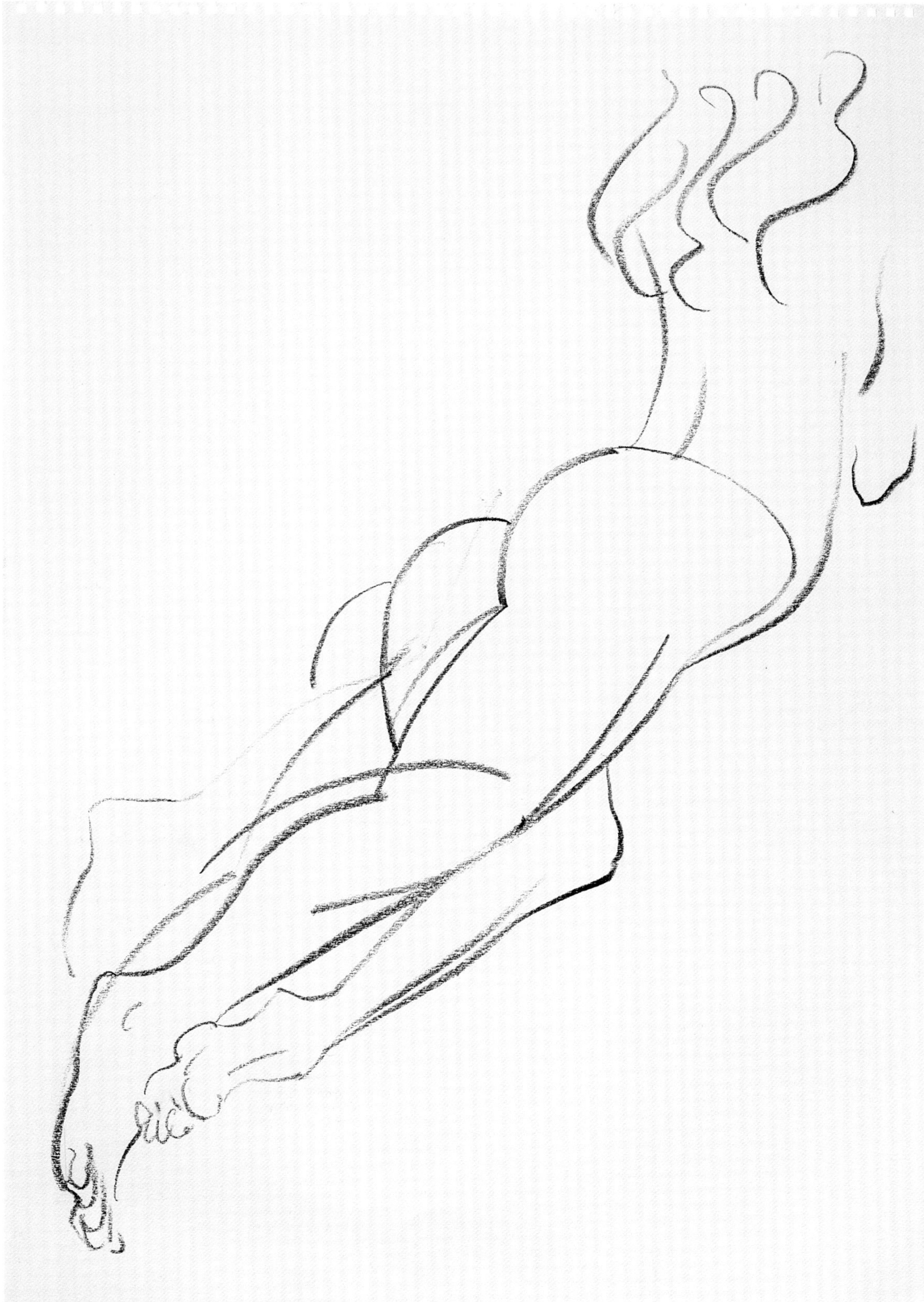

PREVIOUS PAGE: *Picasso Study* | 2004 | charcoal and pastel on paper | 152.5 × 122 cm
ABOVE: *The Bum* | 2009 | charcoal on paper | 58 × 41.5 cm
OPPOSITE: *Nude Study (Phone Art)* | 2009 | mixed media on canvas | 152 × 101 cm

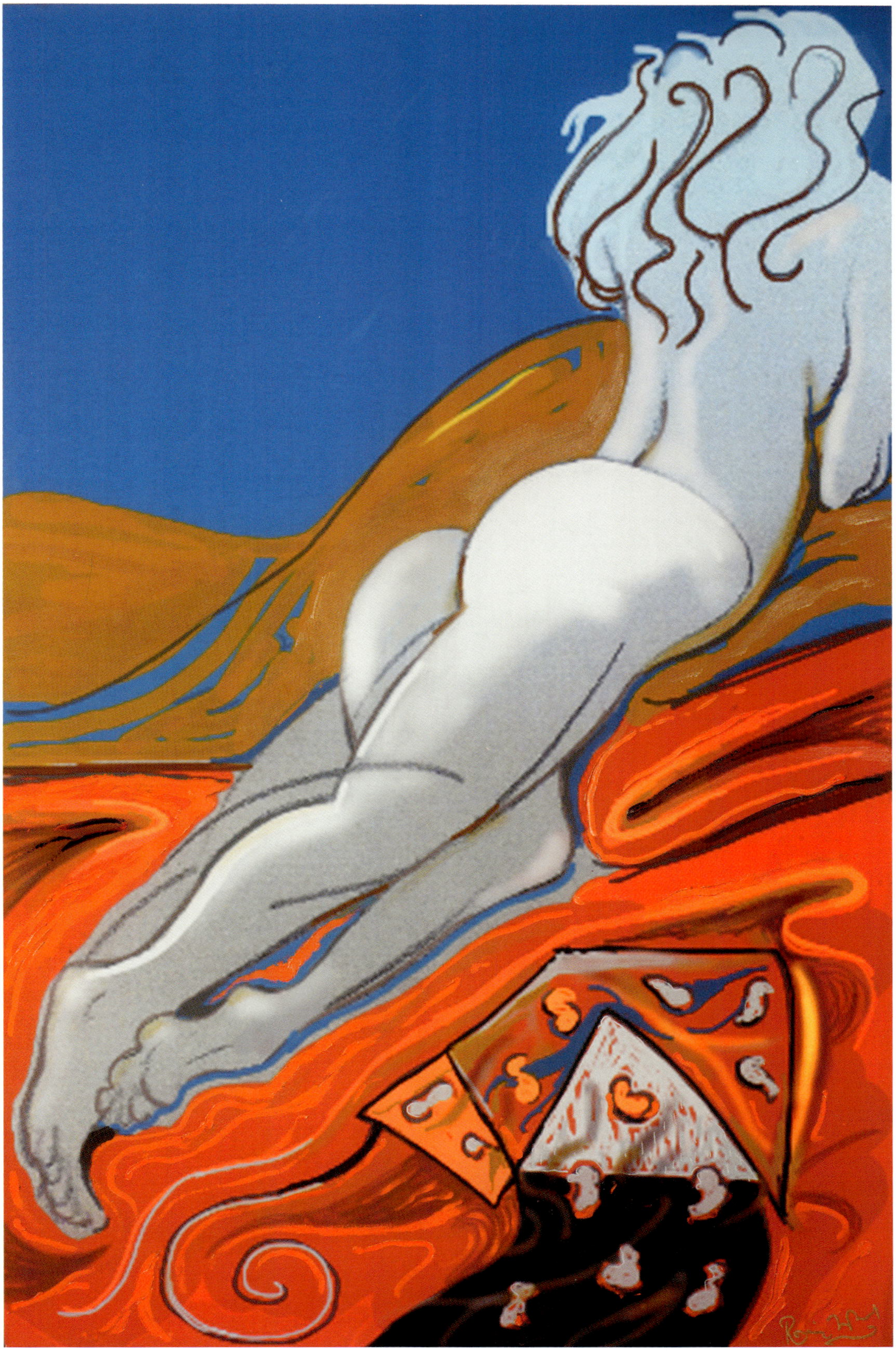

"I did a series of nudes that started as line drawings. I made this one into phone art and then into a painting; I've also had it made into a rug!"

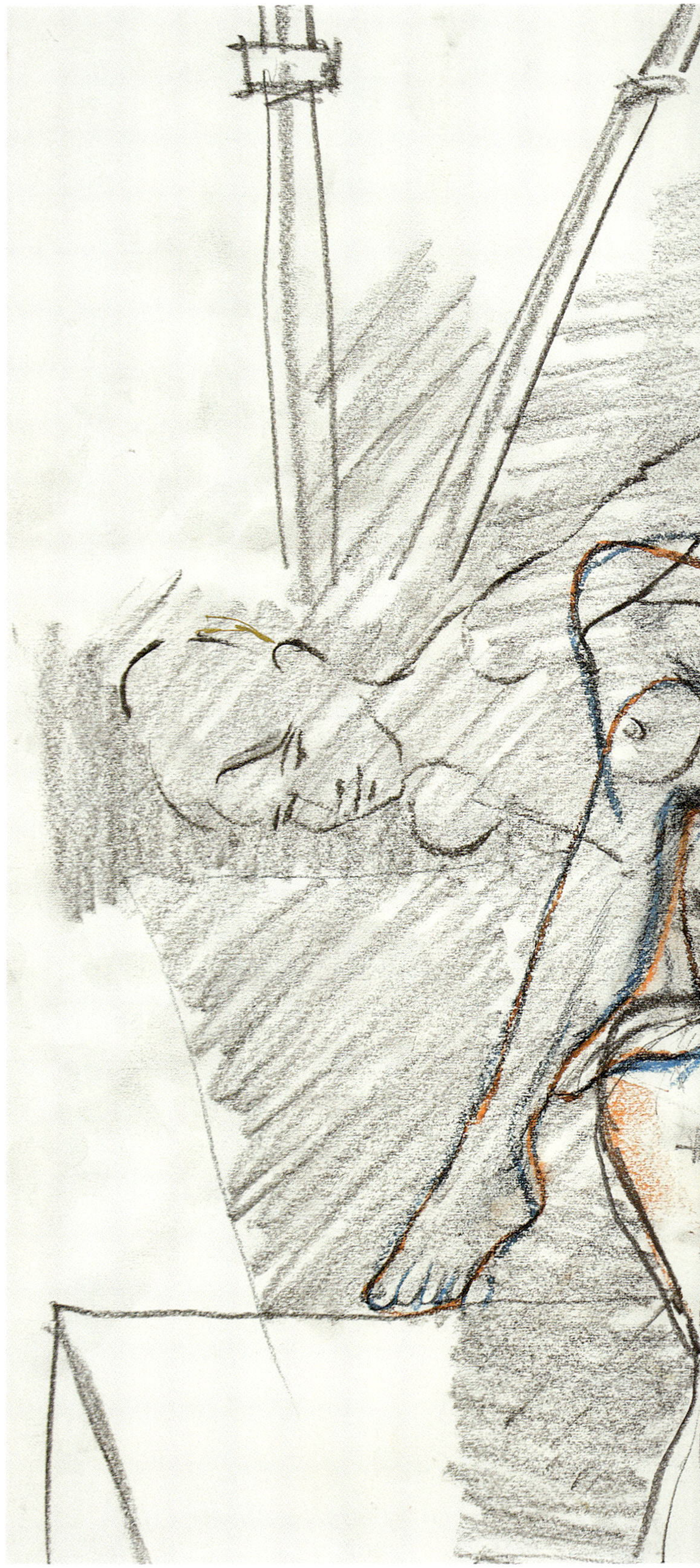

"Artist Maurice Cockrill, the Keeper of the Royal Academy Schools, invited me to sit in on classes, which is where I made this study. He asked me to help some of the students and I ended up buying some of their works of art!"

RIGHT: *Nude Study IV* | 2008 | mixed media on paper | 60 × 84 cm

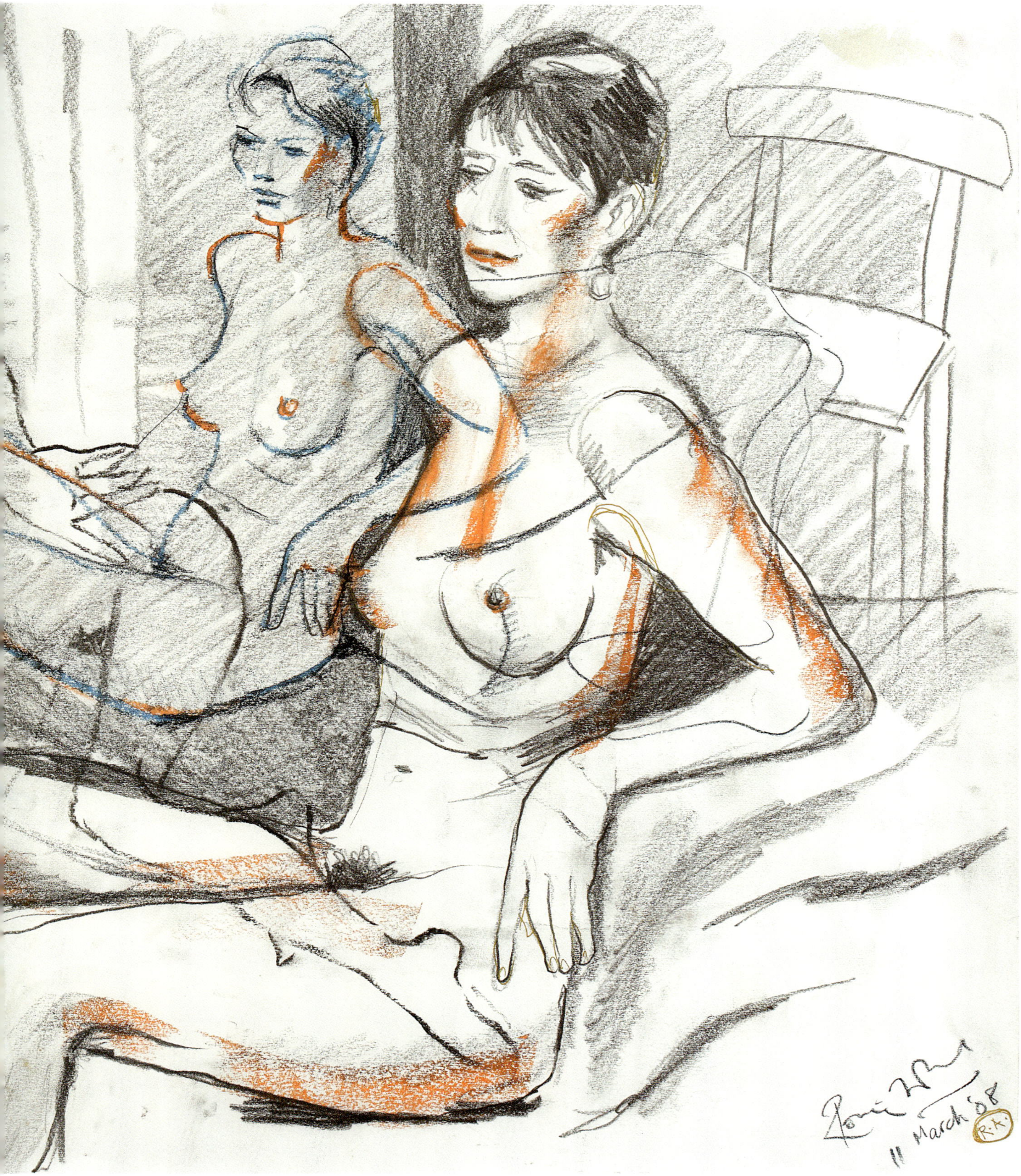
11 March '08
R.A.

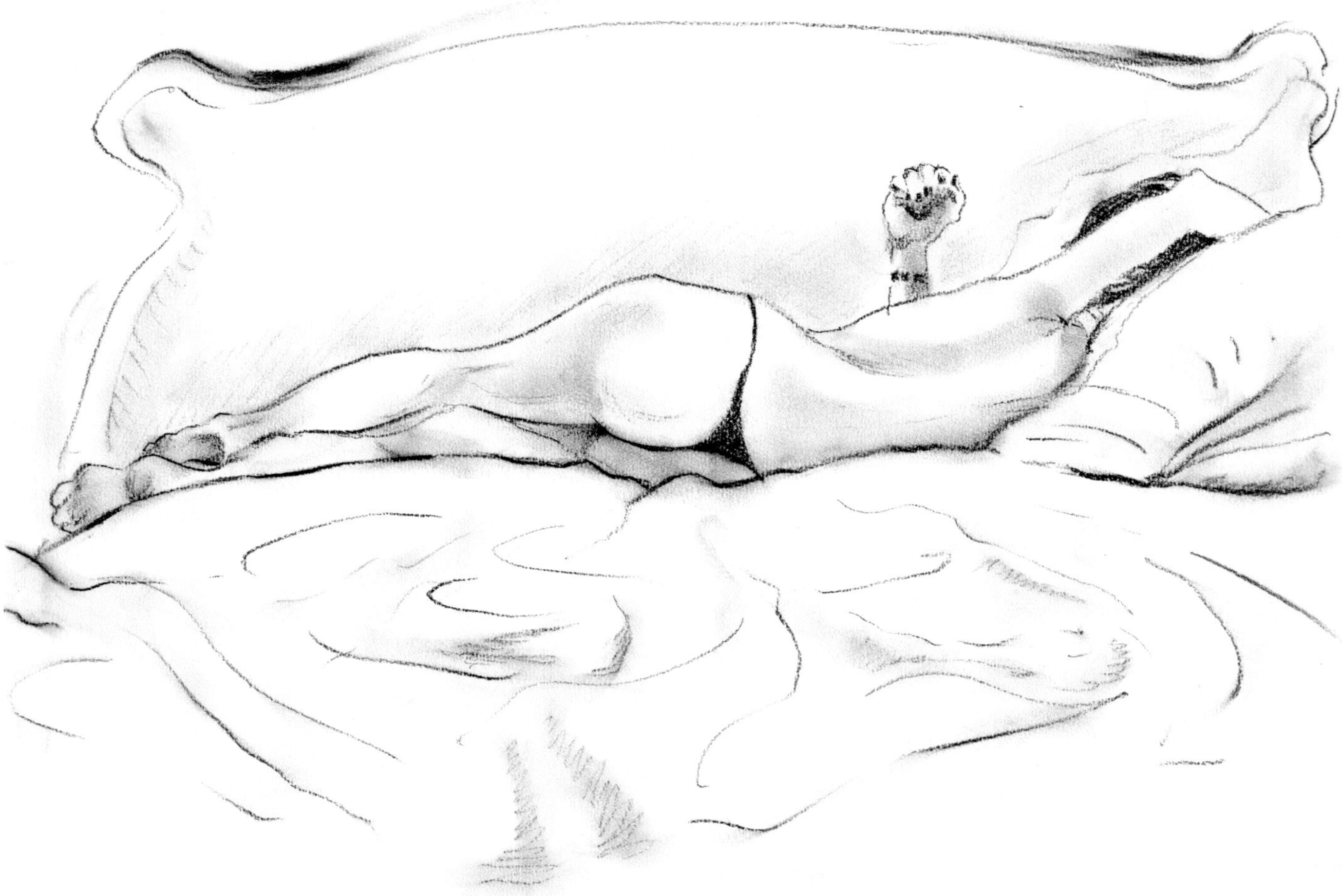

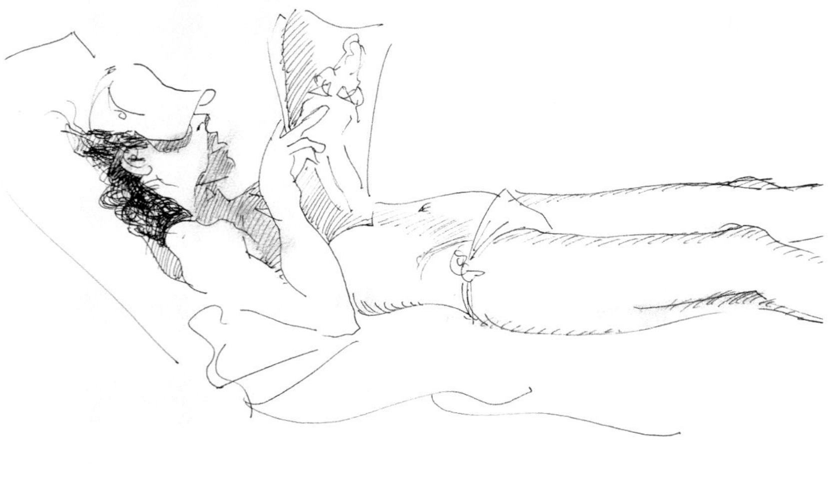

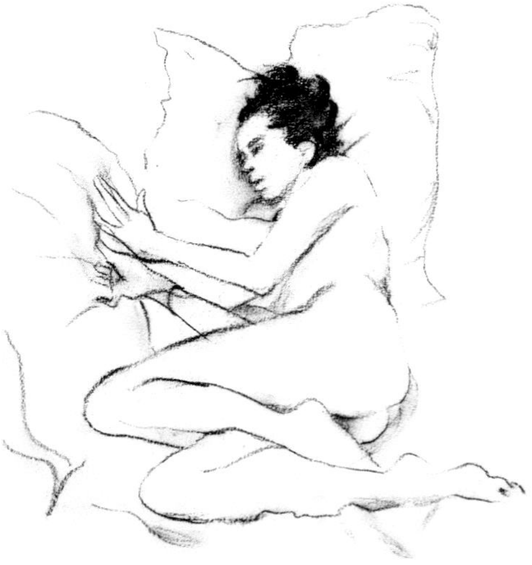

TOP: *Sally V* | 2016 | charcoal and pencil on paper | 30 × 42 cm
ABOVE LEFT: *Sally III* | 2016 | pen and ink on paper | 21 × 30 cm
ABOVE RIGHT: *Sally IV* | 2016 | charcoal and pencil on paper | 42 × 30 cm
OPPOSITE: *Nude Study* | 2005 | charcoal and pastel on paper | 50× 37 cm

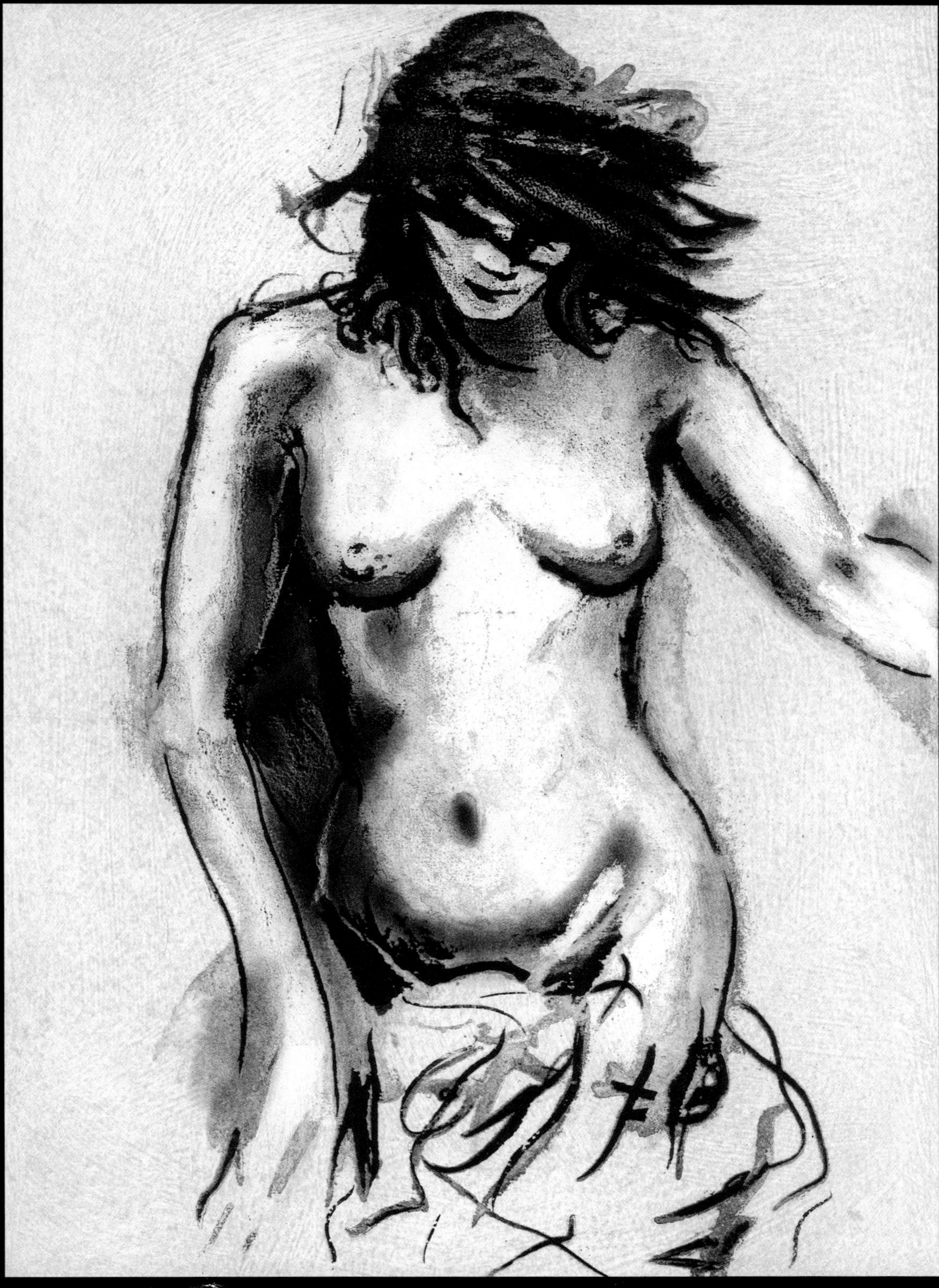

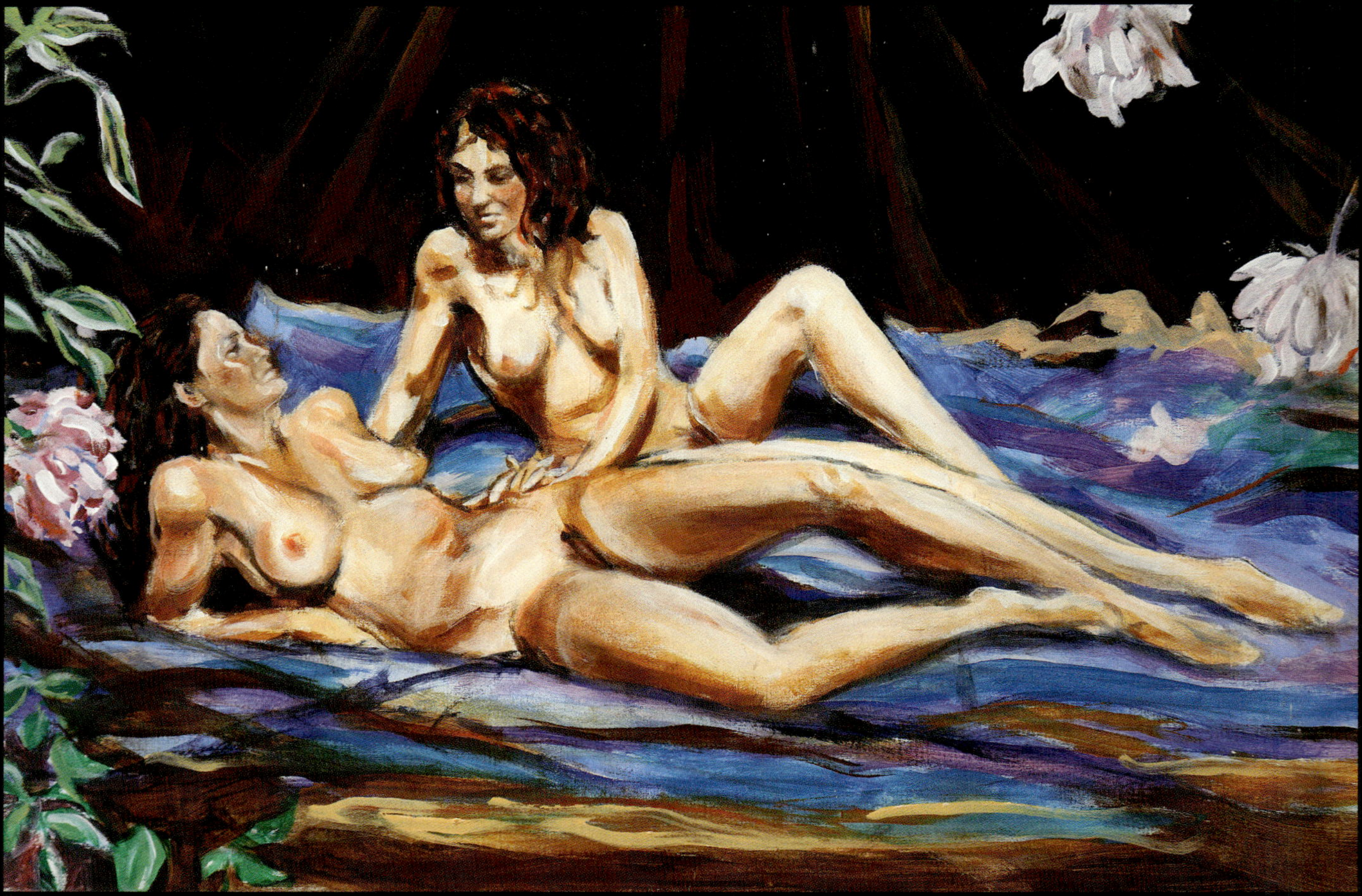

"Two Reclining Nudes was painted in my studio in Ireland and I coloured it to give the figures a more exotic feel. I was probably subconsciously paying tribute to Gauguin and his Tahitian paintings."

ABOVE: *Two Reclining Nudes* | 2004 | oil on canvas | 61 × 91.5 cm
OPPOSITE ABOVE LEFT: *Study in Movement 1* | *c.* 1995 | pencil on paper | 30 × 21 cm
OPPOSITE ABOVE RIGHT: *Study in Movement 2* | *c.* 1995 | pencil on paper | 30 × 21 cm
OPPOSITE BELOW: *Study in Movement 3* | *c.* 1995 | pencil on paper | 29 × 42 cm

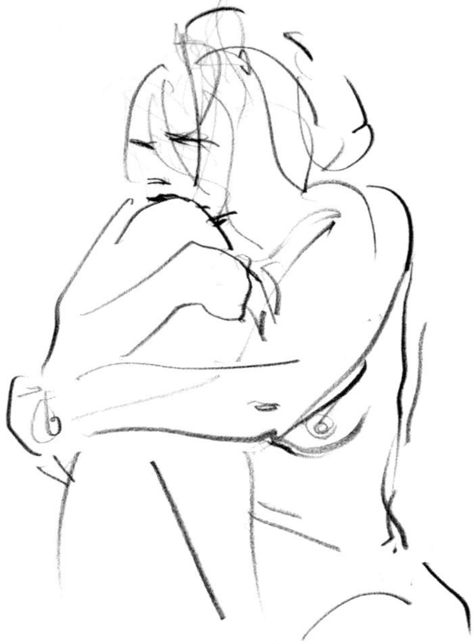

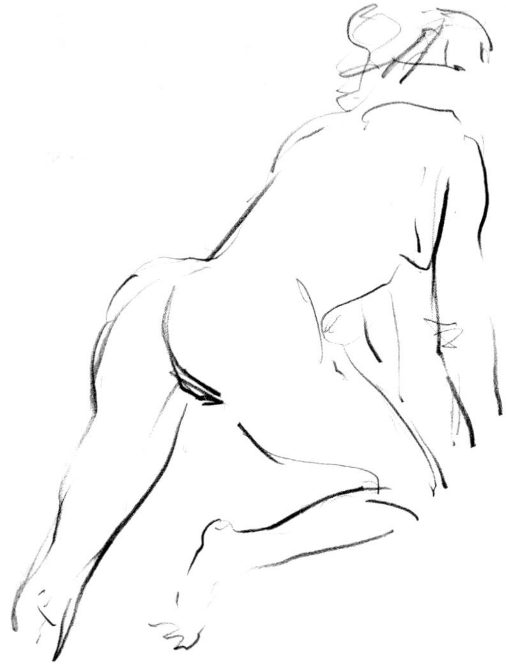

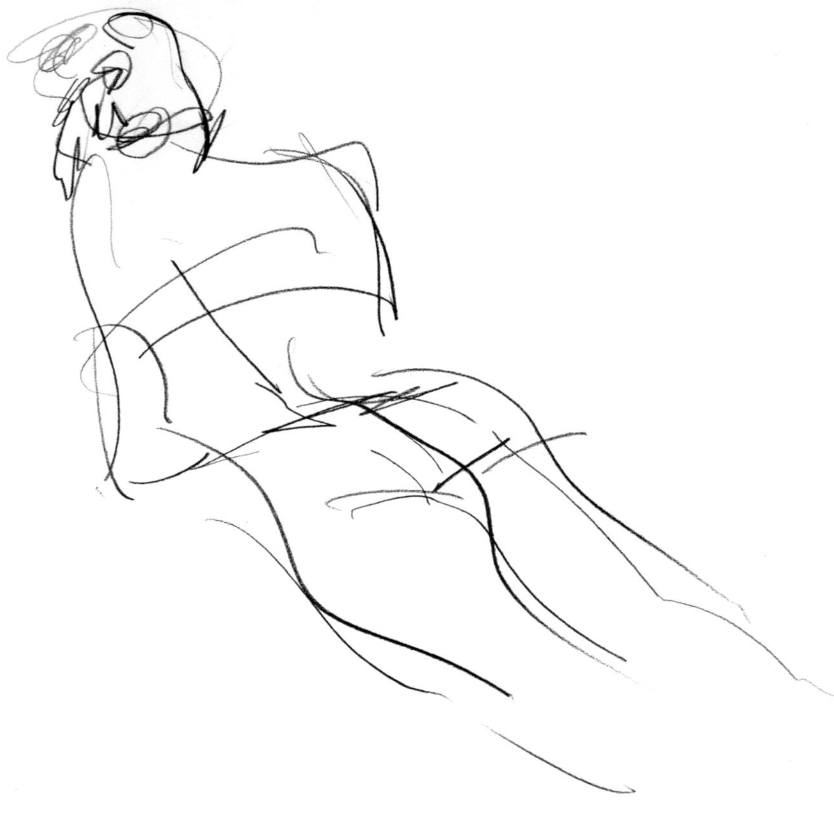

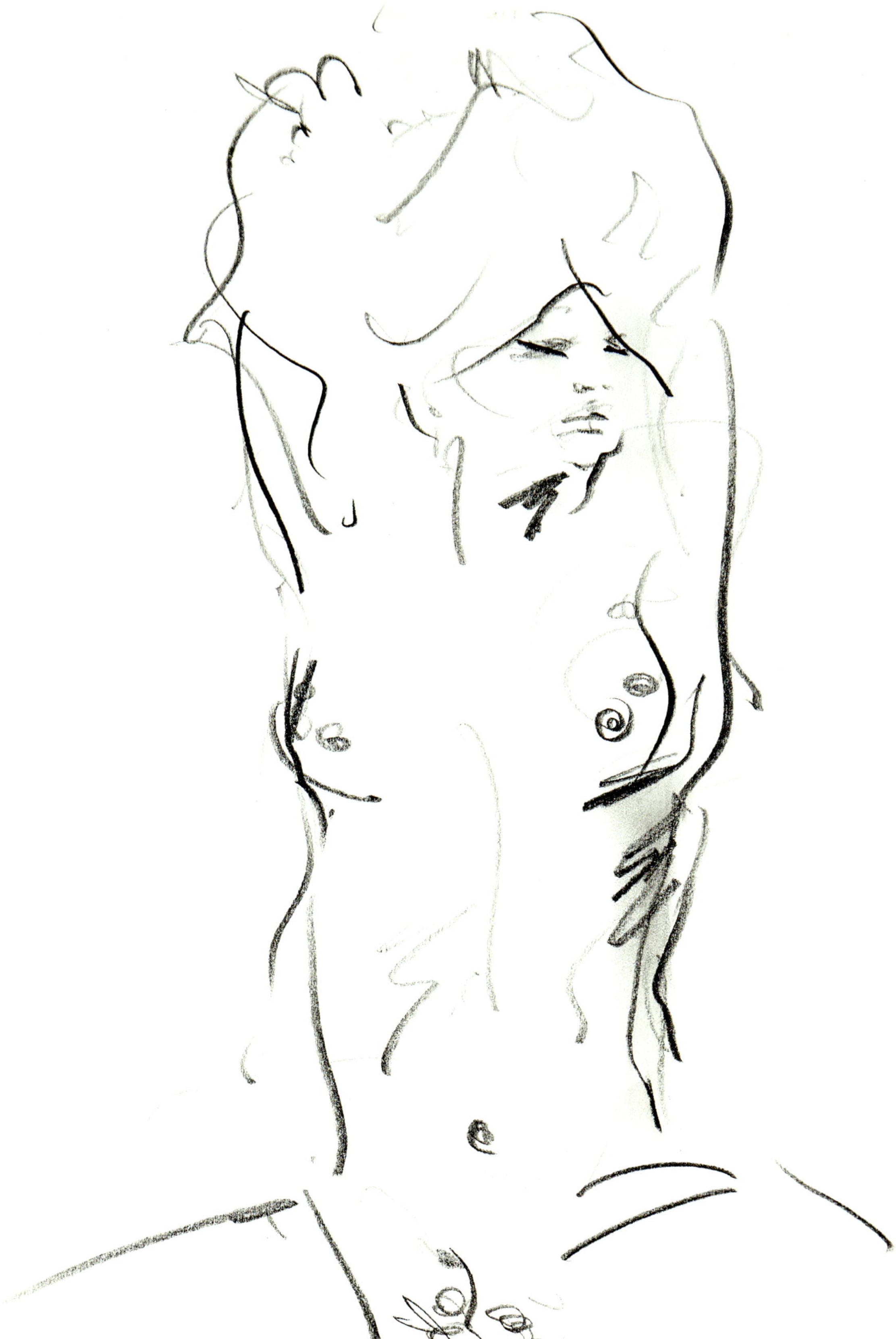

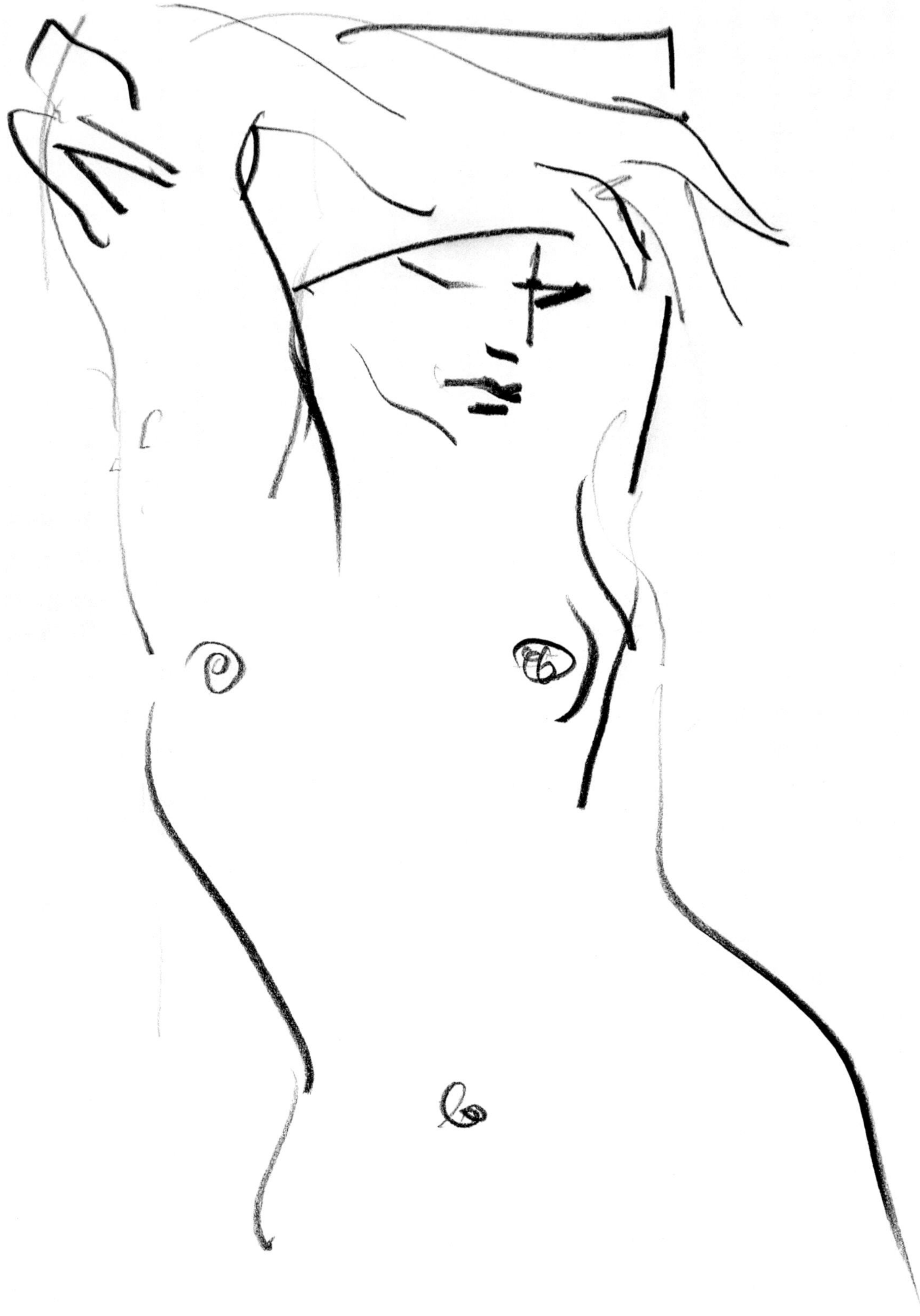

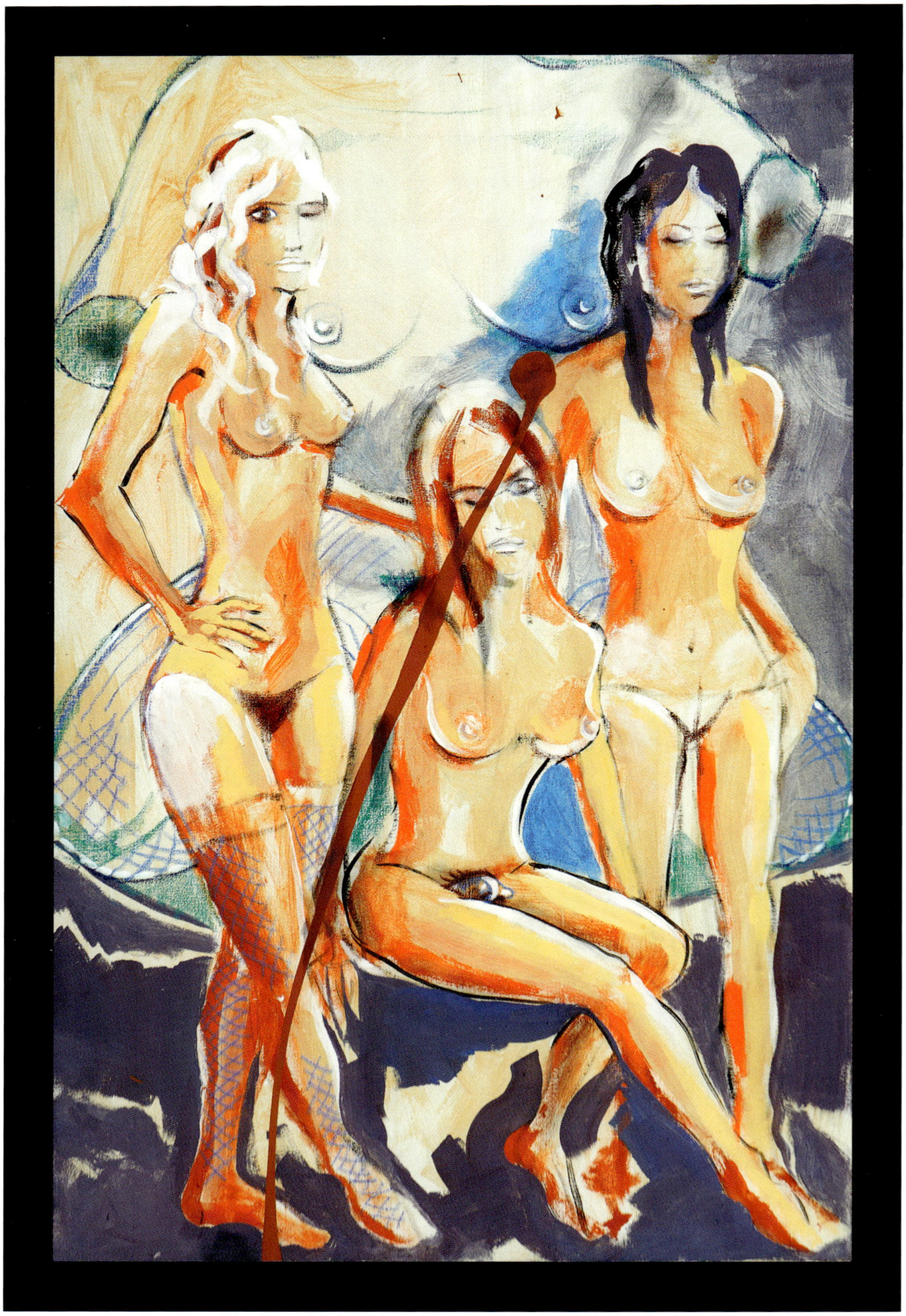

PREVIOUS PAGE LEFT: *Pencil Study II* | 2005 | pencil on paper | 30 × 21 cm
PREVIOUS PAGE RIGHT: *Pencil Study* | 2005 | pencil on paper | 30 × 21 cm
ABOVE: *Three Nudes in Vegas* | 2005–06 | oil on canvas | 90 × 61 cm
OPPOSITE: *Two Nudes in Hampstead* | 2010 | oil on canvas | 76 × 46 cm

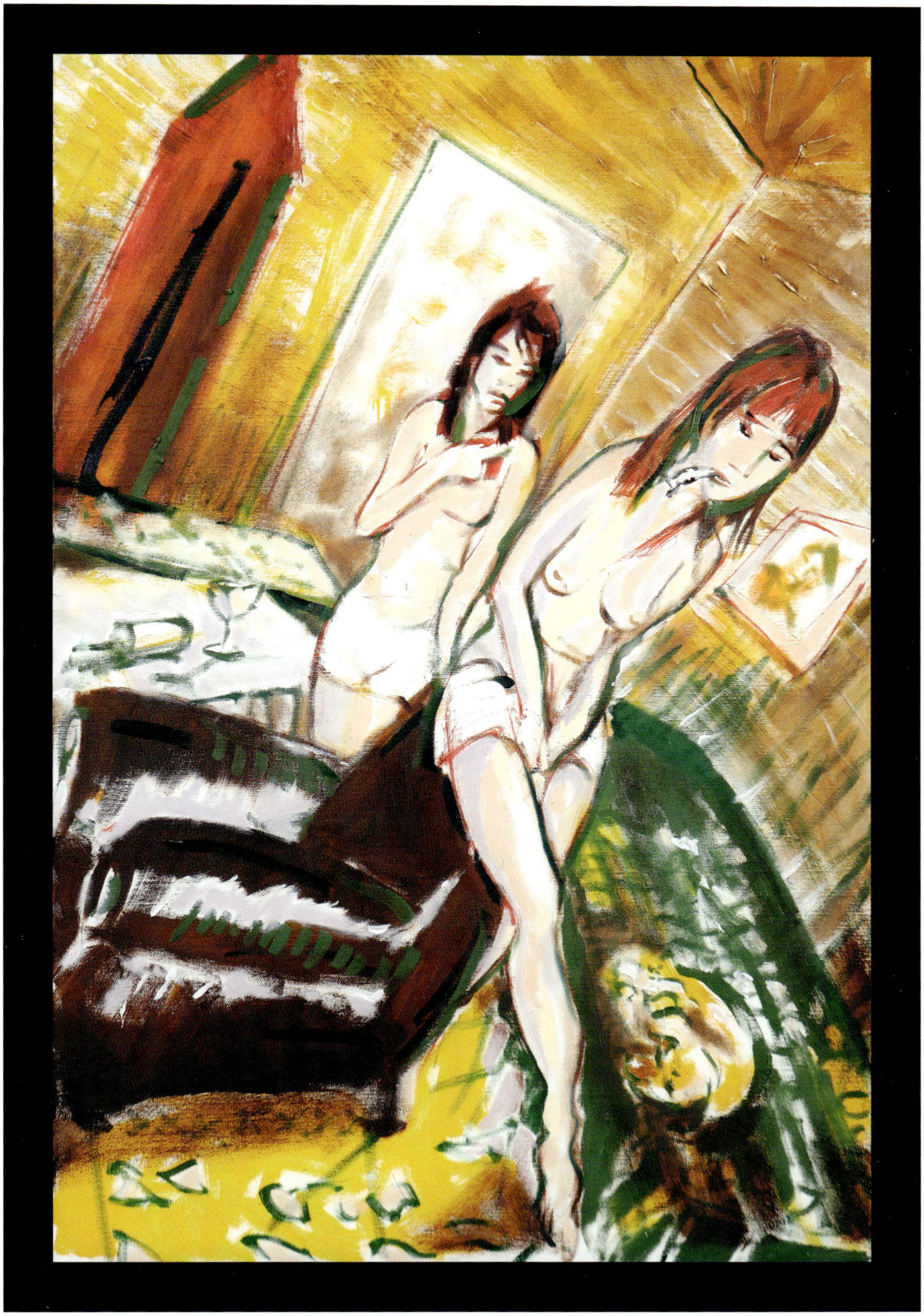

"Three Nudes *was painted in Las Vegas. I had my whole family there with me, which made it all rather embarrassing. It was a little like the Windmill Theatre in war-time London, with the naked girls standing motionless to create a tableau."*

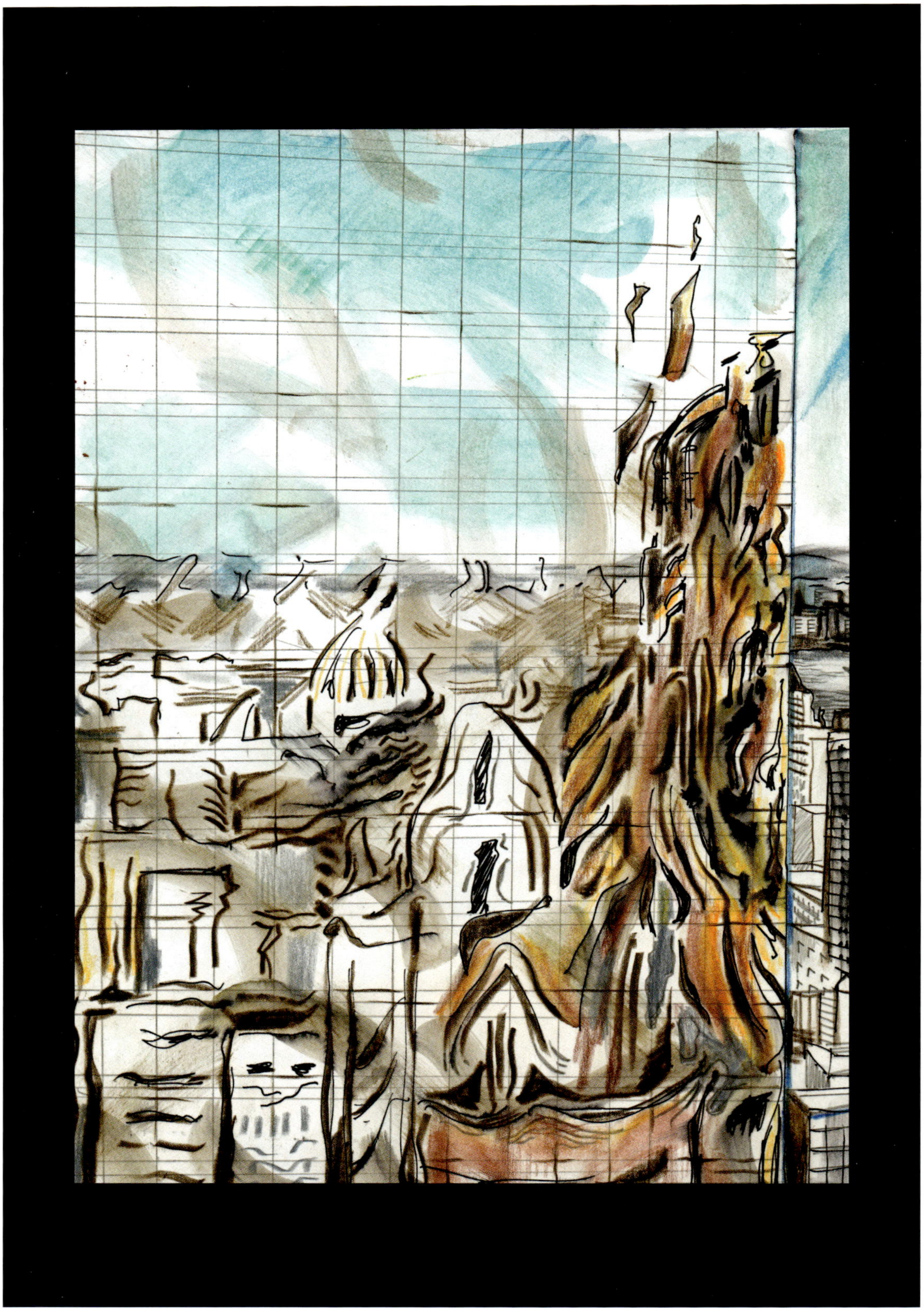

8

VIEWS

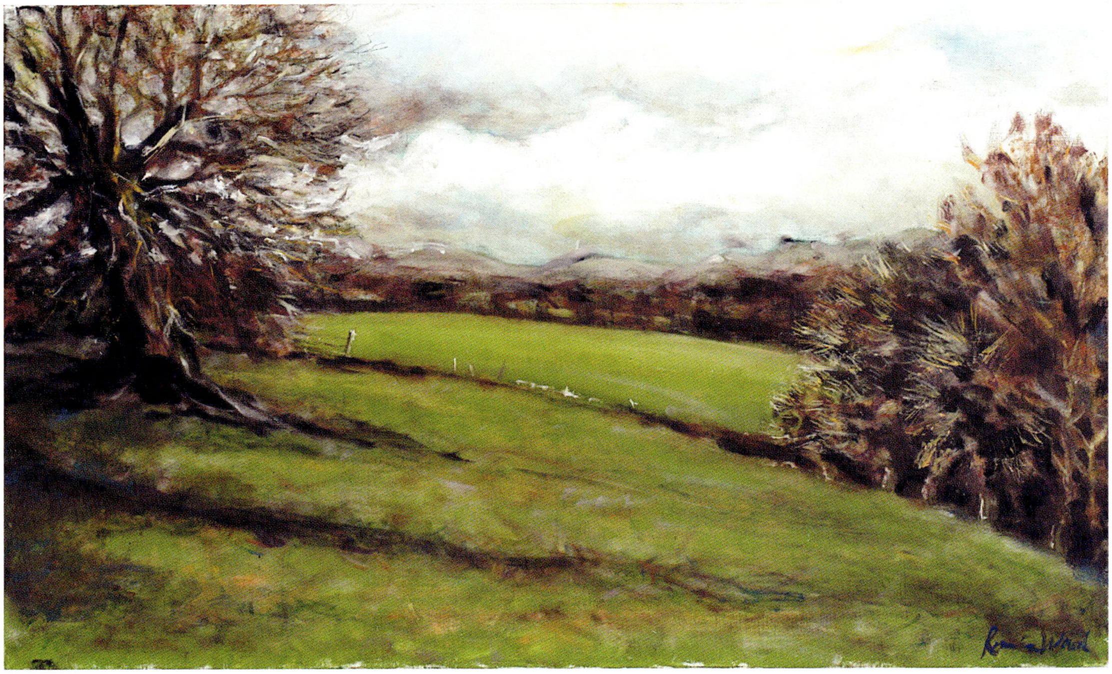

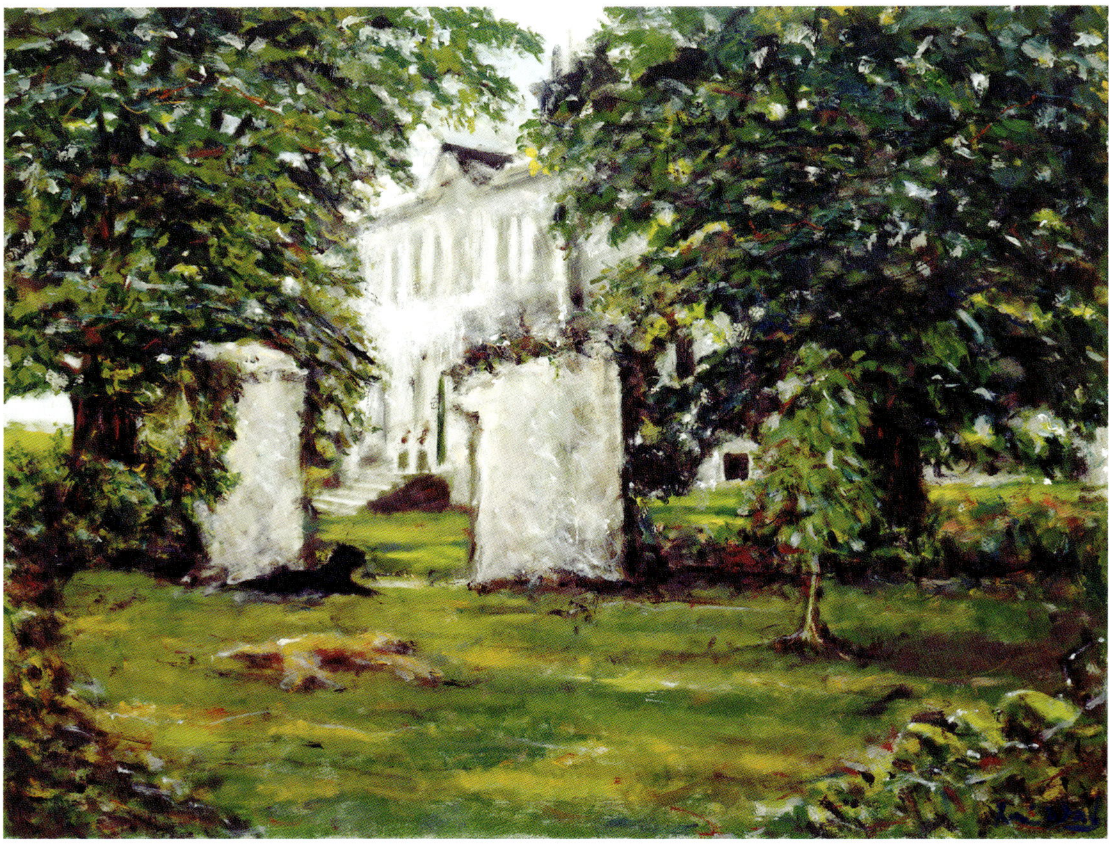

PREVIOUS PAGE: *New York Cityscape* | 2005 | mixed media on canvas | 29 × 21 cm
TOP: *Irish Landscape* | 2005 | oil on canvas | 60 × 101 cm
ABOVE: *Sandymount II* | 1996 | oil on canvas | 68.5 × 91.5 cm
OPPOSITE: *Ireland View from the Studio* | 2008 | pastel on canvas | 84 × 59 cm

I love painting outside and being among the elements. Ireland in particular is so inspiring, because of the vibrancy of the greens."

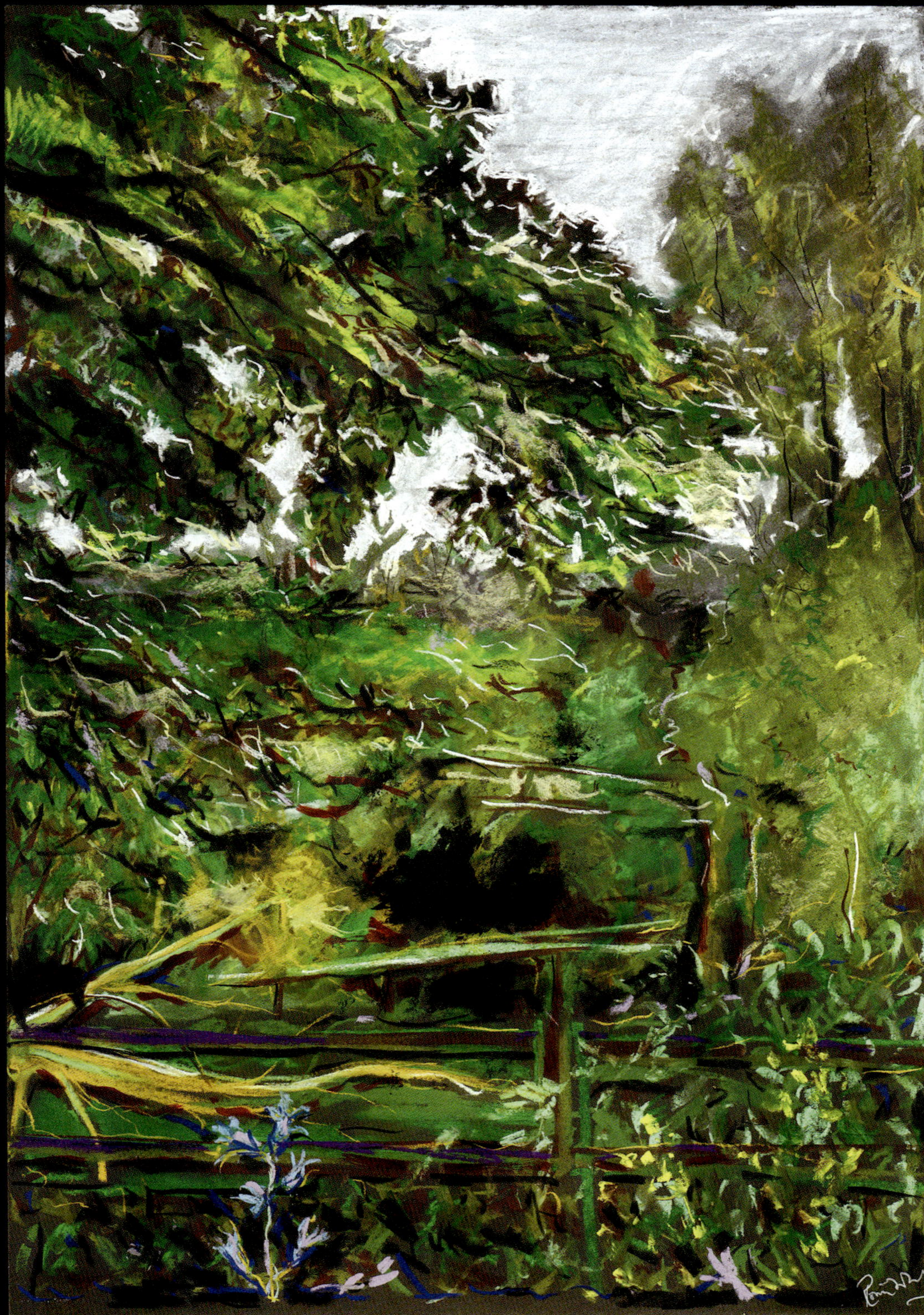

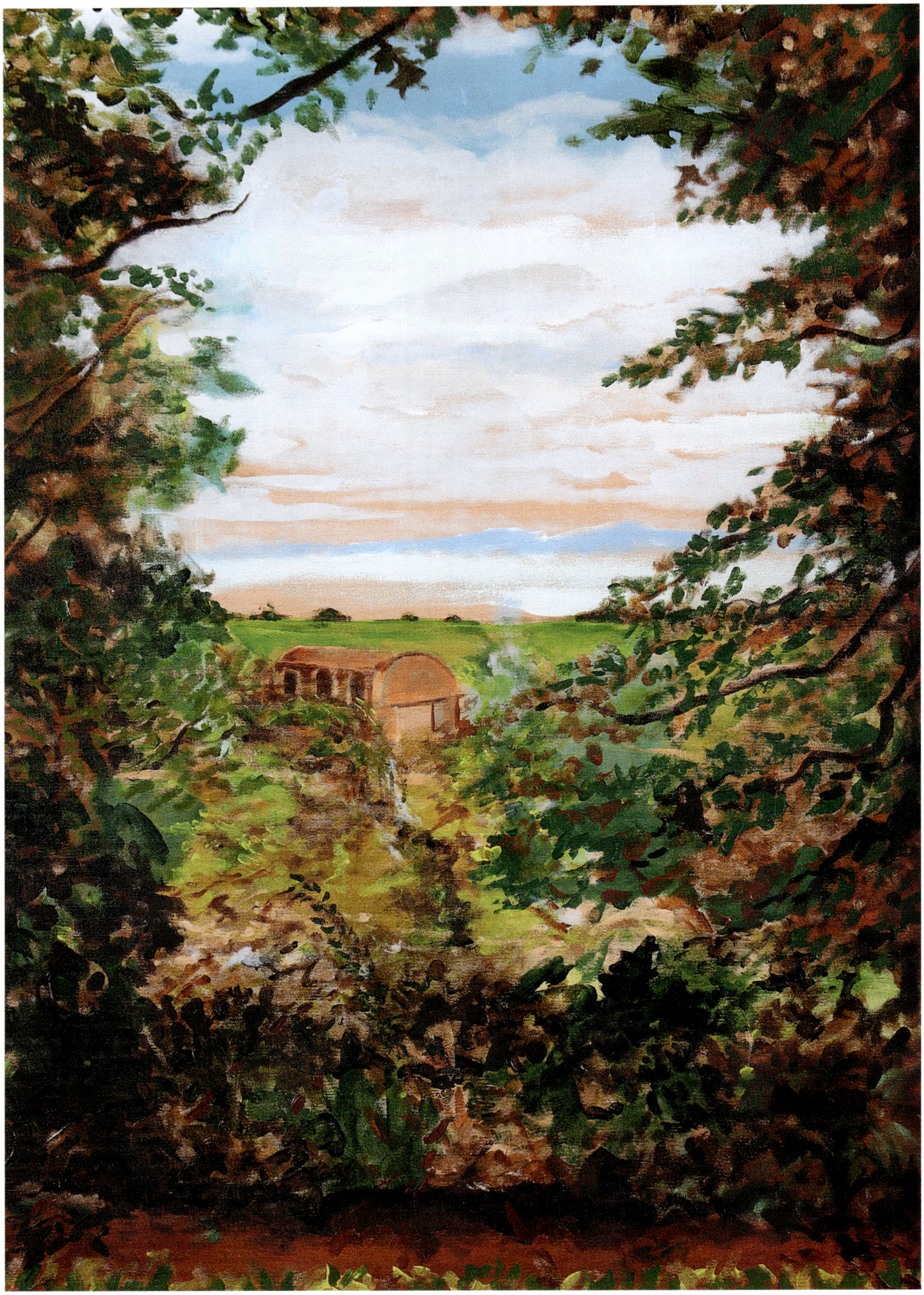

ABOVE: *Irish View* | 2010 | acrylic on canvas | 112 × 90 cm
OPPOSITE: *Landscape* | 2010 | acrylic on canvas | 112 × 90 cm

"When I'm in Ireland, I'm most inspired to paint landscapes. Everywhere you look there are beautiful views."

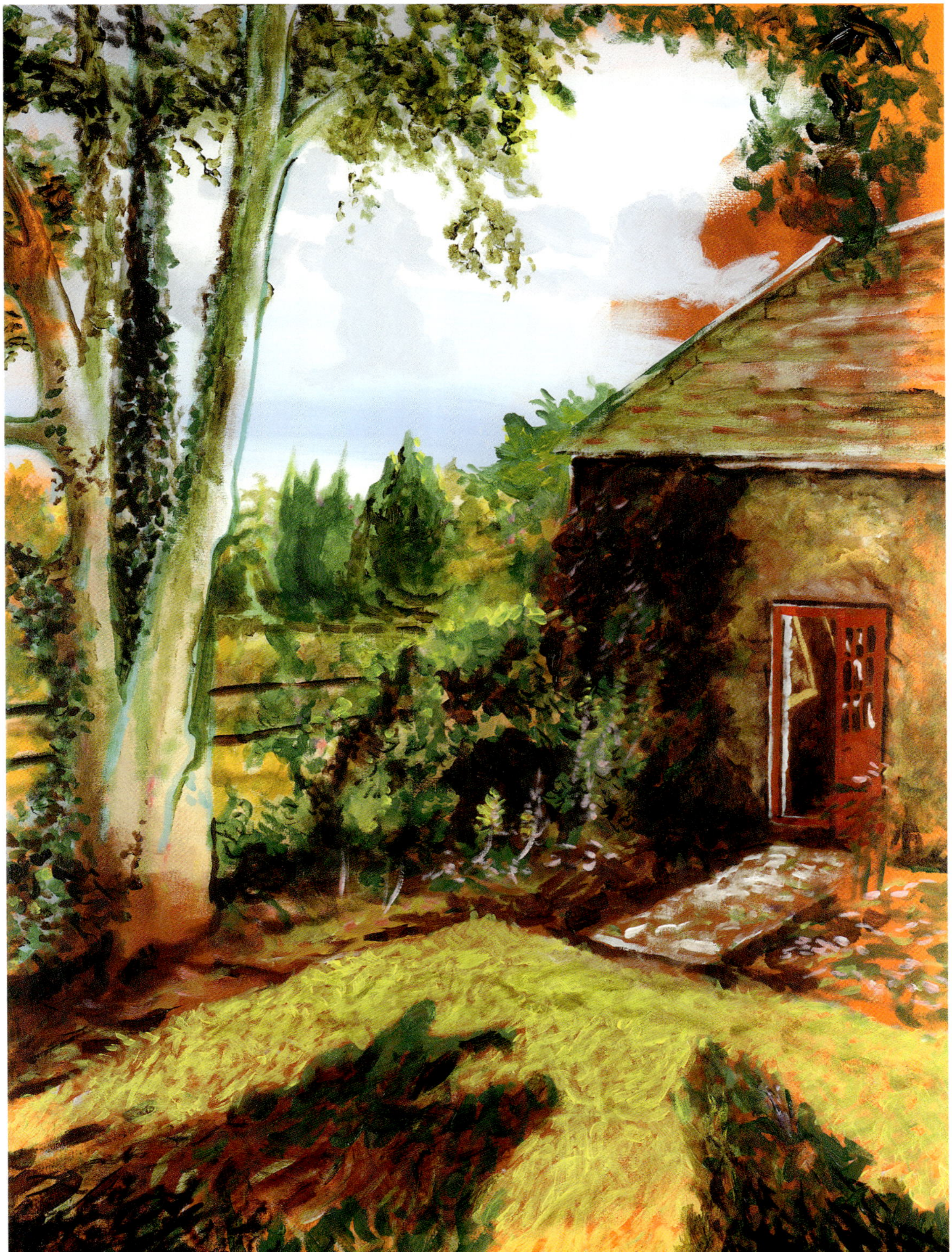

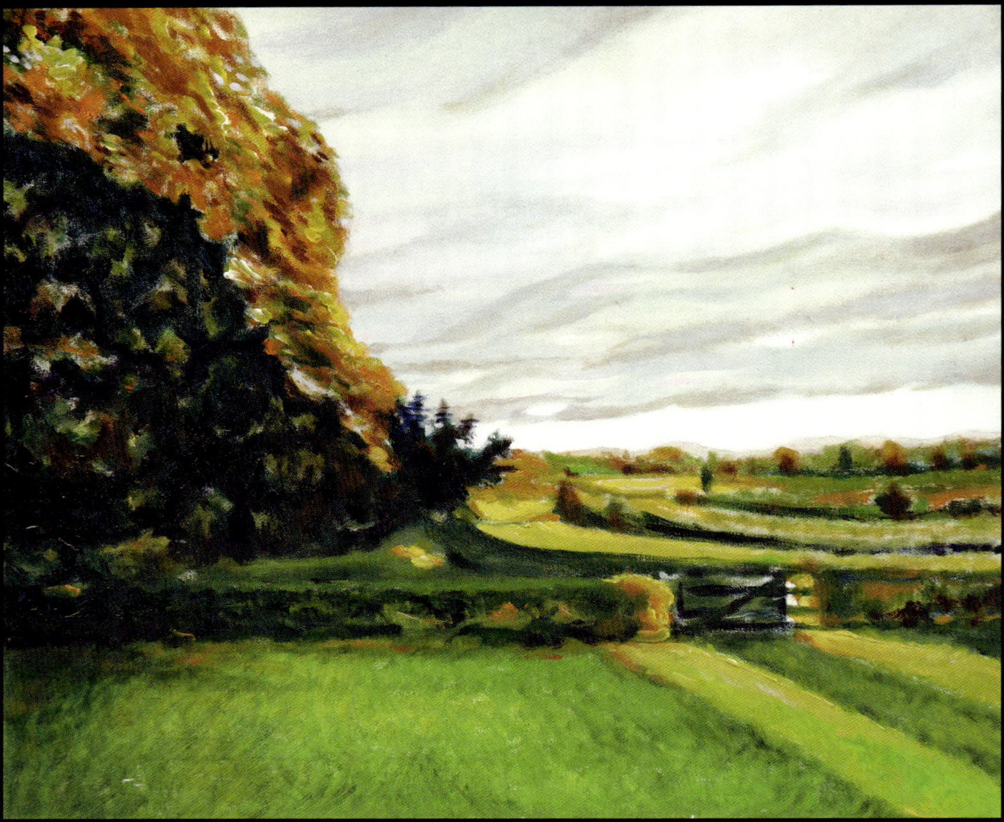

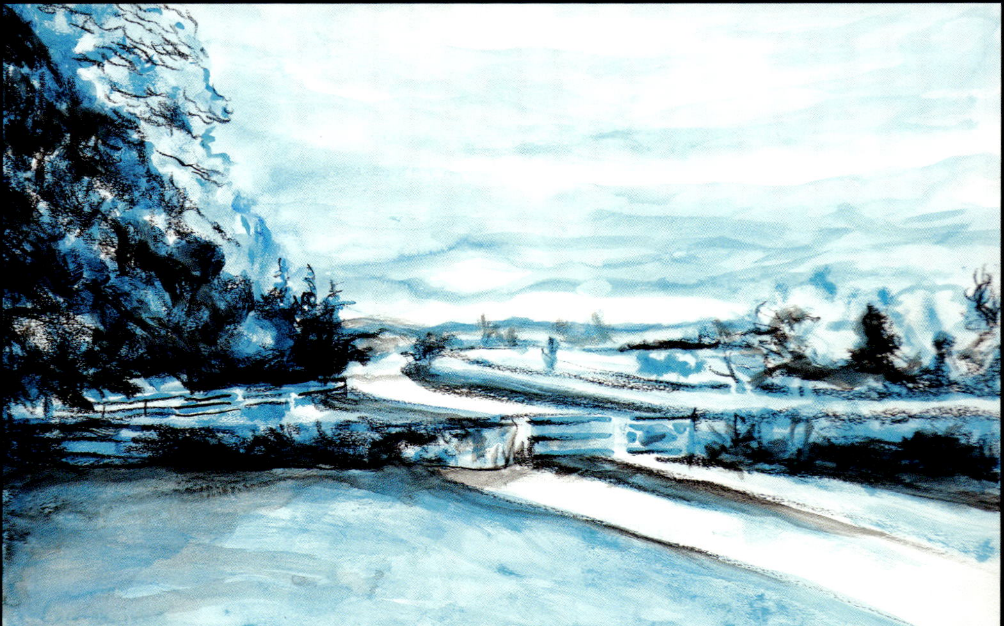

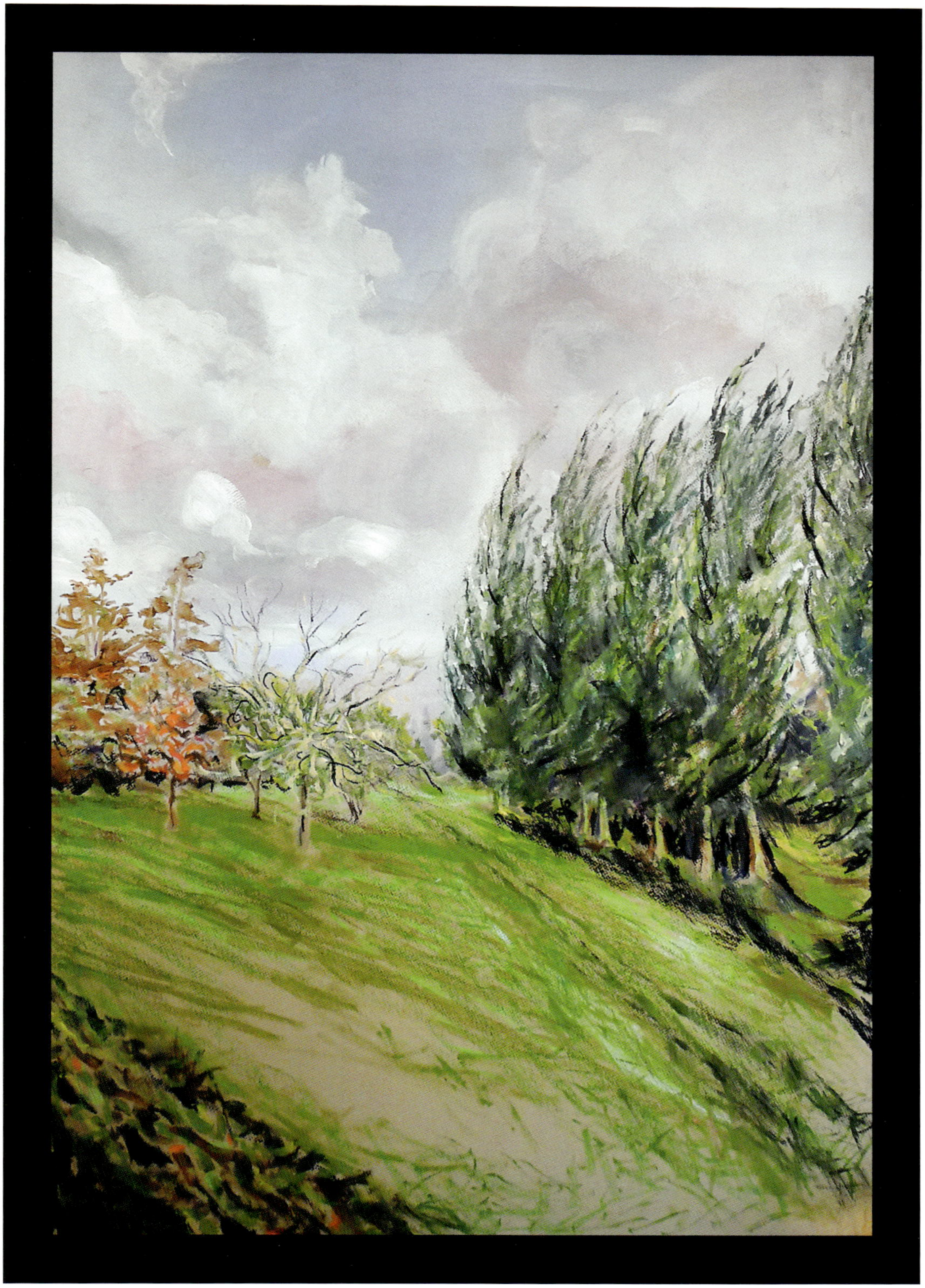

OPPOSITE ABOVE: *Ireland Green* | 2014 | acrylic on canvas | 46 × 55 cm
OPPOSITE BELOW: *Irish Landscape (Blue)* | 2015 | mixed media on paper | 29 × 42 cm
ABOVE: *Landscape* | 2014 | mixed media on board | 120 × 81 cm

'This is the view from my bar at Sandymount, looking towards the house, in the dead of winter."

BELOW: *Bare Trees at Sandymount* | 2001 | mixed media on canvas | 35.5 × 21 cm
OPPOSITE: *Untitled II* | 2007 | mixed media on paper | 112 × 76 cm
OVERLEAF: *Tree Tunnel at Ashridge Forest* (detail) | 2015 | acrylic on canvas | 46 × 55 cm

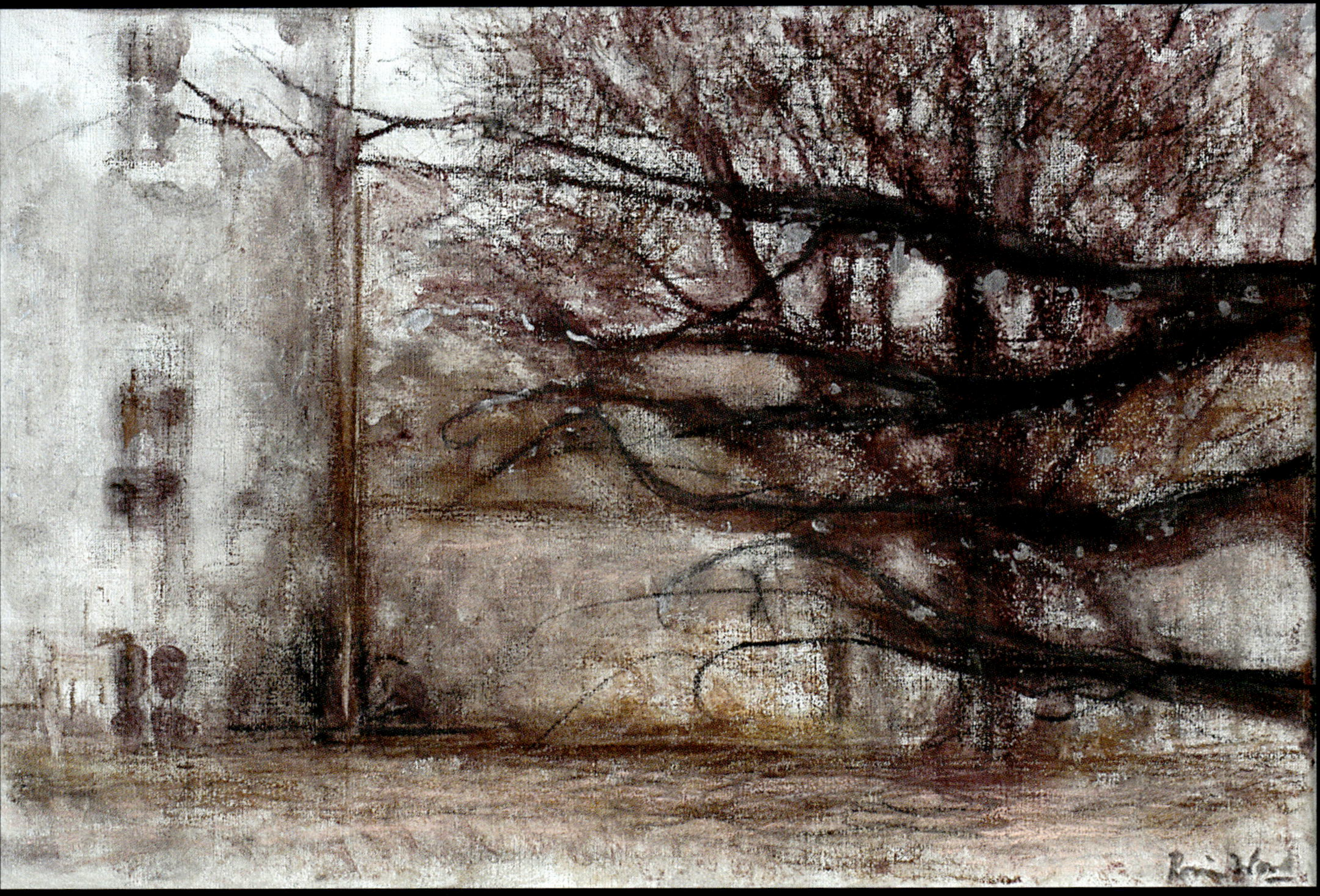

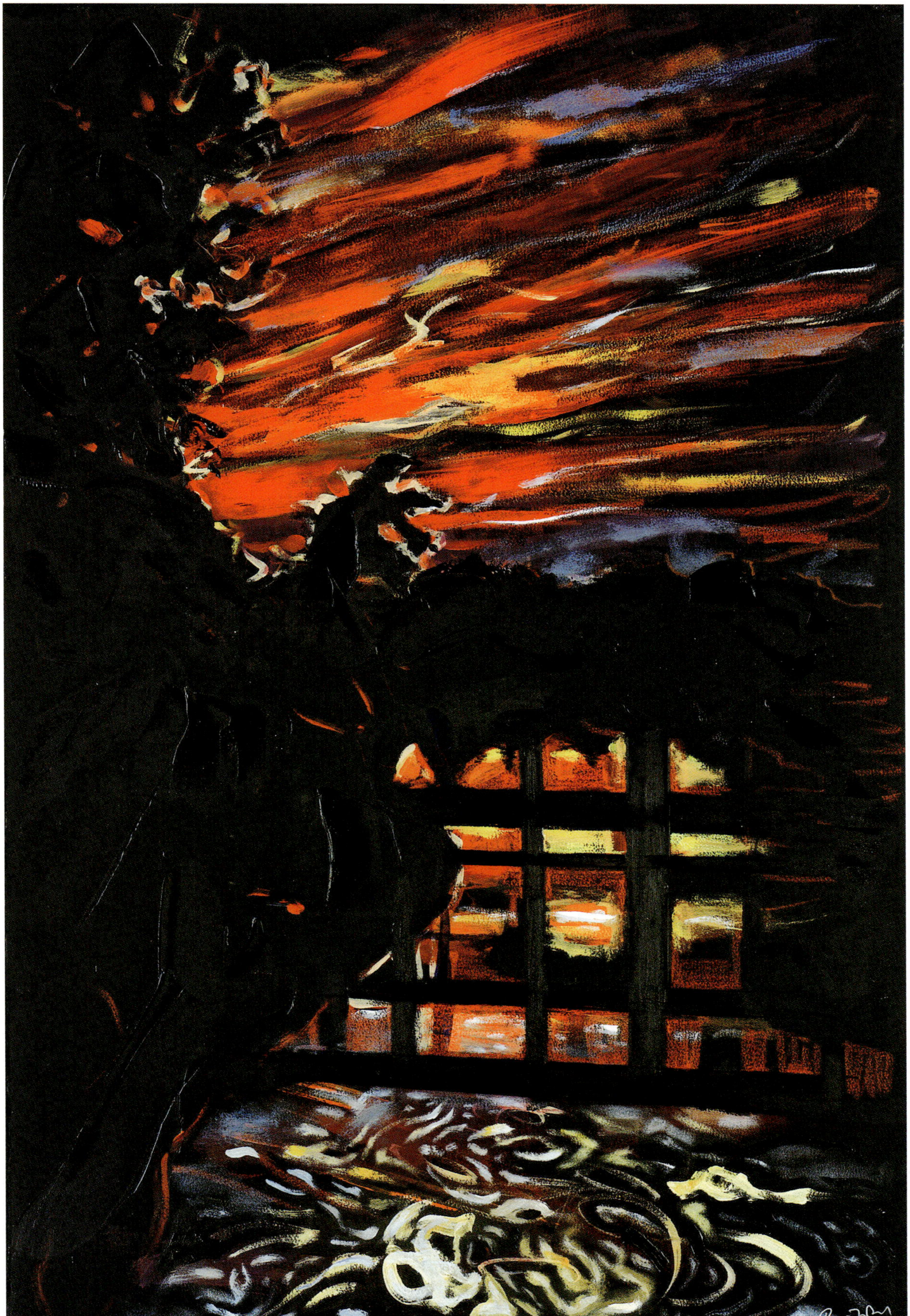

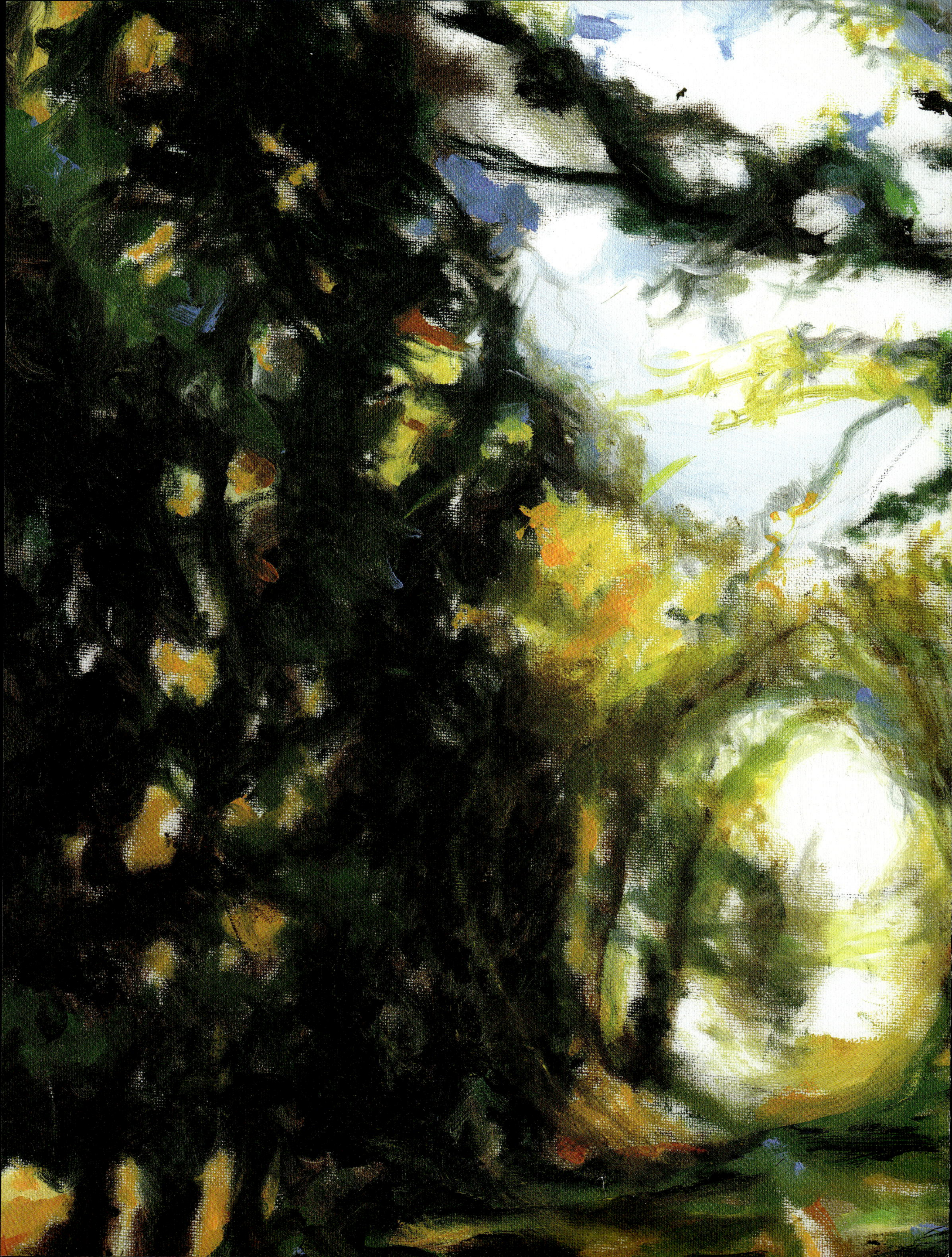

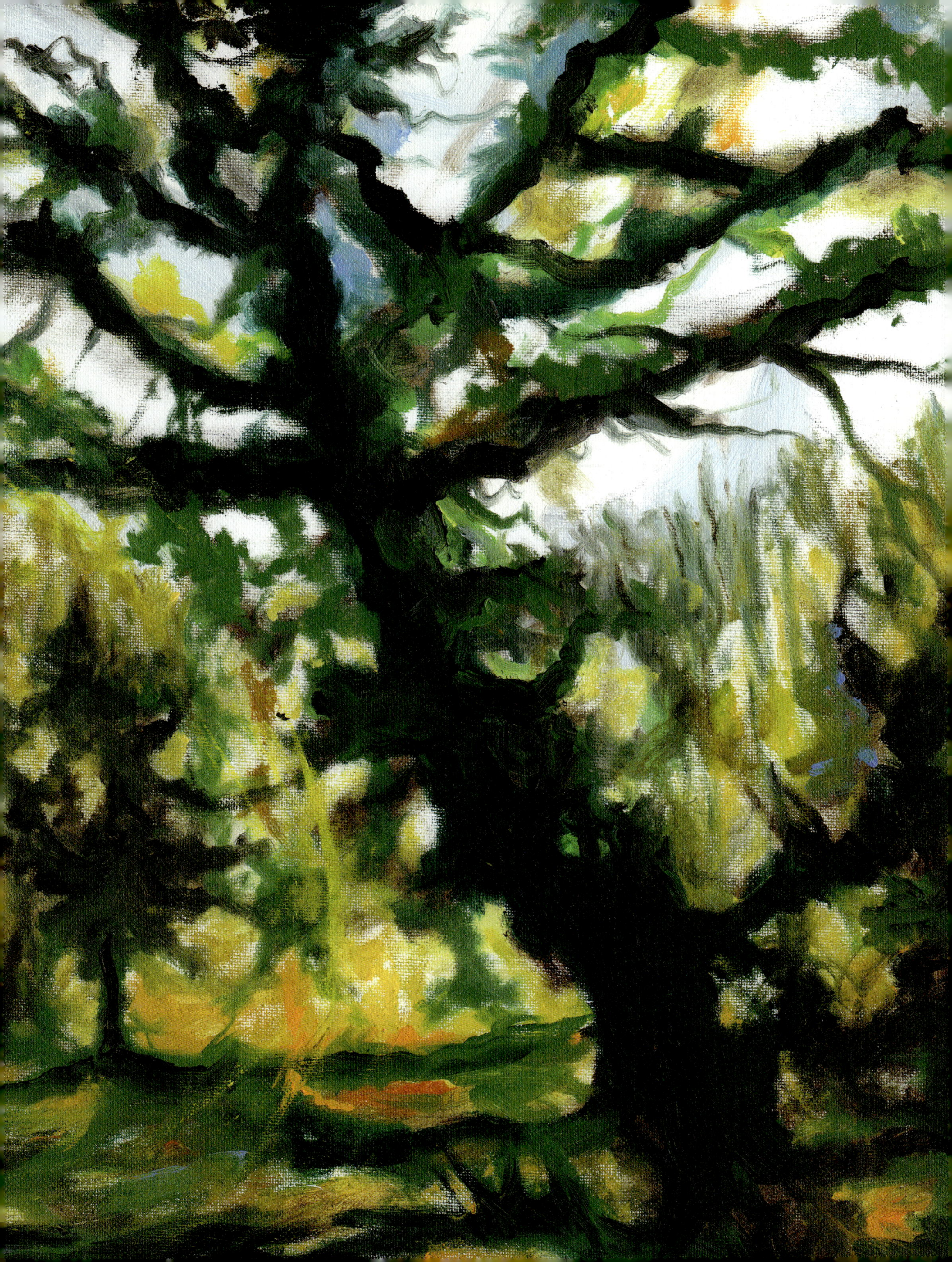

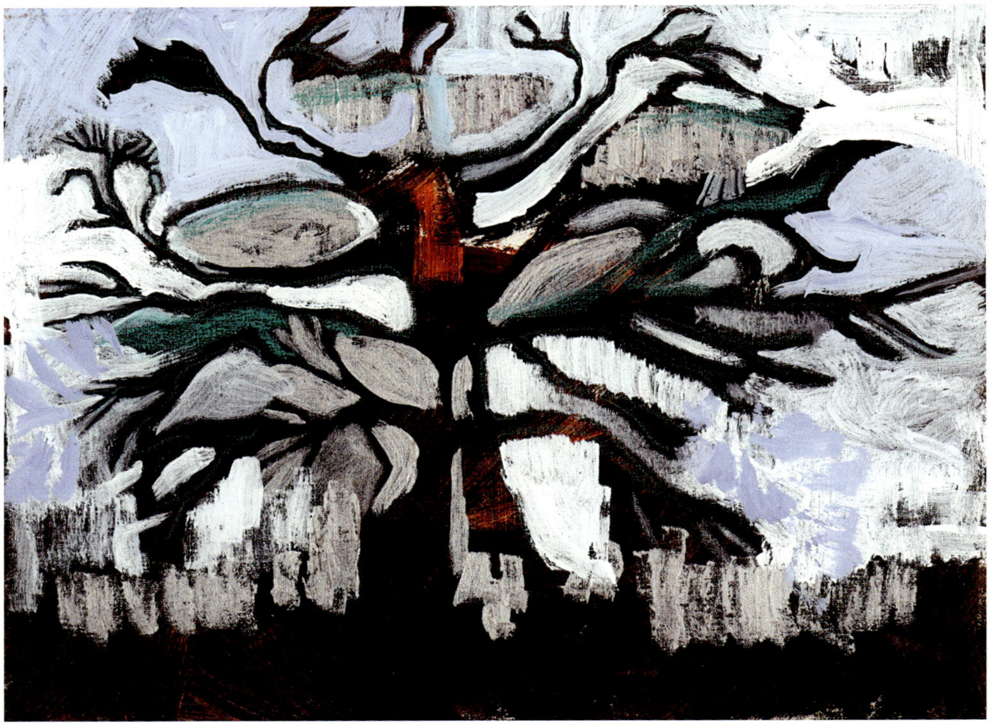

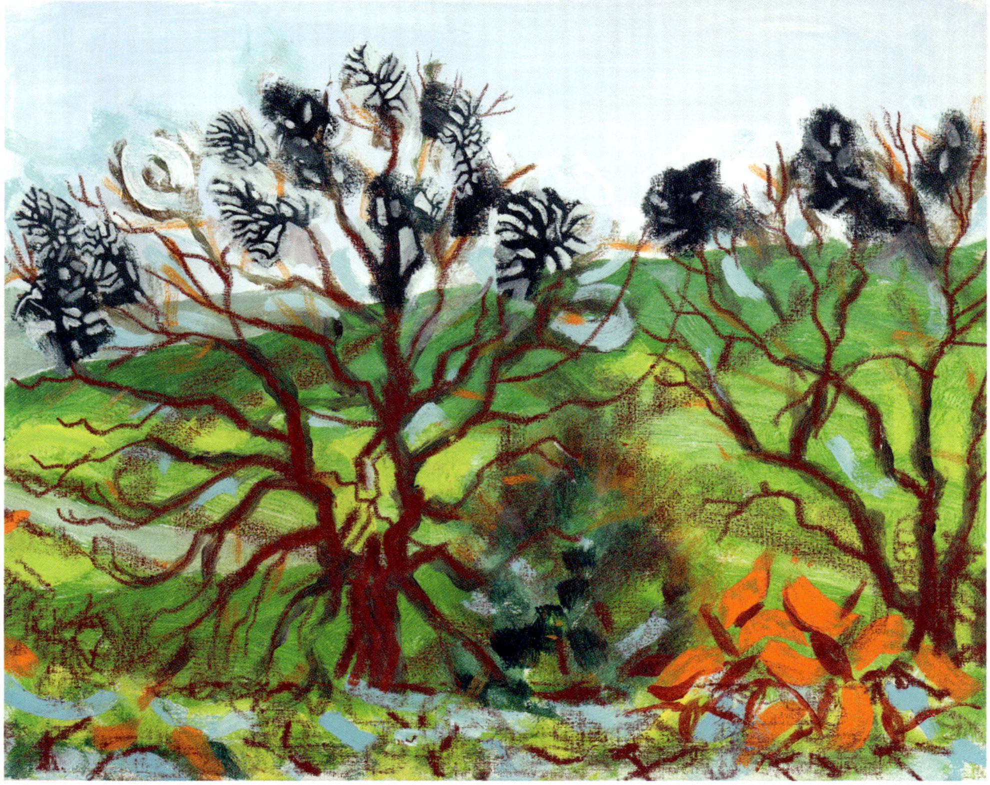

TOP: *Winter Tree* | *c.* 2005 | acrylic on canvas | 30 × 46 cm
ABOVE: *Winter Abstract Tree* | *c.* 2005 | acrylic on canvas | 30 × 46 cm
OPPOSITE: *Tree From Below* | 2008 | mixed media on paper | 81 × 65 cm

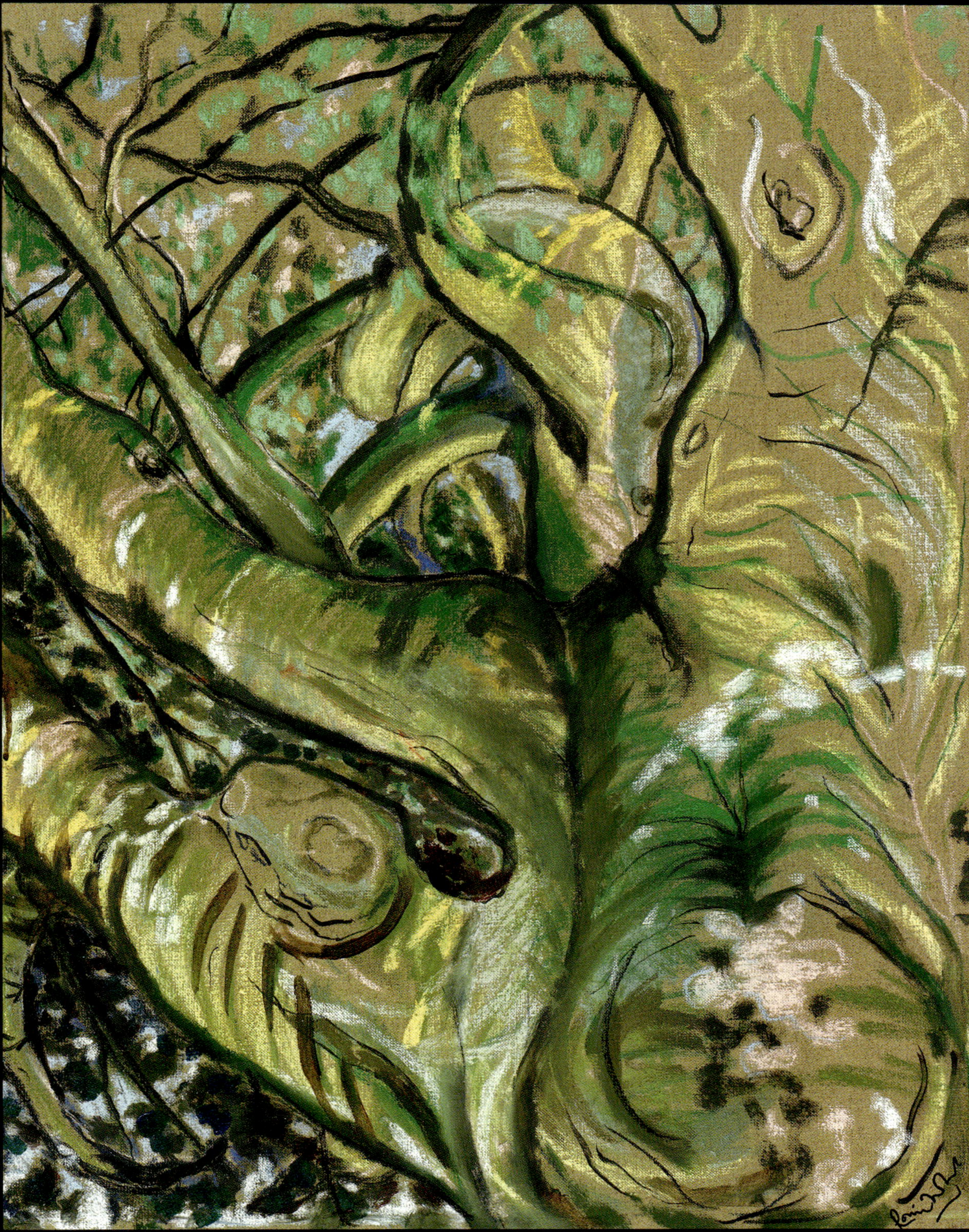

"There is a photograph at the beginning of this book, showing me painting in a pair of stripy trousers; Tree From Below *is the end result."*

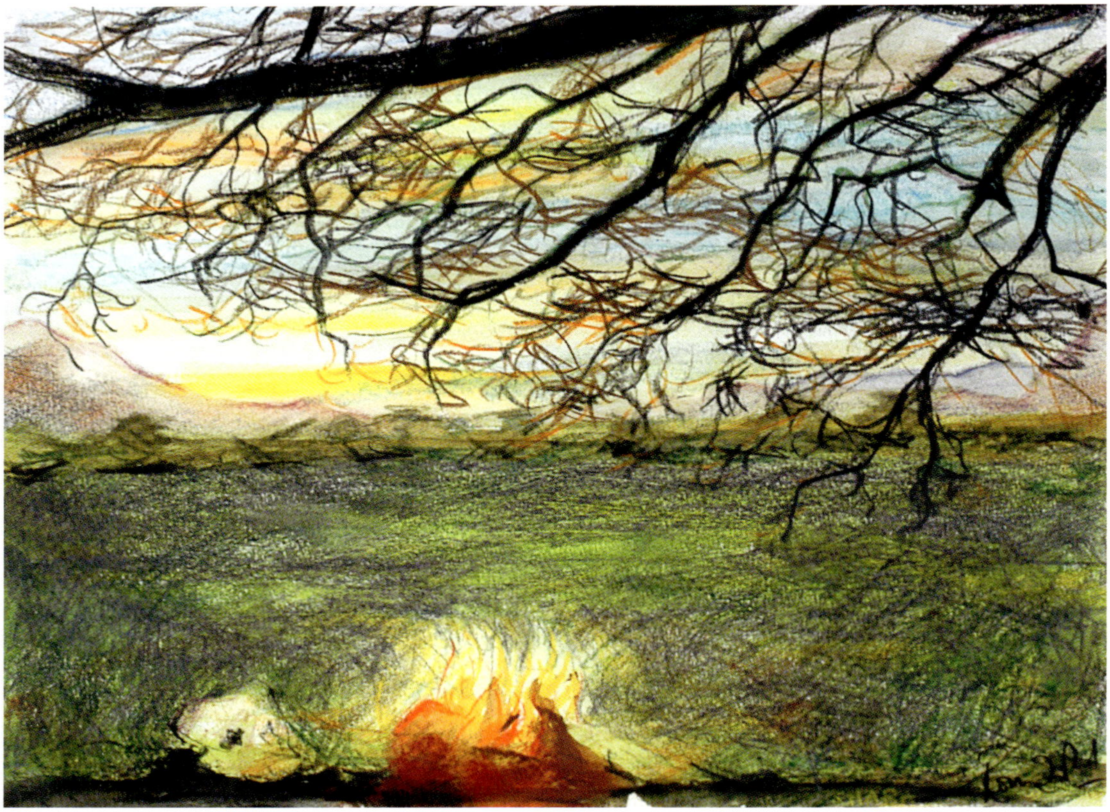

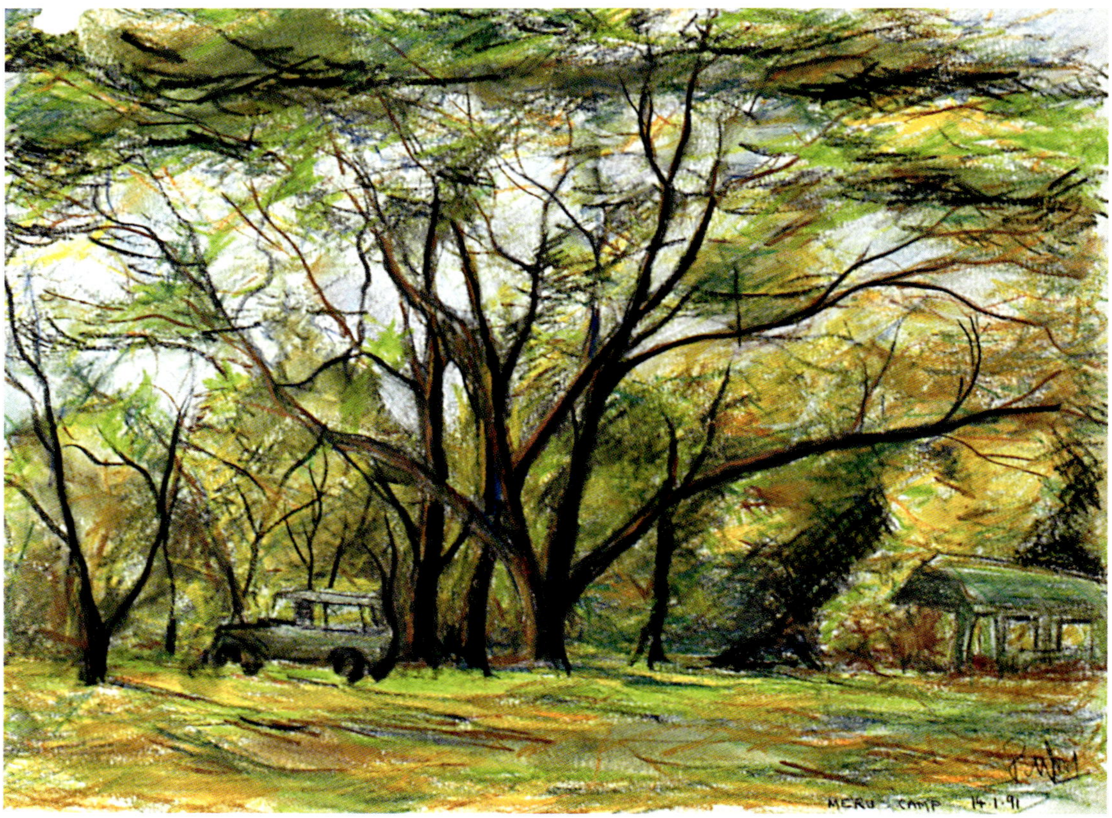

TOP: *Africa I* | 1970 | pastel on paper | 21 × 29.5 cm
ABOVE: *Meru Camp* | 1970 | pastel on paper | 21 × 29.5 cm

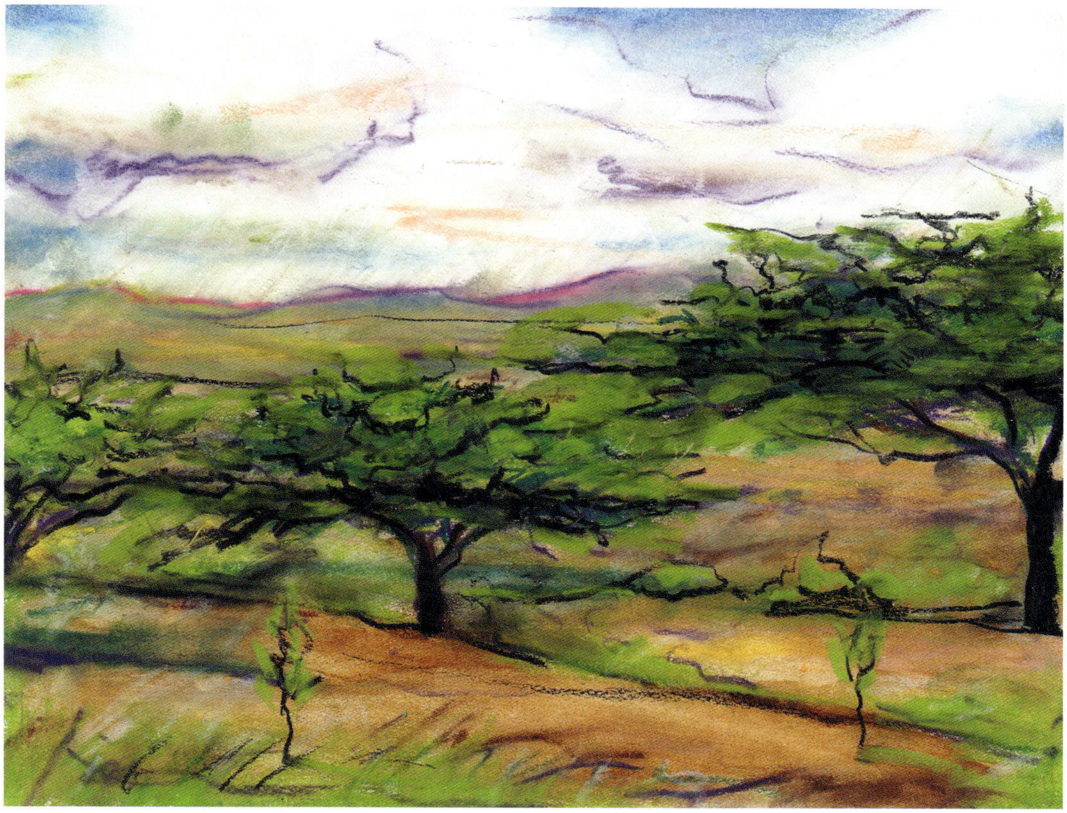

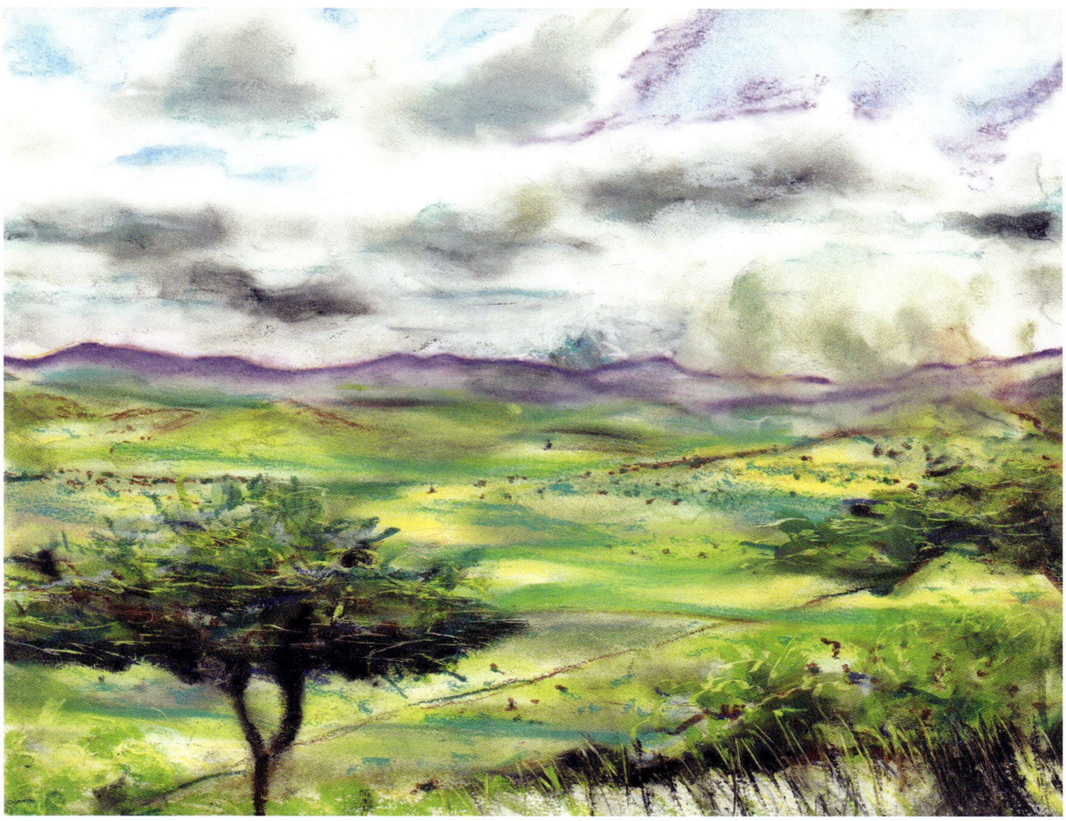

TOP: *Africa IV* | 1970 | pastel on paper | 21 × 29.5 cm
ABOVE: *Africa V* | 1970 | pastel on paper | 21 × 29.5 cm

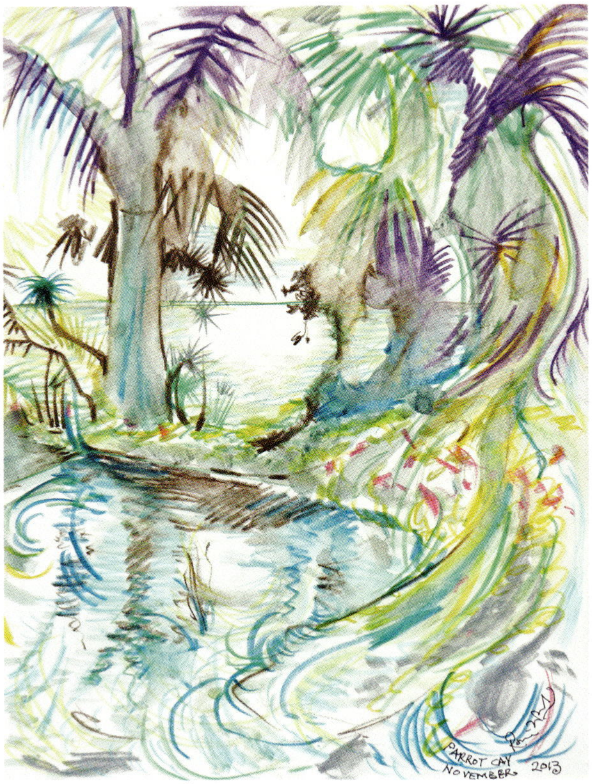
PARROT CAY
NOVEMBER 2013

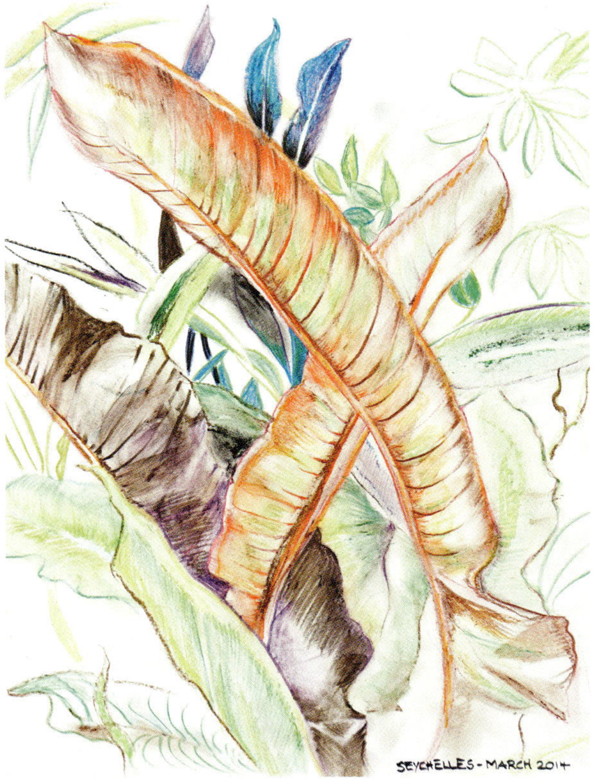
SEYCHELLES - MARCH 2014

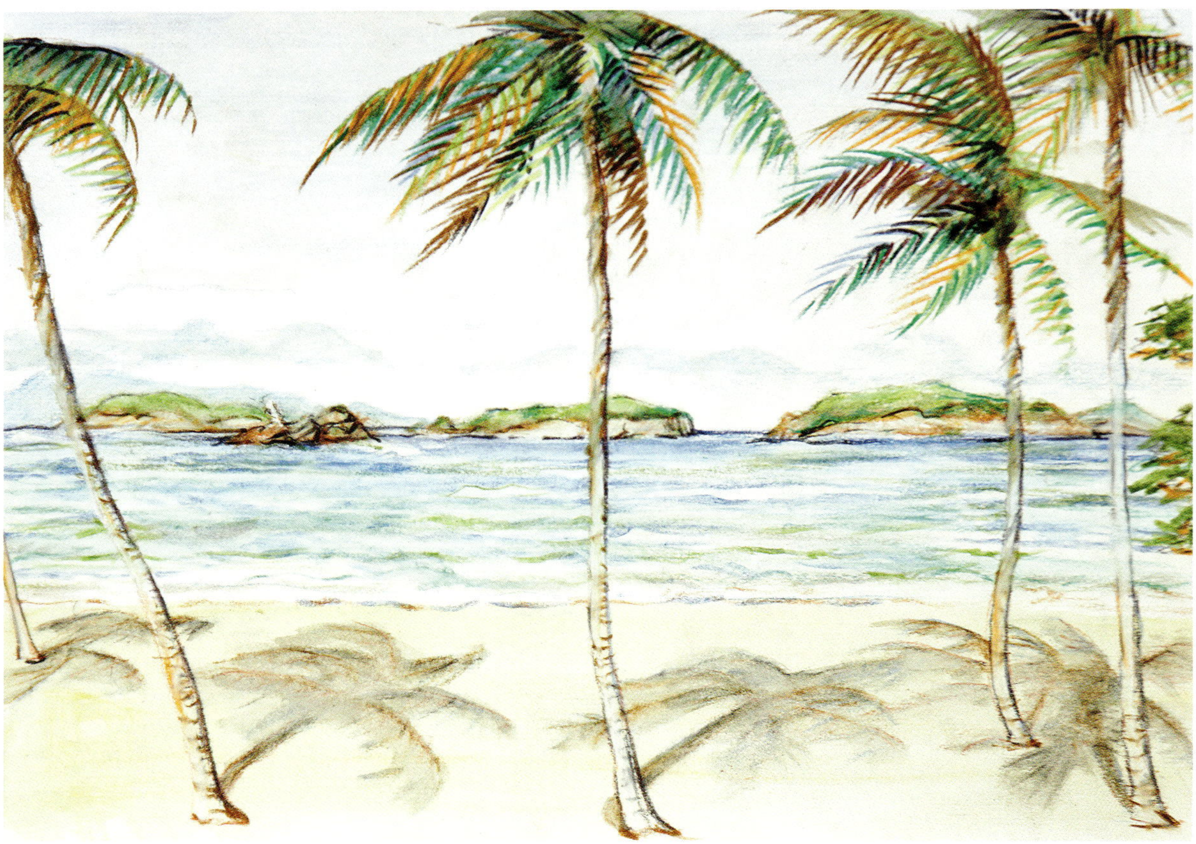

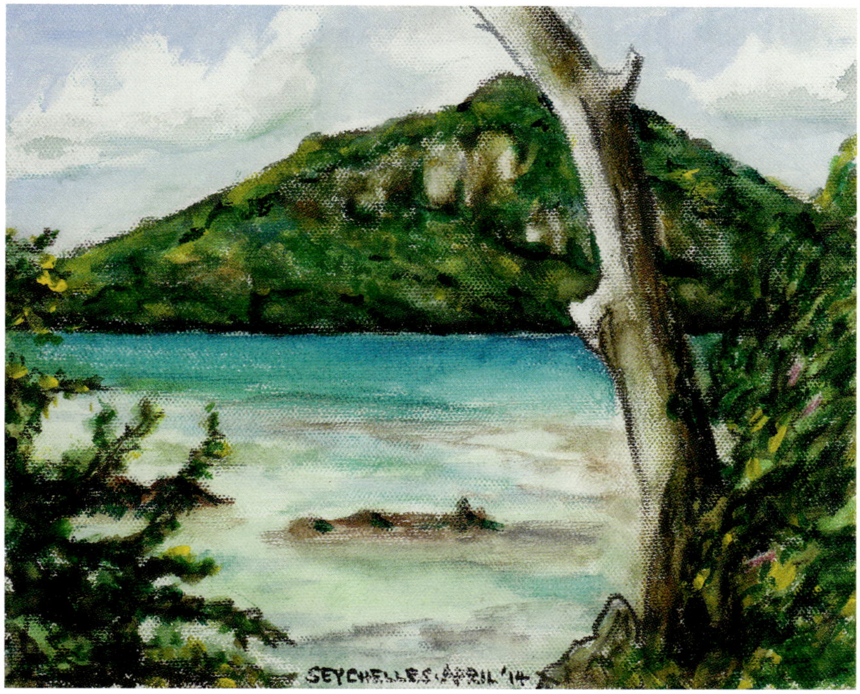

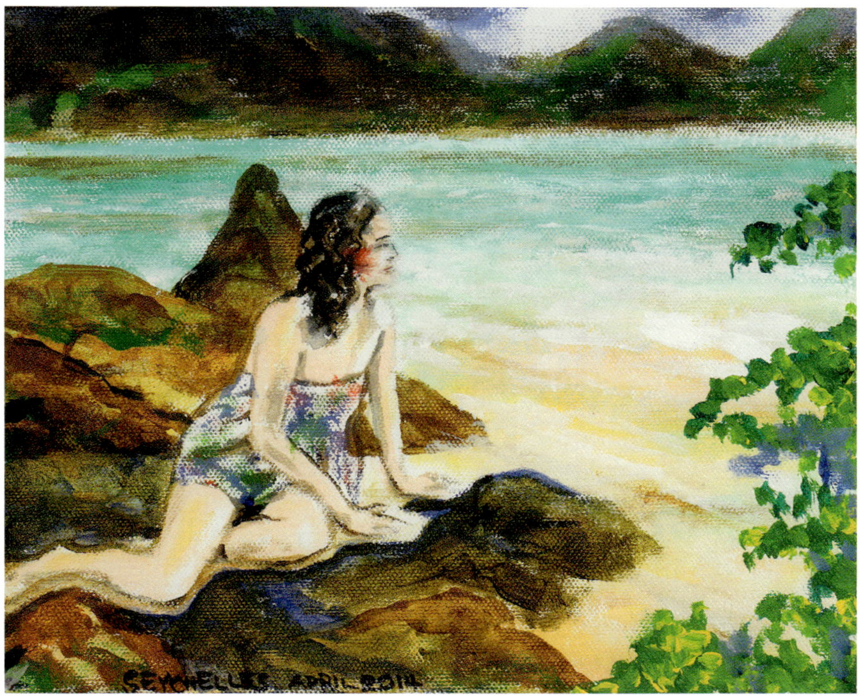

"The Seychelles paintings were done following the Stones' 14 On Fire tour. I love being on the road, but it's great to get back to my art. I did the Parrot Cay painting sitting next to Keith – you can see his vibes in it!"

OPPOSITE ABOVE LEFT: *Parrot Cay* | 2013 | mixed media on paper | 29 × 21 cm
OPPOSITE ABOVE RIGHT: *Seychelles* | 2014 | pastel on paper | 30 × 40 cm
OPPOSITE BELOW: *Mustique Landscape Study* | 2013 | coloured pencil on paper | 21 × 29 cm
TOP: *Seychelles Study I* | 2014 | acrylic on canvas board | 26 × 21 cm
ABOVE: *Seychelles Study II* | 2014 | acrylic on canvas board | 26 × 21 cm

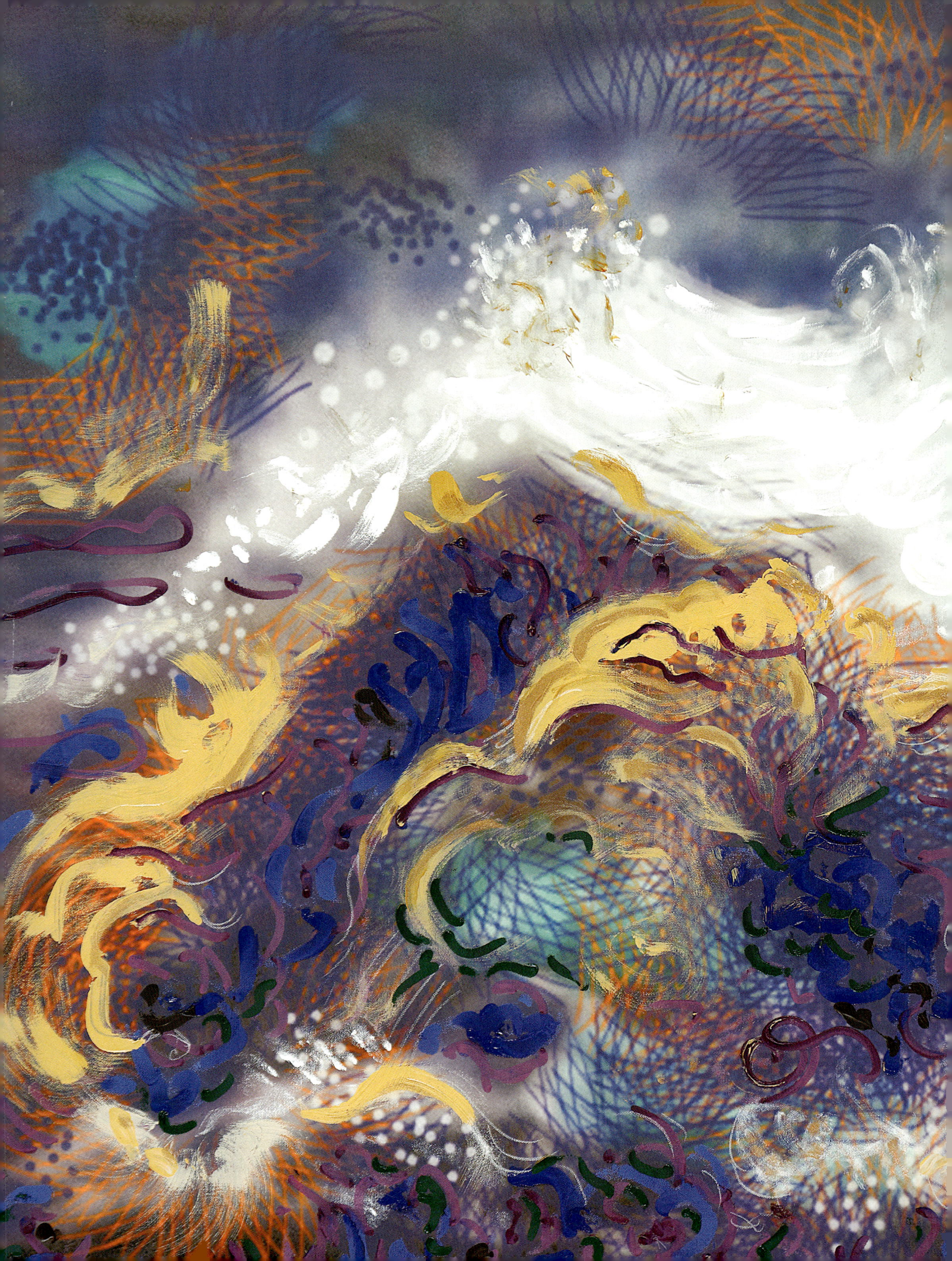

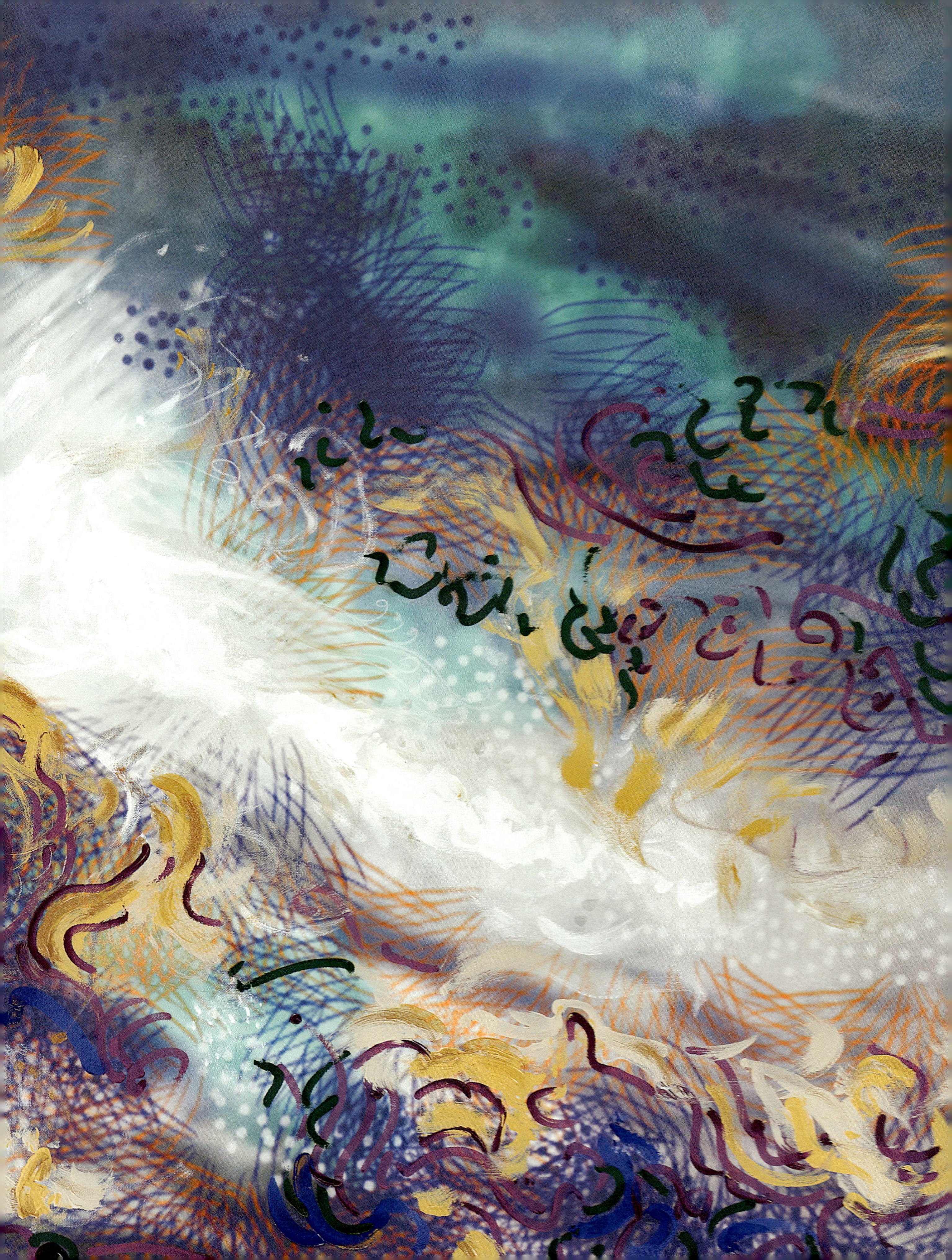

PREVIOUS PAGE: *Abstract River* | 2010 | acrylic on digital phone art canvas | 44.8 × 67.5 cm
BELOW: *Majorca* | 2016 | pen and ink on paper | 30 × 21 cm
OPPOSITE: *Majorca Garden* | 2016 | mixed media on paper | 30 × 21 cm

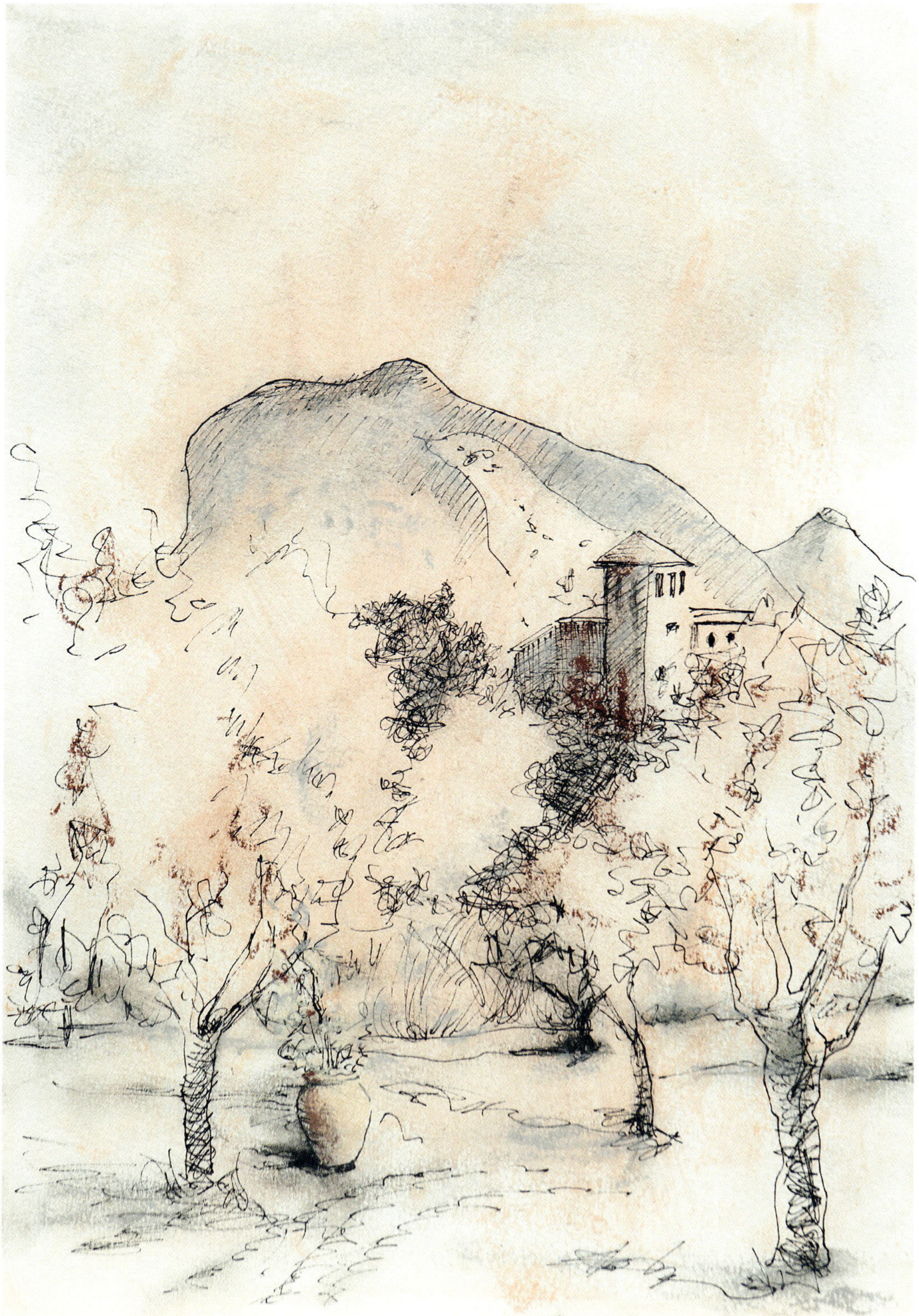

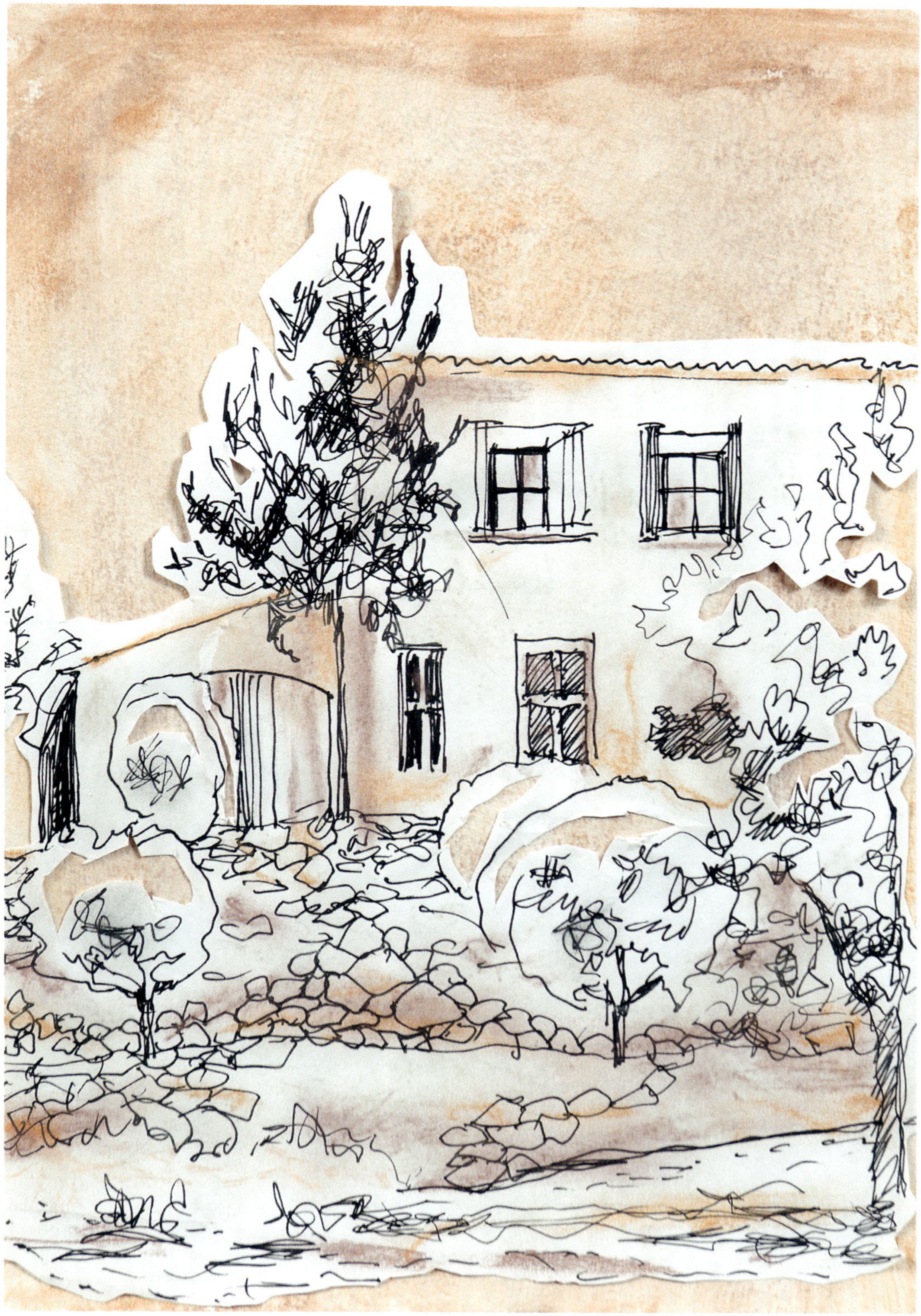

"Abstract River *(previous page) started out as a photo I took, which I then worked on as phone art, before finally adding paint.* Majorca Garden *is a collage of cut-out sketches; for me it captures the feel of this garden."*

BELOW: *Plants from Barcelona Apartment* | 2014 | acrylic on canvas | 65 × 54 cm
OPPOSITE: *Barcelona Balcony* | 2014 | acrylic on canvas | 65 × 54 cm

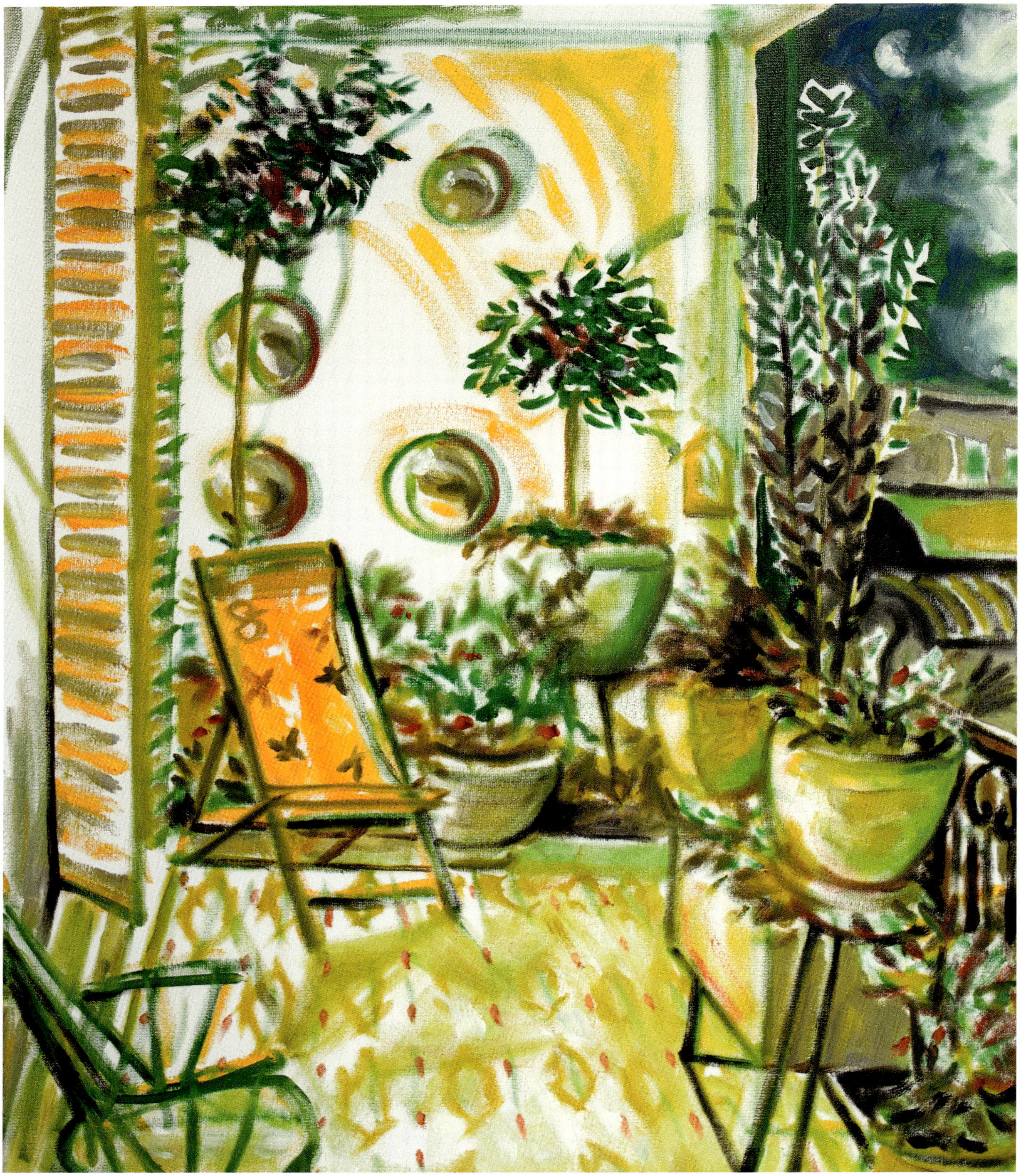

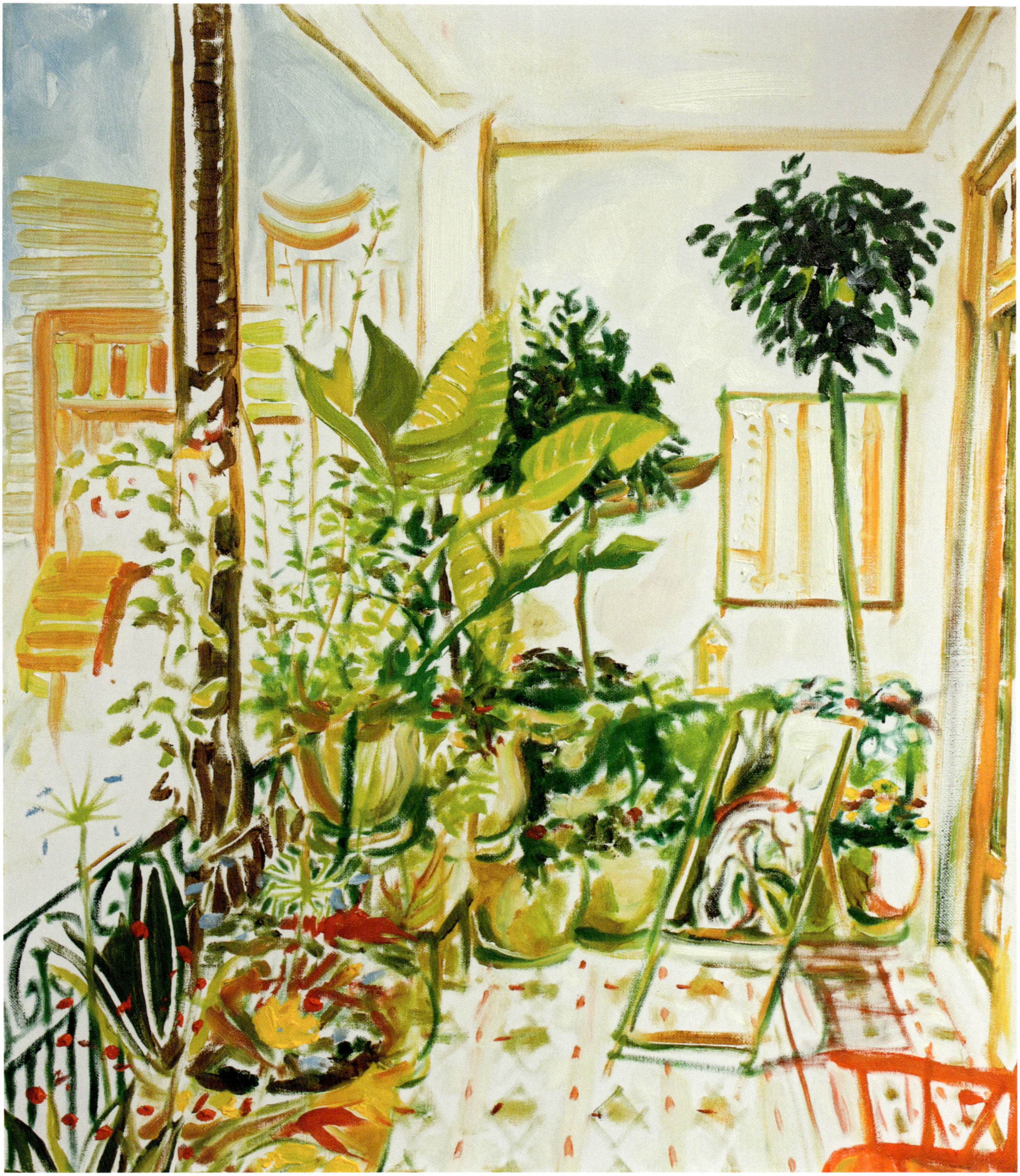

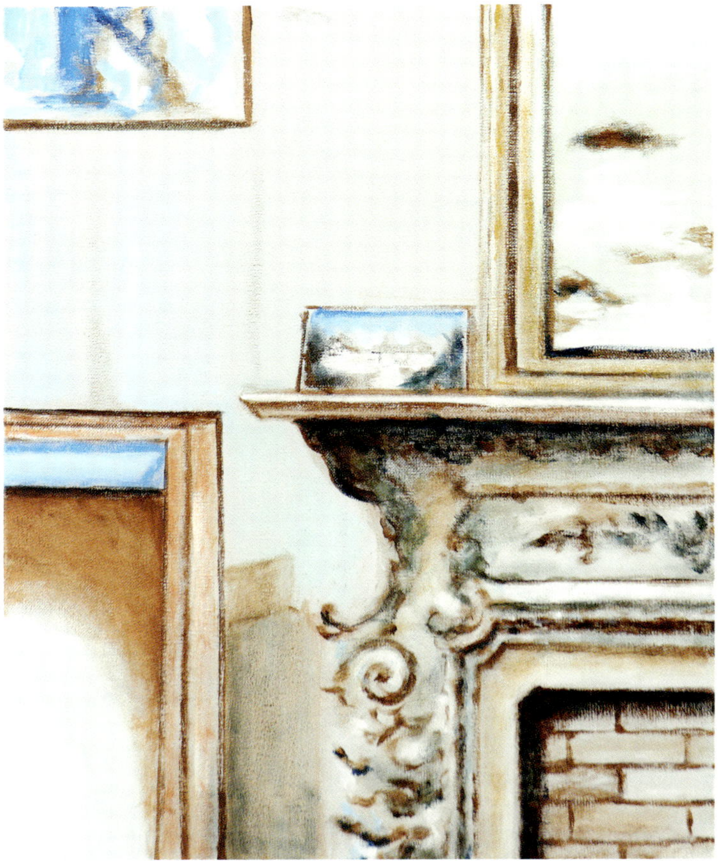

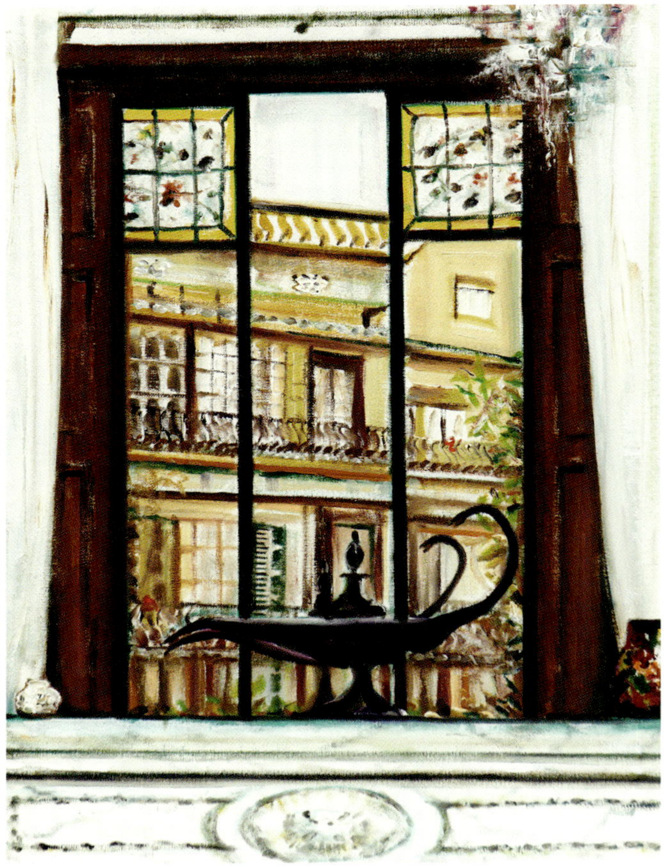

"I'm affected by my environment. And this means my art is transformed by my surroundings. For example, my Irish landscapes are completely different in style from my Barcelona paintings, and that's a reflection of more than just the subject matter itself."

ABOVE LEFT: *Barcelona Apartment Detail* | 2015 | acrylic and pastel on paper | 46 × 38 cm
ABOVE RIGHT: *Barcelona Reflection in the Mirror* | 2015 | acrylic on canvas | 45.5 × 38 cm
OPPOSITE: *From My Barcelona Apartment* | 2015 | acrylic on canvas | 61 × 50 cm

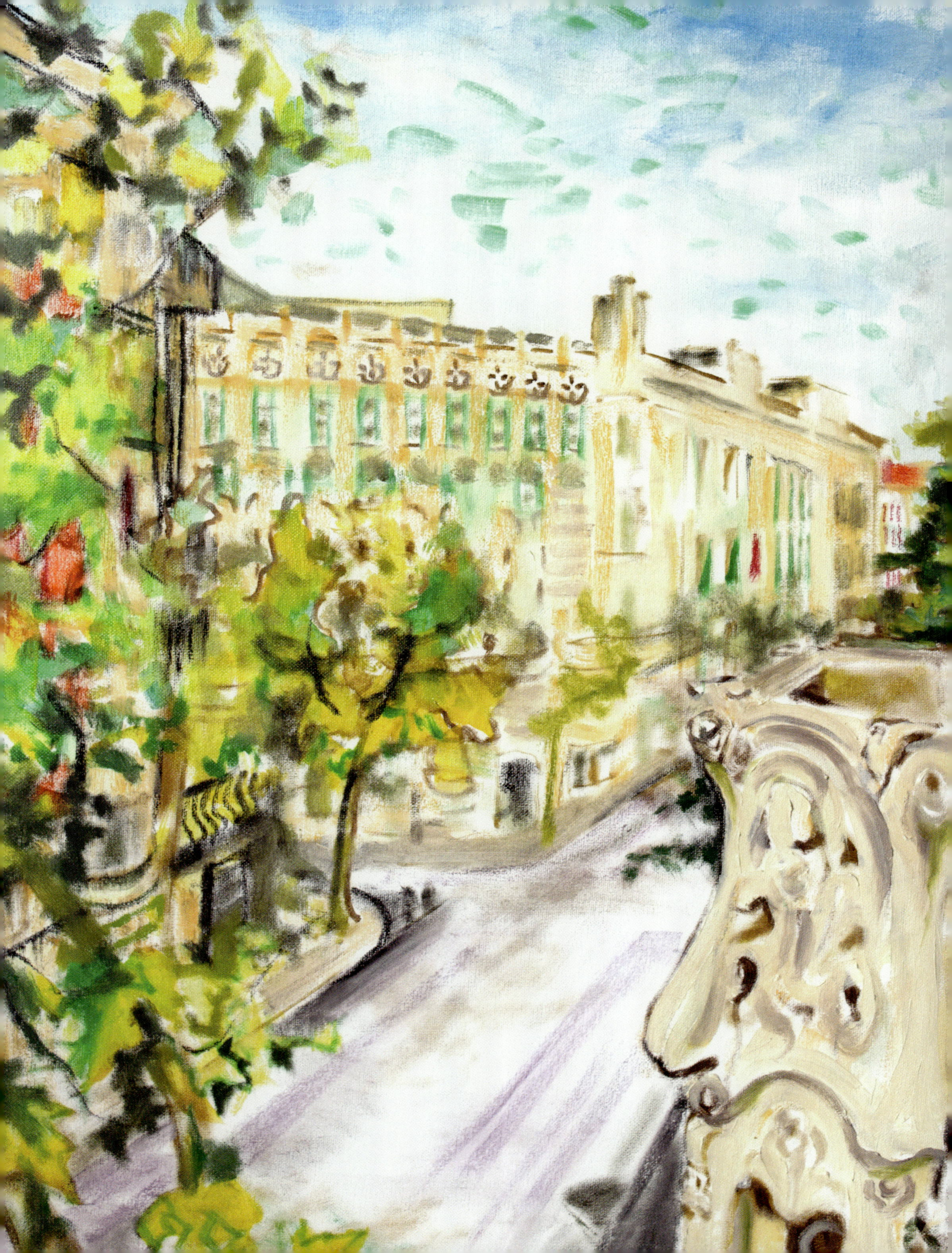

"The whole city of Barcelona, and especially Gaudí's work, is an inspiration to me."

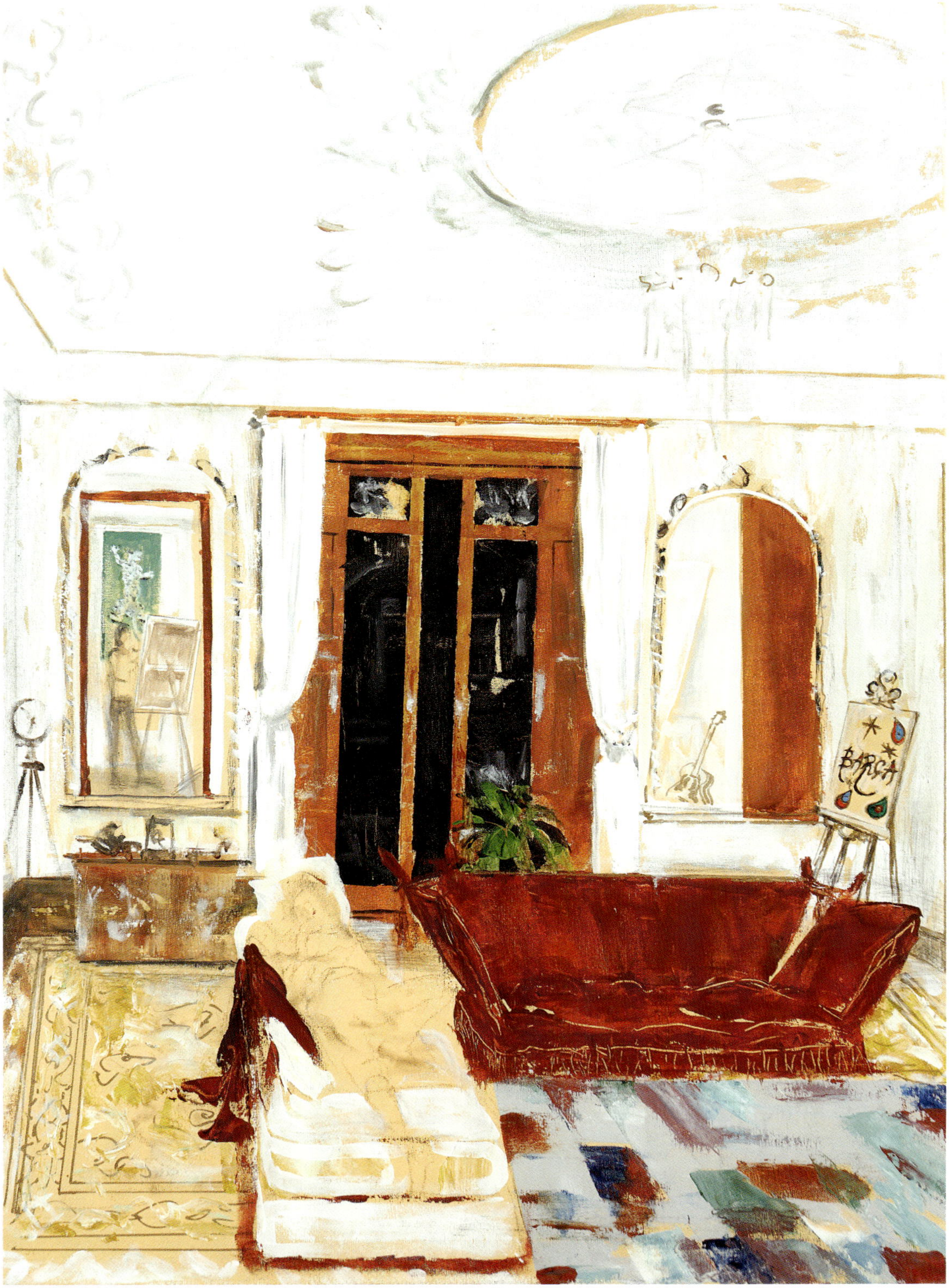

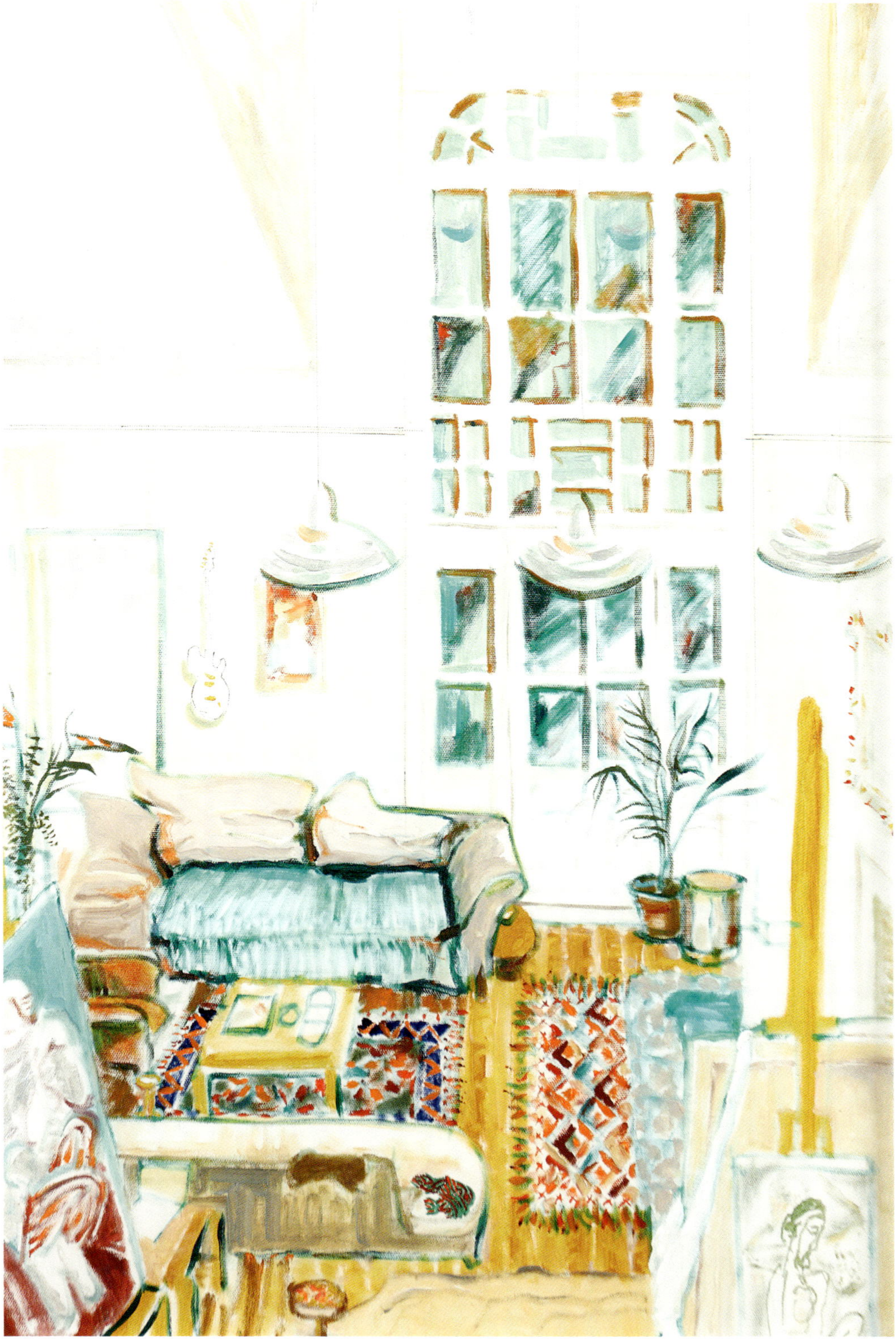

"This is the studio that Damien Hirst equipped for me when I came out of rehab; there was enough equipment for an art school!"

OPPOSITE: *Barca* | 2015 | acrylic on canvas | 100 × 73 cm
ABOVE: *Primrose Hill Studio* | 2009 | acrylic on canvas | 61 × 41.5 cm

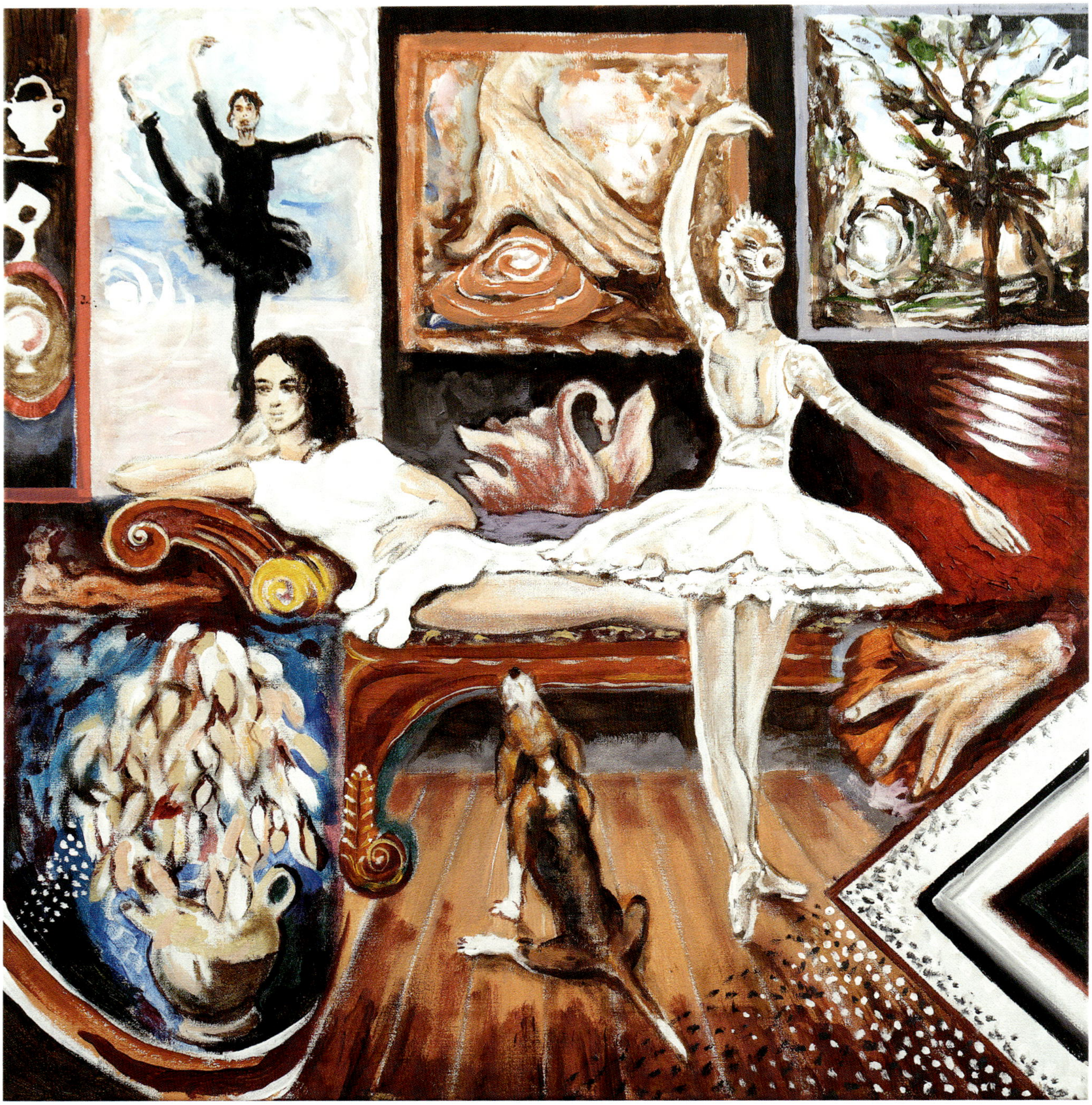

"Here, I let my imagination run free; this work incorporates many of the things I love. There's even a Gauguin and Picasso in there!"

ABOVE: *Sally* | 2015 | mixed media on canvas | 61 × 61 cm
OPPOSITE: *Dolly* | 2016 | mixed media on canvas | 31 × 31 cm

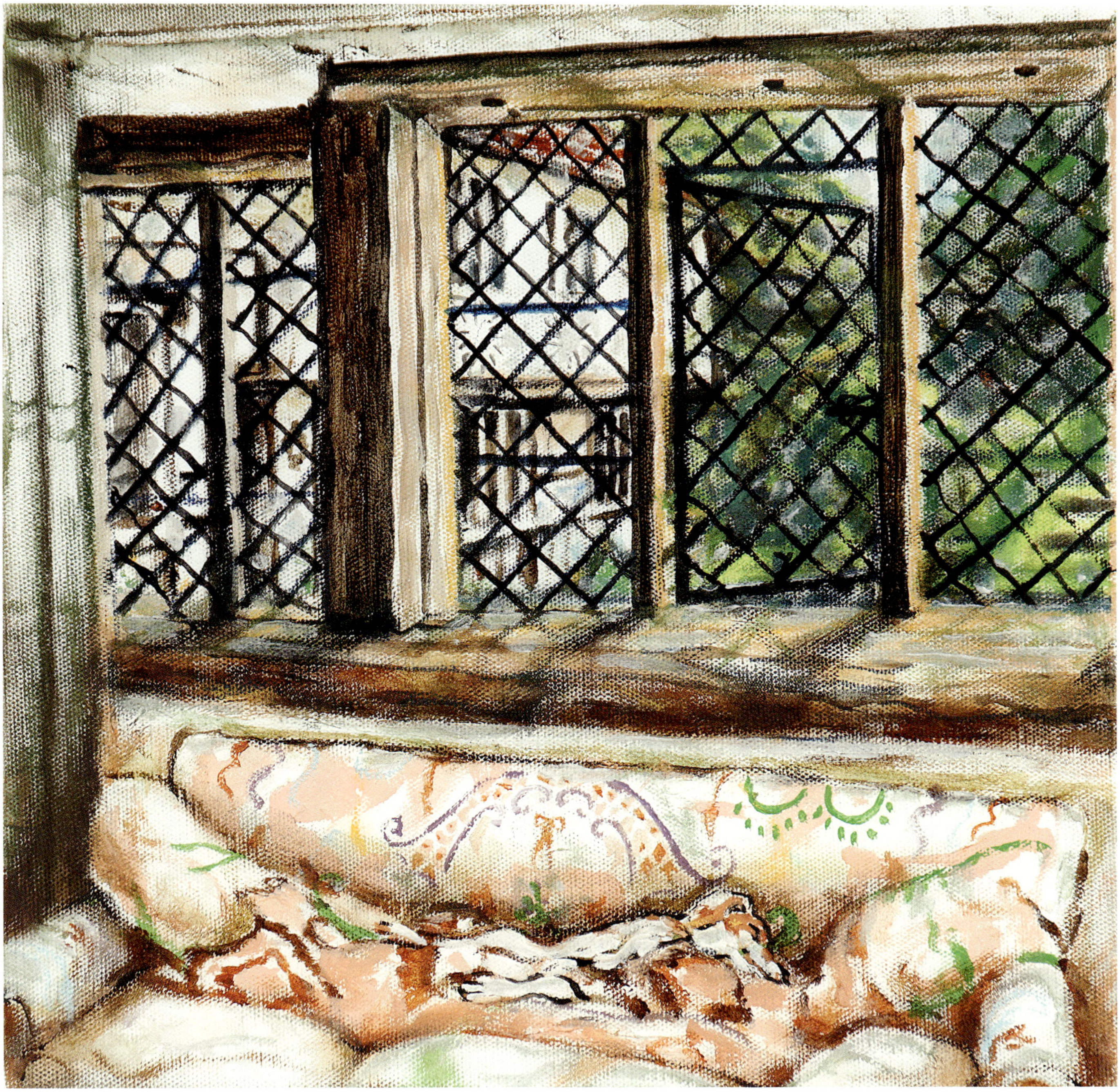

"Dolly gets in the picture, but you really have to look hard to see her. I've had the sofa for a long time but it's finally found its true home."

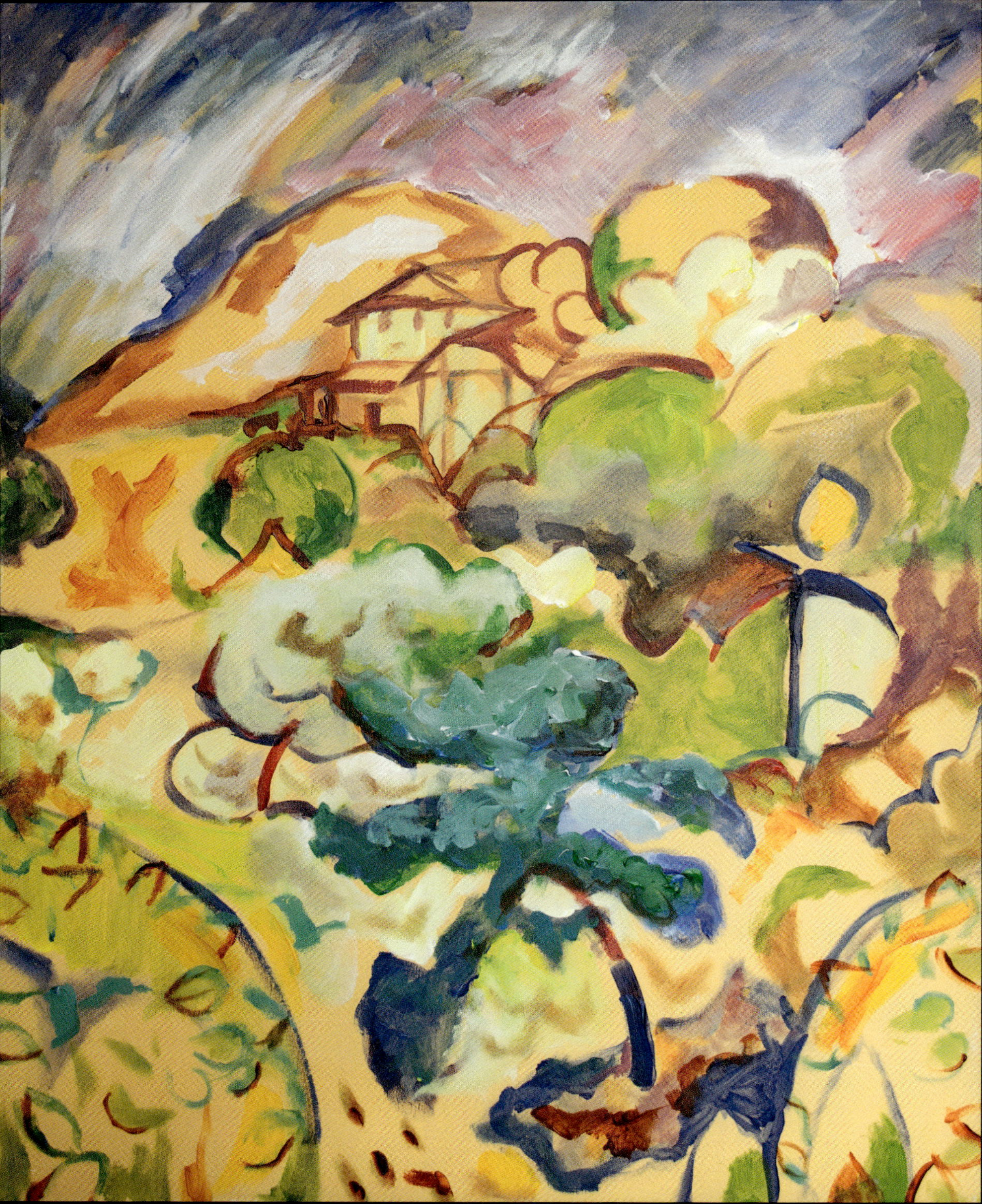

"These paintings are both influenced by Georges Braque; he was one of my very earliest inspirations."

ABOVE: *Landscape Study* | 2017 | acrylic on canvas | 76 × 65 cm
OPPOSITE: *Sunset Ireland* | 2017 | acrylic on canvas | 76 × 65 cm

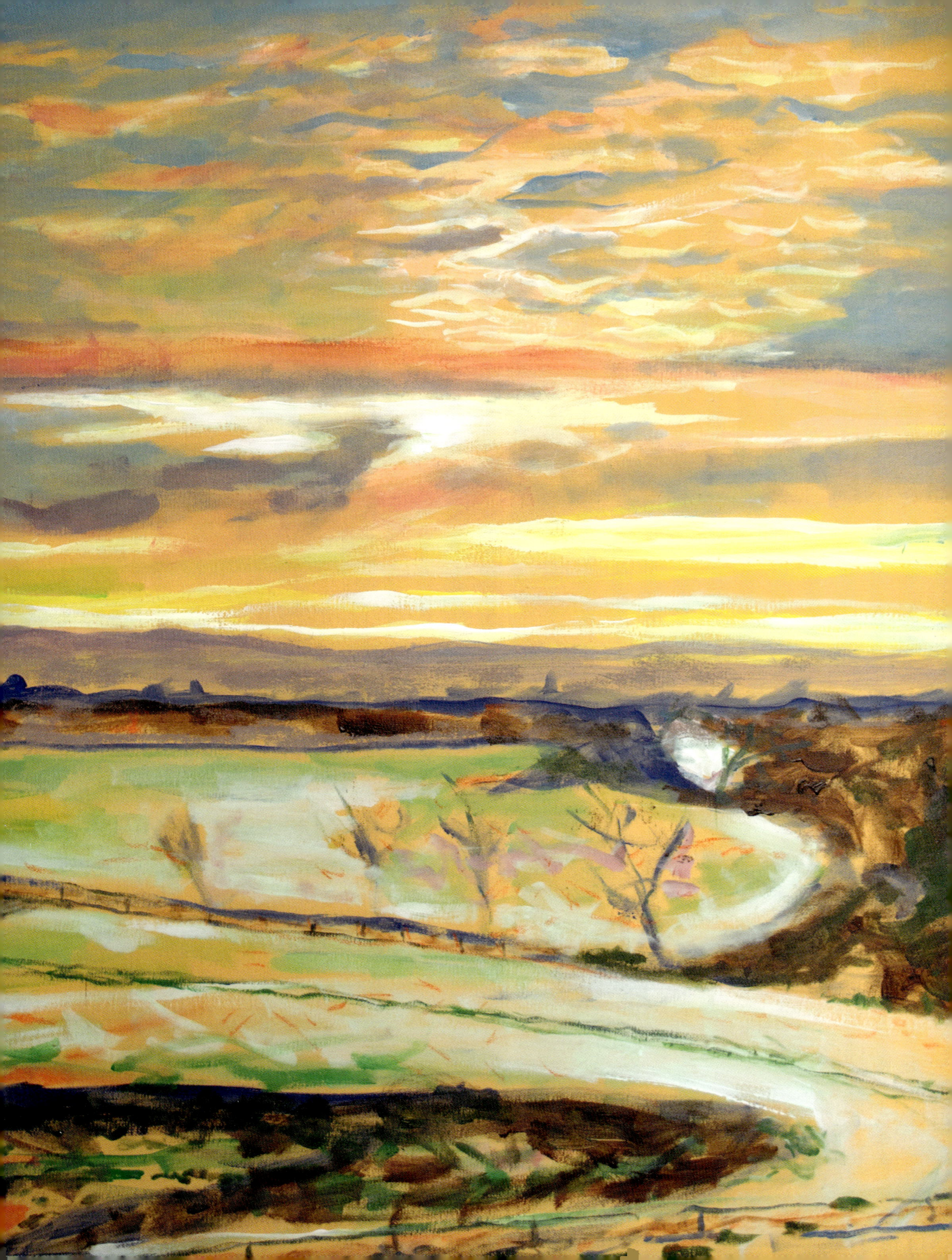

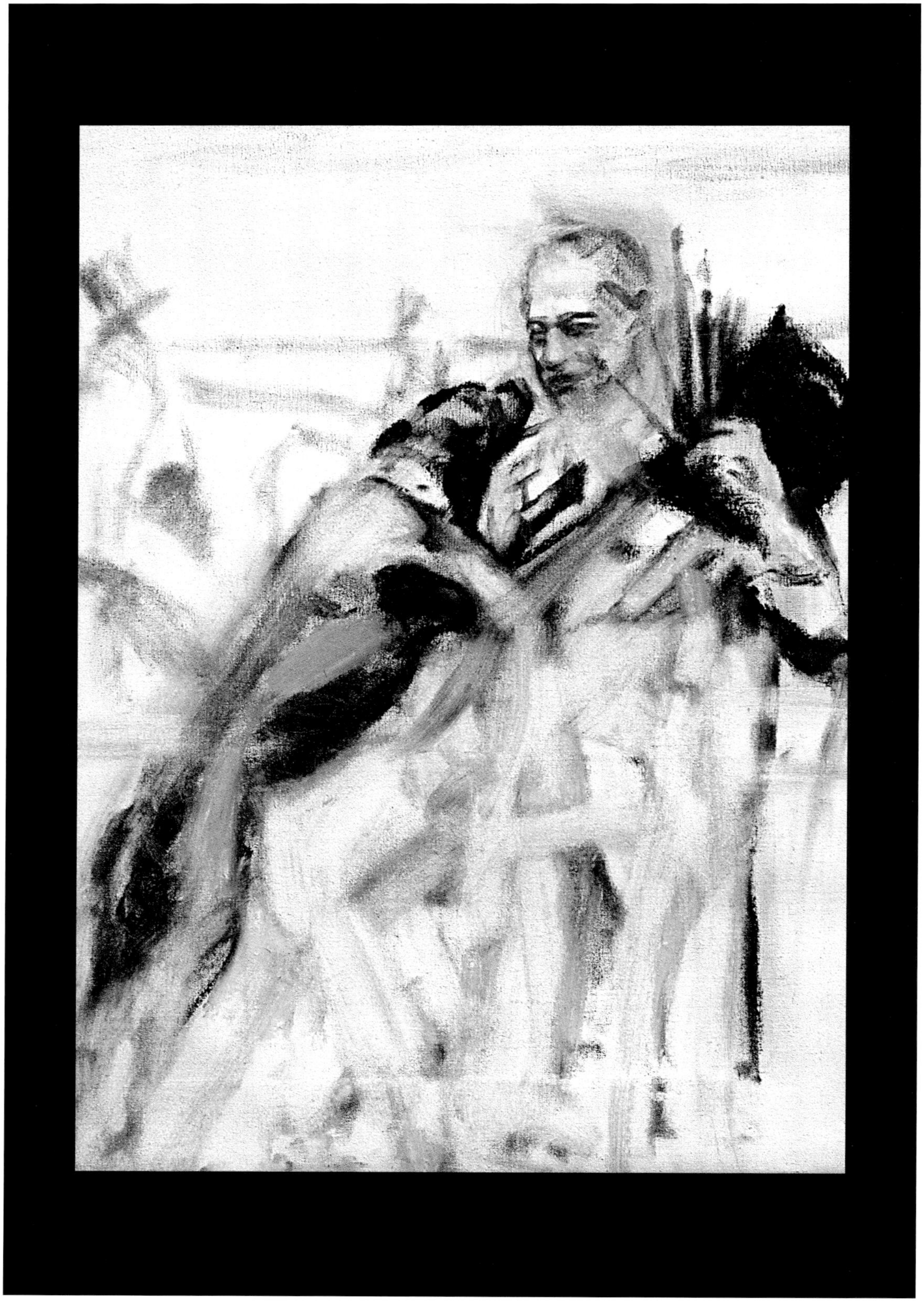

9

ANIMALS

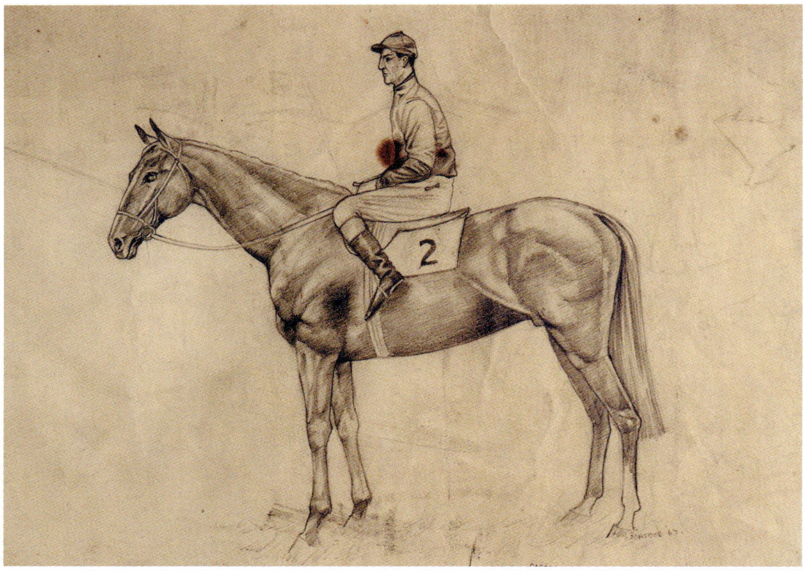

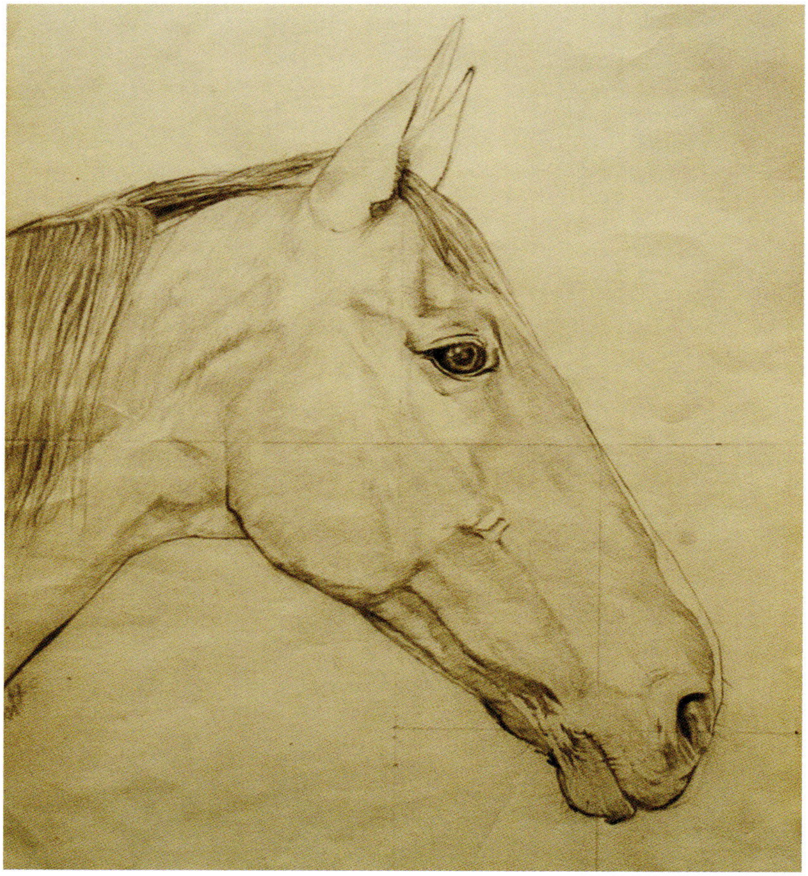

"I began by drawing horses, and these are very early examples. I've never lost my love of drawing and painting them, and have owned racehorses throughout my life."

PREVIOUS PAGE: *Sir Alfred Munnings and his Dogs* | 1995 | acrylic on canvas | 50 ×40 cm
TOP: *Pardao* | 1962 | pencil on paper | 25 × 35.5 cm
ABOVE: *My First Horse Study* | 1959 | pencil on paper | 35 × 35 cm
OPPOSITE: *Moscow Flyer* | 2005 | mixed media on canvas | 40 × 50 cm

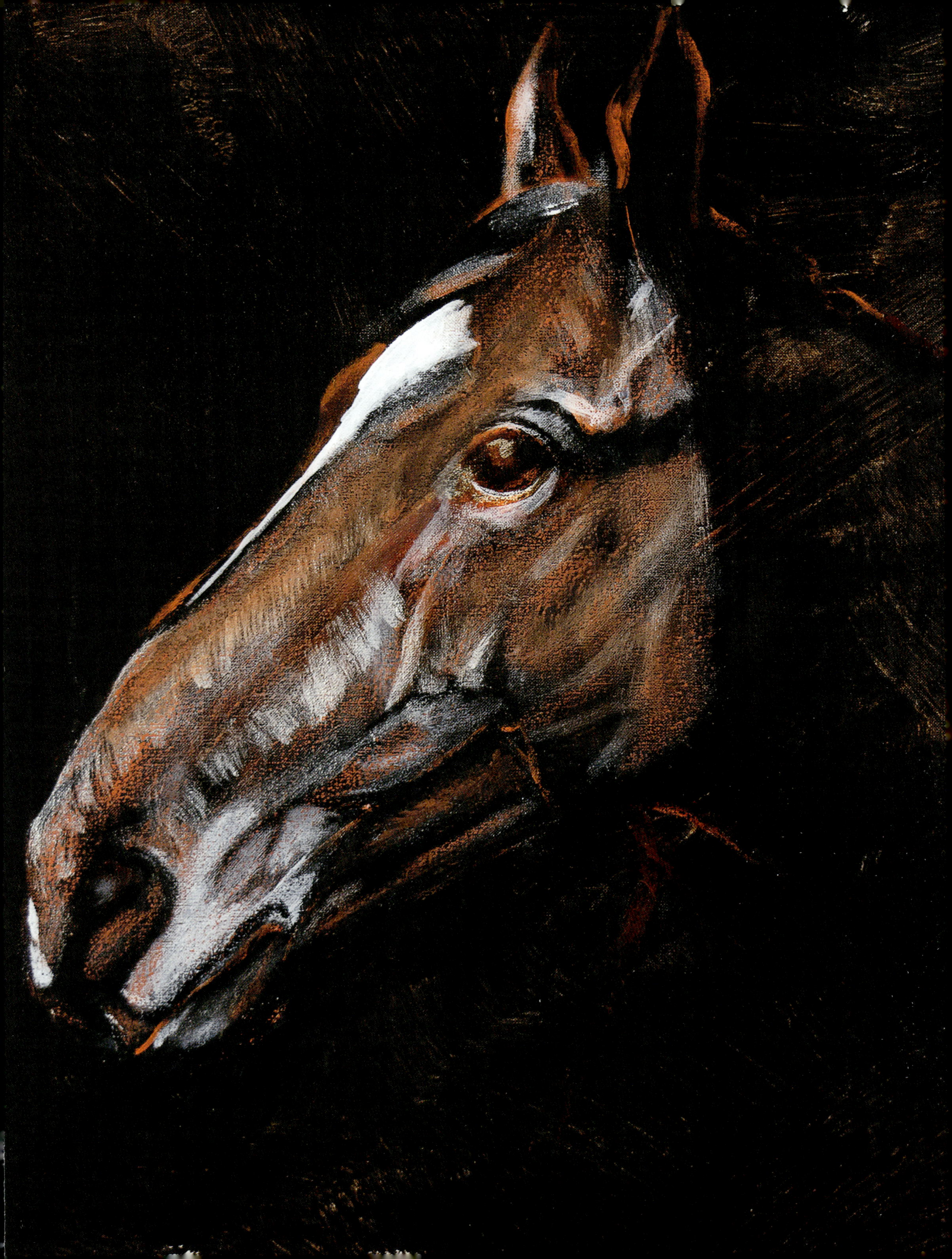

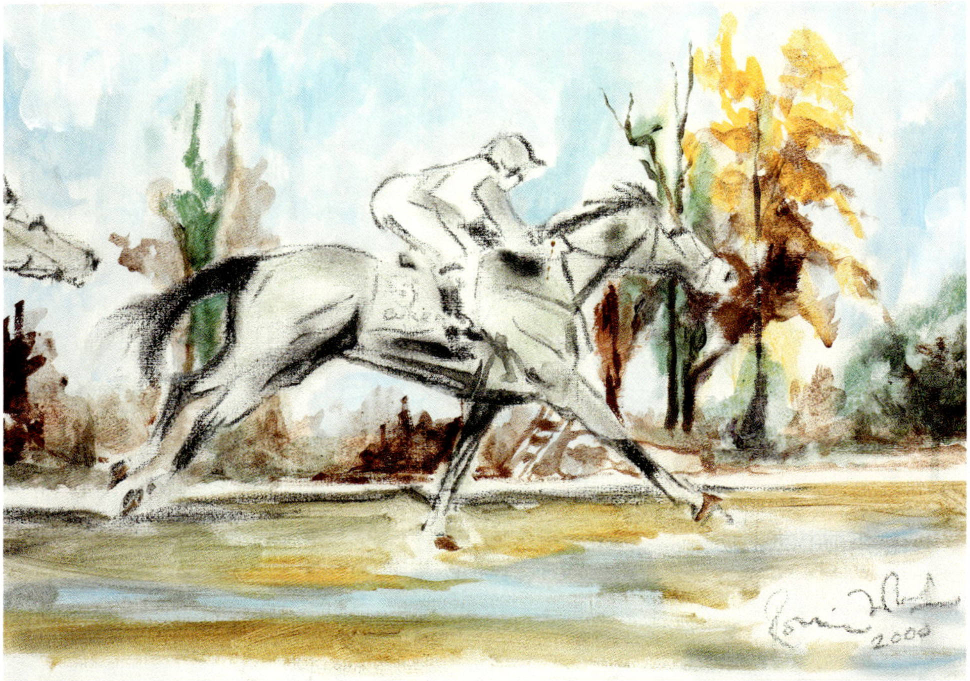

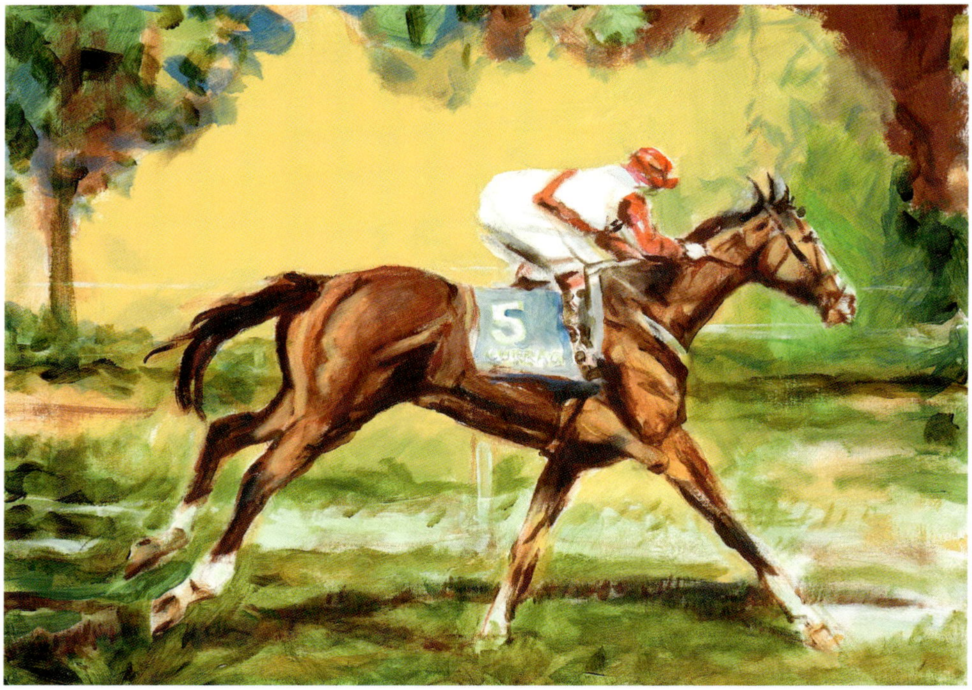

TOP: *Joleah Training* | 2000 | acrylic on canvas | 30 × 40 cm
ABOVE: *Joleah Winning* | 2004 | acrylic on canvas | 60 × 70 cm
OPPOSITE ABOVE: *Horse Study* | 2000 | pen and ink on paper | 35.5 × 51 cm
OPPOSITE BELOW: *Horse Racing* | 2000 | pencil on paper | 30 × 47 cm

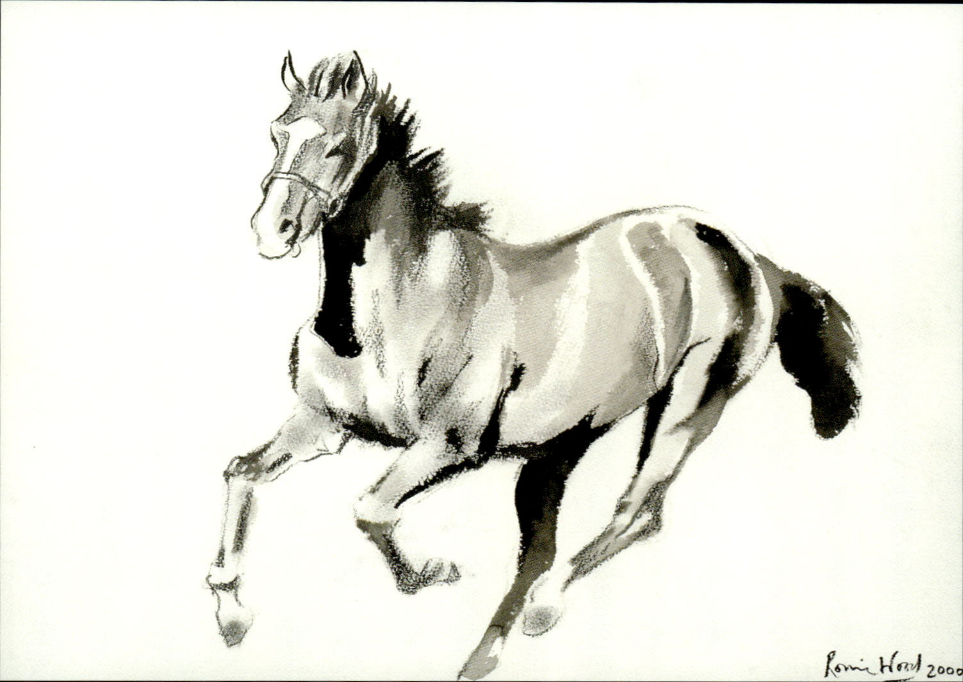

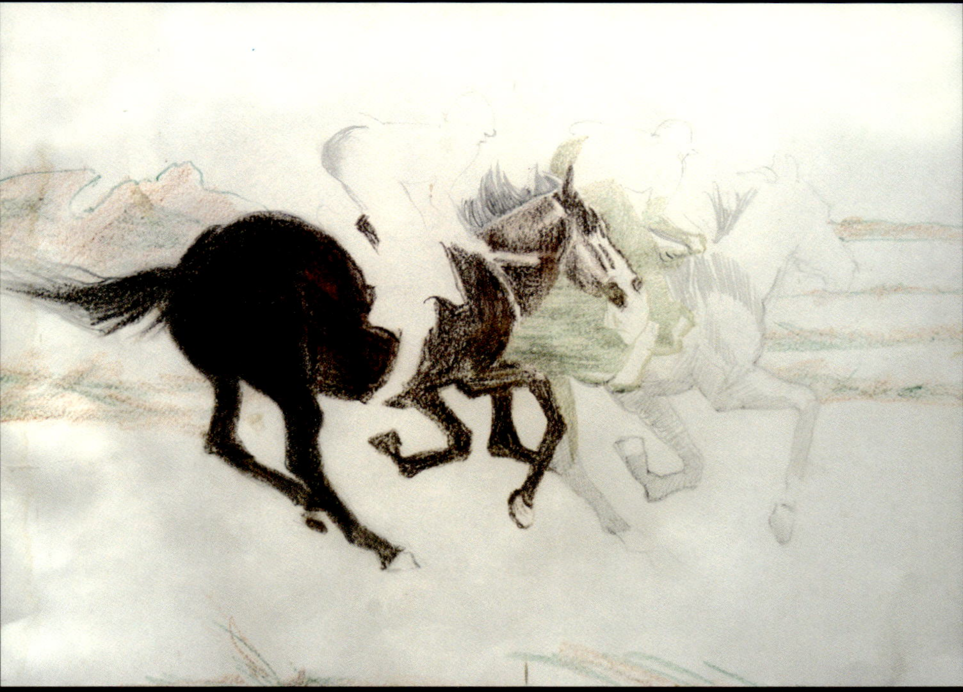

'In 1998 I won Ireland's Small Breeder of the Year trophy. Painting my horses brings back memories of all the ones that I've owned.'

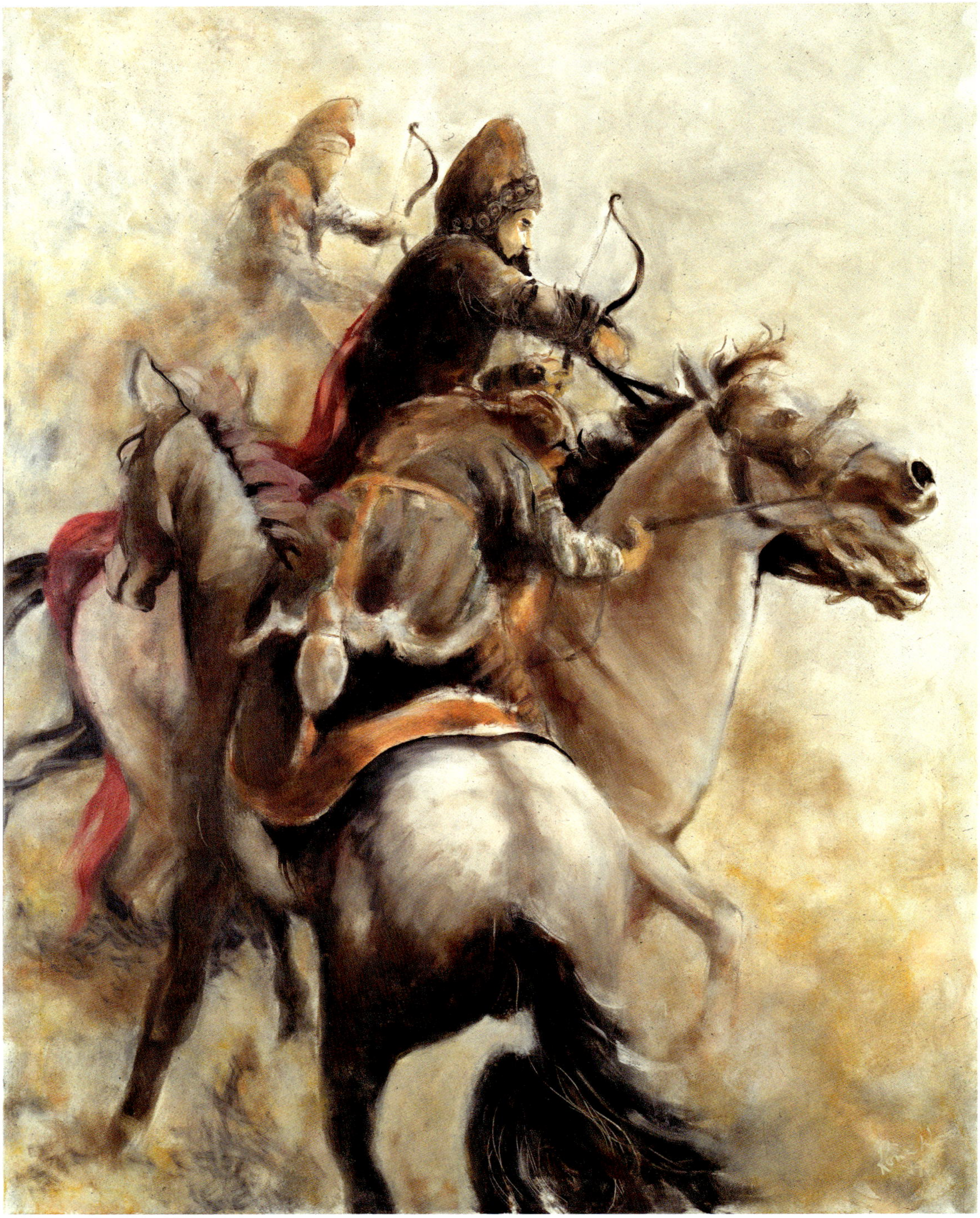

"These were both painted from inspiring photographs I had seen in a book."

ABOVE: *Genghis* | 2005 | mixed media on canvas | 122 × 92 cm
OPPOSITE: *Wild Horses* | 2005 | acrylic on canvas | 122 × 92 cm

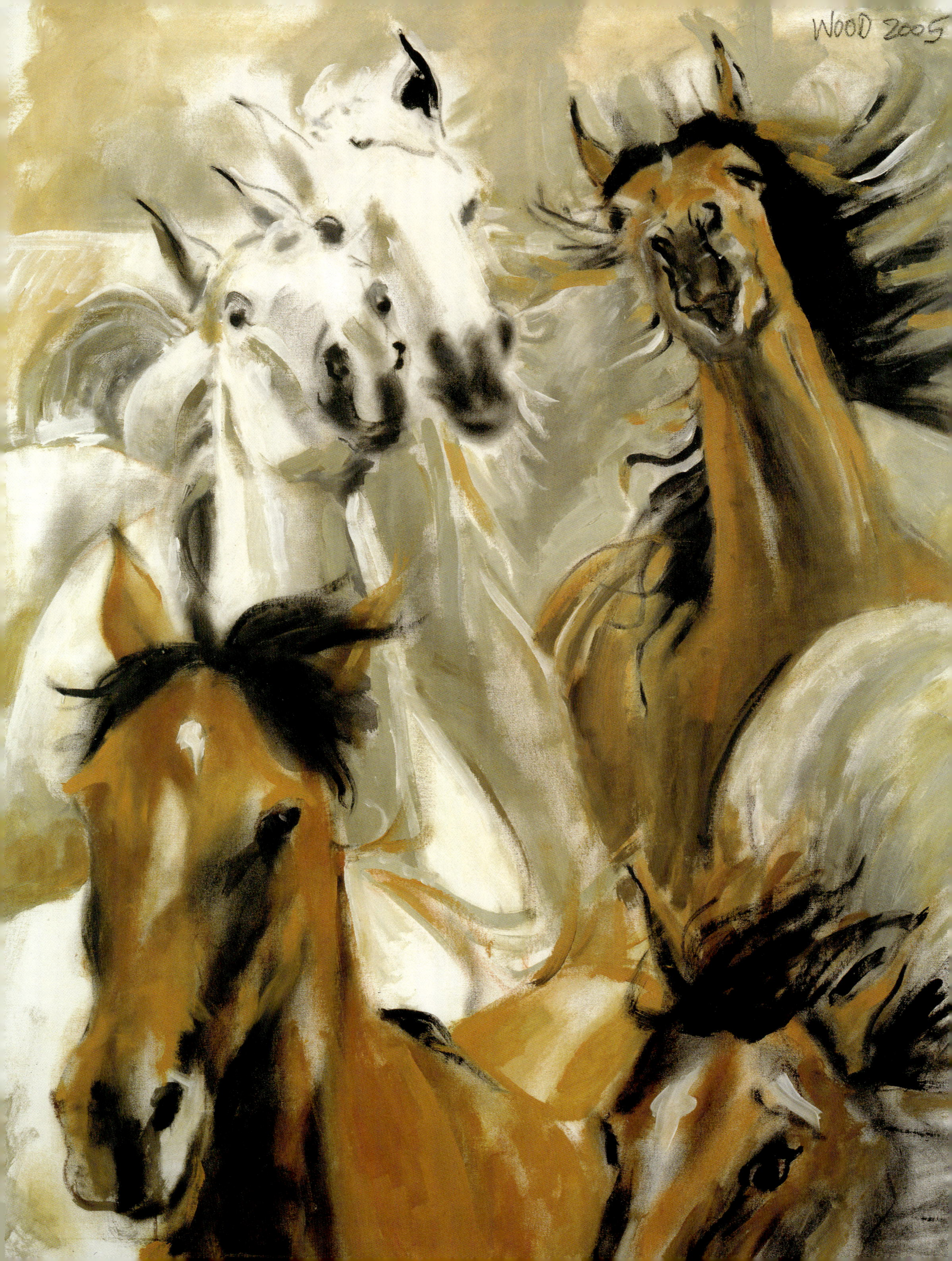
WOOD 2005

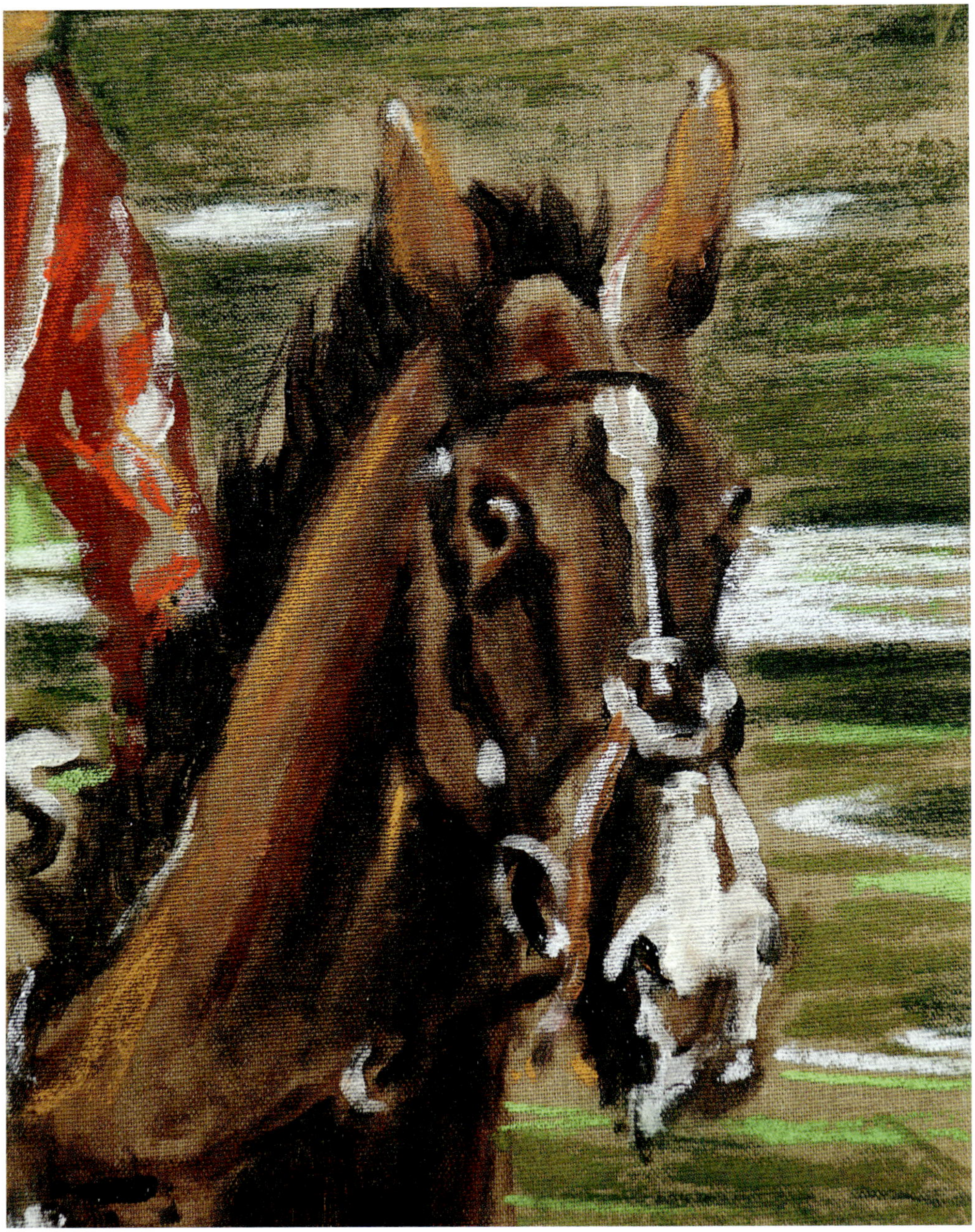

"Wild-eyed Sandymount Duke is the most successful winner I've ever owned – and he's not finished yet!"

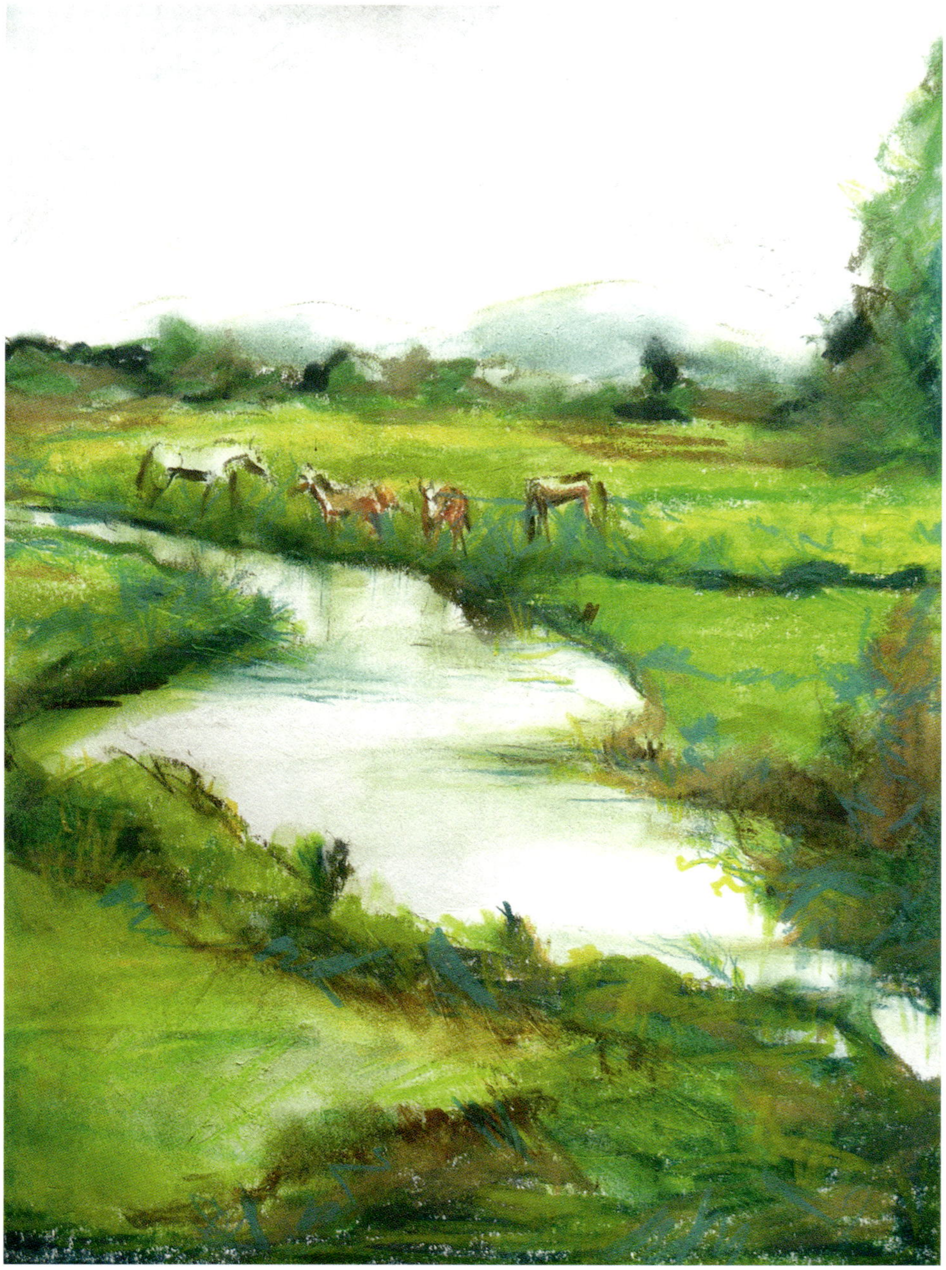

OPPOSITE: *Sandymount Duke* | 2012 | mixed media on canvas | 29 × 21 cm approx
ABOVE: *Irish Riverside Study* | 2009 | pastel on paper | 35 × 28 cm

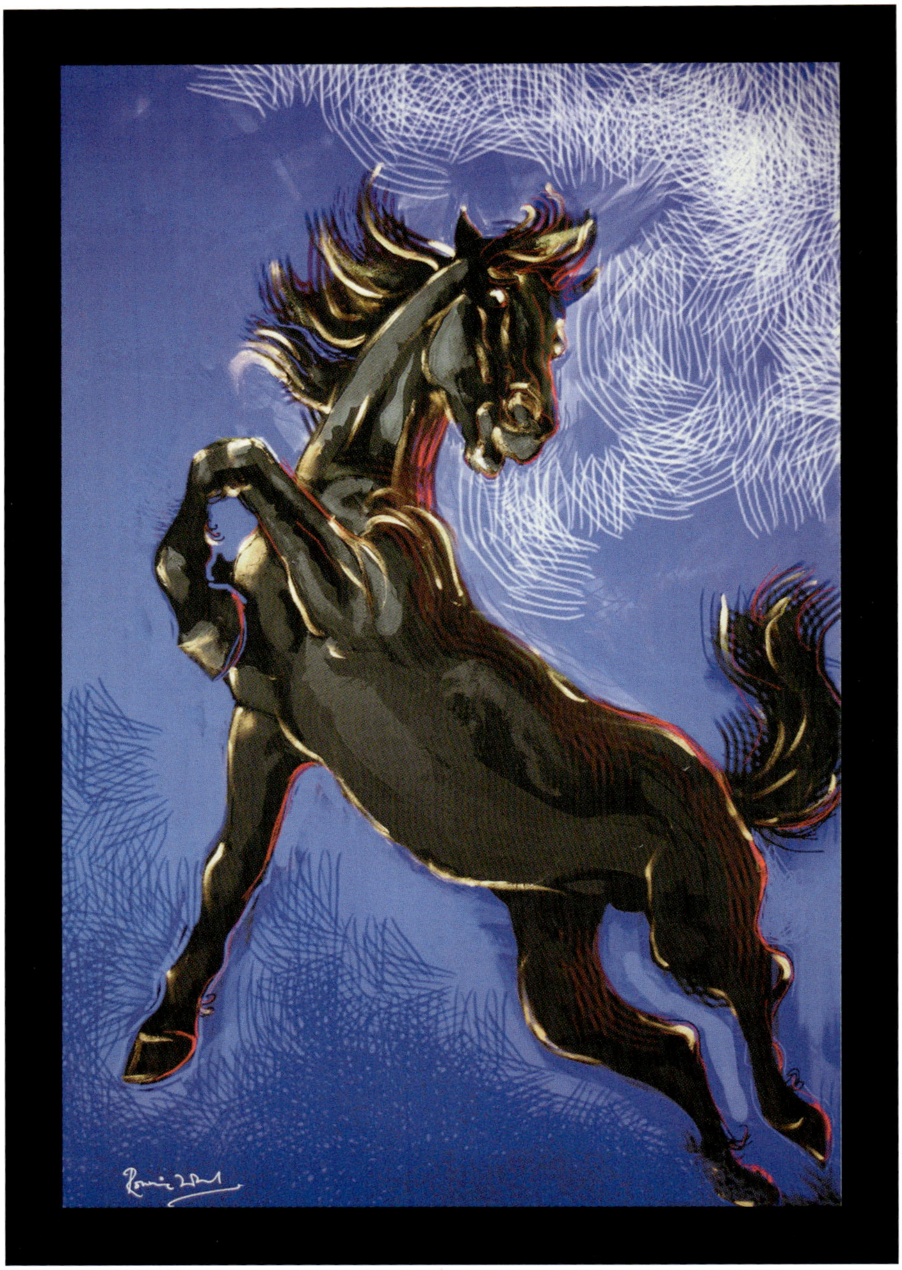

"These are both inspired by Pierre Louis Rouillard's bronze horse outside the Musée d'Orsay in Paris."

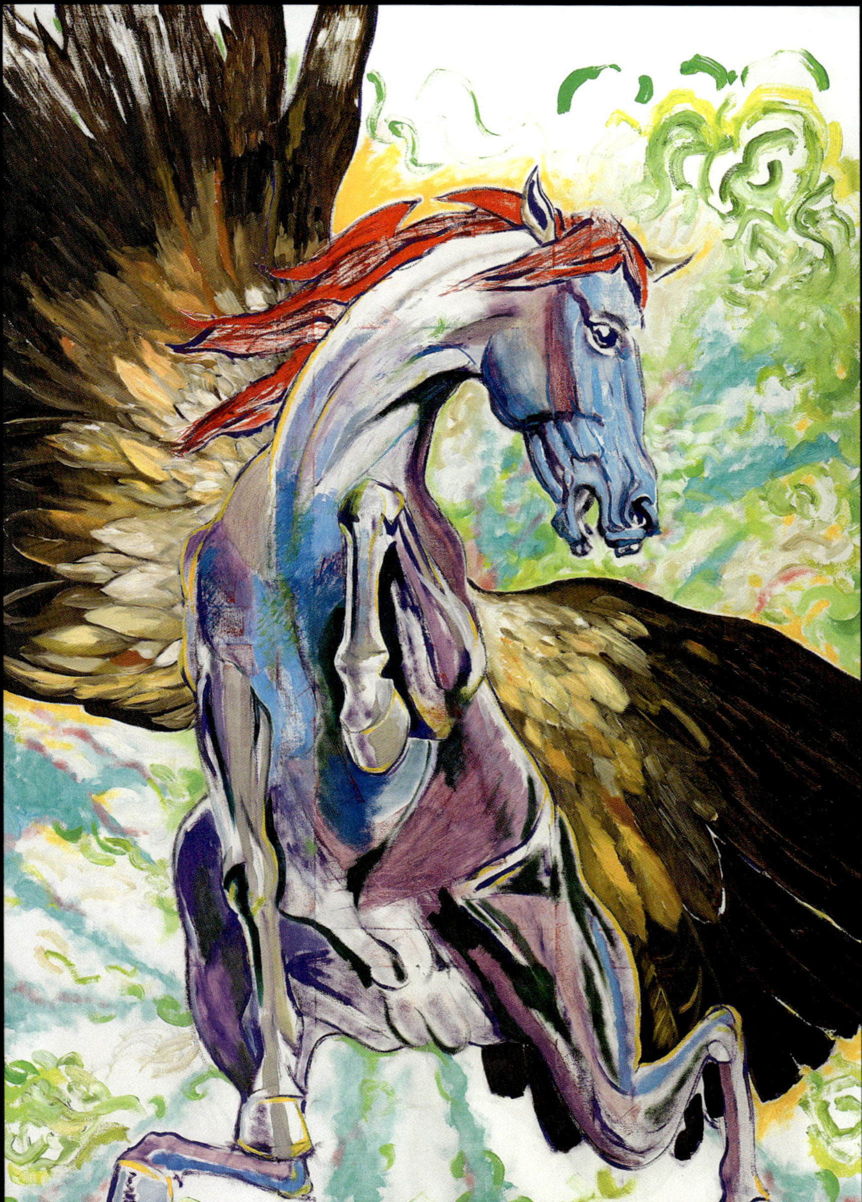

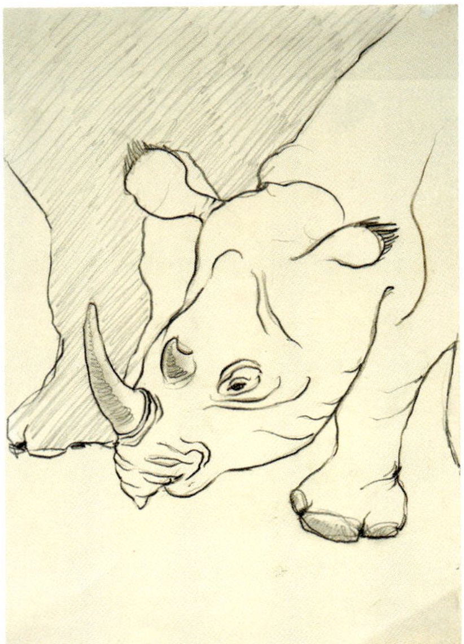

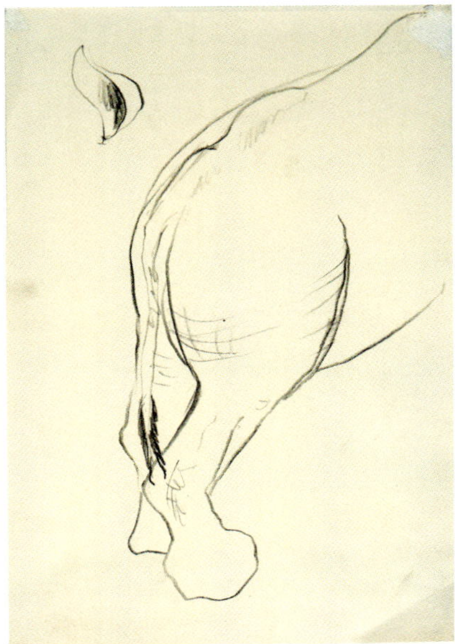

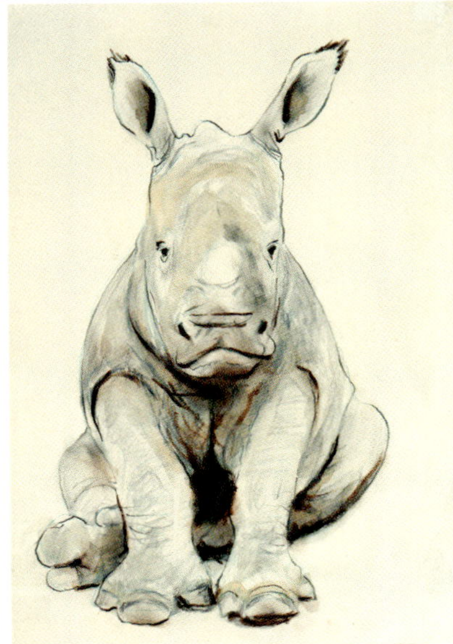

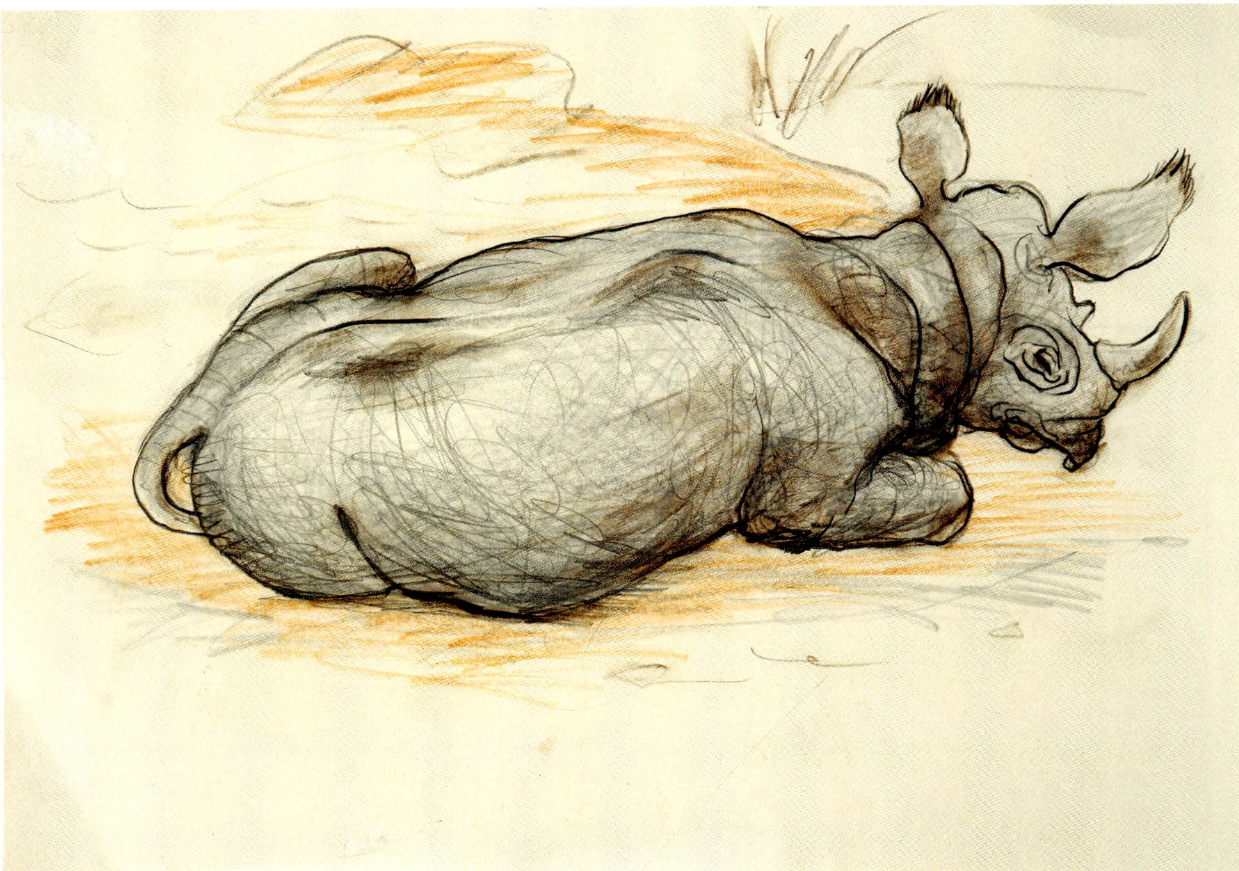

"I did these drawings in 1996 when I went on safari after the Stones' Voodoo Lounge tour had finished. As you can see, I even got splashed!"

TOP LEFT: *Omni I* | 1996 | pencil on paper | 42 × 30 cm
TOP CENTRE: *Omni II* | 1996 | pencil on paper | 42 × 30 cm
TOP RIGHT: *Baby Omni* | 1996 | colour pencil and wash on paper | 42 × 30 cm
ABOVE: *Omni III* | 1996 | colour pencil and wash on paper | 29 × 42 cm
OPPOSITE: *Mud-spattered Omni* | 1996 | pencil on paper | 42 × 29 cm

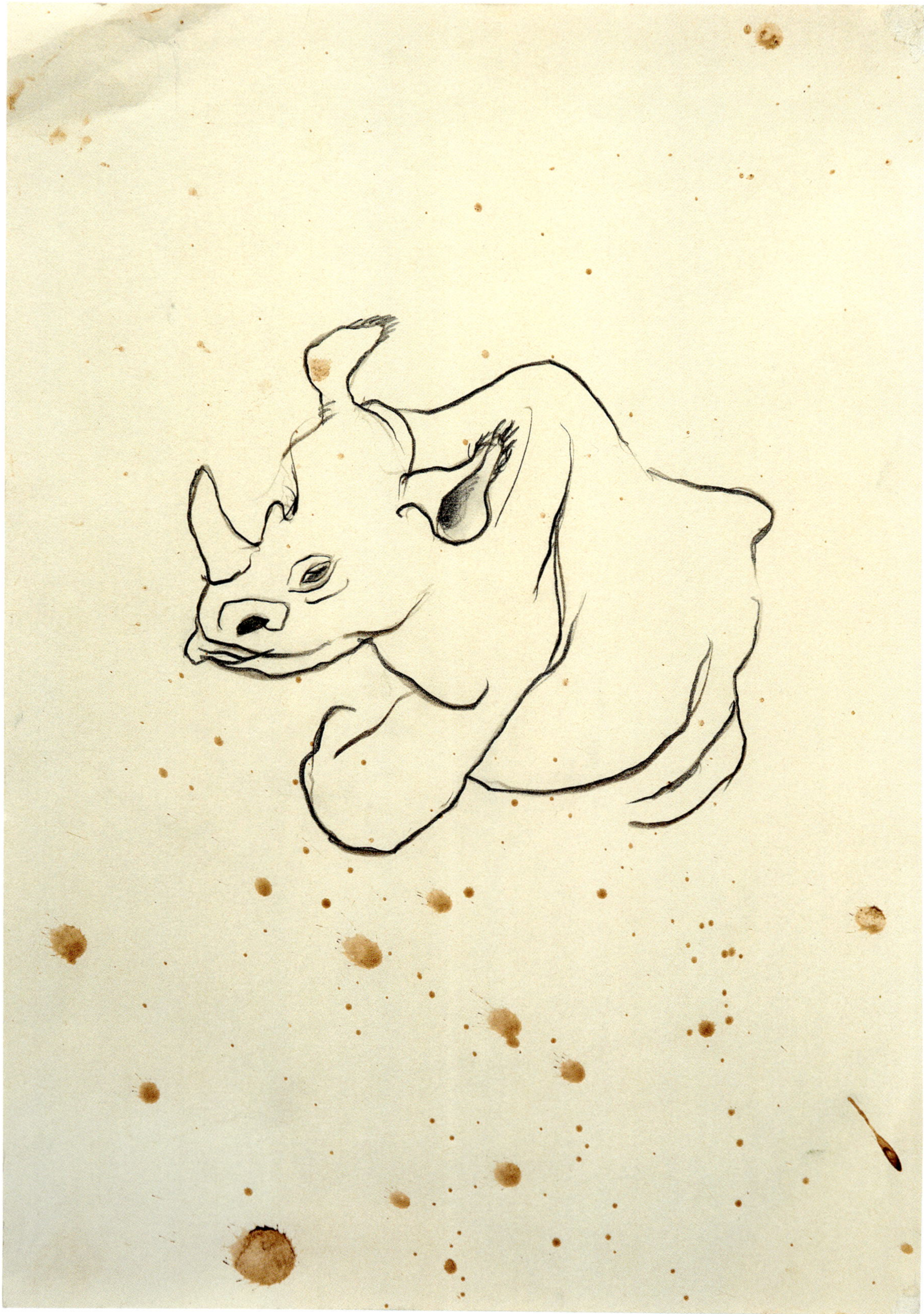

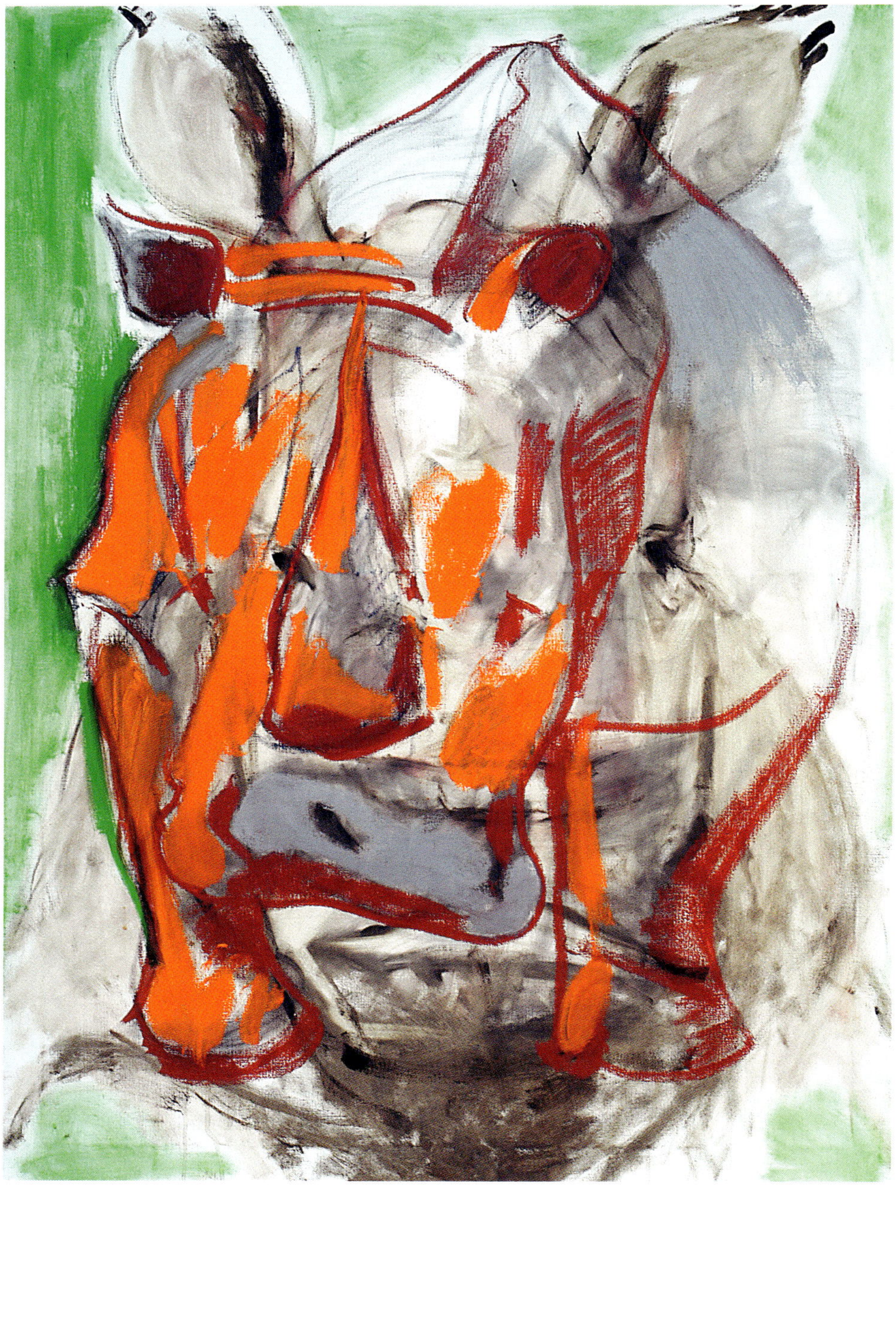

ABOVE: *Rhino I* | 2003 | oil on canvas | 122 × 91 cm
OPPOSITE: *Rhino II* | 2003 | oil on canvas | 122 × 91 cm

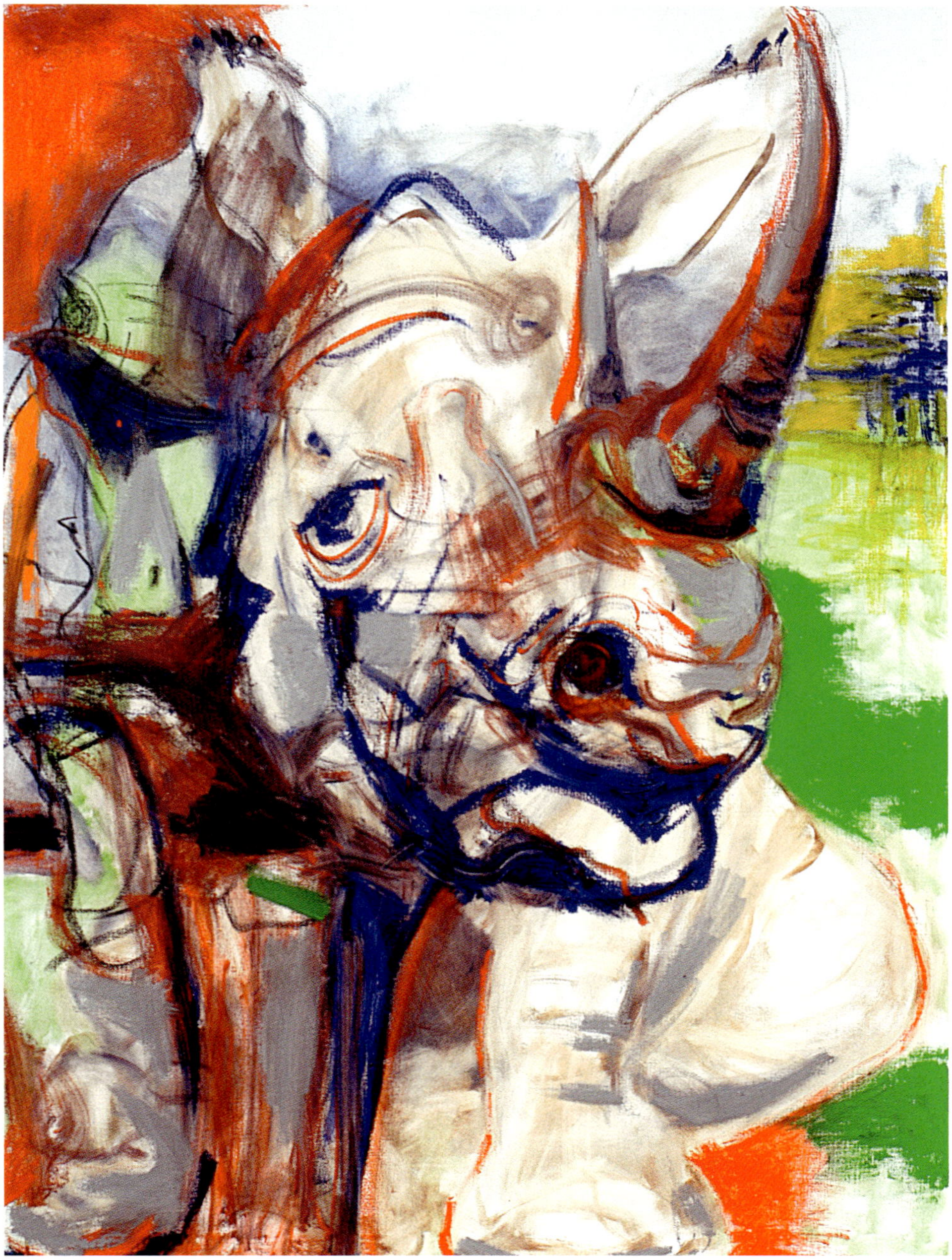

"My love of the rhino stems from the fact that it's the nearest thing to a prehistoric animal to roam the earth. If we don't protect them then poachers will kill them all."

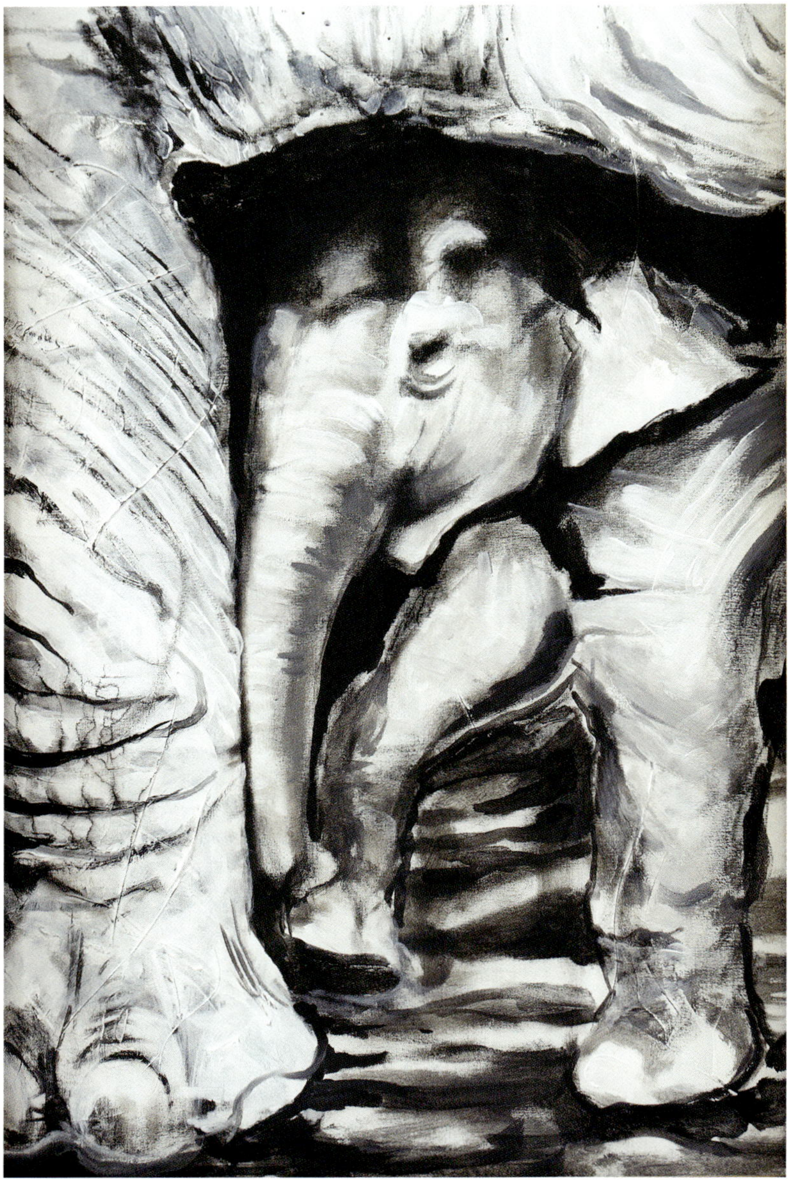

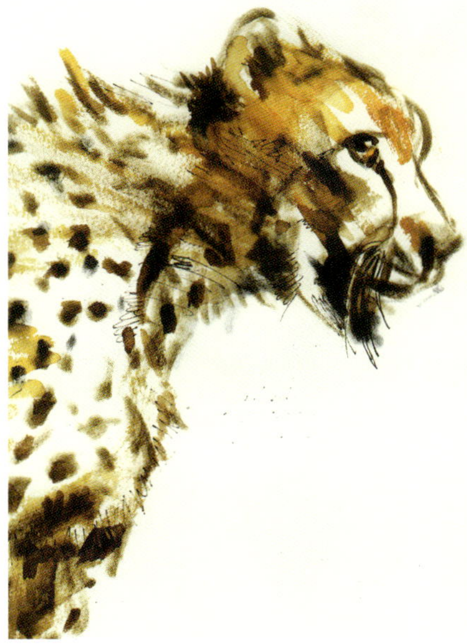

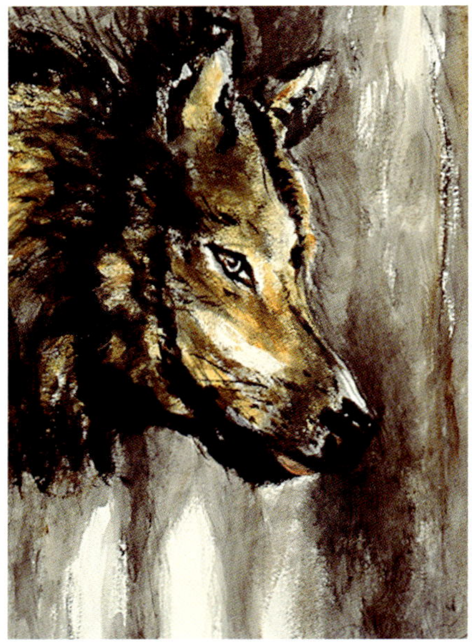

"My love of endangered species extends to all birds and animals. I'm inspired to paint them all."

ABOVE LEFT: *Elephant Study* | 2016 | mixed media on canvas | 91.5 × 61 cm
TOP RIGHT: *Cheetah* | 1994 | acrylic and pastel on paper | 29 × 21 cm
ABOVE RIGHT: *Wolf* | 1994 | mixed media on paper | 29 × 21 cm
OPPOSITE TOP LEFT: *Seal Study* | 1994 | acrylic on paper | 29 × 21 cm
OPPOSITE TOP CENTRE: *Butterfly Study* | 1994 | acrylic on paper | 29 × 21 cm
OPPOSITE TOP RIGHT: *Penguin* | 1994 | mixed media on paper | 29 × 21 cm
OPPOSITE CENTRE LEFT: *Gorilla Study* | 1995 | acrylic on paper | 29 × 21 cm
OPPOSITE CENTRE: *Panther* | 1994 | mixed media on paper | 29 × 25 cm
OPPOSITE CENTRE RIGHT: *Seal* | 1994 | mixed media on paper | 29 × 21 cm
OPPOSITE BOTTOM LEFT: *Panda* | 1994 | mixed media on paper | 29 × 25 cm
OPPOSITE BOTTOM CENTRE: *Eagle Study* | 1994 | acrylic on paper | 29 × 21 cm
OPPOSITE BOTTOM RIGHT: *Chimp* | 1994 | mixed media on paper | 29 × 21 cm

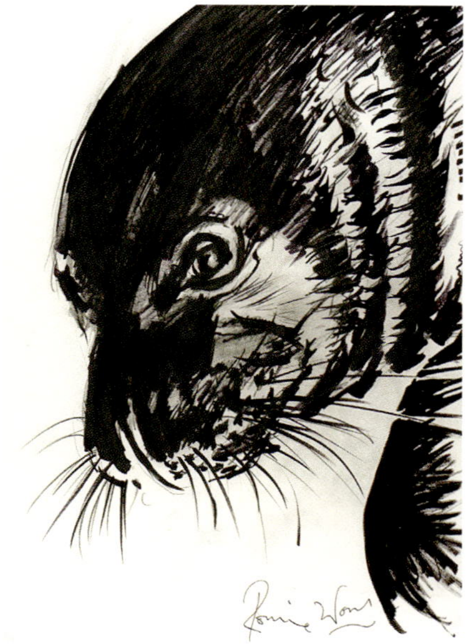
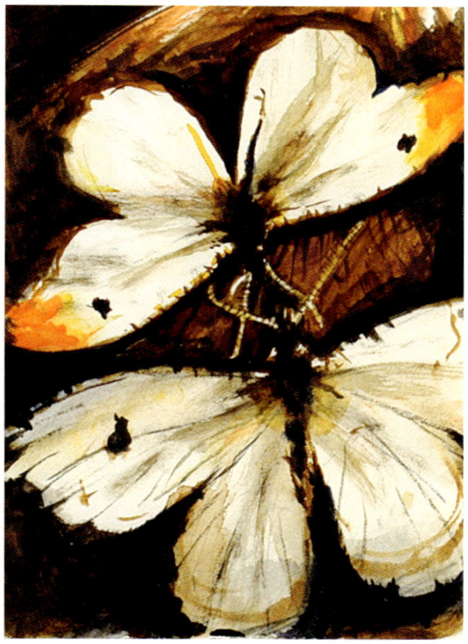
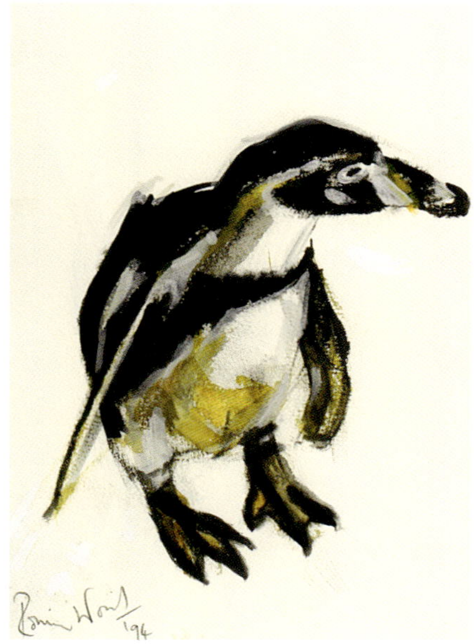
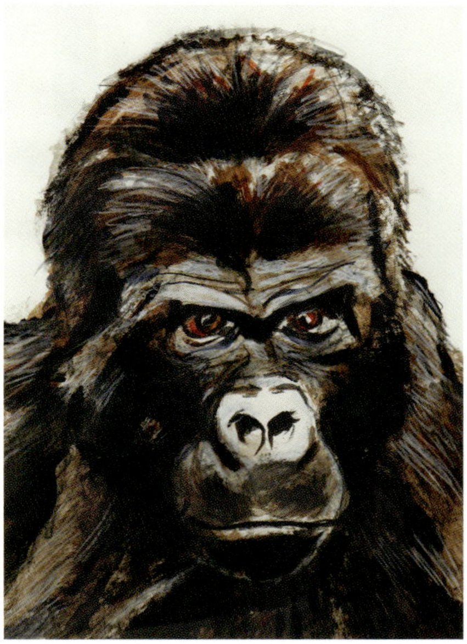
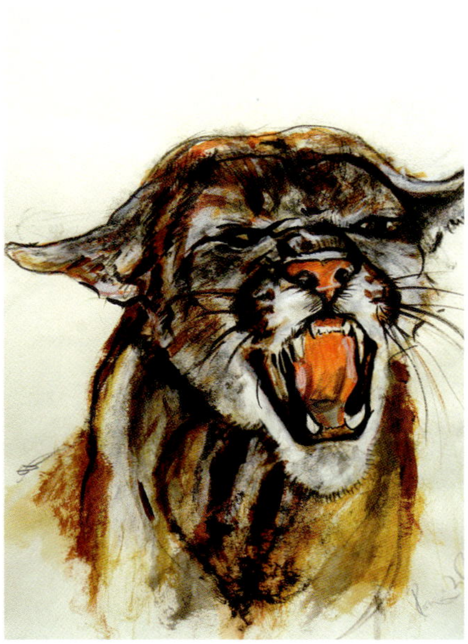
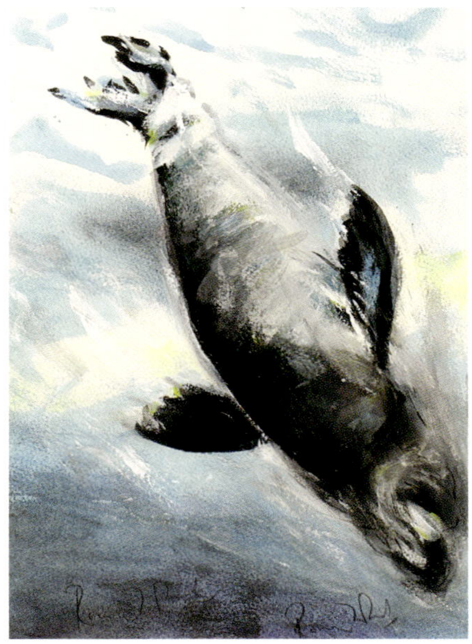
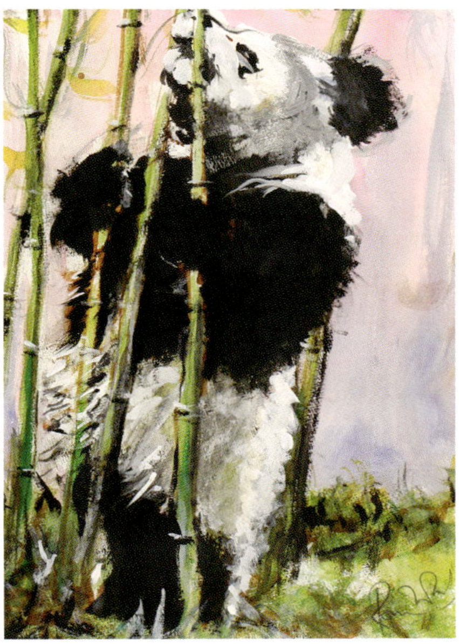
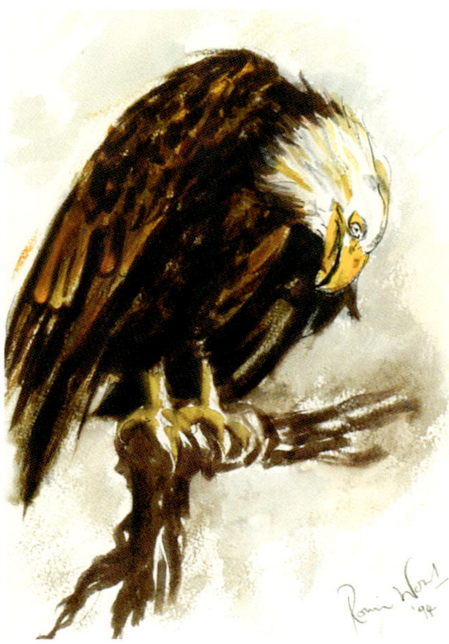
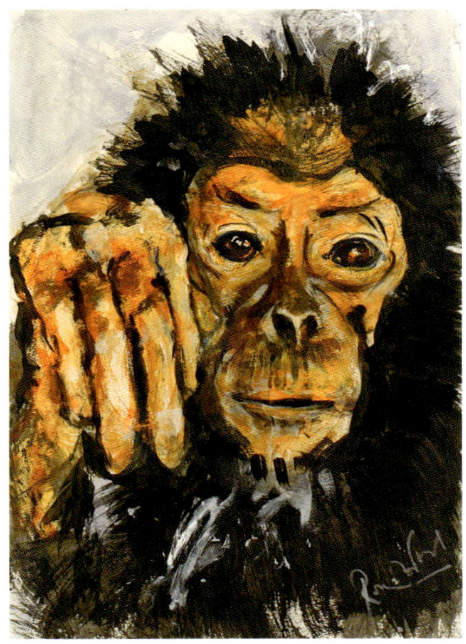

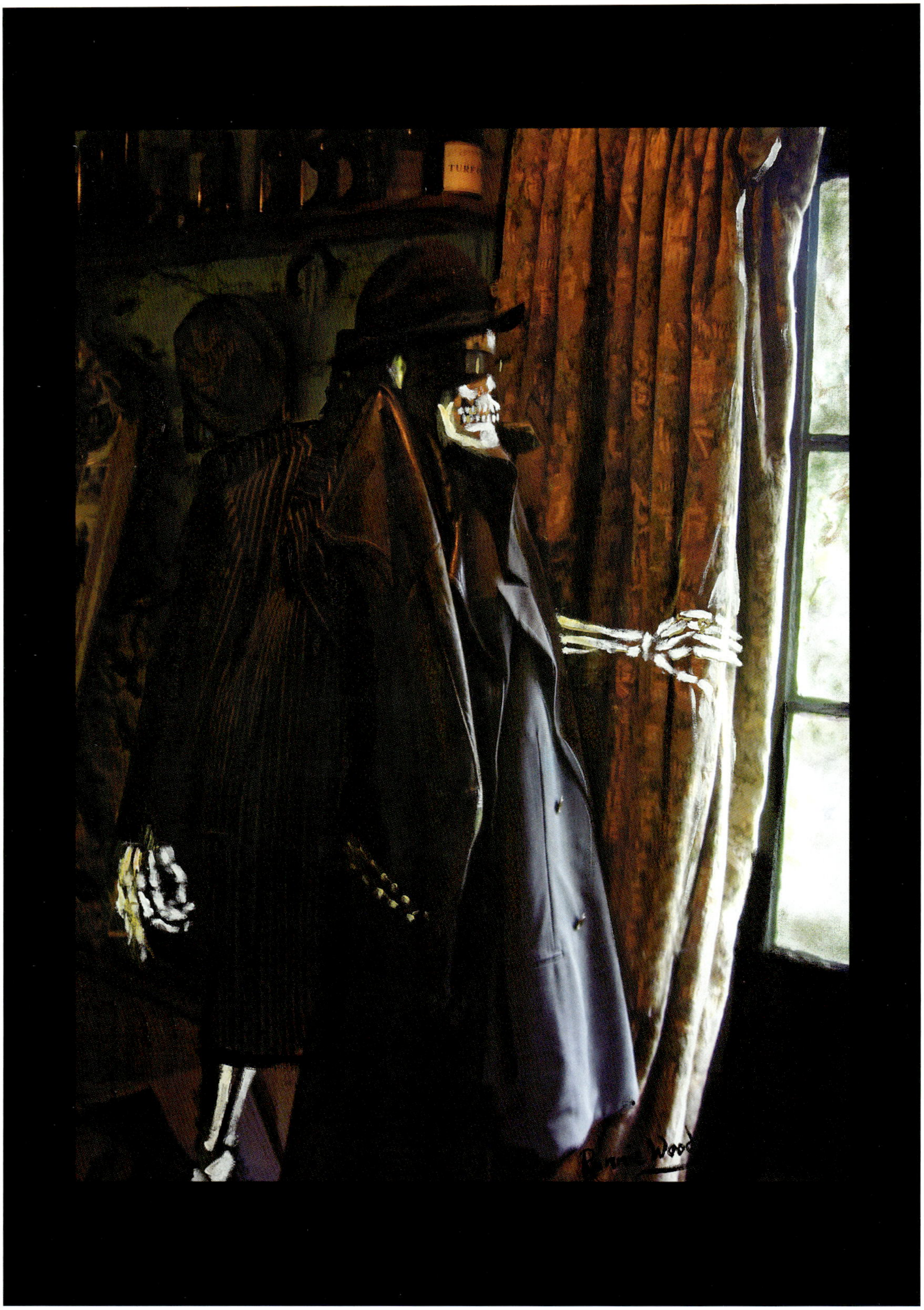

10

BEYOND THE CANVAS

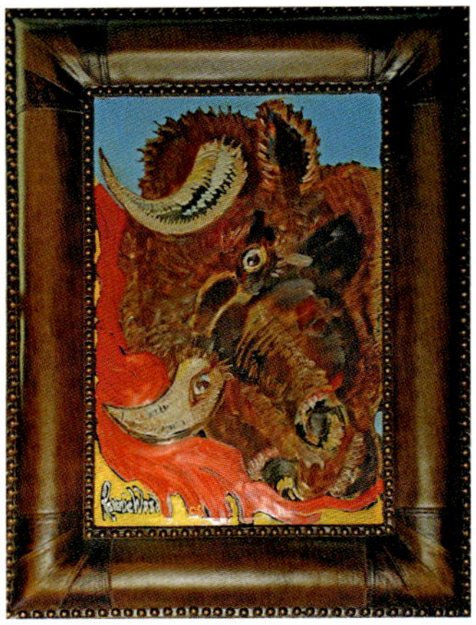
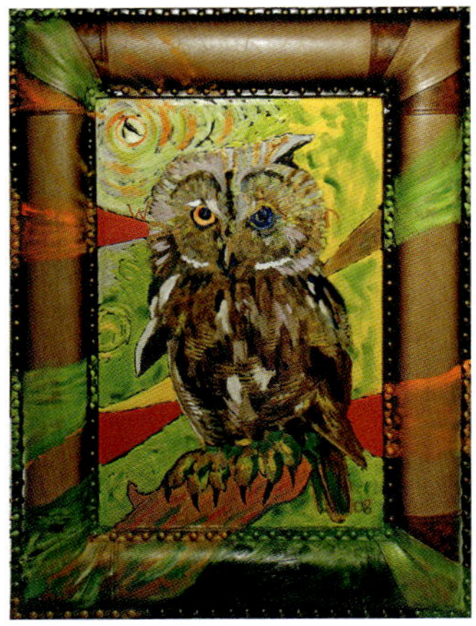
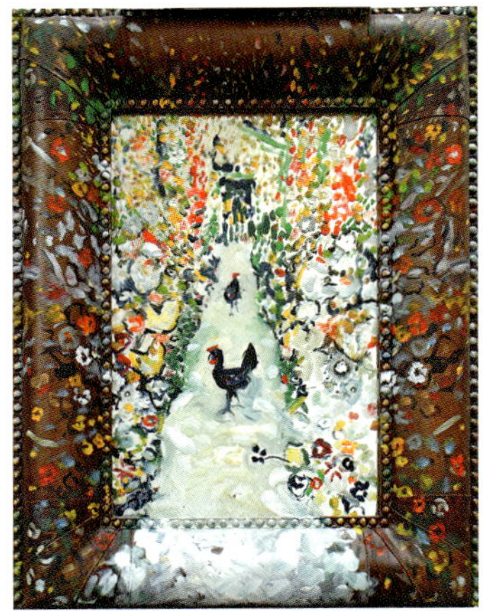
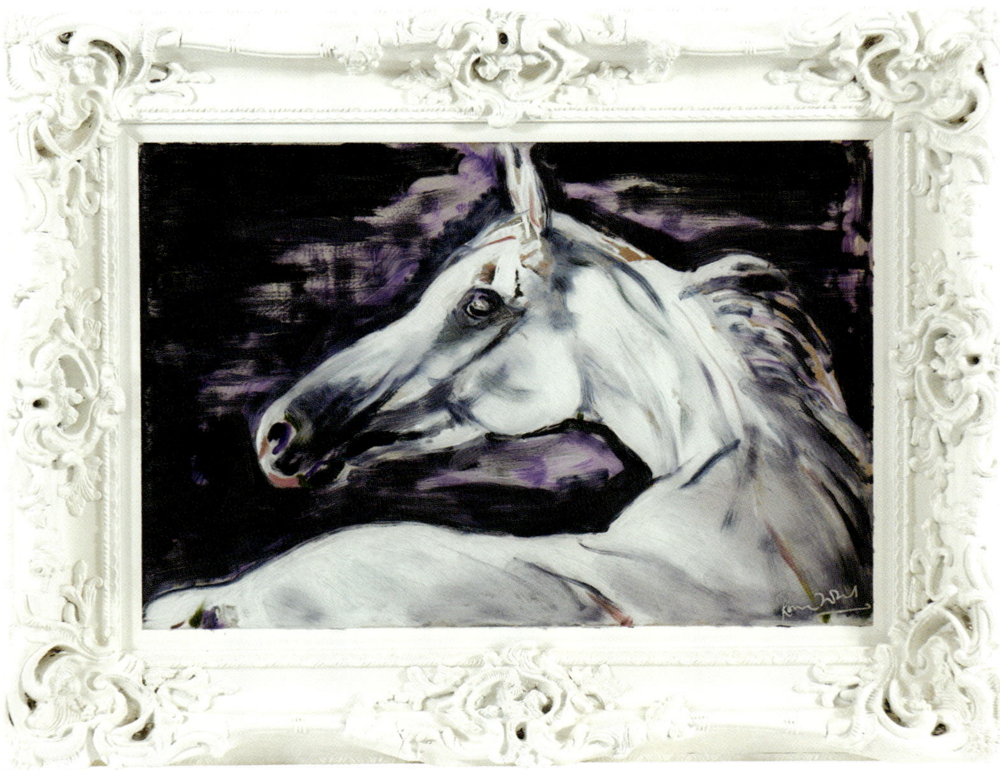

PREVIOUS PAGE: *Ghost, Original* | 2007 | acrylic on pre-printed canvas 99.5 × 84.5 cm
TOP LEFT: *Mirror Painting I* | 2008–09 | acrylic on mirror | 120 × 100 cm
TOP CENTRE: *Mirror Painting II* | 2008–09 | acrylic on mirror | 120 × 100 cm
TOP RIGHT: *Mirror Painting VIII* | 2008–09 | acrylic on mirror | 120 × 100 cm

ABOVE: *Mirror Painting IV* | 2008–09 | acrylic on mirror | 100 × 120 cm
OPPOSITE LEFT: *Door Painting* | 2013–15 | acrylic on wooden panel | 100 × 44 cm
OPPOSITE TOP RIGHT: *Mirror V* | 2009 | acrylic on mirror | 60 × 60 cm
OPPOSITE CENTRE RIGHT: *Mirror VI* | 2009 | acrylic on mirror | 60 × 60 cm
OPPOSITE BOTTOM RIGHT: *Mirror III* | 2009 | acrylic on mirror | 60 × 60 cm

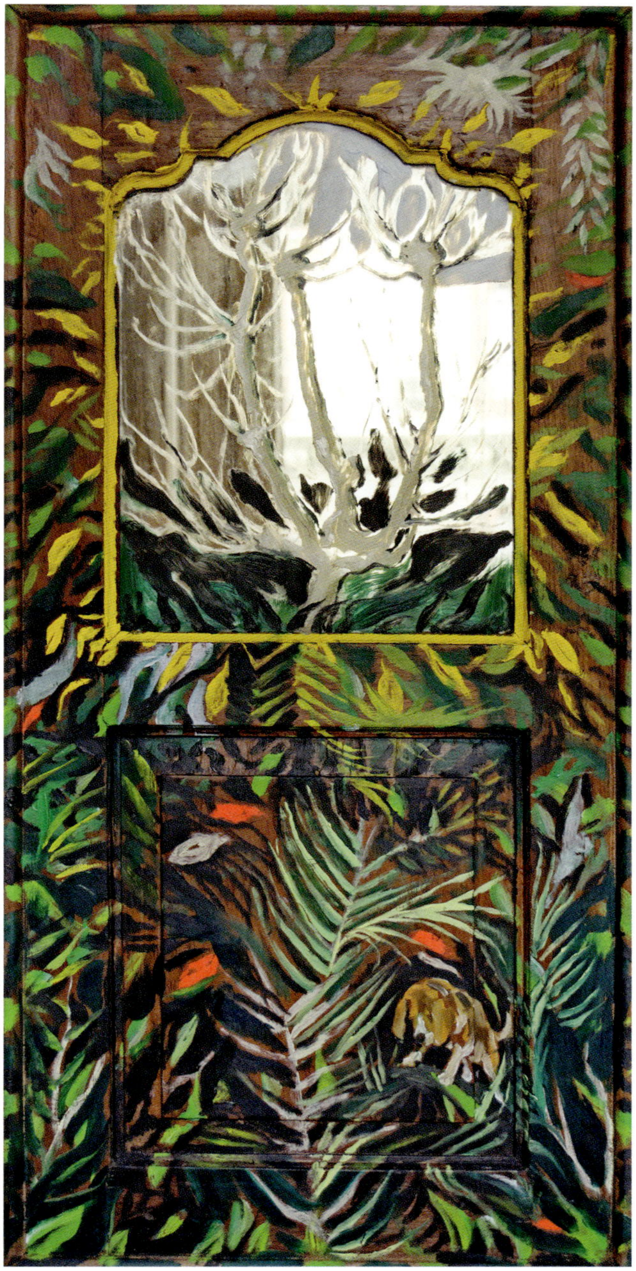

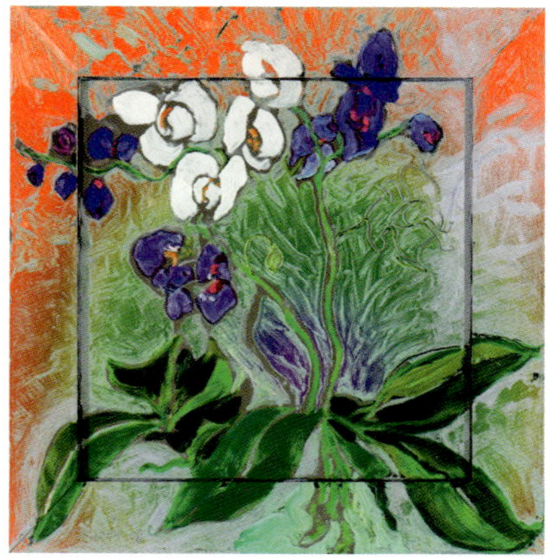

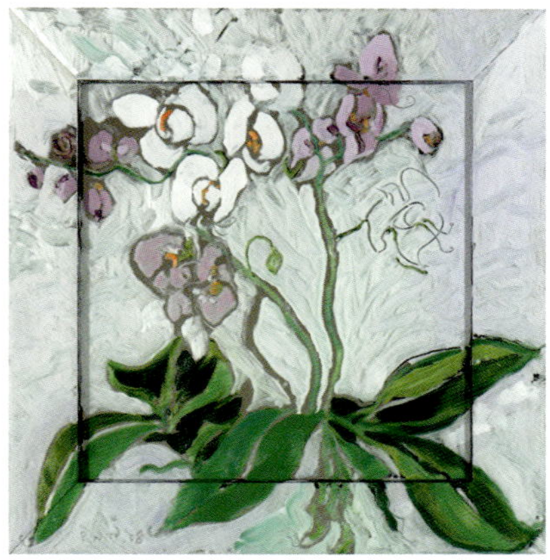

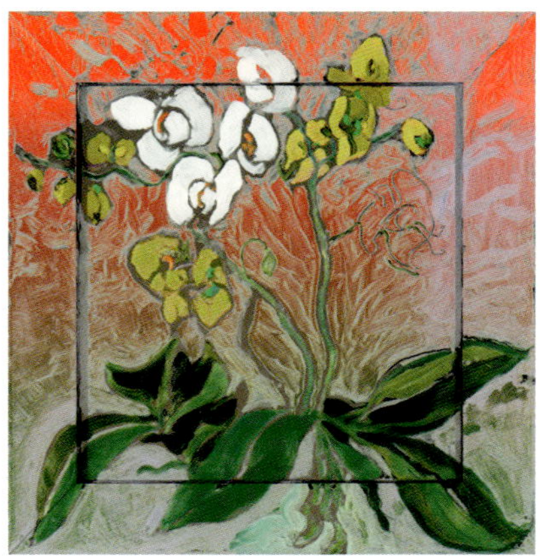

"I really enjoy painting on mirror with oils. Each brush stroke is reflected, taking on a double meaning. Also, each unpainted part of the mirror reflects the person or thing standing in front of it, adding to the magic."

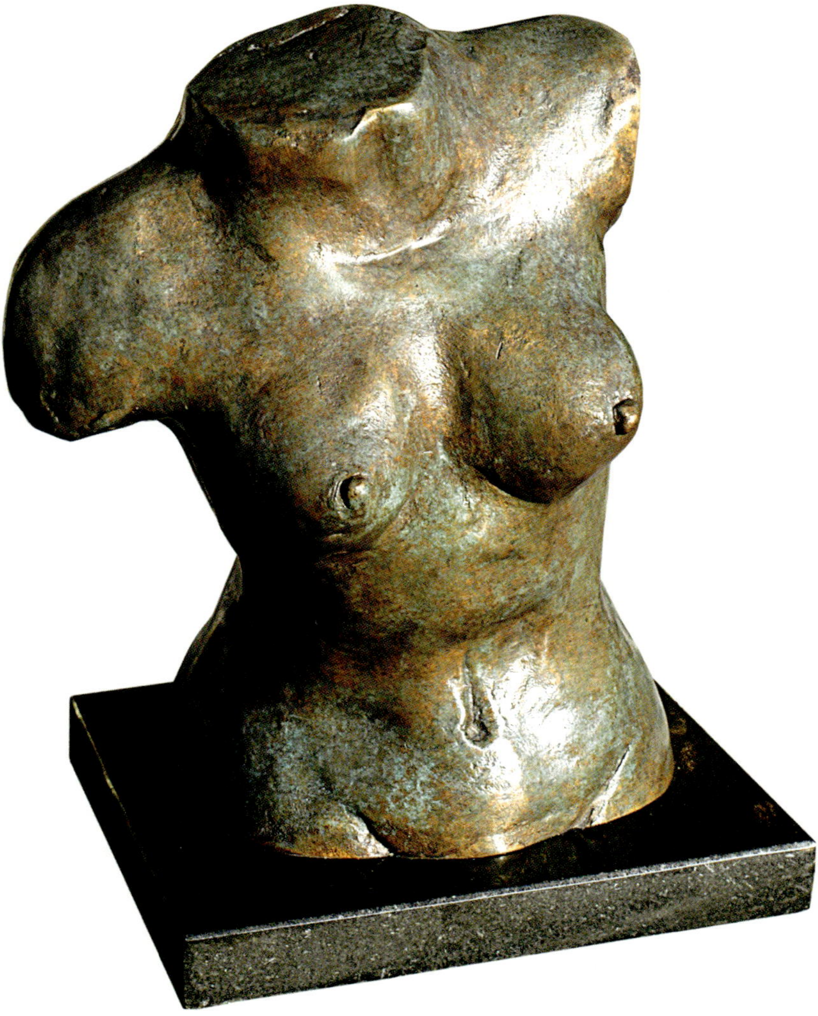

ABOVE: *Torso in Bronze* | 2003 | bronze on a granite plinth | 18 × 14 × 23 cm
OPPOSITE ABOVE: *Bronze Study of Horse and Figure* | 2003 | bronze on a granite plinth | 45 × 40 × 20 cm
OPPOSITE BELOW: *Study of a Head* | 2003 | bronze on a granite plinth | 30 × 18 × 10 cm

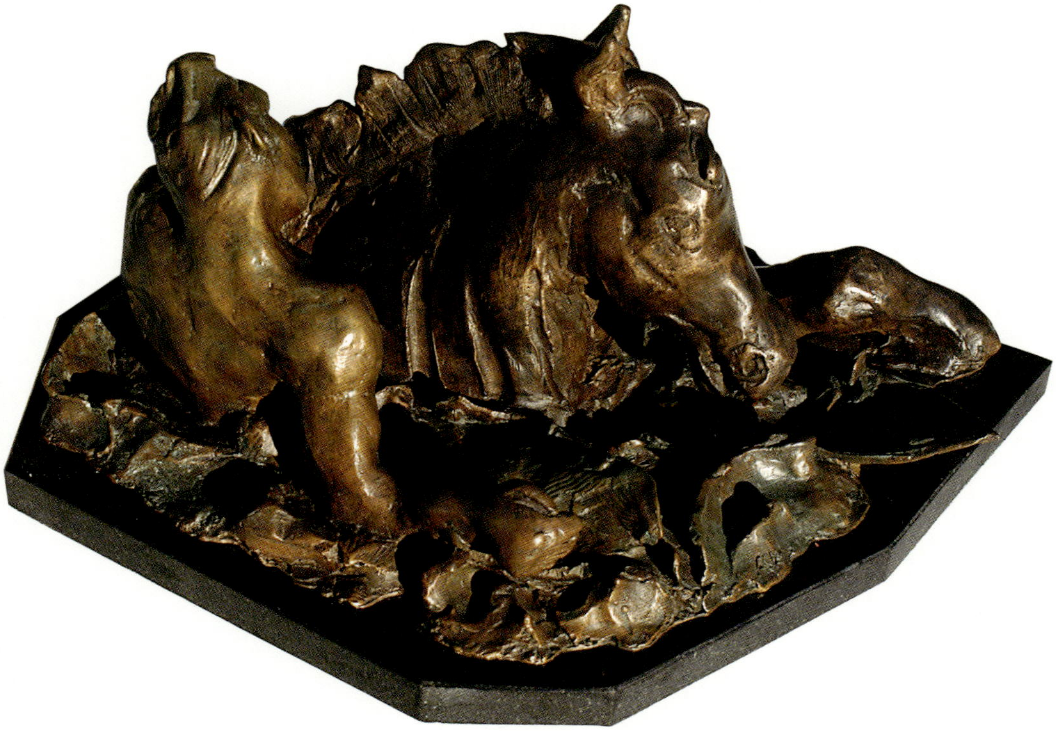

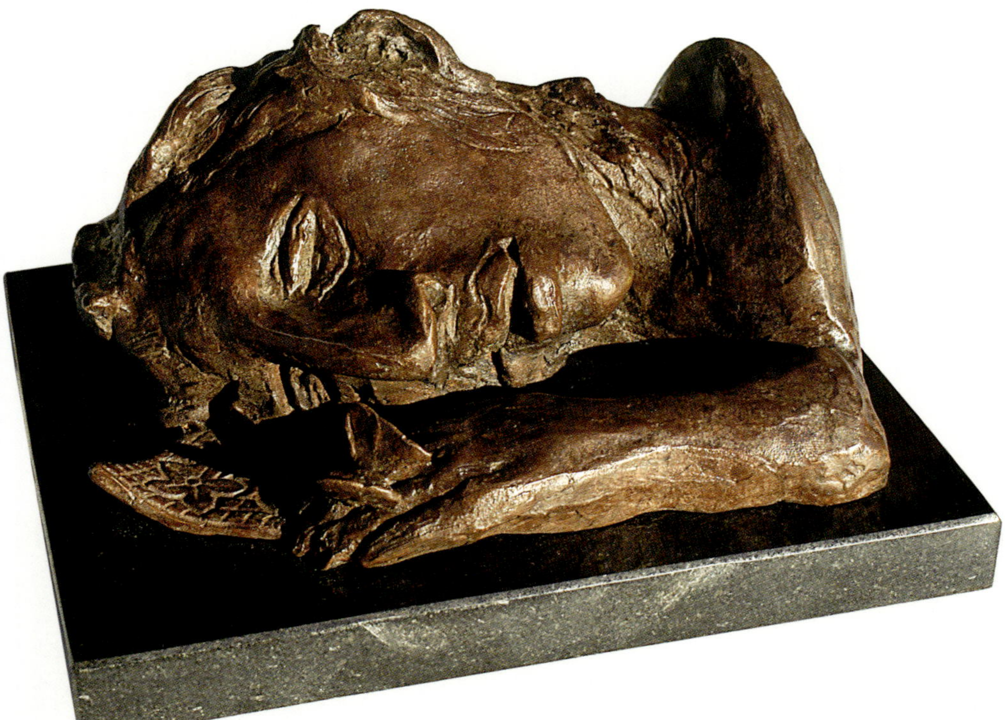

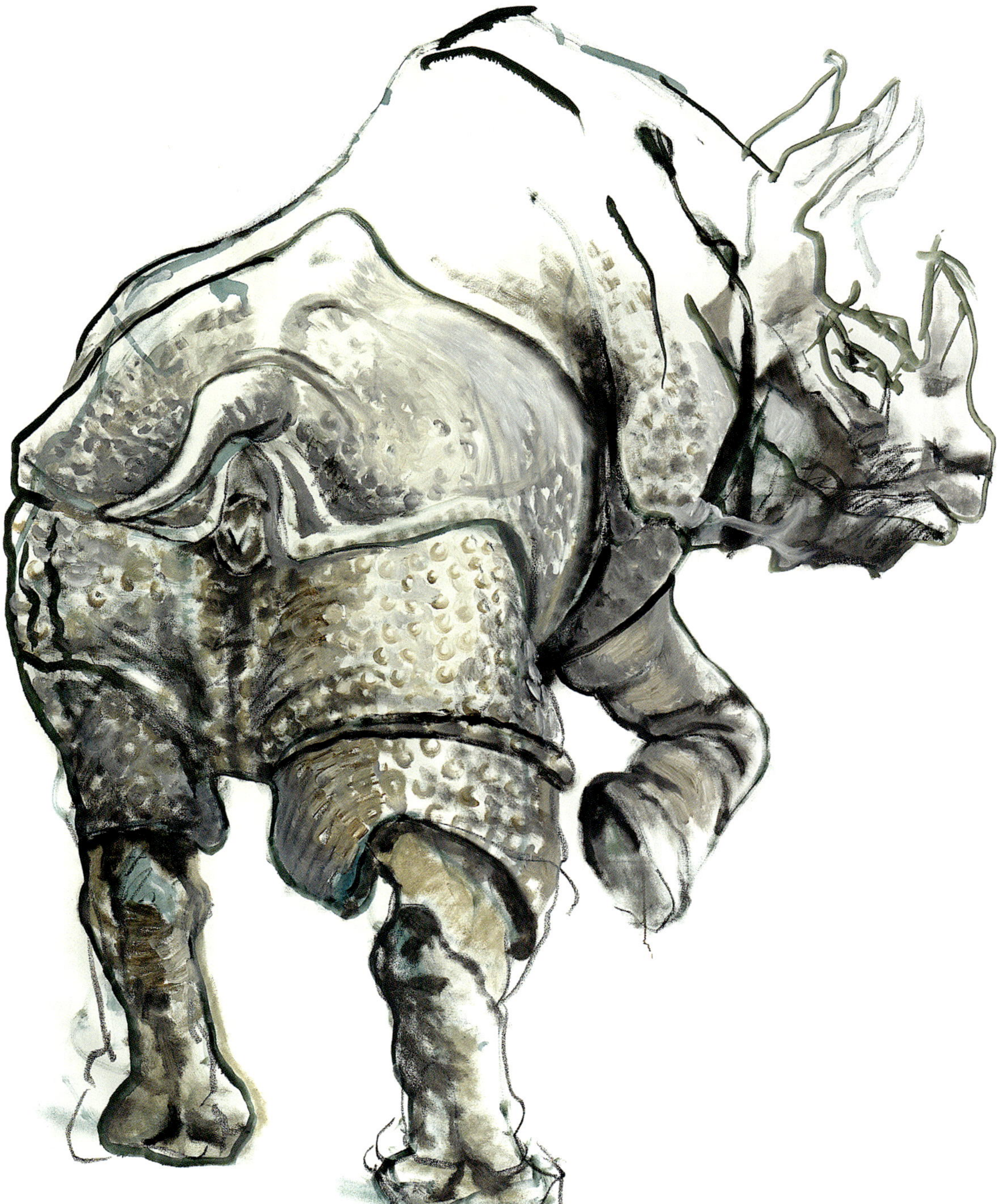

"Inspired by the Alfred Jacquemart's bronze outside the Musée d'Orsay, my Rhino *is exhibited with* Pegasus *at the Butler Institute of American Art. It started out as a drawing, then this painting. From there, I took it on a huge adventure via stained glass, bronze, gold, stainless steel and iron – and the journey's not over yet!"*

ABOVE: *Rhino* | 2009 | acrylic on canvas | 273 × 182 cm
OPPOSITE: *Rhino, Bronze* | 2015 | bronze | 59 × 44 × 15 cm

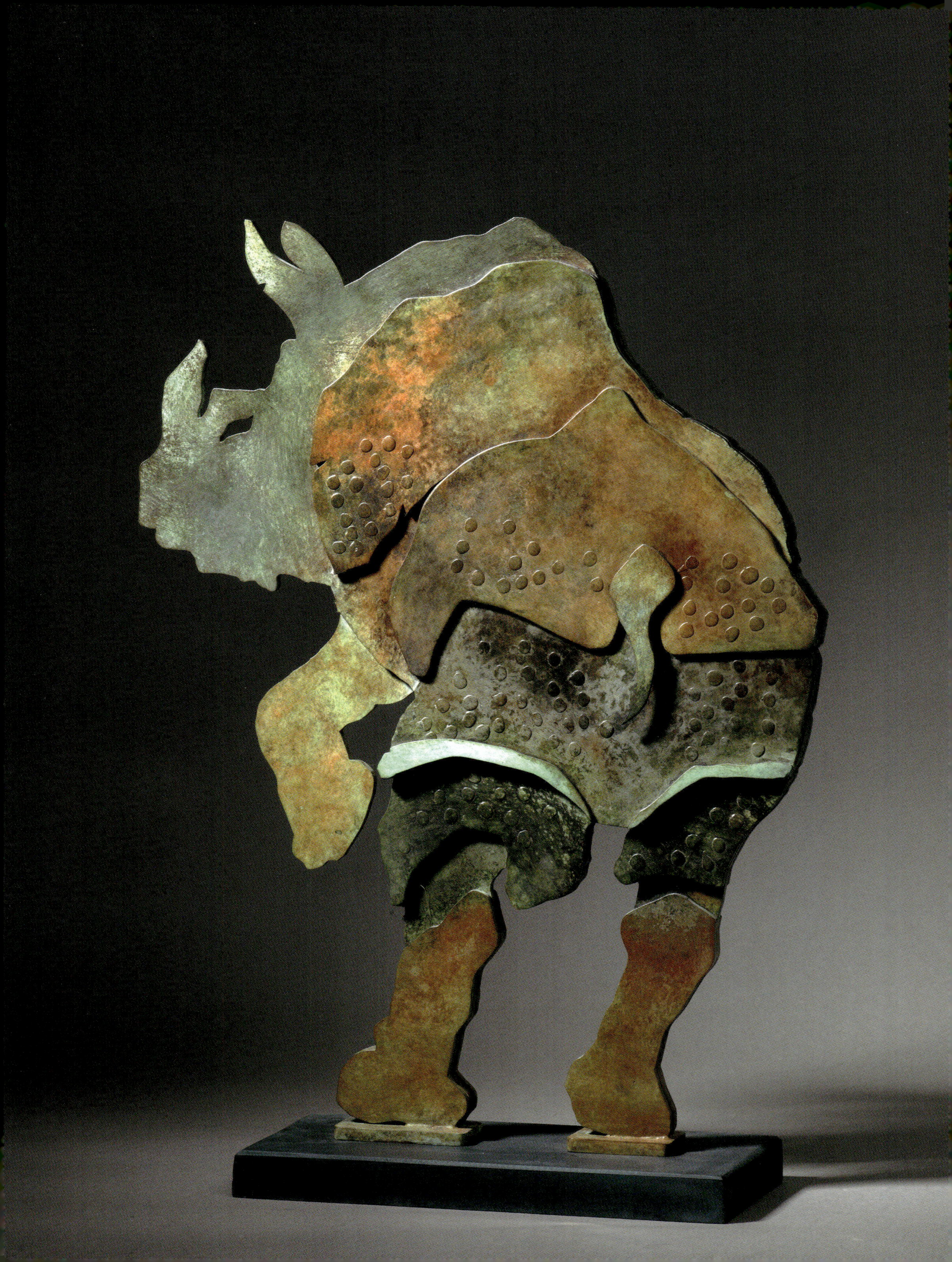

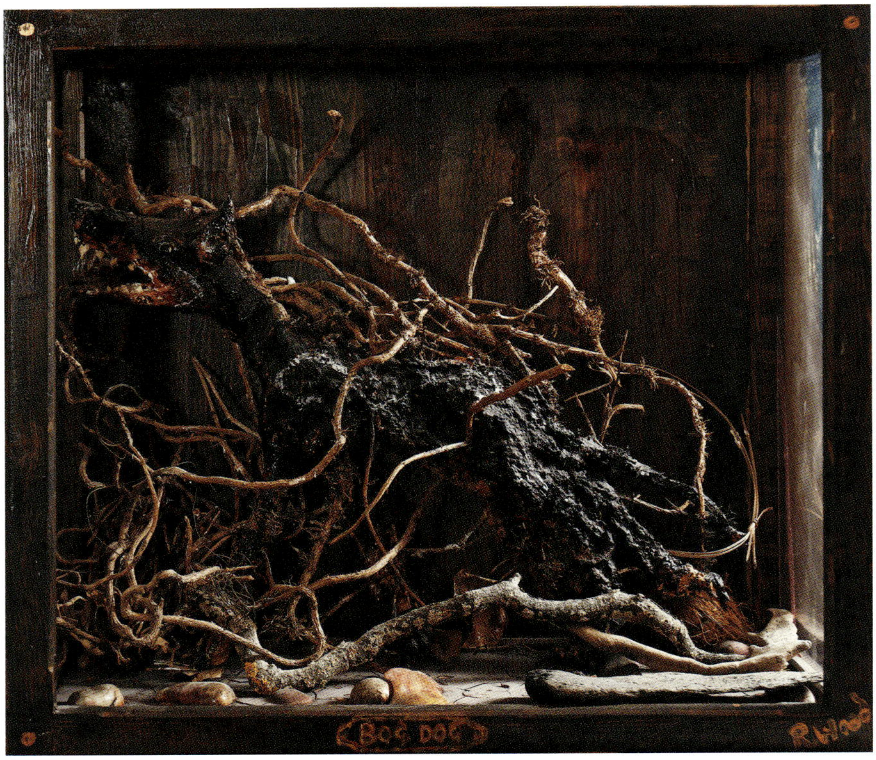

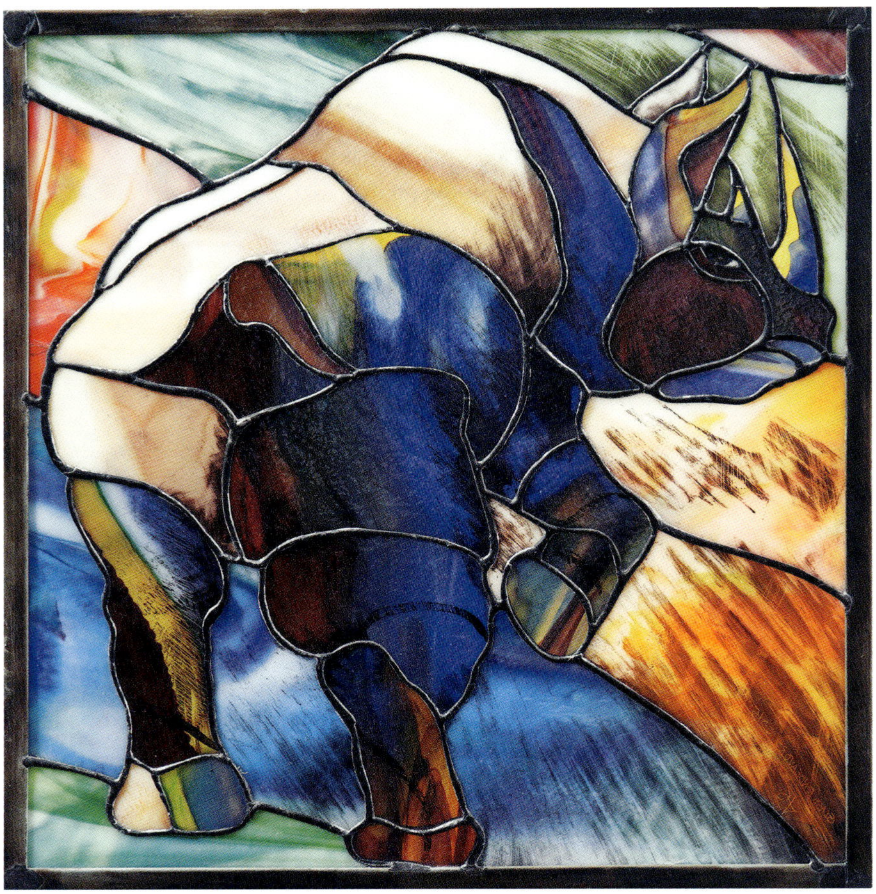

"I love driftwood and dead wood; Bog Dog *is made of creeper torn from Sandymount in Ireland.* Addiction *illustrates how I was feeling before I went into rehab – trapped, but also wanting to change, to escape."*

ABOVE: *Bog Dog* | 2005 | mixed media
76 × 107 × 46 cm
BELOW: *Rhino* | 2015 | stained glass
15 × 15 cm
OPPOSITE: *Addiction* | 2009
acrylic on canvas | 54.5 × 44.5 cm

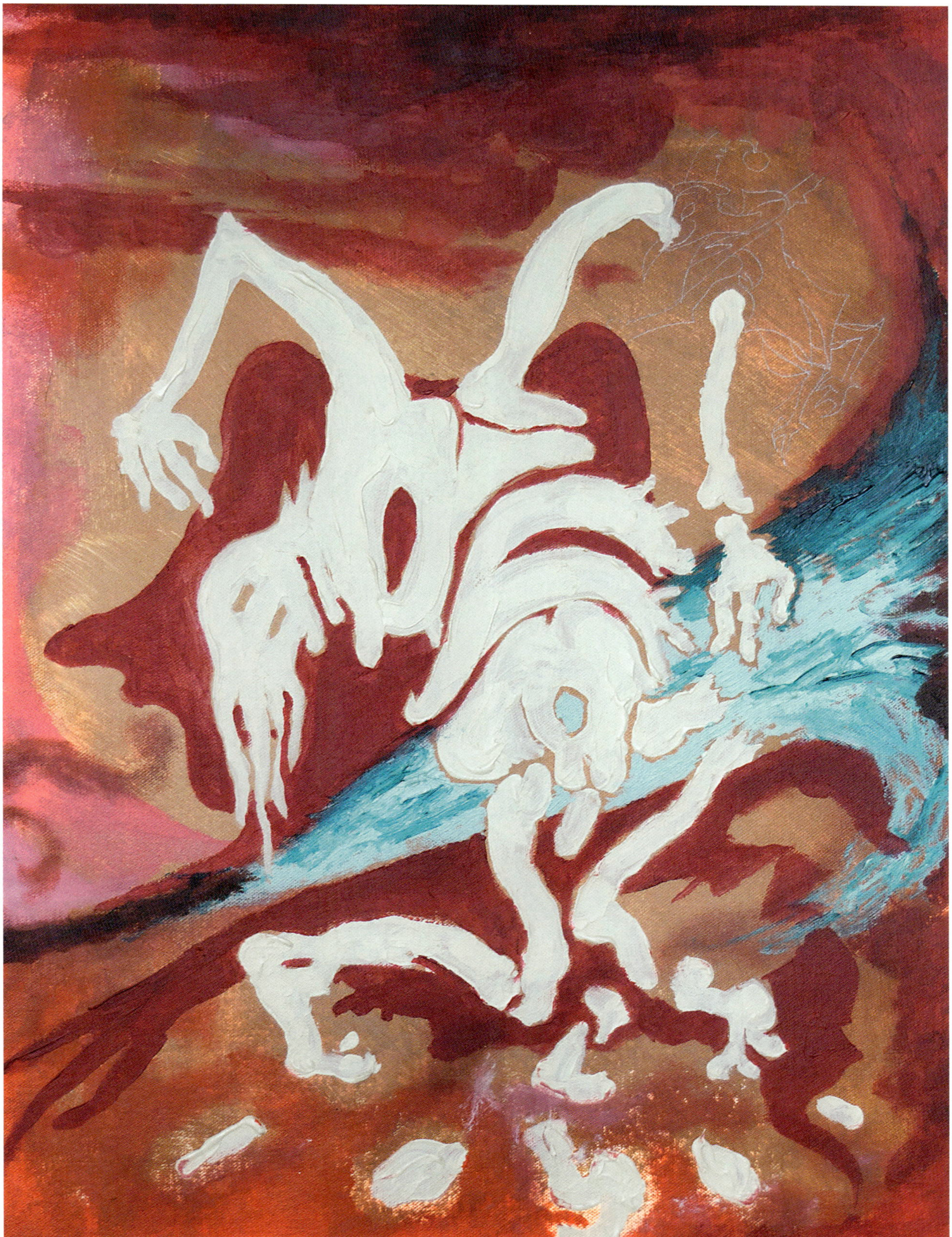

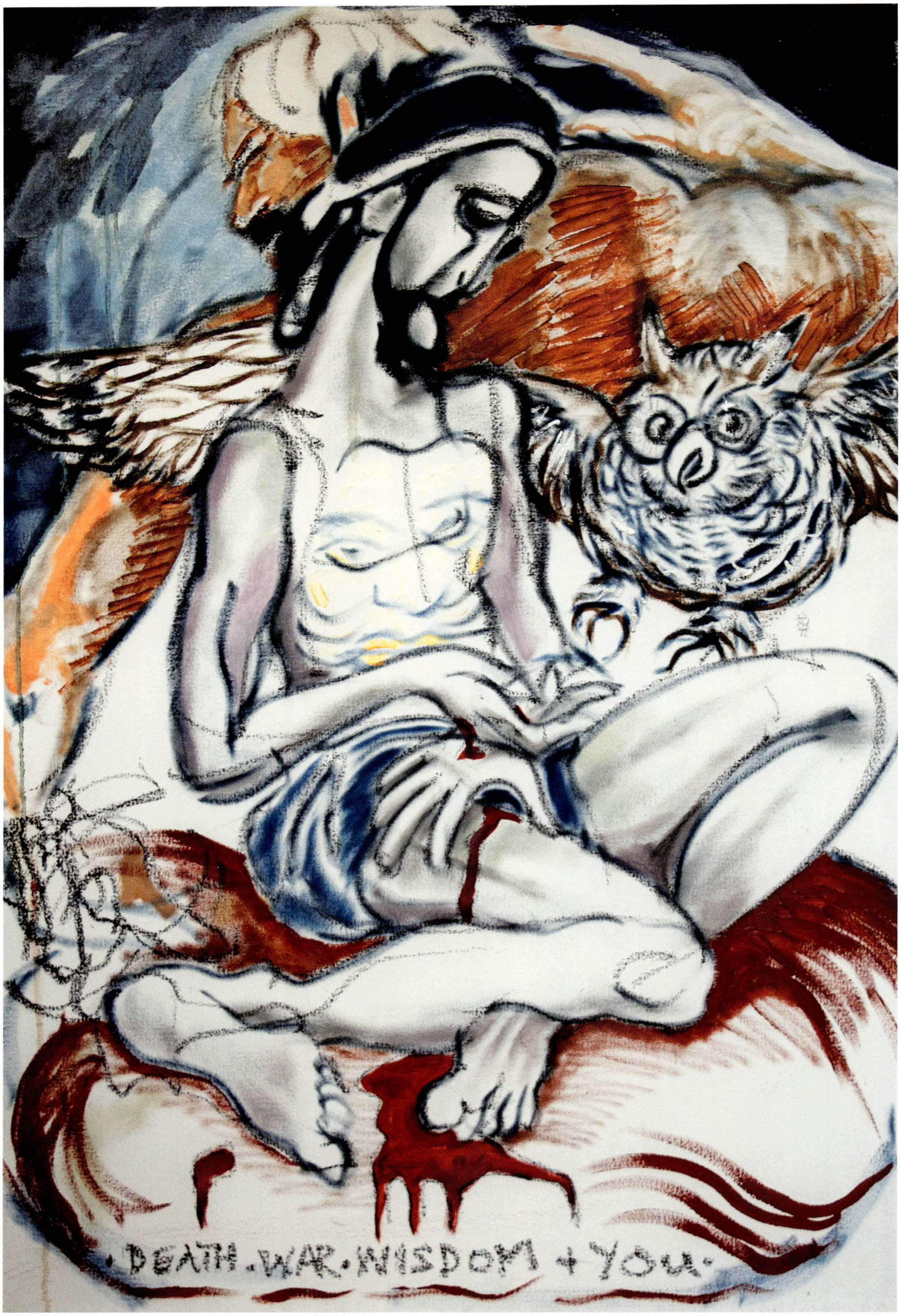
·DEATH·WAR·WISDOM + YOU·

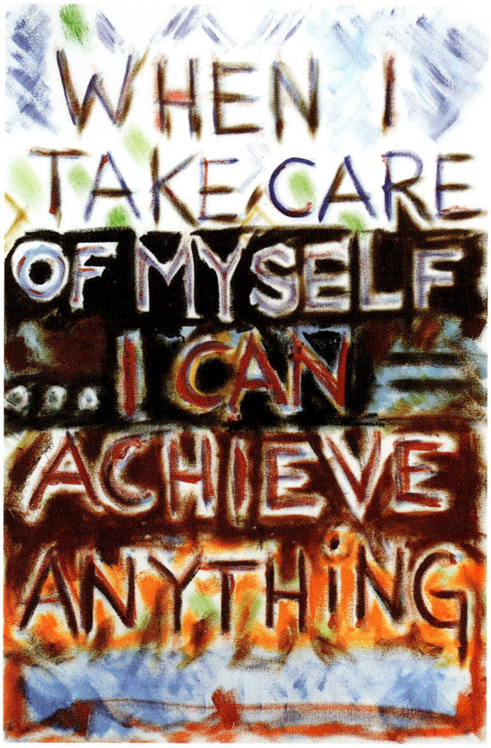

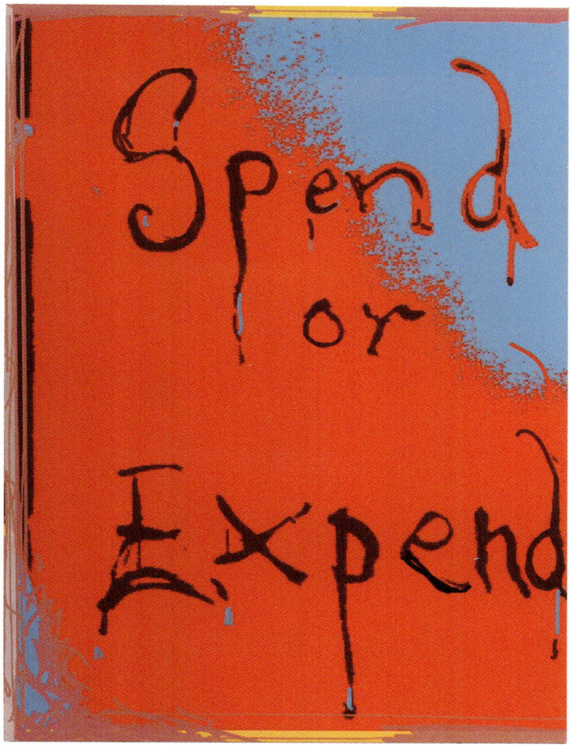

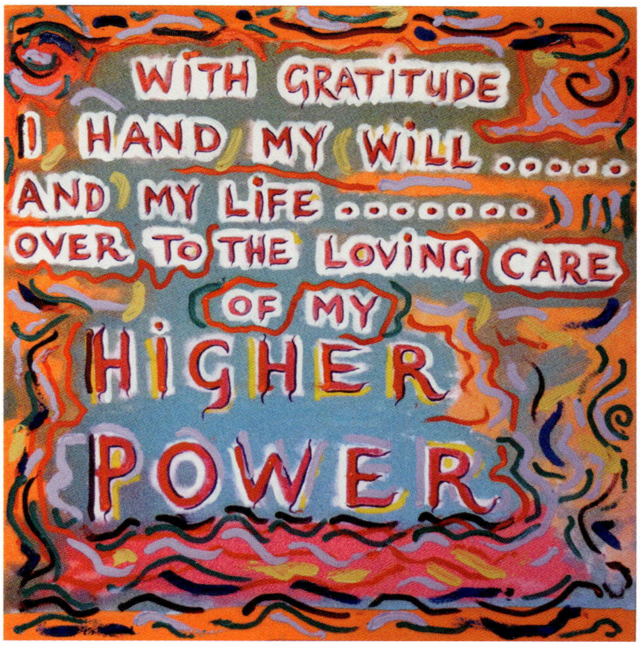

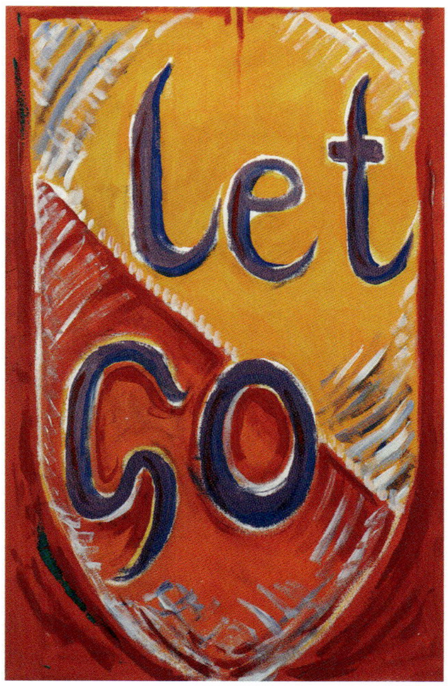

OPPOSITE: *Death War Wisdom & You* | 2009 | acrylic on canvas | 92 × 61 cm
TOP LEFT: *When I Take Care of Myself* | 2009 | acrylic on canvas | 112 × 74 cm
TOP RIGHT: *Spend or Expend* | 2009 | mixed media on canvas | 80 × 60 cm approx
ABOVE LEFT: *With Gratitude ...* | 2009 | mixed media on canvas | 75.5 × 75.5 cm
ABOVE RIGHT: *Let Go* | 2009 | acrylic on canvas | 91 × 61 cm

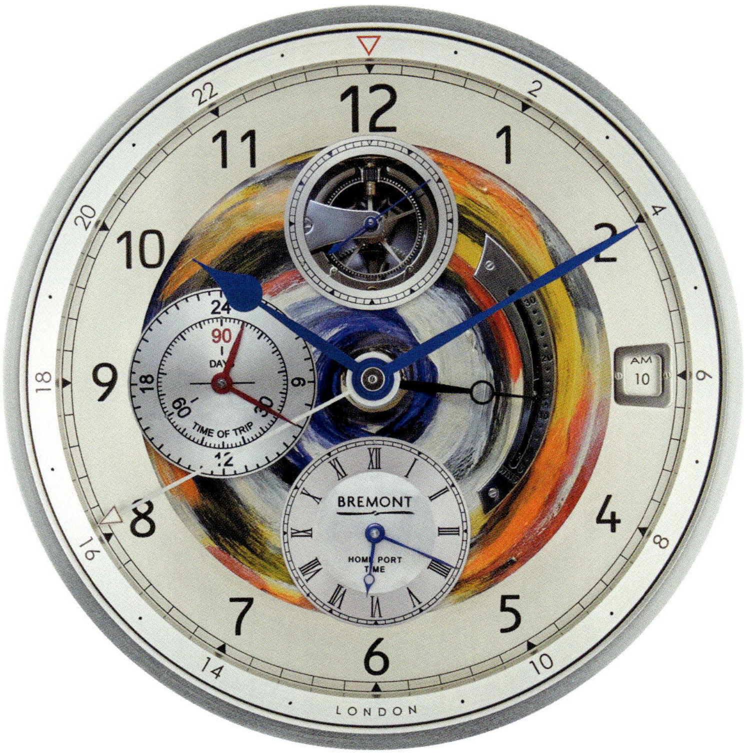

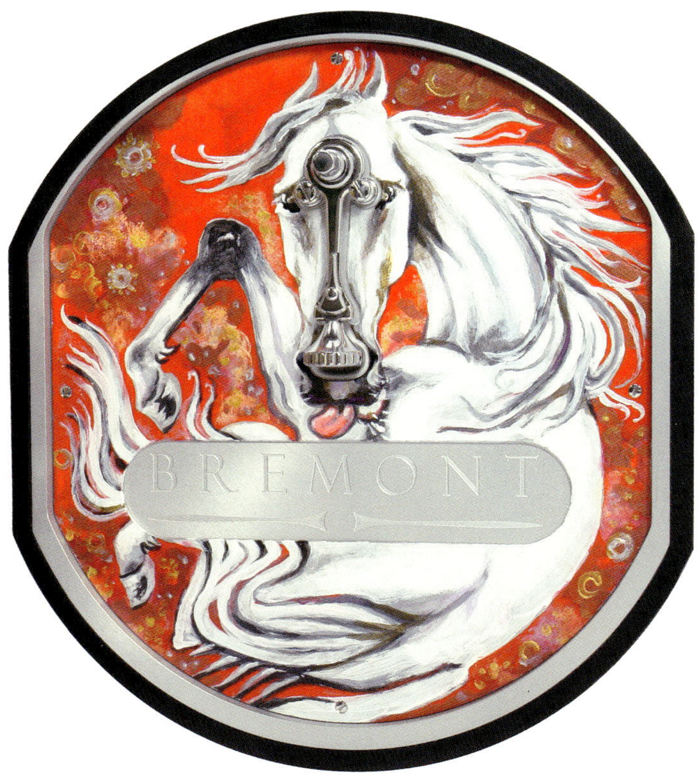

Bremont B1 Marine Chronometer | 2011 | hand-painted chronometer (dial and inside detail) | 25 cm diameter

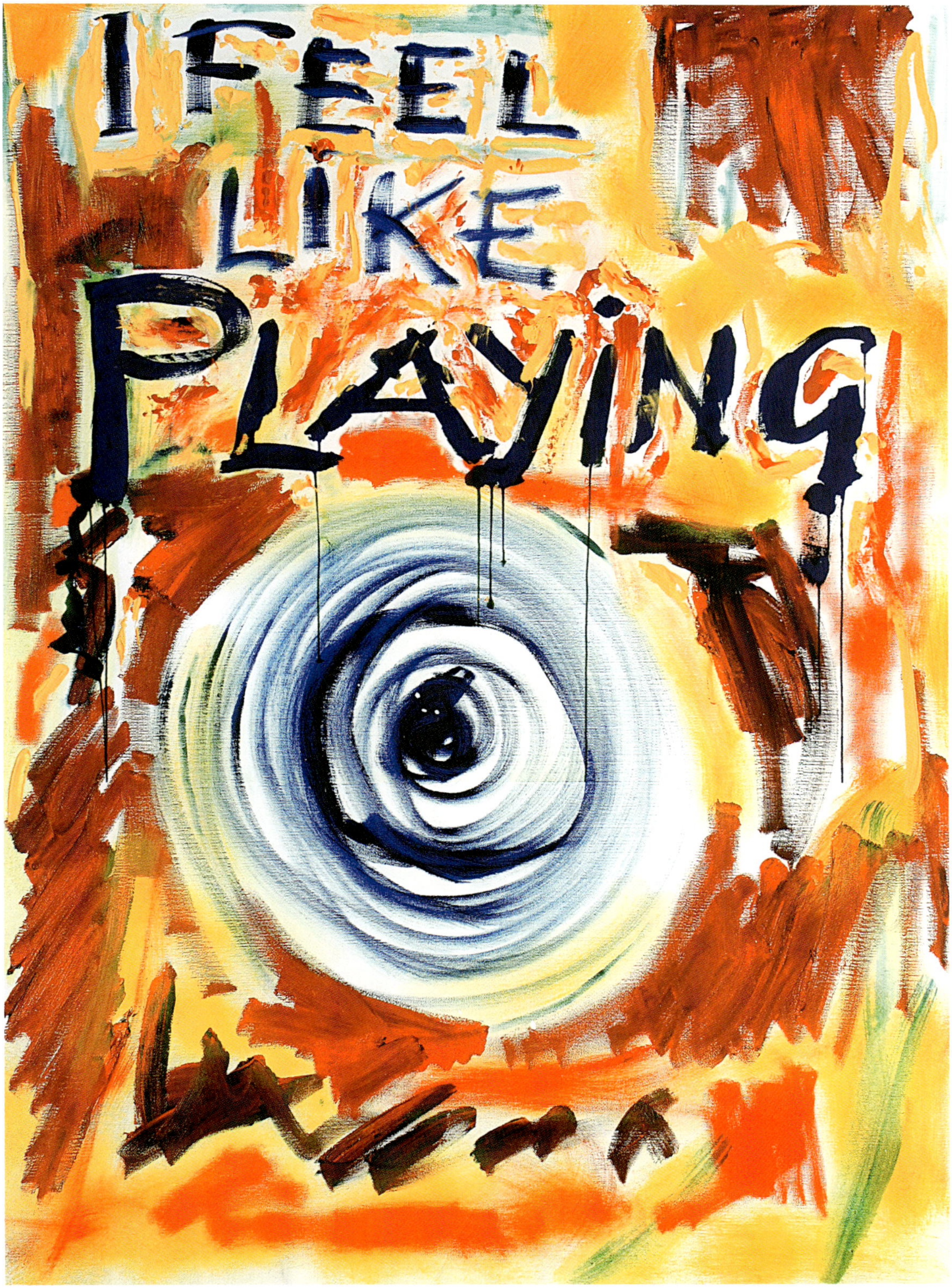

I Feel Like Playing | 2009 | acrylic on canvas | 99 × 61 cm

OUTRO
KEITH RICHARDS ON RONNIE WOOD

It was only when I came upon Ronnie forging his 3rd Rembrandt that I realized that he was a gifted artist.

Swiftness of line, depth of pallette, the fluidity of his etching all pointed out a man of considerable talent.

He followed no rules, just like me. which is why we play guitar.

He paints because he loves it, his joy shows in everything he does and it shows in the handsome bribe he paid me to write this.

Ronnie loves to draw, to paint and is also a sculpture as well.

When the Stones rehearse Ronnie turns every set list into a painting (I help with the spelling) we end a weeks rehearsal surrounded by Ronnie Wood canvasses. He is, in fact a regular picasshole!!

Keith Richards.

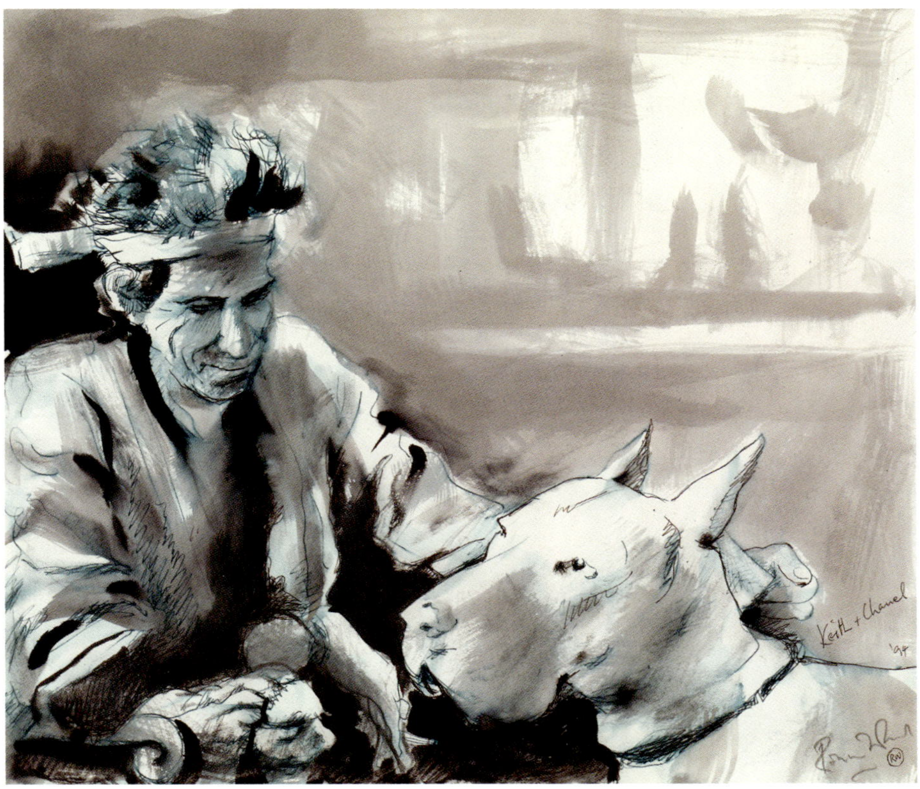

TOP: *Dox Office and Voodoo Lounge* (detail) by Keith Richards | 1994 | pen on paper | 29 × 21 cm approx
ABOVE: *Keith & Chanel* | 1994 | pen and wash on paper | 30 × 40 cm

INDEX OF WORKS

ACKNOWLEDGMENTS

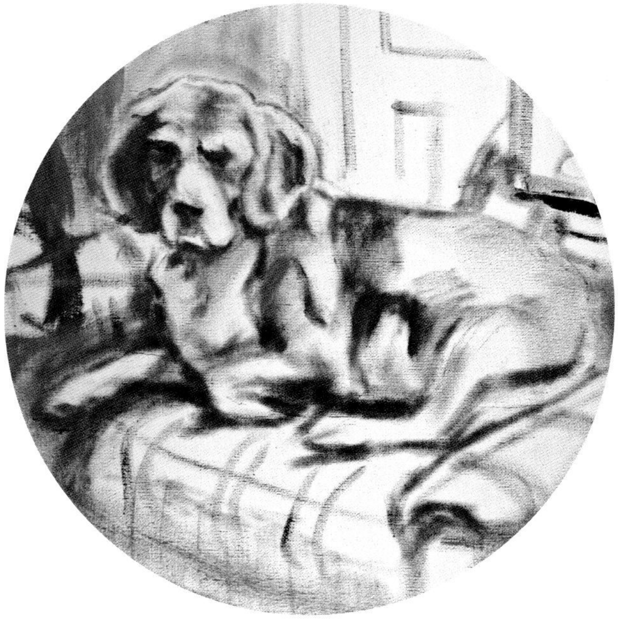

I would like to thank everyone involved for all their hard work. First, a big thank you to Tristan de Lancey at Thames & Hudson for commissioning my book, and to Richard Havers for his invaluable help. Thanks too to the team at my publishers – Jane Laing, Rose Blackett-Ord, Ginny Liggitt, Neil Palfreyman, Becky Gee and Tzortzis Rallis. Also to photographers Simon Pask, who took so many of the images of my art, and Sonny McCartney, who took photos of me in action.

Thanks also to Bernard Pratt, my "art coach" who has looked after my artistic affairs for many, many years and has worked so hard to track down images of old artworks of mine and provided so much behind-the-scenes support; Sherry Daly, my manager; Jenny Taylor, my personal assistant; my children Jesse, Leah, Tyrone, Gracie and Alice; Geraint Humphreys, who did so much of the research; and Sally, my wife and inspiration, who has helped in so many ways throughout the making of this book.

Sources of photographs:
p.21 Top row, left © Matt Cronin.
p.21 Bottom row, centre; p.25 Top row, left, and bottom row, centre and right © Sonny McCartney.
All other images on p.21 and p.25 are from the private collection of the artist.

First published in 2017 in the United States of America by
Thames & Hudson Inc., 500 Fifth Avenue, New York, New York 10110
www.thamesandhudsonusa.com

Reprinted 2017

Library of Congress Control Number 2017934762
ISBN 978-0-500-51989-9

Printed and bound in Slovenia by DZS-Grafik d.o.o.

ABOVE: *Dolly* (detail) | 2014–15 | acrylic on canvas | 45.5 × 38 cm
FRONT COVER: *Forty Licks* | 2004 | mixed media on canvas | 91.5 × 122 cm

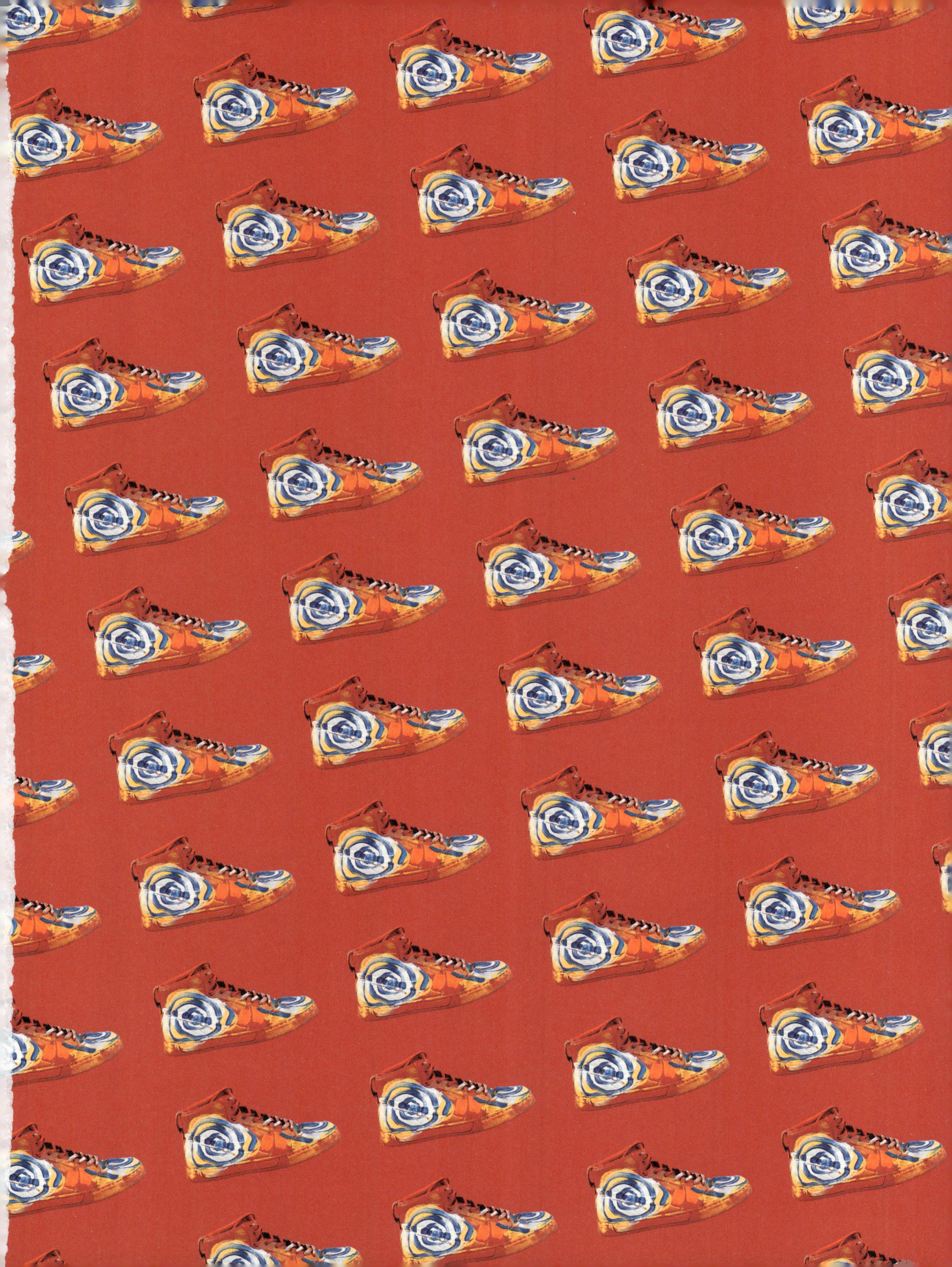

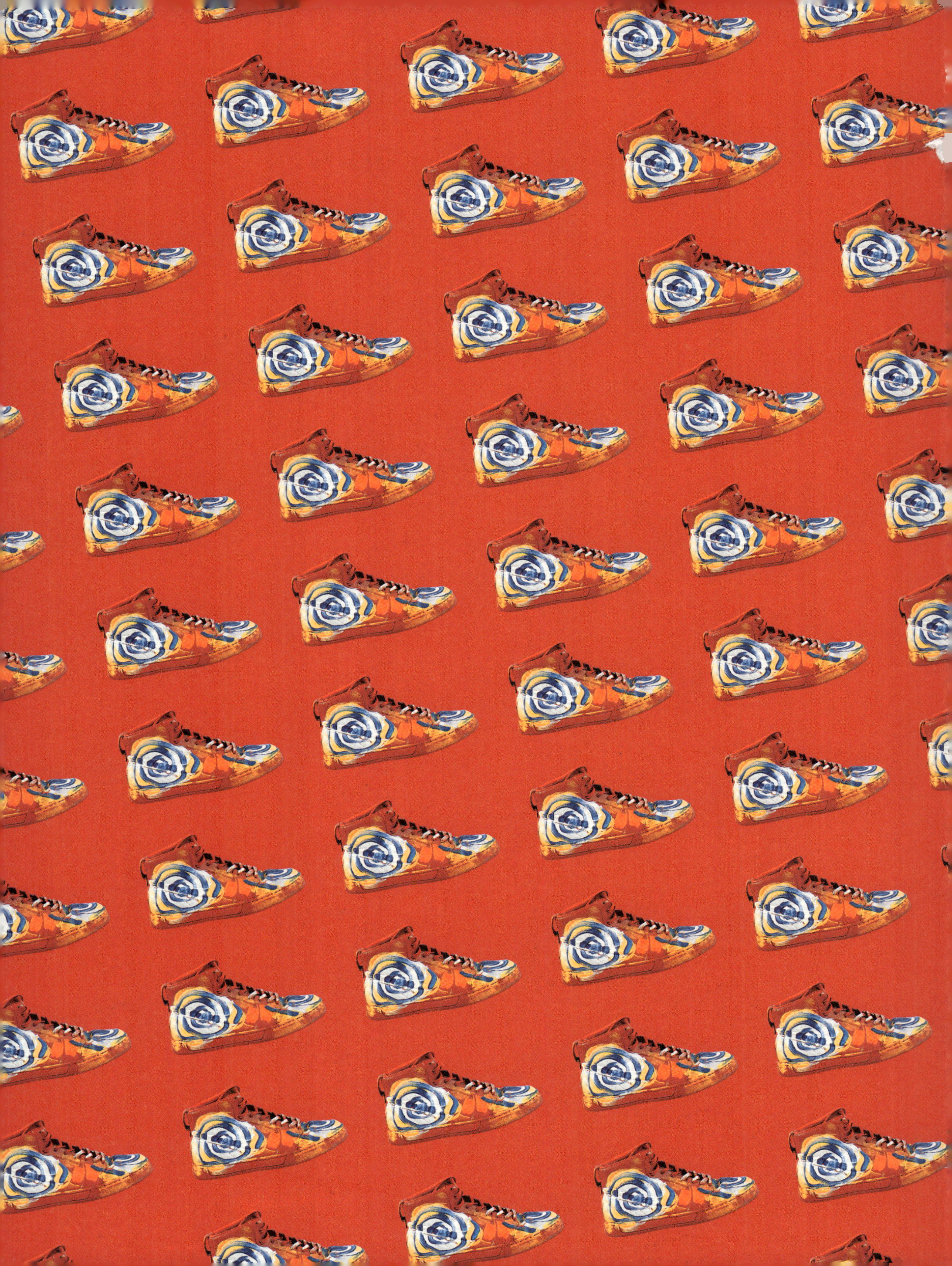